Distant Relations

Distant Relations

How My Ancestors Colonized North America

VICTORIA FREEMAN

Steerforth Press
South Royalton, Vermont

LIBRARY OF CONGRESS CATALOGING-IN-PUBLICATION DATA

Freeman, Victoria (Victoria Jane)
  Distant relations : how my ancestors colonized North America / Victoria
Freeman.— 1st Steerforth ed.
      p.   cm.
Originally published: Toronto : McClelland & Stewart, c2000.
Includes bibliographical references (p.) and index.
  ISBN 1-58642-053-4 (alk. paper)
  1. Freeman, Victoria (Victoria Jane) — Family. 2. Freeman family.
3.Wheeler family. 4. Elliott family. 5. Stanton family. 6. North America —
History — Colonial period, ca. 1600–1775. 7. Indians of North America —
History — Colonial period, ca. 1600–1775. 8. United States — Ethnic rela-
tions. 9. Canada — Ethnic relations. 10. United States — History — Colonial
period, ca. 1600–1775. I. Title.
  CT274.F736 F74 2002
  973.0'092'2 — dc21

                          2002009082

FIRST STEERFORTH EDITION

For my children, Claire and Ariel,
and for Danielle Morrison and Cheryl Mandamin

Contents

Acknowledgements

It is a daunting task to try and thank all the people who have helped, encouraged, and inspired me over the many years of researching and writing this book, but I shall try. I am especially indebted to two people: Dorothy Christian, whose challenging friendship got me started on this project and has seen me through it, and my aunt, Jean Harvey, who sparked my interest in family history and generously shared her genealogical and historical knowledge over many years of correspondence. Without their contributions, *Distant Relations* would not exist.

The support, encouragement, and wisdom of Margaret Christakos, Al Hunter, Helen Thundercloud, Susan Dion Fletcher, Cuyler Cotton, Dorothy Christian, and Mary Alice Smith have carried me through at critical times, and their comments and suggestions have vastly improved the book. I think of them as the grandparents of this project.

My extended family, especially John Freeman, Chris Freeman, Lois Wilson, David Freeman, Bruce Cummings, Stu Harvey, Fraser Harvey, Webb Cummings; my sister, Kate Freeman, and my parents, June and George Freeman, shared their insights about our family culture and history as well as their knowledge of my grandparents, and read various chapters with a critical eye. I want to thank them for their time and trouble and for saying the difficult things; their assistance in no way implies that they agree with my interpretations or conclusions. This project also introduced me to several more distant relations who generously shared family lore with me: John Whit Davis, Bernard Stanton, Bonnie Stover, and the Harris and Ranney cousins on the Internet.

Aboriginal perspectives have been invaluable in shaping this work and in reminding me of why it was necessary. In addition to a number of Native people mentioned above, Walter Redsky, Fraser Greene, and Albert Mandamin, from Shoal Lake #40 and Iskatewizaagegan First Nations; Ada Morrison of the Dalles First Nation; Jody Kechego and Kelly Riley of the Chippewas of the Thames First Nation; Keith Jamieson, Mohawk researcher for the Woodland Cultural Centre, Brantford; Shannon McNair, of the public-relations department of the Mashantucket Pequot Tribe; Gladys Tantaquidgeon and Faith Davison of the Mohegan Tribe; Ray Rogers and Janice Rising of Aamjiwnaang (Sarnia) First Nation; Rev. Aleace Davidson of First United Church, Aamjiwnaang (Sarnia) First Nation; Wendi Starr Brown and the late Lucille Dawson of the Narragansett Tribe; and Mark Peters of the Munsee-Delaware Nation reviewed sections of the book and enlarged my understanding of aboriginal issues. Thanks also to Marge Bruchac and Joseph Bruchac, Joe Morrison, Ada Morrison, Beth Brant, Alfred Redsky, Florence (Mandamin) Redsky, Frank Redsky, Sarah Mandamin, the women in the Iskatewizaagegan band office, Margaret Sault of the Mississaugas of New Credit First Nation, Tom Hill, Jeannette Armstrong, and Emma Paishk. Special thanks to the friends who so lovingly shared traditional teachings and medicine with me. Migwetch.

The following academics and researchers generously reviewed individual chapters related to their fields of expertise: Olive Dickason, University of Ottawa; John Demos, Yale University; Alfred Cave, University of Toledo; Charles Cohen, University of Wisconsin; Richard Cogley, Southern Methodist University; Jim Miller, University of Saskatchewan; Peter Leavenworth, University of New Hampshire; Colin Calloway, Dartmouth College; Donald B. Smith, University of Calgary; Jill Lepore, Boston University; Paul Slack, Oxford University; Susan Dion Fletcher, Ontario Institute for Studies in Education; and Leo Waisberg, Seven Oaks Consulting Inc. I would also like to thank James Axtell, Neal Salisbury, and Reg Good for their assistance, and Nancy Chater, Florence Sicoli, Roger Simon, and the other members of the Testimony and Historical Memory Project, Ontario Institute for Studies in Education, for inviting me to a very thought-provoking colloquium on pedagogy, testimony, and historical memory.

This book would not exist without libraries, especially the John P. Robarts Library at the University of Toronto, and the Toronto Reference

Library, and it has been greatly helped along by librarians. I'd like to thank all the staff at the United Church Archives; Kim Arnold, of the Presbyterian Church Archives; Shirley Wilson of Salford Museum, Salford, Ontario; Joan at the Indian and Colonial Research Centre, Mystic, Connecticut; and Richard Wolfe of the Francis A. Countway Library of Medicine, Harvard.

Because this book was informed by my experience of spending four months in Southern Africa during 1986 and 1987, I'd like to thank Canadian Crossroads International, Byers Naudé, Lois Wilson, Makeda Silvera, Esther Mkhonza, and Phylis Mdluli. I'd also like to express my appreciation to David Marata of the United Church of Canada, Ronald Wright, Susan Crean, Junzo Kokubo, David Rasmus, Athina Goldberg, Elizabeth Langley, Gerry Hallowell, Pablo Idahosa, and Toni and Tom Moran of Mansfield Hollow, Connecticut, for the various ways they assisted this project.

I am indebted to my publisher, Douglas Gibson, my editor, Pat Kennedy, and many other wonderful people at McClelland & Stewart for helping me realize this dream. I am also grateful for the financial support of the Canada Council, the Ontario Arts Council Writers' Reserve Program, and the Toronto Arts Council, as well as the support of various private patrons who helped me with this project or with other projects in the past.

Most of all I want to acknowledge the tremendous support of my parents, who have always helped me, believed in me, and stood by me; my children, who have good-naturedly shared their mother with a computer all these years; and Mark Fawcett, my life-partner, whose insights and feel for language greatly improved the manuscript and whose patience, love, and humour have nurtured me since I first met him twenty years ago. Love to you all.

All of these people and institutions have helped me immensely; none of them is responsible for my interpretations, opinions, or errors.

Author's Note

There are no names for the indigenous peoples of North America that are acceptable to everyone. My ancestors used the word "Indian" and in many sections of the text dealing with early history I have used the same word, though today it is considered inappropriate in many contexts. In Canada we speak of "First Nations" and "aboriginal people," but these terms are unfamiliar in the United States, where Native American is the most common term for the people, and "tribe" – a word rarely used in Canada today – is the norm for their political and cultural entities. I have tried to use the terms appropriate to the country I am writing about, though I have also used the words "Native," "indigenous," and "Native nation" in both territories.

Names of individual tribes or First Nations are equally problematic. The Ojibwa, for example, were known as the Mississaugas in nineteenth-century Ontario, but were and are known as the Chippewas in the United States and in southwestern Ontario, and often today call themselves Anishinabe (spelled various ways), a term which is also used by some related Native groups!

Introduction

In a restaurant deep within a New England casino, amid the whirr and clink of slot machines, under an artificial light that made it impossible to tell if it was day or night, yesterday or tomorrow, an elderly man gave a middle-aged woman a pile of rocks.

As the woman received the rocks, thirty other people – people I'd never met before but who were my very distant American relatives – clapped and smiled, our applause drawing the curious glances of the casino faithful as they lined up to eat before returning to their games of chance. They might have guessed it was a service-club presentation, perhaps a family birthday party – events easily celebrated with a communal gambling excursion. They would likely have been perplexed to know we were there not to gamble but to commemorate a friendship between our common ancestor – a seventeenth-century fur trader – and a Native American sachem.

If you didn't know who was who, you could not tell by appearances who were descendants of Thomas Stanton attending the Stanton Family reunion and who were members of the Mohegan Tribe that had once been led by the sachem Uncas and that now ran the very profitable Mohegan Sun Casino. Time had blurred the racial differences, though the cultural identity of the two groups remained distinct. And it was a Stanton descendant, a colourful Connecticut farmer named John Whit Davis with a keen knowledge of Native-American stone artifacts, who showed the representative of the Mohegan Tribal Council how her Mohegan ancestors had used the ancient tools.

In the context of the flash and energy of the casino – a lucrative money machine for the tribe – the return of these few rocks from the farm of one of Thomas Stanton's sons on what had originally been Mohegan land seemed humble to the point of embarrassment, but it still seemed a positive gesture to give them back, to return this little bit of Mohegan history to its rightful owners. There was something poignant in this unlikely honouring of an ancient friendship between an Englishman and an aboriginal man, for there are so few positive stories from our shared past.

Even today such friendships are not that common: what comes between us still is all that history.

All my life I've felt burdened by this history, a history I didn't know or understand since it was never taught in school: the history of how my people, the people of European ancestry, came to North America, colonized the inhabitants, and ended up with their land. Growing up as a Canadian child of English–Scottish–Irish heritage in Ottawa in the early 1960s, I never knowingly encountered a living, breathing aboriginal person, though I knew from television news reports that they still lived in Canada, mainly under appalling conditions on reserves. I knew vaguely that whatever had happened in Canada had supposedly happened less brutally than in the United States. I struggled with an amorphous sense of guilt that I sensed many other people in North America shared, but which was never talked about.

Within my family, there were two ways to deal with the reality of aboriginal people: to ignore them totally or to "help" them. There was no overt consciousness of aboriginal people on my mother's side of the family at all, as far as I could tell, except for the story of the long-dead relative on the Prairies who drank so much he ended up on the Indian list and was prohibited from buying alcohol – this story told laughingly in a Scots family in which hard liquor had a special place. It was as if aboriginal people didn't exist or, if they did, they no longer had any rights to the land. When questioned, some relatives would express their belief in the hard-luck school of history, a *realpolitik* brutal in its simplicity. *Yes, we took the land. Different nations throughout history have always conquered others; that's just human nature. It's not pretty, but that's the way it is.* They instinctively bristled at uppity Native leaders, with their demonstrations and demands, at the unsettling TV images in those early days of Red Power. Aboriginal people, it seemed, were poor losers; perhaps if no one paid any attention, the troublemakers would simply give up and go away.

On my father's side of the family, it was different. As a child I listened to my father's recollections of summers spent canoeing on Lake of the Woods on the Manitoba–Ontario border with his family, back in the 1920s and 1930s. He used to tell me how his father, a United Church minister, had helped some Ojibwa through hard times; they had thanked him by bringing him fresh venison or moose meat. He described Ojibwa burial grounds he had visited, with the little fenced-in grave plots and the miniature houses and objects – playing cards, cigarettes – left for the dead. He remembered the names of aboriginal children he had played with. I examined the family photographs of my father camping as a little boy, of his twin brother and sister laced up in the tikinaagens (cradle boards) an Ojibwa family had given them.

Many of my relatives on my father's side had tried to help Native people, to do something about the problems they saw. Most were United Church ministers or their offspring, and several had lived far from urban centres close to reserves or other communities of Native people. I admired their caring and compassion and tried to emulate them, though I did not share their Christianity, raised as I was in an atheistic household. It was only much later, when I myself became involved in solidarity work with aboriginal people, that I became aware of the subtle attitude of superiority that could accompany this assistance (and I hasten to add that many members of my father's family also became aware of it, long before me). It was much later still that I learned that my paternal grandfather had been involved with a residential school for Native children. This was a puzzling discovery, for I knew my grandfather had been a good man, one of the most highly regarded of his generation in Manitoba, yet residential schools were everywhere denounced for their legacy of suffering.

Another stream of experience contributing to my awakening consciousness of history was my work in feminist and particularly feminist literary circles, where I first pondered the exclusion of women from conventional historical narratives and also encountered Native women writers and activists. It was hearing them speak about their lives and being confronted by various women of colour about the assumptions and attitudes that bolstered white privilege in the women's organizations to which I belonged (and sometimes being confronted personally) that opened my eyes to the painful reality of racism and how it is perpetuated.

My four-month sojourn in southern Africa in 1986 was also a major catalyst for this book. I taught English in Swaziland under the auspices of Canadian Crossroads International, a secular cultural-exchange program that placed me at a rural, African-run evangelical Christian boarding school that had been founded by Europeans – my own experience of a "residential school." This was followed by an intense three days in Johannesburg, where, through family connections with the World Council of Churches, I toured Soweto and had the opportunity to talk with many anti-apartheid activists, some of whom had been imprisoned and tortured or faced that risk daily, some of whom could no longer return to their homes at night. Their commitment to justice influenced me profoundly and inspired me to try to understand the legacy of colonialism in my own country.

I began the research that led to this book after ten years of involvement in Native issues. One day I was visiting an aboriginal friend's house just outside of Toronto. We had been working together to organize "Beyond Survival: The Waking Dreamer Ends the Silence," an international conference of indigenous writers, artists, and performers to celebrate the International Year of Indigenous Peoples in 1993. She took me for a walk in the woods behind her home, where we passed a sweat lodge that she and her partner had constructed. I was interested in aboriginal spirituality, and remarked that I would like to take part in a sweat with her one day. Immediately our rapport vanished. She turned on me: "Our spirituality is all we have left! Will you take even that?" As we argued, as I felt myself being blamed for the whole history of colonization, I found myself saying hotly, "I didn't ask to be born here!" Which got me really wondering how I *did* get here, who my ancestors were, and how they got me into this mess – you could say it led me to investigate the origins of my citizenship.

Many aboriginal people I knew had an acute sense of the living presence of their ancestors in their lives; I certainly didn't feel the same reverence for my forebears. On the one hand I felt uncomfortable that my ancestors had ended up with someone else's land, though I knew nothing about them or what they had actually done. On the other hand, I was fairly certain that, like most of my extended family today, my ancestors were essentially decent and well-intentioned people. I assumed that it was other people's ancestors who had done the dirty work, not mine; as far as I knew, my people had come to the New World later, in the nineteenth century, and had simply inherited the aftermath of an already accomplished dispossession.

At the same time, I began to notice that many people I knew who were of English, Irish, or Scottish descent like me talked as if they had no connection to their own history. It seemed that most of us were ignorant about how and why our families had ended up on this continent. We knew nothing of our ancestors' struggles overseas (for example, the Highland clearances), although such experiences certainly shaped our forebears and made us who we are today. I was struck by the amnesia of each generation: our family memories often went back only as far our grandparents. They marked the vanishing point of remembered ancestry for most of us – our great-grandparents fell off the edge of the world. In my own case, a few earlier incidents floated in the family memory like isolated bits of flotsam: the Freemans leaving Ireland during the potato famine, the female ancestor who had been an early schoolteacher in Ontario and had ridden a great distance through the wilderness on horseback for some reason, and so on. I have come to realize how much immigrants lose of their family memory because it is tied to physical places – to houses, farms, towns, landmarks, battlefields, and graves. In the case of my ancestors, some families had passed through two other countries before they arrived here; the Freemans, for example, appear to have come from England to Ireland in the 1600s, and then to Canada two hundred years after that.

I began to think about the things we choose to honour, the things we choose to forget, the things we resurrect and re-interpret. "In their sense of identity every people moulds a vessel into which they pour from generation to generation the meanings of their historical experience," anthropologist Edward Spicer once said. This is certainly true for families, even if, in most Western societies, their conscious memories are short. The psychic history of each family is embedded in both what is said and what is left unsaid; what is not talked about, repeated, or passed down can be as important, even more important, than what we are conscious of.[1] There is the silence of those who cannot speak or to whom no one would or even could listen, and the silence of those who choose to remain silent so as not to incriminate themselves. There is also the silence born of the fear of revisiting pain or stirring up anger – our own or that of others.

In the case of the colonization of North America, two kinds of memory, or rather non-memory – that of the family and that of the state – reinforce one other in suppressing our knowledge of our history with aboriginal people. But I believe that this history lives on in us, often unconsciously. Historian Richard Drinnon speaks of the necessity of exploring this "subliminal mind."[2]

There is an Ahnishinahbaeó'jibway[3] writer named Wub-e-ke-niew, who says the Western attitude to history is part of a whole complex of ideas that oppresses others, that our sense of time is basically warped: "In Western European linear time, the past vanishes into obscurity, perceived as dimensionless and infinitely small at the vanishing point of linear perspective." It is the dead past, he says, for most "westerners," who define so much of their experience in terms of evolving technology and the ideology of progress. Life even two hundred years ago, if it's thought of at all, is considered practically prehistoric. We have become detached from our continuity in time, and thus seemingly insulated from our history; we live "encapsulated in a present reality which has been severed at its roots." Time is money, so we focus on this perpetual present, and therefore steal from the future. We do not talk about the past because we wish to escape it. Furthermore, he says, we have created "Indians" as a buffer between ourselves and the true history we share with aboriginal people.[4]

For the indigenous peoples of this continent, on the other hand, memory has been absolutely essential as a means of cultural survival. Their conception of time as a circle offers the hope of justice, "for the circle always comes around and the past is never gone." In Wub-e-ke-niew's view, North American people of European descent cannot escape the consequences of their past, however hard they try, because that past is inextricably part of their present.

Wub-e-ke-niew also contrasts the Euro-American and the traditional aboriginal ways of passing on historical knowledge. Of Euro-Americans he observes that they "are so uninterested in the past they have been convinced by the media that the young know more than their elders. The elderly and the young are polarized and communication across time has been broken for all but the artificial aristocracy who define history as only their own."[5] Certainly the history I learned as a child and young adult focussed on major political figures or generalities about working conditions and the rise of the middle class. I had no connection to this history. I didn't know what various events meant to my progenitors or what their role in those events might have been, and my knowledge of myself was diminished as a result. For most of us in the Western tradition, history appears to be not of our making. Hence, we have no responsibility for it.

It was for this reason that I became interested in family history. I wanted to establish my own personal connection to the history of colonialism on this continent, to explore the role of my ancestors in this process. A comment in Carl Jung's *Memories, Dreams, Reflections* jumped out at me. He wrote: "I feel very strongly that I am under the influence of things or questions which were left incomplete and unanswered by my parents and grandparents and more distant ancestors."[6] I believe our family sagas can be as valid a history as any other kind, and can address some of these long unanswered questions.

This, then, was the context for beginning my research. When I started this book, the only ancestors I knew about were Mercy Jelly (only her name, which I'd seen in a letter my aunt had written my parents many years earlier) and my grandfather, though I didn't know the latter had been associated with a residential school. I was fortunate in that one of my father's sisters had been quietly researching my paternal family's history for twenty years, and she had established several lines of descent that went back to the 1600s and even beyond. From her, I learned that some of my grandmother's ancestors had been on this continent since the early seventeenth century. I began to do research of my own, building on hers, focussing particularly on contacts between my family and aboriginal people. I wanted to understand the attitudes, events, and choices that were part of colonization, to investigate my inheritance in all its complexity. The result of that exploration is this book.

To look back in time and find out about your ancestors means starting from a single person – yourself – and working back through two parents to four grandparents, to eight great-great-grandparents, to an ever-expanding cohort of ancestors in each generation. If I count myself as the first generation, I've traced some branches of my family back fourteen generations, which means I have 8,192 ancestors from that generation – if none of them married any other ancestors of mine. Obviously, I can never really "know" my ancestry, or attribute particular "family" characteristics of the last couple of generations to the handful of sixteenth- or seventeenth-century ancestors whom I can identify, though I must admit, it is fun to try. But if I am trying to understand my relationship to the colonization of this continent, I can at least see that some of my ancestors were in the thick of the processes of dispossession and "deculturation," that I am tied indelibly to that history. And much of what I've discovered applies not just to the individuals I've written about but to many other people of the same generation and time. In that sense, specific ancestors can be emblematic. Also, as each of the first generation of settlers in New England has a huge number of descendants now – well over a million, I believe – a significant number of people alive today on the North American continent share that history. I've tried to illuminate the lives of a few of these thousands of ancestors, tried to trace the criss-crossing paths of their descendants, used their lives to weave together a personal approach to a history that is common to many, many people.

I started with the earliest ancestors I knew about, particularly those who left the British Isles and came to North America. I began with some family names and the places and dates of their births, deaths, and, in some cases, marriages. Early on I decided that I would not just research direct ancestors but also their brothers and sisters and their spouses, so that I would have a sense of the familial culture. I learned about their pastors and community leaders. Then I searched published genealogies and local, regional, and national history books for their names. As I became more familiar with the sources for their times and places, I delved into original records – wills, town records, colonial records of various kinds, the archives of various religious denominations, ships' passenger lists, diaries, letters, registrations of land sales, treaties with various indigenous nations. I was astonished at how much I could find – the Puritans, for example, were meticulous record-keepers, and a wealth of information has survived. Also, it turned out that some of my ancestors and their close relations had been prominent members of their societies, and so were mentioned in history books.

It has been a much greater struggle to find out about the indigenous peoples in the areas where these immigrant ancestors "settled," and to try to find links between the two histories, partly because of the nature of the sources for this history and partly because of my position as a non-Native writer. The indigenous nations in question did not leave voluminous written records of their own actions in previous centuries, though they did record things in other ways, such as through stories, wampum belts, or pictographs.

I knew before I started that history is written by the conquerors, but I was still surprised by the degree of apartheid in many written histories of the period I was researching. Most local histories and genealogies that I consulted made virtually no mention of the indigenous people, except when a white person or ancestor was scalped or killed by them, even though there was usually considerable contact during the first century of European settlement. The town histories generally dispensed with the local Native nations in a paragraph in the first chapter, or implied by their silence that the land had been empty when their towns were founded. These omissions served an obvious purpose: to disguise the uncomfortable fact that the land was already occupied and to minimize the role of the settlers in displacing the indigenous population. So my first task was to try to bring my ancestors and aboriginal people into the same narrative universe.[7]

I did find more information about indigenous people in court records, records of colonial administrations, and in letters and diaries, though, of course, the facts always come "dressed," to use historian James Axtell's word, and all these sources reflect English perspectives on Native actions and motivations. I have done my best to sift through the very evident bias – though, as a non-Native myself, this isn't easy. Sometimes I found direct speech and letters by aboriginal leaders embedded in these sources, and I also came across biographical information. I also discovered Puritan accounts of various wars with the indigenous inhabitants, which were often quite revealing as rationalizations of conquest and dispossession.[8]

Only in the last thirty years have historians such as Francis Jennings and James Axtell begun to write "ethnohistory," which focusses on the interactions between cultures and attempts to understand events from both perspectives. Ethnohistory has its flaws, the greatest being that it is still written mostly by white people. Despite this fact, it's the most useful written historical approach I've encountered.

I have done my best to work from aboriginal sources wherever possible. Unfortunately, Native oral history has not been a major source of information for me. Although much historical information is preserved orally, what is passed on is what is most significant to the people of a particular family or nation, and that does not tend to include the interactions of specific ancestors of theirs with specific ancestors of mine – though in one incredible instance, I was able to corroborate a story of just such a seventeenth-century interaction through a ninety-six-year-old Mohegan elder in Connecticut.[9] This was the story of my ancestor Samuel Rogers and the Mohegan sachem Uncas, told in Chapter 9.

In general, though, I have been unable to spend sufficient time in distant Native communities gradually gaining the trust of elders and learning their languages. To begin with, I'd have to build such a relationship with at least fourteen indigenous nations in Canada and the United States. To complicate matters, some of these nations, such as the Pawtucket, were dispersed and absorbed into other groups long ago and may no longer have an oral history or identity to pass down.

What I have done instead is draw on the expertise of Native and tribal historians wherever possible, though even this has not been easy, because many such people wear several hats and are stretched to the limit. A tribal historian in Connecticut, for example, did not have time to spend with me, because she was extremely busy helping her tribe build a casino to a tight deadline. Luckily, she was able to direct me to her book, and I did find some of what I needed there, as I have in other material written by Native authors. I also sought out aboriginal perspectives from a number of Native writers and friends, who read over and commented on my manuscript. While they may not have had historical knowledge specific to my research, their perspectives, reactions, and questions have been invaluable to me. However, I am still painfully aware of how easy it is to unknowingly perpetuate old stereotypes and misinformation; I think of a comment by Native educator Verna Kirkness: "Every time I hear a white person talking about Indians, I get knots in my stomach."[10]

I was able to interview some Native people about events in the recent past, such as my grandfather's involvement with Cecilia Jeffrey Indian Residential School near Kenora, Ontario. This was useful to me not just for learning historical details but for reminding me of why I was writing this book in the first place. Given my loving memories of my grandfather, it was not easy to conduct these interviews, nor was it easy for my aboriginal informants, who had painful memories or associations with this school and were sometimes suspicious of white writers. Occasionally I had difficulties because of my limited understanding of aboriginal protocol. I had to think hard about why I wanted information, what I would do with it, and what I could give back. Fortunately, I had copies of my grandparents' family photographs to offer people, for sometimes these offered fresh glimpses of life at Shoal Lake during the 1920s to people who had little photographic or written record of it.

As is probably obvious by now, I'm not an academic, a historian, or a theoretician. I have been exploring history at an intensely personal level. It's only after seven years of research and writing that I feel confident that I know enough to tell a credible story. My range of research has been extremely broad – I've had to try to assimilate the histories of three countries, five states, two provinces, several English counties, and fourteen indigenous nations, covering a period of almost five hundred years. I have not always been able to work from original documents and have had to depend on a number of secondary sources. I've tried to be a meticulous fact-checker and I've had my work reviewed by historians whenever possible, but the responsibility for any errors of fact or interpretation is mine alone.

Everything in the following pages is true to the best of my knowledge. I have made nothing up. But one of the interesting things about attempting to write a historical narrative is that you become very conscious that the past has no definitive shape, and no past event has a fixed meaning. To a certain extent, a historian selects the details he or she finds significant and constructs a plot from them; at the same time, as American historian Calvin Martin has said, stories impose themselves on the teller as much as the other way around. The concept of objective truth in history is extremely problematic, since none of us are omniscient or detached from our narratives. Because the remains of the past are so fragmentary and flawed, and all events are placed into constructs of meaning or interpretations that are subjective and to various degrees unprovable, all history is to some extent conjectural. Furthermore, every time we attempt to write or tell history, the meaning changes, much like a house is redone repeatedly to fit different people's needs at different times. As another historian, Robert F. Berkhofer, Jr., has noted, there is always an ambiguity in the English word "history" that falsely implies that the past and the way we look at it are the same.[11]

I've come to realize that my history is different from your history, which is different from another person's history. I like a phrase of writer John Updike: "billions of consciousnesses silt history full, and every one of them the centre of the universe."[12] In my case, I could find information only about some ancestors, and this dictated the shape of my book. All the ancestors I write about, with the exception of my paternal grandfather, are ancestors of my great-grandmother Lydia Asenath Harris, because hers are the only ones I can trace back to the seventeenth century and beyond – her line forms the backbone linking the various episodes of this story. There are many other stories I have not told, such as the history of my mother's Scottish ancestors. Rather than attempt to recount a strictly chronological narrative, I have organized the book family by family, telling stories that concentrate on only a few individuals in each family. There are also significant events, such as the American Revolution, which do not loom as large as they might in other histories because I do not have very much information about how my ancestors and Native people interacted during that period.

My point is that, although I haven't made up anything and I can document all the details, *Distant Relations*, like all written history, is not an accurate representation of the totality of the past. I have selected details, created narratives from a welter of events, and tried to breathe life into people long dead who are now really just ciphers with names. I have tried to conjure up a world that no longer exists and which we in the present can never fully know. "The past is a foreign country," L. P. Hartley wrote; written history, for all its footnotes, is a relative of speculative or science fiction. But it has been my aim in writing this book to be true to George Steiner's definition of history as "exact imagining."[13]

It is a weighty thing to sit in judgement upon one's ancestors, the very people who begat you. It is all too easy to simply condemn them or laugh at their ignorance, as our own descendants may do to us. I did not want to be like an adolescent who suddenly discovers all his parents' faults and contemptuously disowns them, without recognizing either what they have given him or acknowledging how much he is like them. I have wondered how one could honour one's ancestors and at the same time explore their role in colonizing this continent, recognizing their faults, both personal and cultural, and acknowledging the impacts of their actions on the original people of this land. I have tried to see them both as they saw themselves, to the best of my ability, and from this present perspective, as an outsider, seeing them as they could not see themselves. I have tried to view their lives with love, respect, and honest scrutiny.

M A P S

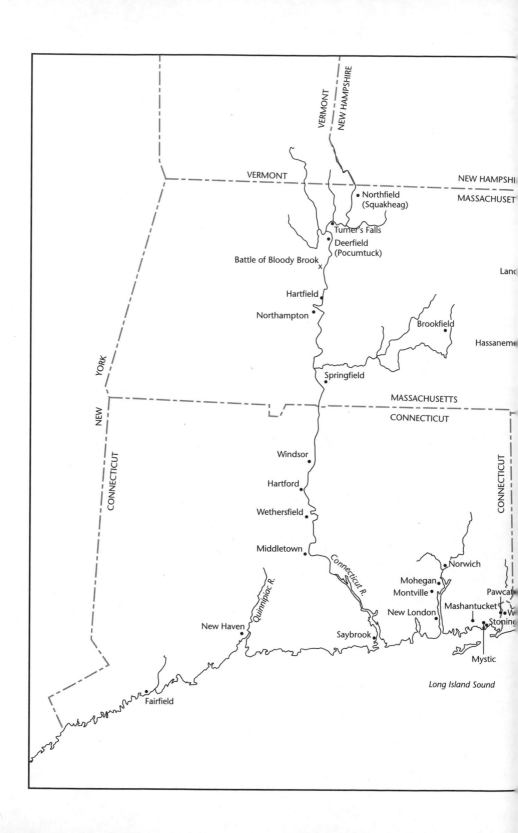

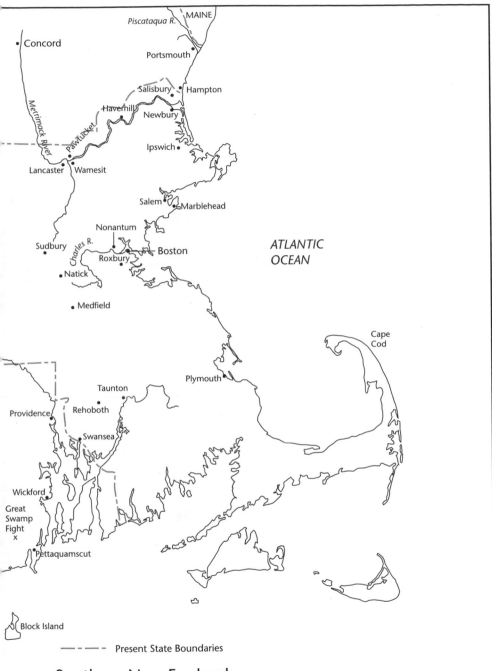

MAINE

Piscataqua R.

• Concord

Portsmouth

Salisbury • Hampton

Haverhill
Newbury

Merrimack River

Pawtucket

Ipswich •

Lancaster) Wamesit

Salem • Marblehead

Nonantum

Sudbury • *Charles R.*

Roxbury • Boston

• Natick

**ATLANTIC
OCEAN**

• Medfield

Cape
Cod

Plymouth •

Taunton •

Providence • Rehoboth

• Swansea

Wickford •

Great
Swamp
Fight
x

• Pettaquamscut

)(Block Island

— — — Present State Boundaries

Southern New England
c. 1676

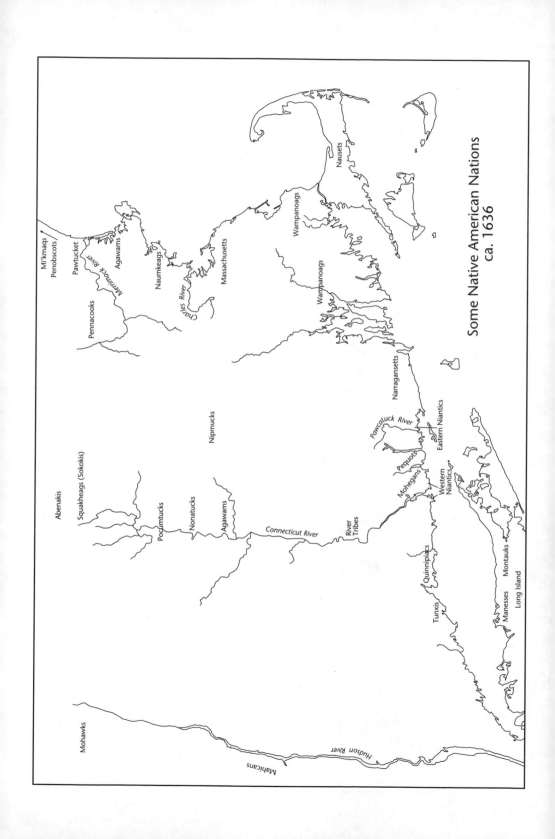

Some Native American Nations
ca. 1636

Mohawks

Mahicans

Hudson River

Abenakis

Squakheags (Sokokis)

Pocumtucks

Nonatucks

Agawams

Connecticut River

Tunxis

Quinnipiacs

River Tribes

Western Niantics

Mohegans

Pequots

Eastern Niantics

Powcatuck River

Narragansetts

Nipmucks

Manesses

Montauks

Long Island

Mi'kmaqs
Penobscots

Pawtucket

Agawams

Merrimack River

Pennacooks

Naumkeags

Charles River

Massachusetts

Wampanoags

Wampanoags

Nausets

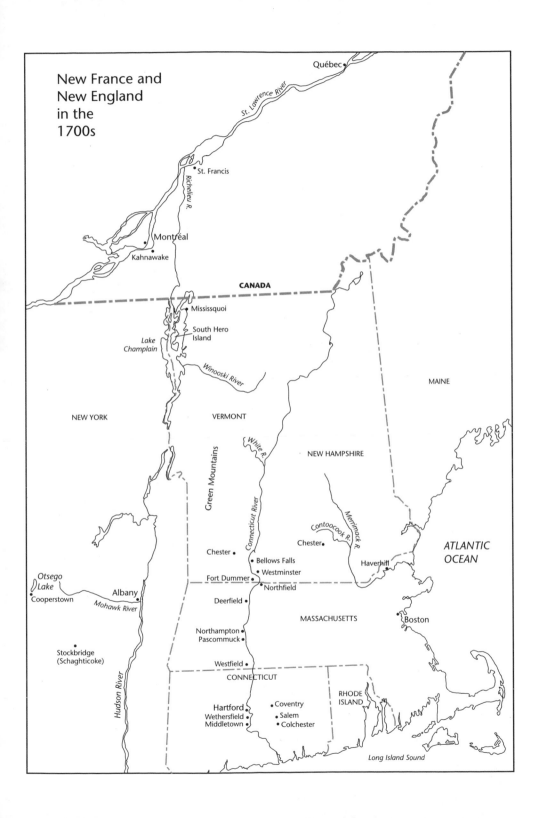

New France and
New England
in the
1700s

Québec

St. Lawrence River

St. Francis

Richelieu R.

Montréal

Kahnawake

CANADA

Mississquoi

South Hero
Island

Lake
Champlain

Winooski River

MAINE

NEW YORK

VERMONT

NEW HAMPSHIRE

Green Mountains

White R.

Contoocook R.

Merrimack R.

Chester

Chester

ATLANTIC
OCEAN

Bellows Falls

Westminster

Haverhill

Fort Dummer

Northfield

Otsego
Lake

Cooperstown

Albany

Mohawk River

Deerfield

MASSACHUSETTS

Boston

Northampton
Pascommuck

Stockbridge
(Schaghticoke)

Westfield

CONNECTICUT

RHODE
ISLAND

Hudson River

Hartford

Wethersfield

Middletown

Coventry

Salem

Colchester

Long Island Sound

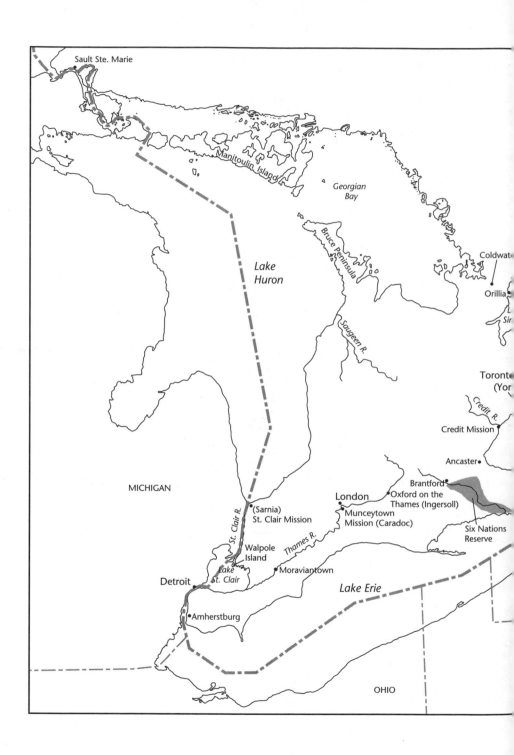

Sault Ste. Marie

Manitoulin Island

Georgian
Bay

Coldwat

Bruce Peninsula

Orillia

Lake
Huron

L
Sir

Saugeen R.

Toront
(Yor

Credit R.

Credit Mission

Ancaster

MICHIGAN

Brantford

London

Oxford on the
Thames (Ingersoll)

(Sarnia)
St. Clair Mission

St. Clair R.

Munceytown
Mission (Caradoc)

Six Nations
Reserve

Walpole
Island

Thames R.

Lake
St. Clair

Moraviantown

Detroit

Lake Erie

Amherstburg

OHIO

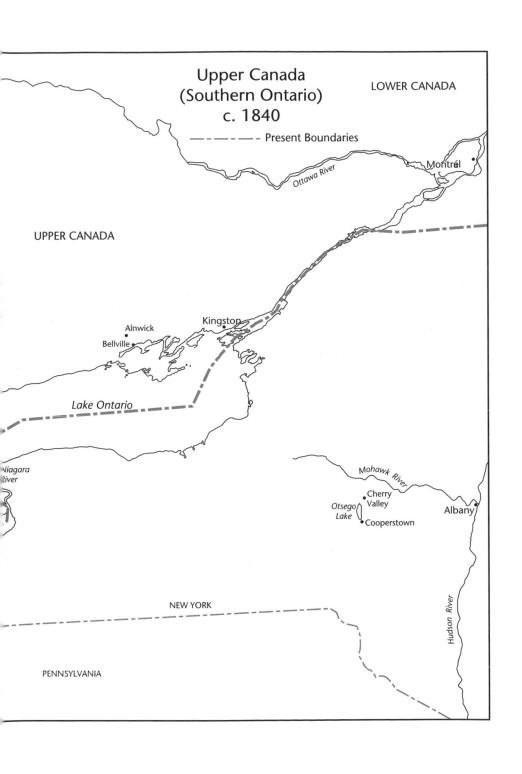

Upper Canada
(Southern Ontario)
c. 1840

— · — · — Present Boundaries

LOWER CANADA

UPPER CANADA

Ottawa River

Montrál

Kingston

Alnwick

Bellville

Lake Ontario

Niagara
River

Mohawk River

Cherry
Valley

Otsego
Lake

Cooperstown

Albany

Hudson River

NEW YORK

PENNSYLVANIA

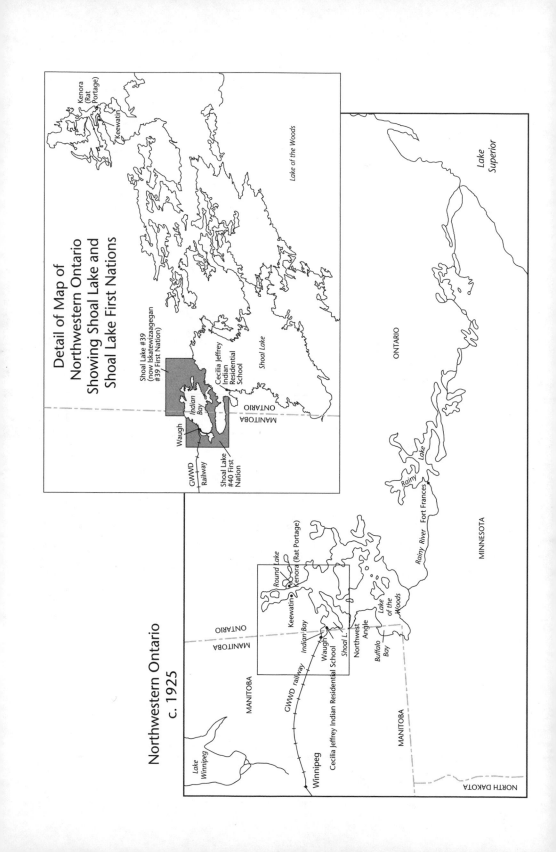

Detail of Map of
Northwestern Ontario
Showing Shoal Lake and
Shoal Lake First Nations

Kenora (Rat Portage)

Keewatin

Lake of the Woods

Shoal Lake #39
(now Iskatewizaagegan
#39 First Nation)

Cecilia Jeffrey
Indian
Residential
School

Shoal Lake

Indian
Bay

Waugh

GWWD
Railway

Shoal Lake
#40 First
Nation

MANITOBA
ONTARIO

Lake
Superior

ONTARIO

Rainy
Lake

Rainy River Fort Frances

MINNESOTA

Northwestern Ontario
c. 1925

Round Lake

Kenora (Rat Portage)

Keewatin

Indian Bay

Waugh

Shoal L.

GWWD railway

Cecilia Jeffrey Indian Residential School

Northwest
Angle

Lake
of the
Woods

Buffalo
Bay

Lake
Winnipeg

MANITOBA

MANITOBA
ONTARIO

MANITOBA

NORTH DAKOTA

Winnipeg

PART I

FIRST RELATIONS

THE WHEELER FAMILY

Ten Generations
of the Wheeler Family

    I. **Mercy Jelly** (1569–?)   married   **Dominick Wheeler** (156?–1616)

   II. **John Wheeler** (1591–1670)   m.   **Agnes Yeoman** (1592?–1662)

  III. **Ann Wheeler** (1620–1687)   m.   **Aquila Chase** (1618–1670)

  IV. Ensign Moses Chase (1663–1743) m.   Anne Vollonsbee (1668–1708)

   V. Moses Chase (1687–1760)   m.   Elizabeth Wells (1688–1755)

  VI. Deacon Seth Chase (1715–1791) m.   Elizabeth Bartlett (1714–1787)

 VII. Bradford Chase (1741–1783)   m.   Abigail Sibley (1745–1824)

VIII. Samuel Chase (1778–?)   m.   Mercy Wilmarth (1783–?)

  IX. Lydia Chase (1800–1900)   m.   Hiram Ranney (1792–1871)

   X. Julia Ranney (1824–1880)   m.   James Harris (1824–1885)

For subsequent generations, see the Harris genealogy in the Harris Family section.

CHAPTER
I
⎯

Home

He was, perhaps, an ordinary, completely undistinguished man, a barber in the English city of Salisbury, who left home for America in 1634. I imagine him as neither good-looking nor ugly, neither tall nor short, neither dominating nor weak – a pleasant enough, reasonably honest fellow who didn't like to stick his neck out or stand out from the crowd. Perhaps he was sober, hard-working, and cautious, a bit guarded in his opinions. His name was John Wheeler, and he was born in 1591 – that much, at least, is fact.

His parents, Mercy Jelly and Dominick Wheeler, were married three years before his birth, on June 3, 1588.[1] That was the summer of the Spanish Armada, when they and all the rest of the population of England lived in terror of being invaded and conquered by their most dreaded enemy. When the Spanish ships were prevented from crossing the English Channel, then blown off course and ruined off the coast of Ireland, the entire English nation rejoiced; national pride and self-confidence soared. One senses that many English men and women then enjoyed their nation's ruthless competition with Spain in religion, exploration, and piracy.

To Mercy and Dominick and their countrymen, the threat of invasion had long been a fact of life; for about one-fifth of its recorded history, England has been a conquered country. The tiny island has absorbed wave after wave

5

of invaders, from the Romans, Angles, Jutes, and Saxons to the Vikings and
the Normans, and some of these invaders were also my ancestors. I try to
remember this as I contemplate the lives of Mercy Jelly, who never left
England, and of her son, who was one of those who invaded America.

Mercy Jelly was my great-great-great-great-great-great-great-great-
great-great-great-grandmother – and one of the earliest ancestors I can
verify. For a long time, her name was all I knew about her, an amusing
curiosity of Puritan times, along with Preserved Fish, Friendly Chase,
Silence Burns, Thanks Lord, Rejoice Long, and Wanton Bump. Yet she is
an anchor in my family's history, from a time when my foremothers and
forefathers were rooted in a place where they had lived for countless generations, before they came to live in someone else's land.

What was this world like that Mercy Jelly lived in, and that her son John
Wheeler left behind? In our mythology it was "Merrie England," a legendary time that we descendants look back to with ethnic pride. In 1588,
the year that Mercy and Dominick married, William Shakespeare turned
twenty-four. It was four years before his first play was performed, eight
years after Sir Francis Drake successfully sailed around the world, four
years since the English first attempted to establish a colony in North
America. From an English perspective, the world was opening up, and
their nation was becoming a great power. The English were now an adven-
turous people, exploring the Far East, Russia, Persia, India, and the Arctic,
though "exploring" is a rather sanitized word for what actually happened
on these expeditions, often to the lasting detriment of the indigenous populations of these "new found landes." For colonization, wars of conquest,
and the exploitation of indigenous peoples and their resources were an
integral part of the flowering of Elizabethan England, as well as of the
other nations of Europe.

That year was the thirtieth of Elizabeth I's reign and fifty-four years
since her father, Henry VIII, had made his tumultuous break with the
Catholic Church; in the eyes of the Pope, now referred to as the Bishop
of Rome, Elizabeth herself was a usurper and a bastard. The English
might have endured religious revolutions, but the sun still moved around
the earth, which was the centre of the universe, and God was undoubtedly
an Englishman.

Mercy Jelly was born about 1569; her husband, Dominick, sometime
between 1565 and 1568. It appears they both grew up in the parish of St.
Edmund's, one of the poorer parishes in Salisbury. The parish registry is

tantalizing. Was the Elizabeth Wheeler who married Thomas Mylls in 1560 Dominick's aunt? Was Francis Wheeler, who married Margery Owens in 1564, his father? (It appears so.) Was William Jellye, who married Enid Atkins in 1565, the father of Mercy?

Like charity, mercy is a Christian virtue. After the Reformation it became a popular name for girls, as saints' names were no longer in vogue among Protestants. Here is an old definition of "mercy" that vividly expresses the world view of her time. *Mercy: God's pitiful forbearance towards his creatures and forgiveness of their offenses.*[2]

The name Dominick derives from Latin, meaning "belonging to the Lord" or "born on Sunday." His last name originally referred to a wheelwright, but there is no record of Dominick's profession. He might have been a grocer, a weaver, a locksmith, a blacksmith, a tailor, a saddler, a hosier, a cobbler, a baker, a haberdasher, a glazier, or a butcher, to name a few possibilities. Most likely he was either a barber, as was his eldest son, John, or a shearer. The latter is suggested by the first sentence of his will, which reads: "Domny Wheller of the Cittye of newe Sarum [Salisbury] in the County of Wiltes, Sherma, . . ."[3] The otherwise incomprehensible word "sherma" may be an abbreviated form of "shear man," apparently the man who cut cloth for a tailor. As city dwellers, Dominick and Mercy would have been less intimately connected to the land than their farming ancestors must have been, though at harvest time, however, Dominick at least would have gone out to the surrounding countryside to help bring in the crops.

New Sarum, as Salisbury was then known, stood at the confluence of the East Avon, Bourne, and Nadder rivers, about three days west of London by carriage. By the time John Wheeler was born, its population numbered about seven thousand people and it was known above all for its wool and woollen cloth trade. Old Sarum, one and a half miles to the north, had been an early Iron Age fort taken over by the Romans, which later became an important Saxon town. Old Sarum later became a bishopric; when the cathedral was built in the valley in 1220, the new town grew up around it. As a cathedral town, New Sarum was also the site of the ecclesiastical courts for the region. The cathedral had the tallest spires in England.[4]

The city centre was in a gridiron pattern and was surrounded by an earthen rampart and gates built in the fourteenth century. Celia Fiennes, a young gentlewoman who visited New Sarum in 1682, left this description of the town:

The houses are old mostly timber buildings there is a large Market
House with the Town Hall over it and a prison just by, there is also a large
Cross in another place and house over it for a constant Market for fruite,
fowle, butter and cheese and a fish Market. . . . pretty large town streetes
broad but through the midst of them runs a little rivulet of water which
makes the streetes not so clean or so easye to passe in, they have stepp's
to cross it and many open places for horses and carriages to cross itt. . . .[5]

Nine and a half miles to the north, on treeless Salisbury Plain, one
could contemplate the mysterious stone circles of Stonehenge. Elsewhere
on the plain rose many rounded barrows, or burial mounds, from neo-
lithic times, silent evidence of a past so remote that all memory of it had
been obliterated.

Mercy was nineteen and Dominick twenty or so when they married.
Husbands and wives should be "two sweet friends," some Puritans said,
emphasizing partnership and the role of the wife in the moral and spiritual
education of children, but love was not considered a necessary prerequisite of sixteenth-century marriages; in fact, it was somewhat suspect to
Puritans, unless it served spiritual ends. Mercy and Dominick's parents
may have arranged their marriage and it likely involved the payment of a
dowry, though some young people, especially those who left their families
to work as domestic or farm servants for a time, were free to choose their
own partners.

Dominick was the head of the household. As his wife, Mercy had been
legally consigned to his custody. Did Dominick beat her? It was certainly
within his rights. Did he drink too much or was he a temperate man?
Everybody drank ale then, even for breakfast; the church made it and sold
it to raise money.

For that matter, was Mercy a scold? Did she live in fear of being called
that? In her day, uppity, argumentative women could be plunked into a
nearby pond in a ducking stool. And women (particularly older, single
women or widows) had to be careful, for they could also be accused of
witchcraft, as were some men. It was during the lifetimes of Mercy and her
children that such accusations – and the horrible tortures that accompanied
them – were at their height.

John Wheeler was not their first child – another son named John had been
born six months after their wedding, but soon died. Other children followed

over the years, from four to fourteen, according to various records, some of which are obviously inaccurate and probably confuse cousins with siblings. The fate of most of these presumed children is unknown. Several may have died in infancy. This was not unusual: it has been estimated that, before 1750, only 25 per cent of the children born in London survived to the age of ten, and their survival rate would have been little better in Salisbury. (Pity Queen Anne a century later: of eighteen children, none lived past adolescence.) In cities such as Salisbury, some mothers were unwilling to breastfeed their babies, since breastfeeding was considered vulgar and it interfered with the mother's work. John Wheeler may have been sent to a wet nurse in the country until he was weaned, a practice that was not always conducive to adequate nourishment, since, to make ends meet, many wet nurses took on too many charges.

Many infants died as a result of the general unhealthiness of English urban life: if a North American aboriginal had visited sixteenth-century Salisbury, he or she would have been horrified by the filth and pollution as well as by the lack of personal hygiene. Indeed, the search for perfumes from the Orient that triggered the Age of Exploration was motivated by the need to disguise the stench of unwashed bodies. Cholera, typhus, smallpox, plague, and dysentery – diseases unknown in the New World, which flourished in crowded, unsanitary conditions – killed many, and the average English diet was less balanced and varied than that enjoyed in America.

In the 1590s, when John Wheeler was a small child, there were several years of poor harvests, and many families in Salisbury went hungry as food prices soared. Malnutrition and disease stalked the poorer areas like the Wheelers' parish of St. Edmund's, where 230 people were buried in 1597, twice the usual number, and baptisms fell precipitously. Desperate, the poor petitioned the bishop for relief, and the city corporation had to enlist help from the queen's Privy Council in London to release imported grain retained in Southampton that was supposed to be on its way to Salisbury. Laws were passed to limit the malting of precious grain for ale in favour of bread production. The famine in the surrounding countryside produced a huge influx of landless "vagabonds," and the town took strong action to get rid of them. In 1598, 96 of these wanderers were literally whipped out of town, 49 of them single women. But the problem persisted: between 1598 and 1638, more than 600 vagrants were whipped out of Salisbury. Many of them were young single men and women from the northern wood-pasture

districts of Wiltshire and adjacent counties who were fleeing covenanted
service or were unemployed craftsmen.

A more serious and direct threat to the Wheeler family than economic
hardship was disease. The bubonic plague had struck earlier, in 1579, when
Mercy was about ten years old, but in 1604, when she was thirty-five and
young John thirteen, it killed about a sixth of the total population of the
town. It had killed 30,000 in London the previous year. The epidemic was
concentrated in the poorer areas of town, such as St. Edmund's parish,
though, as far as I can tell, none of the Wheeler's immediate family were
victims. It is likely, however, that many of their friends and relatives died
horrible deaths or were quarantined for weeks at a time. Did the family flee
the city until the contagion subsided? Or did they live in terror while hundreds died around them?

To prevent too much heartbreak when so many children died, or because
familial affection was considered too worldly, Mercy and Dominick may
have believed that it was harmful to show too much affection for their children. As John grew, they may have beaten him frequently, as they had
likely been beaten by their parents. Some historians assert this was the
normal practice all over Europe at the time – it was certainly a practice far
more prevalent in Europe than in Native America. Most young people
between the ages of fifteen and twenty-four – and some as young as seven
– did not live at home but worked as domestic or farm servants in other
households. In some cases they were sent to work for other families to discourage too close a bond with their own, though generally their work was
not onerous and it was considered part of their education. Puritans were
reportedly harsher than other parents: in theory, they believed children
were born in a "fallen" state, riddled with sin and corruption that had to be
beaten out of them for the good of their souls. If John Wheeler was privileged enough to attend one of the two grammar schools in Salisbury or one
of the small private schools, he was likely beaten there, too. At the same
time he would have learned to read and write, as did many sons, and even
a few daughters, of the emerging middle class. Certainly, if living at home,
he would have joined his family in prayers twice a day, and he may have
assisted with the frequent reading of scripture.

The state of the family's finances during John Wheeler's childhood is
also a matter of conjecture. During the plague of 1604, one-fifth of the
entire population of Salisbury had received some sort of minimal relief
during the epidemic, particularly those in quarantine. This financial drain,

as well as the disruption of trade and the widespread unemployment that resulted from the plague and the flight of the wealthier classes to the countryside, devastated the city economically. Contrary to the hopes of the population, conditions did not improve after the plague, for Salisbury's principal industry, the cloth trade, faced its own crisis, a situation that could have affected Dominick drastically if he wase indeed a shearer. Changes in the markets for cloth abroad had profound repercussions in England, where textiles accounted for 75 per cent of exports. When the Thirty Years' War in Europe cut off many continental markets for cloth after 1618, the situation only worsened, and Wiltshire was particularly hard hit. There were so many impoverished cloth workers and weavers in Salisbury that the town petitioned the lord lieutenant for help.

Salisbury's social upheaval was also part of larger social and economic processes. England's economy was changing with the advent of the "first industrial revolution": the national output of coal increased tenfold, and production of salt, iron, steel, lead, ships, and glass superseded many traditional economic activities. At the same time the weakening of the feudal system left thousands of people masterless, no longer attached by custom and economics to noble families who were responsible for them, and many became destitute, especially since common land was being enclosed and was therefore no longer available for communal grazing by livestock. The magnitude of the changes left many people struggling not only economically but also with a loss of identity and self-worth. Again, an aboriginal visitor from across the Atlantic would have been shocked by the great disparities between rich and poor and the hierarchical land-ownership system that gave huge estates to some and left many others landless. Puritanism, which was to play such a crucial role in the history of my family, was at least in part a response to the social chaos that resulted from these conditions.

Perhaps because of the decline of the wool trade, John Wheeler did not follow in his father's footsteps, but instead became a barber. Until 1605, a barber was a "barber-surgeon" but, by the time John Wheeler was practicing, barbers were restricted from practicing surgery except for bleeding (with leeches) and the pulling of teeth. I like to imagine him as a good and conscientious barber, careful with his razor and considerate of his patients when he extracted molars without anaesthetic.

In 1611, when he was twenty and presumably well-established, John Wheeler married Agnes Yeoman and began his own family. His father died five years later, and in his will made special provision for John Wheeler's eldest sons:

> Domny Wheller of the Cittye of newe Sarum [Salisbury] in the County of Wiltes, Sherma, being in the p'vidence of god stricken Sicke of body but of perfect and good memory thanks be unto god, I do by this my laste will and testament, give unto my wife Mercy Wheller all and singular, my goods and cattell [chattel] . . . during her naturall life and after her life ther Endinge that these things come unto John Wheller the eldeste sonne of the aforesaid Domny Wheller. I will also give unto my sone John Wheller a littel Clock and a plater. I will give unto Edward Wheller, my son John Wheller's eldest sone, one silver spone and to his brother, John Wheller, one pottinger.[6]

The details of the will suggest that the Wheelers were of the middling, rather than the poorest, classes, or else they should never have had such things as clocks and silver spoons to pass on. As such, they were part of that growing and increasingly prosperous class of shopkeepers and small businessmen that was most attracted to Puritanism, with its emphasis on strict moral discipline, hard work, thrift, and the responsibility of the individual for the state of his or her soul.[7]

Puritanism's roots in Wiltshire date back to the Lollards of the fourteenth and fifteenth centuries. Followers of the religious reformer, John Wycliffe, the Lollards attacked the Church for practices such as clerical celibacy, indulgences, and pilgrimages, and criticized the doctrine of transubstantiation. Believing that the Bible was the sole authority in religion, they asserted that every man had a right to read the Book for himself. Growing literacy and the translation of the Bible into English, first by Wycliffe in the fourteenth century, then in 1526 by William Tyndale, inspired increasing numbers of Englishmen to compare what they read with the practices of the Church. Many of the newly literate agreed that the doctrine and rituals of the existing churches deviated greatly from Scripture; what we now call the Reformation was an attempt by these reformers to bring the Church back into line with the Bible.

Once the Reformation was under way, the new emphasis on Scripture set off a series of ongoing theological and political struggles between various strains of the new Protestant Christianity, which differed over the degree to which the Roman Church needed to be reformed. In Salisbury, and indeed all over England, the struggle raged in virtually every church between traditionalists and reformers. The traditionalists, later known as Anglicans, believed that the moderate reform of the old Church in 1558, at the beginning of Elizabeth's reign, was sufficient and definitive. The reformers, on the other hand, believed the English Church had to be completely purged of popish corruption. Some of the reformers were outright separatists who believed that they must leave the Church of England to form a new church; for example, the Brownists followed Robert Brown to Holland in the 1580s, and the Pilgrims founded Plymouth Colony in Massachusetts in 1620. Yet the majority strove to reform the Church from within. Reformers of various stripes were sometimes referred to as "Puritans," a derogatory term of the day used to label a large segment of the population as extremists, much as the word "communist" was used in the 1950s against anyone with social-democratic tendencies.

Rather than simply following the religion of their ancestors, ordinary people like John Wheeler's parents and grandparents suddenly had to decide for themselves which was the true church, a decision which became more and more complicated, not to mention dangerous, as an ever-more-bewildering array of sects and tendencies – Arminian, Calvinist, Lutheran, Presbyterian, Anabaptist, antinomian, Socinian, Society of Friends (Quaker), and so on – sprang up all over Europe, undermining existing beliefs and religious institutions and jockeying for political power. In a world where no separation existed between church and state, religion was not a compartmentalized aspect of life, but was a major determinant of political and social organization. It was generally believed that public order could only be maintained if everyone worshipped in the way that the authorities sanctioned – just as, through much of the twentieth century, states had attempted to control the political beliefs of their citizens to ensure stability. There were many attempts to suppress the radical Protestants: in 1556, for example, a Wiltshire farmer was burned at the stake for reading Tyndale's Bible.

The Puritans had a different conception of human nature and its relationship to the divine than did the traditionalists, for whom ordinary people were linked to God through a series of hierarchical gradations in a Great Chain of Being, with priests, bishops, and ultimately the monarch as head of the church mediating in between. For the Puritans, the words of the Bible formed the sole bridge between God and humanity. Because they recognized Christ as their supreme authority above any secular ruler, followed individual conscience whatever the cost, and condoned dissent from official opinion, the radical Protestants were subversive to government in principle and to conventional hierarchical society – as the authorities were well aware.

What became known as Puritanism thrived in areas of social discontent, particularly in Wiltshire and East Anglia, which were both deeply affected by changes in the wool trade. Despite this, it was really a conservative doctrine. Like fundamentalist Islam today, Puritanism was an attempt to return to the perceived religious purity of an earlier time. All religious and social relations were to be firmly grounded in the Bible.

Interestingly, given differing conceptions of time and history in modern Western and traditional Native cultures, historian Theodore Dwight Bozeman has argued that the Puritans were "primitivists." He describes them as looking not forward, but backward to an "elite long-ago Great, or Strong, Time," the "primal time of special, sacral beginnings" described in the Old and New Testaments, a "primordium when Christianity was revealed in all its fullness." Their conception of history was mythic: the Biblical era was a sacred drama and the basis of the only true history, while all subsequent events were corruptions of that original purity.[8] To the Puritans, the Bible revealed sacred forms of worship and human organization that were complete and applicable to all times and nations.

The Puritans tried to expunge all vestiges of Catholicism from their lives and society and return to the practices of the primitive church of Roman times, when small groups of believers had gathered together in covenanted groups to worship and lead holy lives. Insisting on the centrality of the written word of the Bible and the spoken sermon from the pulpit, the Puritans denounced the symbols and ceremonies of the traditional Church as human inventions corrupting holy ordinances. Puritan divines refused to wear the old vestments, such as the surplice, and objected to genuflecting to the altar in church, to the position of the communion table, and to the use of the sign of the cross in baptism.

In the Wheelers' parish, the struggles between the traditionalists and the reformers within the church seesawed back and forth for years, with endless disputes over church rituals and the conduct of daily life. The vestiges of paganism and Catholicism provided particular targets for the reformers. As John Wheeler grew up, the Church disallowed or disapproved of more and more traditional activities and pastimes: tennis, dice, cards, bowls, parish feasts, saints' days, Hallowe'en, morris dances, maypoles, plays, church ales, and Christmas. Modern debates about Sunday shopping date back to the Puritans' insistence on Sunday as a day of rest and spiritual renewal; King James himself intervened in this debate in 1617, with his publication of the *Book of Sports*, which infuriated Puritans by authorizing a number of activities on the Sabbath.

For much of John Wheeler's early adulthood, the most important people in Salisbury – Bartholomew Tookye, Henry Sherfield, John Ivie, alderman, recorder, and mayor, respectively – were Puritans. They also dominated the vestry of St. Edmund's, the Wheeler's parish. The vestry was a self-perpetuating group of gentlemen and leading citizens who controlled the parish, electing churchwardens and other officers. The historian Paul Slack describes them as "highhanded and implacable in their rule of St. Edmund's parish and in the town as a whole." They tried to create a "godly city," and Salisbury was one of several English towns that "established notable reputations as bastions of moral reformation."[9]

Once this Puritan clique secured its grip on the city council in the 1620s, it embarked on an energetic program to address the city's poverty. By the middle of that decade, nearly half the population was impoverished, and the town was totally unable to afford the burden of relief, for it could support "no staple trade in it, and is so decaied and poor."[10] Salisbury had declined from a major industrial centre to a town that served mainly as a social centre and a stopping place for travellers, many of them vagrants. It is a sad comment on the state of affairs in Salisbury that the only expanding area of the economy was the drink trade – there were more than one hundred licensed inns and alehouses, one for every sixty-five inhabitants, and the brewers became one of the most powerful lobby groups in Salisbury politics.

The Puritans' innovative social experiment combined discipline – whips, stocks, the House of Correction – for the "impudent poor," (that is, those thought to be lazy and up to no good), and a relief program financed by the profits of a municipally run brewery for those considered poor through no fault of their own. The city bought grain and established storehouses from which bread, butter, cheese, beer, and fuel could be exchanged for tokens, which in turn were used to ensure that relief money wasn't spent on drink. Indigents had to demonstrate their moral acceptability to receive relief: it was available to them only if they went to church for morning and evening prayer as well as sermons, and they were compelled to sit on a bench with "For the Poore" written on it in large red letters. While this radical experiment drew much attention, it was undermined by the sheer scale of the problem and the political manoeuvrings of different factions among the ruling elite, especially the brewers.

When another bout of plague struck Salisbury in 1627, everyone who could escape the town did so, and the isolation of the infected town led to more food shortages. At the worst point of the epidemic 2,900 people were on relief out of its 6,500 population, and 88 households were shut up. Once again, the Wheelers' names do not appear on existing lists of those receiving relief or on the lists of the burials during the plague years, so perhaps they were lucky. But the town was full of poor orphans, widows, and broken families. The scale of poverty worsened over the course of the 1630s, when John Wheeler finally left, and more and more formerly-working people, especially weavers, became destitute. There were young beggars everywhere.

At what point did John and his wife, Agnes, begin to think of emigrating? Was it a plan that slowly formed in their minds or did specific events prompt a sudden decision to leave? And why did they choose New England? The Wheelers could have gone elsewhere, as many others did. In fact, of 69,000 people who left England in the 1630s, only 21,000 came to New England, the majority sailing to the Chesapeake and the Caribbean, while others headed for Ireland or Europe.[11]

The American myth is that the country owes its origins to a noble migration of persecuted Puritans seeking religious freedom. Was this true of John Wheeler? Although he lived in a Puritan-dominated parish, I do not know with certainty that he was a Puritan at all; it's just as possible that he was indifferent to religion and only a nominal Protestant, for contrary to the prevailing myth, the vast majority of those who left for New England had not suffered directly from religious persecution in their homeland, though they may have expected worse to come.

During John Wheeler's childhood, Queen Elizabeth had managed to keep closet Catholics, traditional Protestants, and radical reformers together within the Church of England through the Thirty-Nine Articles of 1563. The foundation of modern Anglicanism, the Articles represented an ingenious compromise that combined Puritan adherence to scriptural doctrine with the traditional form of church government and liturgy. However, after Elizabeth's death, this peace did not hold. In 1603, when James I ascended the throne, three hundred preachers were forced to give up their livings (church benefices) because they wouldn't follow the traditional ceremonies. This only intensified the struggle of seventeenth-century Puritans to free the Church from control of the reigning monarch and place it in the hands of the Elect – those who, by God's grace alone, were destined to be "saved" on Judgment Day.

The struggle to establish the true church had implications far greater than one's personal salvation, for many reformers feared a national catastrophe. They believed England "had a special place in the designs of providence"[12] and was joined in a national covenant with God. Failure to complete the reformation of the Church would amount to disobedience of divine law. This would in turn lead to divine punishment as surely as obedience would ensure God's favour – just as it had in the case of the ancient Israelites. A long series of devastating defeats of European Protestants by Catholics in the ongoing Thirty Years' War, which began in 1618, led to the fear that the Lord's punishment would take the form of a Catholic military invasion of England, and the imposition once more of the Catholic faith.

In 1625 the autocratic Charles I ascended the throne and the conflict between the Puritans and the established powers of Church and state came to a head. William Laud, appointed bishop of London in 1628, believed that the Church had the right to decree ceremonies and the authority to decide all religious controversies. Accordingly he tried to enforce social harmony through a royal declaration the same year – which he secured and had approved by the Privy Council and the bishops – that forbade discussion of Church dogma. He decreed that the faithful were required to acknowledge a new issue of the Articles of the Church of England, and not to dispute them. Even universities were forbidden to debate the revised Articles, and Laud and his chaplains gained exclusive control over the licensing of the press. Through a number of measures, he reinstated traditional ceremonies, controlled lecturers, and substituted the *Book of Common Prayer* and the catechism for many sermons. To enforce royal and episcopal authority, he revived the Star Chamber and the Court of High Commission, and both were used to persecute Puritans. In 1630, for example, a fanatical Scotsman named Alexander Leighton, who wrote *Sion's Plea against Prelacy*, was fined £10,000, and sentenced to the pillory and lash at Westminster and Cheapside, "his ears to be cut off, his nose slit and cheeks branded."[13]

Increasingly the Puritans had found a voice in Parliament and, in the 1628 Petition of Right, that body declared that taxes not agreed to by Parliament were illegal. Charles, believing that the sole function of Parliament was to provide the king with financial and other support for his independent and absolute authority, ignored the Petition and dismissed Parliament in 1629. He did not call it again for eleven years, preferring what he termed "personal rule." Others called it eleven years of tyranny. Inheriting a budget deficit, Charles levied taxes without parliamentary support and sought to raise funds by extra-parliamentary means, such as "ship money" – a tax levied on all counties to support the navy.

With the dismissal of Parliament, opposition to the king and the Church turned to sabotage. All over the country bitter disputes arose

> between bishops and their chancellors, their chapters, their neighbours, or their local corporations. Vicars were thwarted by their churchwardens or bullied by their patrons, and local and ecclesiastical authorities encroached upon each other's jurisdiction. To [Bishop] Laud all these petty differences were skirmishes in one great Armageddon. He was determined that the Powers of Light should win in them all and Laud constituted himself court of appeal in all of them.[14]

Henry Sherfield, the Puritan recorder of Salisbury and a prominent member of Mercy's parish, had made himself conspicuous in Parliament, first for his attacks on the duke of Buckingham, the king's favourite, and then during the last Parliament of 1629 by his attacks on royal pardons for the "erroneous and unorthodox opinions" of Richard Montague and Roger Manwaring. The former he accused of being an Arminian, and the latter he attacked for having preached that those who did not pay the taxes imposed by the king without Parliament's consent would face damnation.[15] When Charles suspended Parliament, Sherfield returned to Salisbury in disgust.

By this time, the balance of power in Salisbury had shifted away from the Puritans in favour of a more conservative faction, including the bishop and others associated with the religious traditionalists, but Sherfield and other Puritans refused to recognize their authority. In the Wheelers' church, St. Edmund's, there was a stained-glass window representing God the Father in the guise of an old man in a red-and-blue cloak, measuring the sun and moon with a pair of compasses. The vestry regarded this as blasphemous idolatry and voted to remove it (and also to sell the church organ), but they were forbidden to do so by the ecclesiastical court under the bishop of Salisbury. In fact, the bishop's own views on Predestination had already got him in trouble with Laud. When Recorder Sherfield observed some women parishioners making "low curtsies" before the window, he asked one of them why she did it and was told "that they made them to their Lord God, and to God the Father in the glass window." Sherfield promptly climbed up a ladder and smashed the stained glass with a pikestaff.[16] I can't help wondering if Mercy or her son John witnessed this, if they saw Sherfield slip and fall, injuring himself on a pew beneath. Was Mercy or Agnes one of those curtsying women? Or did the Wheelers approve of Sherfield's actions?

In February 1633, Sherfield was summoned before the Star Chamber to account for his deed. Archbishop Laud wanted a heavier punishment, but Sherfield escaped with a fine of £500, acknowledgement of his misdemeanour, and agreement to pay the not-inconsiderable cost of replacing the window.

A year after passage of this judgment, John Wheeler left Salisbury for good. We'll never know whether he left because of these specific events in his parish or the general suppression of Puritanism, or whether his decision was based more on the hope of better economic prospects for himself and his family. Many people chose to leave for a mixed bag of reasons, including not only religion but various family problems, debts, employment difficulties, and other private hopes and frustrations, as well as perceived economic and social opportunity. For some, there must have been simply a desire for novelty.

Certainly, when William Laud became Archbishop of Canterbury in 1633, he consolidated his power more firmly than ever, and he turned to new measures to bolster the traditionalists and to restrict and persecute the Puritans. These developments must have frightened and discouraged many and led them to believe that God's judgment of England was imminent. Some Puritans chose emigration as a legal and loyal alternative to official separation from the Church of England. They believed that only by leaving the sinners behind in England could true spiritual reformation be fulfilled in New England, and many even planned to return to England to restore the true religion after the time of God's punishment had passed.

If John Wheeler was a devout Puritan, his decision to leave would have been an agonizing one, made only after anxious and prolonged debate with others in his congregation. Many Puritans wondered if it would be "a greate wronge to our owne country and church to take away the godly people," which they believed might increase the likelihood of divine judgment.

Should not Christians "stay and suffer for Christ" in the teeth of such worsening conditions?[17]

John Wheeler left Salisbury nearly twenty years after his father, Dominick, died and fourteen years after the passengers of the *Mayflower* founded Plymouth, the first Puritan colony in North America. The Wheelers were destined for the Massachusetts Bay Colony, which had been chartered in 1629. They departed on the ship *Mary and John*, which sailed on March 26, 1634, under Robert Sayres, master. In a crackdown aimed at controlling emigration to New England, the *Mary and John* had been one of several vessels detained at Southampton on February 13, 1634, by order of the Privy Council. John Wheeler's name – spelled Whelyer – is on a surviving list of passengers, all of whom were required to take the Oath of Supremacy and swear allegiance to the king before being allowed to sail. Furthermore, their captain was required to hold daily services on board ship in accordance with the *Book of Common Prayer* of the Church of England.

Many of the passengers aboard the *Mary and John* were from Salisbury, Amesbury, Newbury, and other Wiltshire towns. So were the two ministers who accompanied them: the Rev. Thomas Parker, only son of Robert Parker, one of the earliest English Puritans, who had served a short time at Newbury before embarking for New England, and his cousin, Rev. James Noyes from Chouldertown. The ship's records indicate that six of the company remained behind to oversee the passengers' chattels, which were to follow them across the ocean on another ship, the *Hercules*.

John was forty-four at the time, Agnes forty-two. Their daughter, and my direct ancestor, Ann Wheeler, was with them when they set out (sources differ on her age); she was accompanied by her sisters Mercy and Elizabeth and two brothers. Three or four older children, the Adam and Edward mentioned in Dominick's will, and possibly another son, William, were left behind, as well as David, who later joined his parents in New England in 1638. One can imagine the scene of their parting, their anguish at the thought that they might never see each other again, their tears and prayers as the ship left the dock.

Whether or not Mercy Jelly was still alive at the time is not known. If so, she would have been sixty-five, perhaps too old to make the trip. Did she stay behind with her grandchildren or with other members of her family, or did John wait till after her death, when his inheritance might have provided the family with the means to emigrate? Perhaps she lived to see the outbreak of civil war in England in 1642, when she would have been seventy-three, but I hope she died before that.

If she was alive, did she encourage them to go? Was she excited about their impending adventure, or fearful for their safety? Did she worry about shipwrecks in violent storms or ambushes by pirates or massacres by the "Indians" she had heard about? Did John and Agnes offer to take her with them and did she refuse? Did she say she would rather die in her own house than live her life among strange heathens in a godforsaken place, that she would rather live with the devil she knew than one she didn't know, that she would never leave England, her home, her roots, no matter how bad things got or how good they might be elsewhere? Perhaps she didn't understand how anyone could leave her history behind and start all over again in a new land, even if a Promised Land, with nothing underfoot but virgin soil, no ancestors buried in the churchyard, no history to stand on. Or did they leave in part to escape her, as the members of my husband's family tried to escape from one another, moving from Europe to Australia and America, contacting each other only to say "she's dead" or "he killed himself."

After John and his family sailed away, did Mercy or her grandchildren ever receive news of them from across the great water? Did they know if John and Agnes were alive or dead, and how they had fared? Did John send back letters, and if he did, what did he tell them?

CHAPTER
2

Dreaming of America

Once at sea, John Wheeler must have been filled with anticipation and apprehension. What did he know or think he knew about the land he was approaching and which he intended to make his home? What had he heard about the "Indians" he would undoubtedly meet? By what right did he feel he could settle on their land? These are crucial questions for me as I try to piece together how basically decent people invaded an already-populated continent. Unfortunately, there is no documentary evidence, no diary or letters that I know of to reveal his state of mind. But I can get a feel for common attitudes, for the lingering consequences of pivotal events, for the ideologies of the time.

Much had happened in the 138 years since Christopher Columbus had first encountered an unknown people on an island he mistakenly believed was in the "Indies" – Asia – and which he renamed Española. News of this and subsequent discoveries, explorations, and adventures in the rich lands across the Atlantic Ocean quickly caught the popular imagination across Europe. The first Europeans who encountered Native North Americans were astonished at their loving, generous treatment of strangers and their ethic of sharing. Their lack of acquisitiveness even led some Europeans to question whether the concept of private property – so central to European society – even existed among the inhabitants of America. (In fact, personal items were individually owned while land was held in common.) The indigenous peoples' social organization was so different from that of Europe that the newcomers wondered if they had any government or religion at all. The early explorers were startled by the Natives' near nakedness and both horrified and fascinated by those peoples who practiced cannibalism.[1] In fact, the word "cannibal" became the most common appellation for these newly "discovered" peoples.

The English had been curious about the fabled inhabitants of North America since three captured Natives had first been presented to Henry VII, reputedly by Sebastian Cabot in 1502, to the wonder of all London. Others would make the trans-Atlantic journey thereafter, usually involuntarily. In 1587, the year before Mercy and Dominick's marriage, for example, Walter Raleigh's captains had brought back two Natives from Roanoke Island off Virginia; five others had been brought to England in 1605. John Wheeler might well have heard of the five Massachusett Indians captured along the coast and on Martha's Vineyard by Edward Harlow (possibly another of my ancestors) in 1608; they created a sensation when they were toured through several southern English cities.

Accounts written first in Spanish or Latin, and later in other languages including English, gave detailed information and misinformation about the "Indians" of the Americas. They spread rumours of islands of giants, incredibly lustful women, and people who lived to 150 years of age. ("I have observed," wrote a Jesuit missionary at Quebec in 1633, "that after seeing two or three Savages do the same thing, it is at once reported to be a custom of the whole Tribe. . . .")[2] In England, massive documentation was provided by Richard Hakluyt and later by Samuel Purchas, much of it invaluable to historians. Then, as now, there was no such thing as strict objectivity in description. How Europeans interpreted what they saw in the so-called New World was greatly influenced by European myths, legends, history, and prophesies dating back more than a millennium, and even far into the mists of prehistory. These included Pliny the Elder's travel writings of monsters and other wonders, Ovid's fantastical *Metamorphosis*, and Tacitus's accounts of the Roman conquest of barbarian Europe, as well as the medieval tales about Prester John. But above all, the Christian Bible was the primary lens through which North America was refracted; biblical language, judgment, and prophecy would greatly influence the way settlers such as John Wheeler or clergymen such as John Eliot, another relation of mine, would interpret what they encountered.

Most European Christians saw the European foray into America as an exodus that paralleled and derived legitimacy from the story of the Hebrew conquest of the "heathen" peoples of Canaan. Just as Jehovah had "subdued all the Nethites, Amorites, Canaanites, Pheresites, Hevites, and Jebusites, . . . and other strange nations besides, whose lands and dominions he wholly divided among God's people" in the Book of Joshua, the Europeans believed that they had been given this new land. This identification with the ancient Israelites was so strong that the biblical patriarch became the Protestant equivalent of a patron saint – Joshua was named an honorary adventurer to Virginia in the 1580s and an honorary member of the Virginia Company from 1606.

Whether the peoples of the Americas were Jews or Gentiles provoked considerable debate among Europeans. Some considered them one of the lost tribes of Israel, but whether descended from Shem or Ham, two of the sons of Noah, was a matter of further dispute. Those who considered them "degenerate Jews" cited supposed similarities in speech and customs, such as the segregation of menstruating women. John Wheeler may well have supported this view. Or he may have believed they were Gentile descendants of Noah through the Tartars, who had entered the New World from Asia as a fallen people in the grip of Satan. In either case, Europeans were convinced that these peoples had to be converted to Christianity.[3]

The impulse to convert the inhabitants of the Americas began with Columbus and has been a part of the European attitude to the indigenous population of the Americas ever since, though the roots of this missionary impulse stretch back to the beginnings of Christianity itself. George Abbot, who was Archbishop of Canterbury during much of John Wheeler's life, wrote that God raised up Columbus and "set his mind to the discovery of a new world," because He remembered "the prophesy of His Son, that the Gospel of the Kingdom should before the Day of Judgement be preached in all coasts and quarters of the world." God looked over America "in his mercy intending to free the people – or at least some few of them – from the bondage of Satan."[4]

The New Testament called for this conversion directly: "Go ye therefore, and teach all nations, baptizing them in the name of the Father, and of the Son, and of the Holy Ghost" (Matthew 28:19). It was not just a compassionate concern for individual souls of Indians that prompted this evangelization; conversion of all non-Christians was necessary to prepare the way for the Second Coming of Christ and the New Jerusalem and thus the salvation of the Elect. "And this gospel of the kingdom shall be preached in all the world for a witness unto all nations; and then shall the end come" (Matthew 24:14).

John Wheeler's justification for joining the invasion of North America would also have drawn on pre-existing ideas of the "savage" and "barbarian" – ideas that, in Western culture, date back to the pre-Christian era. The Greeks coined the word "barbarian" for outsiders such as the Persians and Egyptians. The Romans appropriated the concept for their own uses, applying it to rationalize their imperial ambitions, including their conquest of the "barbarian" Celts of Europe and Britain – the ancestors of many of those Europeans who now came to America's shores.

Indeed, Julius Caesar provides the very earliest glimpse I have of my own ancestors in his *Conquest of Gaul*, written in 52 B.C. In a description that is eerily reminiscent of later Puritan descriptions of North American Natives, he describes British tribespeople clothed in animal skins, dying their bodies blue to appear more terrifying in battle, and apparently allowing women to have sexual partners other than their husbands.[5]

As the historian Francis Jennings has commented, the concepts of heathen and barbarian blended into one during the Christian territorial and religious wars against Islam that became known as the Crusades: "No slaughter was impermissible, no lie dishonorable, no breach of trust shameful if it advanced the champions of true religion. . . ."[6] Shortly after Constantinople's fall to the Moslems in 1453, Pope Nicholas V empowered Portugal's king to enslave the persons and seize the lands and property of "all Saracens and pagans whatsoever, and all other enemies of Christ wheresoever placed."[7] Psalm 2:8 supported this: "Ask of me, and I shall give thee the heathen for thine inheritance, and the uttermost parts of the earth for thy possession." The result was that distant peoples not even known to the Portuguese became targets of bounty- and slave-hunting adventurers. Other European nations soon joined in the plunder.

The European invaders of the Americas and other continents could rationalize this behaviour because they were convinced that God had made them innately superior to all other peoples. In this assumption they were not alone: the Chinese, for example, also had a well-developed sense of their own superiority, and most peoples of the world, including the peoples of the Americas, usually referred to their own tribal group or nation as the "true men," or "we, the people," while their labels for others were often descriptive and sometimes derogatory. In the case of Europeans, however, this attitude of superiority was buttressed by not only the conviction that Christianity was the sole true religion (as many Moslems believed of Islam) but by differences in technological development between Europeans and the inhabitants of much of Africa, the Americas, and Asia. The Europeans could assert their claims of superiority by force.

For centuries, Europeans attributed this technological gap to the superiority of European brains and culture. In fact, Native Americans matched Europeans in ingenuity and expertise, though it was often directed toward different ends.[8] Furthermore, the technology with which the Europeans first awed the inhabitants of North America was often not European in origin:

> Europeans were able to cross the Atlantic Ocean in the first place because they could steer with rudders invented in China, calculate their position on the open sea through trigonometry invented in Egypt, using numbers created in India. The knowledge they had accumulated from around the world was preserved in letters invented by the Romans and written on paper invented in China. The military power they brought with them increasingly depended on weapons using gunpowder, also invented in Asia. The cultural confrontation between cultures in the Western Hemisphere was, in effect, a one-sided struggle between cultures acquired from vast regions of the earth against cultures from much more narrowly circumscribed regions of the New World.[9]

Because of North America's separation from Europe, Asia, and Africa by two huge oceans, the tendency for cultural influences to move most rapidly in an east-west direction, rather than north-south across the differing weather zones (North, Central, and South America are aligned north-south), and the lack of North American draft animals to facilitate travel over long distances, innovations did not spread from one region to another as quickly as they could in Eurasia. The technological superiority that the Europeans enjoyed derived ultimately from advantages in geography and the distribution of potentially domesticable plants and animals.

The Europeans drew many conclusions from this apparent superiority. The revered Greek philosopher Aristotle – whose stature was such that he was considered a final authority – had written of the hierarchy of superior and inferior, and of the right of the superior to rule the inferior and to be served by them. According to his doctrine of natural servitude, "some men are by nature free and others servile."[10] Columbus, therefore, was drawing on a long tradition when he wrote that all Indians were "fitted to be ruled, and should be set to work to cultivate the land," that they should be "taught to go clothed and adopt our customs."[11] To him, their quick intelligence and healthy bodies suggested that they would make good servants or even slaves – especially as it was morally permissible to enslave idolaters. Even those Europeans who expressed concern for the welfare of the inhabitants of this continent rarely seem to have considered that they might be seen as equals.

As historian Olive Dickason documents in *The Myth of the Savage and the Beginnings of French Colonialism in the Americas*, the English word "savage" comes from the French word *sauvage* or "wild," meaning not cultivated, tamed, or domesticated, in turn derived from the Latin *silva*, "of the forest." Originally, it was a more neutral term. In European culture, the concept of the wild man was very ancient, going back even to Enkidu in the Sumerian Epic of Gilgamesh; during the Renaissance "l'homme sauvage" was a well-known figure of folklore. A savage was a person who lived away from society, beyond the reach of its laws, without fixed abode, living according to nature in a manner closer to that of wild animals than to that of man. This became the standard view of the inhabitants of North America, largely because they were seen as nomadic hunters. In fact, in the Americas as a whole, far more aboriginal people were farmers than were purely hunters. Indeed, in some respects, Indian farming at the time of the arrival of the Europeans was more advanced than that of Europe. But due to the lack of animals suitable as sources of domestic meat, even aboriginal farmers had to hunt.

There were two aspects to savagery. One was benign, in which noble savages lived in natural innocence in the "infancy of nature" or a Golden Age, a concept from classical antiquity. The other was bestial and demonic, in which savages lived without knowledge of God and therefore without use of reason. By the time Europe invaded America, such ideas were also coloured by early reports of anthropoid apes: positioned between human and animal, the savage was therefore subhuman and often portrayed as exceptionally hairy.

As Europeans roamed the world, the concept of the "savage" blended with that of the heathen barbarian. While the most frequent differences between so-called civilized and savage societies were feudal as opposed to tribal political organization, the relative importance of agriculture and a sedentary lifestyle over hunting and nomadism, and the presence or absence of Christianity, as Francis Jennings has noted, the actual difference between civilization and savagery was often minor. For example, from at least the fourteenth century, the English considered it their duty to conquer the supposedly savage and uncivilized "wild Irish," although both countries were Christian and Catholic, both were fully agricultural and shared most of the same technology and habits of commerce, and the Irish had their own alphabet and literature. This attitude gave rise to such sentiments as "savages and those rural rascals are only by force and fear to be vanquished," and "The Irish live like beasts . . ., are more uncivil, more uncleanly, more barbarous than in any part of the world that is known."[12] As Jennings has noted, what the word "savage" really meant was "morally inferior." Curiously this perception allowed Europeans to treat other peoples in a manner outside the sanctions of their own morality and law. But even at the time, there were some who understood the cultural relativity of the concept: the French essayist Michel de Montaigne wrote, "Each man calls barbarian whatever is not his own practice."[13]

To Europe's shame, the first savages in the history of Euro-American contact were the Europeans, themselves, beginning with the ruthless and bloody Spanish conquest of the Caribbean, Central and South America, and Mexico. In 1514, the Spaniards adopted the practice of reading the infamous *requerimiento* to the indigenous peoples before battle to justify conquering them: in it "los Indios" were called upon to acknowledge the authority of the Pope and of the rule of Castile over the Indies (by Alexander VI's Bull of May 1493) and to agree to accept the Catholic faith. If they refused, the Spaniards could legitimately proceed by fire and sword, take slaves and seize land and goods, all of which they did. Through the Spanish Conquest, millions of people died by slaughter, imported diseases, and slavery in the silver mines, and the wealth of ancient civilizations, such as those of the Incas and Aztecs, was plundered. It is worth noting, however, that the Spanish treatment of the Indians was vigorously denounced by many Europeans, including the Spanish priest Bartolomé Las Casas, whose work *The Spanish Cruelties* was translated into English in 1555, and Montaigne, whose essays first appeared in English in 1603.

As John Wheeler grew up he would have heard of the brutality of the Spanish Conquest, for the English were only too happy to denounce the tyranny of their enemy, and of the Pope as well. For a while, the English had even considered allying themselves with the "Indians" against the Spanish. Richard Hakluyt, writing to promote the expeditions of Sir Walter

Raleigh and Raleigh's brother-in-law Sir Humphrey Gilbert, for example, reasoned that it was not legitimate to deprive the idolaters of their territory, property, or lives, and argued for conversion through example and persuasion rather than force. The English would treat the Indians with "humanity, courtesy and freedom," he pledged. The Spanish, on the other hand, set "the gloss of religion" upon "mere ambition." All the Indians needed were godly preachers, since they were a simple people in error. Preachers needed only to learn the Native language and "with discretion and mildness distill into their purged minds the sweet and lively liquor of the gospel."[14]

In their denunciation of the Spanish, many English ignored their own history of brutality and the use of terror in the aforementioned colonization of Ireland; perhaps it was less well publicized. In Ireland, the English had met resistance with total war, slaughtering men, women, and children. The same Sir Humphrey Gilbert who would later sail to America had been military governor in Munster in 1569, when he so respected the "humanity, courtesy, and freedom" of the Irish that he decapitated the vanquished and set their severed heads along the path to his tent. In 1587, the year before Dominick and Mercy were married, Elizabeth I had given Catholic priests twenty days to vacate Ireland and had ruled that any priest subsequently caught was to be hanged, cut down while yet alive, disembowelled, and burned. Elizabeth also outlawed Catholic religious services in Ireland, seized 200,000 acres of Catholic-owned land, and distributed it to her English noblemen.

England's condemnation of Spain's activities in the New World also did not prevent Englishmen from recognizing that, if they did not get to America soon themselves, the continent would be colonized entirely by other Europeans. Various nations had been fishing off the Grand Banks of Newfoundland since the late fifteenth century – among them Basques, French, Portuguese, and English – but the French explorer Jacques Cartier attempted to colonize the St. Lawrence Valley in 1541. Accordingly, the English now began to promote the idea of colonization, especially as a way to export local problems, such as overpopulation and unemployment. During Elizabeth's reign, England claimed the eastern coast of North America from Florida to Labrador, and even Baffin Island.

As H. C. Porter outlines in *The Inconstant Savage: England and the North American Indian, 1500–1660*, the Tudor claim to America rested on three extremely shaky arguments. First, there was the legend of Madoc that appeared in ancient Welsh chronicles. The son of Owen Gwyneth, the

Prince of Wales, Madoc supposedly planted a colony in the New Found Lands in 1170 during the reign of Henry II, and afterwards returned to England, leaving certain people there who gave Welsh names to the islands, beasts, and fowls, including the Isle of Penguin. According to the English, the Beothuk of Newfoundland called the Great Auk a "penguin"; hence the inhabitants of North America were descendants of twelfth-century Welshmen. Since the Tudor Kings had Welsh blood, the land belonged to the Tudors! This unsubstantiated story was repeated by most writers on America, and may well have been known to John Wheeler.

England's claim was also based upon the story that Columbus had offered the Indies to Henry VII of England before he turned to Ferdinand and Isabella of Spain. Henry had been either too slow to respond or had rejected the offer. Somehow this previous (rejected) offer gave England first rights to the new land.

Lastly, in 1497, Giovanni Caboto (John Cabot) and his three sons had received letters patent from Henry VII to seek out, discover, and find "isles, countries, regions or provinces of the heathen and infidels whatsoever they be, and in what part of the world soever they be, which before this time have been unknown to all Christians." They could "set up our banners," and "subdue, occupy and possess" as "our vassals and lieutenants, getting unto us the rule, title and jurisdiction." The king was to receive 20 per cent of the net profits. The Cabots left Bristol in 1497, and sailed to Newfoundland. This action was the strongest support, under European law, for the English claim to the eastern coast of North America. Like other European claims, it ignored the claim to ownership of the estimated minimum of eleven million people already living north of the Rio Grande. Because the aboriginal peoples were neither Christian nor seen as fully human, because they were portrayed as roaming the land like animals rather than possessing it, and because Europeans believed that proprietary rights existed only within the framework of an organized state, the indigenous peoples of America were not accorded the same rights as European Christians under developing international law.[15]

By the time John Wheeler peered over the side of his ship and caught his first glimpse of North America in the distance, the English colonization effort, like John Wheeler himself, was about thirty years old. In 1578, in letters patent similar to those issued to the Cabots, Queen Elizabeth had authorized Sir Humphrey Gilbert to seize "remote heathen and barbarous lands"[16] (with the monarch again receiving 20 per cent of any gold or silver mined there), and the English began a number of ill-fated attempts to colonize "Norumbega" (an early name for lands along the northeastern coast of North America). In 1583, Humphrey Gilbert formally took possession of Newfoundland, though a colony was not founded until 1610. In 1584, four years before John Wheeler's parents were married, letters patent were issued to Walter Raleigh "for the discovering and planting of new lands and countries," and two ships explored the coast and islands off North Carolina. "A more kind and loving people there cannot be found in the world," wrote Capt. Arthur Barlow about the North Americans he met on this first expedition,[17] and he portrayed the land as an earthly paradise.

Such a view would soon be tempered by the sometimes harsh realities of early cross-cultural contact. The initial attempt to establish a colony on Roanoke Island, North Carolina, partially as a base for privateering against the Spanish, failed. After several skirmishes with the indigenous population and the near starvation of the settlers, the colonists were rescued by Sir Francis Drake and taken back to England. Subsequent attempts to rekindle the settlement also failed, most notoriously the "Lost Colony" 114 settlers, who disappeared mysteriously during the time that their relief ships were delayed because of the Spanish Armada. Many in England attributed these failures to the behaviour of the colonists: "the hand of God came upon them for the cruelty and outrages committed by some of them against the native inhabitants of that country," wrote Hakluyt.[18]

But popular interest in North America persisted. A 1605 play, *Eastward Ho!* by George Chapman, Ben Jonson, and John Marston, was performed in London and ran through two reprints that year. It satirized Sir Petronel Flash, an impoverished adventurer-gallant with his eye fixed on the gold of the New World. When the royal charter of the Virginia Company was granted in 1606, Michael Drayton's ode "To the Virginian Voyage" of 1606 expressed the widespread "hope to have builded up this heavenly new Jerusalem."[19]

More than anything else, it was probably England's experience in establishing the colony of Virginia that John Wheeler heard stories about as he was growing up. Jamestown had been founded in 1607. Once again the settlement ran into considerable difficulties, from Indian attacks to starvation and sickness. This time, despite great hardships, it persisted and survived. (Today it is recognized as the first permanent English settlement in the United States.) Soon a number of Englishmen brought home accounts of

Virginia, full of details about Native customs – and some extremely unfortunate misinterpretations. William White, for example, described an initiation ceremony of young men as a sacrifice of children – a story that was
widely circulated. He also reported that the Natives worshipped devils.
John Smith published his first book in 1608, and another in 1612, and
repeated the story of the annual sacrifice of children. He also wrote, "They
are inconstant in every thing, but what fear constraineth them to keep."[20]

Opinions in England were divided as to whether force could be used to
convert the indigenous population. The London Council of the Virginia
Company in 1610 instructed the governor of the colony to convert Indians
by "procuring" some of their children, "by force if necessary," to bring
them up with English language and manners. The English could deal
sharply with "priests" (shamans), even unto death "in case of necessity or
conveniency."[21]

Others were more open-minded. Theodore De Bry's engravings of the
watercolours by John White, who had led the 1586 and 1590 voyages,
included thirteen portraits of Native Americans along with portraits of
ancient Britons, to make the point that "the inhabitants of the Great
Britanny have been in times past as savage as those of Virginia." The British
apparently considered themselves better off for having been colonized by
the Romans. In 1624 Rev. Richard Eburne wrote that "we ought to consider,
that time was the old Britons, the ancient inhabitants of this land, were as
rude and barbarous as some of those of foreign parts with whom we have
to do." We are their "offspring": therefore "we ought not to despise even
such poor and barbarous people, but pity them, and hope that as we are
become now by God's unspeakable mercy to usward to a far better condition, so in time may they." Edward Hayes wrote that in older times, many
"holy men" were "stirred up to the converting of us in these north, and then
obscure, regions of Europe"; without them, "we also had continued barbarians unto this day." Similarly, "very many zealous men are moved by the
same charitable spirit towards those paganish Americans."[22]

Was John Wheeler caught up in the fascination with the Native people
of Virginia that was fashionable in London about the time of his father's
death? Did news of such trends ever reach Salisbury? In 1614, *The
Virginian Princess*, a masque with extravagant "Indian" costumes, was performed at Whitehall on the occasion of the princess's birthday. And in 1616
a young Native woman named Pocahontas travelled to England with her
relatives and was presented to King James. She converted to Christianity,

adopted European dress, had her portrait painted, learned to read and write, was entertained by the Bishop of London, and was followed everywhere by mobs of curious onlookers.

I also do not know if John Wheeler was aware of the considerable debate in England over the question of the legitimacy of the English presence in Virginia and the lawfulness of their dispossession of Native land. Some argued that there was lots of room, and the English had to live near Native Americans to convert them. Poet John Donne, dean of St. Paul's Cathedral and an honorary member of the Virginia Company, preached a sermon on the lawfulness of English settlement in the young colony in November 1622. He argued that the Law of Nations stipulated that, if a territory is uninhabited, abandoned, or derelict, it can be rightfully possessed – the principle of *vacuum domicilium*. This also held true if the land was underpopulated as well, for the earth was intended for all men. A man in a fishing boat doesn't own the ocean, he argued; nor do the Indians possess America. The land must be improved, "to the best advantage of mankind in general." If this were not done, "the Law of Nations may justify some force." This was especially true for England, since God was on the side of the English, and directed the English conscience through the Holy Ghost. The Virginia Company had "made this island, which is but as the suburbs of the Old World, a bridge, a gallery, to the New: to join all to that world which shall never grow old, the kingdom of heaven." Donne's was definitely the majority viewpoint, but there were those who disagreed. Even John Smith, at the end of his life, said company officials in London were "making religion their colour, when all their aim was but present profit." Of course, he had also written dismissively at an earlier date: "For a copper kettle and a few toys, such as beads and hatchets, [the Indians] will sell you a whole country."[23]

John Wheeler's attitudes to "Indians" would have undoubtedly been influenced by the Jamestown massacre of 1622, in which Native Americans killed 350 out of probably 1,200 to 1,600 English colonists. The attack was apparently sparked by unfair trading practices and the shooting of an Indian intermediary by two English boys. When the first accounts of the slaughter were published in England later the same year, popular opinion was outraged and held that the English had been too kind, too focussed on winning Christian converts. Commentators spoke of "the bloody and barbarous hands of that perfidious and inhumane people," dubbed the attackers "wicked infidels" and treacherous and vicious "hell hounds." They urged retaliation. The English felt they could now by right invade the country and destroy or conquer the indigenous population. The Virginia Company sent arms and four hundred men, rebuilt and refortified some of the English settlements, and waged campaigns against the Native nations suspected of participation in the massacre. The Indians "who before we used as friends may now most justly be compelled to servitude and drudgery."[24]

But in the same year, Edward Winslow and William Bradford's *Mourt's Relation; or Journal of the Plantation at Plymouth* was published, and it offered a more hopeful view of colonization. The *Relation* described the establishment two years earlier, in 1620, of the first successful Puritan colony at Plymouth, Massachusetts,[25] and was followed by Edward Winslow's *Good News from New England* in 1624 and Francis Higgenson's *New England Plantation* in 1630. At Plymouth, the Pilgrims had stumbled upon truly empty land, the Patuxets having been wiped out in the as-yet-unidentified epidemic of 1617–20. The sole surviving member of the Patuxet welcomed and assisted the newcomers. After initial skirmishes with some neighbouring nations, peace had been secured with a treaty, and the colony appeared to be flourishing. Other Puritan colonies had been founded at Salem in 1626, and in 1629 the Massachusetts Bay Colony had been granted its charter and had established six towns the following year. According to its charter, the Massachusetts Bay Company declared the colony's main object "to wynn and incite the natives of the country, to the knowledg and obedience of the onlie true God and Saviour of mankinde; and this Christian faith, which is our royall intentions, and the adventurers' free profession, is the principall ende of this plantation."[26] This religious pretext was common to almost all of the early grants and letters of commission given by European monarchs to explorers and colonizers alike. The company's seal portrayed an Indian with the words "Come over and help us" issuing from his mouth.

Seventeen ships had arrived in Boston Harbour in 1630, but in its first year, the new colony had suffered so much sickness and hardship that many of the original Massachusetts Bay settlers returned to England in 1631. In 1632, only a few hundred emigrants braved the journey. Then, in 1633, with these outposts more firmly established and the appointment of William Laud as Archbishop of Canterbury signalling greater intolerance of Puritanism in England, the Great Emigration began. When John Wheeler and his family left Southampton in 1634, they were among the three thousand emigrants who headed to Massachusetts that year.

As John Wheeler thought and dreamed of America on that long, long sea voyage, he must have wondered anxiously which of the two well-established stereotypes of North American "Indians" was true. Were they noble, childlike, primitives who lived in a golden world of liberty and happiness, without government or religion, free of the corruptions of "civilization," who would turn willingly to that civilization and Christ? Or were they treacherous savages who would pretend friendship one minute and murder the next? As seen through English eyes, the events in Roanoke and Virginia seemed to support the latter view, which became the most common English attitude: The American Indian was "at first very fair and friendly, though afterwards they gave great proofs of their deceitfulness."[27]

Meanwhile, the subjects of all this speculation and opinion were undoubtedly alarmed by the growing numbers of Europeans arriving on their shores. Indeed, one historian refers to their severe psychic shock, analogous to the way we would feel if we were colonized by extraterrestrials.[28] But for Native Americans there was certainly no reason to question that they were entitled to rule themselves in their own lands as they always had. Yet, as Francis Jennings comments, "All Europeans agreed on the error of that belief. Sooner or later the 'natural' subordination of the Indians was to be translated into formal subjection. For Europeans, the issue was not whether they should rule, but which of them should do it."[29] In all their wild imaginings, the one thing the Europeans apparently never seriously considered was the possibility of the peaceful long-term co-existence of two sovereign, if very different, peoples.

CHAPTER
3

Along the Merrimack

John Wheeler finally arrived in Boston sometime in May of 1634, after a voyage of at least eleven weeks. While I have found no record of John and Agnes Wheeler's first movements upon disembarking from the *Mary and John*, they most likely headed to the northern frontier of the Massachusetts Bay Colony with the other Wiltshire passengers aboard the ship. Already, suitable land was becoming hard to acquire in the Boston area, and new arrivals had to venture ever farther afield. All along the coast new towns had sprung up within the jurisdiction of the Colony. Rev. Thomas Parker and about a hundred of the passengers made their way to Agawam, or Ipswich,[1] which was then the most remote and isolated northern settlement in the colony, some distance from the established town of Salem farther south. To the north, all was wilderness until the tiny outpost of Portsmouth in New Hampshire.

Ipswich had been settled by the English only recently, owing to raids on the local indigenous people, the Agawams, by Mi'kmaqs (then called Tarrantines) from the north. In 1630 the Massachusetts General Court had ordered a group of settlers to desist in their efforts to found a town out of concern for their safety, but three years later the Mi'kmaqs no longer posed such a threat, and the court wanted to ensure its jurisdiction over all the land granted to it in its royal charter. Then, in 1633, the General Court

36

ordered "that a plantation should be begun at Agawam [Ipswich], being the best place in the land for tilage and cattle, lest an enemy, finding it void, should possess and take it from us."[2] In 1634, when the Wiltshire contingent of the *Mary and John* arrived at Ipswich, the settlement was only a few months old. The Wheelers' first child to be born in the New World, Henry, was born there, either in 1634 or 1635.

As they travelled northward from Boston, John and Agnes must have been amazed by the forest, so different from the domesticated English landscape. Alder, poplar, pine, white oak, and hickory stretched across the land as far as the eye could see. Contemporary writers described flocks of birds darkening the sky, fish plentiful beyond imagining, deer in countless numbers, hills covered with blueberries, river valleys thick with strawberries. They may also have come across wolves, bears, and moose. The North American ecosystem, unlike that which they had known in England, was intact and abundant.[3]

How soon after their arrival in America did the Wheelers first encounter the indigenous inhabitants of the country? I have wondered if John Wheeler was curious or fearful, if his mind was open or closed when he first saw one of the "Indians" he had heard about. Was the Native person he saw wearing skin clothes or European cast-offs or almost naked, with a thick layer of animal or vegetable fat or grease to insulate and protect against mosquitoes? Did they make eye contact? Perhaps this first experience contradicted his expectations, for many Europeans had their preconceptions of savagery undermined by the exceptional courtesy, generosity, and hospitality extended them by the Native Americans they encountered.

This initial hospitality may have been due in part to a major difference in world view. The Europeans who first met North Americans could draw on a long history of contact with races and cultures different from their own, ranging from African to Chinese to Arab, and had developed a concept of "others" as clearly unlike Europeans and inferior. But, according to ethnohistorian James Axtell, "the relatively isolated natives of the Americas [whose human experience was limited to other Native Americans] were prepared by experience to see in 'others' largely faithful reflections of themselves or of the anthropomorphic deities who populated their pantheons. . . . the 'others' the Indians knew tended to be similar or even superior [that is, spirit beings]."[4] The unfamiliar technologies the Europeans brought with them were at first seen as evidence of spiritual power.

Also, the spiritual orientation of Native North Americans was toward affirmation of kinship with the rest of creation. According to Axtell, because all living things possessed souls or spirits capable of helping or hindering a person, each being had to be treated with respect and circumspection and was supplicated or thanked in formal ceremonies. Indeed, it was the special responsibility of human beings to maintain proper relationships with all the elements of the cosmos through ceremony, not merely for their own self-interest, but to maintain the beauty and order of creation itself. They defined these relationships in terms of reciprocity rather than domination and submission.

The indigenous nations of what is now northeastern Massachusetts had already had considerable experience with Europeans by the time John Wheeler arrived; in fact, they had been among the first Native Americans to have prolonged contact with English settlers and had had previous dealings with European sailors and explorers for more than a century before that. Whether or not Leif Ericsson or John or Sebastian Cabot ever made it as far south as the Massachusetts coast, coastal Natives were certainly in occasional contact with Basque, Portuguese, English, Breton, and Norman fishermen though much of the sixteenth century, though these rarely landed. Salmon, bass, and sturgeon abounded in the Merrimack River, which flowed into the Atlantic near the Bay Colony's northernmost boundary, and such abundance soon attracted fishermen from distant places. William Wood wrote: "The sturgions be all over the Countrey, but the best catching of them be upon the shoales of Cape Codde and in the River of Mirrimacke where much is taken, pickled and brought for England, some of them be 12, 14, 18 foote long."[5]

Frequent contact began in the 1580s, as felt hats became a European fashion and the demand for beaver furs skyrocketed. The Merrimack Valley was the first important site of the New England fur trade and the local Pawtuckets were friendly and quite eager to trade furs for European commodities. After 1600, large expeditions began to cross the Atlantic, such as that of Samuel de Champlain, who was accompanied by more than a hundred men in 1604, and Matthew Gosnold, Martin Pring, Henry Hudson, John Smith, and others. An account of Gosnold's 1602 voyage describes Native people in European clothes rowing about in a Basque shallop; others were said to speak English so well that one said, "How now are you so saucie with my Tabacco?" In 1620, upon landing at Plymouth Rock, the Pilgrims were greeted in English by a Native American whose first words were, "Welcome, Englishmen!"[6]

Over the decades, the Europeans had acquired a reputation for unpredictability, which had spread from nation to nation along the northeastern coast. Spanish slave hunters had been the first to capture Native Americans from North America; in 1525, Estevan Gomez captured fifty-eight Natives on the New England coast and took them back to Spain, the first of a long series of abductions, murders, and harsh punishments of Native Americans by the Europeans. Between 1600 and 1620, George Waymouth captured five Abenakis on the Pemaquid River to the north; Henry Hudson had explored the coast as well as the river that now bears his name, stealing furs and killing Indians along the way; Capt. Edward Harlow captured several Indians off Monhegan Island in Maine; Thomas Hunt kidnapped twenty-four New England Natives and then sold them into slavery in Malaga; and Thomas Dermer's crew invited some Pokanokets aboard and murdered them without provocation. Such incidents were not quickly forgotten. From an aboriginal point of view, a certain fear and mistrust of the English quickly became a healthy survival tactic. At the same time, though, friendship with the English could also offer benefits, such as the acquisition of trade goods and protection from traditional enemies.

Whether friendly or wary, the Native Americans John Wheeler encountered were almost certainly dejected and sickly, a far cry from their condition before European contact. Many early explorers and settlers had commented on the healthy physique of the Indians and their extensive knowledge of herbal medicine. Before such contact, Native people were believed to enjoy a longer life span than their European contemporaries, and were free of smallpox, malaria, typhus, tuberculosis, plague, diphtheria, measles, and probably syphilis. Their teeth were strong and regular, and they had no rickets or humpbacks from malnutrition, as did so many Europeans. Their diet was healthy and varied: the men hunted moose, bear, turkey, migratory fowl, and many smaller animals, while deer accounted for close to 90 per cent of the wild game eaten. Fishing provided a more reliable source of food than hunting did, and sturgeon, salmon, and shad were major elements in their diet; they also ate beached whales, shellfish, eels, and the occasional seal. The women grew maize, beans, squash, pumpkins, Jerusalem artichokes, tobacco, and sunflowers for oil. They gathered a variety of berries, roots, nuts, and other wild seeds in season. Reliable harvests and the storage of dried maize underground in baskets for the winter months ensured that scarcity was rarely experienced.[7]

The indigenous people of the lower Merrimack are believed to have been the Pawtuckets, who were related to, and spoke the same language as, other Massachusett peoples farther south. The Pawtuckets lived much of the year in small fishing villages along the river, moving seasonally within a restricted geographic area to fishing stations, marsh camps for migratory waterfowl, camps at plant-collecting localities, shellfish camps on the coast, or deer-hunting camps in the forest.

Before contact, their population was numerous. Capt. John Smith, who visited the Merrimack area in 1614, counted at least thirty villages along the river. These villages were occupied during winter, and moved every dozen years or so when local firewood and fields were depleted. The ten or twenty houses in the main villages were covered in bark and were up to thirty metres long and nine metres wide, housing forty to fifty people. Nearby Western Abenaki villages were palisaded for defence, and the Pawtucket villages may have been as well, for the northernmost Massachusett villages appear to have been stockaded in 1600, and the practice became more common at a later date. During the warmer months, small extended families dispersed to farmsteads of single houses surrounded by fields. These houses were large wigwams four to five metres in diameter, and were moved from time to time as the fields were depleted.

Although the Pawtuckets were Massachusett-speakers like the Natives around Boston Bay, politically they were allied with the sachemdom of Passaconaway, the renowned powwow (medicine man or shaman) and sachem (political leader) of the Pennacooks, the leading nation in a small, loosely knit confederacy of mostly Western Abenaki peoples in present-day New Hampshire, northeastern Massachusetts, and southern Maine. The boundary between the Massachusett Indians on the lower Merrimack and the Western Abenakis farther upriver is very unclear. Passaconaway himself lived near what is now Concord, New Hampshire.

Perhaps the greatest and certainly the most celebrated powwow of the age, Passaconaway was a huge man of six foot four, and a sachem of great strength and outstanding ability who had led the Pennacooks to victory over the Mohawks. By the time John Wheeler settled in his former territory, Passaconaway was already elderly. He was known all over New England for performing astonishing supernatural feats. William Wood reported: "if we may believe the Indians who report of one Passaconaway that he can make the water burn, the rocks move, the trees dance, metamorphise himself into a flaming man . . . in winter, when there is no green leaves to be got, he will burn an old one to ashes, and putting those into the water produce a new grean leaf . . . and make of a dead snake's skin a living snake."[8]

Thomas Morton was the first English writer to describe Passaconaway's feats. He recounted that Passaconaway was a "Powah of greate estimation amongst all kinde of Salvages," and concluded that such tricks as swimming underwater across a wide river in a single breath and making ice appear in a bowl of water in the middle of summer were doubtless "done by the agility of Satan his consort."[9]

It is ironic that the Puritans, many of whom came to America for religious reasons, were largely unable to recognize or comprehend the deep spirituality of North America's indigenous inhabitants, for whom every activity had a sacred dimension and in whose world divine power existed everywhere. While some Puritans considered Native American religion simply bogus or non-existent, most Puritans considered its pantheistic vision of spirits in all the elements of nature idolatrous and a form of devil worship. In Puritan theology, witches lurked everywhere, luring men and women into their power, and tricking them into serving the Devil. These same witches soon came to be identified with the powwows (medicine men), who were also the most vehement opponents of the English. As Thomas Morton put it, the younger Indians deferred to the elder, "the Elder [are] ruled by the Powahs, and the Powahs are ruled by the Devill."[10] Many Puritans fully believed that powwows were powerful witches with the ability to peer into and control the spirit world.

Passaconaway reportedly had had prophetic visions of the British conquest of his people, and at first tried to get rid of the English through spiritual means. He went to Plymouth in 1620, after the landing of the *Mayflower*, along with other powwows, to conjure against the invaders, but his efforts proved fruitless. Although his warriors could easily have wiped out the fledgling English settlements within his traditional territories, Passaconaway recognized the newcomers' overall military superiority and apparently decided to treat the English well. From 1631 on, not one Englishman suffered injury at the hands of the Pennacook confederacy.

The effect of the plagues might have led him to take this position, for by the time John Wheeler arrived in northeastern Massachusetts, the Pennacooks and the Pawtuckets had been devastated by European diseases.

Contemporary observers said the epidemic of 1616–1617 (variously hypothesized to be typhus, bubonic plague, or hepatitis), which ravaged Native communities along the New England coast south of the Saco River in Maine down to Narragansett Bay in what is now Rhode Island, killed nine of ten and even nineteen of twenty of the indigenous people who contracted it. In 1622 John Smith had counted only ninety Indians left along the entire Massachusetts coast north of Boston. John White wrote that the plague "swept away most of the inhabitants along the Sea coast, and in some places utterly consumed man, woman and childe, so that there is no person left to lay claime to the soyle which they possessed; In most of the rest, the Contagion hath scarce left alive one person of an hundred."[11] Among the Pennacooks and other Western Abenaki peoples, the mortality rate is estimated to have been 98 percent, leaving only 250 survivors of 10,000.

As physiologist Jared Diamond commented in *Guns, Germs and Steel: The Fates of Human Societies*, this Native American lack of immunity to the "crowd" diseases of Europe, many of which are originally believed to have passed to humans through domesticated animals, was the main factor that enabled Europeans to invade America so easily. (By contrast, in Africa, it was the European invaders who had no immunity to tropical diseases and dropped like flies, delaying colonization on that continent for several generations until the Europeans acquired medicines like quinine.) John Wheeler's arrival in New England coincided with a second great epidemic – this time, of smallpox. Between the fall of 1633 and summer of 1634 several thousand Native people died. Between these two epidemics, the coastal nations of the Pennacook confederacy – the Agawams of the Ipswich area and the Naumkeags of the Salem area – were almost wiped out, and those of the lower and middle Merrimack also suffered terribly.

Thus, the indigenous inhabitants of the coastal Merrimack area were certainly not in a position to assert themselves in the face of this influx of English settlers into their tribal lands, which by 1635 were largely unoccupied. Vulnerable to raids by traditional enemies such as the Mi'kmaqs or by Native nations not yet touched by the plagues (such as the Narragansetts), they may have even welcomed the powerful English as neighbours. It has been suggested that the Pennacooks saw English occupation of the depopulated coastal lands as an "ideal buffer zone" against such raids.

Neither race had scientific knowledge of how such contagious diseases were spread or how populations acquired some immunity through generations of natural selection of individuals with more resistant genes. It seemed to both that the English were untouched by these first plagues, while Native Americans were dying everywhere. Both groups considered disease a manifestation of spiritual influences, and many Puritans interpreted the plagues as evidence of God's intention that the land was meant for His Elect, the Puritans. As Governor John Winthrop put it, "if God were not pleased with our inheriting these parts, why did he drive out the natives before us? and why dothe he still make roome for us, by deminishinge them as we increase?" Later in the century, when racial animosity had deepened, Rev. Cotton Mather remembered that "the woods were almost cleared of those pernicious creatures to make room for better growth."[12]

Because the powwow's (shaman's) ability to cure disease was central to Indian religion, and their efforts were now utterly futile, the plagues undermined Native spiritual beliefs and hence people's sense of themselves and their world – the indigenous people John Wheeler encountered were traumatized survivors of a physical and spiritual holocaust. The loss of most of their elders – the custodians of tradition and their wisest advisors – left a terrible vacuum. Robert Cushman, describing the effect of the epidemic on aboriginal people near Plymouth in 1620, wrote, "I think the twentieth person is scarce left alive; and those that are left, have their courage much abated, and their countenance is dejected, and they seem as a people affrighted."[13] In 1634, the effect on Native people farther north along the coast must have been very similar.

What did John Wheeler think of this devastation, he who had seen so many die of the plague in Salisbury? Did he – could he – question the righteousness of God's judgment against the heathen? If he did, he would definitely have been among a very small minority of Puritans. Some colonists did help care for the dying, buried the dead, and took orphaned children into their homes, but I do not know how widespread this behaviour was. Although they did not know the means of transmission, the English understood that such epidemics were the result of contagious diseases – witness the practice of quarantine in plague-ridden Salisbury and the flight from the city of those who could get away – but I do not know how much of this knowledge was shared with Native Americans.

What opinions of Native people did John and Agnes Wheeler form in their initial contacts? According to historians, most seventeenth-century Europeans coming to the New World did not admit to finding anything admirable in the Natives already here. Indeed, members of both cultures were probably soon acutely aware of what the other lacked. Would John

Wheeler have agreed with William Bradford, who wrote that the land was "devoid of all civil inhabitants, where there are only savage and brutal men which rage up and down, little otherwise than the wild beasts"? "The Indians are Infamous, especially for Three Scandalous Qualities," wrote Cotton Mather, "they are Lazy Drones, and love Idleness Exceedingly: They are also most impudent Lyars, and will invent Reports and Stories at a strange and monstrous rate; and they are out of measure Indulgent unto their Children, there is no Family-Government among them."[14]

Or would he have agreed with the more positive assessment of Native American culture from the commentator who said: "They live in perfect contentment with their present state, in friendship with each other, sharing those things with which God has so plentifully provided them." Did he, like renegade fur trader Thomas Morton, admire their respect for their elders and their willingness to share whatever they had with strangers, acknowledging a "more happy and freer life style, being voyde of care, which torments the mindes of so many Christians"?[15] He would have been in the minority if he agreed with the sentiment expressed in the following poem by the Puritan cleric Roger Williams:

Boast not proud English of thy birth and blood,
thy brother Indian is by birth as good,
Of one blood God made him, and thee, and all
As wise, as fair, as strong, as personal.[16]

Certainly, the cultural differences were immense. Many Natives were not concerned about covering their nakedness, premarital sex was acceptable behaviour in many nations, and women enjoyed more freedom in matters concerning their own bodies, such as sexuality and reproduction. Homosexuality was far more accepted in many Native societies than it was in Europe, and Native marriages were not considered real marriages at all in the eyes of many Europeans, since divorce was so easy. As historian James Axtell phrases it, the Puritans were appalled by the Natives' apparent lack of "order, industry and manners." Aboriginal people did not "labour" in the sense of carrying out regular, compulsory, unpleasant toil. They did not need to – or choose to. The Puritans, on the other hand, enforced laws against idleness in their society and believed, like other Calvinists, that time was a precious gift of God that must be used to serve Him in some productive way. Just as bad was the Indians' lack of humility.

I wonder if John Wheeler would have concurred with another common Puritan criticism, that Native people were not sufficiently mortified and humble before either the Puritans or their Creator, and had to be drawn from "sinful liberty" to "subjection to Jehovah"?[17]

By the time John Wheeler arrived, the lives of the few surviving Pawtuckets in the area had changed markedly, not only because of the epidemics, but also because they had become increasingly dependent on European trade goods over the previous twenty years. They had run out of local furs to trade, and so were no longer useful to the Europeans. New fur-trade routes down the upper Merrimack to the Charles River bypassed the longer Merrimack routes by Ipswich and cut out the Pawtuckets altogether. Increasingly, they were reduced to selling their own labour or their land to maintain their consumption of European implements and other goods, which they preferred to indigenous products. Within a decade, many of these Pawtuckets would became "settlement Indians" living in or near English communities.[18]

John Wheeler and the rest of the group of new settlers from Wiltshire remained in Ipswich over the winter of 1634–35. Finding the town increasingly crowded, some of his group discussed starting their own settlement farther north. The territory lying between Ipswich and the Merrimack River included more than 30,000 acres of fertile meadow, salt marsh, and upland. Reverend Parker and his followers therefore applied to the Massachusetts General Court for permission to establish a plantation a few miles south of the Merrimack River. Their petition was granted on May 6, 1635, and the new town was named Newbury (now Old Newbury). Most of the Wiltshire passengers of the *Mary and John* were persuaded to move to Newbury early in the year 1635. According to tradition, they came by water from Ipswich, and landed on the north shore of the Quascacunquen (now Parker) River.

The Newbury settlers established their new town on the strength of their grant from the Massachusetts General Court, which in turn ultimately derived its authority from the charter granted to the Massachusetts Bay Company by Charles I. The king, in turn, asserted a unilateral royal claim to jurisdiction over eastern North America because of various "discoveries" by explorers serving the English Crown – none of which, of course, was based on the consent of the peoples who had inhabited the land in question since time immemorial. Nevertheless, according to a University of New Hampshire graduate student, Peter Leavenworth, who has made an extensive study of Pawtucket land sales, English settlers who moved onto Native lands in northeastern Massachusetts and southeastern New Hampshire between the 1620s and the 1660s generally viewed Native permission (through deeds or oral agreements) as essential – sometimes even more essential than town or colonial grants. In part they did so to protect themselves against counterclaims by other colonists. At the same time, especially since they were living in areas remote from other English settlements, they recognized that their safety depended on good relations with their Native American neighbours, and there were still survivors among the coastal Natives whose consent may have been obtained at least for form's sake. A law of 1634 prohibiting the purchase of Indian lands without permission from the General Court was often ignored.

It is not known whether there were any negotiations or actual sales of land between the new settlers at Newbury and the Pawtucket owners of the lands in question. No early deeds recording sales of land in Newbury seem to have survived, though deeds from the 1680s retroactively confirm land sales for much of northern Essex County that may have included the Newbury lands. This is not unusual for, in the earliest days of the Bay Colony, there were few formal deeds, and vague (and frequently conflicting) verbal agreements often went unrecorded for decades. Some early deeds were later invented after the fact of English occupation – when legal deeds were required to fend off the claims of other Englishmen.

For their part, the survivors of the plagues initially sold tracts they believed they could do without in exchange for trade goods and cloth. But it appears that at least initially, they did not sell the land in the manner understood and recorded by the English, for the Native concept of land ownership differed fundamentally from that of the Europeans. To them, "land was a basic part of the nurturing environment, part of the shared creation that everyone held in common," like air or sunlight. "It was not a commodity to be . . . controlled by individuals" without reference to other members of the group, though sachems did assign areas to individuals or families for temporary use.[19] Originally, the Pawtuckets probably did not anticipate that the Puritans would want to keep those tracts exclusively for themselves, that title would never revert to the group originally granting the English the privilege of using it, or that the original owners would not have rights of usufruct (the right to use and enjoy the advantages of property belonging to someone else), such as hunting, gathering wood, or planting crops. Certainly they did not understand that Europeans considered private ownership of land a prerequisite for liberty.

To the Pawtuckets, and Native Americans generally, rights to hunt, fish, and gather wild food were far more important than the right to set up one's wigwam or house in a certain place; settlements were moved every ten years or so anyway. They often agreed to sell what to them amounted to rights of habitation, while believing they could share usufruct privileges with the scattered white settlers. Originally, the English, who also had traditions of certain usufruct rights on unfenced lands in England, agreed to the continuation of these rights on the often large tracts of land they acquired, and many deeds spelled out these rights specifically. But some unscrupulous English buyers promised the continuation of usufruct rights to convince Indian proprietors of how little they had to lose by selling their land, and then reneged on these agreements.

However they acquired it, the English were soon dividing up the land in Newbury, following a semi-medieval pattern that was repeated in countless New England towns. Each settler was given a house lot, a planting lot, a wood lot, and a meadow lot. House lots of four acres, with right of pasturage, were assigned to the poorest settlers, fifty acres to every person who paid his own transportation to New England, two hundred acres to everyone contributing £50 to common stock of the Massachusetts Bay Colony, and a larger or smaller amount to others, depending on their individual investments.

The first settlers were soon joined by others interested in stock-raising. In June 1635, two Dutch ships loaded with horses, heifers, and sheep dropped anchor at Boston, and the same day another ship arrived, bringing cattle and passengers, some of whom went on to Newbury. Dwelling houses were erected in the newest town, and a church was organized (the tenth in the colony) under a tree. Reverend Parker was chosen pastor; Rev. James Noyes, who had gone first to Medford in 1634, came to Newbury to become the teacher of the church. (The teacher was the minister whose chief role was to instruct, whereas that of the pastor was to exhort. Typically, the teacher read and expounded on the scriptures and the pastor preached a sermon or made extemporaneous exhortations.) Selectmen were elected and the first taxes were assessed two months after incorporation. Unfortunately, I don't know for sure that John Wheeler was among the

Wiltshire passengers who went from Ipswich to Newbury – he may have stayed longer in Ipswich for at least one other child – son Joseph – was born, or perhaps only registered, in that town in 1636.[20]

That same year, the threat of war with the Pequots farther south in Connecticut and fears that England might unilaterally revoke the Massachusetts Bay Colony's charter and seize direct control of the colonies prompted the colonists to establish a militia. All able-bodied men were divided into three regiments, the third of which included Ipswich and Newbury. Every person capable of bearing arms was obliged to furnish himself with a musket, and also with powder and shot. Early the next spring, a watch guard was established to protect the young town, and when the Pequot War broke out in 1637 eight men from Newbury went to Connecticut with Capt. Israel Stoughton as part of the Massachusetts contingent. I do not know if John Wheeler was among those sent from Newbury or Ipswich to Connecticut, but as an untried member of the new militia, he would have had many thoughts and feelings about the prospect of fighting Indians, especially because of their reputation for savagery. When the English massacred hundreds of Pequots and established clear military superiority in southern New England, many Puritans saw this victory as another sign that God intended them to rule over the Indians and have their land.[21]

Meanwhile, Aquila Chase, the man who would marry John Wheeler's daughter Ann in 1641 (and become my direct ancestor) was involved in the settlement of another town in the area. The original tract of land granted to the Massachusetts Bay Colony by the English Crown extended from three miles south of the Charles River to a vague line three miles north of the Merrimack River, and east and west from the Atlantic to the Pacific Ocean. Confusingly, a portion of the land conveyed by this charter – that part north of the Merrimack that now forms part of New Hampshire – had been granted previously to Capt. John Mason, and a long controversy ensued over the boundary. The Massachusetts Bay Colony was therefore quite anxious to extend settlement north of the Merrimack River to the northern limit of its grant in order to hold its territory against claimants under the Mason grant. In March 1636, the General Court accordingly ordered that "there shal be a plantacion settled att [Winnacunnet] & that Mr Dumer & Mr John Spencer shall have power to presse men to builde a house forthwith."[22] A "Bound House" was soon built at Winnacunnet ("the beautiful place of pines") on a path leading north along the coast from Newbury to Portsmouth. A year later, the inhabitants of Newbury received a conditional grant to Winnacunnet, and those who moved there within one year also enjoyed three years' immunity from taxes. In the fall of 1638 a number of Newbury men presented a petition to the General Court requesting confirmation of the grant and permission to begin settlement there, and in 1639 Winnacunnet, or Hampton, as it later became known, was incorporated.

Aquila Chase was among that first group of settlers who came to Hampton with Rev. Stephen Bachilor in 1638, and he is considered one of the founders of the town.

Almost immediately, title to this land was disputed. Winnacunnet also fell within a thirty-square-mile parcel of land bought by Rev. John Wheelwright and others from the sachem Wehanownowit, his son Pummadockyon, and two other Pawtuckets, Aspamabough and James. These Natives lived on and near the Swampscott River close to Exeter, a few miles inland from the town site. In the Wheelwright deed, "land which is broken up" for Native planting was exempted, and the deed specifically allowed the Indians to hunt, fish, and fowl throughout the tract. Wheelwright had been exiled from the Massachusetts Bay Colony in 1638 for "contempt and sedition" during a religious controversy known as the Antinomian Crisis. He had bought the land because it extended from three miles north of the Merrimack to the Piscataqua River and therefore was considered outside the bounds of the Massachusetts Bay Colony patent. The land was very valuable to farmers, as the salt marshes provided ready hay for cattle. In *New England's Prospect*, published in 1634, William Wood wrote,

> In a word, it [Ipswich] is the best place but one, which is Merrimacke, lying 8 miles beyond it, where is a river 20 leagues navigable: all along the river side is fresh Marshes, in some places 3 miles broad. In this river is Sturgeon, Sammon, and Basse, and divers kinds of fish. . . . So that these two places may containe twice as many people as are yet in New England; there being as yet scarce any inhabitants in these two spacious places.[23]

Wheelwright wrote to the Massachusetts Colony asking the Winnacunnet settlers to cease settlement but the General Court responded that at the time of his purchase, Winnacunnet lay within the Massachusetts patent. Failing that, by the European legal principle of *vacuum domicilium*, Massachusetts had taken possession of vacant land by building a house on it two years earlier. Most important, the court denied the validity of title to unimproved lands derived from Indians, maintaining that they had a natural right to only so much land as they had actually improved, or were able to improve. All other lands were available for occupation and improvement by others. This was an argument that would be used time and time again to invalidate Native title to the land.

It was a disingenuous argument for several reasons, and not all colonists supported it. It was based on the erroneous assumption that the Indians had no fixed habitations and therefore no concept of land-ownership, a view that persisted among the English because it served their interests by limiting Native territorial rights. Roger Williams, who was the minister at Salem for a short period in the early 1630s, pointed out that, while the Natives cultivated only a small portion of their land, they used virtually all of it for hunting. Furthermore, they "improved" their hunting lands by burning the underbrush annually or semi-annually to facilitate hunting. Because they used their land as fully as English farmers did theirs, "no man might lawfully invade their Propriety." If the English were entitled to these hunting lands, Williams argued, then the Indians were equally entitled to the great hunting parks of the English Crown and nobility! He insisted that it was "a National Sinne" to lay claim to Indian lands by virtue of the royal patent, when that title to the land rested with its Indian owners and was lawfully acquired only by purchase. But Williams's views were not tolerated within the Massachusetts Bay Colony, and his insistence on Indian land rights was one of the reasons he was banished from the Colony on pain of death in 1636. The Puritans' proprietary attitude to Native land is captured in an old joke about the Puritans: "Voted, that the earth is the Lord's and the fulness therof; voted, that the earth is given to the Saints; voted, that we are the Saints."[24]

Massachusetts successfully retained possession of Winnacunnet, renamed it Hampton, and ignored Native title to it, and Aquila Chase was among the first wave of settlers to support the Bay Colony in doing so. Chase received the official grant for his land in Hampton in 1640, two years after his arrival in the new settlement, and built a house close to the Landing, where the first settlers had brought their shallops to shore. John Wheeler also moved to Hampton shortly after the settlement of the town, probably in 1638 or 1639. In the spring of 1638, his eleven-year-old son David Wheeler, who had been left behind in England in 1634, arrived via the *Confidence* of London to join him and the family.

There was no Native village in the immediate vicinity of Hampton at that time, although the nearby Merrimack River had long been a major waterway for the Native nations and William Wood's map of 1633–34 showed an aboriginal camping ground or fishing station called "Pentucket" on the south bank of the Merrimack, near the eastern end of Deer Island. But some Pawtuckets apparently lived very close to the English: the name Wigwam Row was given to one of the early areas of Hampton. English oral tradition recorded that in Hampton, "the Indian papooses . . . would, in times of peace, often go to the log-huts of the new settlers, to play with their children."[25]

John Wheeler stayed in Hampton only briefly, for in 1638, the Massachusetts General Court also granted Simon Bradstreet and Daniel Denison of Ipswich, and others of Newbury – including three men originally from Salisbury, England – permission to begin a plantation at "Merrimack," immediately south of Hampton on the north side of the Merrimack River. The first actual settlement dates to the spring of 1639; John Wheeler was one of those original settlers, receiving a house lot in the first division of land at Salisbury, in 1641. He is listed as number 66 on the original list of 69 proprietors. The town was first named Colchester, then Salisbury – ten of the original 60 grantees were from Salisbury, England, and the town's first pastor was Rev. William Worcester, who also hailed from Salisbury.

The land on which John Wheeler homesteaded was very likely open land from Indian fields or cleared village sites, as at Hampton, Amesbury, and other towns founded in the area. First he would have built a temporary shelter, perhaps a cellar roofed with thatch or turf or a rudimentary shack of striplings and clay. Later he would construct a framed house, one room at a time, sheathing the house on the outside with clapboard and thatching the roof with straw or building it of plaster and logs. He either brought with him from England or soon acquired a musket, tools such as axes, a spade, saw, hoe, scythe, sickle, and a froe for cleaving shingles, as well as a harness for a draft animal and utensils such as a frying pan and cooking pot. For the first months at a new location, his family likely lived on salt pork, some molasses and butter, Indian corn and other grains, peas and beans, and perhaps some cheese.

As soon as possible he would have begun to plant the first crop. Most farmers planted wheat, rye, flax, and peas, Indian corn, and beans. They also grew fruit trees, such as apples, pears, and quince. John Wheeler drank beer, then later cider. He may have been able to obtain an ox, cow, bull, or a few pigs. If he owned a horse, he would have needed to obtain bog-shoes for it to enable it to walk on the extensive salt marshes near Hampton and Salisbury, where the salt hay was harvested for cattle. He may also have gathered seaweed for fertilizer.

Soon rude plaster-and-log houses encircled the fenced-in common, as well as the log-cabin meeting house, a court house, stocks, a whipping post, a garrison house, and a jail. By 1643, Salisbury was the shire town for Norfolk County.

In 1642 a rumour circulated that the Indians from the Hudson to Penobscot rivers were conspiring to make war upon the English. As a precaution, a certain quantity of gunpowder was distributed to every town in the colony: Hampton, Salisbury, and Newbury received one barrel each. Governor Winthrop summoned the magistrates and deputies to a special session of the General Court and ordered that all Indians within the colony be disarmed. A warrant was sent to Ipswich, Rowley, and Newbury to disarm Passaconaway.

I do not know if John Wheeler or any of his sons or his son-in-law, Aquila Chase, were among the forty armed men who attempted to carry out this order. The expedition failed because of the heavy autumn rains and other difficulties. In his journal Winthrop recorded that "they could not go to his wigwam, but they came to his son's and took him, when they had warrant for, and a squaw and her child which they had not warrant for."[26] Passaconaway's son Wannalancet was led about by a rope until he managed to escape; he was fired on, wounded, and recaptured. The English then sent a message to Passaconaway, inviting him to come to Boston and confer with officials. He refused to come until the captives had been released.

Fearing a strong reaction by the Pennacooks to the mistreatment of Passaconaway and his son, the General Court ordered the captives released. Two sergeants were instructed to go with guides and interpreters to the Native people living in the vicinity and explain why the order to disarm Passaconaway and others had been issued: "You are to informe them of o^r true intent in disarming the Indians neare us & that wee meane to render them their armes againe when wee are satisfied of their innocensy & that what was done to Passaconnaway his sonne, et. was through his owne p'vocation & not by any order from us (for wee intended only to speake wth him) & that wee have given order to have his squa a& papoose to bee sent whom to him againe."[27] The General Court later ordered that all arms should be restored to their Native owners and that Passaconaway should be compensated or given satisfaction in some way.

It is not known by what means the English propitiated Passaconaway but he later became a "friend" to the English. The Bay Colony's records state that on "May 29, 1644, Passaconnawat & his sonnes offering & desireing to come under this government, according to such articles as Cutshamache & others have formerly bene accepted, they were accepted, & he & one of his sonnes subscribed the articles, & he undertooke for the other."[28] However, it is unlikely that Passaconaway and the English understood their agreement in the same way. According to Peter Leavenworth, Passaconaway did not perceive what he had signed as a capitulation or surrender, although he did agree to place his territories under nominal English control. More likely he anticipated sharing his territories with the English in exchange for their protection.

He had probably also concluded that it was impossible to stop the encroachment of the English, and that more advantage was to be gained through friendship than open resistance. In 1660, when very ill, he addressed a great gathering of his people on the Merrimack River, reportedly to say farewell and to warn them to run away from war with the English should it come. A "Person of Quality" heard the old shaman's oration and recorded an English version:

> I am now going the Way of all Flesh, or ready to die, and not likely to see you ever met together any more: I will now leave this Word of Counsel with you, that you take heed how you quarrel with the English for though you may do them much mischief, yet assuredly you will all be destroyed, and rooted off the Earth if you do. . . . I was as much an Enemy to the English at their first coming into these Parts, as any one whatsoever, and did try all Ways and Means possible to have destroyed them, at least to have prevented them sitting down here, but I could in no way effect it . . . therefore I advise you never to contend with the English, nor make War with them.[29]

Certainly, during Passaconaway's long sachemship the English in northeastern Massachusetts benefited from his commitment to peace. Over the years more and more towns were founded and some were relocated to accommodate larger populations. To resolve complaints about their land, the Newbury settlers at Parker River, for example, decided to move the town of Newbury to the southern shore of the Merrimack River, across from Salisbury, as the new site was believed to offer better commercial advantages. In 1646, the freeholders of Newbury granted John Wheeler's son-in-law Aquila Chase (then of Hampton) four acres of land for a house lot at the new town, six acres for a planting lot and six acres of marsh "on condition that he do goe to sea and do service in the towne with a boate for four years."[30] Aquila is reputed to have sailed between Newburyport and Boston. My ancestors Ann Wheeler and Aquila Chase moved to Newbury before the birth of their second child in 1647; their new house lot was beside that of her brother, David Wheeler. Their move may also have been prompted by an embarrassing moral lapse of the sort only the Puritans could have cared about – it would certainly have mystified their aboriginal neighbours: David, Ann, and Aquila appeared before the Court at Hampton and were admonished and fined for picking peas on a Sunday.[31]

John Wheeler joined them in 1650, and they seem to have flourished in their new home. John, Ann, and Aquila lived there for the rest of their lives. By 1688, a town inventory recorded that Aquila owned 1 house, 10 acres of plough land, 10 acres of pasture, 1 horse, 2 oxen, 4 cows, 1 heifer, 1 calf, 15 sheep, and 2 pigs. His son Moses was also set up by that time with his own house on a more modest scale.

But as the English settlements grew, the Pawtuckets gradually gave up more and more of their land. By the late 1650s, the price for beaver skins had plummeted, and the Pawtuckets sold more land to acquire the trade goods they now relied on. Frequently they bought these items on credit. Over time the English legal acknowledgement of Indian rights grew increasingly superficial, and many settlers blatantly violated previous agreements, particularly with regard to usufruct rights. By the 1660s it was evident that the English would not share in the use of the lands they bought, yet the Pawtuckets continued to sell their lands – by then they did not have a lot of other options. As Peter Leavenworth comments, with hindsight we can see that, as a nation, they were being dispossessed, but at the time land sales seemed to be the best way for individual Natives to sta-bilize their lives and survive in the new world growing up around them. Some ended up moving into the English towns: for example, when house lots and farm lots were assigned in the new settlement of Newbury in exchange for land previously granted at Parker River, one "John the

Indian" received sixty-one acres. In the early days of the new settlement, as many as a dozen Pawtuckets are thought to have lived there. It's quite possible that the eleven children of Ann Wheeler and Aquila Chase played with the children of these "settlement Indians."

John Wheeler's wife, Agnes, died in 1662 in Newbury at the age of seventy. She and her husband had seen their family grow and prosper to an extent that probably would have been impossible had they never left Salisbury, England. That same year, Passaconaway, then well over a hundred years of age and destitute, had seen the land on which he lived granted to an Englishman and was forced to petition the General Court of Massachusetts for help. In a mere eighteen years from the time of his submission to the English, his people had been reduced from prosperity to the verge of starvation, as the fur trade declined and Englishmen armed with grants ordered them off their own lands.

The Court refused all three land grants that Passaconaway had requested to replace the land taken from him. Instead, the court granted the old sachem and his men a tract of land a mile and a half along either side of the Merrimack River in breadth and three miles in length, provided neither he nor they would alienate any part of this grant "without leave and license from this Court first obtained." The grant also included two small islands. In a final insult, Passaconaway was ordered to pay £25 for the surveying of his own land before the deed could be executed.[32] He passed his extreme old age "poor, forsaken and robbed of all that was dear to him, by those to whom he had been a firm friend for nearly half a century."[33] During his last years, a trading post was established at Pennacook (now Concord, New Hampshire) where, against the protests of the sachem Tahanto, another of Passaconaway's sons, unscrupulous traders illegally sold vast quantities of rum to the degradation of the remaining Pennacooks.

John Wheeler may never have set eyes on Passaconaway himself, but the contrast of their fortunes illustrates the dynamics of those early days of white settlement in that area of New England. The Wheelers flourished: numerous descendants bearing the name are still to be found along the northeastern coast. When John Wheeler died in 1670 at Newbury, at the age of seventy-nine, he had lived nine years longer than the average New Englander of the first generation, whose lifespan was itself ten years longer than his counterparts in England, while the lifespans of most Native Americans had plummeted.

THE ELIOT FAMILY

Five Generations of the Family of Jacob Eliot [Brother of John Eliot]

I. **Jacob Eliot** (brother of **John Eliot**)	married	Margery (?)
II. Sarah (Eliot?)	m.	James Harris (1642–1715)
III. Asa Harris (1680–1715)	m.	Elizabeth Rogers Stanton (1673–1750)
IV. Asa Harris (1709–1762)	m.	Anna Ely (1716–1788)
V. Ely Harris (1755–1813)	m.	Lucretia Ransom (1756–1836)

For subsequent generations, see the Harris genealogy in the Harris Family section.

CHAPTER
4

The Saints

If John Wheeler and his family left England as much to better themselves economically as for religious reasons, others, including some members of the Puritan clergy, forsook the comforts and privileges of relative wealth and high social status for the sake of conscience. This was certainly the case for two remarkable ministers from Essex, John Eliot and Thomas Weld, who ended up playing leading roles in the early days of the Massachusetts Bay Colony and sharing the pulpit at First Church of Roxbury, on the outskirts of Boston. Neither of them is my direct ancestor, but I believe I am descended from John Eliot's brother Jacob, who arrived in Massachusetts with his brother on the *Lion* in 1631. Jacob's daughter Sarah appears to have been the Sarah who married my ancestor James Harris of Boston in 1668 (see family chart), though for the past hundred years this Sarah was erroneously believed to be Sarah Denison, a grandniece of Thomas Weld.[1] As the matter is still not resolved conclusively, I claim them both as ancestors; certainly both contributed to my spiritual heritage.

It is hard to imagine two more distinct characters: John Eliot, deemed by some "the gentlest of men" and known for generations, if somewhat cynically now, as "Apostle to the Indians"; and Thomas Weld, known – and respected – by his peers for his uncompromising orthodoxy and intolerance. Weld was Eliot's senior by some years, and may have acted as his mentor. If Weld commanded enormous, even somewhat fearful, respect, of Eliot it has been written, "No man in early New England was so universally appreciated and loved." His sermons were noted for their simplicity and depth, rather than doctrinal sophistication or evangelical fervour. Stories abound of his generosity and self-sacrifice. According to the historian Samuel Eliot Morison, "Faith to him meant three things: love, duty and prayer."[2] Yet both men would play a role in the Puritans' attempts to convert the Indians, and their respective characters illustrate some of the contradictions inherent in this endeavour.

Jacob and John Eliot were sons of Lettese Aggar and Bennett Eliot, who held extensive lands in Hertfordshire and Essex. Bennett Eliot called himself a yeoman (an independent farmer). He was not a member of the aristocracy and his wealth may have been newly acquired. The family was likely related to older Eliot families recorded at nearby Waltham Abbey parish and Roxwell County, Essex, the latter related to one Thomas Eliot, born in Wales, who was known to be alive in 1491. John was baptized in 1604 and Jacob in 1606. Nothing is known of Jacob's early life, but his brother John studied at Cambridge, receiving his A.B. (Artium Baccalaureus) in 1622. He excelled as a scholar, particularly in classics. In 1625, the year the Great Plague struck Cambridge, he applied for orders. He taught for a time at a grammar school near Chelmsford, Essex, where he came under the influence of Rev. Thomas Hooker, later one of the founders of Hartford, Connecticut; there Eliot decided that the ministry was his vocation.

Eliot's decision to emigrate to New England was not the result of direct persecution, but stemmed from his desire to go where he and other church members could expunge "human creations, mere inventions" from the rituals of their church. When a number of his friends were about to leave for New England, they asked him to accompany them as their minister. He accepted, but when he first arrived in Boston a year after its founding, Eliot was initially called by the congregation of the First Church of Boston to take the place of John Wilson at the pulpit during Wilson's absence. It wasn't until 1632 that he joined Thomas Weld as pastor at the First Congregational Church in Roxbury, a small settlement immediately adjacent to Boston, where his friends had settled. His marriage to Hanna Mumford, his "dear, faithful, pious, prudent, prayerful wife,"[3] was the first one performed in the new church. He remained the pastor at Roxbury for fifty-eight years.

Weld, on the other hand, fits the stereotype of the Puritan divine who fled specifically to avoid persecution. As early as November 25, 1630, doubtless because some of his parishioners had complained, Weld's nonconformity had attracted the attention of William Laud, then bishop of London. For his conduct Weld was fined £20 on November 16, 1631, by the Ecclesiastical Commission. Eight day later, the Court of High Commission deposed him "for his contumacy [insubordination]."[4] As his colleague Thomas Shepard described the affair, Weld first appealed to Laud to restore him to a ministry in England, but the place became "too hot" for him, and he and Shepard, who had also been silenced, made plans to leave the country. Happening to be in the neighbourhood of a church where Laud was preaching, they went to listen. The bishop of London suddenly emerged from the church and accosted Weld for trespassing on church property when he was excommunicated. In a heated argument, the bishop accused Weld of intending to go to New England, which Weld admitted. Weld was then committed to the Pursuivant (a warrant officer) and bound to answer charges at the High Commission on a bond of 100 marks. Shepard, on the other hand, managed to escape, and when Laud later tried to arrest him, "away we rid as fast as we could," he wrote, "and so the Lord delivered me out of the hand of that Lyon."[5] Like many Puritans, Weld fled to Amsterdam. A few months later, he left for New England aboard the *William and Francis*. He arrived safely in June 1632 in Boston, and a month later was installed as first minister at Roxbury.

Many of Roxbury's early English settlers, including John Eliot and Thomas Weld, came from Essex. They were "people of substance," rather than "of the poorer sort," and many of the men were farmers or craftsmen. "A note of ye estates and persons" of Roxbury in 1639 – the earliest extant list of its inhabitants – records the number of acres and amount of tax paid by each settler. The sixteen largest landholders included Thomas Weld and his brother Joseph and John Eliot's older brother Philip. John Eliot had fewer than forty acres, while his brother Jacob had remained in nearby Boston.[6]

By the summer of 1632, the first Roxbury meeting house – a "rude and unbeautified" structure, with a thatched roof, no shingles, plaster, gallery pew, or spire – was built on Meeting-house Hill, the site of the present church of the First Religious Society. The First Religious Society of Roxbury was the sixth in New England, after Plymouth, Salem, Dorchester, Boston, and Watertown. Thomas Weld was among its nineteen founders. In

1632 he was ordained pastor and John Eliot was made teacher of the church and society.

I try to imagine the religious excitement that prevailed in Massachusetts during the early 1630s. No longer constrained by the threat of persecution, surrounded by those they considered sinners, or forced to participate in ceremonies they considered abominations, the Puritans of the Massachusetts Bay Colony could finally devote themselves to the task of establishing a truly godly community – a Christian Commonwealth – based on Scripture. Like the Salisbury reformers a decade earlier, they aimed to create their own utopia. Every aspect of human life was to be reconstructed upon the sacred word of God and based upon the settlers' relationship with Him. The Massachusetts Bay Colony governor, John Winthrop, on board the *Arbella*, spoke of the settlers having "entered into Covenant" with the Lord, agreeing to be God's people and to live in a "godly fashion."[7]

Thomas Weld's early experience of the colony was so positive that he wrote home and urged his old parishioners to join him:

> Here we are come into as goodly a land as ever mine eyes beheld. Such groves, such trees, such an air as I am fully contented withal and desire no better while I live. Yea, I see assuredly with industry and self-denial men may subsist as well here as in any place. . . .
>
> All things done in the form and pattern shoed in the mount, members provided, church officers elected and ordained, sacrament administered, scandals prevented, censured, fast days and holy feast days and all such things by authority commanded and performed according to the precise rule. Mine eyes, blessed be God, do see such administration of justice in civil government, all things so righteously, so religiously and impartially carried. . . .
>
> Praised and thanked be God who moved my heart to come and made open the way to me. And I profess if I might have my wish in what part of the world to dwell I know no other place on the whole globe of the earth where I would be rather than here. We say to our friends that doubt this, Come and see and taste. Here the greater part are the better part.[8]

John Eliot also wrote to friends in England, urging them to follow and assuring them that relations between the colonists and the aboriginal population were peaceful:

We are at good peace with the natives, and they do gladly entertain us and give us possession, for we are as walls to them from their bloody enemies, and they are sensible of it and also they have many more comforts by us, and, I trust, in God's time they shall learn Christ.[9]

Although the majority of Puritans who arrived on America's shores were not separatists when they left England (they still considered themselves reformers within the Church of England), the experience of emigration and the unlimited ecclesiastical freedom they found in New England far from the rule of bishops greatly transformed their attitudes and practices. New England ministers referred to England as Rome or Babylon, and described it as a land of idolatry; they accused the Church of England of being a false church and banned the *Book of Common Prayer*. The New Englanders soon evolved a new form of worship and church organization, which later became known as Congregationalism. While they did not overtly portray themselves as a model for the rest of the world to emulate, they believed that their form of worship was most fully in accord with New Testament direction and hoped that one day it would become universal.[10]

Under this new form of church government, membership was limited to the "Saints," those who had explicitly entered into a covenant with Jesus, wherein they agreed to observe and keep all His statutes, commands, and ordinances. After 1636 this was restricted further to those who also testified publicly about their experience of "conversion" – the action of divine grace on their souls. Thus membership was not automatic and excluded a large percentage of the population. (In Boston, fewer than half the adult male population were church members.) Authority over the church rested solely in the congregation and in no higher body; it was the congregation that selected and installed its pastor, teacher, elders, and deacons, all of whose duties could be found in the Bible and in the writings of the primitive church.

Early church services were plain in the extreme: the faithful sat on hard benches, the men and women on opposite sides of the house, with an official called a tithing man to keep them in order. Unaccompanied congregational singing was an important element of the service: rising from their seats, the congregation sang each line in unison from the psalm book as it was "lined out" by an elder.

Several accounts suggest that this could be an excruciating business, especially after the publication of the *Bay Psalm Book*, which had been compiled and translated from the Hebrew by John Eliot, Thomas Weld, and Richard Mather. In 1640 it became the first book published in English-speaking North America. Written in forced rhymes intended to aid memorization, some verses were virtually un-singable. One contemporary complained of "Sentences wrenched about end for end, clauses heaved up and abandoned in chaos, words disembowelled or split quite in two in the middle, and dissonant combinations of sound that are the despair of such poor vocal organs as are granted to human beings. The verses, indeed, seem to have been hammered out on an anvil, by blows from a blacksmith's sledge."[11]

For example:

And sat He would not then waste; had not
Moses stood (when He chose)
'fore him i' th' breach; ye turn his wrath
lest that he should waste those.[12]

Although complaints about the quality of the poetry led to a revision in 1651, the *Bay Psalm Book* was used widely both in public services and family devotions for more than a century, the twenty-seventh and last edition appearing in 1762.

In the colony's first years, the meeting house served not only as the spiritual home of the community but as the centre of political life as well. Here town meetings were held, and outside stood the stocks, whipping post, and pillory. In the holy commonwealth that the Puritans sought to create, church and state would co-operate closely to create a new moral order.

Although there were elements of Puritanism that undermined traditional political authority, such as its emphasis on individual conscience and the supremacy of Christ over secular authority, and Congregational church members had considerable power within their churches, political democracy as we know it today was not endorsed by the Puritan leadership (or any other ruling class in Western society). The government the Massachusetts Bay Puritans created omitted the feudal and hereditary elements of English government and allowed for the election of assistants to the General Court from within the class of freemen of the colony, who had to be full church members. Their leaders, however, still considered the social hierarchy God-ordained and themselves the natural leaders of the people. Most Massachusetts Bay Puritans conceived of their government as "sacred stewardship" and believed that God had commissioned the Colony's leadership to govern the Colony according to Gospel ordinance. Biblical texts such as I Corinthians 6:2 were cited: "Do ye not know that the saints shall judge the world?" The clergy, therefore, played a major role in forming the character of New England; together church and state created a political and religious orthodoxy that was mutually reinforcing.

As already mentioned, Roxbury was one of the original "big six pulpits" in early Massachusetts. The clergy of these churches were expected to articulate and defend Puritan beliefs and practices, and they did so through published sermons and theological treatises, committee work, and visitations. As historian Darren Staloff notes, however, a minister in one of these churches could advance controversial positions with some measure of impunity, as long as he acquiesced to majority opinion when called to do so. Eliot, for example, publicly criticized the 1634 "friendship" treaty with the Pequots: "It was then informed us, how Mr. Eliot, the teacher of the church of Roxbury, had taken occasion, in a sermon, to speak upon the ministry for proceeding therein, without consent of the people, and for other failings, (as he conceived)," wrote Governor Winthrop in his journal. The other ministers considered that no such consultation was necessary in the case of defensive treaties, and Thomas Weld and two other ministers were called in to "bring him to see his error"; Eliot was then instructed to "heale it by some public explanation of his meaning," which he did.[13]

Of the two Roxbury ministers, Thomas Weld was the senior and more orthodox, while Eliot at times expressed radical ideas that other New England divines did not share. Historian Richard Cogley points out that, after the execution of King Charles I in 1649, Eliot belonged to the anti-monarchical "Fifth Monarchy" millennial movement, and his book, *The Christian Commonwealth*, which outlined the political organization of the millennium, was ordered destroyed by the Massachusetts General Court in 1661 to avoid giving offence to the newly restored Stuart government in England.[14] He appears to have been more democratic in outlook than his peers: in *The Christian Commonwealth*, Eliot advocated a nearly universal adult male suffrage rather than suffrage restricted to male church members, and the work "not only ignored New England institutions, but also implied a severe critique of them."[15] By temperament, he was also a conciliator. In both *The Christian Commonwealth* and a subsequent work,

The Communion of Churches, he attempted to bring together different factions, such as the Congregationalists and the Presbyterians, so that they would co-operate in preparing for the millennium. "All difference of opinion," he wrote, "is apt to breed alienation of attention and give entrance to Satan, and grief to the spirit of life and peace."[16]

Yet Eliot was no advocate of religious tolerance, and Weld most certainly was not. The religious freedom that the Puritans came to America to enjoy is sometimes erroneously assumed to have been based on a belief in religious toleration. In fact, the Puritans did not sanction extending religious freedom to all religions. Rather, they saw America as a safe place to live and worship according to their own interpretation of divine law and they acted harshly against those whose interpretations were different. Like most of their contemporaries, the New England Puritans believed tolerance constituted a dangerous complacency toward evil and a sin against God. Indeed, most Europeans believed that a society would not be stable unless it was founded on the one true faith; so crucial was religion to the well-being of society that it simply could not be left to individual choice.

The government of the Massachusetts Bay Colony openly reinforced the power of the Puritan clergy in compelling conformity. And nowhere was this more evident than in the trial and banishment of Anne Hutchinson, in which both Eliot and Weld were deeply involved.

The Antinomian Controversy,[17] as the crisis involving Hutchinson and other "opposers" came to be called (*antinomian* means opposed to the law), came to a head in 1636, after a new requirement for Church membership was instated that involved publicly testifying about one's experience of "conversion." (In Puritan usage, "conversion" was the personal experience of divine grace that led a person to know he or she was saved and therefore a member of the Elect.) The new requirement provoked intense debate over how a saint was to know whether he or she was saved – an agonizing question since the alternative was eternal damnation. No one could take personal salvation for granted, and many people felt deeply anxious about their fate, searching relentlessly for signs of their own election. The "unprecedented inner loneliness"[18] of the Puritans that resulted from such introspection was too much for some: one desperate Boston woman threw her baby into a well, so that she would finally know she was damned. To assist their congregations, Puritan preachers wrote voluminous descriptions of the process of conversion in which the Elect came to know "experimentally" of their salvation. Some ministers spoke of the outward signs of "sanctification," that is, the leading of a righteous life, as evidence that Christ had redeemed, or "justified" a person's soul.

They were soon challenged by Anne Hutchinson, a Boston church member who held well-attended religious meetings in her home, influenced many people with her unorthodox theological interpretations, walked out of sermons she didn't like, and dared to criticize the ministers openly. Provocative as her behaviour was, it was intolerable from a woman, since women were not even allowed to speak in church except under certain circumstances. But Hutchinson had supporters in high places, including Massachusetts governor Sir Harry Vane, and other prominent citizens, including my probable ancestor, Jacob Eliot, John Eliot's brother.

Hutchinson charged that most of the Massachusetts Bay ministers, including Weld and Eliot, were preaching a covenant of "works" rather than "grace," leading people to believe that if they did good works and led a virtuous life they would find salvation, whereas, according to orthodox Puritan doctrine, only God knows who is saved, and good works have nothing to do with God's decision. The ministers, in turn, denounced Hutchinson for distorting their preaching, and they were incensed when she accused them not only of neglecting to teach the covenant of grace, but also of teaching only the forms and not the spirit of religion.

The dispute between the two factions raged through the Colony, affecting even the Massachusetts soldiers on their way to the Pequot War. Wrote Newbury chronicler Joshua Coffin:

It will serve to give the reader some idea of the all-pervading influence of the theological discussions, which were then agitating the whole community, to inform him . . . that these very troops deemed it necessary to halt on their march to Connecticut, in order to decide the question, whether they were under a covenant of grace or a covenant of works, deeming it improper to advance till that momentous question was settled.[19]

The threatened ministers soon retaliated. In 1637, the first church synod in New England condemned eighty-two "erroneous opinions" that were spread in the country, together with numerous "unwholesome" expressions. A number of resolutions were passed to silence dissent, such as prohibiting disorderly meetings of female church members, and the heckling of parsons from the meeting-house floor. Then, in the fall of 1637, Hutchinson was examined by the magistrates of the General Court; the judges were Governor John Winthrop, John Endecott, and Deputy-Governor Thomas Dudley. Eight of the most prominent preachers, including John Eliot and Thomas Weld, served as witnesses; Weld distinguished himself as one of her strongest and most persistent opponents.

Although Hutchinson defended herself effectively against most of the charges, her worst offence was her claim that she had received divine revelations directly – something that would have been completely acceptable and understandable to the original Native inhabitants of New England, who understood that spirits spoke to individuals through dreams and visions, but was intolerable to orthodox Puritans. The General Court banished her, and she was imprisoned for six days at the house of Joseph Weld, Thomas Weld's brother. Thomas Weld, "a holy inquisitor," and other ministers spent that time trying in vain to convince her of her error. Then, in March 1638, the Boston Church held a disciplinary hearing, in which she was admonished. At a second hearing she was excommunicated, and Pastor John Wilson read aloud her excommunication: "In the name of our Lord Jes[us] Ch[rist] . . . I doe cast yóu out . . . I doe deliver you up to Satan . . . I doe account yow from this time forth to be Hethen and a Publican. . . . I command you in the name of Ch[rist] Je[sus] and of this Church as a Leper to wthdraw your selfe out of the Congregation."[20] She subsequently left New England and five years later was killed in an Indian raid near what is now Rye, New York.

Followers of Hutchinson and of Rev. John Wheelwright, her brother-in-law and another figure in the controversy, also faced censure and excommunication. "The Church at Roxbury," wrote Winthrop, "dealt with divers of their members there who had their names to the petition [against Wheelwright's banishment], and spent many days in public meetings to have brought them to see the sin in that, as also in the corrupt opinions which they held, but could not prevail with them; so they pronounced to two or three admonitions, and when all was in vain they cast them out of the church."[21] Similarly, in Boston, John Eliot's brother Jacob was disarmed – though two years later he recovered sufficient community support to be appointed deacon of his church.

It's worth exploring European notions of truth and the resistance to religious toleration more fully, as these were almost diametrically opposed to the ideas and practices of those Native Americans whom John Eliot would later attempt to convert, and greatly influenced how Native Americans were treated by the colonists.[22] To most seventeenth-century Europeans, there was an absolute distinction between truth and untruth. It therefore followed that only one form of church could express the truth. Any other form of church was misguided and dangerous, since whole-hearted acceptance of the true doctrine was the only means to salvation. While acceptance of doctrine didn't guarantee salvation, rejection of it ensured damnation; furthermore, the defection of one member injured the Church as a whole.

In order to save Christianity and its followers from damnation, it was the duty of the State to stop heretics. This was why Pope Paul III had reconstituted the Holy Office of the Inquisition in Rome in 1542. Later, John Calvin used the same reasoning to get Michael Servetus burned at the stake in Geneva in 1553, thus replacing one dogmatic system with another. Calvin later defended this execution by citing God's command to the Israelites to slay the blasphemer and the idolater and pointing to such examples as the destruction of the prophets of Baal by Elijah. This sorry history of intolerance continued well into the seventeenth century, despite the ridiculous spectacle of so many sects – Baptists, Quakers, Jansenists, Jesuits, Catholics, Anglicans, Lutherans, Calvinists, Stoics, Arminians, Anabaptists, Ranters, Puritans – all claiming a monopoly on truth.

There were those who advocated toleration, but they were a small and often persecuted minority during most of the sixteenth and seventeenth centuries. An Italian engineer, Giacomo Acconcio, argued in his 1561 *Strategematum Satanae* that the belief that one has found truth to the exclusion of all others is a trick of the devil to make men commit the sin of pride, and he rejected the basic assumption of an absolute and objective truth that could be denied only out of perversity. Similarly, the Socinians said that those who are so convinced that they alone know the truth that they persecute others who do not agree with them are committing the very error that the Pharisees did in crucifying Christ. In *Heptaplomeres*, political philosopher Jean Bodin stated that, if the test of truth is universal agreement, then Christianity was no more verifiable than any other religion, but he dared not publish this conclusion. In 1619 the atheist Lucilio Vanini was burned as a heretic in Toulouse for saying that a human being was a biological phenomenon whose character was formed by the natural circumstances of his life, and that religion kept poor people in servitude.

In New England, Roger Williams argued for religious toleration and founded the colony of Rhode Island, the first tolerating state in the English-speaking world, but his books were burned by Puritans in England in 1644. In the Massachusetts Bay Colony, Puritans whipped, imprisoned, and banished Quakers, in some instances hanging them on Boston Common for their religious beliefs.

Even in such an intolerant age, the Puritans were known for their "rage for purity."[23] Two aspects of Puritan thought greatly reinforced this intransigent zealotry. Their belief that the Bible was the only word of God, and the whole word of God assumed that the entire world could be described and fixed through biblical language for all time and that truth could be known absolutely. By their doctrine of the Elect, education and reason could not bring salvation (although the Puritans highly valued both); the only means of knowing divine truth was by revelation, and this privilege was largely reserved for the biblical Patriarchs. Human beings could not be virtuous save by God's divine grace. Thus only the Elect and justified knew God's truth; the rest of humankind were damned, existing in darkness, spiritual ignorance, and sin.

The Puritans' willingness to do battle with heretics was further fuelled by their belief that, before the heavenly city could appear upon earth and before redemption could begin, the godly had to engage with Antichrist in a long and bloody battle.

It is hard to imagine a more contrasting world view than that of the Native American peoples into whose land the Puritans were now flooding. According to Henry W. Bowden and James P. Ronda in *John Eliot's Indian Dialogues: A Study in Cultural Interaction*, while Christian leaders tried to determine proper conduct according to a rigid biblical standard that they considered valid for all circumstances, the Native world view was far more flexible and less dogmatic in its theology.[24] Native Americans did not perceive such a sharp and mutually exclusive distinction between good and evil, nor did they expect all people to act in the same way or think alike. They put great value on personal initiative as well as the well-being of the group. While their social values were built on an ethic of communalism, individuals had great freedom to act on their own as they saw fit. In fact, one of the things that made the indigenous people uncivilized in English eyes was their lack of a strong centralized authority to enforce conformity.

Similarly, political authority depended to a great extent on the character of the leader, and not on coercion. While sachems could exercise control over a large geographic area, their influence depended upon their diplomatic skill, personal charisma, and ability in warfare rather than on laws defining a traditional office. Although their positions were usually hereditary, sachems could be discredited, and they had nowhere near the same authority or supporting infrastructure that European kings did, though Europeans mistakenly equated the two. Even warfare was a volunteer effort; there was no sanction against those who did not join the usually small-scale attacks and counterattacks characteristic of Native warfare in pre-contact America.

Although Weld, Eliot, and the other New England divines tried to reassert their power to enforce religious conformity in the wake of the Antinomian Controversy, events in England aroused new anxieties among the settlers. In the summer of 1640, Charles I lost the second Bishops' War, leaving himself in a very weakened position. The Long Parliament was convened in November 1640 and abolished ship money, the High Commission, and the hated Star Chamber. The English Puritans grew daily more powerful, and they succeeded in impeaching the King's ministers and excluding bishops from the House of Lords. State persecution of Puritans ceased, and as a result so did the Puritan emigration to New England. A severe colonial recession ensued. With the English Puritans now ascendant in England, the Mother Country appeared to be on the path to true reformation at last. Many colonists packed up and returned to England permanently, leaving those remaining in New England both economically and psychologically depressed.

As ever-more-dramatic events unfolded in England, a new millennial doctrine gained currency on both sides of the Atlantic that would greatly influence John Eliot: the belief that the "Middle Advent" of Christ was now at hand. A generation earlier, a Puritan theologian, Thomas Brightman, had reinterpreted the Book of Revelation and popularized the notion of the threefold coming of Christ. According to him, between the traditional first coming of Christ in the flesh and His last coming to preside over Judgment Day, there would be a second coming. This would not be a personal appearance of the Lord but an outpouring of His "brightness" – a huge manifestation of supernatural power that would revolutionize the course of world history, resulting in a renewal of the church and the world.[25]

The two chief events of this second coming would be the miraculous conversion of the Jews to Christianity and the defeat of Catholic and

Muslim armies – the forces of Antichrist – by the Protestants in the final battle of Armageddon. The whole world would then turn to Christ and a Golden Age of many generations would follow (Brightman said six hundred years). During this worldwide millennial reign of Christ just before the end of history, the world would partially realize the Kingdom of God and a New Jerusalem would appear, not in Heaven but as the trans-figured church on earth. Human government would no longer be necessary, as all things would be done by divine direction and all human innovations and novelties would be discarded.

This outburst of fervent millennialism marked an important change in Protestant historical thinking. According to historian Theodore Dwight Bozeman, "Thomas Brightman's *Revelation of the Apocalypse* became the eschatological *magnum opus*, in which the full force of an optimistic expectation concerning history [was] first felt."[26] Yet, as Bozeman contin-ues, there is a curious paradox in this development. Although such think-ing eventually gave rise to the idea of linear progress and the orientation to the future so characteristic of Western culture today, the future the Puritans envisaged was actually a climactic return to primordial purity, to that great First Time of the Bible that they so earnestly desired to experience – fun-damentally, it was a return to the past.

While some scholars have argued that the Puritan leaders in New England believed that the Massachusetts Bay Colony was God's Elect Nation and would be the site of the New Jerusalem, more recent scholarship has cast doubt on this thesis and suggests that the New England Puritans generally thought that the ruin of Rome, the rise of a Jewish church, and the inauguration of the millennium would take place far from America. Many thought a newly reformed England would play a special role in these events. What, therefore, would New England's role be?

According to Bozeman, ministers in the Massachusetts Bay Colony such as John Cotton (who greatly influenced John Eliot) considered the New England churches at the forefront of the Protestant Reformation, because of their relatively purified and covenanted congregations. But they stopped short of advocating Congregationalism as a model for England, because they knew the New England form of church government was not acceptable to most English Puritans, who wanted to preserve the Church of England as the national church. Nevertheless, some ministers in New England were eager to help English Puritans in the work of reformation.

Accordingly, in early 1641, when Thomas Weld, Hugh Peter, and William Hibbins were asked to travel to England "to seek financial aid for the colony," they were also instructed to help "further the work of English church reformation."[27]

. Upon their arrival in England, Weld, Peter, and John Winthrop, Jr., who had travelled to England on the same ship, were offered the opportunity to participate directly in the war against the Antichristian forces: they were invited to participate in a semi-official campaign of retaliation against the Catholic Irish for their slaughter of Protestants in Ireland earlier in the year. Peter and Weld accepted at once. They were duly enrolled as chaplains with the forces of Alexander Forbes, "a tough and humourless Scottish baron with a background of religious warfare," who set out in the summer of 1642 with six ships and twelve hundred men to sack coastal Munster and Connaught, "a quite pitiless performance in the spirit of Israel smiting the Canaanites."[28] Hugh Peter served as Lord Forbes's personal chaplain during his expedition, and his lordship was apparently much guided by his advice. Peter would later remark that "the wild Irish and the Indian do not much differ."[29]

Although Weld and Peter did raise money for New England until 1645, they never returned to America. As Parliament gained the upper hand and imprisoned the king's ministers, Weld and Peter became active supporters of the new Commonwealth and rose to influence with Oliver Cromwell; Hugh Peter became his personal chaplain and walked by the side of the Protector's secretary, John Milton, at Cromwell's funeral. After the Restoration, Peter would be executed.

During the Interregnum, Thomas Weld obtained a comfortable parish in the north of England. He served as rector at Wanlip, Leicester, for a time in 1646, and on February 1, 1649, was installed at St. Mary's, Gateshead, Durham. He continued to attack heresy wherever he perceived it, co-authoring a number of pamphlets denouncing Quakerism, "Jesuit plots," and Anabaptists.[30]

Although Oliver Cromwell enforced religious toleration in England during the 1650s, Weld did not comply. He alienated the majority of his parishioners by excluding all but the "Elect" from the sacraments. According to a historian of Durham,

Weld's own parishioners complained bitterly in 1657, that he had for 8 years refused the favour of administering the Sacrament to any of the

parish but to eight women and two men, weak and unstable persons that
(were) sublimed [?] his converts; nor would he permit his excommunicated flock consisting of 1,000 persons, to engage a lecturer to adminis-
ter the means of Salvation.[31]

   But my favourite story about Thomas Weld goes back to 1643, shortly
after Archbishop Laud fell from power and was imprisoned in the Tower of
London. Laud recorded in his diary that Thomas Weld came to visit him,
apparently to taunt him and gloat over their change of fortunes:

> *On Thursday Decemb.* 28. [1643], which was *Innocents day*, one Mr.
> *Wells* [sic], a *New England* minister, came to me, and in a boisterous
> manner demanded to know, whether I had Repented or not? I knew him
> not, till he told me he was Suspended by me, when I was Bishop of
> *London* and he then a Minister in *Essex*. I told him if he were Suspended,
> it was doubtless according to Law. Then upon a little further Speech, I
> recalled the Man to my Remembrance, and what care I took in confer-
> ence with him at *London-House*, to recall him from some of his turbulent
> ways; but all in vain: And now he inferred out of the good words I then
> gave him, that I Suspended him against my Conscience. In conclusion he
> told me, I went about to bring *Popery* into the Kingdom, and he hoped I
> should have my reward for it. When I saw him at this heighth, I told him,
> he and his fellows, what by their Ignorance, and what by their Railing,
> and other boisterous Carriage, would soon actually make more *Papists*
> by far, than ever I intended; and that I was a better *Protestant* than he or
> any of his Followers. So I left him in his Heat.[32]

The irony, of course, is that Thomas Weld, like so many others, was easily
as intolerant as Archbishop Laud himself. In those days it was the mark of
a good Christian.

CHAPTER
5

First Fruits

With the political ascendancy of the English Puritans after 1641, there was increased criticism in England of New England's lack of progress in converting the Indians. In fact, until 1646, very little if any proselytizing took place and the "principall ende" of the plantation seemed to be that of acquiring land and maintaining security for those who had fled England as a persecuted minority. Thomas Lechford, a lawyer who lived in the Bay Colony from 1638 to 1641, stated on his return to England that no one had been sent out by any church to learn the Natives' language, or to instruct them in religion: "They have nothing to excuse themselves in this point of not laboring with the Indians to instruct them but their want of a staple trade, and other businesses taking them up."[1]

The Colony's agents, Thomas Weld and Hugh Peter, addressed this public relations problem head on by using the Indian cause as a rationale to raise money in England for the Massachusetts Bay Colony. In 1643, they published a pamphlet, *New England's First Fruits*, the very first of what would be many fundraising tracts produced in support of missionary work among the Natives of New England. They appealed for English donations to the newly founded Harvard College by "stirring up some to shew mercy to the Indians, in affording maintenance to some of our godly active young schollars, there to make it their worke to studie their language, converse with them, and carry light amongst them, that so the gospell might be spread into those darke parts of the world."[2] The pamphlet also appealed for funds to send poor children to New England as indentured servants.

First Fruits was also written to revitalize the emigration movement to New England. "Thus farre hath the good hand of God favoured our beginnings," the pamphlet reads, and cites examples of the "remarkable passages of His providence. . . . In sweeping away great multitudes of the natives by the smallpox, a little before we went thither, that he might make room for us there." Another sign of God's providence was

> In giving us such peace and freedom from enemies, when almost all the world is on a fire that (excepting that short trouble with the Pequits) we never heard of any sound of warres to this day. And in that warre which we made against them God's hand from heaven was so manifested, that a very few of our men, in a short time, pursued through the wildernesse, slew and took prisoners about 1,400 of them, even all they could find, to the great terrour and amazement of all the Indians to this day: So that the name of the Pequits (as of Amaleck) is blotted out from under heaven, there being not one that is, or (at least) dare call himself a Pequit.

The authors also saw God's hand

> in settling and bringing civil matters to such a maturity in a short time among us, having planted 50 towns and villages, built 30 or 40 churches, and more ministers houses, a castle, a colledge, prisons, forts, cartwaies . . . and all these upon our own charges, no publique hand reaching out any helpe: Having comfortable houses, gardens, orchards, grounds fenced, corne fields &c. and such a forme and face of a Commonwealth appearing in all the plantation, that strangers from other parts, seeing how much is done is so few years, have wonderd at God's blessings on our endeavors.[3]

Within a year the agents had collected nearly £2,000 in money and supplies, although their subsequent efforts were less successful. Only about £75 were earmarked for the conversion effort, and most of this came from a single donor, Lady Mary Armine, who made annual contributions of £20 for about twenty years. Curiously, the colonials distributed English donations to missions but did not themselves contribute to the cause, even once the colonies were well established – all of the missionary financing came from England. In fact, the New England colonists actually produced the smallest number of missionaries and exhibited greater indifference toward missions than did other Europeans.[4]

For reasons to be explored below, the Puritans did not begin their evangelizing for another three years. In 1645 an English Presbyterian minister, Robert Baylie, attacked the Congregationalist New Englanders, saying that of "all that ever crossed the American Seas . . . [the New England colonists] . . . are noted as most neglectful of the work of Conversion."[5]

A number of theories have been put forward to explain this apparent lack of interest. First of all, in Congregationalism, an individual was recognized as a clergyman only as long as he was associated with a specific church and provided satisfactory service for local parishioners. He could proselytize only when he could afford time away from his primary duty as minister of that church. Because he had to be ordained by full church members and depended on his congregation for his livelihood, it was not possible to be ordained by and preach only to pagan Native Americans. As a result, missionary efforts were always secondary to a minister's other activities, and Puritan missionaries did not live among local tribes in the seventeenth century as the Jesuits did in New France. While the Jesuits were often the first to establish contact with various Native peoples, Puritan missionaries began their work long after fur traders and others had been on the scene and indigenous cultures had already undergone significant change.

Secondly, the goal of evangelizing the Indians was a "public motive with a long history" and appeared in many royal charters, grants, and commissions from Elizabethan times onward, but was often included more out of convention than genuine missionary fervour.[6] There is no evidence that any of the colony's civil or religious leaders – not even John Eliot – emigrated primarily because they wanted to convert Native Americans. Nonetheless, they did consider the advantages such conversion would bring: it would "raise a bulwark against the kingdom of Antichrist which the Jesuits labor to rear up in all parts of the world" (especially New France) and increase the glory of Protestant England at the expense of Catholic France and Spain.[7] As historian Henry Bowden writes, "Puritan evangelical work seems generally to have been an afterthought, not a primary motivation, in the enterprise of colonizing the New World."[8]

The historian Richard Cogley, in his recent study of Eliot's missions, advances the theory that one aspect of the Puritans' religious belief explains the long delay in attempting to convert the Natives. Most political leaders and ministers in the Bay Colony, including John Eliot, considered the Indians to be non-Christian Gentiles, who could be converted, en masse, only after the Middle Advent of "Christ's brightness" had resulted in the Battle of Armageddon and the mass conversion of the Jews. The Jews would then liberate Palestine from the Ottomans and return to Jerusalem, where they would inaugurate the millennial reign of Christ. Missionaries appointed by the Lord of the Middle Advent would be responsible for converting the pagan peoples of the world (Thomas Shepard tentatively predicted that this mass conversion would come to pass in 1690), and the world would then endure until the traditional Second Coming, the resurrection of the dead, and the Last Judgment brought the earth's history to a close. According to Shepard, who would work alongside Eliot in the earliest missions, "till the Jews come in there is a seal set upon the hearts" of the Indians, although occasional conversions would be possible beforehand and were still worth the effort of proselytizing.[9] Nonetheless, the "Jews before Gentiles" sequence of this millennial philosophy probably delayed the founding of missions in New England.

In September 1646 – sixteen years after the founding of the Massachusetts Bay Colony – John Eliot, the brother of my probable ancestor Jacob Eliot, journeyed to the village of Cutshamekin, the regent for the under-age grand sachem of the Massachusett Indians, and preached his first sermon to aboriginal people. Apparently, it was not a successful meeting. "When I first attempted it, they gave no heed unto it, but were weary, and rather despised what I said," wrote Eliot.[10] Six weeks later, however, he tried again at Nonantum, the village of a man named Waban, and this time his audience was more attentive. Eliot was encouraged and began to preach to the Indians regularly. His sermons became more effective as his facility in the Massachusett language increased – his teacher was a Native servant or slave from Long Island who had been captured in the Pequot War.

There has been much debate among historians about the nature of Eliot's mission and the degree of coercion used to persuade Native Americans to accept it. In one view, argued first by Francis Jennings, the work to save souls was mingled with the desire of Massachusetts Puritans to assert their political authority over the indigenous inhabitants of New England.[11] In

1644, after rumours of a pan-Indian conspiracy and the English action of disarming the Natives, six sachems within the territory of Massachusetts, including Cutshamekin and Passaconaway, submitted to the Puritan government of Massachusetts, which enabled the settlers to gain control of their lands. As part of this treaty, they had to agree "to bee willing from time to time to bee instructed in the knowledg and worship of God."[12]

According to Jennings, actions the Boston authorities took to ensure conversions demonstrate the political importance of Eliot's undertaking. They introduced laws suppressing Native religion and providing for a missionary reservation where Christian Indians could be segregated. In November 1646 – soon after Eliot's first successful preaching at Nonantum – the General Court passed laws that no person within the jurisdiction of the Bay Colony, whether Christian or pagan, should commit blasphemy against God "either by wilful or obstinate deniing the true God, or his creation or government of the world, or shall curse God or reproach the holy religion of God . . . if any person or persons whatsoever, within our jurisdiction, shall break this lawe they shalbe put to death." The Court also outlawed the rituals of indigenous worship "that no Indian shall at any time pawwaw, or performe outward worship to their false gods, or to the devill," under penalty of heavy fines. The Court provided that two ministers would be chosen by elders at each annual court of Election to "make knowne the heavenly counsell of God among the Indians in most familiar manner," and also arranged for the purchase of land for a missionary reservation.[13] As Jennings points out, Native lands were acquired without compensation in 1644, through the submission of the sachems, distributed to towns and individuals, and then bought back with mission money in order to set up the reservation towns.

By all accounts, John Eliot was a dedicated, self-sacrificing person, who saw himself saving souls for the greater glory of God. Yet the government's motives for establishing Indian missions do appear to have been decidedly mixed. Jennings suggests that the missions emerged as the by-product of an attempt by Massachusetts to seize the territory on the west shore of Narragansett Bay from both the Narragansetts – its rightful owners – and the English colony in Rhode Island that claimed it as well. Certainly John Eliot began his missionary career immediately after an incident that demonstrated that Massachusetts had lost favour with England while Rhode Island had gained it. Massachusetts began loudly trumpeting Eliot's achievements, even claiming credit for converting Natives with whom

Eliot had never had contact. A week after Eliot's first meeting in Waban's village, the Massachusetts General Court had already instructed its new London agent, Edward Winslow (Weld and Peter were fired in 1645), to report to the English Parliament that settlers in Rhode Island were threatening the Indians in the Narragansett country who supposedly had submitted themselves to Massachusetts. Winslow complained that the Rhode Island colony was threatening the success of Eliot's proselytizing mission, "all which hopeful beginnings are like to be dashed."[14] This statement was deliberately misleading; Waban's village was nowhere near the Narragansett lands.

Recently, historian Richard Cogley, while agreeing that Massachusett's territorial designs in the Narragansett country played a role in the Bay Colony's decision to begin the mission, suggests a radically different explanation for its timing. According to Cogley, "Puritan missionary activity was not an early form of the aggressive evangelism so familiar to twentieth-century Americans."[15] He argues instead that the Puritans believed that Native Americans would be drawn to Christianity once they had witnessed the virtues of the Puritan way of life; cultural envy would lead them to ask for the Gospel. Thus, a mission could not begin until the Indians wanted to receive one. Numerous sources confirm that the Natives showed no collective interest in Christianity before the mid-1640s. As Eliot later wrote, at that time, the easiest way to get rid of burdensome Indians was to speak of Christianity to them. At least initially, the Puritans accepted this lack of interest; in the mid-1630s, John Cotton wrote, "we acknowledge and accordingly permit [them] to remain in their unbelief."[16]

According to Cogley, the submission of the six sachems to the Bay Colony in 1644 was what prompted the Massachusetts colony to initiate a mission. In reviewing the documentary evidence, he concludes that their submission was not forced, but came about at the instigation of the sachems themselves, especially the Massachusett sachem Cutshamekin, as a means to gain protection from the Massachusetts Bay Colony against enemies. According to Cogley, the sachems feared Narragansett reprisals for their support of the English and two renegade Narragansett undersachems in disputes over the Narragansett lands. This threat was especially great after the English approved the Mohegans' execution of the Narragansett grand sachem Miantonomo in 1644.

Cogley theorizes further that the Puritans interpreted the voluntary submission of the six sachems to English authority as Indian recognition of the superiority of English law and government, as well as a sign they were ready for religious instruction. John Winthrop, Sr., stated that "we now began to conceive hope that the Lord's time was at hand for opening a door of light and grace to those Indians."[17] Cogley points out that the enactment of the laws against blasphemy and idolatry may have been intended more to placate God than to force Native Americans to accept a mission, since no one was ever prosecuted under them – the Puritans simply feared that open toleration of these practices might bring the wrath of God upon their own Colony.

There is no evidence that Eliot had any particular interest in evangelizing before the onset of the mission in 1646. He may have been only the first in a planned rotating roster of ministers who were to preach to the Indians on a regular basis. However, it seems that his experience of preaching to them affected him deeply and gave him a new vocation. Two weeks after he preached at Nonantum, Eliot's first prayer in a Native language moved one Massachusett man to tears. After the meeting, the Englishmen spoke to the man, who "fell into more abundant renewed weeping, like one deeply and inwardly affected indeed, which forced us also to such bowels of compassion that wee could not forebeare weeping over him also: and so wee parted greatly rejoycing for such sorrowing."[18]

Over the next several years, Eliot visited Waban's village and that of the sachem Cutshamekin on alternate Thursdays, and also began to receive visits of the Natives to his home. Some offered him their children for Christian education or offered their own services as servants in exchange for religious instruction. The sachem of Concord, hearing of Eliot, came to see the minister for himself, was impressed, and invited Eliot to preach in his own village. In the summer of 1647, Eliot brought a number of Indians to a religious synod at Cambridge, where he preached to them in their language, and impressed the ministers, magistrates, and other people present.

Meanwhile, the Bay Colony's representative in England, Edward Winslow, described the colony as too poor to be able to support Eliot's work without English help, ignoring the considerable amount of wampum tribute paid to Massachusetts by various Native nations. At first he did not succeed in his efforts to obtain a licence to solicit funds in all the churches of England, mainly because of complaints about the poor accounting for donations collected in 1643. The money remitted by Thomas Weld had vanished and had

not been used for Indian missions. Finally, in 1649, Parliament authorized
Winslow to collect missionary funds nationwide. A new organization, the
Society for the Propagation of the Gospel in New England, was established
to transmit the funds to Eliot's mission. "The New England Company [as it
became known] stood as a perpetual testimonial to the colony's presumed
benevolence toward the Indians, and it regularly published tracts extolling
Eliot and his associates."[19]

Initially, such efforts attracted few donations, because of the suspected
misappropriation of funds by the two former agents, Weld and Peter. Weld
claimed that most of the money had gone to cover the expenses of bringing poor children (probably orphans) to New England as indentured servants. He later submitted statements to the General Court and the English
corporation and in 1649 wrote "Innocency Cleared," a defence of himself
and Peter. (They were finally cleared of wrongdoing in 1654.) "Innocency
Cleared" offered "A just defence of mr Weld and mr Peters . . . To silence
the malitious, to satisfie the Sober & to remove the obstruction of ye contribution for propagateing the Gospell to ye Natives in New England."
Weld exhorted all to open their minds and purses so that

> there may be no obstruction, either in good peoples contributing, or in
> godly ministers exciting their people to contribute freely to this glorious
> worke . . . houlding fourth the Lord Jesus Christ to those wofull soules
> that now sitt in utter darknes & goe downe to hell by troopes for want of
> light who heare are [no?] more[.] It will be no greife of heart to you . . .
> in time to come to remember . . . that you have bene happy instruments
> in Gods hands to advance ye kingdome of yr deare Lord & pull poore
> heathen soules out of the very mawe of yt Great Devourer . . . who by yr
> meanes, may, one day, come to meet you in ye highest heavens a& blesse
> god for you & wsp [worship] you to all eternitie.[20]

Inadequate bookkeeping continued to plague the company. Mission
records did not properly account for much of the money sent to New
England, and the company was forced to revise its financial procedures.
Much to the embarrassment of the company's officers, the colony spent
mission funds on arms and ammunition; mission funds also financed the
construction of a two-storey brick building at Harvard, which became
known as the Harvard Indian College – although it seems there were never
more than two Indians in residence there at a time.

In spite of these political uses of Eliot's missionary work, the New England Puritans do seem to have made a real effort, however feeble and unsuccessful, to provide education and Christian teaching to a small group of young Native American men at Harvard. Prospective Native students were first given a grammar-school education, an effort which drew upon the skills of several teachers, including Thomas Weld's brother. In 1642, John Eliot had founded, and Daniel Weld become a teacher and then master of, the Roxbury Grammar School. The institution still exists today. Weld enrolled his first Indian pupils in 1656, in his final decade of teaching, and taught until he died at the age of eighty. In 1662, he was paid by the authorities to prepare a number of Indian boys for Harvard. The Harvard entrance exam was quite challenging: in 1645, one had to be able "to understand Tully or such like classical Latin author extempore," and write and speak Latin "in verse and prose . . . and decline perfectly the paradigms or nouns and verbs in the Greek tongue."[21]

But the hopes of both the missionaries and those Native people who wanted their children to acquire skills to protect them in the colonists' world were in vain. The Harvard Indian College was an utter failure, as four of the five Native boys who are known to have attended soon died, and the experiment was abandoned after a few years. Nevertheless, for those who cared to notice, the students demonstrated extraordinary adaptability and persistence in spite of an unfamiliar sedentary life, corporal punishment, homesickness, a totally alien curriculum, the ethnocentrism of their teachers, and social isolation. Caleb Cheeshateanmuck, one of two Native students from Martha's Vineyard, graduated with a B.A. in 1665 and could write Latin and Greek and compose poetry in those languages; unfortunately, he died of consumption shortly after graduating. Eleazar (class of 1679) also wrote Greek and Latin poetry, but did not graduate, and Joel Hiacoomes (class of 1665) would have graduated had he not been murdered during his last college vacation.

Eliot himself was somewhat more successful in his own missionary efforts, though this success was always greatly exaggerated for propaganda purposes. In the early days of European settlement he made few conversions, as Native cultures were still relatively intact and strong enough to resist the imposition of a foreign belief system. Conversions increased as it became more and more difficult for Native Americans to maintain their traditional way of life, as epidemics, loss of land, increasing dependence on European trade goods, and the erosion of sovereignty took their toll. The missionaries depended upon and may have accelerated the pace of this cultural disintegration and also contributed to it.

As Native Americans saw that Christians apparently had the advantage in warfare and seemed immune to the new diseases that their own shamans were powerless to cure, their traditional understanding of how the world worked and how to control its workings was increasingly undermined. The English god appeared to be more powerful. William Wood said the Indians near Massachusetts Bay admired the English god, "because they could never yet have power by their conjurations to damnify the English either in body or goods," and also because "they say he is a good God that sends them so many good things, so much good corn, so many cattle, temperate rains, fair seasons, which they likewise are the better for since the arrival of the English, the times and seasons being much altered in seven or eight years, freer from lightning and thunder, long droughts, sudden and tempestuous dashes of rain, and lamentable cold winters."[22]

Some of the shamans themselves lost confidence in their abilities. As mentioned earlier, Passaconaway, the most powerful and revered powwow in New England, admitted to his followers that he had failed to rid them of the English through spiritual means. In 1649 he avoided Eliot when the latter came to proselytize him, but many of his people came to listen to Eliot and his "praying Indians," as the Christian Indians came to be called. A year later, Passaconaway himself, "exceedingly earnestly and opportunely," asked Eliot and Simon Willard to settle near his village and teach them,[23] perhaps to stave off the loss of many of his people through a secessionist Christian movement and, again, probably to gain greater protection against enemies, such as the Mohawks. Eventually, a number of Pennacooks and Pawtuckets became praying Indians and moved to the "praying town" of Wamesit (now Lowell), on the lower Merrimack. Eliot converted Passaconaway's son, Wannalancet, in 1674.

The English generally did not fear bewitchment by the shamans – although, on at least one occasion, they suspected that the powwows had bewitched their dogs. Thomas Weld and Hugh Peter, the authors of *First Fruits*, assured their readers that "we are wont to keep them at such a distance, (knowing they serve the Devill and are led by him) as not to imbolden them too much, or trust them too farre; though we do them what good we can."[24] John Eliot attacked healers as "great witches having fellowship with the old Serpent, to whom they pray," and he and other missionaries forbade converts to take part in traditional healing ceremonies.

Not surprisingly, most powwows reacted to this challenge to their authority by strenuously resisting the efforts of the English missionaries. Most sachems were just as hostile, though occasionally, when all else failed, they appealed to the English deity. For example, the Mohegan sachem Uncas, who resisted all efforts to introduce religious instruction among his people, summoned powwows to end a drought, and when they failed, he asked Rev. James Fitch of Norwich to pray (which appeared to be effective, as it rained soon after).[25] Yet most aboriginal leaders and elders were intensely aware that the missions represented a serious attack on their sovereignty and they fiercely opposed them. Those nations with the strongest leaders proved most resistant.

In retrospect, what is most surprising is that Native Americans listened to the missionaries as much as they did, for John Eliot and other missionaries denounced most aboriginal ideas and rituals as abominations and usually referred to Native traditions as barbarous, heathen, and uncivilized. The Puritans characterized Indian religion as devil worship and accused Native Americans of laziness, thievery, drunkenness, blood lust, and sexual promiscuity. Eliot hoped to "civilize" them, for he believed that they "must have visible civility before they can rightly injoy visible sanctitie."[26]

According to historians Henry W. Bowden and James P. Ronda, Eliot's message was in many ways a condemnation, a warning of God's wrath and a threat of eternal torment for those who disobeyed God's laws as expounded in the Bible. One can only imagine the reactions of Native people to the news that they were depraved and without hope unless God forgave them, and that they could do nothing to influence their fate. If they did not experience grace, they were doomed to everlasting punishment.

This way of thinking was utterly foreign to them. While the indigenous people of New England believed that sacrilegious acts would prompt retaliation from their gods almost immediately, they also believed that after death all people would dwell together in the same pleasant place. They never imagined a hell for those whose misdeeds called for punishment. John Josselyn commented: "they dye patiently both men and women, not knowing of a Hell to scare them, nor a Conscience to terrifie them."[27] But the new faith declared that only individuals could be saved, and that all beings were permanently separated into the Elect and the non-Elect. Converts would be separated from their friends and relatives, and from their own community for all eternity. This division was emphasized in this life by Eliot's insistence on the establishment of praying towns for

Christianized Natives. There, beyond the influence of heathen tribesmen, the praying Indians were expected to repudiate both their traditional cultures and communities.

The first and largest praying town was Natick, about eighteen miles by bridle path from Roxbury, established in 1650. Over the next quarter-century, fourteen more towns were established, all located an average of twenty-five miles from Boston. In each, would-be converts cut their hair, washed the bear grease from their skin, donned European clothes, and lived as nuclear families in separate houses, which were sometimes built in the English style. They adopted European farming techniques and tended domestic animals, planted orchards, used European tools, and even enclosed private plots of land with fences. They were required to become like Europeans in sexual behaviour, marriage, economy, and government, as well as religion. John Josselyn wrote, "They go clothed like the English, live in framed houses, have flocks of hogs and cattle about them, which when they are fat, they bring to English markets."[28]

Those seeking religious instruction in the praying towns were also required to subject themselves to the government of Massachusetts. The praying Indians were placed under the authority of an English military officer, who appointed Indian commissioners to enforce the laws Eliot drew up to promote virtue and discourage vice. These included punishments for such sins as unemployment, wearing long hair, and killing lice between the teeth. Fines and floggings ensured that town residents lived up to the new standards of piety.

The impetus to "civilize" the Natives came from several sources. As historians Henry Bowden and James Ronda observe, Eliot did not disavow Native culture simply because it was aboriginal: the Puritans were religiously and culturally opposed to all behaviour they considered ungodly, regardless of its origin. Having left England because they were not willing to compromise their own beliefs and conduct, they were as zealous in their efforts to transform the behaviour of fellow colonists as in changing the customs of Native people. While they believed that salvation depended on divine foreordination and not on human attempts to influence God's judgment through acts of virtue (remember the Antinomian crisis), they maintained that godly living had to follow as tangible evidence of the inner regeneration already begun through God's forgiveness. The English generally did not value or respect Native cultures, yet they thought aboriginal people could respond to grace and change their habits. They were "willing to admit that the Almighty could touch a Massachuset soul with the experience of saving grace as easily as He had apparently redeemed a select number of Cambridge graduates."[29]

There were, perhaps, other less-conscious motives. If aboriginal people settled as farmers rather than hunting, they would require much less land for their livelihood, and their military capabilities might be reduced. Certainly one of the purposes of proselytizing was to create firm allies among the Natives, who were otherwise expected to oppose the English. Cotton Mather reflected a common attitude when he wrote:

These parts were then covered with nations of barbarous indians and infidels, in whom the prince of the power of the air did work as a spirit; nor could it be expected that the nations of wretches, whose whole religion was the most explicit sort of devil-worship, should not be acted by the devil to engage in some early and bloody action, for the extinction of a plantation so contrary to his interests, as that of New England was.[30]

The ethnohistorian James Axtell has commented on the Puritan need to transform the culture of the Indians:

To convert the Indians of America was to replace their native character with European personae, to transmogrify their behavior by substituting predictable European modes of thinking and feeling for unpredictable native modes. By seeking to control the Indians' thoughts and motives, the missionaries sought to control – or at least anticipate – their actions, which could at any time spell life or death for the proliferating but scattered settlements on the farming frontier. Unwittingly or not, they lent powerful support to the European assault upon America by launching their own subversive invasion within.[31]

Once some Natives were converted, the praying towns served as the bases from which praying Indians could be sent to convert – some would say subvert – independent tribes.

Also totally foreign to Native culture was the actual process of conversion that John Eliot insisted upon, and it accounts for much of the reason that the Puritan missionaries met with less success than the Jesuits. The Puritans emphasized doctrine and stressed cerebral activities such as sermons, study classes, and reading the Bible, all of which made their religion less accessible to Native Americans. As Ronda and Bowden comment, it was a conception of religion that gave almost exclusive priority to cognition; Eliot and other Puritan missionaries "insisted that understanding must precede confession and that rational assent prepare the way for ritual participation. . . . The Puritans made little use of pictoral art, dance, rituals, dreams, or individualistic communion with spirit beings," as Native spirituality did. It was a measure of the "remarkable inner change" in the Indians who did convert that they agreed to abandon these practices.[32] The Jesuits, by contrast, focussed on children, appealed to both the senses and the emotions, and acculturated themselves to the aboriginal way of life; they attempted to reshape and reorient Native beliefs and practices rather than destroy them.

To facilitate Bible study, John Eliot devised a written form of the Massachusett language and over a number of years translated the Bible. Eliot's Bible, printed by a Nipmuck convert known as James Printer, was the first Bible to be published in North America. The press that printed it was housed in the building of the Harvard Indian College. Eliot also published a grammar of the Massachusett language, *The Indian Grammar Begun: or, An Essay to bring the Indian Language into Rules* (1666) that is believed to be "the first published attempt . . . at a description of an 'exotic' language which can justifiably be called scientific."[33]

Historians have differed markedly in their judgment of Eliot's praying towns and of the Indians who chose to live there. Some speak of conversion as such a negation of traditional cultural identity as to constitute a form of "cultural suicide."[34] Others argue that the praying Indians used the mission towns to counteract English domination rather than abet it, that conversion was a creative and pragmatic choice to adapt to an irrevocably changing world rather than to die resisting such changes. Thus, argues Richard Cogley, the praying Indians, who came largely from the most devastated tribes, overcame the collapse of the coastal fur trade and the loss of their land bases, and bettered their economic conditions through wage labour, apprenticeships, and cottage industries, as well as through consumer goods supplied free of charge from the New England Company. Because they retained some aspects of their traditional culture, such as living in wigwams, and were largely self-governing once they accepted Eliot's laws and forms of government, Cogley goes so far as to argue that the proselytes were more successful at maintaining their vitality, integrity, and independence than Eliot was at restructuring the Native way of life in line with his cultural goals – that the Natives defined the mission towns as much as Eliot did, and that he in turn had to adjust himself to their culture.

However, because Eliot's missions separated the converts from their clans and other tribal institutions and brought together individual converts from many bands into new political entities, tensions and factions soon arose among Native people in those towns. New loyalties were forged that attenuated or replaced kinship relations and weakened traditional spiritual ties to the land. The church was the source of the converts' new identities, and the visiting minister and local exhorters and elders became their new leaders.

In 1650 the Massachusett sachem Cutshamekin confronted Eliot, "because the Indians that pray to God, since they have so done, do not pay him tribute as formerly they have done. . . . And further [Cutshamekin] said, this thing are all the Sachems sensible of, and therefore set themselves against praying to God." In 1665, an English royal commissioner noted that missionaries in Massachusetts proselytized Indians "by hyring them to hear sermons, by teaching them not to obey their heathen princes, and by appoynting rulers amongst them over tenns, fifties, etc." The intention to subvert traditional Native political institutions was quite overt. Daniel Gookin, John Eliot's assistant, wrote, "Religion would not consist with a mere receiving of the word. . . . Practical religion will throw down their heathenish idols and the sachem's tyrannical monarchy."[35]

But Eliot's opposition to traditional Native political organization came from more than a desire to assert the Bay Colony's authority over the Natives; it had more to do with his misidentification of sachems as kings and his growing millennialism. For, as Richard Cogley reveals, Eliot believed that the execution of Charles I was an event of "world-historical significance." In this act he saw the beginning of the destruction of the universal dominion of kings and a reversal of the ongoing degeneration that had been proceeding since the time of the biblical patriarchs. He came to believe that Nimrod had invented the institution of monarchy against God's will and that kings governed with their own interest in mind, not God's. Like the Fifth Monarchists in England, he anticipated that the fall of monarchical governments around the world would lead to the collapse of human political and religious institutions and to their replacement by millennial ones founded on the word of God.

Eliot expounded these and other radical ideas in 1651 in his book, *The Christian Commonwealth*. He wrote specifically to convince the revolutionary leaders in England to establish the biblical civil polity throughout the country, create a congregational state church, and adopt a biblically based code of laws. At the time he wrote it, he believed that England would be the inaugural location for the millennium, because England stood at the "end of the earth" (Deuteronomy 28:64), westward from Mount Ararat. He no longer believed that England had to wait for the conversion of the Jews or the Battle of Armageddon: Christ was the only rightful heir to the Crown of England.

Eliot believed that the praying Indians, like the revolutionaries, had dismantled their traditional political order by ending the "former tyranny" and "usurpations" of their sachems. In this Eliot vastly overestimated the power of the sachems, who did not exert enough authority to maintain either tyranny or servitude. To assist the praying Indians in preparing for the millennium, which he considered imminent, he installed its institutional forms: he reorganized the Natick Indians according to the system of rulers of tens, fifties, and hundreds that is found in Exodus 18. His aim was to "set up the kingdom of Christ fully . . . both in civil and spiritual matters."

He found his Native proselytes extraordinarily receptive to these plans and he declared himself deeply impressed by their spiritual progress. Unlike European Christians who were reluctant to "lay down their own imperfect starlight . . . for the perfect sunlight of the Scripture," the Natives did not "cavil at divine wisdom." He told Edward Winslow, "These poor Indians . . . have no principles of their own, nor yet wisdom of their own (I mean as other [European] nations have) wherein to stick, therefore they do most readily yield to any direction from the Lord, so that there will be no such opposition against the rising kingdom of Jesus Christ among them." He also wrote to Winslow in 1649 that "the Lord Jesus is about to set up his blessed kingdom among these poor Indians."[36]

His experience with the praying Indians, his reinterpretation of certain biblical texts, and his reading of Thomas Thorowgood's *Iewes [Jews] in America*, which advanced the theory that Native Americans were descendants of the lost tribes of Israel and thus degenerate Jews, led him to a startling and controversial conclusion. He began to advance the view that there would be two inaugural locations for the birth of the millennium – a western one in England for the descendants of Noah's son Japheth and an eastern one in New England for the Indian descendants of Shem.[37] Rather than contenting himself with sporadic and isolated Indian conversions as he waited for the conversion of the Jews elsewhere, he now embraced the exhilarating prospect of massive conversions among Native Americans that would become the catalyst for the millennial reconstruction of America and Asia. Thus, as Cogley points out, for a few years Eliot believed that "the Indians – not the Saints – were the ones who made New England a special place in biblical prophesy."[38]

But for these prophesies to be realized, the praying Indians had to be organized, not only into tens, fifties, and hundreds, but into a true Congregational church. In 1652, Eliot invited representatives of local churches to Natick to evaluate the conversion narratives of a group of praying Indians in the hope that they would be judged ready to form a church of their own. The colony's church representatives were impressed with the Natives' progress, but rejected the narratives, concluding that the Indians were not yet ready for the final step in the conversion process. Nevertheless, Eliot clearly felt encouraged, and published the narratives in *Tears of Repentance* (1653), with two prefaces, one for the general public and one dedicated to Oliver Cromwell.

Yet, by the time the Natick church was finally accepted in 1659, this period of millennial excitement had passed. Eliot no longer claimed publicly that the millennium was imminent, and his letters reveal that he was less sure about the lost-tribes theory. The following year the Stuart monarchy was restored, apparently by God's will; a violent rebellion by English Fifth Monarchists against it was put down, and the ringleader, Thomas Venner (who had lived in New England for a time), was hanged. The leaders of the Massachusetts Bay Colony, fearful of losing their royal charter, ordered Eliot's *The Christian Commonwealth* destroyed, and Eliot himself seems to have genuinely repudiated his earlier anti-monarchical stance. Yet Cotton Mather wrote that Eliot remained intrigued with the lost-tribes theory and with the hope of an imminent Indian millennium, which he maintained to the end of his life; apparently this helped him to continue "his travails . . . the more cheerfully, or at least, the more hopefully."[39]

Such were the beliefs of the missionary – but what were the beliefs of the praying Indians? Why did they abandon so many of their traditional ways to join the praying towns? It is impossible now to know how deep and sincere were the Christian beliefs of those aboriginal converts. In some cases, they were likely adding the white man's god and Christian teachings to their traditional belief system, just as they were assimilating the material objects they acquired through trade. Some may have hoped to acquire some of the white man's power by learning to pray to the English god, and to acquire practical skills in the new world of English hegemony. Others adopted Christianity in times of crisis, when their traditional lives had been blasted by disease, dislocation, and depopulation, and when the alternatives were few. According to Bowden and Ronda, "Many who seemed to choose a new way of life over old preferences were actually indicating the impossibility of maintaining their traditional lifestyle under English domination, politically, economically and now religiously."[40]

Christianity also offered some protection against further losses of land and other abuses from English neighbours, for the missionaries often served as protectors – in fact, historian Richard Cogley argues that those who joined the missions were materially better off and acquired more rights to land than other Natives in the early post-contact period. Certainly some of Eliot's success among the Nipmucks, who lived inland from the coastal Massachusett tribes, rested on his ability to protect their communities from demands for tribute and military attacks by the Niantics and Mohegans, who lived farther south along Long Island Sound.

Undoubtedly some aboriginal converts were as genuinely Christian as their white nieghbours. As Cogley points out, there was no material incentive for the praying Indians to aspire to full church membership, yet many chose to do so, and their published conversion narratives compare favourably with those of their English counterparts. To the missionaries, the fact that some Natives responded positively to their preaching confirmed their Calvinistic view of the world: divine grace had touched the souls of those predestined to join the saints.

There were no more than thirty families living at the praying town of Natick in its early days, with about 145 persons willing to explore Christianity. In 1674, "the high point of mission success," about eleven hundred Natives lived in fourteen praying towns, and of these most were considered only potential Christians. Eliot's missions had baptized only 119 Natives, with a mere 74 of them in full communion with a covenanted church. Eliot's associate Daniel Gookin said most of the praying Indians had "not yet come so far as to be able to be willing to profess their faith in Christ and yield obedience and subjection to him in church."[41]

In fact, most Native people in New England were far less interested in Christianity than the Puritans had expected. By and large, they rejected the newcomers' faith and its notions of sin, guilt, heaven, and hell, and considered their own cultural values superior. Some saw the missionaries as sorcerers with evil powers. According to James Ronda, most Native American religions had nothing analogous to the Christian concept of sin as either a "primordial fault" or a "moral transgression against the will of God." Though they certainly recognized personal wrongdoing, they did not agree that it would be punished with eternal damnation. While the Puritans emphasized the depravity of human nature and "viewed natural man as totally incapable of living up to God's righteous demands," the Indians "considered everyone capable of interacting harmoniously with the divine powers who regulated their universe. . . . Local tribesmen found it hard to appreciate salvation because they saw no need of being rescued from an essentially positive state of existence, so full of practicable ways to enjoy it."[42]

Most Natives also rejected the European heaven because they would not find their ancestors there; their own conception of an afterlife was morally neutral. A Huron woman in New France, when asked why she refused to accept the offer of eternal life, expressed a common belief: "I have no acquaintances there, and the French who are there would not care to give me nothing to eat."[43]

The Puritans recorded many pagan Native Americans' objections to Christianity in the numerous fundraising tracts published to support John Eliot's mission, in Eliot's mission reports, and in *The Indian Dialogues* (1671), a series of imaginary dialogues between the praying Indians and other Natives. Eliot wrote the latter work as a training manual for Native missionaries: the dialogues were based on Eliot's own experience and distilled the important issues that recurred frequently in his ministry. The dialogues reveal that some Natives were suspicious of the Christian obsession with death and punishment. One astute Massachusett noted that "God made hell in one of the six dayes. Why did God make Hell before Adam sinned?"[44] A sachem charged that the concept of punishment in hell was designed by Englishmen "to scare us out of our old Customs, and bring us to stand in awe of them."[45]

Many Natives clearly recognized both the ethnocentrism and imperialism of the missionaries and were suspicious of the missionary project. After all, as Francis Jennings points out, one's being a missionary implies that one assumes superiority in the knowledge of the most important Truth in the world. In *The Indian Dialogues*, two pagans wonder if the Bible is really God's word or just an English trick to conquer them. If this religion is so good for them, why did their ancestors not adopt it, transmitting salvation through their own tradition? When Christian Natives from Natick attempt to convert their traditionalist kinsmen, the latter responded, "Our forefathers were (many of them) wise men, and we have many wise men now living, they all delight in these our Delights: they have taught us nothing about our Soul, and god, and Heaven, and Hell, and Joy, and Torment in the life to come. . . . We are well as we are, and desire not to be troubled with these new wise sayings."[46]

Native Americans were also put off by the rigidity and exclusivity of Puritan Christianity. Their own spiritual tradition encompassed a wide variety of beliefs and was flexible in approach.

> The idea of a single religion shared by all peoples seemed to the Indians an absurdity. In their perspective, religious affiliation was determined by tribal birth, not by rebirth in Christ. Most Indians endorsed a philosophy that can be best described as a "two roads" or "two ways" approach. A Huron explained it to Jesuit Jean Brébeuf in this way: "Do you not see that, as we inhabit a world so different from yours, there must be another heaven for us, and another road to reach it?"[47]

While Eliot did not make a large dent in the "heathen" Native population, his summer school at Natick was more successful as a seminary for Native teachers and pastors than the Harvard Indian College had been. Eliot actively encouraged Natives to become ministers. By 1671 every large praying town had at least one lay exhorter, several had Native preachers, and a number of Indian missionaries taught regularly in praying-Indian schools; some Native ministers even occasionally administered communion to neighbouring colonists.

The *Indian Dialogues* also permits a modern reader some insight into the attitudes and reasoning of Native Christians. In one dialogue, the Native missionary describes pre-contact life as depraved "filth and folly," which he hopes to replace with correct beliefs and true piety. "Let us alone," replies the powwow, "that we may be quiet in the ways which we like and love, as we let you alone in your changes and new ways."[48]

Apparently Eliot used more than gentle persuasion to ensure conversions. Roger Williams of Rhode Island complained to the Massachusetts General Court about Eliot's strong-arm tactics:

At my last departure for England [1653], I was importuned by the Narragansett Sachems, and especially by Ninigret, to present their petition to the high Sachems of England, that they might not be forced from their religion, and, for not changing their religion, be invaded by war; for they said they were daily visited with threatenings by Indians that came from about the Massachusetts, that if they would not pray, they should be destroyed by war.

Williams complained to Oliver Cromwell, who was pleased "to grant, amongst other favours to this colony [Rhode Island], some expressly concerning the very Indians, the native inhabitants of this jurisdiction."[49]

Eliot's own correspondence suggests that he also used financial inducements in some cases. "Messengers and instruments look for their pay," he wrote to the treasurer of the New England Company, "and if that fail, the whole moves very heavily and will quickly stand still."[50]

The Puritans' initial high expectations of rapid and widespread Indian conversion proved to be wishful thinking. Although Eliot, Gookin, and a few others persisted in their efforts at conversion, sometimes with the assistance of members of the Roxbury congregation, many Puritans became disillusioned and cynical about such efforts; "most Puritan pastors regarded the Indian churches as comic or blasphemous caricatures of their own."[51] Even Thomas Weld's colleague and fellow agent in England, Rev. Hugh Peter – who wrote *First Fruits* with him and engineered the first collection of missionary funds for New England Natives – remarked that he had heard that the mission work "was but a plain cheat, and that there was no such thing as a gospel conversion amongst the Indians."[52]

Yet a letter written to Eliot by a Native pastor, Daniel Tokkohwampait, in March 1684, shortly before Eliot's death, and signed by fifteen other Natick residents, indicates that some of the praying Indians genuinely loved him and greatly valued his work on their behalf:

You are now grown aged soe that we are deprived of seeing your face and hearing your voice (especilly in the Winter Season) soe frequently as formerly. . . . God hath made you to us and our nation a spiritual father, we are inexpresably ingaged to you for your faithful constant Indefatigable labours, care and love, to and for us, and you have alwaies manifested the same to us as wel in our adversity as prosperity, for about forty years making know [*sic*] to us the Glad tidings of Salvation of Jesus Christ.[53]

Thus, there were strongly divergent contemporary assessments of Eliot's mission, as is still the case today. For a small number of Natives, it was a source of powerful and transformative new ideas that gave a radically different meaning and direction to their lives. For others who joined the praying towns, it offered a means to gain material advantage or protection from the colonists. Yet the vast majority of New England Natives rejected Eliot's message and invitation to join the Christian fold. To them, the mission was dangerously divisive and subversive of their own culture and society. Non-Christian Natives often scorned and sometimes abused aboriginal Christians, as aboriginal Christians denigrated and sometimes threatened them.

Added to the already existing enmities and divisions between the various indigenous nations, the Puritan missionary movement created a new factionalism in Native societies that made co-ordinated responses to English colonialism even more difficult. Furthermore, although New England colonists paid lip-service to Eliot's mission, few settlers were genuinely interested in the welfare of the Christian Indians, many disparaged Eliot's efforts, and most would not accept Christian Indians as equals. Thus, the mission left the Christian Indians in a strange limbo between the two cultures, and extremely vulnerable to the hostility and suspicions of both English and non-Christian Natives, as we shall see in later chapters.

THE STANTON FAMILY

Eight Generations
of the Stanton Family

I. John Stanton (1530–?)   married   ?

II. Thomas Stanton (1560–?)   m.   ?

III. Thomas Stanton   m. 1597   Catherine Washington

IV. **Thomas Stanton**   m.   **Ann Lord** (1614–1688)
(1616–1677)   (sister of **Richard Lord**)

V. **Mary Stanton** (1643–?)   m.   **Samuel Rogers** (1646–1713)
(son of **James Rogers** and
Elizabeth Rowland)

VI. Elizabeth Rogers   m.   (1) Theophilus Stanton
(1673–?)   (2) Asa Harris (1680–1715)

VII. Asa Harris (1709–1762)   m.   Anna Ely (1716–1788)

VIII. Ely Harris (1755–1813)   m.   Lucretia Ransom (1756–1836)

For subsequent generations, see the Harris genealogy in the Harris Family
section.

CHAPTER
6

"These Now Insulting Pequots"

Of all my ancestors I have been able to research, the fur trader Thomas Stanton probably had the greatest number of relationships – including friendships – with aboriginal people. If John Eliot was memorialized as the "apostle" to the Indians, Stanton has been remembered as their "friend," implying both that he helped them and that he formed personal relationships based on affection and respect. "No man in New England at that time professed so accurate a knowledge of the Indian character and language as Mr. Stanton," wrote Frances Manwaring Caulkins in her *History of New London*. "He exerted a wonderful influence over them, and they reposed unlimited confidence in him."

This characterization may be true or it may be what various descendants of the colonists would like to believe. It is hard to separate the man and the myth, to know what is fact and what wishful interpretation. Certainly it appears that he was more able than most Europeans to break through significant cultural barriers and earn a measure of trust and even affection from some of New England's indigenous inhabitants, both for his personal character and in his role as a mediator between the colonists and the Natives. As one of the few English colonists to learn an indigenous language, he would have had far more access to the thoughts and feelings of many Native Americans and they to his than was the case with most of his countrymen.

One wants to find out that some of the Europeans managed to break through the prejudices of their time, that some tried to influence the course of events to the benefit of Native Americans, that true friendship was possible, just as in our day there are sometimes bonds of solidarity and friendship. Yet I suspect that his relationships with the various Native nations in southern New England were more complicated and layered than this – indeed, that they were as fluid, various, and ever-changing as the fluctuating political landscape of the day.

If he was indeed a friend to "the Indians," it is important to ask, Which Indians? As an interpreter and diplomat for the English, Stanton did not see all Native Americans as the same, and he had very different relations with different nations. To a modern researcher, the colonial records reveal many contradictions in Stanton's long involvement with Native peoples: the most glaring is that this "friend to the Indians" began his career in New England by participating in a genocidal war – the 1637 campaign against the Pequots. Indeed, his life, like John Eliot's, illustrates the full range of both the possibilities and limitations of English–Native American interactions among the first generation of colonists.

Thomas Stanton was born in 1616 in Wolverton, Warwickshire, where a well-to-do Stanton family had lived since at least the time of his great-grandfather, John Stanton, born in 1530.[1] A year after John Wheeler left England, Thomas Stanton is believed to have sailed from London to Virginia. He would have been only nineteen when the *Bonaventure* cast off near the Tower of London on January 1, 1635, and he may have lied about his age to gain passage as an unaccompanied adult, since the age of majority was twenty. I do not know why he left England, but it was probably not for religious reasons, as his family do not appear to have been Puritans. It may have been a simple case of a young man seeking adventure and fortune.

There is some speculation as to whether the ship actually went to Virginia or used that destination merely to satisfy the authorities and facilitate departure from England.[2] Thomas Stanton's whereabouts and activities in the year following his arrival in North America are unknown. The only thing we know with certainty is that, in a matter of months, he appears to have picked up a considerable amount of a Native dialect that did not differ substantially from the indigenous languages spoken in New England. If he was indeed in Virginia, he may have obtained some furs before heading north to Boston in 1636. It is not known why he left Virginia.

He did not stay in Boston, either. Perhaps he preferred life in less-settled areas, or that was simply where his skills could be used to best advantage. Perhaps he had already decided that he wanted to be a fur trader and had set his sights on the Connecticut River Valley, where furs were rumoured to be plentiful. Or perhaps it was his facility with language that prompted him to leave, for within a matter of months he became the interpreter for John Winthrop, Jr., the first governor of the fledgling colony of Connecticut. At that time the colony consisted of a fort on a vaguely defined grant of land at the mouth of the Connecticut River and disputed claims to a few towns upriver. It was as Winthrop's interpreter that Stanton became involved in the first major confrontation with a Native nation in New England.

As Stanton would later discover, the Connecticut Valley was a region of bewildering political complexity. Before Stanton had even arrived in the New World, England and the Netherlands had both claimed the Connecticut Valley by right of discovery while the Pequots, who lived farther east in the drainage area of what is now the Thames River of southern Connecticut and were the most powerful aboriginal nation in the region, claimed it by right of conquest over the indigenous "river tribes." In 1633, the Dutch had established the first trading post on the Connecticut River at Hartford after purchasing land from the grand sachem of the Pequots – the first known deed of sale of Native territory in the region of lower New England. Later that same year, English fur traders from Plymouth Colony established a rival trading post several miles upriver from Hartford, near Windsor, where the English hoped to acquire furs coming from the interior before they reached the Dutch. Settlers from Massachusetts soon arrived and took over much of the English land at Windsor.

The Europeans were by no means the only ones vying for control of the Connecticut. The Narragansetts of Rhode Island, who had emerged as the most populous Native nation in New England after the plagues of 1619–20, had established a trading relationship with the Dutch at an early date, and now sought to undermine the Pequot tributary system in the Connecticut Valley, which threatened their role as middlemen in the trade.[3] In addition, the local and not very numerous "River Indians" – the Pocumtucks, Nonotucks, and others small bands – had invited the Puritan leaders to send settlers as early as 1631 for protection against the Pequots. They repeated their invitations in 1633 and again in 1634.

The Pequots, for their part, were determined to maintain control over the exchange not only of trade goods and furs along the Connecticut, but also of valuable wampum – strings of small, cylindrical shell beads, which Native Americans used as a form of currency, in diplomatic negotiations, in recording information, and to symbolically express status and allegiance. The Pequots acted aggressively against other aboriginal nations that challenged their hegemony. Interestingly, although later Puritan historians vilified the Pequots, portraying them as the most barbarous, cruel, treacherous, and universally hated Natives in New England, the Puritans' impression of them in the early 1630s was far more positive. William Wood, for example, compared them favourably to many other Native nations and described them as courteous, friendly, and trustworthy, "just and equal in their dealings, not treacherous either to their countrymen or English."[4]

With all these conflicting ambitions and alliances, and with a fortune to be gained, violence soon flared. Shortly after the Dutch established their House of Good Hope at Hartford in 1633, the Pequots had killed several rival aboriginal traders, possibly Narragansetts or their tributaries, who were visiting the Dutch trading house. In retaliation, the Narragansetts declared war on the Pequots, and the Dutch abducted the Pequot grand sachem Tatobem. When the Dutch killed him, even though the Pequots had paid a substantial ransom, a group of incensed Pequots, including Tatobem's son, along with one or two Western Niantics, murdered one Capt. John Stone and his crew on the Connecticut River. It appears to have been an act of retribution in accordance with Pequot custom, whereby a revenge execution was carried out by the kinsmen of a murder victim to restore communal harmony – apparently, they mistook Captain Stone for a Dutchman. Stone, a West Indian "trader cum pirate," stirred up trouble wherever he went. He had been banished from Massachusetts Bay for committing adultery and for threatening magistrates, and Plymouth had demanded his death for his attempt to abduct a ship. He had provoked the Pequots by abducting two Indians, whom he apparently hoped to sell into slavery. In carrying out this culturally sanctioned form of limited retribution, the Pequots did not anticipate that their act would end their trading relationship with the Dutch. But the Dutch, incensed by the killing of a white man, fired on a group of Pequot traders who approached the House of Good Hope, killing a sachem, and banned any further commerce with their former trading partners.

Faced with the collapse of their commercial alliance with the Dutch, internal power struggles following the death of their sachem, and a war with the Narragansetts, the Pequots then turned to the English in their efforts to maintain control of the Connecticut trade. And so, two years before Thomas Stanton arrived in Connecticut, the Pequot chiefs went to Boston to negotiate a military and trading alliance. They asked Massachusetts to mediate peace for them with the Narragansetts; two years later, when these negotiations and the unratified treaty they produced were revisited by the English, Stanton became intimately involved with the events that led to the outbreak of war. It is worth a detailed look at the circumstances of this treaty to understand Stanton's subsequent role in the first significant military action in New England's post-contact history.

The 1634 "friendship" treaty with the Pequots – there is that slippery word "friendship" again – appears to have been a compromise that really pleased no one. The Pequots had come to Boston seeking trade, peace with the Narragansetts, and a commitment from the English to come to their defence in the event of attack. In exchange, they brought a substantial gift of wampum and furs and made an extraordinary offer – they would relinquish their rights of conquest over the Connecticut Valley in favour of the English – and even volunteered to assist them with settlement. At the end of the negotiations, what they ended up with was trade with the English and peace with the Narragansetts – but also two English demands that they apparently could not or would not fulfil.

The first English demand was that they hand over the murderers of the renegade Captain Stone. To the English, although Stone was someone they were undoubtedly glad to be rid of, and he had been killed outside the jurisdiction of Massachusetts, the murder of a Christian white man by a heathen "savage" was a work of Satan that had to be countered decisively. While the Pequots admitted responsibility for Stone's death, all but two of Stone's murderers were dead of smallpox. The emissaries also indicated that, though they were willing to approach the sachem of the two surviving murderers, the sachem might be unwilling to surrender them, given that Stone had taken two of their people as captives and mistreated them. The Pequots asserted that they had killed Stone "in a just quarrel."[5]

The Puritans had also declared the wampum present of two bushels of wampum inadequate. They demanded four hundred fathoms (six-foot strings) of wampum, as well as forty beaver skins and thirty otter skins, an amount equivalent in value to approximately £250 sterling, or nearly half of the colony's property taxes levied in Massachusetts Bay in 1634. This was an exorbitant amount, which the Pequots could not pay without considerable hardship.

What happened next is a matter of some conjecture, as the treaty itself has not survived and colonial records are scanty. Apparently, the Pequot ambassadors were not authorized to agree to such demands, so they promised to take them back to their councils for consideration. On that basis, the governor and magistrates concluded the treaty negotiations. The treaty then failed to be ratified by the Pequot council, and the Pequots did not deliver up Stone's killers. Nor did they pay the additional wampum – most likely they were unwilling to pay such an amount for an agreement that offered only trade and not military protection, and they believed they had already paid a sufficient quantity of wampum to atone for Stone's death. It has also been suggested that the Pequots rejected the demand for more wampum because their "present" had been transformed into a demand for tribute, which implied subordination to the English.[6]

For their part, the magistrates were inclined to believe the Pequots' explanation of Stone's death: the Pequot account "was related with such confidence and gravity, as, having no means to contradict, we were inclined to believe it," wrote the governor of the Massachusetts Bay Colony, John Winthrop.[7] They referred the matter to the clergy – almost certainly including John Eliot and Thomas Weld – who apparently advised against compromise. Although the Pequots and the English traded peacefully for the next two years, and the English began to establish towns on the Connecticut, the English did not give up their demand for the surrender of Stone's killers.

The fertile Connecticut Valley with its wide, treeless meadows quickly attracted settlers from several towns in Massachusetts Bay who sought better land or wished to live beyond the Bay's authority. Several towns moved en masse to re-establish themselves. In 1634, a fur trader, John Oldham, led a small group of settlers from Watertown, near Boston, to establish the town of Wethersfield. In 1635 a group of settlers under John Eliot's former mentor, Rev. Thomas Hooker, founded a settlement at Saukiog, a large Native village on the site of the future city of Hartford, near the Dutch trading post. The local Native people welcomed them and they purchased land from Sequassen, the grand sachem of the "River Indians." By the time Thomas Stanton arrived in Boston in 1636, the population of Hartford, Wethersfield, and Windsor numbered about eight hundred inhabitants.[8] At some point over the next year, Thomas Stanton settled there too, and began trading along the Connecticut River.

The settlers' lands were held without any kind of legitimizing patent from England, so political jurisdiction and legal title to the land in these new settlements along the Connecticut was shaky. Massachusetts claimed the land through the unratified friendship treaty with the Pequots, while the settlers themselves acquired their titles from the local River Indian sachems. Meanwhile, another group of Englishmen had taken possession of land at Saybrook, at the mouth of the Connecticut, under a patent from the Earl of Warwick; they appointed John Winthrop, Jr., governor of the fledgling colony of Connecticut and laid claim to the entire Connecticut Valley. The Pequots were caught in the middle: Massachusetts and Connecticut colonies vied for possession of the valley, and both sought to bring the Pequots under English control.

A final element increased tensions in the region. A new and bitter rivalry arose between the Pequots under their new sachem Sassacus and the Mohegans under the sachem Uncas. The Mohegans had been a subgroup or tributary of the Pequots; their leader, Uncas, who had a claim by birth and marriage to both Mohegan and Pequot sachemships, had broken with the Pequots and established his own rival nation, with the help of the English and the Narragansetts, either out of personal ambition, as the colonists believed, or over differing approaches to relations with the English.[9] While the Pequots were wary of the English, Uncas quickly positioned himself as their closest and most loyal ally.

It appears to have been Uncas who started rumours that the Pequots were conspiring to attack the English. In June 1636, he told a Plymouth trader named Jonathan Brewster that the Pequots had been planning attacks on Plymouth's trading ship. Brewster sent a warning to Fort Saybrook that "the Pequents have some mistrust, that the English will shortly come against them, (which I take is by indiscreet speaches of some of your people here to the Natives) and therefore out of desperate madnesse doe threaten shortly to sett both upon Indians, and English, joyntly."[10] Uncas also told the trader that the murder of Stone three years before had been planned by a Pequot council-of-war and carried out by Sassacus, the new Pequot grand sachem, himself. Both of these accusations appear to have been entirely unfounded, but with little experience of the nations involved and with an ingrained belief that Native Americans were agents of Satan who would inevitably try to thwart the people of God, the Puritans were deeply alarmed.

It was in this context that, after two years of peaceful co-operation with the Pequots, Massachusetts suddenly revived its demands for Stone's killers and the additional wampum, although these conditions had been set aside after their rejection by the Pequots in 1634. It was also at this juncture that Thomas Stanton makes his first appearance in the New England records. For in early July 1636, the Connecticut governor, John Winthrop, Jr., was commissioned by the Massachusetts Bay Colony to meet with the Pequots at Fort Saybrook. He was instructed to renew the demands for Stone's murderers and the additional wampum, and to confront them with the accusations that they had killed two shipwrecked English traders on Long Island and had also planned the rumoured attack on Plymouth's trading ship (both apparently false). If they could not prove themselves innocent of the Long Island murders or refused to surrender Stone's murderers, Winthrop was to tell them the English would take their revenge. In effect, as the historian Alfred Cave has commented, "Winthrop's instructions were to threaten war if he could not secure Pequot submission."[11] His interpreter in this confrontation would be the young Thomas Stanton.

Stanton and several others travelled overland from Boston to Saybrook, carrying with them the otter-skin coats and beaver and skeins of wampum that had been the original good-will present from the Pequots in 1634. Among those attending the Saybrook conference were Connecticut Governor John Winthrop, Jr., Thomas Stanton, Rev. Hugh Peter (later to be Thomas Weld's colleague in England), Fort Saybrook's commander, Lieut. Lion Gardiner, and possibly the trader John Oldham, as well as Sassious, the sachem of the Western Niantics, and unidentified representatives of the Pequots. Governor Winthrop, through Thomas Stanton, asserted that the rejected demands of 1634 were "the very condition of the Peace betwixt us"; otherwise the English would "revenge the blood of our countrimen as occasion shall serve."[12] He advised the Pequots that the Bay Colony would not accept their excuse that the tribal elders had not ratified the 1634 treaty.

The Pequots, however, still believed they had already given a reasonable quantity of presents to compensate for Stone's death; they refused to pay additional wampum or to extradite Stone's killers. The English, in turn, interpreted their refusal as treachery and a sign of hostility towards the English. The commissioners, signalling the termination of friendly relations, returned the Pequot presents of 1634, in spite of the opposition of Lieutenant Gardiner, who foresaw that, in the event of war with the Pequots, he and his men would be left isolated in the undermanned Fort Saybrook after the commissioners had retreated to the safety of Boston. (Gardiner might also have been somewhat more sympathetic to the Pequots' position.) Such was the pressure on the Native participants during the conference that the Western Niantic sachem Sassious suddenly granted his entire territory to Connecticut governor John Winthrop, Jr., personally and transferred allegiance from the Pequots to him.

Throughout these tense discussions, twenty-one-year-old Thomas Stanton was the only conduit for communication. Did his own support for the English colour his translations? Did the participants fully understand each others' positions? One can only wonder how accurately he was able to translate from one language to another after only one year in North America, and what nuances of meaning were lost along the way. It seems unlikely that Stanton could have understood and conveyed the subtleties of Pequot speech, based as it was on an understanding of life totally foreign to his own. Indeed, how could one translate between what historian Calvin Martin has referred to as these "mutually unintelligible thought worlds?"[13] As it became clear that the two sides could not or would not comprehend each other, as they moved inexorably closer to war, did Thomas Stanton sense that English intransigence, not Pequot belligerence, was preventing conciliation – that power, not justice, was the fundamental issue? Or did he believe as firmly as the others in the Puritan stereotype of Indian malevolence and interpret every Pequot action in that light?

A few days later, John Oldham, a fellow fur trader close enough to Stanton to mention Stanton as a beneficiary in his will, was killed by Narragansett Indians on Block Island in Long Island Sound, after returning from a trading mission on the Connecticut. Unlike Stone, Oldham had been a valuable and trusted friend of the Massachusetts government, and his death was taken far more seriously. The motive for the killing was unclear: the Narragansetts may have blamed Oldham for a devastating smallpox epidemic that killed seven hundred members of their nation, a plague that they believed had been deliberately sent by the English.

The Narragansetts themselves understood the gravity of the crime; Roger Williams, the Puritan cleric who had been banished from the Massachusetts Bay Colony and had then founded Providence Plantation in what is now Rhode Island, had extensive contact with the Narragansetts and reported that the Narragansett sachem Miantonomo had sent two hundred warriors to Block Island to mete out revenge on behalf of Massachusetts. But Williams and the Massachusetts authorities later became suspicious of the Narragansett leaders' claims of innocence when a Narragansett taken prisoner at the scene of the murder implicated many prominent Narragansett leaders in the killing. The colonists then demanded that six undersachems be turned over to the English. Miantonomo, seeking to sidetrack the English, claimed that the true murderers had found refuge with the Pequots. This was untrue, as Miantonomo knew. He himself sent six fathoms of wampum to the Eastern Niantics (who were affiliated with the Narragansetts) to execute a sachem who was purportedly the leader of the party that had murdered Oldham. But Miantonomo's accusations were enough to fan the flames of English hostility toward the Pequots.

The news of Oldham's murder and of the Pequots' refusal to comply with the rejected demands of 1634 reached Boston at almost the same time. The colonists interpreted these events as evidence of an Indian conspiracy against the English. Remembering the massacre of colonists in Virginia in 1622, the Massachusetts governor and his Standing Council assembled all the magistrates and ministers, including Thomas Weld and John Eliot, "to advise with them about doing justice upon the Indians." They decided to carry out a pre-emptive strike to ensure their own safety. Thus, contrary to later Puritan historiography, the English were actually the aggressors in the war; evidence of any Indian conspiracy against them was very slim indeed. In fact, as Alfred Cave has commented, "The Pequot War was not waged in response to tangible acts of aggression. It cannot be understood as a rational response to a real threat to English security."[14] Sadly, as Cave explains, it was Puritan misinterpretations and false assumptions about the character and actions of the Pequots – stereotypes of Indian treachery and savagery fuelled by rumours from rival aboriginal leaders – as well as the Puritans' goal of regional hegemony that seem to have been the real causes of the war.

On August 25, 1636, Captain John Endecott left Boston in command of five ships, eighty men, and four officers. "They had commission," wrote John Winthrop, Sr., "to put to death the men of Block Island, but to spare the women and children, and to bring them away and to take possession of the island, and from thence to go to the Pequods to demand the murderers of

Capt. Stone and other English, and one thousand fathom of wampum for damages, etc. and some of their children as hostages, which if they should refuse, they were to obtain it by force."[15] The unpaid volunteers who made up the expedition's forces expected to profit from plunder and the sale of captured women and children in West Indies slave markets.

The expedition was not a success. The men of Block Island managed to evade the English volunteers, so the English torched crops and abandoned villages, leaving the island empty-handed. Then, reinforced by Lieut. Lion Gardiner from Saybrook and his force of twenty men, Endecott headed east along the coast toward the Pequots. Hundreds of the latter appeared on the shores, apparently unaware of having given the Puritans cause for hostility, calling out, "What, Englishmen, what cheer, are you hoggery, and will you cram us?" (Are you angry? Will you kill us, and do you come to fight?)[16] The English renewed their demands, but the Pequots stalled for time and retreated. Once again the English looted empty villages and destroyed crops, before abandoning their expedition and setting sail for home with neither wampum nor hostages. I have no evidence that Thomas Stanton was part of this expedition.

The main outcome of this exercise was the very situation the pre-emptive strike was supposed to prevent: the outbreak of Native hostilities against the colonists. The Pequots were incensed and appalled at the burning of their villages and crops: this European practice of "total warfare," waged against combatants and non-combatants alike, appears to have been foreign to their own rules of war, and it kindled bitter hatred of the English – especially since, in their eyes, they had done nothing to provoke it. The Pequots attacked Gardiner's men on their way back to Saybrook and then approached the Narragansetts to form an alliance against the English. Initially, the Narragansetts were sympathetic to the Pequots in their grievances, even though they had long been competitors and enemies, but finally Roger Williams persuaded them to join forces with Massachusetts Bay instead. To the intense relief of the latter, Narragansett sachem Miantonomo agreed to remain neutral, and later supported the English against the Pequots, asking Williams only to notify Boston "that it would be pleasing to all natives, that women and children be spared, etc."[17] Miantonomo's decision would prove to be a fateful one.

Endecott's expedition also angered Lion Gardiner, who afterwards was left behind in Fort Saybrook with few provisions and only twenty men to deal with the enraged Pequots. His fears were proved all too prescient, for the Pequots soon began a series of horrifying attacks on his men and a couple of traders, sometimes torturing them within sight and hearing of the fort, attacks that in turn outraged English notions of the proper conduct of war and made the tiny band of soldiers afraid to leave the fort throughout the winter of 1636–37. In April 1637, Thomas Stanton sailed downriver from Hartford, bound for Boston, and was becalmed at Saybrook. A large party of Pequots, attracted by the ship, surrounded the fort. Gardiner's account of this incident vividly illustrates the precariousness of their situation and also gives a strong sense of the character of young Stanton:

A few days after, came Thomas Stanton down the River, and staying for a wind, while he was there came a troop of Indians within musket shot, laying themselves and their arms down behind a little rising hill and two great trees; which I perceiving, called the carpenter whom I had shewed how to charge and level a gun, and that he should put two cartridges of musket bullets into two sakers guns that lay about, and we levelled them against the place, and I told him that he must look towards me, and when he saw me wave my hat above my head he should give fire to both the guns; then presently came three Indians, creeping out and calling to us to speak with us: and I was glad that Thomas Stanton was there, and I sent six men down by the Garden Pales [stake fence] to look that none should come under the hil[l] behind us; and having placed the rest in places convenient closely, Thomas and I with my sword, pistol and carbine, went ten or twelve pole without the gate to parley with them. And when the six men came to the Garden Pales, at the corner, they found a great number of Indians creeping behind the fort, or betwixt us and home, but they ran away. Now I had said to Thomas Stanton, Whatsoever they say to you, tell me first, for we will not answer them directly to any thing, for I know not the mind of the rest of the English. So they came forth, calling us nearer to them, and we them nearer to us. But I would not let Thomas go any further than the great stump of a tree, and I stood by him; then they asked who we were, and he answered, Thomas and Lieutenant. But they said he lied, for I was shot with many arrows; and so I was, but my buff coat preserved me, only one hurt me [he had been wounded while retrieving lumber two weeks before]. But when I spake to them they knew my voice, for one of them had dwelt three months with us, but ran away when the Bay-men came first. Then they asked us if we would fight with Niantecut [Western Niantic] Indians, for they were our friends and came to trade with us. We said we knew not the Indians one from another, and therefore would trade with none. They said, Have you fought enough? We said we knew not yet. Then they asked if we did use to kill women and children? We said they should see that hereafter. So they were silent a small space, and then they said, We are Pequits, and have killed Englishmen, and can kill them as mosquetoes, and we will go to conectecott and kill men, women, and children, and we will take away the horses, cows and hogs. When Thomas Stanton had told me this, he prayed me to shoot that rogue, for, said he, he hath an Englishman's coat on, and saith that he hath killed three, and these other four have their cloathes on their backs. I said, No, it is not the manner of a parley, but have patience and I shall fit them ere they go. Nay, now or never, said he; so when he could get no other answer but this last, I bid him tell them that they should not go to Conectecott, for if they did kill all the men, and take all the rest as they said, it would do them no good, but hurt, for English women are lazy, and can't do their work; horses and cows will spoil your corn-fields, and the hogs their clam-banks and so undo them: then I pointed to our great house, and bid him tell them there lay twenty pieces of trucking cloth, of Mr. Pincheon's, with hoes, hatchets, and all manner of trade, they were better fight still with us, and so get all that, and then go up the river after they had killed us. Having heard this, they were mad as dogs, and ran away; then when they came to the place from whence they came, I waved my hat about my head, and the two great guns went off, so that there was a great hubbub amongst them. Then two days later, came down Capt. Mason, and Sergeant Seely, with five men more, to see how it was with us; and whilst they were there, came down a Dutch boat, telling us the Indians had killed fourteen English.[18]

The Dutch were wrong about the number of dead and a later report that the Pequots, after leaving Wethersfield, had massacred all the inhabitants of Springfield, was totally false, but Pequot aggression against settlers in the Connecticut Valley had indeed begun.

Earlier in April, the settlers at Wethersfield, located south of Hartford, along the Connecticut River, had driven the local Natives from their homes within the town's boundaries. This action violated the original agreement made when they bought the land. The refugees appealed to the Pequots, who, in retribution for the poor treatment of the sachem Sowheag, killed six Englishmen and three women working in the fields and took two girls hostage. The Pequots then went to Saybrook to flaunt their hostages and the clothes of the dead settlers and to taunt the soldiers in the fort.

The English were now convinced of the necessity for decisive punitive action. After the attack on Wethersfield, Rev. Thomas Hooker, the founder of Hartford, warned that any delay would lead other Indians to conclude that the English were cowards; and if that happened, all the tribes would turn against the English. Rev. John Higginson, who was at Fort Saybrook, wrote to John Winthrop, Sr., that "the eyes of all the Indians of the country are upon the English. If some serious and very speedie course not be taken to tame the pride and take down the insolency of these now insulting Pequots . . . we are like to have all the Indians in the country about our ears."[19]

Connecticut did not wait for Massachusetts, which had been planning a joint attack of both colonies later in the spring or summer. The newly formed General Court of Connecticut declared war on the Pequots on May 1, 1637. Connecticut mobilized a force of ninety Englishmen from the three Connecticut River towns and Fort Saybrook under Capt. John Mason, a veteran of the continental wars, and about seventy Mohegans and "River Indians" under the sachem Uncas. Before leaving Hartford, the Connecticut troops were exhorted by the local minister to "execute those whom God, the righteous judge of all the world, hath condemned for blaspheming his sacred majesty, and murthering his servants . . . execute vengeance upon the heathen." Among the soldiers was Thomas Stanton; he was a "great friend and supporter of Captain Mason," and would act as his interpreter during this campaign.[20]

Captain Mason's strategy was to avoid a direct attack on Weinshauks, the main village of the sachem Sassacus. There was no chance the Puritan forces could mount a surprise attack from the well-guarded Pequot harbour in the Thames River, so he planned instead to march overland from the east. Accordingly, the troops sailed eastward along Long Island Sound, past the Pequot villages, to Narragansett Bay, where they planned to recruit a large contingent of Narragansetts to their cause before heading west and marching back to the Pequot villages. Massachusetts, meanwhile, sent forty soldiers by land to Narragansett Bay.

On reaching Narragansett Bay, the Connecticut soldiers marched up to the chief sachem's residence, where Mason, through Stanton, requested free passage through the Narragansett country. Miantonomo agreed to allow it, but warned the English that "our Numbers were too weak to deal with the Enemy, who were (as he said) very great Captains and Men skilfull in War."[21] The next day, Mason, Stanton, and the troops marched west to an Eastern Niantic village on the edge of Pequot territory. After an initially cool reception, the sachem Ninigret contributed more warriors to the Narragansetts already joining forces with the English. The English then continued their march accompanied by about five hundred warriors, some of whom later deserted.

Ahead of them lay two fortified Pequot villages, the westernmost of which, Weinshauks, "was so remote that we could not come up with it before Midnight, though we Marched hard." Although Sassacus, the Pequot grand sachem, was at this more distant fort, Mason and Capt. John Underhill decided to attack the nearer fort, Mystic, as their troops were exhausted, suffering from the intense heat, and lacking provisions for an extended campaign. Spending the night by a swamp near the fort at Mystic, Stanton and the other soldiers heard loud singing from the Pequot encampment. Their Native allies explained that the Pequots were celebrating – they had seen the English ships sailing by them a few days earlier and concluded "that we were afraid of them and durst not come near them."[22]

Shortly after daybreak on May 26, 1637, Stanton and the other English and Native soldiers were led to Mystic fort by Wequash, a sagamore of the Niantics; Wequash had formerly been a Pequot tributary who, like Uncas, had broken with them after the murder of Tatobem.

What happened next has been vividly recorded by the English commanders:

Then Capt. Underhill came up, who Marched in the Rear; and commending ourselves to God, divided our Men: There being two Entrances into the Fort, intending to enter both at once: Captain Mason leading up to that on the North East Side; who approaching within one Rod, heard a Dog bark and an Indian crying Owanux! Owanux! which is Englishmen! Englishmen! We called up our Forces with all expedition, gave Fire upon them through the Pallizado; the Indians being in a dead indead their last Sleep: Then we wheeling off fell upon the main Entrance, which was blocked up with Bushes about Breast high, over which the Captain passed, intending to make good the Entrance, encouraging the rest to follow. . . .

The captain also said, We must Burn them; and immediately stepping into the Wigwam where he had been before, brought out a Firebrand, and putting it into the Matts with which they were covered,

set the Wigwams on Fire. Lieutenant Thomas Bull and Nicholas Omsted
beholding, came up and when it was throughly kindled, the Indians ran
as Men most dreadfully Amazed. And indeed such a dreadful Terror did
the Almighty let fall upon their Spirits, that they would fly from us and
run into the very Flames, where many of them perished. And when the
Fort was throughly Fired, Command was given, that all should fall off
and surround the Fort.[23]

Though caught by surprise, the Pequots resisted fiercely, and several of
Underhill's men were wounded in a barrage of arrows as they broke
through the barrier at the gate. But fire gave the colonists the advantage:

Captain Mason entering into a wigwam, brought out a firebrand, after he
had wounded many in the house. Then he set fire on the west side, where
he entered; myself set fire on the south end with a train of powder. The
fires of both meeting in the centre of the fort, blazed most terribly, and
burnt all in the space of half an hour. Many courageous fellows were
unwilling to come out, and fought most desperately through the pal-
isades, so as they were scorched and burnt with the very flame, and were
deprived of their arms – in regard the fire burnt their very bowstrings –
and so perished valiantly. Mercy did they deserve for their valor, could
we have had opportunity to have bestowed it. Many were burned in the
fort, both men, women and children. Others forced out, and came in
troops to the Indians, twenty and thirty at a time, which our soldiers
received and entertained with the point of the sword. Down fell men,
women, and children; those that scaped us, fell into the hands of the
Indians that were in the rear of us. It is reported by themselves, that there
were about four hundred souls in this fort, and not above five of them
ecaped out of our hands.[24]

When the massacre was over, only seven Pequots remained, and these
were captured by the English. Captain Mason estimated the number of
Pequot dead at six or seven hundred; Underhill claimed the Pequots themselves had reported losing four hundred, but Mason's estimate may have
been more accurate. Two Englishmen were killed, one possibly from
friendly fire, and twenty out of seventy-seven English soldiers had been
injured, as well as twenty Native allies; several of the latter complained

that they had been shot by the Englishmen in the intense musket fire. The wounded had to get along as best they could on their own, for the ill-prepared army had left its only surgeon, who was "not accustomed to war," on board ship at Narragansett Bay.[25]

CHAPTER
7

"Destroy Them . . . and Save the Plunder"

I can only imagine the emotions of my ancestor as he stood – shaking perhaps or wounded – outside the smouldering ruins of the Pequot fort, surveying the nightmarish scene around him, the dead and dying everywhere, the overpowering stench of burning flesh heavy in the air. He would not have known how many children, women, and men he and his fellow soldiers had burnt alive or slaughtered, but he must have known the number was in the hundreds. For days afterwards, that first cry "Owanux! Owanux!" (Englishmen! Englishmen!) must have echoed in his ears, or maybe it was the terrible screams of children in the fire, or the triumphant yells of the warriors and soldiers, just as the repeated motion of plunging his sword into flesh must have been a vivid memory in every muscle and sinew of his body. I wish I knew if he was elated or horrified.

He had been in North America for barely two years and was only twenty-one. He had spent a year training as a cadet at a military college in England, but this massacre of hundreds of innocent people was his first experience of war. The fact that he stayed so short a time at cadet college suggests that he hadn't particularly cared for the military.[1] One of his commanding officers, Capt. John Underhill, later remarked, "Great and doleful was the bloody sight to the view of young soldiers that never had been in war, to see so many souls lie gasping on the ground, so thick, in some

116

places, that you could hardly pass along."[2] Stanton had been angered by Pequot insolence at Fort Saybrook, and he may have felt the English were justified in making war on the Pequots, but his later actions suggest that he was horrified by the cold-blooded slaughter of women and children fleeing the conflagration.

If he was not badly wounded, my ancestor had likely been with the others in the field afterwards, when they had come upon a handful of living Pequots near the ruined fort – the ones they left to their allies, the Narragansetts and Mohegans, out of curiosity, because they wanted to see "the nature of Indian war." Did he agree with Captain Underhill, in whose contemptuous opinion "they might fight seven years and not kill seven men. They came not near one another, but shot remote, and not point blank, as we often do with our bullets, but at rovers [random], and then they gaze up in the sky to see where the arrow falls, and not until it is fallen do they shoot again. This fight is more for pastime, than to conquer and subdue enemies." His own friend and leader in the fight, Capt. John Mason, declared it "did hardly deserve the Name of Fighting."[3] Did the young man join the scornful laughter or did he stop to contemplate the difference, not only in the style, but in the meaning of their fighting?

Historians dispute whether the English had planned to massacre non-combatants all along, and whether the torching of the fort was a spontaneous action. "We had formerly concluded to destroy them by the Sword and save [take] the Plunder," recorded Captain Mason. Certainly the decision to shoot or impale non-combatants fleeing the burning village was an act of terrorism intended to break Pequot morale, rather than a military necessity. It horrified the colonists' aboriginal allies. As Underhill recorded, "Our Indians came to us, and much rejoiced at our victories, and greatly admired the manner of Englishmen's fight, but cried Mach it, mach it; that is, It is naught, it is naught, because it is too furious and slays too many men."[4] According to Francis Jennings, the word "admire" was used to express astonishment and wonder rather than respect, and "naught" meant bad or wicked. Their Native allies were astounded by the ruthlessness of the English; they had sought victory, not extermination.

Such wholesale slaughter of non-combatants appears to have been a European rather than an indigenous North American custom. The English had previously waged this kind of war in both Scotland and Ireland, and it was certainly practiced by all sides during the Thirty Years' War then raging on the other side of the Atlantic. Although there is some evidence that pre-contact Native warfare could occasionally be intensive and genocidal – as in the case of the Laurentian Iroquois, who were annihilated in the sixteenth century – such behaviour is believed to have been far less common than in Europe, until conflicts with Europeans changed traditional patterns. The Native allies of the English in the Pequot War certainly had their own bloody practices, however, though these were definitely not on the same scale: the Mohegans reportedly roasted and ate a Pequot victim.

Meanwhile, the Pequot women survivors of the Mystic conflagration, recognizing the spiritual power of the victorious English, shouted, "Much winnit Abbamocho" – that is very good Devil! – to the English soldiers who had devastated their fort, a cry that usually honoured the guardian spirit of a shaman after a successful cure.[5] The victorious troops, meanwhile, sang their own hymns of thanksgiving to God.

The more seasoned commanders of the English forces appear to have suffered no qualms about their tactics, and justified the massacre as God's judgment on the heathen. John Underhill wrote:

It may be demanded, Why should you be so furious? (as some have said). Should not Christians have more mercy and compassion? But I would refer you to David's war. When a people is grown to such a height of blood and sin against God and man and all confederates in the action, there he hath no respect as to persons, but harrows them and saws them, and puts them to the sword, and the most terriblest death that may be. Sometimes the Scripture declareth women and children must perish with their parents. Sometimes the case alters; but we will not dispute it now. We had sufficient light from the word of God for our proceedings.[6]

The fight was apparently over. The Narragansetts had decided to leave their English allies and return home, but were attacked on the way by Pequots from their other fort at Weinshauks and driven back to the English. The English killed "in the space of an hour . . . above a hundred Pequeats, all fighting men."[7] With the departure of most of the remaining Narragansetts, and low on food and munitions, the English did not have the strength to attack the second Pequot fort itself. Buoyed by the timely arrival of their ships in Pequot Harbor, at the mouth of the Thames River, the English began their evacuation with some difficulty, given the number of wounded and the tired and hungry condition of the men. On their way they encountered three hundred more Pequot warriors from

Weinshauks, who momentarily backed off when confronted by the better-armed English.

The Pequots then sent a contingent to the Mystic fort. At the sight of the devastation and the mounds of corpses, they succumbed momentarily to a terrible grief, crying and tearing their hair, before vowing vengeance on the English. According to Mason,

> Thus were they now at their Wits End, who not many hours before exalted themselves in their great Pride, threatning and resolving the utter Ruin and Destruction of all the English, Exulting and Rejoycing with Songs and Dances: But God was above them, who laughed his Enemies and the Enemies of his People to Scorn, making them as a fiery Oven. . . . Thus did the Lord judge among the Heathen, filling the Place with dead Bodies.[8]

After the original shock, rage revived the Pequots, and they set off after the soldiers. The men in the rear of the marching English turned and fired, hitting several Natives; the remaining Pequots then scattered, shooting their arrows at random as they retreated into the woods. They continued to harass the soldiers along the trail for some time. The English managed to kill several by firing blindly into the underbrush; these were then beheaded by the Mohegans.

Thomas Stanton must have been very relieved to see the English ship awaiting them in Pequot Harbor, but this mood would not have lasted long, as a dispute between Mason and the ship's captain, Daniel Patrick, ended up with Mason, Stanton, and the troops forced to return to shore and march by land the twenty miles to Fort Saybrook. On the way, they burned and plundered the territory of the Western Niantics, who, in spite of their deal with John Winthrop at Fort Saybrook earlier in the year, had not been accepted as English allies. The Western Niantics then sided with the Pequots after the English had burned the Pequot villages.

Although the surviving Pequots from Sassacus's village still outnumbered the English troops then in Connecticut, they appear to have been overcome by panic and despair at the Englishmen's ruthlessness. Sassacus, the grand sachem, could no longer muster a fighting force, and only the intervention of his counsellors saved him from the wrath of his people, who blamed him for the disaster at Mystic. In their rage, the Pequots killed instead Mohegan relatives of Uncas, who were still living among them. But they did not undertake further attacks against the English, having apparently concluded that they could not win such a war against them. Desperate, they fled into the woods, some heading to Long Island, some surrendering to the Narragansetts, the majority heading west in the hope of finding refuge with the Mohawks in New York, but moving slowly because of the children and the need to secure food along the way. Rumours spread that the Pequots and the reputedly cannibalistic Mohawks had "slaine many both English and Native" in Connecticut.[9] Accordingly, the English and Mohegans went in search of them, picking off or capturing stragglers.

Whatever the English originally intended, the war had escalated into more than a matter of capturing and executing a few Pequots who had committed criminal acts. Now the English determined to annihilate the whole nation. Thomas Stanton was even sent to Long and Shelter Islands in search of them, "but there was none," Lion Gardiner wrote, "for the Sachem Waiandance . . . had killed so many of the Pequits, and sent their heads to me, that they durst not come there; and he and his men went with the English to the Swamp."[10]

The swamp was the Sasco Swamp near Fairfield in the present-day New Haven area. There the largest remnant of the Pequot nation hid, until, on July 14, the English surrounded the swamp and began firing into the thicket. Apparently hoping to avoid further non-combatant casualties, Thomas Stanton offered to enter the swamp and negotiate with the enemy. Many advised against such a hazardous venture, but Stanton insisted. "Indians desired parley and were offered by Stanton that if they would come out and yield themselves they should have their lives, all that had not their hands in ye English blood."[11] Several hours later, he walked out of the swamp followed by 180 women, children, and old men.

But approximately two hundred warriors decided to remain in the swamp, and take their chances, declaring that they would rather die than be captured. Stanton re-entered the swamp once more to attempt negotiation; the warriors "shot at him so thicke as, if he had not cried out, and been presently rescued, they had slaine him."[12] Stanton then took part in the fight that ensued, known as the Swamp Fight, which lasted throughout the night. The English entered the swamp and shot down many Pequots, many of whom drowned in the mud. The Pequots resisted strenuously: forty escaped and fled to the Mohawks, but since the Mohawks were allies of the Narragansetts, they later put Sassacus and several other refugee sachems to death, cut off Sassacus's head, and sent it to the Connecticut authorities as a token of friendship to the English.

The soldiers seized Pequot wampum, kettles, and trays as booty and then divided up among themselves those Pequots who had followed Stanton out of the swamp. Mainly women and children, the captives were divided among the colonies and the Native allies as slaves: some were given to the soldiers, either gratis or for pay. Two women and fifteen boys were sent to Bermuda to be sold as slaves, but were blown off course and landed on Providence Isle, a Puritan colony off the coast of Nicaragua. Thus my ancestor was party to one of the earliest instances of Indian slavery in New England, which predated African slavery there.[13] No records survive to show whether he received any slaves himself or approved of their enslavement. Most Puritans did: many prominent men, including Roger Williams and Thomas Weld's future colleague, preacher Hugh Peter, asked for the slaves, whom they used mainly as domestic servants.

The other Native nations must have contemplated with horror the thoroughness of the English victory. Several sent representatives to the colonies offering friendship or promising tribute or curried English favour by killing Pequot refugees.

On September 21, 1638, the Connecticut General Court assembled at Hartford and concluded a peace treaty between the colonies, the Narragansetts, and the Mohegans. I have not been able to establish if Thomas Stanton was the interpreter for this agreement or not, though he might well have been, or at least have been present. The Hartford Treaty stipulated that the Pequot captives were to be divided between the colonists' Native allies, who agreed to deny sanctuary to any remaining warriors who had engaged in combat and to execute any they apprehended. The surviving Pequots were to abandon their villages and pay an annual tribute to Connecticut colony of a fathom of wampum for every warrior, half a fathom for a youth, and a handful for a child.[14] The genocidal intentions of the colonists were made abundantly clear by their stipulation that all the surviving Pequots give up their tribal identity and take on that of the Mohegans, the Narragansetts, or the Eastern Niantics. The surviving Pequots were compelled to sign a treaty that declared them extinct as a people and forbade the use of their name forever.

Massachusetts celebrated the end of the Pequot War with a Day of Thanksgiving on October 12, a date I find uncomfortably close to Canadian

Thanksgiving. The conviction of God's approval of the massacre became a commonplace among the Puritans: Thomas Weld's friend and colleague Thomas Shepard, for example, called the victory over the Pequots "a divine slaughter,"[15] and later Puritan writers were equally certain that English troops had been instruments of divine judgment. The early Puritan historians portrayed the Pequot War as an unfolding of God's plan for New England, the first of many Indian wars they would see as providentially ordained events. To the English, the Pequot War was proof that they had both the power and God's sanction to impose their will on the Native nations.

It is easy to regard this as cynical, self-serving propaganda, but to understand the Puritans' actions on their own terms, I have to recognize their spiritual motivations, and this is much more difficult for me – the Puritan world view is so utterly alien, so completely different from my own. It appears that the colonists sincerely believed they had acted in their own defence, that their righteous violence was necessary to rout the forces of Satan in the wilderness and to further the work of God. They had long expected such conflicts, just as the Old Testament Jews had faced them. They assumed that Native Americans were by nature untrustworthy and treacherous; since they were heathens, they were the natural enemies of Christians. As historian Alfred Cave writes, "Puritan ideology precluded long-term co-existence with a 'savage' people unwilling to acknowledge Christian hegemony. Clarification of Pequot intentions in the short run would not necessarily have changed the long term outcome. . . . Although they feared Indian war and prayed that they be spared its horrors, they also suspected that it was both necessary and inevitable."[16]

The Puritans would remember the war of 1637 as a mythic struggle of good over evil, of light over darkness, of Christian civilization over heathen savagery. The Pequots were Satan's minions and the Indian fighters, the agents of God. Unfortunately, these characterizations would prove to be very durable, "a vital part of the mythology of the American frontier," applied throughout American history to justify the appropriation of aboriginal lands and the extinguishing of Native sovereignty as security measures.[17]

Several decades later, the Puritan historian Cotton Mather wrote that through God's providence, the Puritans achieved not only "the utter subduing" of the Pequots but also "the affrighting of all the other Natives" as well, and so assured several decades of peace. Among the indigenous nations, the Pequot War confirmed the English reputation for treachery and cruelty. As Francis Jennings notes, they had learned that agreements with the English lasted only as long as they did not compete with English self-interest, that the English showed no mercy in warfare, and that their own weapons were no match for those of the English. After the war, three hundred Niantic warriors suspected of hiding Pequot refugees refused a challenge from forty of Mason's men, saying "they would not Fight with English Men, for they were Spirits."[18]

The sachems of the Narragansetts, the Mohegans, the Pequots, and the Niantics had made a serious blunder in trying to use the English in their power struggles with each other. It appears that they did not foresee how they would be used against each other in a divide-and-conquer strategy. The balance of power had now shifted to the English: after 1637, all New England aboriginal nations south of Maine acknowledged, if sometimes unwillingly, the authority of the Puritan colonies. Even the colonists' allies suffered an erosion of their own sovereignty after the war, for by the Hartford Treaty, the Mohegans and the Narragansetts agreed to submit all inter-tribal disputes to the English for settlement, and to be bound by the decision of the colonists. They had not known that the Puritans would respect Indian independence only when it was advantageous, and that with their greater firepower and expanding population the Puritans would wield power over the Native nations with increasing impunity.

Only Uncas, the Mohegan sachem, showed himself capable of manipulating the colonists to his own advantage. The war marked the beginning of a long alliance between the English and the Mohegans, which Thomas Stanton often facilitated.

With the defeat and removal of the Pequots, immigration into the Connecticut River Valley surged. The Connecticut River tribes also ceded vast tracts of land to the English. The colonies annexed most of the conquered Pequot territory and parcelled out lots to Connecticut veterans of the war: Thomas Stanton was one of those who received a grant of land for his services.[19]

The English may have gained control of Pequot land, but the attempted genocide of the Pequot nation did not succeed, for as soon as those Pequots assigned to the Narragansett sachem Miantonomo reached Rhode Island, they left him and were later joined by those assigned to Ninigret; these two groups moved to a place near the Pawcatuck River called Massatuxet, now Westerly, Rhode Island, where they built a wigwam village and

planted corn. To compel these Pequots to live with Miantonomo and
Ninigret according to the treaty obligation of 1637, Connecticut sent
Capt. John Mason and forty men, including Thomas Stanton, and Uncas
and a hundred Mohegans to break up the settlement and drive them back
to their overlords.

> And presently beating up our Drum, we Fired the Wigwams in their
> View: And as we Marched, there were two Indians standing upon a Hill
> jeering and reviling of us: Mr. Thomas Stanton our Interpreter, Marching
> at Liberty, desired to make a Shot at them; the Captain demanding of the
> Indians. What they were? Who said, They were Murtherers: Then the
> said Stanton having leave, let fly, Shot one of them through both his
> Thighs; which was to our Wonderment, it being at such a vast distance.
> . . . We then loaded our Bark with Corn; and our Indians their Canoes;
> And thirty more which we had taken, with Kittles, trays, Mats, and other
> Indian Luggage.[20]

Even this assault did not uproot the determined Pequots; they rebuilt
their wigwams and planted crops. The English finally gave up their effort to
remove them, and the Pequots remained at Massatuxet from 1637 to 1661.

The Hartford Treaty specified that all Indians who harboured or were
assigned Pequot refugees were to pay wampum tribute to the colonists.
Various historians have suggested that these stipulations reveal another
economic motive for the Puritan war against the Pequots – namely, control
of the wampum trade, for the Pequots and Narragansetts made or controlled much of the wampum in southern New England. Historian Lynn
Ceci notes that war was declared a few months after wampum was
declared legal tender in the colonies. As the English conquered the Pequots
and gained control of other wampum-makers, the value of English pence
doubled to six beads per penny and the colonists were able to maintain that
rate by controlling the quantities of wampum in circulation after 1638. It
has been conservatively estimated that payments of wampum tributes and
fines to the English between 1634 and 1664 amounted to more than 21,000
fathoms (six-foot strings) of wampum, worth about £5,000 in English currency, and more if double-value purple beads were included. "Thus a second
outcome of the Pequot War was, in effect, the partial underwriting of New
England colonization costs by the conquered natives. A third outcome was
the creation of a new, more advantageous English trade triangle, one that

began . . . with free tribute wampum gained without trade goods, and ended with credit – including final payment of the Puritan indebtedness – and badly needed supplies from Europe."[21]

The Pequot War certainly benefitted Thomas Stanton. In 1638, the General Court of Connecticut appointed him as the official Indian interpreter in all public transactions with the Indians, with a salary of £10 per annum. He was to attend courts on all occasions, both general and particular courts, as well as meetings of magistrates, wherever and whenever issues arose between the English and the Indians. His connections would also prove extremely influential: his friend Capt. John Mason became deputy-governor of the colony, and Stanton was for many years the intimate friend of Governor John Winthrop, Jr., of Connecticut.[22]

I do not know if Thomas Stanton acted as interpreter for the Hartford Treaty that concluded the Pequot War. According to the author of the Stanton family genealogy, however, he was a delegate at an "English and Indian Council meeting" at Hartford the same year, along with Roger Williams, Uncas, and Miantonomo, which may have been the treaty negotiations. He was definitely the interpreter for another treaty, later in 1638, that governed the original land purchases for the colony of New Haven. The local Quinnipiac Indians sold the lands (while retaining hunting and fishing rights for themselves) for twelve coats of English cloth, twelve spoons, twelve hatchets, twelve hoes, two dozen knives, twelve porringers, and four cases of French knives and scissors.[23]

To that deed Stanton added the following declaration:

> I, Thomas Stanton, being interpreter in this treaty, do hereby profess in the presence of God that I have fully acquainted the Indians with the substance of every article and truley returned their answer and consent to the same, according to the tenor of the foregoing writing, the truth of which, if lawfully, called, I shall readily confirm at any time.[24]

Sometime in 1636, as English–Pequot tensions escalated, Thomas Stanton had begun trading furs in the Connecticut Valley. It is thought that he acquired his land in Hartford early in 1637, before the war began, through his future father-in-law, Thomas Lord. Today Stanton is recognized as one of the original proprietors of Hartford; his livestock grazed on land that is now the site of the present State Capitol building.[25] In 1638, Thomas Stanton and William Whiting, one of the town's most prominent merchants, obtained exclusive fur-trading privileges at Hartford from the Connecticut General Court.

It was just after the war that Stanton married Ann, the daughter of Dorothy and Thomas Lord, all of whom had come to Hartford with the group led by Thomas Hooker; they soon started a family, which would eventually number ten children. One of Ann Lord's brothers was Dr. Thomas Lord, the first physician and surgeon in Connecticut. Another brother, Richard Lord, became a partner of Stanton's, and the two were licensed to trade with the Indians on Long Island for a period of twelve months in 1642, though this business relationship was short lived – two years later Richard Lord was fined £5 for drawing his sword and making threats against Stanton in a dispute about trading for corn with the Indians.[26]

In the wake of their victory, the English, Thomas Stanton included, enjoyed almost forty years of prosperity and relative peace. The Pequots, haunted by the massacre and the loss of their land, scrambled to survive and became more and more determined to resist annihilation. Meanwhile, the aboriginal allies of the English manoeuvred to stake out their positions in the power vacuum left by the decimation of the Pequots.

CHAPTER
8

Ambassador to the Indians

As fur trader, interpreter, and a man of public affairs, Thomas Stanton was now very busy. "He himself appears to have been always upon the wing, yet always within call," as the historian Frances Caulkins described him. His influence only increased in 1643, when the colonies of Plymouth, Connecticut, Massachusetts, and New Haven formed a federation called the United Colonies of New England and appointed Thomas Stanton as Interpreter-General of New England. "From 1636 to 1670," Caulkins writes, "his name is connected with almost every Indian transaction on record."[1]

It was during this period that he acquired his reputation as "friend to the Indians," and it is worth pondering the significance of this appellation. In what ways was friendship possible between a seventeenth-century Englishman in a position of power and an indigenous American, or, to put it bluntly, between a colonizer and someone who was trying to avoid being colonized? What was the nature of his numerous and various interactions with aboriginal people?

The first thing to consider is that, as the main conduit for aboriginal people in complicated negotiations over land purchases, boundary adjustments, trade treaties, war alliances, and the arbitration of disputes between rival chiefs, he was not a man to get on the wrong side of. Some gestures of friendship on the part of Native Americans undoubtedly were politically motivated. He may have been an able and useful intermediary for many Native people in their efforts to maximize their influence with the English yet minimize English challenges to their sovereignty; at the same time, they may have regarded him with some caution and recognized that his interests were fundamentally different from theirs. For example, it's clear from Stanton's letters that one of his essential functions was to provide intelligence to the English authorities about the political dynamics between various nations that the English were always scrambling to understand, and he often supplied information to the English about rumoured uprisings and plots against them. He clearly kept his own interests in mind – whether the issue at hand was furs or land or the security of the English. Yet many Native people seem to have respected him and trusted him over other Englishmen – and it's interesting to speculate why.

Stanton was somewhat hot-headed in his youth and blunt in his speech, as the two incidents with the Pequots related by Mason and Gardiner demonstrate. As the years passed, however, various Puritan leaders turned to him for his wisdom and skill in negotiating with various Native leaders. With his growing knowledge of local languages, he must have understood more about Native cultures than most Englishmen, though he undoubtedly still considered his own culture superior. Unlike most English people in New England, he travelled extensively through Indian country, and must have slept in many a wigwam. He also appears to have been less pious than most of the Puritan gentlemen who played leadership roles in the colonies – he was not a regular church member through most of his life, and was considered "not godly enough" to help John Eliot in his translation of the Bible into Massachusett[2] – and this may have been a plus in the eyes of Native Americans, for it would have made him slightly less judgmental. He also could be compassionate, as demonstrated by his actions at the Sasco Swamp during the Pequot War.

Throughout his long period of service to the colonies, Thomas Stanton was sent on missions to the Mohegans, the Narragansetts, the Pocumtucks, the Mohawks, the Montauks, the Tunxis, and other nations. He developed ongoing relationships with many aboriginal leaders, most notably Uncas, sachem of the Mohegans; Ninigret, sachem of the Eastern Niantics, who were allies and relations of the Narragansetts; and Harmon Garrett (Wequashcook) and Robin Cassacinamon, the leaders of the two groups of Pequots who eventually managed to re-establish themselves on land of their own following the war. In the case of Uncas, at least, it appears that the men enjoyed a real if difficult friendship, and a positive relation between the Mohegans and the Stanton family and their in-laws persisted over several generations. Thomas Stanton's relations with the Narragansetts were much more problematic – at one point the grand sachem Miantonomo even plotted to kill him.

Probably the most crucial role Thomas Stanton played was as emissary of the United Colonies in the ongoing disputes between the Mohegans and the Narragansetts. Under the Hartford Treaty, as we have seen, the two most powerful of the independent nations that remained, the Narragansetts and the Mohegans, had agreed that neither was to make any appeal to arms in any quarrel between themselves or against other tribes without first referring the case to the arbitration of the English. The colonies' decision was to be binding. The English obviously had no idea what they were getting themselves into. Even without a major war between the English and the indigenous people of New England from the end of the Pequot War in 1637 until 1675, the English found themselves deeply involved in innumerable conflicts and confrontations between the Mohegans and the Narragansetts and their allies. Thomas Stanton in turn found himself at the centre of English efforts to mediate these disputes.

English intrusion in the region greatly exacerbated the tensions between these Native nations. The near elimination of the powerful Pequots and the selective fury of the plagues, which initially spared the Narragansetts and devastated most other New England Native groups, disrupted the regional balance of power. In the new and uncertain political climate, the indigenous nations competed for access to furs, wampum, European goods, and English favour. In addition, the very presence of the English led to profound and bitter disagreement between the nations regarding strategies for dealing with them. It has been suggested that tensions between the Mohegans and the Narragansetts and their allies may also have been exacerbated by a divide-and-rule strategy on the part of the English; certainly they were inflamed by the conflicting ambitions of the various English colonies.[3]

For example, although many English detested the Mohegan sachem Uncas, the Puritans tended to side with him in his disputes with the Narragansetts. Uncas was an immediate neighbour of the colony of Connecticut, then mainly centred in the Connecticut River Valley and around New Haven. His enemies, the Narragansetts, on the other hand, lived in the vicinity of Providence, Rhode Island, the much-detested, tolerant colony of

Roger Williams, who had been banished from the Massachusetts Bay Colony in 1635 for his unorthodox opinions about Indian rights, the Massachusetts patent, and the churches. Thus, as historians such as Francis Jennings and Neal Salisbury have pointed out, rivalry between the Mohegans and the Narragansetts reflected that between Rhode Island and the United Colonies, and also hearkened back to the earlier struggle over trade with the Dutch. On top of all this, although the Narragansetts had helped the English win the Pequot War, Connecticut, Rhode Island, and Massachusetts all sought control of Narragansett territory.

As Jennings puts it, the Mohegans were Connecticut's surrogates against the Narragansetts, and also against the Bay Colony's claims to Narragansett land. (Massachusetts claimed it as its share of the spoils of the Pequot War.) The Narragansetts became more and more hostile as English designs on their sovereignty and land became clear. At the same time, Uncas positioned the Mohegans as the most reliable allies of the English and aggressively helped them in their efforts to reduce Narragansett autonomy. Tensions between the Narragansetts and the Massachusetts Bay Colony on the one hand and Connecticut and the Mohegans on the other also stemmed from competing efforts to control the distribution of wampum.

It is impossible to know now to what extent Thomas Stanton, so often the mouthpiece for the United Colonies in dealings with the Mohegans and the Narragansetts, was aware of these various underlying motivations, but he was certainly initially perceived by the Narragansett sachem Miantonomo as biased in favour of the Mohegans. Roger Williams wrote that Miantonomo had asked him to accompany him to a meeting with the magistrates at Hartford, not only because he did not trust the magistrates "who have bene (I feare) to [too] full of threatnings," but also because "he can not be confident of Tho. Stantons faythfullnes in points of Interpretation." This mistrust was more than a question of difficulties with the Narragansett dialect; in fact, Williams had reported a few weeks earlier that there were rumours circulating that Miantonomo was planning to assassinate Stanton (though Williams regarded these reports as slanders planted by the Mohegans). Three months later, Williams reported, "I allso in case I should listen to Indian Reports shall bring many who will affirme that Tho. Stanton hath received mighty Bribes," and that Uncas was the source of those bribes, though Williams refused to believe it.[4]

Uncas, the Mohegan sachem, with whom Thomas Stanton had many dealings over a span of forty years, is one of the most interesting figures of the time. To me, he's somewhat larger than life, and would have made a great Shakespearean character. In theory and at the end of the day he was the most loyal aboriginal ally of the English, but he seems also to have been the slipperiest. In fact, the English probably regarded him as more trouble than any of their enemies. He kept them in a state of constant confusion and mistrust; it is safe to say he infuriated them, outmanoeuvred them, and always kept them guessing. He was often able to manipulate the colonists to his own advantage or to the advantage of the Mohegans; clearly he made the most of whatever power he had. Appropriately, his name supposedly meant "fox."

It seems he recognized sooner than many Native American leaders that the English had the will and the means to dominate the region, and his survival strategy was to use and appease them rather than openly resist them. Interpretations of his behaviour and motivations differed wildly at the time and are still in dispute. Although most Puritan historians saw his earlier break from the Pequots as a matter of thwarted personal ambition, Melissa Jayne Fawcett, the current Mohegan tribal historian, attributes the break to a dispute between Sassacus, the son of the murdered Pequot sachem Tatobem, and Uncas over how to deal with the English; Uncas favoured political alliance as the best way to flourish in the new political environment, while mainstream Pequots did not support this strategy. But Uncas's strategy worked: the Mohegans, unlike most of the nations in New England, were never conquered. During his lifetime, the English never encroached on Mohegan territory, though shortly after the Pequot War, Uncas signed over a deed to most of eastern Connecticut to the English in an apparent effort to maintain English favour and win support for his own struggle for dominance among the sachems of the region.

The most common contemporary English assessment of Uncas was that he was "grasping, ambitious and thoroughly amoral." A prominent Puritan described him in his later years as "an old and wicked, wilful man, a drankard and otherwise very vitious . . . who hath always been an opposer and underminer of praying to God." Even though Uncas had played a vital role in the Pequot War, the English initially suspected him of harbouring the enemy, though he soon managed to convince the government of his loyalty. Capt. John Mason, who had led the English and Native forces in that war, remained his staunch supporter through thick and thin, and described him as a man of exceptional bravery and "a great Friend."[5]

From his recorded comments, Stanton appears to have had a clear sense of the less-reliable aspects of Uncas's character – in 1657, he wrote, "ye

English have no sooner qualified any thing by their interposing but Uncas presently undoes all by his proud & high words,"[6] yet he apparently remained on friendly terms with him. He was undoubtedly useful to Uncas, as he had the ear of the highest authorities, especially Mason and Connecticut Governor John Winthrop, Jr. The authorities for their part may have encouraged Stanton to maintain a good rapport with Uncas, their most difficult ally.

Many leaders of other Native nations detested Uncas. Some regarded him as a traitor for his role in the Pequot War. Others were jealous of his good relations with the English and the power and resources he wielded as a result. Most Pequot survivors of the war had been given to Uncas and, through his alliance with the English, the Mohegans were allowed to assume jurisdiction over most Pequot territory. For the next fifteen years he was subject to numerous attacks from the Narragansetts, the Niantics, the Pocumtucks, Tunxis, and other nations and he escaped more than one attempt to kill him. If he had not enjoyed English protection and the support of people like John Mason and Thomas Stanton, it is doubtful he would have survived.

These conflicts were often quite complicated, involving not just the Mohegans and the Narragansetts, but their allies. For example, in 1643, Uncas reported to the magistrates at Hartford that Miantonomo, the Narragansett grand sachem, had hired a Pequot to kill him, and that some of the followers of Sequassen, a River Indian sachem and ally of the Narragansetts, had assassinated another Mohegan sachem; they had also shot arrows at Uncas as he canoed down the Connecticut River. The Connecticut governor at the time, John Haynes, tried to make peace between Uncas and Sequassen, to no avail. Uncas was then granted permission to avenge the wrong. He assembled a large number of warriors, invaded the territory of Sequassen, killed a large number of Connecticut River Indians, and drove Sequassen into exile.

As Sequassen was his relative, Miantonomo was indignant. The Narragansett grand sachem asked Governor John Winthrop, Sr. (father of John Winthrop, Jr., frequent governor of Connecticut) if the Massachusetts Bay Colony would be offended if he made war on Uncas. The colony agreed to allow him to choose his own course. In 1643, six hundred to a thousand Narragansett warriors marched from Rhode Island to Mohegan territory in southeastern Connecticut. Although the Mohegans were greatly outnumbered, Uncas tricked and surprised the Narragansetts and captured Miantonomo, held him prisoner at Fort Shantok, south of Norwich, then took him to Hartford. After considerable consultation with many prominent Puritans, including five of the most distinguished clergymen in Massachusetts (whose identities I have not been able to ascertain, but who may well have included John Eliot), the United Colonies, in a move later denounced as "cold-blooded murder," voted in favour of Miantonomo's execution. Cleverly, they arranged for the Mohegans to carry it out, ensuring that there would be sufficient enmity between the two Native nations to prevent any future alliance against the English. The commissioners granted Uncas permission to kill the Narragansett sachem and agreed to assist him should the Narragansetts make war on him. After a short captivity, Uncas's brother killed Miantonomo in 1643.

The Narragansetts were understandably outraged. They demanded satisfaction, and threatened to call in the powerful Mohawks to attack the United Colonies if the English did not withdraw their garrison protecting Uncas. They were particularly incensed because they claimed that they had made an agreement to pay ransom and had made a first payment, and that Uncas had not only killed their sachem but refused to return the ransom. Thomas Stanton and Nathaniel Willett were sent to both the Narragansett sachems and Uncas to try to sort out the truth of the matter. They were further instructed to "remind [the sachems] of the treaty of Hartford, reread each article, take answers in writing, then read them back to them that they may understand how ye understand their answere and that we may know they owne it and there is no mistake."[7]

In due course Stanton reported that he could find no evidence that a ransom had been paid. The Narragansetts asked permission to fight the Mohegans, but Stanton informed them that the English would stand by Uncas, and he succeeded in getting them to sign a peace bond in 1644. It didn't last, for in the spring of 1645 the Narragansett sachem Pessacus, Miantonomo's brother, came to Mohegan country with a large force and destroyed wigwams and crops; the Mohegans retreated to their own Fort Shantok, where they were under siege for some time, without food, and were almost forced to surrender. A group of English settlers under Thomas Leffingwell rescued them, and Uncas gratefully made a grant of lands to his saviours that became the site of the present town of Norwich, Connecticut. The English then declared war on the Narragansetts and the Narragansetts withdrew. Another peace treaty was concluded in August 1645: the Narragansetts and their tributary, the Niantics, agreed to pay the English

two thousand fathoms of wampum and to send four children of their chiefs
to Boston as hostages. When they later reneged, the English again threatened to declare war.

The calculating nature of Puritan involvement in these disputes is
revealed in a letter written in 1645 by Emanuel Downing, a member of the
Massachusetts General Court, to his brother-in-law John Winthrop, Sr.,
governor of Massachusetts. In it, he contemplated the benefits of a war
against the Narragansetts:

> Sir . . . If upon a Just warre [with the Narragansetts] the Lord should
> deliver them into our hands, wee might easily have men woemen and
> children to exchange for Moores [African slaves], which wilbe more
> gaynefull pilladge for us then wee conceive, for I doe not see how wee
> can thrive untill wee get into a stock of slaves sufficient to doe all our
> buisiness, for our children's children will hardly see this great Continent
> filled with people, soe that our servants will still desire freedome to plant
> for them-selves, and not stay but for verie great wages. And I suppose
> you know verie well how wee shall mayneteyne 20 Moores cheaper than
> one Englishe servant.[8]

While the Massachusetts Bay Colony was busy with the Narragansetts, the
Connecticut magistrates were investigating yet another plot against Uncas.
Thomas Stanton interpreted for a man who accused Sequassen, the
Connecticut River Indian sachem who had now returned from exile after
Uncas's raid, of plotting to kill the two Connecticut commissioners to the
United Colonies. These were Edward Hopkins and John Haynes, who took
turns serving as governor of Connecticut in alternate years from 1643 to
1654, as well as William Whiting, Stanton's original business partner, who
was now a magistrate. Sequassen's plan, the man alleged, was to frame
Uncas as the murderer. When the plot was discovered, Sequassen fled
to the village of Pocumtuck on the upper Connecticut (now Deerfield,
Massachusetts). Uncas captured him and took him to Hartford, where he
was later released for lack of evidence.

Meanwhile, Pessacus, brother of Miantonomo, had decided to look
farther afield for allies against Uncas, and made overtures to the Mohawks
and the Pocumtucks. The Pocumtucks readily agreed, for they were angry

at Uncas for invading their territory and carrying off Sequassen, and planned to join a large campaign planned for July 1648. The English found out about a huge gathering of warriors at the village of Pocumtuck and sent Thomas Stanton to discover what was going on. He found "one thousand warriors at Pocumtuck, 300 or more having guns, powder and bullets," building a "very large and stronge fort." According to Deerfield historian George Sheldon, Stanton then gathered together the sachems and warned them that the English were bound by treaty to defend Uncas against the Narragansetts and their allies. This warning, as well as the news that the "French," or "Eastern," Indians (Abenakis) had attacked the Mohawks, induced the sachems to give up their expedition.[9]

Mohegan–Narragansett hostilities, with their attempted assassinations, raids, and counter-raids, suspected alliances, English threats of war, and so on, continued for years. The United Colonies sent Stanton on innumerable missions to the Narragansetts and Mohegans; he delivered English ultimatums, informed them of charges against them by either the English or other Native nations, notified them when previous answers were unsatisfactory, demanded wampum fines, investigated rumours of conspiracies, summoned the sachems to meetings of the United Colonies, and recorded their testimonies and responses for the commissioners. He also contributed his own assessment of the veracity of various statements (such as remarking that a sachem who claimed to be too sick to come to a meeting looked perfectly healthy) and on at least one occasion he got into trouble with the authorities for criticizing their actions toward Uncas.[10] At times he was in considerable danger, as when he was sent to speak with Ninigret after the latter led a Narragansett/Niantic attack on the Montauks of Long Island. In sworn testimony he related how

Ninigret's men disturbed them, asking whether they went, shouting and hallowing and using scornfull words saying they cared not for the English nor did they feare them; And when therupon Thomas Staunton with his Rapior in the scabbert struck att the wolfes tayle on the head of a Pequot Indian most active in the said offencive Carriage demaunding why hee did soe Reuile the English whoe Intended them noe harme; A Narraganset Captaine cocked his gun and the said Pequot drew his Bow with an Arrow in it presented att him Wherupon Thomas stood still and tould them they might doe their pleasure hee had a Messaage to deliver to Ninigrett which hee would doe though hee lost his life before he returned home After which when Thomas came to Ninnegrett and read his Message from Mr Winthorpe Ninnegrett Asked what the English had to doe to desire or demaund his prsoners and tould Thomas they should neither see them or have them; And Ninnegrett's men expressed themselves very tumultuvsly and would hardly suffer any spech betwixt Ninnegrett and Thomas Staunton.[11]

Thomas Stanton was not the only interpreter and ambassador used in these situations, but he appears to have been one of the most successful. For example, when, in 1658–59, hostilities escalated between the Mohegans and the Pocumtucks (Narragansett allies) there was once again the danger of a general war. Another interpreter was initially sent to parley with the Pocumtucks; he was threatened and assaulted. A second messenger was sent to try to set up a meeting with the Pocumtuck sachems and Connecticut authorities, but the English were not satisfied with the Pocumtucks' reply. A week later, Thomas Stanton sallied forth with the following instructions: "You are to let them know that wee received theire answare but in several particulars are unsatisfied as first that they desire to keep peace yet have committed several outrages against several English and pretend excuses not to come and answer for them; or give satisfaction." He returned several days later with a written message from the sachems that contained a clear, dispassionate view of the troubles between the parties and answers to all the charges against the Pocumtucks. It concluded: "Wee desire the English Sachems not to perswade vs to a peace with Vncas although hee promeseth much hee will performe nothinge; wee haue expereince of his falcenes; alsoe wee desire that if any Messengers bee sent to vs from the English they may bee such as are not lyares and tale carryers but sober men; and such as wee can vnderstand."[12] Presumably they counted Stanton as one of these sober men, for this diplomatic effort bore fruit; there were no further troubles between the Pocumtucks and the Mohegans.

Another element in the complicated relations between the English, the Mohegans, and the Narragansetts was the situation of the surviving Pequots. On several occasions, Stanton was sent to confront Uncas and Ninigret concerning the treatment of their captives or overdue wampum tribute payments. Uncas was repeatedly accused of extorting wampum payments from the Pequots to support his ongoing wars with the Narragansetts and Pocumtucks, and Ninigret's failure to send the required tribute for his captives led the United Colonies to demand payment at once or face an English force that would seize Narragansett goods and release Ninigret's Pequots from his subjection.

When a group of Pequots under Uncas petitioned the United Colonies to be allowed to live independently, Stanton's friend John Winthrop, Jr., who had become a good friend of the Pequot leader Robin Cassacinamon, championed the motion. As the United Colonies contemplated yet again the possibility of war with the Narragansetts, they realized that Pequot fighters subject directly to the English could be quite useful to them as warriors and also for gathering information about conspiracies against the English. In 1650, the United Colonies permitted the Pequot leaders Robin Cassacinamon and Harmon Garrett to establish their own independent settlements near New London and on the Pawcatuck River and stipulated that, for the next ten years, all wampum tribute would be paid directly to Thomas Stanton. That same year, the Pequots assisted the United Colonies in a brief action against the Narragansetts.

In 1656, Stanton's neighbour George Denison (whose children would marry three of Stanton's), John Winthrop, Jr., and Maj. John Mason (he had been promoted to Major-General of the Connecticut forces shortly after the Pequot War) were appointed to assist the Pequot "governors" of the two independent communities in carrying out the commissioners' instructions. The following year, Stanton was also appointed to the same role, and he and Denison continued in these positions year after year. In 1662, the two men were first described as "overseers" who, among other responsibilities, were to "do what may best reduce them [the Pequots] to civility and the knowledge of God as well by causing due punishment to bee inflicted on them in their injuiries and offensife demeanors."[13] I believe they were the first tribal overseers of an indigenous nation in New England.

Given all these examples of the ongoing tensions between the Narragansetts and their allies on the one hand and the United Colonies and the Mohegans on the other, it is surprising that none of these incidents erupted into a major war. Part of the reason is that, although they coveted Narragansett land, the Puritans still had land to expand into that they had obtained from other indigenous nations in the 1620s and 1630s. But an even more important factor in maintaining relative peace and stability in New England for three decades was the existence of exchange networks of furs, wampum, and European goods that linked English traders to the Narragansetts and their allies, such as the Pocumtucks, and, through these, to the powerful Mohawks to the northwest – the English needed the Mohawks as allies in their competition with New France and *its* Indian allies (such as the Algonquin and Montagnais). Thomas Stanton, as one of the most prosperous fur traders in Connecticut, was at the centre of these exchange networks.

Indeed, for a time, the fur trade drew Natives and Europeans together. From the end of the Pequot War in 1637 to the early 1660s, Europeans and aboriginal people were interdependent partners in the New England economy. Native people produced the local currency (wampum) as well as the American trade item most in demand in Europe – dressed fur pelts for felt hats (Europe already having decimated its own population of fur-bearing animals) – and also provided other services for the colonists, such as hunting wolves, building fences, and other such tasks. The Native nations with whom Thomas Stanton had the most contact – the Mohegans of southern Connecticut, the Eastern Niantics in the disputed border region with Rhode Island, and the Narragansetts of Rhode Island – flourished as middlemen in the fur trade, and were largely able to retain their autonomy during this period.

In 1649, Stanton perceived new prospects in the trade. He had accompanied John Winthrop, Jr., as interpreter to Wequetequock Cove along the Pawcatuck River in southeastern Connecticut to consult with Ninigret, "with a view to conciliate his Indian neighbours, and come to a fair understanding in regard to bounds and trade."[14] While there, Stanton visited the Pawcatuck Valley, and was so impressed with its potential for trading purposes that, when he returned to Hartford, he obtained an exclusive licence from the General Court for the trade along the Pawcatuck River for three years, along with six acres of planting-ground, and liberty of feed and mowing for three years. He received the licence in 1650 and soon erected a trading-house along the river, where he began a profitable trade with the Indians. In 1651 he moved his family to Pequot Plantation, a new plantation started by John Winthrop, Jr., at the mouth of the Thames River several miles to the west of the Pawcatuck River, and in 1656 took them east to the new settlement of Pawcatuck, near the present-day town of Stonington. Stanton was the first white settler on the Pawcatuck River and the second in the area. (Both Pawcatuck and Stonington were originally part of Pequot Plantation, and later formed a new plantation that was known as Pawcatuck, Stonington, or Southerton at various times.)

Whether Stanton knew it or not, the vast economic network that included him and the Native Americans he traded with profoundly altered the internal economies of the Native nations, as had happened with the Pawtuckets along the Merrimack River years earlier. Because most Native people preferred European implements and cloth to their own products – they bought iron axes, hatchets, awls, ice chisels, butcher knives, swords, fish hooks, brass and copper kettles, blankets, and articles of clothing, among other things – they became enmeshed in and dependent upon the European market economy. Without constant practice at their own labour-intensive production techniques, their traditional skills and detailed craft knowledge were soon lost – a process readily observable today among many Inuit – and were not replaced with the means or skills to make or maintain the European trade items. Worse, they often bought European goods on credit supplied by the trader.

With this increasing dependence on trade goods and the continued high demand for furs, many hunters abandoned tradition. Now they hunted beaver and other fur-bearing animals intensively, moving beyond their traditional territories in search of more fur. Guns became necessary for commercial hunting and to gain the upper hand in fierce competition between various Native nations for control over the movement of goods and access to suppliers. The Mohawks, for example, had earlier access to firearms than most nations, buying them first from the Dutch in the mid-1630s and then from English traders on the Connecticut River (likely including Thomas Stanton) in 1639; they quickly established their military and trade supremacy through much of northeastern North America. Other nations were then drawn into the trade to ensure their own survival.

To my knowledge, there are no surviving records of Thomas Stanton's trade either in Hartford or Pawcatuck, but it is possible to get a sense of the scale of the trade by looking at the figures for another prominent trader, John Pynchon of Springfield in the Connecticut Valley. In the five years between 1652 and 1657 he sent to England 8,992 beaver skins, valued at £5,520 and 16 shillings sterling, 320 otter skins, 148 muskrat skins, 11 moose skins, beaver bags containing castor, and a variety of other furs including sable, mink, fox, raccoon, wildcat, and fisher. This was relatively small change in the continental trade: by the late 1650s, 46,000 pelts were being brought in to Fort Orange (near modern Albany, New York) annually, for example.[15]

Historian Francis Jennings has noted the paradox of the fur trade, that "contact with the more complex culture of Europe did not stimulate the development of greater complexity in Indian culture and industry, but rather the opposite, as the trade with Europeans subordinated and eliminated all crafts except those directly related to the fur trade, while inter-tribal trading relations survived only if they served the purposes of intersociety trade [e.g., the production and trading of wampum]."[16] Where the ceremonial exchange of goods had once reinforced equality among bands, the new trade relations created greater inequality by giving advantages to some bands, while disadvantaged bands paid tribute to Indian middlemen, just as they did for hunting rights or protection against their enemies.

Many Europeans, including Thomas Stanton, got rich on the fur trade, but aboriginal people never did, chiefly because Native cultural values did not promote the accumulation of wealth. Indeed, in healing and other rituals, many Native nations (notably the Narragansetts) gave away or destroyed large amounts of personal property in the belief that such distribution improved their collective well-being; some even tried to interest the English in doing the same. The indigenous nations traded more for social and political reasons than to make a profit: many traded for wampum and cloth, which were valuable as symbols of status and for cementing social and political relations. As Francis Jennings succinctly puts it, "The Indian's culture permitted and encouraged him to become a trader, but it forbade him to be a merchant."[17]

At the time, Native Americans appear to have considered the fur trade a good thing, at least initially, but in fact, as another historian, Colin Calloway, noted, the trade proved to be "a Trojan horse." It spread the diseases that decimated and weakened aboriginal populations, leaving them vulnerable to English ambitions. It introduced alcohol to many nations, with devastating results (like many other traders, Thomas Stanton sold alcohol to the Indians, which was illegal). The commerce precipitated and exacerbated a crisis in belief among many Native Americans, for in hunting with such intensity, hunters violated powerful taboos – traditionally, conservation for future generations was an essential element of spiritual practice and animals were respected as sources of spiritual power, who could withhold their gifts if not properly addressed and treated. This new basis of the Native economy was also self-defeating, for in exterminating the beaver, the very basis of the trade itself was destroyed, while Native dependency on European trade goods continued. These were not the intentions of the English traders or the Native beaver hunters, but these were the results.

By 1660 the local fur-bearing animal population was largely extinct, and the indigenous nations of New England became increasingly irrelevant to Europeans in economic terms, except as intermediaries for furs from farther north or as owners of land that the settlers coveted. Some traders began to sell and rent land acquired from fur-poor Indians who could not pay for the supplies they had bought on credit. For example, between 1650 and 1670, the Natives of the upper Connecticut River incurred such debts at John Pynchon's stores that they were forced to sell major portions of their lands along the river. The pattern was apparently repeated elsewhere, though I do not know if this happened in the Pawcatuck area where Thomas Stanton lived – certainly, he did end up with a large amount of land. Then, in the 1660s, beaver hats went out of fashion in Europe, and even the role of intermediary was suddenly redundant. The demand for furs plummeted. Once the settlers were no longer dependent on the aboriginal nations, they relegated Native Americans to the margins of New England society and increasingly sought to displace them.

In the early days of the colonies, wealthy New Englanders had invested in the fur trade, but in the second half of the seventeenth century the beginning of trade with the West Indies offered better opportunities, such as exporting fish and lumber, ship-building, and distilling rum. The Stanton family pioneered in this trade as well, though it is not clear exactly when they began. The *Stonington Chronology* pinpoints the date as 1670, without providing sources or details as to what ship Stanton used; it is possible that he engaged in this trade with whatever shipping arrangements he used in his regular trade for furs.[18] According to Frances Caulkins, the trade opened up by Thomas Stanton and Sons was the first between New London and Newport, Rhode Island, and laid the foundation of commercial relations between New London and the West Indies.[19] It is known that, in 1681, four years after Thomas Stanton's death, Jos. Wells built a forty-one-foot sloop for Daniel Stanton, Samuel Rogers (another direct ancestor), and Alex Pygan, and Daniel Stanton relocated to Barbados, where the firm of Thomas Stanton and Sons shipped corn, beans, sun-dried fish, and jerked venison to him from Pawcatuck.

Through this shipping venture, the Stanton family may also have engaged in a more unsavoury trade. According to John Whit Davis, a descendant of Thomas Stanton who grew up in Thomas Stanton's third house, there is a family story that the Stantons occasionally brought back African slaves through their trade with Barbados, the main source of slaves in New England, though I have not been able to substantiate if and when this actually occurred. It is known that, by 1680, there were still fewer than thirty African slaves in Connecticut; Governor William Leete reported: "As for Moors there comes sometimes 3 or 4 in a year from Barbadoes."[20] Certainly by 1677 Thomas Stanton owned one African slave: a letter written that year by Rev. James Noyes, Stonington's minister and Thomas Stanton's son-in-law, mentions "Ruth, Father Stanton's negro," who herself bought a Pequot girl slave from the Pequot leader Catapezet for two truck-ing-cloth coats and five yards of painted calico.[21]

The Connecticut Court also authorized Stanton to sell Native Americans into West Indian slavery on two occasions. When Cuskatome and the sachem's brother-in-law stole "a considerable estate" from Stanton, the General Court ruled in Stanton's favour, ordering that he be paid £27, 12 shillings within fourteen days. If the fine was not paid, Stanton was author-ized "to dispose of these Indians by selling or sending them to Barbadoes or any other English Island." In another instance, Thomas Stanton and his neighbour George Denison were directed by the court to demand payment of a fine by a Narragansett sachem for stealing a neighbour's horses and verbally abusing him when he tried to get them back. If no payment was made in thirty days, they were to apprehend two of the sachem's men and sell them for £20 and transport them out of the country (to Barbados) or otherwise dispose of them as they saw fit.[22] I do not know whether either of these incidents resulted in the threatened enslavement, but Stanton was well positioned to arrange such sales through his shipping contacts.

The success of the overseas trade brought New England merchants a new influx of English currency, and the demand for wampum declined as a result; by 1661, wampum had ceased to be legal tender. Deprived of the wampum trade and with the fur trade in decline, the interests of whites and Natives began to diverge sharply. As the dynamics between the two soci-eties changed – to the detriment of Native people – the possibility of Native American hostility grew. The English became more suspicious of possible pan-Indian uprisings and acted to sabotage such efforts. Thomas Stanton's intelligence network became crucial in the efforts of the colonies to antic-ipate conspiracies.

In the winter of 1668, Robin Cassacinamon, leader of the Nameag, or western, group of Pequots, had hosted a dance at Noank. This was the first reservation for the Pequots, on land donated by John Winthrop, Jr. Both Mohegans and Narragansetts attended the dance. Thomas Stanton wrote to John Mason, now deputy-governor of Connecticut, that to see Uncas and Ninigret together at Robin's dance was a "wonderment," "they who durst not looke upon the other this twenty years, but at the missell of a gun or at the pile of an arrow."[23] Stanton and a number of militia men broke up this dance and attempted to arrest Ninigret, who was suspected of conspiring against the English. Robin Cassacinamon objected to Stanton's actions and sent a petition to the Connecticut authorities, which described Stanton as recklessly throwing his weight around and creating an incendiary situation where none had existed previously:

> this winter that Unckas and NinyCraft and A great Many other Indians mett together in the place where we Dwell to make a Dance after the Indian fashon, Intending no hurt at all to the Inglish and when we were about to Dannce Mr. Stanton cam with some souildiers to Cary Away Ninigraft. Mr Stanton said he would Dye in that place but he would have him and chargd the pequott Indians to Asist the English and the thing being sudaine to us and I knew not whether the Indians would Asist the Inglish or noe I was much afraid that some men would be kild becuase I then saw Ninicrafts men, Almost one hundred of them, have clubs in their hands and the Inglish men layd their hands upoon their swords Redy to draw. then I cryed out to them and asked them what would satisfy them. At last Mr. Stanton told me he must have A great deal of wampom. then I told him he should have what he would and that wampom was like the grass when it was gon it would com againe but if men be once kild they will live noe more. then I Agreed to pay Mr. Stanton Twenty pound to satisfy him for I was Afraid that Ninecrafts men might have fyrd Inglishmens houses and that A great dell of hurt might A com of it, and it may be the pequot Indians and other Indians might A bein blamd that had noe hand in it. . . .[24]

As we've seen, then, Thomas Stanton's relationships with Native Americans were by no means only of a "friendly" nature; power was an essential element of the dynamics shaping his business, political, and judicial activities. But there was yet another, if somewhat unlikely, aspect of Thomas Stanton's interactions with Native people – religion.

As I mentioned earlier, the commissioners of the United Colonies at one point suggested that Thomas Stanton assist John Eliot in his translation of the Bible, since Stanton was the best linguist in New England. He was not accepted, reputedly because he was considered "not godly enough . . . for the spirtuall parte of this worke." Connecticut evidently had lower standards for godliness, for in 1650 the General Court assigned Stanton and one elder to proselytize the Indians twice a year, apparently to no avail. Because Eliot's Massachusett Bible would be incomprehensible to Mohegans and Pequots in Connecticut, Rev. Abraham Pierson of Branford, aided by Thomas Stanton, prepared a bilingual catechism suited to Connecticut dialects. Stanton or one of his sons also acted as interpreter for Mr. William Thompson, who in 1657 was appointed missionary to the Pequots at Mystic and Pawcatuck, but after 1661, Thompson's stipend was withheld with the comment that he had "neglected the business."[25] Stanton was also instructed to select young Pequot boys to go to study with Daniel Weld in preparation for religious studies at Harvard, which he presumably did.

There is no evidence that Stanton was ever very religious; his name never appears in local records of church attendance. He appears to have remained "aloof" from religion until 1674, when he joined with others to build the First Congregational Church of Stonington. (Bernard Stanton, family historian for the Stanton Society, theorizes that, like many people facing death, he "got religion" when he became ill toward the end of his life; another possibility is that his son-in-law, Rev. James Noyes, pressured him into contributing to the founding of the church.)

The commissioners of the United Colonies also hoped to train Thomas Stanton's sons to serve as missionaries to the Indians. In 1653 they voted to send two sons of Thomas Stanton – Thomas junior and John – to Harvard to prepare them to be consultants for the Harvard faculty at the expense of the Society for the Propagation of the Gospel in New England. Although they were proficient in the Mohegan–Pequot language, neither was academically inclined. "Nor do they seem to have had the missionary zeal necessary for lives dedicated to uplifting the heathen," writes historian Alden T. Vaughan. "Like their father, they were probably more akin to the later American frontier type than to the Puritan reformers." In fact, John Stanton's misbehaviour and neglect of his studies came to the attention not only of Harvard President Charles Chauncy but also of the commissioners of the United Colonies, who wrote to him in 1659: "John Stanton We have Received information from Mr. Chansye of yor intolerable neglect in yer studyes And of Severall Miscarriages wch may not be borne."[26] Because of his father's intercession, and a vote of confidence from Reverend Thompson, the college gave him another chance, but he did not complete his studies, nor did his brother.

I was once told by another Stanton descendant that Thomas Stanton converted Uncas to Christianity – an interesting story but very unlikely. Everything I've read about Uncas describes him as hostile to Christianity. John Eliot's assistant, Daniel Gookin, for example, noted that he had "always been an opposer and underminer of praying to God."[27] Certainly, if Stanton did convert anybody, it was not through the usual preaching and exhorting but as a result of more vigorous and unorthodox action, such as that described in the following curious anecdote, which was told about a "Mr. Stanton" – likely Thomas Stanton or one of his sons:

> Sometime after the English lived at Stonington, there came an Indian (of that place) to Mr Stanton (who had the Indian tongue) and told M^r. Stanton there was an Indian (of that place) that had a quarril with him, and had sent for a greate powaw from Long Island, who had undertaken to revenge the quarril; and thereupon shewed a greate feare; whereupon M^r. Stanton sent for the powaw, and desired him to desist, telling that Indian was his pertecaler friende, but the powaw refused without so greate a rewarde might be giuen, that the Indian could not be able to giue, and the Indian powaw grew still more high and positive in his language, until he told M^r. Staton he could immediately tare his house in pieces, and himself flye out at the top of the chimney; and grew at length to be so daring that he raised the old gentlemans Temper, so that he started out of his greate chayre and layed hold of the powaw, and by main strength took him, and with a halter tyed his hands, and raised him up to a hook in the Joyse, and whipped him until he promised to desist and go home, which he did and the poore fearefull Indian had no harm from the powaw; there were many Indians without the house, who came as neare as they dare, and saw the disipline, and expected the house to be tore in pieces (as they said), who, when they saw the matter so concluded went away much Surprised.[28]

To me, that is completely consistent with my own picture of Thomas Stanton and his relationship to Native Americans – a man of action who would vigorously support his "particular friends" among the Indians, but on English terms – someone who would not hesitate to turn traditional Native society or its power relations upside down if he thought them wrong or if they interfered with English plans, and who, whether he intended to be or not, was himself an agent of change among Native people.

CHAPTER
9

Land

I've known since I was a child that the English ended up with the land that originally belonged to aboriginal people and I often heard that white people "took" or "stole" the land. But it wasn't until I began to research relations between my family and aboriginal people that I began to understand how such transfers actually happened. Outright conquest was undoubtedly the means by which some of the land was acquired, as in the case of the former Pequot lands that were granted to Thomas Stanton for his service in the Pequot War,[1] but as I've discovered, the process of dispossession in many other cases was more gradual and subtle, accompanied as it was by a veneer of legality. The Puritans proudly claimed that they had treated the Indians fairly and had acquired land deeds through sale, yet a closer look at the process by which many deeds were acquired reveals a more disturbing pattern. An examination of some of the land deals involving Thomas Stanton and his children and the Native nations with whom he had the most contact – the Narragansetts, the Pequots, the Mohegans – illustrates the various ways that English land hunger impinged on Native Americans. Thomas Stanton himself became a large landowner in southeastern Connecticut and southwestern Rhode Island – it is estimated that his holdings eventually totalled approximately 20,000 acres.[2]

The struggle for the Narragansett lands across the Pawcatuck River to the east of Pawcatuck – in which Stanton played a part – is one of the most notorious examples of Puritan greed, speculation, and unscrupulous treatment of the aboriginal inhabitants on record. The "Narragansett country" (now the southwestern third of Rhode Island) was roughly four hundred square miles of largely rocky and marshy terrain; the only good agricultural land lay in a strip along the western shore of Narragansett Bay and rose in a chain of low hills. "Boston Neck," as it was called, contained some of the choicest pasture in all New England, and would later support great stock farms in the eighteenth century. Because of the terrain and the independence of the Narragansetts, who valued it for its protected waters and excellent fishing, the Narragansett country was one of the last sections of the New England seaboard to remain "undeveloped" and out of the hands of the English. Connecticut, Massachusetts, and Rhode Island all vied for possession of this land and held – or claimed to hold – English land patents that included the Narragansett country; incredibly, all three patents had been issued under the seal of the same man, the Earl of Warwick, who was the head of the Parliamentary Committee for Foreign Plantations, in England.[3]

Connecticut had in many ways the weakest claim on paper, since even its legal status as a colony was on shaky ground. In 1632, a patent was purportedly issued to Lord Saye and Sele, Lord Brooke, and other gentlemen who were planning a colony on the Connecticut River by the Earl of Warwick, then president of the Council for New England. This Warwick patent was never brought to New England, and it has been suggested that it may not have existed at all. In 1644, one of the partners of Lords Saye and Brooke, George Fenwick, sold the patent to the Connecticut government; as historian Richard S. Dunn notes, "Even if the patent did exist, Fenwick was not legally qualified to convey it. So Connecticut's legal status rested on an illegally transferred patent of which she did not even possess a copy."[4]

While the exact eastern boundaries of this patent were unclear, Connecticut also claimed all the former Pequot land by right of conquest. But then there was considerable disagreement over the precise bounds of the former Pequot territory; some asserted it had reached almost to Narragansett Bay, while others cited the Mystic or Pawcatuck Rivers as the eastern limit of their jurisdiction. The area between the Mystic and Pawcatuck Rivers, where Thomas Stanton had chosen to settle, was subject to competing colonial claims for years: the Pawcatuck settlement was subject at various times to the jurisdiction of Massachusetts or

Connecticut, depending on which river was considered the boundary between them. While under Massachusetts's jurisdiction it became known as Southerton, and later, under Connecticut's, as Stonington. (Today, Pawcatuck and Stonington are two adjacent villages on the Connecticut side of the Pawcatuck River.)

The Massachusetts Bay Colony, for its part, unilaterally claimed the Narragansett territory west of the Pawcatuck River as its reward for participation in the Pequot War, although once again whether or not Pequot domination had ever extended as far as the Narragansett country was a matter of considerable controversy. In 1643 the Rev. Thomas Weld had tried unsuccessfully to get a "Narragansett Patent" from Parliament in England for Massachusetts. His proposed patent set forth that Massachusetts should expand over Narragansett Bay, not only because of its rapidly increasing population but also so "that the gospell may be speedier conveyed and preached to the Natives, that now sit there in darkness, which by Planting further into the heathens Country they [the Massachusetts colonists] may have better opportunity to doe."[5] As Francis Jennings argues, conversion of the Natives was clearly a pretext: the Puritans had at that point shown no interest in missionary activity even among the Native people living within the existing boundaries of the Massachusetts Bay Colony. For whatever reason, the patent was not secured.

The Massachusetts colony's magistrates had then tried another tack: they persuaded four squatting settlers on the west side of Narragansett Bay to "submit" themselves to Massachusetts's authority and also procured the submission of two undersachems of the Narragansett nation. Then, to "protect" these new settlers, troops were sent from Massachusetts to dispossess and imprison other English settlers in the area (most of whom were considered heretics by Massachusetts), although they had purchased their lands directly from the Narragansett grand sachem Miantonomo. Both the captured English and the Narragansetts appealed to England, the Narragansetts formally submitting to the English Crown as a direct dependency to avoid conquest by Massachusetts (unfortunately, the king would soon be beheaded).

Roger Williams of Rhode Island appealed to Parliament the same year and succeeded in 1644 in getting the Narragansett lands included as part of the Rhode Island patent. Rhode Island then had the best claim, because its patent was the only properly registered and authentic legal document from Warwick's Parliamentary Committee on Foreign Plantations.

But the leaders of Massachusetts continued to claim that the Narragansett land was their share of spoils from the Pequot War and resurrected a doctored version of Thomas Weld's rejected Narragansett patent, which they then pretended was legitimate. The General Court of Massachusetts Bay sent a letter to Roger Williams claiming that they had received "lately out of England a charter" which included "Providence and the Iland of Quidny [Aquidneck]" and warning Williams and others of their countrymen to "forbeare to exercise any Jurisdiccion therein otherwise to appeare at our next Gennerall Court." This order outraged the Rhode Islanders, but was disregarded because the patent was so obviously a fake. Even then, Massachusetts did not give up. In 1645, after Thomas Weld and Hugh Peter had been dismissed as the Massachusetts colony's agents in England, two new commissioners were appointed to join others "in negotiating for us before the earl of Warwicke and the rest of the Commissioners of Plantations or before the High Court of Parliament, if occasion require, concerning the two late grants or charters for government or jurisdictions in the lands adjoining Narragansett Bay."[6]

The Narragansetts and their allies, the Eastern Niantics, naturally became very wary of the English, and must have been only too conscious that many Englishmen would go to great lengths – even starting a "defensive" war such as that waged against the Pequots – in order to gain access to Narragansett land. The possibility of such a war, you may remember, was discussed by Winthrop's brother-in-law Emanuel Downing, with the added suggestion of getting rid of the owners of the land by making slaves of them. And in fact, the United Colonies (which did not include heretical Rhode Island) did declare war on the Narragansetts in 1645 for breaching a peace agreement they had made with the Mohegans, though the colonies did not act on this declaration, perhaps out of fear of the Mohawks.

Thomas Stanton was sent on several missions to Ninigret and other Narragansett sachems over the next few years to cajole them into coming to meetings of the commissioners or to get them to pay their overdue wampum tribute and wampum fines for breaching the peace agreement. Some of the reluctance he encountered was undoubtedly due to the Narragansetts' entirely justifiable suspicion of the English, particularly since they had approved the murder of Miantonomo, the Narragansett grand sachem, without cause, and favoured Uncas in any dispute. Stanton was also sent to investigate rumours that the Narragansetts were plotting war against the English.

A final complicating factor in the competition for the Narragansett lands was the involvement of land speculators. The most notorious was Humphrey Atherton, a captain in the Massachusetts militia, who gathered together a group of investors, which came to be known as the Atherton Company, consisting of some of the wealthiest and most prominent gentlemen in the United Colonies, including the Connecticut governor John Winthrop, Jr., and eventually Thomas Stanton. Atherton, who also served as superintendent of the praying Indians for three years, began to aggressively seek out opportunities to seize or buy the Narragansett lands. He first tried to get the land through Rhode Island's Roger Williams, but Williams refused, since Atherton was flouting Rhode Island's jurisdiction and upsetting the Narragansetts. Atherton persisted in his efforts and threatened the Narragansetts with a full-scale war, expecting to be backed by the United Colonies, since they were continually at odds with the Narragansetts.

In 1650, when trouble brewed between the Mohegans, Narragansetts, and Pocumtucks, and the Narragansetts were ordered to pay a wampum fine, there was again talk among the English of a war against the Narragansetts. Atherton quickly suggested an early assault and was commissioned by the United Colonies to lead a force of twenty Massachusetts men to collect the overdue wampum by force. Others were more cautious; John Winthrop, Jr., joined Roger Williams in warning Atherton not to start a war.

I thought fitt to informe you what I heard this morning from the relation of M^r. Stanton, who had confered in my hearing wth a Narogansett Indian, who is counted sobor and wise and one that hath shewed much fidelity to the English; and he demanded of him what he heard the Naragāsett to determine of. He answered that they did really intend to pay the peage [wampum] as fast as they could gather it; but he thought that there was noe possibility that all could presently be gathered, and that if the English should therupon goe about to sease vpon the person of Nenekunnath [Ninigret], or any of the other sachems, he thought they would be madd, and rather hazard all, wives & children & lives and all that they had. S^r, I hope your wisdome will lead you rather to accept of any reasonable termes of peace then beginne a warre of such doubtfull hazard.[7]

While there was talk of military action in 1652, 1653, and 1654, and even plans for a force to muster at Stanton's house at Pawcatuck, an English conquest of the Narragansett lands did not materialize.

It wasn't necessary. In 1659, things came to a head when Humphrey Atherton arranged a private deal with some Narragansetts to purchase the best Narragansett land; Connecticut governor John Winthrop, Jr., was one of his partners, as were Thomas Stanton and George Denison. (Winthrop later claimed that his name had been used without his knowledge or consent, but other evidence suggests that he was at least a passive partner.) Although the previous year the Rhode Island General Court had declared that purchases from Indians must be approved by their court of commissioners or be forfeit, the Atherton Company secured Boston Neck and a second more northerly tract along the shore of Narragansett Bay from local sachems by drawing up the deeds for these purchases in terms of deeds of gift rather than of sale. Critics of Atherton charged that he had kept one signatory (Narragansett sachem Pessacus's feeble-minded younger brother) drunk for several days and taken him to Boston before buying the land for almost nothing. John Winthrop, Jr., used his authority as the governor of Connecticut in the company's interest, and signed a conciliatory letter in November 1659 to the outraged Rhode Island court, along with other Atherton partners – he later received one of the eight farms on Boston Neck; Stanton received another.[8]

The same year Stanton acquired five thousand acres in Charlestown, Rhode Island, thirteen miles east of the Stanton farm on the Pawcatuck River. The land was conveyed as a deed of gift from the Pequot leader Harmon Garrett (Wequashcook) to Thomas Stanton; some sources describe it as a reward for Stanton's rescue of Garrett's daughter from a rival tribe, the Manesses Indians of Long Island. Stanton took possession of the land and built his son Joseph a house, but his title to the land was subsequently called into question, since the Pequot leader, though the son of a Niantic sachem, was not entitled to dispose of the tribal lands of the Niantics.[9] Furthermore, the land in question had been previously purchased by the Atherton Company (of which Thomas Stanton was an associate member) from the Niantic sachems Ninigret, Suncquash, and Scuttup, on the condition, introduced by the purchasers, that no associate member should sell out his share until he had given the company opportunity to buy it. After some consultation, Stanton agreed to hold the land for himself and the company, so that his share of Atherton company land should include the Harmon Garrett purchase. This arrangement was subsequently agreed to by the company.

That same year the Atherton Company found an ingenious way to acquire the title to the whole of Narragansett country from the Narragansetts. The latter had been creating disturbances in eastern Connecticut and Long Island in their long-running dispute with the Mohegans: in 1659 Ninigret had attacked the Mohegans and killed the Native servant of Plymouth trader Jonathan Brewster "at Mistris Brewster's feet, to her great affrightment." The following spring, shots were fired at the new English plantation of Mohegan near the Mohegans' encampment on the west bank of the Thames River, allegedly to kill Maj. John Mason (who had just moved there, and was reputedly hated by the Narragansetts). The Connecticut authorities urged the United Colonies to take punitive action. The commissioners of the United Colonies (among them John Winthrop, Jr.) agreed "to require and force the Narragansetts to a just satisfaction" and appointed Thomas Stanton and his neighbour and relative by marriage George Denison to demand that Ninigret and other Narragansett sachems deliver those Indians responsible for the trouble or pay 595 fathoms of wampum. They gave the Narragansetts an ultimatum: unless the Narragansetts paid the wampum within four months to the governor of Connecticut (Winthrop), the Connecticut government would be authorized to exact the sum by use of armed force. If the Narragansetts could not produce such a large supply of wampum, they were permitted to mortgage the whole of the Narragansett country to the United Colonies.[10]

Thomas Stanton, George Denison, and their neighbour Thomas Minor confronted the Narragansetts, but found that they could produce neither the culprits nor all of the wampum (though it does appear that they paid some of it). Then, in an astonishing move, Humphrey Atherton stepped in, purportedly to help the Narragansetts. He wrote to Winthrop that he found the sachems "in a very sad condition not knowing how to discharge their engagement to the commissioners: & they intrated mee to heelpe them . . . which upon sume condissions I have undertaken wherein your selfe is interested," and undertook to furnish the wampum at once in return for a mortgage on the land. The cost of the "loan" was then increased by the addition of a service fee of 140 fathoms. In the presence of one member of the Atherton Company, Ninigret and two associate sachems pledged "all our whole country" as a guarantee of payment of the fine within six months. Atherton paid the wampum to Governor Winthrop himself, on condition that the mortgage on the Narragansett country be transferred to the Atherton Company. Winthrop was apparently reluctant to do so, but was eventually persuaded. When the Narragansetts failed to redeem the mortgage within six months, it was foreclosed, and the company, which now included eighteen associates, including Winthrop, Thomas Stanton, Stanton's brother-in-law Richard Lord, and George and Daniel Denison, claimed ownership of the entire southwesterly quarter of what is now Rhode Island. As historian Robert C. Black III comments, "It was a procedure such as would be repeated, with variations, across the continent."[11]

Rhode Island – not surprisingly – refused to recognize the validity of the transaction, so the Atherton proprietors then began to campaign for Connecticut's jurisdiction over the area. They knew the younger colony would be more sympathetic to their interests. Meanwhile, a "renegade" Pequot captain named Sosa, who lived with the Narragansetts, claimed the half of Southerton/Stonington that lay east of the Pawcatuck River. He claimed the land belonged to him as a gift from the Narragansett sachems for his services on their behalf in their previous wars with the Pequots (before the Pequot War with the English). Others argued that the land had never belonged to the Narragansetts, but was tribal land of their tributaries, the Niantics. Whatever the truth of his claim, Sosa sold the land to a number of planters from Rhode Island, who took possession of it under the jurisdiction of that colony. The result was that, in several cases, the same land was sold to different people under two different colonial jurisdictions – and the tensions became explosive. Stanton, Denison, and other residents of Southerton complained to the government of Massachusetts (which still had jurisdiction over Southerton at that point) that they were not receiving adequate protection, "it haueing bin Giuen out that they [the Rhode Islanders] will have Capt. denison alive or dead, and that there will bee many widowes and fatherless Children amongst vs are long."[12]

At this point, the 1660 restoration of Charles II in England changed the whole situation. It threw the colonies into a panic, as only Massachusetts had a royal charter and Connecticut's legal status was extremely uncertain – which meant that its right to self-government was in jeopardy. Rhode Island sought royal protection against the predations of the other colonies and wanted to confirm the patent it had received in 1644, and both Rhode Island and Connecticut sent agents to London to acquire royal charters favourable to them. John Winthrop, Jr., was the agent for Connecticut and arrived in London with instructions to have the "lost" Warwick patent of 1632 confirmed or to petition for a charter incorporating the colonies of New Haven, Rhode Island, and Dutch New Netherland, as well as the Narragansett country, into Connecticut. His Atherton Company partners sent letters entreating his protection; it is a measure of their desperation that they also sent him a copy of Thomas Weld's defective Narragansett patent of 1643 (mentioned previously in chapter five), which annexed to Massachusetts the whole of Narragansett Bay along to New London, even though they knew it was not properly enrolled, sealed, or dated.

Winthrop managed to obtain a royal Charter for Connecticut in 1662, which secured his colony's legal status and also put the Connecticut boundary at Narragansett Bay, thus annexing the Narragansett lands. (Thomas Stanton's brother-in-law Richard Lord was one of the corporate body to whom King Charles granted the Connecticut charter.) The agent for Rhode Island retaliated by managing to persuade the Lord Chancellor to hold up the Connecticut charter for review, and the two agents agreed to arbitration over the boundary dispute by Sir Thomas Temple, the governor of Nova Scotia, and Robert Boyle, the scientist, who was named governor of the New England Company that year.

After several months of failed mediation, the agents finally accepted an unworkable compromise: the Pawcatuck River was to be the boundary between the two colonies, leaving Narragansett as part of Rhode Island, but the Atherton proprietors of the Narragansett lands (including Thomas Stanton, George Denison, Richard Lord, John Winthrop, Jr., and Winthrop's son Wait) were permitted to join Connecticut's jurisdiction if they chose. This they soon did, naming their plantation Wickford and requesting the protection of Connecticut. The Rhode Islanders rejected the compromise and tried to force the Narragansett proprietors to accept their colony's jurisdiction.[13]

With the granting of the Connecticut charter, the Massachusetts Colony lost its jurisdiction over the town of Southerton (Stonington) and the town was split in two by the setting of the boundary between Connecticut and Rhode Island at the Pawcatuck River. Skirmishes once again broke out between Rhode Island and Connecticut settlers on either side of the river.

The disputes over the boundary seemed so intractable that finally, in 1664, a royal commission was sent over from England, and the disputed territory was taken away from both colonies and awarded directly to the king on the grounds that the Narragansetts had submitted to the king's protection in 1644 to ward off Massachusetts's designs on their territory. The new jurisdiction was named King's Province, and since this arrangement had taken over half of Rhode Island's territory Rhode Island was authorized to govern the province until further notice. The commission listened to Rhode Island's charges that Atherton and his partners had defrauded the Narragansetts when they bought their land in 1659 and concluded that the foreclosure on the Narragansett mortgage could be voided whenever the Narragansetts managed to raise their 735 fathoms of wampum. They ruled that the land purchases were void and ordered the proprietors, including Thomas Stanton, to vacate.

When they refused, the Rhode Islanders attempted to evict them forcibly, and once again they were rebuffed. Finally Rhode Island agreed not to disturb the property owners, but hostilities continued. A rather hypocritical 1668 petition by the town of Stonington against the encroachments of Rhode Island was written by Thomas Stanton: "Neither can anye true harted & fellow-feeling Christianes chuse but to mourne to see & heare of our Neighbouring disorders & acknoledge our condition is trulie deploarabl, to have parsones [persons] of such Corrupt prinsipalls & praktises to Live so neer us, & on our owne. Tis not of smalle concernment, the bad Exampell yt is given to the Indianes."[14] Stanton was sent to Rhode Island to treat with the governor concerning Narragansett, apparently with no lasting result. In another incident, Stanton and Thomas Minor were laying out lands east of the Pawcatuck River – in the disputed territory – when they were met and opposed by a group of Rhode Island men armed with clubs. One was later arrested and imprisoned at New London for this assault. Tempers cooled somewhat in 1672, when Rhode Island validated all the previous transactions of the Atherton Company, but Connecticut continued to try to gain control of the Narragansett territory until 1728, when it finally accepted the Pawcatuck River boundary. By then, the Narragansetts had lost most of their population through King Philip's War and were no longer contenders for ownership.

Meanwhile, Stanton was embroiled in another land dispute that contributed to local tensions: the presence of a group of Pequots who had originally been assigned to Ninigret's people, the Niantics, as their share of war captives after the Pequot War. In 1650, these Pequots, like the Western Pequots, of Nameag, under Uncas, had been granted independence from their Native overlord and had settled on the eastern shores of the Pawcatuck River. In 1661, settlers in Rhode Island, coveting this land, drove them off and across the river, into the town of Stonington. The Pawcatuck Pequots numbered 120 warriors (about four to seven hundred people) and were led by Harmon

Garrett, the Pequot/Niantic sachem who had granted land to Thomas Stanton and whose father or brother Wequash had guided the English to the fort at Mystic during the Pequot War. In Stonington, the Pequots squatted on land owned by the settlers (which had, of course, originally been Pequot land). Massachusetts intervened and granted the Pequots a parcel of land in Stonington, but Connecticut did not recognize this grant, when it was granted jurisdiction of Stonington in 1662. The Pequots were in a desperate situation, not knowing where they could live or plant their corn, and were harassed continually by their English neighbours.

Thomas Stanton, as we've seen, had long been involved with the Pequots and, with George Denison, had been an assistant or overseer of the Pequots for several years. In 1663 the commissioners of the United Colonies instructed Stanton, Denison, and James Avery to assign eight thousand acres of land in the Pawcatuck area for Harmon Garrett and his people, the land to be known as the Cossaduck Reservation. This was to be the first reservation for Native Americans (as opposed to praying town) to be granted by a colonial government in New England (the first reservation, for the Western Pequots at Noank, although assigned earlier, had been on land donated by John Winthrop, Jr.; the colonial government merely gave its permission for the Pequots to live there apart from Uncas).[15] Although later reservations often were assigned the worst land and tribal overseers became notorious for cheating indigenous nations of what remained, Stanton, Denison, and Avery chose good land for this reservation – partly wooded hills and part of a fine river bottom, about ten miles back from the coast. Unfortunately, the land they selected fell within the limits of the township of Stonington and included some land that English settlers already owned. The residents of Stonington protested vehemently that the Indians should be located farther inland, back in the rocky hills, away from the settlements, and they formed a committee to evict the Pequots. There ensued a long and bitter dispute with a host of angry colonists and considerable waffling by the authorities, who repeatedly confirmed the Cossaduck Reservation but were unable to enforce this decision in the face of numerous counter-actions by the Stonington residents. The Pequots set up their wigwams and began planting at Cossaduck in spite of constant harassment and intimidation.

A letter written by George Denison to John Winthrop, Jr., expressed his concern for the presing and opresing nessesity of the poor Indians: who can find no resting place for the sole of there feet, not with standing the many ingadgements, orders and grants thay have (by your helpe) obtained, and have relyed upon, yet as it seems all in vaine, for as I and the Indians are informed (by what means I know not for none ware imployed by the towne) there is this Court in your worships absenc an order, makeing voyd all the former orders and that the Indians must be removed next Aprill of from Cosattuck, not with standing the last order by the Commette. . . .

Denison asked Winthrop to stay the order until the next meeting of the General Court,

when they may have an oportunity to speake for them selves, and that thay may not bee put of from there improvements and the land which thay have (by order) broken up for there lively hud, for it will be all one to them to cut of there heades as to take away the means of there subsistanc – the very hearing and fearing what will bee is almost a distroying thing unto them, and ocations great morning amongst them, who have labered hard to get food.

And I wish they had not caus to reproch the faith or truth of the English. . . . I pray Sir doe sume thing which may bee effectuall for there relefe, that there lives and comforts may not bee offred in sacrifise to the wills of men.[16]

While Denison and Stanton spoke passionately in favour of the Pequots at Cossaduck, Stanton's son-in-law, Rev. James Noyes, was one of those writing to Governor John Winthrop about the untenability of their presence.[17]

After much negotiation, Connecticut agreed to give the Pawcatuck Pequots a smaller tract of land, but the Pequots refused to move to it. By 1669, the Pawcatuck Pequots were suspected of joining a rumoured pan-Indian conspiracy to attack the English. Thomas Stanton's son John described their condition in the following deposition to the General Court: "Nesomet sometimes last summer did say to mee, that they were now desperate. They did not now care where they now went to live or where they died, – speaking about their being removed from Cowissattuck."[18]

Stanton reported to John Mason that he had "diverse and strange information concerning the Indians in these parts." Harmon Garrett, leader of the Pawcatuck Pequots, had told him that Ninigret had sent messengers to all the leading sachems of the different tribes, inviting them to a great dance. He also promised Garrett that "if hee would Come and Yoyn wth him in it, it should bee the means of his rising upp." A white youth named Osborne who had lived at Cossaduck and understood the Pequot language had been told by a Native woman to warn his mother, "in pity of her," as the Indians intended to wipe out the English. The dance was only a pretext, so all of the Natives could meet and plan the attack. Goodwife Osborne had been persuaded by her husband not to tell the authorities, for fear that "she should be counted a Twattler [prattler]." A Pequot named Mosomp had confirmed the conspiracy. He told the boy, Osborne, that the Indians would regain Cossaduck, "or it should cost the English their blood. . . . The truth is thye are verie hie of late and slite all athorietie of the English, but such as sutes with their own 'umores.' "[19]

Stanton also noted that Ninigret had invited only fighting men to the festivities, sending others back, and that some Long Islanders had brought large sums of wampum to Ninigret to finance a war. Also that the Narragansetts were well furnished with ammunition, and that a "credible Indian" had told him that Robin Cassacinamon's assistant had visited the Mohawks in the spring with a great sum of wampum, and since his return had "uttered discontent and yt hee would live no longer under the English. If thaye do anything it will bee wthin these few dayes, and if god prevent them not, our town is Like to undergoe the first of there Cruelltyes."[20] But this time, at least, the rumours were only that, and no attack materialized.

Finally, in 1685, long after Thomas Stanton's death in 1677, Connecticut purchased a mere 280 acres for the tribe near Lantern Hill in North Stonington, the site of the present-day Pawcatuck Pequot reservation (though they were subsequently defrauded of some of that land). The Nameag or Western Pequots had fared somewhat better; they had been granted a reservation of 2,000 acres called Mashantucket, near the present town of Ledyard, Connecticut, in 1667. I believe this may be the oldest surviving reservation in New England; it is certainly one of the oldest in the United States.

Even the Mohegans, the aboriginal nation most favoured by the English, were subject to considerable pressure to give up land. After the Pequot War, they had received all the former Pequot territory, from the Connecticut River to the Narragansett territories. In 1640 Thomas Stanton had been the witness and translator of a document whereby Connecticut, hoping to strengthen its case for the granting of a royal charter by gaining legal title through purchase, persuaded Uncas to deed the entire Mohegan country to the governor and magistrates of Connecticut for the trifling amount of five and one-half yards of trucking cloth, with stockings and other articles as a gratuity. The true nature of this deed was not clear, for as historian David Conroy notes, Connecticut continued to recognize Mohegan ownership of all unincorporated lands and Uncas continued to believe he owned or possessed the right to use the land. It appears that what Uncas gained was Connecticut's unswerving support, even as he increased his power over other indigenous nations, and Connecticut gained confirmation of land it had already settled or claimed, in the absence of a royal patent. But in later years this transaction and Uncas's original intentions were disputed. Uncas had not signed the deed and the Mohegans said it hadn't been intended as a true bill of sale but a right of pre-emption, and that Connecticut was supposed to act as guardian or trustee of the land, but Connecticut maintained that, with the deed, the Mohegans had extinguished claims to all or most of their territory. In 1655, Uncas appealed to the commissioners of the United Colonies to confirm his "liberty to hunt and fish in all such lands and territories of lands which he hath sold to the English."[21]

It's worth wondering about Stanton's role in this. He had known Uncas for only a few years at the time he translated and witnessed this deed. Was there a genuine confusion or misunderstanding of the wording or intention between the English and Mohegans? Or was there a deliberate fuzziness in the written version of the deed (Uncas being nonliterate), so that it could be re-interpreted in favour of Connecticut later on? What did Stanton understand of Connecticut's motives? And did Uncas fully understand the English notion of "selling"? Did he, like Passaconaway or Cutshamekin, sign over title to maintain English favour and protection or to win support for his own struggle for dominance among the sachems of the region? Or did he understand that his people would retain usufructuary rights and so be able to continue to hunt and fish on the land forever? Did he believe he was merely agreeing to share it?

The first deed was in sufficient dispute that, in 1659, Connecticut considered it necessary to acquire a second deed to the lands. This time, the Mohegans, recognizing the threat of land-hungry colonists, sought in John Mason a powerful protector and deeded the land to him personally, essentially creating a Mohegan land trust controlled by Mason, who formally relinquished jurisdiction over the land to Connecticut the following year. Mason received five hundred acres for himself and the authority to lay out new plantations on land sold to settlers. The tribe was assured it would be supplied with sufficient planting ground at all times, and Mason set aside an eight-by-four-mile tract of land between New London and Norwich for the tribe's use in perpetuity.

But Uncas, who has been scornfully referred to as the "first real estate agent" in Connecticut, also gave large tracts of land to individual colonists, partly for his own protection. It is not clear whether he intended to give them lands simply for their use, or lands to own in the European sense. In 1658, he made his first grant of land to English settlers within the Mohegan reservation: the recipients were one Richard Haughton and James Rogers, another ancestor of mine. (Rogers had arrived in North America in 1635 on the *Increase* and had been one of the men from Saybrook to take part in the Pequot War in 1637 under Capt. John Underhill. Later he became a prosperous baker and tradesman and the largest property-holder in New London.[22])

The first actual settlers on the Mohegan sequestered lands were my direct ancestors, James Rogers's son, Samuel Rogers, and his wife Mary, daughter of Thomas Stanton. Samuel Rogers had been on intimate terms with Uncas for many years, and Uncas had given him a valuable tract of land upon Oxoboxa Brook.[23] Uncas's gift was almost certainly strategic – having Thomas Stanton's daughter and son-in-law living in close proximity to Uncas would have encouraged Stanton and his powerful friends to side with the Mohegan sachem in disputes with the Narragansetts. Rogers and Uncas agreed to a mutual defence pact that was the basis for the following story about their friendship, which has survived among the Mohegans as well as in the historical records of the colonists:

Uncas promised Rogers that in case of emergency or attack by enemies [Narragansetts] he would hasten with warriors to his assistance. In this area Rogers built his house of hewn logs, surrounded by a strong wall or stockade with a small cannon mounted in front of the place, firing of which was to sound the alarm. Uncas, from his Indian village about four miles away, would often visit his friend at his home in the wilderness and together they would smoke the pipe of peace and "take a social glass."

On one occasion, and to try out the fidelity of Uncas, the colonist fired the signal gun of alarm, which was two reports in succession. This plan had been previously agreed upon. In half an hour's time many of the Mohegan warriors rushed over the hills and up the valley, with the sachem leading, to rescue their white friend at the block house. Rogers, as a surprise, had arranged a banquet or barbecue for the entertainment of his Indian allies and had killed and roasted an ox for the occasion. The Indians not only enjoyed the feast, which was a bountiful one, but applauded and relished the trick which had been played upon them.[24]

Samuel Rogers and Mary Stanton became large landholders in the English settlement of Mohegan. They were given or sold deeds of land not only by Uncas but by his sons Owaneco and Josiah, in recompense for services rendered to them and their tribes. (Samuel Rogers's land transactions far outnumbered those of any other man in the colony.)

But Uncas and succeeding sachems made lavish grants and transfers of land to many other settlers as well, and the boundaries of different grants were found to be constantly overlapping each other; the same tracts were often granted to different parties by the same sachem, or by rival sachems; the resulting confusion and conflict took more than a hundred years to untangle. And while the Mason trusteeship worked while both Uncas and Mason were alive, after their deaths Connecticut began to make grants of land without consulting the Mason family. After Uncas's death in 1683, most of the Mohegans, along with John Mason's descendants, fought a lengthy and ultimately unsuccessful legal battle to place the tribe under royal rather than colonial authority, in order to provide the tribe with greater autonomy in selecting its leaders and conserving its land, a struggle that some of my later Harris ancestors would actively oppose. The court finally ruled in favour of Connecticut in 1773, seventy years after the Mohegans and Mason family had originally launched their suit. By that time the Mohegans were a tiny and virtually powerless minority overwhelmed by the burgeoning English population that had settled on their lands in southeastern Connecticut. The colony meddled in the internal politics of the nation, interfering with the succession of the sachemship and favouring leaders who sold off tribal lands to white settlers.

By the 1660s, the demographics of the New England colonists had changed significantly. Like Thomas Stanton, many of the first generations of European settlers had been in the twenty to forty age group when they arrived in New England and had brought or soon produced young children. Because of the long and difficult process of settling farms and towns, few of these children became independent at an early age; many of the men did not marry until their mid-twenties or later. When they did, a baby boom ensued, and that, helped along by mortality rates far lower than the European norm (none of Stanton's ten children died in childhood, for example), meant that, by the 1660s, there was a huge backlog of families seeking land of their own, with increased concern for precise titles and boundaries. The 1660s and 1670s saw the settlement of countless new towns in former fur-trading areas, and many Native nations that had previously been relatively autonomous, like the Narragansetts, the Niantics, Wampanoags, and the Mohegans, found that their neighbours, and even their supporters among the English, desired land above all else.[25] In fact, land – not religion – was now the central concern of the Puritans.

MY ANCESTORS AND

KING PHILIP'S WAR

CHAPTER
10

God's Wrath

By 1675, the English colonies were well established and expanding. The various branches of my family and their in-laws – the Wheelers, Chases, Stantons, Lords, Denisons, Eliots, and others, such as the Ranneys, Edwardses, and Janeses, whose descendants I shall introduce later in this narrative – had all established their homes and farms in New England and settled in to stay. They were no longer a tiny minority in an Indian multitude; of the approximately 78,000 people who now lived in New England, three-quarters of them were English.[1]

The estimated 18,000 indigenous inhabitants of the area had seen their world dramatically altered by the settlers' presence. While Thomas Stanton and others had investigated expressions of hostility towards the English and the odd rumour of a pan-Indian conspiracy, there had been no serious challenge to English hegemony in the almost forty years since the colonists' easy victory in the Pequot War. The English had become complacent about their ability to control the indigenous population, convinced as they were of their own military and cultural superiority. Native Americans had not formed a united front to resist the English, since they had little pan-Indian consciousness and the arrival of the English had deepened existing divisions within aboriginal societies; instead, small groups of Natives had used a variety of strategies to counteract or compete for advantage with the newcomers. Some had chosen cultural adaptation through the Christian missions as the way to prosper within the new dispensation, while others had attempted to preserve their independence and enhance their power through diplomacy.

That there was no rigid frontier separating these two very different peoples was an indication of how much they had adjusted to each other. English and Native settlements were interspersed throughout each colony in close proximity to one another, and many Native Americans now worked in English homes or on English farms. In fact, as the historian James Drake has noted, the invaders and indigenous people had forged a single "covalent" society in which both groups, while maintaining their distinct cultures and wielding unequal power, were linked in localized webs of social relations based largely on mutual obligations. English cultural intermediaries such as Thomas Stanton and John Eliot had been instrumental in developing and maintaining these links, as had Native individuals, like Uncas and some praying Indians, who had perceived how elements of English society could be used to Indian advantage. In the short term, these relations were mutually beneficial, at least for those directly involved: Thomas Stanton had helped Connecticut obtain title to land from Uncas to legitimize itself as a colony in the absence of a royal charter; Uncas had made the Mohegans pre-eminent among aboriginal nations through his alliance with the English.

But in 1675 this hybrid society with its web of intricate relationships would be blown apart, violently and irrevocably, in the conflict that has come to be known as King Philip's War. It would prove to be one of the bloodiest wars in American history, and its consequences so long-lasting that its reverberations still affect Native–non-Native relations today.[2]

King Philip's War has often been popularly described as a "race war," a last-ditch attempt by Native Americans to preserve their way of life from English domination, and for those fighting on the side of the Wampanoag sachem Metacom – or King Philip, as he was known to the English – this was undoubtedly true. Yet the fact that many aboriginal groups sided with the English reveals a much more complex dynamic. James Drake has suggested that the war should more properly be viewed as a civil war that divided, engulfed, and shattered the unique society that had been created in the first years of colonization.

What is most curious and most telling about King Philip's War is that the English were so totally unprepared for it. I don't know whether any of my ancestors, other than Thomas Stanton, were aware of the frustration and resistance that was building within some Native nations: one senses such a wilful blindness on the part of the English, such an unwillingness to consider Native Americans – particularly pagans – as people, that many colonists were apparently oblivious to their rage or other human feelings. Very few Englishmen, usually dissenters and outsiders such as Thomas Morton and Roger Williams, seem to have glimpsed some of the value of traditional aboriginal life; I suspect that my ancestors, like most English people at the time, could not step outside the Puritan mindset and their certainty of God's plan in order to apprehend the worth of a different way of being, and so it was almost impossible for them to comprehend passionate reactions to the threatened loss of it. Most likely, they were completely unprepared for the ensuing explosion of virulent hatred of the English and their culture.

Incredible as it may seem today, most colonists believed that Native Americans had no reason to harbour ill feelings against them. According to the English, they had dealt fairly with Native Americans in land purchases and legal proceedings. They seemed largely oblivious to the fact that both had been carried out according to English practice and completely disregarded the needs, values, traditional practices, and world view of Native people. In part, this was because the English had a different understanding of the nature of the "submissions" the various sachems made: to the colonists, the Indians had become "subordinate subjects," never equals, though the second-class status assigned to Native Americans was not yet attributed to race but to history, culture, and religion. As James Drake comments, the colonists perceived their relationship to the Indians as "tutelary." John Eliot epitomized the most benevolent face of this paternalism: to him, Natives were dependents, to be instructed in civilization and the one true faith. In fact, within this context of assumed superiority, the English had prided themselves on treating Indians more fairly than had the Spanish; they strove to be morally superior colonizers.

Yet, the experience of the Wampanoags contradicted this English self-perception. Just before the war broke out, Metacom explained to a Quaker Rhode Islander (a potential mediator in his conflict with Plymouth) that the English used underhanded methods to acquire Wampanoag lands: they claimed more land than had been agreed upon; they "made [petty chiefs] drunk and then cheted them in bargens." If sachems refused to sell land, the English sought out or created "another king that would give or sell them there land." With English settlement, he continued, the Natives found their corn was continually destroyed by wandering English livestock. When Indians sought redress in the courts or from the colonial authorities, they were denied justice, "all English [being] angered against them, and so by arbetration they had much rong. . . . If 20 of there [h]onest indians testefied that an Englishman had dun them rong, it was as nothing, and if but one of their worst indians testefied against an indian or other king when it plesed the English that was sufitiant."[3]

Think about hatred for a moment, that most unpleasant of human emotions. It is the emotion of last resort, when all else has failed, when all one can do is hate with every fibre of one's being, when resistance is the only life-affirming action. The war that broke out in 1675 was not a Machiavellian jockeying for power among relative equals, nor even a settling of scores, but a war of resistance, power, terror, and hatred. King Philip's War marks the point at which some of the original people of the land confronted their loss of autonomy and the absolute necessity of taking action before it was too late. It is not surprising that young people started it, for in their future they would have seen only the prospect of second-rate status in an alien state that denigrated everything about them and lived off their land.[4]

Yet the outbreak of war was not inevitable – nor, apparently, was Metacom the master conspirator the English imagined him to be. In fact, it seems that the war was started by young militants over whom he had lost control, as has been the case in so many of the incidents that have erupted in Indian country in my own lifetime, such as Oka or the 1973 standoff at Wounded Knee. Once hostilities broke out and spread, Native Americans and Englishmen were forced to choose sides. Virtually all English settlers ended up supporting the colonies, though some, particularly in Rhode Island, were very critical of Plymouth and Massachusetts for starting the war and tried to limit their involvement. For Native Americans, given their various ties to the English colonies and the reality of English military might, the decision of which side to support was an agonizing one.

All my New England ancestors were affected significantly by the war's devastation and terror, and many joined in the fighting. For John Eliot and Thomas Stanton, however, the fourteen months of killing and destruction represented more particular failures. For John Eliot had a personal connection with the man whose forces would interrupt his own evangelical work and would destroy the praying towns and all that he had laboured so long to bring about. And, although Thomas Stanton played a crucial role in maintaining the neutrality of one key sachem, and his earlier relations with the Pequots and the Mohegans helped to build the foundation for their support of the English, the diplomatic network that he had spent almost forty years of his life building and maintaining could not contain the war's outbreak or stop the horrendous loss of human life and property.

There is something very sad and telling in the fact that it was the Wampanoag sachem Metacom whose name is associated with the war. His father Massasoit had concluded the first peace treaty with the Plymouth Pilgrims in 1621 after the landing of the *Mayflower* and had been their most constant ally. The Wampanoags had at that time "Constraened other indians from ronging the English and gave them Coren and shewed them how to plant," as Metacom would later remind the settlers.[5] Metacom's nation, the Wampanoags, lived in what is now southeastern Massachusetts and was then Plymouth Colony, and had been outnumbered by the English in their own traditional territory since the 1630s or 1640s.

Most Native nations, as we have seen, had tried to protect themselves against enemies or the loss of their land by submitting to English authority; they had viewed colonial governments as a kind of sachemship, in which they gained protection in exchange for their allegiance. Metacom's father had been one of the first sachems to submit to a colonial authority, in 1639. Metacom would formally renew this submission in 1662 and 1671. As Plymouth Colony had never been granted a royal charter, it depended on its role as a protectorate over the Wampanoags for its legal existence in England.

But over the course of the 1660s and early 1670s, a number of factors created tension between the Wampanoags and Plymouth, and led Metacom to conclude that his position and power within Plymouth Colony were increasingly tenuous. Even before Metacom became sachem, the Wampanoags had become suspicious of the English, for Metacom's elder brother Wamsutta (also known as Alexander), who preceded Metacom as sachem, had died in 1662, after being called to Plymouth and questioned about a suspected plot against the English; rumours spread in Indian country that the English had poisoned him, though this was never substantiated. After Metacom succeeded his brother, disputes with the settlers over land became increasingly bitter, and appeals to the English court system failed to protect the Wampanoags.

Plymouth threatened Wampanoag sovereignty further by approving the settlement of a new town called Swansea at the base of the Mount Hope peninsula, where the main Wampanoag village of Sowams was located, and authorized the town of Swansea to purchase and annex additional land from the Wampanoags. In March of 1671, Metacom had led a group of fully armed warriors to the town of Swansea and made a threatening show of arms, but did not attack. When called to Plymouth to account for this behaviour, he admitted that he had been preparing for war. Metacom was ordered to turn in his weapons and sign a treaty later known as the Taunton Treaty, which stipulated that he could not sell land or go to war against another tribe without Plymouth's consent. He was forced to sign a declaration that read: "I having of late through my Indiscretion, and the Naughtiness of my Heart, violated and broken this my Covenant with my Friends, by taking up Arms, with evil intent against them, and that groundlessly. . . ."[6] On top of this indignity, the English and the Wampanoags understood the terms of the treaty differently: Metacom thought that he was to surrender only the weapons he and his warriors had carried at the time, whereas Plymouth demanded the surrender of all weapons owned by the Wampanoags. When the Wampanoags refused to comply, the colonists insisted that all other nations associated with the Wampanoags, such as the Seconetts, should also give up *their* weapons, and threatened a military expedition to "reduce them to reason."[7]

Metacom then appealed to Massachusetts for assistance in his dealings with Plymouth, but was politely rebuffed. He then agreed to accept the arbitration of a group of prominent colonists, including Thomas Stanton's close friend, John Winthrop, Jr., but the arbitrators ruled against the sachem and he was forced to accept the Taunton Treaty. Because he was fined £100, he was forced to sell more land to pay the fine. After this, the frustrations of Metacom and the Wampanoags simmered until 1674, when several disputes about land sales re-ignited dormant tensions.

All of these events not only threatened the Wampanoags, they also threatened Metacom's leadership. Individual Native leaders were able to maintain their own power and hold on to their followers only if they were able to protect their people and their interests and were perceived as coping effectively with the various threats posed by English colonization. According to James Drake, Metacom was increasingly seen by his people as less able to deal with the English than other Native leaders (such as

Uncas or Ninigret) or the other rival group that threatened to draw off his followers – the praying Indians.

The role of the praying Indians in the events leading to the outbreak of war is of considerable interest to me as I try to piece together the historical impact of John Eliot's missionary work on Native–Non-Native relations. By 1675, there were fourteen praying towns, and more and more praying Indians; the missions posed an increasing threat to traditional Native leaders. In 1659, Rev. John Cotton had begun preaching regularly to the Wampanoags in Plymouth Colony, and Metacom could not have failed to notice the growing influence of praying Indians with the English compared with non-Christian Natives. In fact, the actual onset of hostilities was closely connected with the tensions between missionized and non-missionized Natives – and the death of John Sassamon, a former advisor of Metacom's, who was a praying Indian and had served as one of John Eliot's chief assistants. In the view of James Drake, the events surrounding Sassamon's death and the trial of his supposed murderers convinced the Wampanoags that all the colonies, with the exception of weak Rhode Island, were allied against non-Christian Indians.

John Sassamon had been orphaned at a young age; it is possible that his parents died during the smallpox epidemic of 1633 and converted to Christianity on their deathbeds. They left their son in the care of an English family, as several Natives had done, apparently interpreting their illness as proof of the superior power of the Christian God.[8] Raised in an English household, Sassamon might have attended the Indian school in the town of Dorchester (now part of Boston). During the Pequot War he had joined the English forces and appears to have acted as an interpreter. He had probably known John Eliot even before that war, for the preacher visited the Indian school every lecture day. Later, Sassamon helped Eliot translate the Bible, and undoubtedly assisted Eliot in his own language studies; he appears to have known Eliot for more than forty years. Although many praying Indians learned to read the Massachusett language and a few to write it, Sassamon was among a very small élite who could read and write English with any competence.

Sassamon helped build the chief mission town of Natick in 1650 and was made a schoolteacher there. He appears to have been one of Eliot's favourite and most talented students, for he was sent to Harvard for at least one term in 1653 (before the building known as Harvard Indian College had been built), where he was a classmate of the sons of some of the most privileged men in the Massachusetts Bay Colony as well as John Eliot's own son. He was one of only two Indians who are known to have survived the experience of attending Harvard. Eliot characterized him as "a man of eminent parts and wit," though there is some evidence that Sassamon was ambivalent about his position as a Christian Indian in Puritan society – neither completely English nor completely Indian. According to the Puritan historian William Hubbard, Sassamon received "frequent Sollicitations of Mr. Eliot, that had known him from a Child, and instructed him in the Principles of our Religion, who was often laying before him the heinous Sin of his Apostacy."[9]

Sassamon, along with Job Nesutan, assisted Eliot in the translation of his Indian primer, two books of psalms, and the entire Bible, the first Bible to be printed in North America, as mentioned earlier. But Sassamon may have had a falling out with Eliot or become disillusioned with English society or Christianity in 1662, for in that year he left Natick and joined the Wampanoags, where he apparently served as scribe and translator for the young sachem Alexander (Wamsutta), and then for Metacom after Alexander's death. He assumed a role of considerable importance, acting as a secretary, interpreter, advisor, and go-between for the sachem and colonial officials; William Hubbard said that the young man had "upon some Misdemeanour fled from his Place [at Natick] to Philip, by whom he was entertained in the Room and Office of Secretary, and his Chief Councellor."[10] According to Cotton Mather, Sassamon "apostatiz[ed] from the profession of Christianity, [and] lived like a heathen in the quality of a Secretary to King Philip; for he could write, though the King his master could not so much as read."[11]

Perhaps Metacom hoped that Sassamon, as one of the élite of Natick, could help the Wampanoags achieve the same success in preserving their lands that the Natick Indians had enjoyed, for the latter had obtained the security of a grant from the General Court, which protected even unimproved lands, and they had even been granted land belonging to the English town of Dedham, against the town's wishes. Sassamon's name appears numerous times as a witness in Metacom's land transactions.

Yet it is also possible that Sassamon was sent to the Wampanoags at John Eliot's request, for the Puritan missionary had a strong desire to convert Metacom. In 1664, Eliot asked the commissioners of the United

Colonies to "give incouragmt to John Sosaman, who teacheth Phillip and his men to read," and claimed that Metacom had asked him to send books, so that he could learn to pray to God.[12]

Daniel Gookin, one of Eliot's English assistants, made the following assessment of Metacom:

> There are some that have high hopes of their greatest and chiefest sachem, named Philip. . . . Some of his chief men, as I hear, stand well inclined to hear the gospel: and himself is a person of good understanding and knowledge in the best things. I have heard him speak very good words, arguing that his conscience is convicted: but yet, though his will is bowed to embrace Jesus Christ, his sensual and carnal lusts are strong bands to hold him fast under Satan's dominions.[13]

Metacom did apparently consider becoming a Christian for a while, but later vehemently rejected the white man's religion. In a section of Eliot's *Indian Dialogues* that must have come back to haunt him, written before King Philip's War, Eliot introduced Metacom and presented him to the book's readers as interested in learning more about Christianity. However, according to Puritan legend, there was an altogether different encounter between Eliot and "Philip, the ring-leader of the most calamitous war that ever they made upon us," that illustrates Metacom's spirit of resistance: "our Eliot made a tender of the everlasting salvation to that king; but the monster entertained it with contempt and anger, and after the Indian mode of joining signs with words, he took a button upon the coat of the reverend man, adding, That he cared for his gospel, just as much as he cared for that button."[14]

Eliot's hopes of converting Philip were soon thwarted; most Wampanoags firmly rejected Christianity, and in 1671 John Eliot wrote that he could not recall "such violent opposition" to the preaching of the faith.[15]

After several years as Metacom's assistant, Sassamon left the Wampanoags for reasons unknown, although they have since been widely speculated about. Sassamon appears to have been a "slippery character," as James Drake says: he had apparently written the illiterate Metacom's will at the sachem's request, adding a provision of his own that much of Metacom 's land was to be left to Sassamon, which Metacom later discovered. Other accounts say Sassamon returned to Natick at John Eliot's request or because Metacom decided against becoming a praying Indian.

It's also possible that Sassamon was discovered to be a spy. During Metacom's dispute with Plymouth over the terms of the Taunton Treaty, John Eliot and three praying Indians, including John Sassamon, had intervened to try to defuse the situation and met with both Metacom and Plymouth officials. During these meetings Sassamon revealed to the English that Metacom had been meeting secretly with Narragansett sachems in the hope of making an alliance against the English. It's not known if his claim was true or if he was trying to undermine Metacom, for there are hints that Sassamon had ambitions of his own and was competing with Metacom for followers.

At any rate, Sassamon left the Wampanoags and returned to the praying Indians, acquiring land from one of Metacom's advisors and, in 1673, setting up the Indian church in the nearby praying town of Namasket, where he hoped to attract some of Metacom's followers.

Then, in January 1675, Sassamon travelled to Governor Edward Winslow's house in Plymouth Colony to say that Metacom was preparing for war – and a week later Sassamon disappeared. His body was later discovered under the ice of a pond, and his death originally deemed accidental. Plymouth officials became suspicious a few months later, when a praying Indian named Patuckson claimed that he had witnessed Sassamon's murder and named three pagan Indians who were Metacom's chief councillors as the murderers. Plymouth officials exhumed Sassamon's body and became convinced that there had been foul play.

Metacom was suspected of having contrived the murder as revenge for Sassamon's disclosure of the plot against the English, though it is impossible now to know if this was indeed what happened. There is some doubt about the credibility of Patuckson's testimony, for it was said that he owed the three Indians in question a gambling debt, "and not to pay so accused them, and knoing it wold please the English so to think him a better Christian."[16] Nevertheless, there was a quick trial, in which six Indians – most likely Christian Indians – were sworn in as associate jurymen, in addition to the twelve English jurymen – a very unusual move by the Puritans. The three Natives were convicted upon very flimsy evidence and hanged, one confessing after the rope broke that the two others were responsible for the crime. (He was later executed.)

If Sassamon was murdered, the motive cannot be ascertained now with any certainty. Puritan commentators believed that his betrayal of Metacom's plans against the English was not the only reason he was killed.

Increase Mather (father of Cotton), said it was "out of hatred against him for his Religion, for he was Christianized, and baptiz'd, and was a Preacher amongst the Indians . . . and was wont to curb those Indians that knew not God on the account of their debaucheryes." Daniel Gookin called Sassamon the first Christian martyr among the Indians, for he "suffered death upon the account of his Christian profession, and fidelity to the English." Nathaniel Saltonstall said that Metacom's men had killed Sassamon because they – and Metacom – did not want to be converted.[17]

The executions enraged militant young Wampanoags. They pressured Metacom to plan a large-scale assault and began to utter threats toward the English. Because the murder trial had been conducted by Plymouth Colony, which was supposed to protect Metacom in exchange for his submission, and hinged upon evidence submitted by Christian Indians, and because previous attempts to appeal to other colonies for assistance had failed, the non-Christian Wampanoags concluded that they could not depend on any English colony for protection and had to find some other way to protect their autonomy. They became convinced that violence was the only means available to them, and soon there were numerous signs and rumours that the Wampanoags and their allies were mobilizing for war.

Metacom himself may have been pushed into war somewhat reluctantly, for he agreed to an attempt at reconciliation. The Rhode Island deputy-governor, Quaker John Easton, headed a Rhode Island peace delegation that met with Metacom and his councillors and heard their grievances. The Wampanoags enumerated their complaints about land dealings and poor treatment in the courts (quoted earlier). In addition, Easton reported, "they had a great fear to have ani of ther indians should be Caled or forced to be Christian indians, thay saied that such wer in everi thing more mishivous, only disemblers, and then the English made them not subject to their kings, and by ther lying to rong their kings." Easton's comment was "We knew it to be true."[18]

Given Metacom's previous experience with arbitration, it is not surprising that he first rejected it when Easton first proposed it. But then Easton, demonstrating an impartiality rare among the English colonists, suggested that there be only two arbitrators: an Indian sachem to be chosen by the Wampanoags and Edmund Andros, then governor of the colony of New York. The proposal appeared to be agreeable to the Wampanoags, but violence broke out before it could be implemented. On June 20, 1675, a few days after the peace conference and less than three weeks after the executions, a group of young Wampanoags looted some abandoned houses in Swansea and set two on fire. It may be that they considered Metacom ineffectual in his dealings with the English and so took matters into their own hands.

Terrified settlers spread the alarm, and the town of Swansea sent messengers to Plymouth for military aid. Plymouth warned Boston that the Narragansetts and the Nipmucks were believed to be ready to join the Wampanoags, and requested help in stopping them. Massachusetts sent out three missions: one to the Nipmucks, one to the Narragansetts, and a peace mission to the Wampanoags. Rhode Island promised a boat patrol to keep the Wampanoags hemmed in on the Mount Hope peninsula.

On June 23, a Swansea youth, angered by the shooting of his cattle and the attempt to loot his house, shot and killed one Native – the first death in the conflict. The next day the Wampanoags attacked Swansea, killing six settlers who were trying to retrieve corn from an abandoned farm, including the boy who had shot the Wampanoag; later they killed another settler and wounded several others who were returning from church. Other killings followed. A peace delegation from Massachusetts, which was on its way to the Wampanoags to make more proposals for arbitration, found horribly mutilated corpses on the road and returned home, recognizing that their mission was now pointless.

There is no evidence that the Wampanoags who killed the settlers were following a fully developed military strategy, or intended to start such a massive war. If Metacom had indeed been preparing for war, it broke out before he was ready, for his forces had not yet acquired sufficient guns and ammunition or succeeded in cementing alliances with other Native nations against the English. However, rumours proliferated of a general uprising against the colonists: the English believed the Indians would act as they would themselves and form an alliance with their countrymen. But the indigenous nations, with their individual tribal loyalties, would prove far more difficult to unify than the English colonies, who all shared an allegiance to their English homeland and king and who now, with the exception of Rhode Island, prepared for war. In fact, there is some evidence that Native Americans initially perceived this as a local matter between Plymouth and the Wampanoags; the Narragansetts, for example, had no intention of joining Metacom and were surprised by the co-ordinated efforts of the colonies to act against Metacom's people. In their previous experience, the English colonies had been competitive and combative with each other, so the Narragansetts had not appreciated that there was an underlying ethnic identity that unified all Englishmen.

The combined armies of Plymouth and Massachusetts were so disorganized that they could not contain Metacom in the Mount Hope peninsula. When a force of almost five hundred English soldiers finally left Swansea and pushed into the peninsula in pursuit of Metacom, it found the area deserted, for he had escaped by water. What they did find were the smoking ruins of the settlers' houses, a Bible "torn in pieces in defiance of our holy religion," and the severed heads and hands of eight settlers stuck upon stakes.[19] The campaign of terror had begun. Like so many disempowered minorities of our own era, terrorism was one of the few options available for a group that knew it was no equal to the English in military terms.

Once violence had erupted and spread, aided by a total lunar eclipse that both sides interpreted as an omen of destruction, people all over New England faced the dilemma of which side to support, and many – especially Native Americans – were torn by multiple allegiances and considerable ambivalence. In the beginning, many colonists were wracked by doubts about whether their prosecution of the war was just. Edmund Randolph, an agent for the Crown, contended that the Wampanoags had been provoked into war by the actions of the colonists in repeatedly calling Metacom to court on contrived charges. John Eliot also expressed a certain scepticism: "What the causes of the warre were, I suppose Plimoth will declare." Quaker Edward Wharton wrote,

> Our Rulers, Officers and Councellors are like as men in a maze, not knowing what to do: but the Priests spur them on, telling them the Indians are ordained for destruction; bidding them go forth to Warr, and they will Fast and Pray at home in the mean time; yet their General, with some other Officers, complain and say, with tears, "They see not God go along with them."

Others worried that "the dishonour would redound to the Name of God, if New England should goe to war in a bad cause, or not very way justifiable in the sight of God & all the world."[20]

Quakers in Rhode Island opposed armed resistance to the Indians' violence.

Similarly, many Native Americans reacted to the outbreak of war with caution and hesitation. Puritan historian William Hubbard echoed

Wharton's comments, describing the Indians "in a kind of Maze, not knowing well what to do; sometimes ready to stand for the English, as formerly they were wont to do, sometimes inclining to strike in with Philip."[21] According to James Drake, their decision to join or oppose Metacom depended on many, often local, variables. In general, their choice appears to have been based on to what degree an individual or group had enjoyed success in dealing with the English or felt marginalized by the colonial political structure, rather than simple ethnic loyalty. Those who supported the English did not necessarily fight for the same reasons that the English did – they had their own motives. Families, communities, and former allies sometimes found themselves on opposite sides, or were drawn into the war in spite of their ambivalence because of their loyalties. Nevertheless, many Natives began to rally around Metacom, and he came to symbolize their resistance to English domination and their determination to save their cultural autonomy.

Through the following days and months of their waking nightmare, the English – my ancestors included – believed Metacom and his warriors were bent on their annihilation. Perhaps this eventually became the warriors' aim, but, as Francis Jennings has observed, Metacom's original intentions appear to have been far more modest: to regain self-government and to live according to traditional Wampanoag values and beliefs in their own secure territory.

Metacom first headed for Nipmuck country in central Massachusetts. To the utter horror of the English, and especially John Eliot, he attracted allies from the praying towns, particularly Nipmucks who had just been in the process of joining the Christian towns when war broke out. The terrible attack on the Puritan village of Mendon, for example, was led by a Nipmuck sachem who had been constable of one of the mission towns. Over the next few weeks, every missionary town lost at least a few of its men to Metacom's cause, apparently including even James Printer, the Nipmuck who had helped print Eliot's translation of the Bible.

When it became clear that Natives from many New England nations – and even praying Indians – were joining Metacom in his attacks on the colonists, the English were stunned. Their state of shock was exacerbated by the ongoing use of terror by Metacom's forces. Terror became a potent weapon of the war early on, and the ordeals and heroism of the colonists quickly became legendary as horror stories passed from one small community to another. I'm sure that most of my ancestors would have heard the story of what happened at Brookfield, for example.

In early August of 1675, an attempted parley between Massachusetts troops and supposedly friendly Nipmucks near that settlement in central Massachusetts turned to disaster, as the troopers were nearly wiped out in a terrible ambush. The survivors escaped, and the entire village of about eighty people, mainly women and children – including women in labour – was cooped up in one house for two days while the Nipmucks besieged them. The Nipmucks captured one settler, cut off his head, and used it as a football, before mounting it on a pole in full view of those in the house. The Nipmucks then attempted repeatedly to set the house on fire, at one point building an ingenious mobile torch, using a barrel and long shafts on wheels from appropriated farm vehicles. Remarkably, the colonists were saved by a sudden rainstorm and the arrival of reinforcements, and the Nipmucks disappeared after setting the remaining buildings of the town on fire. The town was soon completely abandoned. It was from experiences like this – and the stories that emerged from them – that the stereotype of the savage Indian was greatly reinforced, for, to most English, the Indians' actions had no conceivable motivation other than mindless savagery. To the colonists, "violence itself was the Indians' only vocabulary."[22]

The words of Mary Rowlandson, who was captured and held for several months by Metacom's forces and whose narrative of captivity would prove tremendously influential, described the Puritans' attackers as depraved and inhuman: "It is a solemn sight to see so many Christians lying in their blood, some here, and some there, like a company of Sheep, torn by Wolves. All of them stripped naked by a company of hell-hounds, roaring, singing, ranting, and insulting, as if they would have torn our very hearts out."[23]

Yet, as Jill Lepore argues in *The Name of War*, her study of King Philip's War, cruelty is a symbolic language. In mutilating the physical bodies of the colonists, in stripping naked these always-fully-clothed people, in destroying all the possessions that were so central to their identity – their houses, their churches, their mills, their grinding stones, their crops, their cattle, and their Bibles – Metacom's warriors attacked everything that was English and that had made the landscape English. They frequently attacked colonists on the Sabbath, as they went to church, or on special days of religious observance, ripping apart their Bibles, making their taunting blasphemies about doing good by sending the colonists to heaven so soon, and

desecrating their churches – they went into the church at Brookfield and
made hideous noises, then called out "Come and pray, & sing psalmes."
The Indians consistently defied the fundamental beliefs of the Puritans and
exulted that their hated God had abandoned them.[24]

The colonists recorded such atrocities in meticulous and horrifying
detail. Metacom's men and their families, on the other hand, left no written
record of their experiences at the hands of the English, and so the nature
and scope of English atrocities are largely unknown, except for those
instances when the Puritans decided to record them for themselves. It's
known, for example, that many atrocities were committed by buccaneer
mercenaries under Capt. Samuel Mosely, a former pirate hired by the
Puritan forces. I've also read that the English forces often simply replaced
the English heads on poles with those of Native casualties, and that they
had their own bloody practices, such as beheading notable victims and
drawing and quartering their bodies. According to Lepore, mutilated body
parts were often displayed in public spaces of colonial towns to reassure
the English that their enemies were indeed dead and punished, whereas
Metacom's men committed their atrocities for the benefit (and terror) of
the English survivors who would come upon the scenes of battle.

Metacom's use of random terror, against which the colonial army was
generally useless, brought settler life to a standstill. Colonists sought
shelter in their garrison houses, never knowing where or when the next
attack would come. For fourteen months, my ancestors and all the other
settlers lived in a state of collective terror, an experience that indelibly
marked their psyches and affected their attitudes toward the Native population for generations to come – just as the slaughter and attempted genocide of the Pequots thirty-eight years previously had lived a subterranean
life in the minds of many New England Natives, even those who had sided
with the English. For the colonists, King Philip's War was the war that fixed
"Indian" as "enemy," even though many Native people had fought on the
English side.

Some of my relations were victims in these attacks and others were part
of the militia that came to the rescue. In the tiny, isolated settlement of
Squakheag, later known as Northfield, which was then the most northerly
English settlement on the Connecticut River, two teenage sons of my
ancestor William Janes were among eight settlers surprised and killed in
the fields as they worked to bring in the harvest. The next day a Capt.
Richard Beers and his Massachusetts company of about thirty-six men

were sent north to evacuate the town, unaware of the previous day's ambush. Among his soldiers was John Wheeler, the grandson of Mercy Jelly's son John Wheeler: he had been impressed at Newbury on August 5, 1675, and served as trumpeter.[25] Just two miles from Northfield, the soldiers were ambushed and twenty killed, including Captain Beers, though young John Wheeler survived. The survivors fled back downriver to Hadley, and Maj. Robert Treat and a hundred Connecticut troops successfully evacuated Northfield the next day, encountering on their way the severed heads of some of Beers's soldiers mounted on poles.

Two weeks later John Wheeler saw action again, on the day that contemporary New England historian William Hubbard called "the most fatal Day, the Saddest that ever befel New England," when Wheeler's new commander, Capt. Thomas Lathrop, and his company were ordered to form convoy teams bringing loads of grain from Deerfield to Hadley. "The company, consisting of eighty men, arrived safely at Deerfield, threshed the wheat, placed it in eighteen wagons, and while on their return through South Deerfield, as they were stopping to gather grapes, which hung in clusters in the forest that lined the narrow road, they were surprised by an ambuscade of several hundred Indians who poured upon them a murderous fire." Sixty-four Englishmen died in the battle of "Bloody Brook," but John Wheeler was again one of only eight survivors. It is possible that his cousin, Thomas Chase, the son of my ancestors Ann Wheeler and Aquila Chase of Newbury, was also among the survivors; if not involved in the battle, he was certainly in the vicinity.[26] Wheeler and the other survivors were rescued when Captain Mosely and his raggle-taggle troop of buccaneers arrived from Deerfield and charged the Indians, driving them into the woods and swamps. When the Indians began to regroup and surround them, they were rescued in turn by Major Treat's forces from Connecticut.

The wildfire spread of the war, a succession of terrible defeats, and the total destruction of so many towns shook the English to the core and left them fearful and pessimistic. The unthinkable – that they could be defeated by uncivilized Natives – now seemed entirely possible. With the evacuations of Northfield, Deerfield, and Brookfield, there remained only five inhabited English towns in all of western Massachusetts.

An October 5 attack on Springfield was another terrible blow, for this largest and most prosperous of the Massachusetts towns along the Connecticut River had enjoyed excellent relations with the neighbouring Agawams, and many of the inhabitants had refused to believe that the local

Indians would ever deviate from their loyalty to the English. But the Massachusetts army, by blaming the neutral Agawams for an earlier attack by the Nipmucks, and by seizing their weapons and demanding their children as hostages, may have precipitated their flight to join Metacom. In Hatfield, near Northampton, English panic and anti-Native feeling ran so high that an elderly female Indian captive was ordered "to be torn in pieces by dogs."[27]

The actions of the Springfield Indians made the English increasingly suspicious of neutral or friendly Indians everywhere. Daniel Gookin pointed out that the treacherous Indians of Springfield and Hatfield had never been Christians, but this fell on deaf ears, and the situation of "friendly" Natives became ever more perilous. Gookin later wrote "the animosity and rage of the common people increased against them, that the very name of a praying Indian was spoken against, in so much, that some wise and principal men did advise some that were concerned with them, to forbear giving that epithet of praying." The question of policy toward them became the subject of heated debate. All praying Indians were ordered to concentrate in five towns "for their own security" and were deprived of weapons and forbidden to hunt. Praying Indians had fought in the first months of the war; now the authorities disbanded their companies to appease popular opinion, a decision that left Massachusetts in peril. Many ambushes against the colonists were successfully carried out because the English lacked Indian scouts, and many towns were burned because the Massachusetts authorities refused to believe reports from friendly Indians and their own spies. (Connecticut, in contrast, by employing Mohegans and Pequots, was never ambushed.)[28] It was only much later in the war that Massachusetts realized its error and employed some praying Indians as scouts and warriors.

In fact, the number of praying Indians turning on the English was greatly exaggerated in the general hysteria of the time. Their situation bears some similarity to that of Japanese-Canadians and Japanese-Americans during the Second World War, for the English feared that their loyalty would not transcend the ties of blood and culture. Most praying Indians were "greatly ambitious to give demonstration to the English of their fidelity and good affection," according to Daniel Gookin, and remained peacefully in their towns, at risk of attack by other Indians.[29] In spite of the shocking defection of some praying Indians, he and John Eliot strenuously defended them against English hostility. But many colonists felt no Native could be trusted: with the praying towns located close to white settlements, and many Christian Natives related by blood to those fighting with Metacom, the loyalty of the praying Indians could have life-or-death consequences for the English.

Defenders of friendly Indians, such as John Eliot, were definitely in the minority. When Capt. Samuel Mosely, the notoriously cruel former pirate and Indian hater, accused fifteen Christian Indian suspects – including Eliot's former printer at the Cambridge press, James Printer – of murdering seven colonists at Lancaster, he interrogated them roughly, obtained a confession from one of the Indians through torture, and marched them to Boston, tied together with a rope around their necks. John Eliot and Daniel Gookin bravely tried to prevent their unjust prosecution by helping to conduct their defence, since the evidence presented against them was totally unreliable. Largely through their efforts, all were acquitted except one, who was sold into slavery to appease public clamour, but was afterwards released. The population was so incensed at the acquittals that the authorities were forced to smuggle some of the Indians out of town at night to save them from a lynch mob, and both Gookin and Eliot were threatened.

A week after the attack on Springfield, the praying Indians of Natick, the largest of the praying towns, were ordered deported to bleak, windswept Deer Island in Boston Harbor on pain of death, because of unsubstantiated suspicion that the Naticks had "some designe against the English." John Eliot visited them before they left to offer what support he could; he "comforted and encouraged and instructed and prayed with them, and for them." While Massachusetts legislators initially instructed the provincial treasurer to provide for them, these resources were totally insufficient for the nearly five hundred men, women, and children, who had to endure the bitterly cold winter of 1675–76 without adequate food, clothing, or shelter. Indians who tried to escape could be killed, and others were kidnapped from the island and sold into slavery. The now-elderly John Eliot, Daniel Gookin, and a few others protested against such harsh treatment and visited the Indians on several occasions. They found "the Island was bleak and cold, their wigwams poor and mean; their clothes few and thin," and again the missionaries were almost lynched for their efforts. It became increasingly dangerous for any New Englander to defend the praying Indians. Feelings ran so strongly against Eliot and Gookin that they were openly accused of treason. Gookin recorded that "he was affraid to go along the Streets."[30] But the situation of the praying Indians was even worse, for they had forsaken their families and original culture only to be rejected by their adopted one, and now were so hated by both cultures that they could be threatened by violence from either.

The prospect of starvation and death on Deer Island terrified those Christian Indians who were not yet incarcerated there – and their fears were well founded, for more than half of those exiled there died over the winter. The inhabitants of the praying town of Wamesit decided to leave the Bay Colony altogether to avoid such a fate and withdrew northwards up the Merrimack to land controlled by the French. They explained their decision in a letter, which said "as for the Island, we may say there is no safety for us, because many English be not good, and maybe they come to us and kill us. . . . We are not sorry for what we leave behind, but we are sorry for the English have driven us from our praying to god and from our teacher."[31]

James Printer's story is a telling illustration of the dilemmas faced by the Christian Indians. After surviving his capture by Captain Mosely, the murder trial, and the hatred of the Boston mob, he returned to the praying town of Hassanemesit, only to be captured by three hundred Nipmucks allied with Metacom. According to Jill Lepore, the praying Indians were given a stark choice: if they would go with the warriors, their lives would be spared; otherwise the warriors would take all their corn. If the praying Indians did not go with Metacom's men, they faced the prospect of starving or of being shot by the English if they left their town to find food. If they actually reached another town, they would likely become the victim of Indian-hating vigilantes, be sold into perpetual slavery in the West Indies (as had already happened to hundreds of Christian and enemy Indians), or be shipped to Deer Island where they would freeze and starve. James Printer evidently considered Metacom's men to be the lesser evil, but many colonists did not believe that the inhabitants of Hassanemesit who went with the Nipmucks were true captives, and after devastating attacks on Lancaster and Medfield by the Nipmucks, in which the Hassanemesit captives were believed to have taken part, a group of colonists sought further revenge on the Christian Indians at Deer Island.

John Eliot defended several of the Hassanemesit captives when they ended up in English hands. James Printer's brother, Tukapewillin, who had been the minister at Hassanemesit, at first also went along with the Nipmucks, but after several months planned his escape with an Indian from Deer Island who had been sent by the English to spy on the Nipmucks. They also hoped to free the children and wives of both men. Unfortunately,

Captain Mosely found out about their plans and arranged for their capture by the English as soon as they left the Nipmucks; they were robbed and abused. Although Tukapewillin's wife and eldest son escaped into the woods, Tukapewillin and the spy (also a preacher) were sent to Deer Island. During a brief release from the island, Tukapewillin was allowed to visit John Eliot. He emphatically declared his loyalty to the English and described his impossible situation:

> Oh Sir I am greatly distressed this day on every side, the English have taken away some of my estate, my corn . . . my plough, cart, chaine, & other goods. The enemy Indians have also taken a part of what I had, & the richest Indians mock & scoff at me, saying now what has become of your praying to God. The English also censure me, & say I am a hypocrite. In this distress I have no where to look, but up to God in Heaven to help me.[32]

Another praying Indian from Hassanemesit, known as Captain Tom, suffered a worse fate. He had also been taken captive by the Nipmucks, then captured by the English in June 1676 and tried for treason. His story of Nipmuck captivity was not believed, and Eliot reported "a great rage was against him." An English captain testified that he had seen Tom at the attack on Sudbury in the Bay Colony, but Tom denied this, saying that he had been sick during the attack and had never fought against the English. Although the testimony of another praying Indian, who was a spy for the English, corroborated Tom's story and provided evidence that he had gone with the Nipmucks out of fear of being sent to Deer Island, several Englishmen contradicted this account and claimed to have seen him in the fighting. John Eliot evidently believed his story, for he visited Captain Tom in prison and later went to the governor "& intreated that Capt. Tom might have liberty to prove that he was sick at the time when the fight was at Sudbury & that he was not here." Governor John Leverett would not be swayed and described Tom as a bad man. Eliot responded angrily that "at the great day he should find that christ was of anothr mind." Eliot accompanied Tom to his execution and reported that Tom addressed the crowd, saying, "I did never lift up hand against the English, nor was I at sudbury, only I was willing to goe away with the enemise that surprized us."[33]

For all that one can criticize John Eliot's cultural imperialism in attempting to civilize and Christianize the indigenous population of New

England, his actions during King Philip's War were brave and difficult. One can imagine how heavy his heart must have been, for his life's work was threatened, his successes in "civilizing" no longer recognized, his sense of justice outraged by the treatment of the Christian Indians, and his genuine concern for the people he had come to know was now considered almost treasonous.

Most notable was his petition to the Massachusetts General Court against the sale of Indian captives into slavery and the policy of Indian extirpation, one of only two such protests that the English colonists are known to have made. The Puritans had sold some captured Pequots into slavery after the Pequot War in 1637, and the colonists had formally established, in a 1641 document known as the "Body of Liberties," that it was legal to sell captives taken in just wars. Apparently, many Puritans considered slavery a "compassionate compromise," since these Indians were not executed, as were ringleaders and those known to have killed English people. In becoming enslaved, however, they received a severe punishment.[34] Women and children and those not considered dangerous were forced into servitude in New England for a number of years, while many others were sold into foreign slavery in the West Indies and beyond.

The Humble Petition of John Eliot Sheweth:

That the terror of selling away such Indians unto the Islands for perpetual slaves, who shall yield up themselves to your mercy, is like to an effectual prolongation of the war, and such an exasperation of them, as may produce we know not what evil consequences upon all the land.

Christ has said, blessed are the merciful for they shall obtain mercy. This usage of them is worse than death. The design of Christ in these last days is not to extirpate nations, but to gospellize them. His sovreign hand and grace hath brought the gospel into these dark places of the earth. When we came we declared to the world (and it is recorded) yea, we are engaged by our Letters Patent from the King's Majesty, – that the endeavour of the Indians' conversion, not their exteripation, was one great end of our enterprise in coming to these ends of the earth. The Lord hath so succeeded that work as that, by his grace, they have the Holy Scriptures, and sundry of themselves able to teach their countrymen the good knowledge of God. And however some of them have refused to receive the gospel and now are incensed in their spirits unto a war, against the English, yet I doubt not that the meaning of Christ is to open a door for the free passage of the gospel among them.

My humble request is, that you would follow Christ's design in this
. matter, to promote the free passage of religion among them, and not destroy them.

To sell souls for money seemeth to me a dangerous merchandise. To sell them away from all means of grace, when Christ has provided means of grace for them, is the way for us to be active in the destroying their souls. . . .

All men of reading condemn the Spaniard for cruelty upon this point, in destroying men, and depopulating the land. The country is large enough; – here is land enough for them and us too. . . .

I desire the Honored Council to pardon my boldness, and let the case of conscience be discussed orderly, before the King be asked. Cover my weakness, and weigh the reason and religion that laboreth in this great case of conscience.

John Eliot[35]

This petition seems to have been totally ignored. There is no record of any debate about it and, in July 1675, after an attack on the Plymouth town of Dartmouth, all but six of one hundred and sixty Natives who had not been part of the attack agreed to surrender to local military authorities under a promise of protection and amnesty. They were then sold out of the country and into slavery. It was the same story with two hundred Maine Indians. According to Capt. Benjamin Church, "had their promises to the Indians been kept, and the Indians farely treated, 't is probable that most if not all the Indians in those Parts, had soon followed the Example of those that had . . . surrendered themselves; which would have been a good step toward finishing the War."[36]

Eliot's argument against slavery focussed chiefly on the necessity of saving the souls of the Indians, who would have no access to proselytizing in the West Indies. At the same time, the authorities, Eliot included, were also thinking long and hard about the state of their own souls, or at least the souls of their fellow citizens. Believing as they did that the English were innocent of any wrongdoing against the indigenous nations, they attributed the outbreak of war and the fierce determination of the Native forces not to serious grievances that might have provoked the Natives but to God's punishment of the colonists for their own spiritual corruption – their sins of worldliness and inconstancy. "Why should we suppose that God is not offended with us when his displeasure is written in such visible and bloody characters?" asked Increase Mather.[37]

The Massachusetts government declared:

> The Righteous God hath heightned our Calamity and given Commission to the Barbarous Heathen to rise up against us, and to become a smart Rod, and severe Scourge to us, in Burning and Depopulating several hopeful Plantations, Murdering many of our People of all sorts, and seeming as it were to cast us off . . . hereby speaking aloud to us to search and try our wayes and turn again unto the Lord our God from whom we have departed with a great Backsliding.[38]

During the fall of 1675, the Governor's Council of Massachusetts published a catalogue of offences prevalent among the population that had supposedly led to this retribution. These included "Neglect of discipline in the churches," "Evill or pride in apparrell" and hairstyles, toleration of Quakers and their "damnable haeresies [and] abominable idolatrys," "much disorder and rudenes in [the] youth," profanity, contempt for authority, and idleness. The most "shameful and scandalous" sin was "the loose and sinfull custome of going or riding from towne to towne. . . . oft times men and weomen together, upon pretence of going to lecture," when their true purpose "meerely to drincke and revell in ordinarys and tavernes."[39] The remedy was for the people to repent and reform, and so many days of humiliation and fasting, as well as regular self-examination, were prescribed.

Some Puritans believed that extraordinary expressions of faith were called for: one colonist expressed this piety by sitting in the town common reading the Bible in the middle of an Indian attack – and so became the only casualty of the day. In a similar instance, one Goodman Wright "had a strange Confidence, or rather Conceit, that whilst he held his Bible in his Hand, he looked upon himself as secure from all kinde of Violence." He too was killed, the Indians "deriding his groundless Apprehension, or Folly therein, rippe[d] him open and put his Bible in his Belly."[40]

In attributing the Indian war "in this good Land, which the Lord hath given us," to divine wrath, my ancestors and their fellow colonists failed to recognize Native motivations, strategies, and expertise. Most English could not view aboriginal people as rational, fully human, beings with human needs and desires, not to mention legitimate grievances; in English eyes, they were basically God's pawns, being used by Him to punish his chosen people. When his chosen ones had reformed, God would then turn on and destroy the Natives, even though they had been carrying out His plans.

In the meantime, the Puritans felt themselves justified in fighting the enemy, believing as they did that they acted in self-defence against unprovoked attacks by the forces of evil. The fact that the Christian English were fighting non-Christians was as significant to the English as it was to Metacom's men, for, in the eyes of some influential Puritan writers, even offensive wars were just if waged over religion, and the normal rules of conduct in war did not apply when fighting heathens. They saw the enemy as inhuman, as "Wolves and other Beasts of Prey, that commonly do their Mishchiefs in the Night, or by Stealth" – or animals who would fight to the death. New Englanders viewed all Indian society as guilty, regardless of sex or age. They were all "serpents of the same Brood."[41]

CHAPTER
11

Thomas Stanton's War

Let us return to the beginning of the war again, to those first fateful days in late June 1675, and look at these events through another prism – that of Thomas Stanton and his neighbours in Pawcatuck. It appears that no one in Connecticut heard the news of the outbreak of war until several days after the killings in Swansea. The following letter was sent to Thomas Stanton and may have been the first report of the killings sent to Connecticut:

> June 29, 1675: Mr Stanton – Sar Thes are to give you notis of ye News I say you with ye rest of my Nebors and frinds that 12 housis of Swanse are borened and on of them was a garison hous and sivera men killed Saiconke also is boroned or a good part of it and men kild by Nep mock [Nipmuck] indean hear on house is robed as wesopos and the last night another house brooken up and another boroned on more Neare Mr Smeths and intend to have two heads from Suamacott the pepel heare are gon and going of towods Island I wish and desier you to take car of your silvs I have hired this barer I hear filis is bound for Mohigin [Mohegan] I am in hast for fear of ye mesenger
>
> Yours yet
Henry Stephens
Jun 29 75[1]

192

One can imagine Stanton's reaction upon receiving this letter. The dreadful situation he had spent decades trying to prevent had finally come to pass. Did he think back to the murders of settlers on the Connecticut River in 1637 that had marked the point of no return in dealings with the Pequots? Or the screams of women and children burning in the Pequot fort? Were either the English victims at Swansea or the Wampanoag assailants people he knew? Or were his first thoughts for the safety of his family and their exposed position along the Pawcatuck River? Certainly, given his wealth of experience with Native peoples, and his relatively good standing among them, he must have felt a heavy responsibility to do all he could to contain the war and prevent other aboriginal nations from joining Metacom. Did he, more than others, understand the seriousness of the situation?

Stanton immediately sent word to New London and to Governor Winthrop in Hartford. He then began to gather intelligence. Although the Wampanoags were not attacking towns within Connecticut, there were rumours of "strange Indians" (that is, not local Indians) in the woods. Connecticut's eastern frontier, particularly Pawcatuck/Stonington and Norwich, would be terribly exposed if the Narragansetts, who could muster about a thousand warriors, joined Metacom. The Narragansetts had long been enemies of the Wampanoags, but their ally Ninigret, whose territory was on the other side of the Pawcatuck River from Stonington, had been suspected of a plot against the English in 1669, when, as you may recall, Thomas Stanton had seized him at a dance and created a tense standoff only dispelled by the actions of the Pequot leader Robin Cassacinamon. And ever since the disputes about the Atherton Company land claims, the English had seen the Narragansetts as troublemakers and potential enemies.

Luckily for the English, Ninigret immediately "sent one of his counsill to Mr Stanton to tell him yt he has no hand in this business of Philip [Metacom], tho six of his men weare there contrary to his mind, and thre of them weare killed."[2] For the next year it would be Stanton's special mission to maintain Ninigret's neutrality, and he would succeed in doing so. In fact, both Thomas Stanton and George Denison played a major role in inducing the Native nations of southeast Connecticut – the Pequots, the Mohegans, and the Niantics – to remain neutral or to actively support the English. Thomas Stanton and his son-in-law Rev. James Noyes of Stonington acted as the usual liaisons between the United Colonies and the Pequots and Niantics for the duration of the war.

How did Stanton and the other intermediaries persuade these nations to side with the English? The personal relationships that had developed over the years probably played a large part in cementing these alliances, but it is not clear under what circumstances they did so. Were the Native nations also threatened by the English? Did they simply side with them out of a belief that Metacom's cause was hopeless and their best chance for survival was to be on the winning side? Or were they pursuing their own agendas, as had those, like Uncas, who had sided with the English in the Pequot War four decades earlier? Were these alliances, as historian James Drake maintains, "as much an opportunity to enhance one's position in a complicated shell game among the English, the Mohegans, the Niantics, and the Pequots as a war against Philip"?[3]

Certainly Ninigret came to believe that he was in a position to play the role of peacemaker, a role that he may have sought for altruistic reasons, but which definitely would have increased his prestige and power with the English; he "let it be known that he could and would end the war between the two races, using even his own wampum if necessary," and over the course of the war he dreamed up several schemes to carry out this intention. At the same time he also demanded material inducements and solicitous attention from Stanton, whom he sought out on several occasions. In early November, for example, Stanton returned home to find Ninigret "at my house with his men eating and pestring of my house." And though Ninigret declared his neutrality at the beginning of the war, there would be tremendous pressure later to change his position and support Metacom. Stanton, for his part, clearly felt he had to do all he could to ensure that did not happen. The following May, Stanton would write a letter to the secretary of Connecticut colony, asking that he be reimbursed for

> my Great expenses of Estate & time wch hath bin of 12 months standing, where in wch time many a good sheepe & peeses of porke & beefe hath ben Eaten & indeede my hous was open to him and his Men Constantlie & Extreamlie Combred, bee sides severall Jurnies I made to him and for him being sent by him to the house of Mr Smithes & other plases to please & Humore him & to Counsell & keepe his Men from out breaking as appears under thar handes, . . . and & Let me tell you playenlie yt it is a great Marsie to Nengrat & to uss if god made mee an instrument of any good amongst them for things were upon a tickell pin.[4]

Ninigret's neutrality and friendliness to the English were confirmed early on, but no one knew who the rest of the Narragansetts would support. When news of the attack at Swansea became common knowledge, a Connecticut regiment under Maj. Robert Treat was summoned and some three hundred men gathered at Capt. George Denison's stockade. A council-of-war dispatched forty men to Connecticut's eastern frontier, and the governor's second son, Capt. Wait Winthrop, was authorized to act as both military commander and commissioner.

Pequot loyalty to the English was a given, as the two Pequot communities were too small and vulnerable to act independently (though the Mashantucket Pequots built a military fort on their own land for defence), but the Connecticut authorities were initially unsure of the loyalty of Uncas and the Mohegans. By now they were a powerful and numerous tribe of perhaps 2,500 or 3,000 people, living in the very midst of the English. This was a life-or-death question for many, including Thomas Stanton's daughter Mary and her husband Samuel Rogers, who lived right next to Uncas himself on land he had granted to them.

The same day that he heard the news of the attack on Swansea, Daniel Wetherell, commissioner of New London, visited Uncas to ascertain his loyalty – and did not come away reassured. He wrote to Governor Winthrop on June 29:

> We have reason to believe that most of his men are gone that way, for he hath very few men at home nor did I see more than three guns Amongst them tis certain he hath lately had a great correspondence with Philip, and many presents have passed: Hon Sir my humble request is that a speedy and effectuall order maye be sent us for the putting all these parts in a posture of defence for it is reported that Philip is very near us and expects further assistance from Uncas.

The next day he visited Uncas again and sent a second report to Winthrop: "We have great reason to believe that there is a universal combination of the Indians, and fear you cannot aid us timely."[5] Indeed, news of outbreaks of violence farther south in the area of the Chesapeake and Delaware Bays coincided so closely with the outbreak of war in New England that the English momentarily feared a general uprising of all the indigenous nations against them.

After leaving the colonists in a state of agonizing uncertainty for several days, Uncas demonstrated his loyalty to the English by sending six envoys to Boston to offer Mohegan military assistance. Just to be sure, the English insisted that the sachem send the wife and child of his son Owaneco to Boston as hostages. The English were cautious because they were receiving conflicting information: the Narragansetts were telling them that Uncas was secretly involved with Metacom, while the Mohegans were accusing the Narragansetts of the same thing (this was an old pattern of accusation and counter-accusation dating back to the period just after the Pequot War). Uncas again assured the Colonies of his loyalty and sent his son Owaneco and fifty warriors to Boston. They were escorted there by a group of soldiers that included Asaph Eliot, the son of John Eliot's brother Jacob (my probable direct ancestor), and were soon joined by another company of fifty-two praying Indians (this was in the early days of the war, before the praying Indians' company was disbanded).[6] Attawanhood, another son of Uncas, and thirty Mohegans joined the colonial forces in the western part of Massachusetts. The Mohegans were promised they could keep any plunder they seized from Metacom as their wages.

A few days later, Wait Winthrop reported to his father that he had met with Thomas Stanton, Thomas Minor, and others of Stonington, who had advised him that it was imperative that the commissioners of the United Colonies gather immediately and devise a plan to prevent the Narragansetts from joining Metacom. After consultation, the commissioners decided to send an English force, along with Mohegans and Pequots, to parley with Ninigret and the other Narragansett sachems. Winthrop hoped "the appearance of a considerable force might strike the greater aw and put a suddaine issue to any thoughts of joining against the english. . . . we have intellegence that 30 or 40 of Philips men are com for releife to one of the narroganset Sachems who has sent to nengraft for aduise whether he shall bind and deliver them to the english or let them goe."[7]

While Stanton and the others were justifiably concerned with the safety of their community, there were additional motives for an expedition to the Narragansett country, especially for Connecticut. Given the previous history between Connecticut, Massachusetts, and the Narragansetts, it is evident that the settlers also saw the war as an opportunity to assert their control over the Narragansetts and their land once and for all. In fact, as Francis Jennings notes, almost all colonial troops were diverted from the pursuit of Metacom to deal with the Narragansetts. In the official records, Connecticut's troops had been sent "to Stoneington and New London to ayd and secure the good people of those townes against the Indians," but Connecticut falsely asserted that the Narragansetts were belligerents and sent its troops into Rhode Island. There they joined those from Massachusetts who had got there first – while Metacom was busy attacking towns in Plymouth Colony a considerable distance away.[8]

The government of Rhode Island had not asked for assistance from either Massachusetts or Connecticut, but this did not stop their advance into Rhode Island, which had no army of its own. Rhode Island's governor, William Coddington, complained to New York governor Edmund Andros that the reason for "contention against these Indians" was to invalidate "the king's Determination for Naraganset to be in our Colony," but he could do little. A local magistrate who was overheard protesting that "the Indians had given no cause of warre" and the troops' "coming here did more hurt than good" was arrested by the commanders of the invasion for his "Mutinous and scurrilous and abusive Carriages towards the Massachuset and Connecticute Government." Connecticut's council ordered him jailed for "retarding and delaying their procedure."[9]

The Narragansetts arrived at the parley with the Massachusetts forces with a large number of armed warriors. The sachems were "noticeably cool" to the mission. Massachusetts was almost ready to call in the rest of the army and attack when Capt. Wait Winthrop arrived from Stonington with a force of sixty English troopers and sixty Pequots and persuaded them to postpone any military action. Winthrop, who had been warned by his father, Gov. John Winthrop, Jr., not to provoke violence, had spoken with Ninigret on the way, probably through Thomas Stanton or one of his sons. Ninigret promised friendship and also promised to turn over to the English those Wampanoags who were seeking refuge with the Narragansetts.

The incident reveals the more cautious and appeasing approach of the Connecticut authorities, who enjoyed better relations with their Native neighbours than did the leaders of the Massachusetts Colony – partly because of Stanton's diplomacy. Winthrop's advice was "It's best to keepe and promote peace with them, though with bearing some of their ill manners and conniving at some irregularities." One Stonington man suggested that the negotiators should "winke at small faultes" for the present, and attack if necessary in the winter, when there were no leaves to provide cover in the forest and the ice facilitated travel over the swamps.[10]

Wait Winthrop, Rhode Island's Roger Williams, and the commissioners from Boston then met with the Narragansett sachems, who told the English they had no agreement with Metacom, although they did want to avenge themselves on Uncas for a murder committed by Uncas's son. The English insisted on Narragansett submission and, with the aid of Thomas Stanton's son Joseph as interpreter, drew up a "peace treaty," which was duly signed not by Canonicus, the grand sachem of the Narragansetts, but by four "subordinate counsellors" who had no authority to sign for their people and did so under duress. The treaty obligated the Narragansetts to treat the Wampanoags as enemies and refuse them sanctuary; it also offered bounties to the Narragansetts if they would bring in the heads of Wampanoag warriors. But another provision is most telling: by it the Narragansetts supposedly confirmed *all* previous land grants to the English, which clearly included the still-disputed lands claimed by the Atherton Company of mixed Massachusetts and Connecticut partners, including Thomas Stanton and Connecticut governor John Winthrop, Jr.[11] Canonicus later regarded this treaty as farcical.

After this confrontation with the English, the Narragansetts retreated to a large swamp, where they apparently hoped to wait out the war. The colonists' expedition into Rhode Island had wasted precious time by delaying the war against Metacom by about ten days. They then withdrew their armies from Rhode Island as Metacom began a series of devastating surprise attacks in Plymouth and Massachusetts colonies. When the Massachusetts and Plymouth armies finally went after Metacom's forces, a series of blunders led once again to his escape. The English forces, encumbered with heavy muskets and poor supply lines, and unfamiliar with much of the territory, were no match for fast-moving aboriginal warriors with an intimate knowledge of the land.

In fact, the whereabouts of Metacom and his warriors was a mystery. On August 6, he was reported to be within eighteen miles of Stonington, starving and sick, but this was probably his allies, the Pocassets under the female sachem Weetamoo, who were seeking refuge with the Narragansetts.

Only ten days after the treaty with the Narragansetts was signed in July 1675, Ninigret had sent the severed head of a Wampanoag to New London and demanded a coat as promised. Ninigret and his aide Cornman kept in close contact with Thomas Stanton at Stonington, and also with Richard Smith, another fur trader and Atherton partner at Wickford in the

Narragansett country (where Stanton also had land). Within three weeks, another Narragansett sachem, Pessacus, had also delivered the heads of several of Philip's followers. But as the towns in the upper Connecticut Valley burned, the English expressed increasing suspicion of the Narragansetts, especially when Weetamoo and her people were not held prisoner by the Narragansetts, as the terms of the treaty stipulated, but were given shelter.

When Ninigret heard that the Narragansetts were now sheltering as many as four hundred refugee Indians (Weetamoo's Pocassets and, if Uncas's accusation was correct, the women and children of Metacom's Pokanoket band of Wampanoags), he passed this information on to Thomas Stanton, promising that the fugitives would be surrendered upon demand. Ninigret's trust of Stanton is demonstrated by a proposal he made to him, that he bring a few Wampanoags to Stanton, whereupon Stanton would give them back to him, urging that they be well treated. This, Ninigret felt, would encourage the refugees to surrender themselves, and they could then be persuaded to go to Aquidneck Island, where they could be quickly taken into custody by the English. Stanton was intrigued by this scheme, but it was never put into effect.[12]

I imagine these two men, realists both, as they sit across Thomas Stanton's table of an evening. Ninigret is the consummate politician – weighing his choices, his words, manoeuvring for position, seeking information of his own from Stanton without appearing too curious. Yet I wonder about his state of mind, if he felt any doubts in breaking ranks with the other Narragansett sachems, his close relatives, if his stand put him in mortal danger. Stanton is his affable host, himself appraising and wary, ever mindful of the delicate balance between conveying English wishes and alienating the powerful sachem whose neutrality could earn them victory and whose hostility could cost them their lives. I wonder how much they could trust each other, if they were ever able to strategize together over how to end the war, or if the distances between them were such that they could merely listen to each other's proposals and convey reactions. How much were they each acting as conduits for other people not present: the Narragansetts, the colonial authorities? *Go back and tell them, if your people do this, we will do that.*

Thomas Stanton attended an important meeting between the English leaders and the Narragansetts on September 22, 1675, at Wickford, where the Narragansetts were urged to surrender the fugitives. Thomas Stanton reported that he found "a great strangenes in the sperites of the sachems heare, sutch Strangnes as I never observed bee fore or since I knew them and I conceive it is in refference to the Wampanoacks wch are com in to Canonicos, Quanapm, Nanantenow and the oulde queene." Ninigret told Stanton that he was resolved to keep his agreement with the English, and if the other Narragansett sachems did not do the same he would remonstrate with them and declare himself an English ally, and turn to the English for assistance.[13]

The apparent split between the Niantics and the other Narragansetts worried the English, and Cornman signed a formal re-affirmation of the July treaty for Ninigret and a young sachem known as Canonchet, on behalf of the other Narragansett sachems. Canonchet promised to deliver every enemy Indian in their custody no later than October 28. But October 28 came and went and the prisoners were not given up to the English. Rumours began to circulate that the Narragansetts were supporting Metacom and even participating clandestinely in the war. At the end of October an Indian of Plymouth Colony who returned from visiting the Narragansetts was said to have confirmed that the Narragansetts were already giving aid and support to Metacom, and he claimed that Canonchet was planning to attack the English in the new year. It appears that there were internal generational differences among the Narragansetts, with Canonicus favouring neutrality, but unable to stop Canonchet and other younger Narragansetts from supporting Metacom. (Also, given that their arch-rivals, the Mohegans, were the chief Native allies of the English, the Narragansetts would have found it difficult to join the English without furthering Uncas's goal of Mohegan dominance.)

When the commissioners of the United Colonies met early in November, they had to decide whether to use force to get the Narragansetts to release the prisoners, at the risk of provoking them into joining the war as well. If they didn't press the Narragansetts and the latter did secretly support Metacom, the enemies of the English would have time to gather their strength, accumulate weapons and ammunition, and plan their campaign. If the English waited until spring or summer to decide the matter, they would face a further disadvantage, for the leaves on the trees would conceal the Native warriors in the woods.

Connecticut – perhaps because of its history of better relations with its Native neighbours, or because the colony of New York was attempting to seize western Connecticut, and Connecticut did not want to be engaged in two different wars at the same time – was less willing than the other colonies to take extreme action against the Narragansetts, and argued for diplomacy. Finally, the United Colonies agreed to send an army of a thousand men to force the Narragansetts to observe the treaty and surrender the fugitives. The plan was that, if they refused to co-operate, they would then be treated as enemies, but what later transpired suggests that most of the English considered military action a foregone conclusion and even desirable.

The United Colonies notified Rhode Island of their plan to send a campaign into their territory in December, and Rhode Island was invited to contribute a contingent of men, and to make ships available for the transport of men and supplies, which it agreed to do. Maj.-Gen. Daniel Denison, the brother of Capt. George Denison of Stonington, was named supreme commander, until illness forced him to give up this position to Edward Winslow. Major Treat was named second-in-command of the united forces, as well as commander of the Connecticut forces. Exposed plantations such as Stonington were warned to be ready for trouble. In the meantime the commanders began to plan an expedition into the Narragansett country in the middle of winter; Wickford, where Thomas Stanton had considerable land, was the terminus for vital supply lines, and Richard Smith's garrison house was chosen as the base of operations.

All over New England, men enlisted or were conscripted, though there were also many draft-dodgers, such as Stanton's young son Robert, who was impressed along with eight other Stonington men, but at first did not appear. The Massachusetts foot companies included several of my ancestors or relations: young John Wheeler (a grandson of the original emigrant ancestor) in Capt. Joseph Gardiner's company; Thomas Chase, another grandson of John Wheeler and the brother of my ancestor Ensign Moses Chase, in Maj. Samuel Appleton's company; and James Harris of Boston under Capt. James Oliver. The Massachusetts government offered its troops an additional inducement. On December 10 the governor issued a proclamation that "if they played the man, took the fort, and drove the enemy out of the Narragansett country, which is their great seat, they should have a gratuity of land, besides their wages."[14]

Thomas Stanton's role as trusted intermediary proved critical at this juncture. He and Tobias Saunders (a resident of Westerly, Rhode Island) wrote to Winthrop on December 10 with their own assessment of the situation:

wee thought it very sutable to acquaint you with what Discors wee have
had this day with Nencraft [Ninigret]. it was proposed first what he
thought conserning the Naroganset sachems wheather they war
Resolved to stand war with the english yea or no. . . . he saith That he
thinks that they will not begin with the english first but if in Case the
english begin with them thay are Resolved to stand upon thair Defence.[15]

John Winthrop, Jr., wrote back to Stanton two days later expressing his
desire that Stanton effectively secure a peace treaty or military alliance
with Ninigret, the Mohegans, and the Pequots:

and [I] know no better person whome they may repose trust in for ye
attempting such an essay than your selfe, of whose wisedome & pru-
dence they have had good experience. . . . Doubtless they canot but judge
yt ye lengthning out of the warr will be bitternes to ye Indians as well as
ye English in ye latter end: and it surely a considerable opportunity yt
both Ninigret and Mohegens now have to provide for yr owne futur set-
tlemt & peace . . . and as you have beene greatly instrumentall to keepe
Nenecrat fro engaging agt ye English so I doubt no but you will prudently
endeavour to continue in fidelity to them, by representing to him the
good fruit he hath and will have in it, and by acquainting him how
acceptable his peaceable deportment is to them and of great benefit to
themselves. . . .[16]

There is, however, no evidence that Stanton or anyone else was instructed
to negotiate with the rest of the Narragansetts, as was the stated purpose of
the campaign. Their intent from the moment they came to Rhode Island
seems to have been simply to crush them. As the noted historian Douglas
Leach puts it, "the stated purpose of the expedition seems to have dissolved
in the general urge to smash the potential foe as quickly as possible."[17] As
the Massachusetts and Plymouth forces made their way to Wickford, they
killed a number of Narragansetts, and about seventy were taken captive.
On December 14, Winslow of Plymouth led a large force against two
Narragansett villages, killing a number of people and burning wigwams,
again apparently without provocation. One Rhode Islander, Samuel
Gorton, warned the Connecticut governor John Winthrop, Jr., of his fears
about where things were headed:

> I remember the time of the warres in Ireland (when I was young, in Queen Elizabeths dayes of famous memory) where much English blood was spilt by a people much like unto these [Indians] . . . where many valiant souldiers lost their lives, both horse and foot, by means of woods, bushes, boggs, and quagmires. . . . And after these Irish were subdued by force, what treacherous and bloody massacres have they attempted is well knowne.[18]

As the colonists saw it, they were waging a preventive war. The United Colonies reported that those Indians were "deeply accessory in the present bloody outrages of the Barbarous Natives," yet historian Francis Jennings notes that "its bill of particulars was a flimsy and feeble justification for neglecting a swarm of furious enemies to attack the only peaceful tribe in sight."[19]

Most of the Narragansetts as well as the Wampanoag refugees had retreated by then to a secret and nearly completed great "fort," or fortified village, on a small island in the middle of a large cedar swamp, where they planned to pass the winter undisturbed. The English were poor swamp fighters and the secret island was difficult to approach, but among the captives picked up by the English forces was one "Peter," a Narragansett who avoided the common fate of being sold as a slave in the West Indies by turning traitor and agreeing to guide the English to the fort. (He wasn't the only traitor: Joshua Teft, a white man, joined the Narragansett side – though he may have been a captive as he claimed – and was later captured by the English, convicted of treason, hanged, and quartered.)

The English now faced difficult decisions. Hostilities had escalated on December 15 when a Narragansett by the name of Stonewall John came to negotiate for peace. Immediately suspected as a spy, he irritated the English officers with his boastfulness, and was sent away with instructions that his people should send their sachems if they wished to negotiate. The colonists' mistrust was confirmed when, minutes after he departed, Narragansetts in the vicinity mortally wounded three English soldiers, and later two more were killed at a house about three miles away. Still, the English were not ready to launch a large-scale attack, as there was as yet no sign of Major Treat and the Connecticut army, and additional supplies from Massachusetts hadn't arrived as expected, so provisions were scarce. To make matters worse, the temperature had plummeted and it was bitterly cold. The following day, the Narragansetts killed most of the people in a garrison house at Pettaquamscut, a small settlement about nine miles south of Wickford, and burned down the building. Finally, Major Treat arrived with more than 300 Connecticut soldiers as well as 150 Mohegans and Pequots under Uncas's son Owaneco and the Pequot leader Catapezet. Capt. John Mason of Norwich, the son of the renowned John Mason of the Pequot War, led 70 men from southeastern Connecticut, including Thomas Stanton's sons Samuel, Daniel, and Joseph Stanton (I'm not sure if Robert participated in this campaign). Their older brother, Capt. John Stanton, and Capt. George Denison, father-in-law to several of the Stanton men, were also present.[20] The English troops now constituted the largest military force ever assembled in New England.

On December 18, they marched to Pettaquamscut, where they camped without tents or any other shelter around the ruins of the garrison in a blowing snowstorm. It was the coldest winter the English had ever encountered in New England, and the weather had fouled up their supply lines. They had only two days' rations with them when it began to storm and snow heavily. By the next day, a number of soldiers were suffering from frostbite and had to be left behind. In an act of blind faith, the armies followed Peter, the Narragansett captive, through miles of unfamiliar terrain, to the edge of the swamp, where they encountered several Narragansetts, fired on them, and, without waiting for further orders, chased after them. Ordinarily almost impassable, the swamp was now completely frozen, and was easily crossed. Ahead of them, the troopers saw the fortified village, surrounded by a wall of upright stakes, reinforced with a hedge and inner rampart of rocks and clay, and guarded by numerous block-houses and flankers (side fortifications). Inside were at least a thousand men, women, and children.

Fortuitously, the English had arrived at the most vulnerable part of the fort, where the palisade was not finished and had been blocked by a tree trunk. With a rush the Massachusetts soldiers ran over the frozen swamp and charged this breach; the first who climbed over it fell in the heavy fire, including two captains (in fact, many casualties in the first companies were the result of careless shooting by the troops farther back). The survivors of the first three companies drew back in confusion, while two other companies, including that of John Wheeler, pressed forward. Wheeler's captain also fell. Major Appleton, with the remainder of the Massachusetts forces, including Thomas Chase, dashed forward and stormed through the gap, driving the Narragansetts out of the nearest flanker. The Connecticut forces then followed him in under heavy fire, and Captain Mason was mortally wounded.

In a reprise of the English massacre of the Pequots at Mystic, the order was given to set the wigwams on fire. Capt. Benjamin Church tried to countermand this order for he thought the army should keep the village intact for its own use that night, since the troops lacked shelter and the village was well stocked with grain and other food. But, as had happened almost forty years earlier, the fort became an inferno. No one knows how many Narragansetts died inside their wigwams. The usual figure cited for Narragansett deaths is 1,000 total, with at least 97 slain and 48 wounded warriors, the rest non-combatants; the lowest estimate reported is 300 non-combatants. Certainly many women, children, and elderly counted among the dead. The "shrieks and cries of the women and children, the yelling of the warriors, exhibited a most horrible and appalling scene, so that it greatly moved some of the soldiers. They were in much doubt and they afterwards seriously inquired whether burning their enemies alive could be consistent with humanity and the benevolent principle of the gospel."[21]

By nightfall the English had secured their victory and beaten back those warriors who had escaped the fort and fired on the English from the woods. The victors had lost at least 20 men and about 200 were wounded, 80 from Connecticut (not including Native allies, for whom I have no figures). As there was no shelter in the swamp, the troops began to retreat all the way back to Wickford in the darkness, ever fearful of attack – a harrowing journey that my relations must have later described to their families many times, the exhausted men buffeted by icy winds and snow, and many of the wounded perishing on the way. A number of men suffered frostbite and were permanently disabled because of frozen hands and feet. The largest group of soldiers reached Wickford about two hours after midnight, but others got lost and didn't arrive until seven the next morning. Eventually the number of casualties was more than 80, including seven of the 14 company commanders.

Almost one-half of the casualties had been suffered by the Connecticut forces. The shortage of supplies and bad weather prompted Major Treat to urge that his troops be allowed to return home temporarily. At first Winslow denied this request, but morale was so terrible that a number of men deserted their units. Treat was then permitted to take his men back to Stonington to recuperate. The cold weather continued: it was so cold that the mills were frozen, and millers couldn't grind wheat into flour.

Meanwhile, those Narragansetts who escaped the conflagration in the swamp were forced to evacuate their own territory and face the bitter cold without food or shelter. Vowing revenge on those who had murdered their families, the surviving warriors then joined Metacom's struggle, but they did so without their winter cache of food. Hunger would be their constant companion.[22]

The English victory over the Narragansetts had come at great cost, but was the first major break for the colonists after months of disasters. The defeat of the Narragansetts was also a major setback for Metacom's hopes for a pan-Native front against the English and was followed by a second setback: Metacom could not persuade the Mohawks to join the uprising, despite his trip to the colony of New York to negotiate with them. (The Mohawks were allies of New York governor Edmund Andros and, toward the end of the war, actively supported the English.)

How did the relationship between Ninigret and Thomas Stanton change after the Great Swamp Fight, in which Stanton's own sons had fought and in which so many of Ninigret's relatives had been burned alive? Before that battle, they had shared a hope that Ninigret could deliver the refugees, or even convince the other Narragansetts to abstain from fighting the English; perhaps they had hoped that by working together they could achieve a lasting peace. Now everything had changed. What pain, what doubts, must Ninigret have felt, knowing that his relatives were murdered in the swamp while he was still courted, fed, and attended by the English, by Thomas Stanton? Did he look at Stanton differently? Did he feel tainted by their association? What, if anything, could they share after that? Was he tempted to join the rebels, and avenge so many deaths, as the surviving Narragansetts had done, despite what he surely now knew of the terror of English power, or did he accept the consequences of his own and the other sachems' choices?

The new year, 1676, began with a string of Native victories in Massachusetts, Plymouth Colony, and Rhode Island. It still appeared that they would win. The colonial army regrouped in January, and once again numbered 1,000 men, with 315 from Connecticut under Major Treat, including George Denison and perhaps Thomas Stanton's sons. They passed through Stonington into Narragansett country, and then farther north into the Nipmuck region, accompanied by Uncas and the Mohegans, in pursuit of the Narragansetts, but the campaign was largely ineffective. It was later remembered as "the hungry march," for supplies ran out and the men had to kill and eat some of their horses. The Narragansett war chief Canonchet, now the effective military leader of the uprising, took advantage of the withdrawal of most of the colonial troops to the western front. He attacked and burned six English settlements, killing men, women, and children, and his forces ambushed and wiped out two different Massachusetts companies of fifty men each. It was said that his exultant warriors proudly displayed more than two hundred scalps.[23]

To counter these incursions, Stanton's neighbour and relative by marriage, Capt. George Denison, enlisted a company of seventy-five dragoons – mounted volunteers and regular soldiers each armed with musket and sword – and called together a hundred Pequot and Mohegan allies, who travelled on foot. Relying on information received from his Indian spies, Denison and Capt. James Avery carried out three raids that winter, against Narragansett villages. In the third of these excursions, launched March 28, 1676, they captured Canonchet. This success was later considered one of the great exploits of the war and cemented Denison's reputation as "the most distinguished soldier of Connecticut in her early settlement, except Major John Mason [who as a captain had been the Puritans' hero in the Pequot War]."[24]

Canonchet was then about thirty-six years of age and a son of Miantonomo, who, as we've seen, had been killed by Uncas with the approval of the colonial authorities in 1644. The murder of his father had made him understandably hostile to the colonists, and when he joined Metacom in rebellion he became a formidable enemy. But early that spring, spies reported to Denison that Canonchet and thirty warriors had gone on an expedition into the Pawcatuck Valley to gather seed corn for planting. Without waiting to muster the rest of his troops, Denison had set off with forty-seven English soldiers and about fifty Indians and commenced his attack. Most of the Narragansetts fled, leaving Canonchet almost entirely alone. The Indian allies of the English and a few English soldiers pursued him, and as he saw his pursuers gaining on him, he threw off first his blanket, then his silver-laced coat and belt of peage (wampumbelt, the insignia of his rank). As he forded a river he fell and wet his gun, "which so embarrassed him in his flight that he was soon overtaken," first by Monopoide, a Pequot, and then by twenty-one-year-old Robert Stanton. Canonchet was tackled, thrown, and quickly bound.

Being questioned by the young man [Robert Stanton], whom he personally knew, about the treaty of peace, between the English and Indians, and
not wishing to recognize the authority of his youthful inquisitor, he
looked upon him with lofty and defiant contempt and said you are a child,
you cannot understand matters of war; let your brother, Capt. John
Stanton, or your chief, Capt. George Denison, come, then I will answer.
But when the officers whom he had requested to see came up, he refused
to enter into any negotiations with them, so he was brought a prisoner to
Stonington, where a council of war was held, which he declined to recognize, and after his absolute refusal to enter into and abide by a treaty of
peace with the English . . . he was condemned and ordered to be shot, and
when told of his fate he said that "he liked it well, and should die before
his heart had grown soft or he had said anything unworthy of himself."[25]

His execution was approved by George Denison, who ordered that he die
without being tortured and, according to Indian custom, at the hands of
three sachems of rank as high as his own. These were Uncas's son Owaneco,
and two Pequot sachems (probably Cassacinamon and Momoho) who were
the nearest to his own rank among the conquerors.

That all might share in the Glory of destroying so great a Prince, . . . the
Pequods shot him, the Mohegans cut off his Head and quartered his
Body, and Ninnicrofts Men made the fire and burned his Quarters, and
as a Token of their Love and Fidelity to the english, presented his Head
to the Council at Hartford.[26]

Denison's men also killed the forty-three Narragansett warriors they had
captured.

In the weeks following the capture of Canonchet, the Native campaign
began to falter, and within six months the power of Metacom was broken.
Hunger, disease, severe losses in battle, successful English defences of a
couple of Connecticut River towns, growing English military superiority
with the help of friendly Indians, and their greater depth of resources, discouraged Metacom's warriors, who began to "scatter about in small
Parties, doing what Mischief they could." Small groups of disillusioned
Indians began giving themselves up to the colonists or Indian allies. In a
letter from Stonington was a report that "about two hundred Indians had

sent to Vncas, signifying they were willing to come ine [surrender], if might have assurance of their lives," and Stanton was sent to investigate. Thomas Stanton acted with Maj. Fitz-John Winthrop (brother of Wait Winthrop) and Hon. Samuel Willys as a commission to negotiate peace, if possible, between the English and Indians in April 1676, but apparently their efforts went nowhere.[27]

Stanton was also kept busy trying to dampen old rivalries between the colonists' allies, which continued to flare and impede the war effort, and intensified as the opportunities for plunder increased. For example, when Ninigret accused the Mohegans of taking wampum from his wife and brother-in-law, Thomas Stanton backed his complaint, and warned the authorities of "Uncas' pride and aroganzie and covtiousness," adding that "it will bee well if hee prove not as bad as Phillip to the English. . . ." On another occasion Stanton and his son-in-law, Rev. James Noyes, persuaded Ninigret to send a peace offering to the Pequots as a sign of their willingness to forget past wrongs; they were even persuaded to carry the offering to the Pequots themselves, but to no avail. In May, Stanton was granted "20 pounds for his good service and expense in securing the fidelity of Chief Ninigret to the English and as partial recompense for damages of war to his estate."[28]

In May, the colonists won their most decisive victory; they heard of a large encampment of hungry Sokokis (allies of Metacom) who had gone to the falls about five miles north of Deerfield, Massachusetts, to fish. With their warriors absent, those at the site were unprepared for attack. With no militia units available, English garrison forces and volunteers – men and boys – from various Connecticut Valley towns were mustered, under the command of Capt. William Turner. Two of my relations, Benjamin Edwards of Northampton and John Chase, son of Aquila Chase and Ann Wheeler and grandson of John Wheeler, were among those who responded to this call. The English marched through the night to attack the unsuspecting camp and fired on the sleeping Natives – mainly women, children, and old people – at first light. The Sokokis mistook the English for their most dreaded enemy, the Mohawks, and panicked. The English then slaughtered "several hundreds of them upon the Place," destroyed all the ammunition and food, "demolisht Two Forges they had to mend their Armes," and generally created mayhem.[29] The survivors were driven into the turbulent river and over the forty- or fifty-foot drop of the falls – known since as Turner's Falls.

Metacom's warriors counter-attacked swiftly and with considerable casualties. The militia were ambushed as they retreated, and thirty-eight Hadley and Northampton men were killed by the first volley from the enemy. The English scattered in a disorganized rout as men fled through the woods towards Deerfield. Metacom's warriors circled along the flank, killing at least forty of the men, about one-quarter of their number. Some of the militia lost their way – one sixteen-year-old boy was wounded in the leg and wandered alone for two days before reaching Hatfield. Captain Turner was shot as he tried to cross the Green River and was left to die; my relation John Chase later helped bury his commander.[30]

The battle of Turner's Falls resulted in many English casualties, but it was far worse for Metacom's forces. The slaughter of their relatives was a devastating blow from which Metacom's followers never recovered. More and more of them were demoralized and starving, and as they began arguing among themselves many dispersed.

Connecticut organized a new force of 440 Englishmen and aboriginal auxiliaries under Maj. John Talcott, with instructions to "kill and destroy [Metacom's warriors], according to the utmost power God shall give you."[31] Capt. George Denison commanded the company raised in New London country. This army killed many Narragansetts and then moved up the Connecticut River to the upper towns, destroying food caches without finding many warriors before returning in early June.

As more and more of Metacom's men surrendered or fled, the colonies became confident that complete victory was theirs. On July 3, Connecticut troops killed or captured 67 more Narragansetts, making a total of 238 in only two days. But the English also became more and more ruthless, massacring women and children almost without qualm, sating their appetite for revenge by looking on as their Native allies tortured their captives. English optimism was strengthened by news of a series of Mohawk attacks on Metacom's forces, which terrified and further demoralized the enemy. Finally, on August 12, 1676, Metacom himself was killed in a swamp on his ancestral lands in the Mount Hope peninsula, not far from where the war had begun. He was shot, beheaded, and quartered. His head was sent to the governor and council in Boston and was later mounted on a pole in Plymouth, where it remained for decades. His death marked the end of Native resistance in southern New England.

For the rest of the summer, the English forces rounded up the starving remnants of their once formidable enemy, who, "thus dispersed several Ways, were strangely confounded" by their sudden defeat. Hundreds of Wampanoags, Narragansetts, and Nipmucks were sold as slaves in Spain, Portugal, Bermuda, the West Indies, the Azores, and Virginia, including Metacom's wife and child. John Eliot and Daniel Gookin argued that captives, and especially children, should be placed with Christian families as servants. The General Court eventually agreed to this, and in May 1677 devised a system to ensure that Native youth bonded as servants "be instructed in civility & Christian religion" by their masters. The court also decreed that these children remain in servitude until the age of twenty-four, at which time they would gain their freedom.[32] But by the time this legislation was enacted, many had already been sold out of the region.

Certainly my Stanton ancestors and perhaps others were involved in this trade: Thomas Stanton's son, Captain John Stanton, "gained much on the sale of captives."[33]

Because the English considered the Indians subjects of the colonies, they thought of those who surrendered as rebels who had committed treason and murder, not as prisoners of war from other nations. Hence they deserved execution. As James Drake has pointed out, in selling many who were not leaders into slavery instead, the Puritans believed they were dispensing mercy – as well as making a profit – because slavery was considered akin to banishment. Also, slavery solved the problem of what to do with the former rebels and eliminated any potential for ungodly idleness.[34] Yet the enslavement of so many Natives was also possible because they were non-Christians, and therefore, in the eyes of the colonists, inferior.

By the time the war ended, Thomas Stanton and Ninigret must have been very weary old men. Neither of them had been young at its outset, and the events of the war must surely have aged them. They had seen too many young men die, too many women and children massacred, too much blood and fear. Thomas Stanton was probably ill, for he would die within the year at age sixty-two. Ninigret lived long enough to provide a haven to many Narragansetts and some Wampanoags, but he saw his own power greatly diminished. For the power of all the Native nations in New England was now broken; from the time of the arrival of the English, it had been the threat of combined action by independent nations that had given the Indians – even those who supported the English – their power, and that was gone. The world that Stanton and Ninigret had known and in which they had prospered, the society in which they had needed to convey information to each other, assess motives, and manoeuvre within their relationship, had been destroyed. There was a void where their old purposes had been.

CHAPTER
12

Among the Ruins

The war was over. As my ancestors and their neighbours surveyed their smoking ruins, tended their injured, and buried their dead, the full meaning of what had happened began to filter through their consciousness. Everything had changed. The physical landscape had been utterly transformed and was tainted now by memories of fire and violence. Nearly all that was English had been destroyed; all that the English had arduously tamed was wild again. Almost one of every ten men in the English colonies was dead and huge numbers of non-combatants, too; no one knows how many English had lost their lives, perhaps 800, perhaps 2,500. There were widows and orphans everywhere. One colonist wrote, "Every person, almost [in the colony] lost a relation or near friend, and the people in general were exasperated."[1] New England had become a land haunted by blood and ghosts – by history.

Twenty-five colonial towns had been pillaged, and more than half of these had been burned to the ground, resulting in a loss of over a thousand homes. The Crown's agent, Edmund Randolph, reported in October 1676, "losses of 600 men and 150,000 pounds, there having been about twelve hundred houses burnt, eight thousand head of Cattle great and small, killed, and many thousand bushels of wheat, pease, and other grain burnt . . . and upward of three thousand Indians, men, women, and children destroyed,

213

who if well managed would have been very serviceable to the English; which makes all manner of labour dear."[2]

The war affected the colonists profoundly, especially in the frontier areas. The towns along the Connecticut River had been hit especially hard, as they had been the scene of most of the fighting and had suffered the greatest number of casualties. Many towns, such as Northfield and Deerfield, were abandoned altogether, while others absorbed large numbers of refugees. In Hampshire County alone, 225 people lost their lives in three years. In Deerfield, over one-third of the adult men had been killed at Bloody Brook – fourteen men in all, leaving nine widows and over forty fatherless children.

This was the world that a new generation of my ancestors inherited. For example, Hannah Edwards, whose grandfather Alexander Edwards had initially settled in Springfield in 1640, was born during those years of terror. Her family had huddled for safety within the palisade erected to protect the centre of the town of Northampton, enduring and surviving two attacks by enemy Indians. Her uncle, Benjamin Edwards, participated in the massacre at Turner's Falls, where twelve of thirty-one Northampton men died. In the years 1675 and 1676, forty-three townsfolk died, many of them killed by Indians. Hannah undoubtedly grew up on the hatred and bitterness of those around her, for that town, like Springfield, had enjoyed excellent relations with the neighbouring Native people for at least a generation before the war – at least so the English had thought. Now they spoke of the "faithless and deceitful Friendship" of "those perfidious, cruel and hellish monsters."[3]

Likewise Benjamin Janes, her future husband, would grow up in a world disordered and distorted by fear and hatred. Benjamin was three years old when his two teenage half-brothers, Ebenezer and Jonathan, had been among those killed in the fields outside of Squakheag (also called Northfield) on September 2, 1675, as mentioned earlier. (His father, William Janes, had been one of the town's founders, and had previously been one of the original settlers at New Haven, Connecticut, in 1638.) The rest of the terrified townspeople – including Benjamin, his parents, and other siblings – had barricaded themselves inside their fort and cowered there for days, unable even to retrieve the bodies of their dead, while Metacom's forces killed their cattle, destroyed their grain, and burned every building outside the fort. The first soldiers sent to rescue them were massacred on the way; they were not rescued until September 7, when they were finally able to abandon the town they had only recently established and were escorted to Northampton under heavy guard.[4] A three-year-old might not remember these experiences, but surely their impact on Benjamin and his family persisted for years and formed the foundation of his attitudes toward Native Americans throughout his life. All through his childhood, and that of Hannah Edwards and others of their generation, the people around them mourned their dead and struggled to rebuild their communities, in many cases starting all over again.

So many people were poor again, and the colonists were left with a huge long-lasting deficit that was still not paid off when a new war, King William's War, broke out in 1689. The authorities greatly increased taxes, which would prove hard to collect, as the colonists' incomes would not recover their 1675 levels until 1775. In fact, they would not exceed pre-1676 levels until after 1815. Those who had fought in the colonial army or militia with hopes of plunder were also cruelly disappointed. Massachusetts did compensate its soldiers, but it took fifty years to distribute the promised land, and all the governments were flooded with petitions for various sorts of compensation by veterans. Among my ancestors, Moses Chase's son Sam claimed land in Buxton, Maine, for his father's service in King Philip's War. John Wheeler was due wages for his service. John Chase and Thomas Chase petitioned the town of Newbury for a thousand acres of land, but there was no action on these claims for many years; only in 1727 was a committee appointed to survey the land in question. Connecticut was almost as bad, granting land to veterans only in 1701. Robert and Daniel Stanton received land in the cedar swamp where the Narragansetts had been defeated, as did Capt. John Stanton and Samuel Stanton. Although Thomas Stanton, Sr., had been rewarded earlier for his success in keeping Ninigret from joining Metacom, he died in 1677 at the war's end; his will – and therefore the rights to all the property he had amassed – was not settled for forty years, in 1718, because of challenges to various deeds, family disputes, and other problems.[5]

Of course, the military heroes of the war were handsomely and quickly rewarded. Capt. George Denison, the father-in-law to three of Thomas Stanton's children, was honoured with large land grants by the Colony of Connecticut and the Town of Stonington. Owaneco, the Mohegan sachem (and son of Uncas), who had led Denison's Indian allies, held a great feast in Denison's honour and presented him with two thousand acres of tribal lands. Denison tore down his old stockade and built a fine new "mansion

house," where he gave famous dinner parties to friends, family, old com-
rades in arms, and even sachems, until his death in 1694. That house
burned in 1713, but the new house, which incorporated some of the old
timber, still stands today.[6]

The various colonies were largely disappointed in their hopes of conquest from the war, for they failed to expand their territories. The "rights
of conquest" over the Narragansett country, which at first had seemed to be
the great real-estate prize of the war, were later nullified by the courts
and disputed until 1724. Although Massachusetts Colony gained control
over Nipmuck territory in what is now northern and central Massachusetts,
it lost Maine. Plymouth Colony failed to retain even the territory of
Metacom's village of Sowams, where the war started, and within a dozen
years Plymouth Colony was absorbed into Massachusetts. Worse, the New
England colonies also lost their independence from England, for the British
Crown took advantage of the situation to reassert its authority, cancelling
the Massachusetts charter, and installing Sir Edmund Andros as the governor of the Dominion of New England. Speaking of the war, Andros himself
said, "The advantages thereby were none, the disadvantages very greate
and like to be more, even in the loss of said Indians."[7]

The lot of "said Indians" was far, far worse than that of even the worst-
off colonist, and, to my ancestors and their neighbours, that must have
seemed only just. Sherburne F. Cook has estimated that, of the approximately 11,600 rebels, between 5,160 and 6,880 died, approximately 1,000
were sold into West Indian slavery, and another two thousand fled the
region – a total loss of 60 to 80 per cent. John Eliot's assistant Daniel
Gookin reported that almost half the praying Indians died in the war, and
the non-Christian allies of the English, such as the Mohegans, are believed
to have suffered equally heavy losses.[8]

This drastic change of fortune was very evident to my ancestors.
Puritan historian William Hubbard reprinted the following comment in his
postscript to his history of the war:

> Thomas Stanton and his son Robert, who having a long Time lived
> amongst them, and best acquainted with their Language and Manners of
> any in New-England, do affirm, that to their Knowledg the Narhaganset
> Sachims, before the late Troubles, had two thousand fighting Men under
> them, and nine hundred Arms; yet are they at this Day so broken and
> scattered, that there is none of them left on that side of the Country,

unless some few, not exceeding seventy in Number, that have sheltered themselves under the Inhabitants of Road-Island, as a Merchant of that Place worthy of Credit lately affirmed to the Writer thereof. It is considerable by what Degrees they have been consumed and destroyed.[9]

Those who fled New England created new multi-tribal communities elsewhere, such as at Schaghticoke (later known as Stockbridge) in the upper Hudson Valley, which soon included Sokokis, Nonotucks, Pocumtucks, Agawams, Pennacooks, Narragansetts, Nipmucks, Wampanoags and others. Cowass, at the great oxbow of the Connecticut River in Vermont, would become another melting-pot settlement, and one that some of my relations would later visit as Indian captives. Many refugees – now confirmed and bitter enemies of the English – headed farther north, to Canada, where they became willing allies of the French, many of them joining communities around the Jesuit mission villages, such as Chambly, Sillery, and St. Francis, near Montreal.

Even many of the Abenakis and Pennacooks, who had remained neutral during the war but who had still been mistreated by the English, were forced by hunger and fear of Mohawk attacks to flee to Canada. By about 1686 the Pennacooks had sold their remaining lands in New Hampshire and begun to disperse. Most went with their sachem Wannalancet to St. Francis, Quebec, others to New York and Maine and even the Midwest, while some remained in New Hampshire and Vermont.

The war had destroyed the old New England society that had consisted of both English and Native Americans. As James Drake has commented, a new society, with a fundamentally different form, took its place. In 1670, Native Americans had accounted for approximately 25 per cent of the population of New England; by 1680, they had plummeted to between 8 or 12 per cent. By 1750, the visible Native American population of New England was a few thousand.

If there was one thing that Hannah Edwards and Benjamin Janes learned as they grew up, it was that Indians could never, ever be trusted. This was now unquestioned dogma and the New England colonies adopted new policies toward the remaining Native population to ensure that they would never again be obliged to trust them; their own safety was paramount. A sharply demarcated frontier now separated English and Indian settlements. Even Indian allies were restricted to their remaining tribal lands, which

were put under close supervision and hemmed in by English communities
– these became an early form of reservation. In Massachusetts, any Natives
not serving as servants or apprentices in English towns were forced to live
at four of the old praying towns, Natick, Punkapaog, Hassanemesit, or
Wamesit, "where they may be continually inspected." Although approximately 40 per cent of John Eliot's Massachusett converts had survived the
war with their faith in the Christian God intact, the old praying towns were
no longer restricted to believers – praying Indians and pagan supporters of
Metacom were now thrown in together. In both the praying towns and the
new multi-tribal communities outside New England, Natives from different
tribes were jumbled all together and had to reconstitute their identities.

The residents of the remaining praying towns eked out their living on the
margins of English society. At least once each year, the authorities compiled
a list of all the residents of each town, so that the government could monitor
them, and those who would not comply with the new restrictions on their
freedom were incarcerated in their local House of Correction. Under such
circumstances, many traumatized survivors became dispirited, and their
communities fractured under the strain. The four surviving praying towns
suffered an ever-dwindling land base; the number of church members
declined as many of the inhabitants turned to drink rather than God. As
Francis Jennings commented, their transformation into a subject people
now appeared to be complete.

Only a few Puritans remained in contact with them, for most of the relationships that had bound the region's Native and English groups together
had been broken. John Eliot continued to evangelize after the war, but he
was in his seventies by then, and no young missionaries of his stature took
his place. Once the remaining Natives were confined to the praying towns,
the English lost interest in Christianizing them, and Indian missions were
never revived in Massachusetts. Nonetheless, Eliot persisted in his humanitarian efforts. In 1685 he wrote to Robert Boyle in England, begging him
to locate and arrange the return to America of some Native captives who
had been dumped at Tangier by a slave trader. When he became too old to
proselytize at the praying towns himself, he proposed that African servants
should be sent to him for religious instruction. One of his last recorded acts
was to deed, in 1689, land for "the maintenance, support, and encouragement of a school and schoolmaster at that part of Roxbury commonly
called Jamaica or the Pond Plain, for the teaching and instructing the children of that end of the town (altogether with such Indians and negroes as

shall or may come to the said school)." Shortly before his death in 1690 he is reported to have said, "There is a cloud, a dark cloud upon the work of the gospel among the poor Indians." His last prayer was "The Lord revive and prosper that work, and grant it may live when I am dead."[10]

The older generation of people like Thomas Stanton, George Denison, Roger Williams, and others who had formed friendships with Native Americans, negotiated with them, learned their ways, and protested their ill treatment, were soon dead or dying. There is a certain poignancy in Richard Anson Wheeler's description of Thomas Stanton shortly before his death: "After the close of King Philip's War, and when he had become an old man, he was frequently visited by Sachems of various tribes, who manifested for him unabated confidence and esteem. Uncas, in his old age, went from Mohegan to Pawcatuck for Mr. Stanton to write his Will, taking with him a train of his noblest warriors to witness the same, giving to the occasion all the pomp and pageantry of savage royalty."[11] A story that has been passed down in the Stanton family is that the Mohegans stayed and partied with the Stantons for three days.

Native leaders like Uncas and Ninigret, who had chosen alliance with the English as their best survival strategy, now found themselves with fewer and less powerful English allies. Even Uncas, who lived quietly and remained on good terms with the Stantons, the Rogerses, the Masons, and many other Connecticut families, and of whom Maj. John Mason in his memoirs wrote, "He was a great friend and did us much service," only managed to keep Mohegan land safe from English predations during his lifetime (he died about 1683), though he managed to keep power longer than all his rivals.[12]

As Hannah Edwards, Benjamin Janes, and others of their generation grew up, they absorbed the image of the Indian savage that war had apparently confirmed, and which now became a racist stereotype. The word "heathen" continued to be used to identify Native people for another half-century in New York and Pennsylvania, but in New England, the term of choice was now "savage," and my ancestors would have used it and believed all that the word implied. Fear and hatred of alien races was becoming embedded in American culture; "Indians," as Michael Puglisi comments, had become symbols of everything alien to English civilization and Puritan spirituality – the scapegoats for Puritan fears, the projections of their own desires, guilt, and aggression.[13]

It is worth taking the time to explore this notion of "savagery" further, for, although the war-time atrocities of the Indians are well documented (as opposed to those of the English), there were many aspects of seventeenth-century English society that from today's vantage point appear equally "savage."

Some widely reported Native customs, such as the prolonged ritual tortures of war captives sometimes practiced by the Iroquois and other groups – including applying brands, embers, and hot metals to various parts of the body, putting hot sand and embers on a scalped head, tearing out hair and beard, setting fire to cords bound about the body, cutting off one joint of the body after another, or driving skewers into finger stumps, all while forcing the victim to dance – appear to have been far less common among the Native people of New England, except in direct retaliation against the Iroquois. In fact the Iroquois were especially feared by the aboriginal peoples of New England because of these practices.[14]

Also, as James Axtell and others have argued, European societies in the sixteenth, seventeenth, and early-eighteenth centuries were far more coercive than the Native nations of New England, with physical punishment the necessary tool. In Europe, a tradition of torture went back to at least Greek and Roman times and perhaps reached its zenith during the Inquisition; the rack was not abolished till 1640. Burning at the stake and many ingenious forms of torture were inflicted by Church and State on thousands of Europeans for religious and other crimes, chiefly to obtain information on treason or heresy, and also to extract "confessions," so that the soul of the victim could be saved. In contrast to torture in Native societies, where captured warriors from other nations usually provided the victims (although some Christian Mohawks were tortured after returning to their home – and pagan – villages), European nations tortured mainly their own citizens.[15]

And then there were the punishments. Col. Daniel Axtell received the following treatment in 1660 for his part in the beheading of King Charles I in London: he was "drawne upon a hardle" to the "Tyborne gallow tree," where he was "hanged, cut downe, his body quickly opened and his intrealls burnt; hee was quartred and brought back to Newgate Prison to be boyled and then, as the [nine] others, [his head] to be sett up as his Majesty pleased." In the mid-seventeenth century, a man who slightly wounded Louis XV with a penknife had his right hand, which had held the knife, consumed in burning oil before lead and resin were poured into the wounds; then he was torn apart by four horses, while the lords and ladies of the court as well as the general populace surrounded the scaffold.[16] Although these were both punishments for high treason, and thus were particularly savage, they give some idea of the imaginative brutality employed. And, as we have already seen, English forces engaged in numerous instances of barbarity and terrorism during military campaigns in Ireland.

In New England, violence to the body served as both a form of punishment and a way to terrorize the indigenous population. When the celebrated soldier Miles Standish wished to intimidate the Massachusett Indians who threatened the fledgling Plymouth Colony in 1623, he killed their leader and set his head on the top of the Plymouth fort with a blood-soaked flag. Such treatment was not reserved only for Indians – if Quakers returned to Massachusetts after having been banished, they would be whipped and have their ears cut off. If they repeated this offence a third time, they would have their tongues pierced by hot irons. Some were hanged on Boston Common. As historian James Axtell has remarked, "In the seventeenth century, the standards of English Justice and Indian revenge were never far apart, and the objects of both had little chance of survival."[17]

Yet to the colonists who survived King Philip's War and their children, the savagery of Native Americans was what set them apart from Englishmen. Ugly expressions of racial animosity became commonplace. In increasingly aggressive language, colonial leaders advocated the elimination of Indians who could not be directly controlled. "As long as any hostile bands remain unconquered," said Rev. Increase Mather in 1676, "we cannot enjoy such perfect peace as in the years which are past [i.e., before the war]." In his *Magnalia Christi Americana* (1702), Cotton Mather argued that "the most scrupulous persons in the world must own, that it must be the most unexceptionable piece of justice in the world for to extinguish them." Acts of violence directed against Natives were rarely punished or even censured; on the contrary, they were often openly applauded.[18]

The Puritan association of witches and Indians was greatly strengthened after the war. When, in August 1676, a violent storm damaged much property and caused injuries, many colonists believed a boast by some Indians "that they had caused it by their Pawwaw." Many of those testifying in witchcraft trials, who claimed to have had contact with the devil, described spectres that were "tawny colour." According to Cotton Mather, one of those executed for witchcraft at Salem had confessed that French-Canadians and Indian sagamores [sachems] had been present at their chief "witch-meetings," at which they conspired to ruin New England.

Englishmen attributed supernatural evil powers to Catholic priests, just as they did to Native American shamans, viewing both as spiritual enemies bent on subverting the Puritans' godly community in America.[19]

But however much the Puritans made scapegoats of Native Americans, the colonists were also left with a conviction that God had punished them for their own sins. Some believed that their leniency toward Quakers was the reason for God's anger. Others began to question their beliefs and practices and searched for signs of degeneracy within their communities, such as witchcraft, ungodliness, and lack of discipline. In September 1679, a synod of Puritan ministers was held to enquire into the causes of God's displeasure against New England and to reverse the general decline in godliness and religious zeal. For the rest of the century, in countless jeremiads and homilies, Puritan ministers denounced contemporary evils and transgressions and tried to re-invigorate the religious mission into the wilderness.

In their view, the colonists had not learned any spiritual lessons from the experiences of King Philip's War. As time passed, the clergy noticed that many people were all too "apt to forget the fears and sorrows which have been upon us," and neglected to observe the Sabbath, took excessive pride in their personal appearance, and dressed in a "flaunting" manner. In 1676, the county court of Hampshire along the Connecticut River charged sixty-eight people from five towns, some for wearing silk (by law, one had to have an estate worth £200 to wear silk hoods or scarves), and others for long hair and "other extravagances."[20] "Revelling" and "rioting," swearing, fornicating, and being too preoccupied with acquiring real estate were other common sins.

Some ministers, like Increase Mather, blamed the younger generation for New England's woes. He wrote that God had no reason to punish New England with "so dreadfull a judgment, untill the Body of the first Generation was removed, and another Generation risen up which hath not so pursued, as ought to have been, the blessed design of their Fathers, in following the Lord into this Wilderness."[21] But it was not just the younger generation that was straying: in 1682 the errant and aging Capt. George Denison was fined 15 shillings for not attending public worship.

It was in this context of declining piety that Mary Rowlandson wrote the first of what was to become a flourishing literary genre in New England: the captivity narrative. Published in 1682, *The Sovereignty and Goodness of God* related the story of the bloody Indian attack on the Plymouth town of

Rehoboth in 1675, and her weeks of captivity, as a warning to those straying
from religion. "My conscience did not accuse me of unrighteousness toward
one or other: yet I saw how in my walk with God I had been a careless crea-
ture."[22] Her account, laced with biblical quotations, aimed to be morally and
spiritually uplifting and to inspire godliness. But such captivity narratives
– and Rowlandson's was only the first of many – reinforced the colonists'
tendency to see Native people in allegorical terms, as devils tormenting the
faithful or heathen Canaanites, obstructing God's chosen people. With
fewer and fewer New Englanders having day-to-day contacts with Native
people, let alone friendships, there was little to counteract this perspective.

Over the next quarter-century, the effects of all these changes of attitude
and circumstance deeply affected even those Native groups, such as the
Mohegans, who had most loyally supported the English in peace and war.
While Uncas lived, they had continued to enjoy their lands unrestrained
and maintained their friendly relations with many of the English families
of southeastern Connecticut, including my Stanton, Rogers, and Harris
ancestors. Upon the death of that extremely able politician, the fortunes of
the Mohegans began to slide. His son Owaneco became an alcoholic, and
unscrupulous Englishmen took advantage of him: in an intoxicated state he
sold a large tract of Mohegan hunting grounds to settlers at Colchester –
where my Ransom and Harris ancestors later moved – for five or six
shillings. The Mohegans tried to get this land back, but even with the help
of Maj. Samuel Mason (another son of the John Mason who attacked the
Pequots), they were unsuccessful.

Owaneco became destitute, and often visited the nearby settlements
begging for food. One of the colonists furnished him with a card on which
was written:

> Owaneco, king, his queen doth bring,
>   To beg a little food;
> As they go along his friends among
>   To try how kind, how good.

> Some pork, some beef, for their relief,
>   And if you can't share bread,
> She'll thank you for pudding, as they go a gooding,
>   And carry it on her head.[23]

In 1710, just before his death, Owaneco granted a sweeping deed to John Livingston, Robert Denison, and two of my relations, Samuel Rogers, Jr., and James Harris, for all the Mohegan lands between New London and Norwich that he had not previously granted or sold. The property comprised many thousands of acres. Owaneco reserved only a small portion to himself and the tribe in the eastern part of the area known as Montville, along the Thames River. The price was only £50. At the same time a deed of feoffment, or trust, was executed in favour of Gordon Saltonstall, Capt. John Mason (grandson of the original John Mason), Maj. John Livingston, Capt. Daniel Fitch, and Capt. John Stanton (son of Thomas Stanton). By it, the eastern reserved tract was to be held forever by the Mohegan tribe, under the regulations of the feoffees and their successors, "so long as there shall be any Mohegans found or known or alive in the world" (except for some small parcels in the possession of others, which were to be confirmed to them). This deed was signed by Owaneco and several of the chief men of the tribe. These proceedings aroused the ire of the inhabitants of New London, who regarded the Indian land as granted to them by an act of addition to the town, passed by the General Court in May 1703 and expressly guaranteed by their patent. The town tried to prosecute Livingston and his associates for breach of law. The court cases dragged on for sixty years, and arguments to benefit the Indians were basically a pretence for a struggle among various whites vying for Indian land.

When Owaneco died in 1710, he was succeeded by his young and intemperate son Cesar amid disputes over whether chief authority was vested in Ben Uncas, Cesar's guardian, or Cesar himself. The Connecticut authorities and some of my Harris relatives became more involved in arguments over the sachemship and intervened to support their own puppet candidates: "the Connecticut assembly and the English overseers (overseers were first appointed in 1719) supported a particular lineage of hereditary sachems who sold, leased and rented tribal lands to whites for individual profit."[24] The Mohegans continued to lose more and more land, without compensation.

The Pequots faced a similar erosion of their lands and sovereignty. Robin Cassacinamon remained leader of the Mashantucket Pequots until he died in 1692. Other nominal chiefs followed, but most affairs were handled by overseers appointed by the legislature – the successors to Thomas Stanton and George Denison. The Mashantucket reservation was

The 1629 seal of the Massachusetts Bay Colony is a wishful depiction of a Native American appealing to English Puritans to "Come over and help us." Reproduced by courtesy of the Massachusetts Archives.

This cover of the 1938 commemorative magazine for the tercentenary of Hampton, New Hampshire, depicts the Puritan mythology of the early settlement of the Massachusetts Bay Colony. (Reproduced by courtesy of the New Hampshire Historical Society.)

OFFICIAL PICTORIAL MAGAZINE

1638 · *Hampton Tercentenary* · 1938

COMPLETE PROGRAM
25 Cents

John Eliot (1604–90) was the brother of my probable ancestor Jacob Eliot and the foremost English missionary in seventeenth-century New England. This 1659 portrait is by an unknown artist. (Reproduced by courtesy of the Huntington Library, Art Gallery and Botanical Gardens, San Marino, California.)

In August 1995, descendants of Thomas Stanton gathered at his house in Pawcatuck, Connecticut, for their second family reunion. Dating to the 1670s, this house was Thomas Stanton's third in the area, and has been owned continuously ever since by Stantons or members of the inter-married Davis family. (Photo courtesy of Bernard Stanton.)

This portrait of Ninigret II, the son of seventeenth-century Niantic sachem Ninigret, dates to c. 1681 and is by an unknown artist. My ancestor Thomas Stanton was instrumental in maintaining Ninigret's neutrality during King Philip's War, and quite likely knew and was perhaps visited by his son as well. (Reproduced by courtesy of the Museum of Art, Rhode Island School of Design, Providence, Rhode Island.)

Monument of the Great Swamp Fight of King Philip's War near West Kingston, Rhode Island. Many of my ancestors took part in this 1675 battle, which resulted in the slaughter of several hundred non-combatant Narragansett men, women, and children and the entry of the survivors into the war on the side of the Wampanoag sachem Metacom.

The author in front of the statue of Hannah Dustin, who, in 1697, became a Puritan heroine for scalping ten Abenakis, including six children. Dustin married a grand-son of my emigrant ancestor John Wheeler. The statue is on an island at the confluence of the Merrimack and Contoocook Rivers in New Hampshire.

Kahkewaquonaby, Reverend Peter Jones (1802–56) by the English portrait artist Matilda Jones, 1831. Jones and other Methodists converted many Ojibwa in Upper Canada. Elijah Harris, brother of my ancestor James Harris, was a colleague of this celebrated Ojibwa/Welsh missionary. (Reproduced by courtesy of the National Gallery of Canada, Ottawa.)

Portrait of Rev. James Evans. In 1834, Evans, the famous Methodist missionary and later inventor of Cree syllabics, was posted to the St. Clair mission in Sarnia, Ontario, where Elijah Harris was the teacher of a school for Ojibwa children. (Reproduced by courtesy of the United Church Archives.)

A dreamcatcher left at the stone in Sarnia, Ontario, that commemorates the establishment of the St. Clair mission by Thomas Turner in 1832. Although Elijah Harris was there before Turner, he is not mentioned. In various native traditions, dreamcatchers screen out the bad and let in the good.

(Above, left) My grandfather, Rev. Edwin Gardner Dunn Freeman. (Above, right) Cora Mandamin, an Ojibwa graduate of Cecilia Jeffrey Indian Residential School, who lived with my father's family in Winnipeg while studying nursing, and who became a family friend.

Conference of Chiefs and Headmen, Kenora, 1928. At this conference, numerous chiefs voiced their worries about the relocation of Cecilia Jeffrey Indian Residential School. A very young Walter Redsky is second from the right in the front row of children. Captain Frank Edwards, the Indian agent, is seated at the table, as is F. H. Paget, of the Department of Indian Affairs. (Reproduced by courtesy of the Lake of the Woods Museum, Kenora.)

My grandfather took this photograph of my grandmother and their children standing in the long grass in front of the abandoned Shoal Lake school in 1936 on one of their many camping trips to the region. My father is second from right.

John "Whit" Davis (right), of the Thomas Stanton Society and owner of Thomas Stanton's house in Pawcatuck, Connecticut, presents ancient Mohegan stone tools to Loretta Roberge, a representative of the Mohegan Sun Casino, Montville, Connecticut, during a 1998 reunion of Thomas Stanton's descendants.

eventually divided in two, leaving only 989 acres for the Pequots, while the rest was distributed to settlers.[25]

The generation that grew up in the years following King Philip's War would also have learned new attitudes to non-English peoples through their community's increasing acceptance of slavery, the incidence of which surged after the war, particularly with regard to African slaves. While there were some slaves in the Connecticut River towns, and it is known that Hannah's relative Nathaniel Edwards had a slave in the 1720s, southeast Connecticut and Rhode Island, where my Stanton and Denison ancestors lived, became the largest slave-holding section of New England, with the chief slave-holding plantations in Narragansett County – the vast majority of Americans involved in the slave trade came from Rhode Island. African slavery gradually replaced Indian slavery, as Native slaves escaped too easily. At first African slaves were brought from other English or Dutch colonies, but New England gradually became directly involved in the slave trade, and many families amassed fortunes as a result. By 1690 approximately one in every nine families in Boston owned at least one black slave, and by 1720, there were two thousand slaves in Boston, or one-sixth of the total population. In Connecticut, many descendants of Thomas Stanton and George Denison owned slaves, and many slaves took the name Stanton as their surname; by 1761, of a total population of 3,900 people in Stonington, 254 were African slaves, and 309 were Indians (presumably servants). Legend has it that Gen. Joe Stanton, one of Thomas's great-grandsons, who inherited Thomas Stanton's land in Charlestown, Rhode Island, had "forty horses and as many Slaves," but I've found no evidence to corroborate such a large number.[26]

The new generation of New England Puritans saw slaves and indentured servants bought and sold in the public market and inventoried as property. In the inventory of the effects of my ancestor James Rogers at the time of his death (1687) is listed "an Indian servant and his wife, a negro woman having about 3 years to serve valued at 8 pounds. Adam a Malotta [servant] about 3 years to serve (5 pounds), A Negro woman deaf and dumb (2 pounds)."[27]

When I visited Thomas Stanton's third house, built in Pawcatuck in the 1670s and still standing, I also saw the huge 442-pound boulder that commemorated a feat of Venture, an African slave well over six feet in height, in carrying a cask of molasses of equivalent weight. Venture's published narrative of his capture in Guinea, Africa, and his years of slavery under the Stantons and other masters documents his mistreatment (including his near-murder by Thomas Stanton's grandson of the same name) and his eventually successful efforts to obtain freedom for himself, his wife, and his children and to establish his own farm.[28] I saw the grave of Venture's son Cuff Stanton, who had been a house slave, then was freed by his father, but apparently continued living with and working for the Stantons, enjoying more amicable relations with them than his father had. He lived to be ninety-two and was buried off to the side in the Stanton–Davis family burial ground; the inscription on his tombstone reads: "We believe he was a Christian."

As Jill Lepore comments, the enslavement first of Native Americans and then of Africans was a "critical step in the evolution towards an increasingly racialized ideology of the differences between Europeans and Indians [and other non-white people]."[29] The differences that the first generation of settlers had interpreted as mainly cultural and owing to a lack of exposure to Christianity were now attributed increasingly to biology and race. After King Philip's War, more and more colonists suspected Native Americans were less than human, and this suspicion hardened into conviction in subsequent generations.

I cannot think of King Philip's War without feeling a profound sense of failure, as if it were my own. The naïveté that had prompted the Massachusetts Bay Colony to put "Come over and help us!" in an Indian's mouth on the company seal was gone forever, as was that of those Native American nations who invited the English to come and live in their midst to protect them from their enemies. The fragile trust that had formed the basis of Thomas Stanton's diplomatic efforts for forty years and of John Eliot's missions was broken, perhaps irretrievably.

Yet, despite the hatred and prejudice that now became the norm among the colonists, and most likely among my own ancestors, I know that not all of the colonists reacted in the same way or held such attitudes to the same degree. My Harris ancestors and relations, for example, continued in their friendship with various Mohegans. Sarah, the daughter of my ancestor Samuel Rogers and sister of my direct ancestor, Elizabeth, became a special friend of Owaneco. She and her husband James Harris (a brother of my ancestor Asa Harris, who married Elizabeth) received large grants of land from Owaneco, and James Harris also became "an especial favorite of the whole tribe" (at least until he became involved in a dispute between rival sachems). Indeed, the cordial relationship between the Mohegans and the Harrises persisted into the nineteenth century and was recorded by the family genealogist, Nathaniel Harris Morgan: "I have often when a boy heard my grandfather Nathaniel Harris [not a direct ancestor of mine] relate instances of this friendship and have seen many of the sad remnants of this tribe on their frequent and friendly visits to his old homestead in Salem [Connecticut], where they always found a welcome. My honored mother, in her early childhood, had acquired so considerable a knowledge of their dialect as to be able to converse with them, to a fair extent, in their own language."[30]

There were indeed such exceptions, but overall King Philip's War profoundly altered the relationship between Native Americans and the English – and hence between Native Americans and my ancestors. It was not a "race war," as we have seen, but it spawned a race hatred and a fortress mentality that would only begin to ease three hundred years later. Both groups had seen the worst of each other, and the conditions that might have allowed them to see the best in each other no longer existed. Hatred, fear, violence, and bigotry had prevailed over the possibility of peaceful co-existence. The generic "Indian" of stereotype – a despised and suppressed "shadow self" projected by the Western mind – now lived a murky, subterranean existence in English culture and memory and would obstruct Native–white relations for generations.[31] In spite of the crowing of the English and their conviction that the land was now rightfully theirs, they too had lost – or so it seems to me from my modern perspective.

PART II

ITERATIONS

THE JANES FAMILY

Six Generations
of the Janes Family

I. **William Janes**   married   (2) Hannah Broughton
    (1610–1690)   (1638–1716)

II. **Benjamin Janes** (1672–?)   m.   **Hannah Edwards**
                                                      (1675–1755)

III. **Seth Janes** (1713–?)   m.   Sarah Larabee (?–1801)

IV. **Elijah Janes** (1744–1826)   m.   Anna Hawkins (1742–?)

V. **Heman Janes** (1765–?)   m.   Abigail Burdick (?–?)

VI. Laura ("Lorainy") Janes   m.   Rev. James Harris (1785–1858)
    (1791–1873)

For subsequent generations, see the Harris genealogy in the Harris Family section.

CHAPTER
13

Hannah's Scalp

She was sitting against a log on the side of Pomeroy's mountain, wiping the blood from her forehead and eyes when they found her; no skin or hair left on the crown of her head. She fainted dead away and was carried in a litter to Northampton, and later to Wethersfield, where the famous Dr. Gersholm Bulkley tended her. Miraculously, she survived, and after a long convalescence gave birth to four more children, including my direct ancestor. She lived to the age of eighty.

I have tried to imagine the sound in the woods that morning, after the killing: first a great silence, and then the wind rustling through the tall trees. The air was cool still and the ground was wet and muddy – there were no buds yet, even in mid-May, for spring was very late that year in northern Massachusetts. I imagine it as one of those days when the sky was blue and absolutely clear of clouds, when the early-morning light was golden. Were there birds: the flash of a cardinal or scarlet tanager, the tapping of a woodpecker? Did all the other life of the forest carry on, as if nothing had happened, or were the forest's creatures shocked and frightened, too, by the unfamiliar sounds and smells, the aura of fear and death?

Did she sit in a kind of giddiness from the shock, a hyper-reality? Did time stretch and bend as she noticed each detail in all its sharpness: the black ant struggling then drowning in the scarlet rivulet that flowed down her dress and across the moss and scratchy lichens onto the rock beside her? Did she notice her shadow falling harmlessly on the muddy ground, the warmth of sun held in the bark of the log she sat on, the smell of mud and blood? Did she struggle to remain conscious through bouts of vertigo? Was she shaking? Did the fear still cling to her or had it worn off, only a frisson remaining from the charge, the primal terror?

Could she remember what had happened? Or did she sit in a dull stupor, numb, dumb, everything blotted out by intense, throbbing pain. They had murdered her children in front of her, first four-year-old Miriam and then eight-year-old Hannah, her namesake, back at Benoni Jones's house, smashed their skulls with their tomahawks, before tearing Nathan, her baby, out of her arms, and dashing his brains out against the doorpost. She had been forced to leave him lying there in a bloody, crumpled heap, could not stop to pick him up and say goodbye, for they had been marched through the woods, the women and boys and Benjamin, her husband, till he managed to escape. Did she know that he had managed to sound the alarm, or did it seem to her that he had simply disappeared and left her to her fate? It was because of him that the troops had given chase, and her captors had panicked, scalped her, and left her for dead.[1]

The story of the scalping of Hannah Janes (née Edwards) is difficult to talk about with any kind of balance. The issue of scalping is so political that some people, Native and white, deny that it was an indigenous practice at all and claim that the Europeans brought it over from Europe, in spite of overwhelming evidence to the contrary.[2] Aboriginal people resent the way scalping is taken as proof of Indian "savagery"; in fact the primal image of the "savage" is that of a scalping Indian – the stereotype of the warrior who engages in war to satisfy an instinctual love of violence persists to this day. Some whites use it to justify their fear of Native people and their sense of moral superiority. If you are trying to be politically correct, scalping is something you don't mention at all. But the true story of what happened to Hannah Janes is fraught with all the contradictions of the time.

She was twenty-nine years old that day when her world changed utterly. Four years earlier, in 1700, she and her husband Benjamin had moved from the thriving town of Northampton, Massachusetts, on the Connecticut River – where her grandfather had been one of the original "planters" – to the small frontier settlement of Pascommuck three miles away. The new settlement lay just northeast of Mount Tom where the Connecticut River sweeps around the point now known as Mount Nonotuck. There were six families living there: the Janes families of Benjamin and Hannah and of Benjamin's brother Samuel; the family of Benjamin's sister Ruth Janes, who had married John Searl; and also the families of Benoni Jones, John Webb, and Moses Hutchinson. The Janeses were certainly related to the Searl and Jones families, and may have been related to the others as well.

It was there, in the early morning of May 24, 1704, that the inhabitants of Pascommuck were "ambushed by Indians," only three months after fifty colonists had been massacred and a hundred taken into captivity in the more famous attack at nearby Deerfield, Massachusetts. For months the settlers of the Connecticut Valley had been living in fear – particularly those who, like Hannah, lived in outlying areas – never knowing when or where the next ambush would come. They knew full well what kind of treatment to expect in the event of Indian attack: the men of Pascommuck had most likely been among the forty men from Northampton and Hadley who had set off to Deerfield after seeing the "orange glow [of burning buildings] on the horizon" and hearing the first reports of atrocities. They had seen with their own eyes the devastated town, the dead and dying everywhere and, although they had skirmished with the enemy, they had not routed them. In the days following, many of the surviving women and children of Deerfield had been sheltered at Northampton.[3]

But now it was Pascommuck's turn. The story related in several Puritan sources is that a group of unspecified "Indians" on the verge of starvation had gone over to the Merrimack River in the hope of finding game or fish, without success. Returning westward they had planned to go to Westfield, but all the rivers had overflowed their banks and the Westfield River was impassable. In fact, the floods of that spring were the greatest recorded in New England up to that time, covering thousands of acres. The night before the attack, the Natives climbed Mount Tom to gain a good view of Pascommuck and found that the nearby land was almost entirely covered by water. The settlement was cut off from Northampton by the flooding, so its inhabitants were essentially defenceless.

According to some sources, the settlers were careless in protecting themselves from attack. Only the Benoni Jones house was surrounded by a low palisade, and no watch was kept. Just before dawn the inhabitants were wakened in their beds by the noise of their attackers rushing towards the house. The Indians got their guns into the gun-holes and shot Patience

Webb through the head when she looked out the window. Those in the house tried to defend themselves, but the Indians set fire to the building and the settlers surrendered. Most of the dazed settlers – the men and most of the children – were killed, but the women and youths were spared so that they could be taken to Canada, where they would be held for ransom.

Benjamin Janes alone of the men was spared to carry provisions. He was ordered to empty his straw bed and carry food in the casing. As the captives marched through the woods, he lagged a little behind, as if encumbered by his load, "and near a small ravine leading down to the water where he knew a boat was tied, he dropped quite suddenly his burden and escaping observation by the friendly covering of shady trees and running down leaped into the boat and pushed away toward the other side." He managed to paddle to Northampton and raise the alarm.[4]

Capt. John Taylor and a troop of cavalry immediately set off in pursuit. They had to detour around the extensive flood to intercept the Indians, who suddenly turned to kill and scalp as many of their hostages as they could before facing the militia – presumably so they could escape more easily. They tomahawked all the youths they had saved for captives, except for eight-year-old Elisha Searl, whose "quick wit prompted him to grab one of the Indian's packs and run with it to show that he would be no hindrance to them." The attackers were not able to scalp all of their victims, as the soldiers were too close. In the brief skirmish, Captain Taylor, "more bold than prudent," was killed by the Indians' first fire, and they made their escape over Pomeroy's mountain. There they tomahawked and scalped Hannah Janes and left her for dead.[5]

At least nine of the Janes family had been killed, including three or possibly four of Hannah's children; two of Samuel Janes's sons were stunned by tomahawk blows but not killed. Elisha Searl's father and three younger siblings died; his mother survived a "murderous" blow from a tomahawk and safely delivered her baby four months later. Mrs. Moses Hutchinson managed to escape before they had gone far. But Esther Jones, wife of Benoni Jones; Margaret Huggins, her eighteen-year-old niece; and Elisha Searl were forced to walk to Canada, where they joined other New England captives waiting to be "redeemed" – ransomed by either their families or their colonial government.

So far the story matches most such accounts: savage Indians attack defenceless settlers, brutally kill innocent women and children, and the militia ride to the rescue. And that is the version given in many Puritan accounts of the incident and in the genealogy of the Janes family. The attackers – "Indians" – are rarely identified by nation, nor are their motives explained, other than the reference to starvation. But if they were hungry, why would they take captives? The actions of the attackers appear terrifyingly irrational, the inhuman acts of morally deficient, scarcely human beings.

Scratch the surface and another story emerges. The first thing that is clear is that Hannah's attackers were not the indigenous Nonotucks, a small band of "River Indians" sometimes included by scholars in the Pocumtuck tribe, whose village had been located on the west bank of the Connecticut River at what in 1656 became Northampton. In 1653 the English colonists purchased the Nonotuck meadowlands and twenty-one families from Springfield and Windsor, Connecticut, eventually settled there. Save for a dispute in 1658 over inadequate compensation for the land sold to the settlers in 1653, which was remedied, the English and Nonotucks had lived side by side in relative peace for twenty-two years, the "Indians often coming into the village for traffic and other purposes, and the salutation of Netop (my friend) was often heard in the street. . . . The men sold fur and venison, and the women made and sold baskets and other things."[6]

Their relations were only superficially cordial, however. In 1675, the year that Hannah was born, the Nonotucks joined Metacom. The following year, Northampton was attacked by a force of three hundred Indians, and before they were repulsed they killed five Englishmen, wounded six, and burned down a number of houses and barns. When King Philip's War ended in 1677 with the defeat of Metacom's forces, most of his warriors, including the Nonotucks, fled to New York or New France, or, if captured, were sold into slavery in the West Indies. The Nonotucks were never able to return to their ancestral lands.

Even transient Indians were unusual in Hannah's time, for legislation passed by the Massachusetts General Court in the 1690s had outlawed trade of any kind with Natives in the upper Connecticut Valley and declared that any Indians found within twenty miles of the west side of the Connecticut River would be treated as enemies. By 1704, the Nonotucks were present only in the dimming memories of the older generation of Northampton settlers.

The county record of the massacre is brief but provides important clues to what was really going on that day in Pascommuck:

Pascomok Fort taken by ye French and Indians being about 72. They took, and Captivated ye whole Garrison being about 37 persons. The English Pursueing of them caused them to knock all the captives on the head, Save 5 or 6. Three they carried to Canada with them; the others escap'd and about 7 of those knocked on the Head Recovered, ye Rest died.[7]

I find it curious that the fact that there were Frenchmen in the raiding party is rarely mentioned in other accounts of the event.[8] Nor is the fact that the killings took place in the context of a war, Queen Anne's War (also known as the War of the Spanish Succession), which lasted from 1702 to 1713, the real enemies being France and England. They were fighting over whether King Louis XIV's grandson, the Duke of Anjou, would become the next king of Spain. In fact, the war party that raided Pascommuck was led by Seigneur Jacques Testard de Montigny, reputedly the greatest warrior of New France, who was sent to the Connecticut Valley with a party of French and Indians. The French had also been behind the much larger Deerfield massacre the previous February, when the raiding party had consisted of 250 Frenchmen, Abenakis, and Kahnawake Mohawks. The Abenakis (including some Pennacooks) lived north and east of the southern New England colonies in what is now New Hampshire, Vermont, and Maine (as well as in Nova Scotia and New Brunswick) and had long been allies of the French; the Kahnawake Mohawks lived in a Catholic mission village near Montreal.

The reasons for these attacks are given in a letter sent to Versailles on November 17, 1704, by the governor of New France himself, Pierre de Rigaud, Marquis de Vaudreuil, and his intendant. They wrote that they had to satisfy the Abenakis by sending Hertel de Rouville to Deerfield, but "the Indians of Penaske [also Abenakis, likely Penobscots from Maine] having likewise sent us word at the same time . . . that the English had killed some of their people, M. de Vaudreuil sent Sieur de Montigny thither, with four or five Frenchmen as well to reassure them in the fear they entertained of the English, as to engage them to continue the War. . . . Sieur de Montigny distinguished himself particularly on that occasion." In fact, it was French policy to incite hatred between the English and the Abenakis, for the latter inhabited the vast uncharted borderland separating New England and New France.[9]

A remark by the Deerfield captive, Rev. John Williams, in his captivity narrative, *The Redeemed Captive Returning to Zion*, confirms that the

French led the attack on Pascommuck: "They [the French] were wonderfully lifted up with pride after the return of Captain Montinug from Northampton with news of success."[10] Thus it is conceivable that Hannah Janes was scalped by a Frenchman.

Indeed, the ambushes of Deerfield and Pascommuck were only episodes in a long series of bloody attacks and counter-attacks that raged across New England and New France for most of Hannah's lifetime. These intercolonial wars began in 1689, with King William's War (1689–1697), followed by Queen Anne's War (1702–1713), Grey Lock's War between the Abenakis and the English from 1722–1725, King George's War (1744–1747), English–Abenaki skirmishes from 1750 to 1753, and the French and Indian War (or the Seven Years' War, as it was known in Europe), which broke out in 1754 and was still convulsing the region at the time of Hannah's death in 1755. She did not live to hear of the English conquest of the French and their Indian allies at Quebec in 1759, by which the English secured their hold on eastern North America.

Although most of these conflicts originated in Europe, they were bitterly fought in North America as well. In the New World, the English and French colonies egged on their Indian allies in a manner that reminds one of Third World proxy wars during the twentieth-century's Cold War. Every colonial government engaged Indian auxiliaries – mercenaries – for they were mobile and effective fighters and they could act as spies. Indian allies were a bargain from the European point of view: they were paid half to two-thirds of the wages of white soldiers – if they were paid at all – otherwise they were rewarded with plunder and captives. They did not disrupt the economy when called into service, could live off the land or survive on parched corn, were easily disbanded, and drew no pensions. In New England, the militia was too small and inexperienced to defend towns across three hundred miles of frontier without the help of Mohegan, Pequot, and other Native warriors. Following the raid on Pascommuck, for example, Capt. John Livingston led a volunteer party of fifty-one Natives, mainly Mohegans from southern Connecticut, and twenty-nine whites to defend western Massachusetts.[11]

The aboriginal nations formed alliances with the French or English colonies for their own reasons, often to ensure the best positions they could in the new world of European domination. As they gradually lost control of their lands, military service became a valuable source of income. It has also been suggested that, compared to other forms of employment available to

Natives in white society, fighting allowed young Indian men to earn their manhood in more traditional ways. But with escalating intercolonial hostilities that inevitably involved the Abenakis, war took on a disproportionate importance in Abenaki society, and produced a distorted image of them as inherently war-like. The reality was that the Abenakis had to fight to survive.

With the exception of the Pequots, the Mohegans, the Niantics, and the praying Indians – and at times, the powerful Iroquois Confederacy – most indigenous nations in northeastern North America were allies of the French. It has been said that, if Samuel de Champlain had not alienated the Confederacy when he sided with their enemies, the Hurons and the Algonquins, in an attack in 1609, the English might very well have been driven from the continent. The French did not hold themselves as aloof from their aboriginal allies as did the English; among the Abenakis, "French missionary and fur-trading activities produced interdependence, intermarriage, and a network of relationships . . . that the English never allowed or appreciated." As a result, by the eighteenth century, "many Abenakis had French names, wore French clothes, were baptized, wore crucifixes, and were buried in French cemeteries."[12]

But the Abenakis were in the unfortunate position of living between New France and New England, and their homeland in Vermont and New Hampshire was the main thoroughfare for Native raiding parties and European campaigns. Each war disrupted their subsistence activities and sometimes forced them to evacuate their villages; during Queen Anne's War, for example, some Abenakis had to appeal to the French to stave off starvation. They were also vulnerable to reprisals: a week after the massacre at Pascommuck, Caleb Lyman led a small expedition of English and Mohegans north from Northampton to Cowass, a well-known Abenaki gathering place where the Pascommuck captives had stopped for a while. There they surprised a party of nine Natives, broke up the encampment, and killed eight of them, taking six scalps. But, according to the governor of New France, Vaudreuil, "of all the Indians, the English feared the Abenakis most [as the French had feared the Iroquois], and they had never been able to gain the advantage over them except by perfidy."[13]

For Hannah and Benjamin and their families, this near-century of violence left a legacy of personal tragedies – the Pascommuck massacre was by no means the only such incident. As we saw in the last chapter, Northampton was attacked during Hannah's first year of life, and many

Northampton men died in other skirmishes during King Philip's War. Benjamin's half-brothers had also been killed at Northfield that same year. Although Northampton was spared in King William's War, which began in 1689, the town lived in constant fear of attack, and both Hannah's father and grandfather (as well as Benjamin's aged father, William Janes) died during the war's second year, likely in the deadly epidemic that swept through the Connecticut Valley in 1690. Three years later, Hannah's maternal uncle, aunt, and three cousins died in another attack by enemy Indians. And in the years after the Pascommuck raid, there would be other losses, too.

By the late seventeenth century, scalping – cutting the crown of hair from a fallen enemy – was familiar to most European colonists. It's worth exploring this practice in more detail, since it represented such conclusive evidence to them of Indian barbarity. Archaeological, historical, linguistic, and cultural evidence indicates that it was a practice indigenous to North America, and was also practiced less widely in pre-Columbian South America. Numerous Europeans encountered scalping among various eastern First Nations in the earliest stages of contact and expressed surprise at the practice. On Jacques Cartier's second voyage up the St. Lawrence in 1535, the explorer was shown "the skins of five men's heads, stretched on hoops, like parchment," when he visited the village of Stadacona, now Quebec City. His host Donnacona told him they were from enemy Toudamans (Mi'kmaqs) from the south.[14] Other Europeans encountered the practice in Florida, Nova Scotia, Virginia, and Alabama, to name only a few regions. (The only European reference to scalping is found in the writings of the fifth-century B.C. Greek historian Herodotus, who noted it among the Scythians of Asia Minor; his work was first published in England in 1502 and was not widely known at this time.)

The origins of scalping are obscure. It was not a local custom among New England aboriginal nations when the English arrived – though they did take heads (as did the English) – but it had extended into New England by the time of King Philip's War in 1675. (Metacom's warriors suffered considerable consternation when the rough buccaneer, Captain Samuel Mosely, removed his wig during battle and hung it on a tree.) It was employed by the Eastern Abenakis, but not originally by those Western Abenakis who lived on New England's borders. Scalping may have originated among peoples who lived near the Gulf of Mexico; the Iroquois had also practiced it from early times. Originally, only enemies slain a considerable distance from home were scalped, the more common practice being to sever the heads, hands, and/or feet of victims. These customs reflected a widespread aboriginal practice of mutilating the dead of enemies and a common conception that a part of the body represented the whole.

The rationale for scalping varied. Some aboriginal people believed that the spirit of the victim would have no rest in the afterlife. Others believed the spirit was bound to serve that of the victor, while still others believed it was wholly annihilated. Among some nations, enemy scalps were used to appease the ghosts of slain warriors and ease the mourning of relatives, while, among the Iroquois, it appears to have been mainly a proof of valour (though the capture of enemies – some for torture, but most for adoption into the tribe – was usually preferred to the taking of scalps).

Elaborate customs were associated with scalp-taking. Warriors of many nations in eastern and western America wore scalplocks, a small braid or lock of hair on the crown of the head, often decorated with paint, feathers, and jewellery, and considered a mark of manhood and defiance. Once a scalp was taken, it was dried with hot ashes and stretched on a hoop, sometimes decorated, then used to adorn the warrior, his tent, weapons, garments, poles, or lines, or even fastened to canoes. In some nations, it was handed over to the chief or presented to the community at large, after appropriate ceremonies. Each scalp was then greeted with a special scalp cry and was often buried with a warrior among his other honours. Scalp dances, usually performed by women who held the scalps aloft or carried them on poles, were an important part of victory celebrations in many Native cultures.[15]

There were various techniques for scalping, which could result in a larger or smaller portion of the scalp being removed. In some, a circular incision was made first; in others, the head was seized by the hair and jerked to loosen the hair from the bone and then the scalp was removed in one swooping cut.

Gruesome as it sounds, scalping was actually a rather tame form of physical mutilation by the standards of the day – as we saw in the last chapter, there were worse forms of violence in both Native American and European cultures. But there were important cultural differences in the way the two societies were violent. For example, both Native Americans and the English devised horrific tortures, but in some Native societies torture of outsiders was an activity carried out by the community as a whole, and was related to trials of bravery and ancient religious rituals of human sacrifice, whereas in English culture it was often carried out in secret by professionals in the service of the state or the church or constituted a state-sanctioned public punishment for a crime. While European soldiers and Native warriors were equally creative and brutal in killing their enemies – and equally cavalier about displaying severed heads – scalping contravened English cultural norms for the conduct of warfare and Europeans held strong taboos about desecrating Christian corpses (except as punishment meted out by a court), since the body was necessary for the Christian resurrection.[16] (Interestingly, the pagan Irish also mutilated corpses.) Scalping, even though no more intrinsically horrifying than many other practices, sickened and terrified the New England colonists, and even professional soldiers. To them it was a sign of Indian depravity.

As war followed war, the colonists' desire for vengeance grew and they came to adopt the "savage" behaviour they condemned in their enemies, believing that "necessity pleads an Excuse for following so inhuman an Example, as the shortest way . . . to put an End to such Barbarities."[17] In addition to scalping, the militias began slaughtering and torturing Indian prisoners, even women and children.

When the Rev. Solomon Stoddard of Northampton recommended in 1703 that dogs be used to track Indians and to guard towns, he justified this departure from "Christian practice" as follows:

> If the Indians were as other people are, and did manage their warr fairly after the manner of other nations it might be looked upon as inhumane to pursue them in such a manner. . . . But they are to be looked upon as thieves and murderers, they doe acts of hostility, without proclaiming war, they don't appeare openly in the field to bid us battle. . . . they use those cruelly that fall into their hands. . . . In short, they act like wolves and are to be dealt withall as wolves.[18]

Hannah Janes may well have shared these attitudes; Reverend Stoddard was her minister.

We know from Hannah's story that the victims of scalping occasionally survived their ordeals to live to a ripe old age. In fact, the German historian Georg Friederici found references to forty-eight survivors, thirty-three white and fifteen Indian, and several other instances have been documented as well.[19] If only the crown of the head was scalped, one's chances of survival were better, since little blood was lost. In cases of total scalping, the loss of blood was considerable and difficult to control, and complications, such as infections or necrosis (where the bone rotted and brain tissue seeped out), were more frequent.

After Hannah was scalped, she was taken downriver to Wethersfield (or Westfield, depending on the source). Her husband stayed with her there for some time, and the governor and council gave him a brief, dated May 8, 1707, craving the charity of the people of Branford, Guildford, Killingworth, and Saybrook to support them, as he was now "so impoverished that he is unable to satisfy the surgeons in whose hands she hath been and is like to be, for their cost and pains therein." At last, "under the care of Dr. Gersholm Bulkley and other surgeons, she finally rose from a long confinement and years of suffering, to the comforts of life."[20]

Gersholm Bulkley (1635?–1713) was a noted clerical physician with a large consulting practice in all parts of Connecticut and western Massachusetts. He had graduated from Harvard in 1655, and during King Philip's War was appointed surgeon to the 350 Connecticut men marching under Major Treat, where he likely treated many victims of scalping. He undoubtedly met many of my Stanton, Denison, and Rogers relations during the war, and it is documented that he slept on at least one occasion at Thomas Stanton's house. Later he became famous as a chemist and alchemist. His son James served as pastor of the huge colonial army[21] that defeated the Narragansetts in the Great Swamp Fight.

How did Bulkley and the other doctors treat Hannah? In spite of the frequency of scalping, there is little first-hand information about contemporary treatment of victims by either Native or English healers. Laurence Heister's A General System of Surgery, a standard reference work published thirty-one years after Hannah Janes was scalped, was based on "thirty years' experience." It prescribes the following treatment:

Having discovered the injured Part of the Cranium, and cleared away the grumous Blood and Matter with a Sponge, you are next to remove any Splinters of bone that may come in your way, with your Fingers or the Forceps. . . . When you have discovered by the alteration of the colour of the Bone what Part of the Cranium has received a Contusion, . . . you must bore several small Holes through the external Lamella of the Bone, till you find Blood proceed from the wounded Diploe; after this you may dress the Part up with balsamic Medicines; but where any violent

Symptoms come on, which demonstrate an Extravasation of Blood in the Cavity of the *Cranium*, the *Trepan* [a drill that cuts circular discs of bone from the skull] is to be called for without delay.[22]

A paper published in 1806 by Dr. James Robertson of Nashville described several instances of successful treatment; when the exposed skull began to turn black, he bored holes in the bone, about one inch apart or less, until a reddish fluid appeared on the point of the awl. Flesh began to rise in those holes and above the skull and sometimes raised a black scale from it, which had to be scraped off. According to Robertson, the scalped head healed very slowly, generally taking two years to regrow the skin, and sometimes three or four, as appears to have been the case with Hannah Janes. Remarkably, hair generally regrew over much of the regenerated scalp, although there was always part of the scalped head left with little or no hair growth.[23]

I wonder if Hannah ever tried the following contemporary treatment, which claimed to produce a fine growth of hair on a bald head: "take sum fire flies, sum Red wormes and black snayles & sum bees and dri them and pound them and mixt them in milk or Water."[24] I don't know if this was swallowed or rubbed on the head – I hope the latter!

And what of Hannah's original hair? Where did her severed scalp end up? Was it prepared in the traditional manner, stretched on a hoop, displayed on a wigwam pole, her hair catching the breeze somewhere in Montreal or Quebec? Was it among those that the Abenakis boasted of to Iroquois and Mahican delegates at a meeting with colonial officials in Albany in 1706, when they said, "Nos cabanes sont remplis de cheveleures angoises qui flottent au gré du vent" ("Our wigwams are full of English scalps blowing in the wind.")?[25] How long did it last before it mouldered away? And how much was it worth to the person who took it? For Hannah's scalp would have been of considerable value to whoever presented it to the French and collected the bounty.

And there hangs another tale – the role played by both English and French in encouraging scalping for money. Indeed, according to Friederici, "scalping, in its commonly known form and greatest extent was . . . largely the result of the influence of white people, who introduced firearms, which increased the fatalities in a conflict, brought the steel knife, facilitating the taking of the scalp, and finally offered scalp premiums, which so stimulated the hunt for these objects that the removing of whole heads was abandoned." In fact, the hungry Indians who attacked Hannah Janes had originally thought of giving themselves up to the English in order to eat, but decided that they would do better to get a "reward from Canada" for scalps and captives.[26]

The Puritans were the first to offer bounties for the heads of their Native enemies. In 1637 English colonists and their Mohegan allies brought in large numbers of Pequot heads. During King Philip's War in 1675, the governments of Connecticut and Massachusetts offered their own men thirty shillings for every enemy head, while the Narragansetts were promised one "Coat (that is, two Yards of Trucking Cloth, worth five Shillings per Yard here)" for every enemy "Head-Skin" [scalp].[27] Ninigret, as you may recall, was one of those who took the English up on this offer.

When the first intercolonial war broke out in 1689, the outnumbered French promoted scalping as a means of terrorizing their English neighbours. "While the English took and maintained the lead in promoting the white scalping of Indians," notes historian James Axtell, to "the French goes the distinction of having first encouraged the Indian scalping of whites. In 1688, even before the official declaration of war in Europe, the governor of New France offered ten beaver skins (equivalent to the price of a gun with four pounds of powder and 40 pounds of lead) to the Indians of northern New England for every enemy scalp, Christian or Indian. Not to be outdone, the English took the lead in 1696 when the New York Council '*Resolved for the future*, that Six pounds shall be given to each Christian or Indian as a Reward who shall kill a french man or indian Enemy.'" Even before this, the General Court of Massachusetts passed the Act of 1690: "For better Encouragement to prosecute the French and Indian Enemy," the General Court offered "fifty pounds p[er] head for every Indian man and 25 pounds p[er] head for any Indian woman or Child, male or Female, under the age of fourteen years taken or brought in Prisoner, the Scalps of all Indians slain to be produced." The price per scalp, perhaps because of the relative poverty of the treasury of New France, was always higher among the English than among the French.[28]

As the war progressed, settlers from the devastated frontier settlements were most insistent in demanding higher scalp bounties. They sought revenge as much as financial gain and formed their own volunteer war parties instead of relying exclusively on distant forts for defence. These bounty hunters were further incensed by horrifying descriptions of Indian atrocities, particularly the killing and mutilation of pregnant women and little children, in newly published captivity narratives. (The role and nature of the captivity narratives has been the subject of much study; certainly many were written for propaganda purposes.)

By 1704, concern for "Christian practice" led to a series of graduated bounties, with scalps of men or boys over the age of twelve worth £100 to a volunteer company, women and boys above the age of ten only £10, and no reward for the scalps of children, though live Native children could be sold into slavery.[29]

Over the years of intercolonial warfare, the various governments steadily increased the bounty, especially after the Deerfield massacre of 1704, reaching a high of £100 for a single scalp taken by a volunteer. The results were predictable. On one occasion, the Indians allied with the French surprised an English field hospital and scalped all the patients. In New England, parties of volunteer Indian fighters – usually frontiersmen – turned into professional bounty hunters. A few Puritans protested the development of this "trade," but most New Englanders simply became inured to the sight of enemy scalps. Rows of these trophies were nailed to the wall of the Salem courthouse, and they were probably displayed in a similar fashion in many other towns. Bounty hunters flaunted their prowess: in 1725, for example, Capt. John Lovewell and his company paraded triumphantly through the streets of Boston with ten hooped scalps on poles; Lovewell and his Lieutenant Farwell even wore wigs made from enemy scalps. A visitor from England recorded in his diary in 1760 that "Some people have an Indian's Skin for a Tobacco Pouch."[30]

Puritan ministers stood at the forefront of this call for vengeance. Some even invested in scalping parties and shared in the profits. For example, Rev. Thomas Smith of Falmouth wrote in his journal for June 18, 1757: "I receive 165 pounds 3–3 . . . my part of scalp money."[31]

Administrators of the scalp bounties had to deal with a few tricky problems. First of all, how was one to ensure that a scalp was an *enemy* scalp? To prevent fraud, a three-month prison sentence and fine double the value of the bounty were threatened for trying to pass off a "false scalp," such as one of a friendly Indian. In some instances, scalps were subdivided for greater profit or taken from corpses in graveyards. In 1757, the French curtailed scalp bounties after reports that Indians had passed off French scalps for English ones. In New England about the same time, only whites were allowed to collect the bounties. But the grisly practice was revived during the Revolutionary War, when Englishmen scalped other Englishmen.

One of the most famous scalping incidents in New England involved yet another relation of mine, Hannah Dustin of Haverhill, Massachusetts, wife of John Wheeler's grandson Thomas Dustin, who was captured by Indians on March 15, 1697, during King William's War. A week after she gave birth to her twelfth child – three had died in infancy and a fourth as a youth – Abenaki Indians set her house on fire and captured Hannah, her infant, Martha, and her nurse, Mary Neff, while her husband managed to herd their seven other young children to safety. After dashing out her newborn's brains against an apple tree (later a tourist attraction in the region) and "murdering and captivating thirty-nine persons," the Abenakis forced the two women and the other captives to begin the long trek to New France – in Hannah's case, wearing only one shoe.

En route, Hannah, the widow Neff, and Samuel Leonardson, a young boy captured a year and a half earlier, were assigned to an Abenaki family of two men, three women, and seven children. Hannah devised a plan to escape. One night, along the way, when the family and captives were camped on an island between the Merrimack and Contoocook Rivers, about seventy-five miles from Haverhill, the captives managed to kill all their sleeping captors with tomahawks, save one "favourite Indian lad" and a badly wounded woman who escaped. In their excitement, the captives fled. Then, realizing that they had missed a fiscal opportunity, they returned to scalp all ten of their victims, including the six children. They returned to Haverhill with their bloody trophies; then, on April 21, they visited Boston, bearing with them "as evidence of their achievement" the scalps, the gun, and the tomahawk.

Hannah was dismayed to discover that the bounty on scalps had been cancelled during her absence, and it was only after her husband petitioned the court that she and her colleagues received their payments: "The humble petition of Thomas Duston of Haverhill showeth: That the wife of ye petitioner (with one Mary Neff) hath, in her late captivity among the barbarous Indians, been disposed and assisted by Heaven to do an extraordinary action, in the just slaughter of so many of the barbarians . . ." She also received many congratulatory gifts from friends and strangers, including £50 from the governor of Maryland, as well as great acclaim. Her story so stirred the Puritans and later New Englanders that it was told over and over again for at least a hundred years, by authors such as Cotton Mather and

Nathaniel Hawthorne. A statue unveiled in her honour in 1874 still stands on Contoocook Island to this day.[32]

When the other Hannah – poor, scalped Hannah Janes – was finally "cured" – that is to say, when the wound on her head had closed up and healed – she and her husband moved to Coventry, Connecticut, with other pioneers in 1712 or 1713. Although Coventry was a new settlement, it was some distance from the vulnerable northern Massachusetts frontier, lying due east of Hartford, nestled in gently sloping grassy hills and beside a pleasant lake. The land had been left by Joshua, another son of the Mohegan chief Uncas, to various Englishmen in his "highly irregular" will of 1676. However, disputes about land titles delayed settlement for more than thirty-five years and by the time the Connecticut government ratified the plantation at Coventry in May 1706, twelve of the fifteen legatees had died. Richard Lord, son of Thomas Stanton's brother-in-law and erstwhile business partner, and William Whiting, the descendant of another Stanton partner, sat on the committee that tried to divide the land, but the titles were not fully sorted out till 1718. Benjamin Janes, husband of scalped Hannah, and his relative Ebenezer Searl were among the dozen Northampton men who migrated to Coventry as a group in the spring of 1709. Another former Pascommuck family, Moses Hutchinson and his family, also went to Coventry.[33] Abel Janes, a brother of Benjamin Janes, moved to nearby Lebanon.

In these new surroundings, "God gave them other children to comfort their desolated hearts."[34] Indeed, after the 1706 death of Hannah's first child after the massacre, she gave birth to more children, including twins. The second youngest child of the four was Seth Janes, my direct ancestor, born in 1713.

Hannah must have often pondered the fate of her friends, relatives, and children, and of the captives, Elisha, Margaret, and Esther, as her wound healed and she went on with her life. How did she interpret what had happened to all of them at Pascommuck? To the Puritans, there was no such thing as an accident, something occurring without divine purpose. According to historian John Demos, the Puritans had two predominant modes of understanding affliction. The first emphasized God's punishment in response to human wrongdoing, for the purpose of righting the moral order and encouraging spiritual reform. We know from the captivity narratives that many of the prisoners saw the massacre of their loved ones and their own captivity as God's chastisement for their own individual sins or those of their society; conscious as they were of Old Testament analogies, they accepted that the righteous had to suffer with the sinners when God punished His flock for its accumulated wrongs. They consciously identified with the ancient Israelites, that other chosen people who broke their religious covenants with God, suffered in the wilderness, and struggled for control over a promised land. They saw the Indians as those other heathens, the Canaanites. God's warning to the ancient Hebrews rang in their ears: "I will not drive them out from before you; but they shall be as thorns in your sides." We know that after the Deerfield massacre, the General Court of Massachusetts ordered a day of fasting and prayer, and that all across New England pastors preached on such subjects as "ye awful and dreadful dispensation of God's hand at Deerfield," and on the shameful "sins of a professing people." The year before the massacre, Hannah's own minister, Rev. Solomon Stoddard, had preached that, in their sinfulness, "men are wont to make many pretences and excuses, and by them they mitigate the terror of their consciences, but this does not prevent the displeasure of God: and if God be angry with his people, it will before it be long, break out upon them."[35]

When John Williams and other captives were released from captivity, they saw their deliverance as a sign of God's mercy and proof of His intention that they would ultimately prosper – perhaps Hannah interpreted her survival in much the same light.

The other mode interpreted the misfortune as God's "testing" and "trial," as "a special challenge to bring out the best in the faithful and to present special opportunities for holiness." For example, the preacher Cotton Mather told the captive John Williams that what had happened to him – the murder of his wife and infant, the captivity of several of his children, the devastation of his town – was good for him personally and useful for New England.[36]

Did Hannah see herself as severely tested? Did she search herself for past sins or impiety? Did she see her tormenters as Satan's agents, who with God's help she had thwarted by surviving? Did she ponder the nature of redemption? Perhaps the words of Mary Rowlandson consoled her: "As he wounded me with one hand so he healed me with the other."[37] Did her faith deepen as she turned to her Bible, as she struggled to understand the fate the omnipotent God she worshipped had pre-ordained for her? Or was her faith deeply challenged, so deeply shaken that she could not admit it in the community in which she lived?

Grief, as hard as any there is to bear, must have enveloped her – for months, for years. How ever did she survive the loss of her first baby born after the massacre? How could she have endured it? And as her grief persisted, she must also have felt guilt, for as a Puritan she would have believed that love of family was temporal and should not supersede the love of God. Her dead children were dismal proof indeed of the ephemeral nature of this world.

I keep, in a white linen envelope, a child's lock of hair. It is silky still and golden in the light, my daughter's first curl, the last physical remnant of the child that was, that infant time. It conjures up memories of her soft, sweet-smelling skin, her slow awakening to the consciousness we share, a time when all was fresh and new and innocent beyond all words or knowing.

What is it about hair that speaks to us so? In so many cultures it has spiritual significance, both for good and evil. Think of Samson and Delilah, the shaved heads of Nazi collaborators, the hair shirt worn by penitent monks, the locks exchanged between lovers. In medieval Europe, it was believed that cutting children's hair would sap their strength, and so their hair was left to grow for years. During childbirth, midwives undid women's hair, believing that braids or knots would tie up the birth.[38]

Long hair has had a deep-rooted association with paganism in Western culture. The *Compendium Maleficarum*, a treatise on witches and witchcraft compiled by Francesco Maria Guazzo in 1608, said witches could control rain, hail, wind, and lightning with their hair. Accordingly, inquisitors shaved the heads of accused witches before torturing them. Christians ruled that women's heads must be covered in church, lest they draw demons into the building. So it is hardly a surprise that one of the things that irked the Puritans about their Native neighbours was their hair.

The sin of long hair was pride, the original sin of Adam and Eve; the colonists quoted I Corinthians 11:14, which said a man having long hair was shameful. These attitudes were derived from Scripture and were exacerbated by the English civil war, when long hair and powdered wigs were associated with the monarchist Cavaliers. In North America, eastern Native hairstyles were infinite and various, and would "torture the wits of a curious Barber to imitate."[39]

In New England, John Eliot and his colleagues had pressured their congregations, the university, and colonial governments into outlawing "proud fashions" and "the wearing of long haire after the manner of Ruffians," "wild-Irish," and "barbarous Indians." Indians who became Christians were expected to wear their hair short. "Nothing symbolized the Indian's identity – his independence, his sense of superiority, his pride – more effectively than his long hair. A willingness to cut his hair signalled his desire to kill the Indian in himself and to assume a new persona modelled upon the meek, submissive Christ of the white man's Black Book."[40] (Ironically, in most European depictions, Jesus had long hair.)

Curiously, both Native and European cultures shared the belief that whoever possessed another's hair had power over his soul. Gypsy witches, for example, advised those seeking a relationship to secretly wear a lock of the beloved's hair as a ring or locket.

In a similar vein, the scalplock of a warrior represented his soul or living spirit. To lose that hair to an enemy was to lose control over one's life, to become socially and spiritually dead, whether biological death resulted or not, because power and identity had been transferred into the victor's hands. As a living spirit, the scalplock was not to be trifled with.[41]

And so I wonder, what did the loss of her hair mean to Hannah Janes? What colour had it been, what texture? Perhaps she wondered how many people had touched it, and in whose wigwam that intimate part of herself was now displayed. I wonder if she ever felt completely whole again.

How, beyond religious rationalization, did she deal with the pain of all that had happened to her, the slaughter of her children and relatives before her very eyes? Did she have nightmares or flashbacks? Was a part of her frozen at the scene, as happens to so many traumatized victims of violence? Did she rejoice when Benjamin Church the Indian fighter led a retaliatory attack on the Abenakis in Maine and then the French in Nova Scotia, killing, burning towns, taking French and Indian prisoners? Did she envy the actions of that other Hannah, famous Hannah Dustin, with her ten Abenaki scalps; did her soul twist with hatred and burn for revenge? How did she remember or imagine her attacker? Was he ever human in her eyes?

I wonder if it is only a coincidence that her first surviving child to be born after the massacre was named Silence (as that of her sister-in-law, Sarah, was named Submit). Perhaps she tried to blot out the memory of their faces, their blows. I imagine that sometimes she would just begin to hear their whooping cries, to feel their hands on her, and then she would shut it out again, and go back to the silence, the wind in the trees, the small white perfect puffs of clouds . . . the comforting blessed silence – for then she could go on.

What did she pass on to her children? Did she ever speak of her experience? Did they grew up on a fear and hatred that she never spoke of, did they drink it in her milk? I wonder what inchoate feelings passed through all nine generations to me, her descendant – what painful residue is left from so much violence and hate?

And what about that other person in this story, the man in shadow, whose name we don't know, the man who took her scalp? What did he pass on to *his* descendants? What did he feel as he grabbed her and made the cut, as once more the fabric of human life, of human society, was slashed and rent? Was he seeking revenge for attacks on his own family or relatives, and if so, did the killing and scalping assuage his grief? Or was it money he was after? Did he feel anything other than triumph as he carried her warm and dripping scalp away, as her blood stained his hands. Was she quickly forgotten or did he later look at her scalp and wonder about the person it had come from? Did he wonder at all about the forces that had brought them together, there at the point of that sharp-edged knife?

CHAPTER
14

Gone Indian

As Hannah Janes sat dazed and bleeding on Pomeroy's mountain, three of her relatives were beginning the long forced march to New France, a trip of at least three hundred miles. As they walked, the scene of the massacre must have replayed itself over and over before their eyes. Thirty-nine-year-old Esther (Ingersoll) Jones had lost her husband and two children, though her eighteen-year-old niece, Margaret Huggins, travelled with her. Hannah Janes's eight-year-old nephew Elisha Searl had seen three of his siblings and his father murdered and his mother tomahawked and left for dead. For weeks they were forced to travel with the murderers of their loved ones, to adapt to strange food – what there was of it – and function in a totally foreign language and culture. If they fell behind or sickened, or aroused the anger of their captors in any way, they risked being killed themselves. The group likely travelled up the Connecticut River to the White River, went along the Winooski to Lake Champlain, then north along the Richelieu to the settlement of St. Francis on the Saint Lawrence, and finally southwest to Montreal. Then they joined the hundreds of other New England captives in New France, including those from the Deerfield massacre, who spent their long days praying and hoping to be ransomed.

Unfortunately for all concerned, the negotiations between Canada and New England for prisoner exchanges were interminable and largely inconclusive; prisoners were repatriated, in larger or smaller groups, piecemeal, whenever relations between the adversaries temporarily improved or gestures of good faith were called for. In this way, between two hundred and three hundred captives, including all of the French prisoners in New England – were eventually released, but many English captives remained in New France for considerable lengths of time, many for more than four years and some for much longer. While the French and Indian captives in New England were simply incarcerated, and so understandably formed no attachment to the land of their captivity, the situation for the New England captives in Canada was more complex. Many of the captives were bought from the Indians by Governor de Vaudreuil, who held them until they were redeemed by the English. During their stays in New France, they lived comfortably with French families or in convents; the worst aspects of their lives were loneliness, uncertainty, and the strong pressure on them to convert to Catholicism.[1]

In fact, one of the Pascommuck captives, Esther Jones, and her cousin, Abigail Turbot, who had been captured in a previous raid on Kennebunkport, Maine, became pawns in the propaganda war between French Catholics and English Protestants. Esther became seriously ill in her second year of captivity, as did her cousin Abigail. Fellow captive Rev. John Williams of Deerfield recounted the story in his captivity narrative.

> And when two English women who had always opposed their [the Catholic] religion were sick in the hospital, [the priests] kept with them night and day, till they died, and their friends kept from coming to visit them. After their death, they gave out, that they died in the Romish faith, and were received into their communion. Before their death, masses were said for them; and they were buried in the churchyard with all their ceremonies. And after this, letters [were] sent into all parts, to inform the English, that these two women turned to their religion before their death and it concerned them to follow their example, for they could not be more obstinate than those women were, in their health, against the Romish faith, and yet on a deathbed embraced it. But I shall hereafter relate the just grounds we have to think these things were falsehoods.[2]

Nine months later, young Margaret Huggins, the second Pascommuck captive, was also baptized a Catholic, though it appears that she was soon redeemed and returned to New England.

But of the three captives from Pascommuck, most troubling was the case of Elisha Searl, who stayed by choice in New France until adulthood. He was adopted by a French family, became Michel Searl, was baptized a Catholic, and was on the list of those captives granted French citizenship in an act of 1710. "Being kindly treated, he became fond of the French and the free, unhampered life that he lived with the Indians," recounts Frederic Janes in his genealogy of the Janes family.[3] In fact, he was engaged to marry a young French woman and became, at least to some degree, a "white Indian," visiting the Mississippi River and the Great Lakes with his Native friends, engaging in the fur trade. Elisha was by no means the only English captive to adopt Native ways and to be reluctant to return to New England; this tendency – evident in a minority of cases but widely remarked upon – was strong and disturbing evidence that the indigenous people of North America were not the "savage" and Satanic creatures depicted in Puritan propaganda.

Between 1689 and 1713, the years of heaviest French–aboriginal raiding along the northern and eastern frontiers of New England, approximately 600 men, women, and children were seized, 324 of these during Queen Anne's War (1702–1713). Of these latter captives, 37, or 12 per cent, were killed by Indians or died in captivity, while 122, or 37 per cent, definitely returned to New England, having been ransomed or exchanged for French prisoners or having returned by some other means. Roughly 24 per cent definitely refused to return home and remained in Canada. Another 4 per cent probably remained, and an additional 6 per cent eventually returned to New England after voluntarily staying in Canada for some time, as did Elisha Searl (the fate of the remainder is unknown). While most of those remaining in Canada became French citizens and Catholics, what is perhaps most surprising is that perhaps 7 per cent (some estimates suggest up to 15 per cent) of the captives from Queen Anne's War became full-fledged members of Native societies, and others, like Elisha Searl, appear to have moved in both aboriginal and French societies.[4]

The taking of captives during warfare was an aboriginal practice which the French used to their own advantage but did not control. While the money to be made from selling captives to Vaudreuil undoubtedly proved a major incentive during the intercolonial wars, there were strong traditions among the Iroquois in particular, but also among other nations indigenous to the region, of taking captives either to be adopted into the tribe in order to physically and spiritually replace a dead relative or to be publicly tortured and killed. While notably few New Englanders were tortured by their aboriginal captors – contrary to Puritan propaganda – the need to restock the population was critical in the early eighteenth century, since the arrival of the European settlers in the previous century had resulted in devastating epidemics and more frequent and deadly warfare. According to historians Alden Vaughan and Daniel Richter, adoption of other Natives among the Iroquois was so frequent that, by 1700, the Iroquois Confederacy contained more outsiders and their descendants than ethnic Iroquois.

There is no evidence of New Englanders being captured for adoption before 1675, but in subsequent years, captives of all races, whether white, black, or brown, were treated as relatives and equals, and were thoroughly integrated into the social life and kinship structure of the tribe. Some adopted Englishmen even became chiefs: Timothy Rice of Westborough, Maine, became a clan chief. John Tarbell became the eldest chief and chief speaker of the Kahnawakes; he and his brother were the leaders of the thirty families who left Kahnawake and founded the settlement of Akwesasne on an island in the St. Lawrence in 1754. This acceptance differed markedly from the Puritans' attitudes to their Native captives. Did the colonists "ever adopt an enemy," asked former captive Mrs. James Johnson, "and salute him by the tender name of brother?"[5]

While Native cultures were willing to accept captives as full members of their communities, the gulf between the two cultures was so great that few adult New Englanders preferred Indian society to their own. Most captives had been conditioned from birth to fear and despise aboriginal people; many, of course, had personal experience of war-time atrocities and had witnessed the slaughter of loved ones. Captivity narratives fanned these hatreds and fears, and Puritan theologians and politicians were virtually unanimous in their negative opinion of "savages." Propaganda, like Benjamin Thompson's 1676 poem accusing Indians of sexually abusing captives (which was totally untrue, war-time rape being a European trait), heightened the captives' apprehensions. While infants and those who lagged behind were often swiftly killed on the trek northward, few of the Puritans' other fears were realized.

Yet some captives found among their captors the "most perfect freedom, the ease of living [and] the absence of those cares and corroding solicitudes which so often prevail with us." Some even found Indian life morally superior to English civilization and Catholicism more satisfying than Puritanism. Sylvanus Johnson, who lived with the Indians from the ages of six to ten, "always maintained that the Indians were a far more moral race than the Whites." "In their social bond," Hector de Crevecoeur, a French diplomat in New England, commented, there was "something singularly captivating, and far superior to anything to be boasted of among us."[6]

Adult captives did face one ritual in the process of adoption that they came to dread: the ceremony of running the gauntlet. It was the prospect of this ritual that had made Hannah Dustin so determined to escape from the Abenakis.

> They make a stope [upon reaching their home vilage], and strip their pris-
> oners stark naked, and with their painting stuff red them all over, and sett
> them before the company that has been to warr, who have each of them a
> club in thier hands, who, when the word is gifen, they run and their pris-
> oners run, and what blows they can give them befor they get into the fort
> they have for to welcome them to their new habitation, and . . . there is att
> the entry of the fort gate and heap of squaws and childring who stand
> ready for to receive them with their sticks, clubbs, ols and fire-brands,
> who lay on which all the force and might till he getts into the wigwame
> where he is to live.[7]

Although Natives took captives of all ages, those most successfully adopted into aboriginal societies were children between the ages of seven and fifteen; almost 40 per cent of these were assimilated and another 10 per cent lived for a while as French or Indians before returning to New England either voluntarily or against their will. Among girls of this age group, almost 54 per cent remained with their captors. While the fact that such children were isolated from other captives and taken into homes played a major part in the success of their transculturation, more than one commentator attributed the reluctance of captives to return home to "the liberty and licentiousness with which they are raised."[8] Indeed, Native American child-raising was far gentler than the European practice.

"We may justly reproach them with the way in which they bring up their children," wrote early eighteenth-century traveller Pierre Charlevoix; "they do not so much as know what it is to correct them." Another traveller reported that "the [Indian] child is not troubled in any way; they leave him to do entirely as he wishes." Deerfield captive Joseph Kellogg explained the seductiveness of aboriginal life: "The Indians indulge the english boys abundantly [and] let them have the Liberty they will . . . and so an easy way of life and libertinism is more prevailing with them than any affection they have to religion."[9]

"When an Indian Child has been brought up among us," Benjamin Franklin wrote in 1753, "taught our language and habituated to our Customs, yet if he goes to see his relations and make one Indian Ramble with them, there is no perswading him ever to return." But

> when white persons of either sex have been taken prisoners young by the Indians, and lived a while among them tho' ransomed by their Friends, and treated with all imaginable tenderness to prevail with them to stay among the English, yet in a Short time they become disgusted with our manner of life, and the care and pains that are necessary to support it, and take the first good Opportunity of escaping again to the Woods, from whence there is no reclaiming them.[10]

The few Native people who lived among the English, on the other hand, were never accepted as equals, let alone as relatives. Although a number did become Christians and adopted English customs in the praying towns, they always remained on the fringes of white society. The ingrained English sense of cultural superiority prevented aboriginal people from ever finding a valued place in that society. Also, the many Puritan strictures on behaviour were too onerous for most Natives used to the freedom of their own way of life. Many Native converts apostatized because, as the English themselves admitted, "they can live with less labour, and more pleasure and plenty as Indians, than they can with us." Hence, the eventual acculturation of many aboriginal people into English society in New England was less a choice than a necessity, the result of the increasing imbalance in population, the power of English technology, and the Puritans' cultural aggression.[11]

In 1782, Crevecoeur wondered "by what power does it come to pass, that children who have been adopted when young among these people, can never be prevailed on to readopt European manners? . . . for thousands of Europeans are Indians," he wrote, "and we have no examples of even one of these Aborigines having from choice become Europeans!"[12]

Crevecoeur was both exaggerating the number of converts to "savagery" and ignoring the numbers of New England Natives who had converted to Christianity and moved to the praying towns. Nonetheless, his comments reflect a deep-seated anxiety among Europeans bent on "civilizing the wilderness" that the wilderness would triumph in the end. They were particularly concerned about isolated frontier towns, where fur traders and others living on the margins of Puritan society came into frequent contact with aboriginal neighbours. William Baker, for example, who had been living at the Plymouth Colony's trading post on the Connecticut River, went to Mohegan territory and was described by Roger Williams as "turned Indian in nakedness and cutting of hair, and after many whore-doms, is there married." In 1642 the General Court of Connecticut threat-ened three years' imprisonment in the workhouse and a fine or corporal punishment for "divers persons" who "departe from amongst us, and take up their abode with the Indians in a prophane course of life." Puritan min-isters warned of God's vengeance on those who became Indianized. More generally, the fear of "regression" may have reflected the darker and unconscious parts of the Puritan soul that the Puritans so strictly sup-pressed in themselves and projected onto others. (The English who settled in Ireland were also seen to have "degenerated.")[13]

The phenomenon of Puritans *choosing* to become "heathens" and "savages" deeply shocked the New Englanders and threatened their sense of cultural superiority. The most famous "white Indian" of all was Eunice Williams, who had been captured in the Deerfield massacre two months before the attack on Pascommuck. Eunice was the daughter of the promi-nent Deerfield minister John Williams and granddaughter of Rev. Eleazer Mather, the pastor of Northampton before Solomon Stoddard. Seven years old at the time of her capture in 1704, she was taken to the village of Kahnawake in New France, adopted by a Mohawk family, and sent to a Catholic school. To the horror of all New England, Eunice refused to return to her homeland, in spite of many attempts to reclaim her – including visits to Montreal by her own father after his own release from captivity.

Williams even tried to have her repatriated against her will, but the French couldn't force the mission Indians to yield her up – the Kahnawake Mohawks were allies, not subjects; if they were denied their accustomed rights concerning prisoners of war, they might refuse to fight for the French. John Williams was told by a priest that "the Mohawks would as soon part with their hearts as my child." For years, her situation was followed by the general public in New England, and prayers were said for her deliverance in churches throughout the English colonies. But in spite of all entreaties, she became a Catholic, married a Mohawk man, lived in a longhouse, had two children, and became mother-in-law to Onnasategen, the grand chief of the village.[14]

In 1714, Rev. Joseph Meacham, brother-in-law of this famous "unredeemed" captive, became the new preacher at Coventry. Hannah and Benjamin Janes were probably well acquainted with the ongoing story of Esther Meacham's captive sister, as Hannah's husband Benjamin was a deacon of the church in Coventry for many years, and the ongoing efforts to persuade Eunice to return were fairly common knowledge. Hannah might well have been friends with Esther Meacham; certainly they had much in common, for Esther had been captured during the terrible massacre at Deerfield, and had lived with her Stoddard relatives in Northampton upon her return from captivity; she knew well Hannah's former pastor and home town and the horrors she had endured. In their new lives, in their new settlement, did they ever speak of these things?

One might think, after all they had been through, that the Janes family would have had enough of the frontier, but such was not quite the case. For Hannah's husband Benjamin also held land in the most remote, isolated, and exposed town on the Connecticut River – tiny Northfield, which as its name implies, was north of all English settlement and which, as we've seen, had been attacked by Metacom's forces during King Philip's War, leading to its abandonment. It lay thirty miles north of Pascommuck and Northampton, just south of what is now the Vermont border. This village had been founded by people from Northampton and Hadley; in 1672 the township was granted to a group of associates under the Indian name of Squakheag. The following year, the first settlers built a fort and stockade around a number of small huts roofed with thatch. They had asked Benjamin's father William Janes to accompany them, to be their religious teacher, and it is said that Elder Janes preached his first sermon on the Sabbath after their arrival under the spreading branches of a large oak tree.[15] The spot is still marked with a plaque today.

The indigenous people were the Squakheags, or Sokokis – Western Abenakis whose territory spread from Northfield, Massachusetts, to the great rapids at Bellows Falls, Vermont. It was the Squakheags who had guided the French and the enemy Indians to Deerfield in 1704. Although they were formerly far more numerous, the combination of European diseases and a series of deadly, if sometimes inconclusive, wars against the Mohawks (in 1624, 1650, and 1663) had decimated and scattered them and their southerly neighbours, the Pocumtucks. In the 1660s, the Sokokis had established a fortified encampment near Squakheag, which was attacked in

1663 by Mohawks, Senecas, and Onondagas; although that battle ended indecisively, it marked the beginning of an exodus of Sokokis to New France. In 1664, the Iroquois launched a devastating campaign against the Pocumtucks, destroying their villages, then attacked the Sokokis and the Pennacooks. By 1670 the Native communities in the middle Connecticut Valley had scattered – the first English settlers to arrive at Northfield in the early 1670s, found only a handful of Sokokis still living there.[16]

That was soon to change with the advent of King Philip's War, when Squakheag and its vicinity became a centre of Native resistance. Almost three thousand of Metacom's warriors from all over New England gathered there to pass the winter. The defensive trenches they built on a hill just outside Squakheag are still visible, more than three hundred years later.

The residents of the new town had barely begun to settle in when war broke out in June of 1675. That September, Metacom's men attacked a group of inhabitants and garrison soldiers outside town and killed eight, including Benjamin Janes's half-brothers, as described in chapters 10 and 12. The town was completely abandoned and remained so for ten years.

The family of William Janes was one of the eight families who tried to re-establish the town in 1685, but they were driven away five years later, during King William's War. In June 1690, the General Court authorized the abandonment of the town, "all the inhabitants of Northfield that have any corn or other provision, viz. hogs, horses, cattle, etc. [to] transport it down within the space of 6 or 8 days."[17] No further effort to re-settle Northfield was made for more than two decades. William Janes returned to Northampton and died there.

When Queen Anne's War ended in 1713, the town began to rebuild, and a few years later Benjamin Janes and his nephew Jonathan Janes (who had been stunned but not killed by a tomahawk blow during the attack on Pascommuck) returned. I don't know if Hannah accompanied Benjamin or stayed behind in Coventry with her young children. It seems that Benjamin Janes remained in Northfield for some time, for he was chosen as trustee for the town in 1719 and constable in 1725 and served as an officer in the church. In 1725 he sold out to his nephew. It was at this time, if not earlier, that he was reunited with his other nephew, the former captive, Elisha Searl.

For in 1722 the long-lost Elisha had come "with an Indian companion [or companions] to Northampton seeking his portion of his father's estate . . . and was with reluctance constrained to remain . . . as he was now

strongly attached to his [Catholic] faith and the Indian mode of life."
Speaking no English, he is said to have made himself known to his relatives
by walking with a pair of stilts he had been fond of using when he was a
boy. He wished to return to New France, but "his people to engage him to
abide here & not return to Canada separated him from his companions who
after a few months went back alone." This account suggests that his family
used a degree of coercion and constraint to separate him from his friend
(Abenaki? Kahnawake Mohawk?) and keep him in Northampton, and that
he agreed to remain only after some time. Many people took an interest in
him and used their influence to get him to stay; they gave him presents and
got him a commission. Some inducement seems to have been necessary.
The House of Representatives voted him £10 and desired his Excellency
the governor "to retain him in the publick service as a Sergeant at the
Garrison of Deerfield or Northfield."[18]

One can only wonder about the immense inner adjustment he must have
gone through. Among other things, there was a sweetheart waiting for him
back in New France, a young French woman named "Katreen." How did
he integrate the twenty-one years of life he had spent on the other side of
the religious and cultural divide with the Puritans' view that theirs was the
only righteous way? Apparently he reverted to the religion of his parents –
was this a genuine conversion or simply a matter of survival in New
England, where Catholicism was not tolerated? And how did Elisha reconcile all the conflicting feelings he must have had about Native people and
their way of life? It is known that some returned captives became cultural
intermediaries while others put their former "Indian" lives behind them, or
were caught in a kind of limbo between cultures. I suspect that Elisha
largely disavowed his former life, for he was soon on the front lines of a
war between the English and the Abenakis, serving from late November
1723 under Capt. Joseph Kellogg, himself a returned captive known for his
"unyielding enmity toward the Indians."[19]

The Treaty of Utrecht, which ended Queen Anne's War in 1713, had not
resolved the real issues between either the English and the French or the
English and the Abenakis. The Abenakis were increasingly disturbed by
the substantial growth of the New England colonies in both population and
area, as English settlement spread ever northward up the Connecticut
River, eastward along the coast of Maine, and west into the Berkshires.
In 1713, Connecticut was granted a tract of land on the northern frontier in

exchange for alterations to its southern boundary. These lands were sold by public auction in Hartford in 1716, the proceeds going to Yale College. The land north of Northfield was considered very desirable, lying as it did on the main communications route between Massachusetts and New France, and providing access to the hunting and pelting regions along Lake George and Lake Champlain, in present-day New York.[20] The English proprietors of this huge grant of land began to divide it up for settlement, to the consternation of the Abenakis, who held a prior, if unrecognized, claim to it. The Abenakis looked to the French to defend them against the English invaders of their lands.

Goaded by this steady encroachment on Abenaki land and unfair trading practices by some of the English traders, the Abenakis attempted to stop further settlement. Negotiations between the English and the Abenakis were conducted in 1717 and 1719 but went nowhere. In 1722, following raids on English settlements in Maine, Massachusetts Gov. Samuel Shulte declared war on the Eastern Abenakis of Maine, and the Abenakis of Vermont and New Hampshire soon established a second, western, front of the war. As the English suspected, Vaudreuil, the governor of New France, secretly supported the Abenakis on instructions from Louis XV, encouraged other tribes to assist them, and helped to keep the Iroquois neutral in spite of the efforts of the English (and a substantial increase in the scalp bounty), reminding Indians "that the design of the English is to make themselves master of the entire continent."[21] The families of Abenaki warriors fighting the English were financially assisted by the French king when they retreated from Vermont to St. Francis and Bécancour in New France.

The leader of the Abenaki warriors on the western front was Grey Lock, who was himself not Abenaki but a Woronoake from the Westfield River in Massachusetts, "a chieftain of one of the Pocumtuck confederate clans," and a refugee from King Philip's War. During Queen Anne's War, Grey Lock had been a "French Indian," and had led small war parties against various towns on the Connecticut River. In 1712, he led one of the last raids of the war on Northampton.[22]

By 1723, Grey Lock had a following of refugee warriors and was conducting strikes on the Connecticut Valley; he soon acquired the name of Wawanolewat, "he who fools the others, or puts someone off the track." In August 1723, Grey Lock killed two people near Northfield, and captured two young boys in another raid the next day; he subsequently gave one captive to the Kahnawake Mohawks, and some Kahnawake warriors joined Grey Lock in September. A company of cavalry was posted to Northfield at the end of August and remained for a couple of weeks to protect those harvesting their crops. In October, Grey Lock returned during the corn harvest, killed a man, wounded two others, and carried one unfortunate man into captivity (for the second time). In November of that year, Capt. Joseph Kellogg, who, as we've seen, was a former captive, was ordered to raise a company of soldiers, forty of whom were to be stationed at Northfield and the rest to scout the Connecticut River. Both Elisha Searl and his cousin, Jonathan Janes, were part of this company. Col. John Stoddard, the son of Rev. Solomon Stoddard, endorsed Elisha Searl: "He is now a Sargeant under Capt. Kellogg; was put in at the request of the assembly, on his return from Canada where he had long been a prisoner. He seems to be a discreet and careful man."[23]

As part of its strategy to prevent Abenaki strikes on the vulnerable frontier towns of Northfield, Deerfield, Hadley, and Northampton, along the Connecticut River, the Massachusetts General Court then voted to establish a block-house at a site a few miles north of Northfield near present-day Brattleboro (the site is now submerged by the Connecticut River after a dam was erected at Vernon in 1909). The commanding officer, Capt. Timothy Dwight, was to "post 40 able men, English and western Indians to be employed in scouting a good distance up Connecticut River, West River, Otter Creek, and sometimes eastwardly above Great Monadnock for the discovery of the enemy coming toward any of the frontier towns."

On February 3, Dwight brought four carpenters, twelve soldiers with narrow axes, and two teams over the ice to the site to begin construction of the fort, and requested that Elisha Searl be transferred there. He reported for duty on February 7, three days after Jonathan Janes had arrived on the scene, and Elisha was promoted to lieutenant; as such he was second-in-command of the fort. Both Jonathan and Elisha helped to build the fort, which was of pine timber and contained several buildings within a stockade. It was located near enough to the water to observe any canoes passing by and command the river, and it had one great gun for alarms, which could be heard a long distance, as well as four small swivel guns for defence in the houses. It was completed that summer and named Fort Dummer after Massachusetts Lieut.-Gov. William Dummer. The first English settlement in Vermont, it became the major base of operations for scouting and punitive expeditions into Abenaki country.[24]

From the beginning, friendly Indians were crucial to the fort's construction and defence. Of the original muster roll of 1724, fifty-five men are listed under Capt. Timothy Dwight, a dozen of whom were Native American, mainly from Schaghticoke, Kahnawake, and Hudson River tribes. According to Mary Cabot, the compiler of *Annals of Brattleboro*, "Great importance was attached to the presence of the Indians, and various means were taken to retain them in the service." On June 20, 1724, a committee appointed by the General Court of Massachusetts examining demands by the Mohawks at Fort Dummer agreed that two sachems would be paid two shillings a day, that all Indians be given an allowance for provisions, that their guns be repaired free of charge, that a supply of knives, pipes, tobacco, lead, shots, and flints be made available to them, and that the commanding officer give out one gill of rum a day to each Indian "and some to other men as occasion may require." Daniel Dwight of Northampton, a brother of Timothy Dwight, was chosen as chaplain; in addition to his duties as chaplain he was to "instruct the Indian natives residing thereabouts in the true Christian religion."[25]

The soldiers were on constant alert, as the Abenakis "skulked" in the nearby woods. Although Captain Kellogg's expeditions from the fort succeeded in destroying some Indian villages and crops, the Abenakis adopted evasive strategies, dispersing rather than gathering in palisaded villages, as the Pequots and the Narragansetts had done. In June, Grey Lock's men were seen near Northfield, but made no attack; they later surprised a group of men working in a meadow near Hatfield, then killed two men at Northfield in August, as well as five at Rutland. Over the summer, guards of thirty to forty men were sent out daily when people were harvesting, but some were still careless, such as Hannah Janes's cousin, Nathaniel Edwards, who went to gather flax in Pomeroy's meadow near Northampton without a guard and was killed and scalped. In the fall, Grey Lock was again sighted around the settlements of Deerfield, Westfield, and Northampton. On October 11, 1724, he attacked the fort. About seventy of the enemy and four or five occupants were killed or wounded, but the attack was repulsed, and Fort Dummer does not appear to have been attacked again during the war. The following September, however, a scouting party of six Fort Dummer men travelling west of Fort Dummer were ambushed, only one man escaping. It was the final action of the war.[26]

———

The war ended inconclusively. Grey Lock was never caught or defeated, and he may simply have tired of war. The English and the Abenakis signed a peace treaty at Boston on December 15, 1725. Grey Lock did not meet his objectives: while the peace treaty did result in nearly twenty years without overt hostilities, it didn't stop Puritan expansion up the Connecticut River or into western Massachusetts. In the fall of 1726, Dwight's company at Fort Dummer was discharged, and Captain Kellogg recruited a small company for garrison duty at the fort, where he remained in command until 1740. Kellogg successfully petitioned the General Court for permission to establish a trading post at Fort Dummer, and was appointed agent. The fort became known as the Truck House. Because trade goods were cheaper there than at the French trading houses, Native people came in large numbers, bringing in deer and moose skins and tallow, receiving advances of 50 per cent on rum, sugar, and molasses and 25 per cent on European goods.

Elisha Searl and Jonathan Janes had been discharged on November 30, 1725, and Jonathan returned to his property in Northfield. I'm not sure what Elisha did for the first three years after his discharge, but in 1728 he returned to Pascommuck. After the raid in 1704, the village had been abandoned for thirteen years. Most proprietors or their heirs had sold out, like Benjamin Janes, but a few, like Jonathan Janes's brother Samuel, eventually ventured back. Although his father, mother, sister, and two brothers had been killed there and he had himself been stunned by a blow of a tomahawk, Samuel returned to his father's homestead in 1717 and lived there without a neighbour for three years; he must have been reminded constantly of what had befallen his family there. In 1720, the home of Benoni Jones (husband of the captive Esther Jones) was bought and occupied. Eight years later Elisha Searl married Rebecca Danks and reclaimed his father's farm, but the process of resettlement was slow; thirty-five years after the raid, only six families were resident. Elisha lived to be eighty-five and passed on to his children and grandchildren stories of the attack on Pascommuck, his life in New France, and his visit to the Mississippi River with the Indians, as well as his mother's silver hair pin, which, as of 1905, was still preserved.

So, from the remaining evidence, it appears that Elisha successfully negotiated the transition back to New England Puritan, though I am struck by Colonel Stoddard's description of him as "discreet and careful." I imagine him closely guarding his inner self, which had survived so much turmoil and transformation. What did he think of when he was alone, reflecting on his time in captivity? What had he lost in discarding the identity of the Frenchman Michel Searl and what did he secretly keep? How had the experience marked him? There is one clue that he did not reject all of what he had lived: he named one of his daughters Catherine, in remembrance of the young woman he had loved and left behind in New France.

For some captives, life turned out very differently. In Coventry, Hannah Janes also had several opportunities for reflection upon the horrific events of 1704 and the subsequent captivities of her neighbours, for it is quite likely that Hannah met the most famous Deerfield captive and white Indian – Eunice Williams herself – when Williams visited her sister, Esther Meacham, wife of the minister of Coventry. Williams visited at least twice in the summer of 1741 and again in the fall of 1743. Her visits were public events, attracting crowds of well-wishing friends of the family as well as the curious wherever she went. One can only wonder what Hannah must have felt if she did indeed meet Eunice, who, like herself, had survived the blood and terror of 1704, but who now, thirty-seven years later, wore Native dress, spoke no English, camped in a field with her husband rather than stay in her family's house, and who, despite ongoing pleas, prayers, and exhortations, refused to renounce her life among the Kahnawake Mohawks or her Catholicism, reputedly because she feared that living among heretics would endanger her and her children's salvation.[27]

Was Hannah curious about this near neighbour who had lived so many years on the other side of the deepest divide? Or did she stay away – was it simply too much to contemplate a face-to-face encounter with someone who had joined the "enemy," who had allied herself with those servants of Satan who had scalped her and murdered her children? Did she join in the prayers for Eunice's soul? Did she, as some did, make any connection between the arrival of Eunice and the extraordinary religious revival sweeping up and down the Connecticut Valley? Did she attend the famous sermon at nearby Mansfield, given by a Williams cousin of Eunice's, Solomon Williams, on behalf of Eunice and her husband, where the congregation was so large that only a small portion could be seated inside the meeting house, the rest spilling outside, some coming from as far as twenty miles away?[28]

Hannah and her husband were almost certainly caught up in the fervour and frenzy of the Great Awakening, as the religious revival of the 1740s was called; Coventry was one of the towns deeply affected by this spiritual excitement. Rev. Jonathan Edwards (no relation to Hannah), one of the leaders of the Awakening, reported, "Last spring and summer the word of God was wonderful at Coventry, under the ministry of the Reverend Mr. Meacham. I had opportunity to converse with some of the Coventry people, who gave me a very remarkable account of the surprising change that appeared in the most rude and vicious persons there."[29]

The Rev. Steven Williams, brother of Esther and Eunice, described an outdoor religious meeting held by his brother Eleazar and Coventry's Reverend Meacham "on ye Meeting-House Hill," the congregation "remarkably attentive & Grave." In the evening Meacham preached again, "and there was considerable Crying among ye people in one part of ye House or another."[30] What did this fervour mean to Hannah? What, if any, release or resolve did it bring?

In fact, an initial revival had been sparked a decade earlier among Hannah's relatives in Pascommuck under the leadership of the charismatic Reverend Edwards. It is likely that Elisha Searl and Hannah's nephew Samuel Janes, who now both lived at Pascommuck, were part of this revival. It was also during the Great Awakening that most of the non-Christian Native people still remaining in New England converted to Christianity.[31]

The years of peace that had allowed Fort Dummer to become a trading post, Elisha Searl to become a farmer, and Eunice Williams to visit her New England relatives in Coventry and perhaps meet Hannah Janes, were shattered in 1744 with the outbreak of yet another war – King George's War. Once again, Fort Dummer became a key defensive position, and Northfield a depot for supplies and a place to marshal troops behind the front lines. Once again Abenaki territory became the main war route between New England and New France. As in Grey Lock's War, ill-equipped and poorly organized English militia companies tried to counter surprise enemy attacks as best they could. At Pascommuck, Samuel Janes helped build a fortified garrison house; Jonathan Janes joined a company from Northampton in the attack on the French fort at Louisbourg in 1744. Within five years, every English settler was driven out of Vermont by the French and their Abenaki allies, only Fort Dummer and one other fort, Fort Number Four, remained as English outposts.

CHAPTER
15

Vanishing

Another war followed King George's War – the Seven Years' War, or the French and Indian War, as it was known in America – but it would be the last between New England and New France. The Janes family continued to send its young men into battle: Elisha Janes fought in the Crown Point campaign in 1755 and Nathaniel Searls, possibly a relation of Elisha Searl (there were several spellings of his last name), fought in the same company. Jonathan Janes, the grandson of the Samuel Janes who had been struck by a tomahawk at Pascommuck, was present at the surrender of Louisbourg in 1758.[1]

Hannah Janes died in 1755 at the age of eighty. During her lifetime, the Abenakis, who had been the instrument of so much grief in her family, remained undefeated. When, in 1759, Robert Rogers attacked the Abenaki village of St. Francis (along the St. Lawrence River, east of Montreal), massacring at least thirty of its sleeping inhabitants, he counted six hundred scalps hanging on poles. The Abenakis had resisted the invasion of their land for eighty years, but their resistance was being worn down, as army after army pursued them to their villages and destroyed their families, homes, and crops. Many Abenakis in Vermont had withdrawn from their villages to escape the war, famine, or disease, and a sizeable number moved to Canada. They were assisting the French to defend Quebec, when the

English captured it in 1759; by 1760 Fort Dummer was abandoned, and the Abenakis found themselves treated as a conquered people.[2]

The year 1760 was another turning point in the history of Indian–white relations in North America. With the defeat of the French at Quebec, the British gained a huge new northern empire and were able to expand unchecked. English soldiers returning from fighting in the north told their relatives of vast forests and rich lands suitable for farming; perhaps this is how the Janes family first heard of land in Vermont. With northern New England no longer a war zone, the sons of New England families flooded into the region, seeking new land they could call their own. Many came from western Massachusetts and Connecticut, where the population had increased 500 per cent in thirty years. For the now-typical southern New England farm of fifty acres was barely adequate to support a family. The original farms had become environmentally degraded – they suffered increasingly from crop pests and soil exhaustion owing to overcropping and overgrazing, and firewood was scarce, since the forests had been cleared. The New England way of life was unsustainable on a fixed land base: in the average family of six or seven children, only one could inherit the family farm; the others emigrated to escape poverty.[3]

A number of my ancestors were among the thousands who thronged to Vermont, New York, and other frontier areas, some even going as far as Nova Scotia to the lands of the displaced Acadians. The earliest of my ancestors to head north was Ephraim Ranney (1725–1811), who came to Westminster, Vermont, in 1761, from Middletown, Connecticut, where his Scottish great-grandfather Thomas Ranney had settled in 1658. Numerous Ranney men – Ephraim's uncles, cousins, and brothers – had taken part in the French and Indian War; at least two had died and others had partici-pated in the capture of Louisbourg. Ephraim Ranney bought land on the banks of the Connecticut and opened a tavern. His son Ephraim junior (1748–1835) helped clear much land on the bank of the Connecticut River, and then opened a store in Westminster West – the building and his 1815 account book still exist today.[4]

The migrants were a restless bunch, often moving on from one place to the next, living a rough frontier life similar in hardship to that of the first Puritans – but without the moral discipline of their ancestors. These migrants distinguished themselves instead by a new competitiveness and acquisitiveness that soon became the stereotypical trademark of the Yankee. An important element of this transformation was the reworking of their mythology about their history and destiny. They no longer thought of themselves as refugees from a foreign land; they were victors who had won their right to the land by conquest. As for the original inhabitants of the land, they were either defeated peoples or former allies who were now irrelevant obstacles to be cleared from the path of settlement. Soon they would be mythologized as a vanishing breed, an inferior and dying race.

The Abenakis who returned to their homelands in Vermont after the war found their territories occupied and claimed by English settlers in spite of the fact that the Articles of Capitulation had included a clause protecting the lands, rights, and religion of France's Native allies. The Royal Proclamation of 1763 had established the Appalachian watershed as the western boundary of English settlement, which supposedly safeguarded Abenaki lands west of the Green Mountains; non-Natives could obtain these lands only by purchase through the Crown. But the northern superintendent of Indian affairs for the Crown, Sir William Johnson, contended that the boundary didn't apply to either the Kahnawakes or the Abenakis. Their lands now belonged to King George, although they were still allowed hunting and fishing rights. The Abenakis were able to retain only a tiny remnant of their former lands, the village of Missisquois, at the northern end of Lake Champlain, near the Quebec border, where white people were forbidden to settle. Any bands not living there were regarded as wanderers. Traditionally the Abenakis had used dispersal as a survival tactic, and they turned to that strategy once again. While settlers flooded into their homelands, they retreated deeper into the forest and mountains, to the most marginal lands; the family became the basic unit of survival. Small enclaves survived in Vermont and preserved their cultural and political identity, returning occasionally to their traditional hunting, planting, fishing, or harvesting areas. Some married whites. But many Abenakis left for other parts of northern New England, including New York and Maine; others went to Quebec and the Maritime provinces. Some joined inter-tribal communities at Schaghticoke, near Albany, New York, and Cowass in Vermont, which had been established after King Philip's War. Life was hard for those who remained in their homelands, but those who left lost their connection to the ancestral and sacred sites that linked the people to their past.

I do not know what sort of contact Ephraim Ranney and his descendants had with the Abenakis, for there are no records of any dealings between them. Perhaps he, like most Vermont settlers, subscribed to the self-serving notion that Vermont was "uninhabited" before their arrival.[5] Perhaps he occasionally saw the small family groups that continued to return to the ancient Abenaki fishing site at Bellows Falls near Westminster. While the men fished, the women sold baskets to the townspeople and tourists.

In 1760, the number of settlers in Vermont had not been greater than three hundred, but after the defeat of New France, the English population increased dramatically. In 1761 alone, seventy-eight new townships were granted in the northern Connecticut Valley; six Vermont towns were established that year, six in 1763, and seven in 1764. By 1774, seventy new towns had sprung up in Vermont, "many of them peopled by restless migrants making their second or third move toward the frontier."[6] The non-Native population of northern New England increased from perhaps 60,000 to 150,000 in fifteen years, and the number of settlers in the Connecticut Valley from a few hundred to several thousand.

The peace that attracted the settlers to Vermont was short-lived, for within fifteen years of Ephraim Ranney's arrival, Britain and the colonies were at war. In Vermont, resistance to Britain had started with resistance to the "loyalist" New York Colony's jurisdiction over Vermont, spearheaded by the famed Green Mountain Boys organized by Ethan Allen. In 1772 Westminster was made the shire town of Cumberland County because of resistance to the New York Court in the previous shire town of Chester. When, in 1775, the county court convened under New York's authority and "loyalist domination," a group of Westminster settlers opposed to this took possession of the courthouse. In the ensuing melee, the New Yorkers opened fire, killing one man and wounding four others. When the Green Mountain Boys arrived, heavily armed, they in turn took possession of the courts and threw the judge, the sheriff, his posse, and court officials into jail. News of the "Westminster Massacre," as it became known, spread rapidly and fanned the flames for independence. At a convention held in Westminster on January 15, 1777, Vermont was declared an independent state, which it remained until 1791, when it was admitted into the Union. Deacon Ephraim Ranney and four of his sons – Ephraim junior, Elijah, Daniel, and Waitstill (who was fourteen years old in 1776) – served in the Revolutionary War along with at least ten other Ranneys and eight men of the related Wilcox family. Ephraim's son Elijah was elected to the Vermont legislature in 1783.[7]

During the war, much of Vermont was once again a no man's land, with Lake Champlain the route between the English and their aboriginal allies in Canada and the American colonies. The defeat of an American expedition to Canada alarmed settlers in the Champlain and Connecticut Valleys and a number of towns were evacuated. The Americans wanted the Abenakis to act as a protective barrier, but after a century as enemies, and with the loss of their lands, the Abenakis were understandably wary. Both the English and the Americans threatened them with extinction if they didn't join their side. In the end, the Abenakis fought for both sides, but their support was half-hearted and many tried to remain neutral.

When the war ended with American victory, the Peace of Paris that recognized American independence was negotiated without reference to Native Americans, and the ensuing treaty made no mention of them. Although the Natives from the multi-tribal community of Schaghticoke, who had supported the Americans, were rewarded with a grant of land in Vermont after the war, the Americans refused to acknowledge the continuity of the Abenakis' occupation of Vermont or recognize their ownership of the land. They denied the Abenakis title and any rights to their land, including the village of Missisquoi, and treated them as unwelcome wanderers. Some Abenakis sought refuge in Canada, where they live to this day, and other extended family bands tenaciously remained in northern Vermont to survive as best they could. After the war, the new Yankee settlers "found it easy to believe that the only Abenakis they encountered were trespassers from St. Francis in Quebec who had no business in Vermont."[8] With the end of the war in 1783, there was another period of intensive settlement in Vermont, particularly in the Champlain Valley, and this time my Janes ancestors joined the flood.

Ira and Ethan Allen had formed the Onion River Land Company with Vermont frontiersman Remember Baker in 1777 to acquire the fertile land around Missisquoi and Lake Champlain. They headed the movement to dispossess and deny Abenakis their sovereignty, and spread the fear that the Abenakis were still a threat to white settlers. Tensions increased in 1786, when Abenakis from Missisquoi laid claim to their lands and were told bluntly that they had lost their title. Col. Ebenezer Allen (later one of the first settlers of South Hero Island in Lake Champlain, where my Janes ancestors acquired land) was appointed by Gov. Thomas Chittenden of Vermont to "remove all unlawful intruders by force." Allen and a small detachment of troops patrolled the Missisquoi Bay area, protecting settlers.[9]

Among those who moved into the lands acquired by the Onion River Land Company was my ancestor Elijah Janes, grandson of Hannah Janes.

Serving as first a minuteman at Williamstown, Vermont, in 1776, later as lieutenant in a regiment of dragoons, and then as quartermaster, he had fought in the Revolutionary War from 1776 to 1782. Born in 1744 in Coventry, Connecticut, the son of Hannah's son Seth, he had been among the early settlers of Pittsfield, in western Massachusetts, before moving around 1790 to South Hero Island.[10]

One of "four beautiful Islands . . . which formerly had been inhabited by savages" as recorded by Samuel de Champlain in 1609, South Hero was the southern part of Grand Isle, the largest island in Lake Champlain, which had been granted in 1779 to Ethan and Ira Allen, under the name of Two Heroes (modestly named by Ethan Allen after himself and his brother). Grand Isle was later divided into North and South Hero Islands.[11] The names on the original charter for South Hero include Solomon Stanton, Joshua Stanton, Edward Harris, and George Harris; there is a good possibility that these are relations. The first settlers arrived in 1783, including Col. Ebenezer Allen, who reached the southern end of the island and took possession of South Hero. (The oldest surviving log cabin in the United States, the Hyde Cabin on North Hero Island, dates to that year.)

"Considerable numbers" of Abenakis had occupied Grand Isle during the early years of the war and these and other Abenakis had fought with the British in skirmishes around Lake Champlain. "Quite a numerous body" of Indians wintered on Stave Island off South Hero in 1783, which may have been the same settlement as that recorded at the beginning of the war. The anthropologist Gordon Day recorded an Abenaki oral tradition of an attack on their village located near the southern tip of South Hero Island, possibly in 1777 – an indication that these Abenakis were pro-American. Their assailants were probably Native allies of the British. Some Abenakis were still there when the Janes family arrived on the island around 1790, for the early inhabitants of Grand Isle County recorded that Abenakis continued to live in the region until at least 1800, and after that date bands of eight or ten families spent part of the year at their traditional camping grounds well into the nineteenth century.[12]

When Elijah Janes arrived at South Hero, the population of the township was 280. (Elijah's sons Heman and Humphrey had arrived earlier, as they are included in the 1790 census.) By 1793 there were more than 200 families, including Elijah's wife and children, and by 1800 the population had reached 609. The grant list indicates that Elijah Janes had property worth $6. He was considered a man of substance, owning and selling considerable land. Elijah's son Heman, born in 1765, married Abigail Burdick, likely a daughter or other relation of James Burdick, who ran a ferry from Colchester Point on the mainland to South Hero from 1793. She may also have been a descendant of the Burdicks who lived first at Westerly, Rhode Island, across the Pawcatuck River from Thomas Stanton, and who married into the Stanton family. Numerous Janes cousins, brothers, and sisters also came to Vermont and settled in various towns.[13]

Like their Puritan ancestors of the seventeenth century, Vermont's settlers raised or made almost everything for their daily needs, growing flax for garments, tablecloths, and towels, making candles, soap, butter, cheese, knitted stockings, mittens, carts, sleds, and furniture. Nearly all families made maple syrup. The settlers were also transforming the landscape, cutting down the oak and pine forests of the Champlain Valley, marketing the lumber, especially oak timber for shipbuilding, pine for masts and spans. These ecological changes caused further hardship for the Abenakis;one settler describing a group of Abenakis seen in northern Vermont in 1799–1800 as "being in a necessitous and almost starving condition, which probably arose from the moose and deer (which formerly abounded here) being destroyed by the settlers." This particular group survived by making baskets, birch-bark containers, and trinkets and selling them at the settlements; they left in the spring and did not return.[14]

The Abenakis made numerous attempts through the courts to regain their lands, including those that the Janes family now "owned," but their claims were always denied because they could show no title or proof of ownership. Their efforts to regain their land were complicated by conflicting claims by the Kahnawake Mohawks to original occupancy of the eastern shore of Lake Champlain – the Mohawks claimed parts of western Vermont as hunting territory because of previous raids against the Abenakis. In 1798, five chiefs representing the Six Nations presented the Vermont legislature with a petition signed by twenty chiefs of the different nations, requesting compensation for hunting grounds they had lost in Vermont. The claim included Grand Isle. Their claim was dismissed: "their claim if it ever did exist, has long since been done away and become extinct, in consequence of the treaty of peace in 1763 between the King of Great Britain and the French King, . . . said Indians have no real claim either in justice or equity." Another delegation in 1800, accompanied by a representative of the Abenaki Nation, appeared before the legislature, with authorization to make a final settlement of their claims. Vermont Governor

Isaac Tichenor met with Abenakis and Kahnawakes and said "if ever a claim existed, it is wholly extinguished by previous treaties between other powers." The Abenakis would go to court again in 1812, 1826, 1853, and 1874, to no avail; more and more Abenakis left their old village sites as it became clear that American settlement would engulf their lands and their rights would be denied. "By 1800, in the eyes of the new Vermonters, the Western Abenakis were trespassing nomads with no present rights and no legitimate historical claim to the country that they had inhabited and continued to inhabit."[15]

At St. Francis in Quebec, the influx of Abenakis from Vermont prompted the St. Francis Abenakis in 1797 to request a grant of additional lands in the eastern townships of Lower Canada. They were granted more than eight thousand acres of new land in 1805 in Durham Township, just south of St. Francis, and established a satellite village. But pressure on the land continued and the Abenakis struggled to survive on a parcel of poor land that didn't produce enough crops for them to live on. By the 1830s the community of St. Francis was in dire straits, and many Abenakis were forced to go elsewhere to make a living, some even going to the Pacific Northwest coast in the employ of the Hudson's Bay Company.[16]

In the view of most white settlers, the Western Abenakis seemed to have disappeared from Vermont by 1800, and they told themselves that the sad remnants had all moved en masse to Canada. In fact, several hundred Abenakis survived in northwestern New England after 1800; some still lived along the east shore of Lake Champlain and on the islands. The settlers were largely unaware of those who stayed, because the "vagrants" who appeared on the edges of white communities were usually referred to as "gypsies." Some intermarried. Some worked as day labourers, carpenters, tanners, and traders, in or near the settlements. My Janes ancestor in Vermont likely shared the nineteenth-century Euro-American view that the Abenakis, like all other "Indians," were a vanishing race, doomed to disappear before the advance of "civilization."[17]

THE HARRIS FAMILY

Ten Generations
of the Harris Family

  I. **James Harris**   married 1666   **Sarah (Eliot?)**
      (1642–1715)

  II. Asa Harris (1680–1715)   m.   Elizabeth Rogers Stanton
                                                           (1673–1750)

  III. **Asa Harris** (1709–1762)   m.   Anna Ely (1716–1788)

  IV. **Ely Harris** (1755–1813)   m.   **Lucretia Ransom** (1756–1836)

  V. **Rev. James Harris** (1785–1858)   m.   Laura ("Lorrainy") Janes
      (brother of **Elijah Harris**)   (1787–1873)

  VI. **James Harris** (1824–1885)   m.   Julia Ranney (1824–1880)

  VII. Lydia Harris (1852–1925)   m.   Rev. George B. Davis
                                                           (1848–1918)

  VIII. Ada Minnie Davis (1870–1969)   m.   Rev. E. G. D. Freeman
                                                           (1890–1972)

  IX. George E. Freeman (b. 1921)   m.   D. June Maxwell (b. 1930)

  X. Victoria Freeman (b. 1956)

CHAPTER
16

Repeating Patterns

One thing I have noticed in the course of my research is the way in which patterns of interaction between the English and Native people that were established early on in New England were subsequently repeated, with variations, across great distances and over many generations. If the story of the Janes family reflects the lingering consequences of King Philip's War and the enduring race hatred it engendered, that of my Harris ancestors, who moved from Connecticut to New York State and then to Ontario, reveals a recurring pattern of English frontier settlement: the dispossession of aboriginal people and their marginalization except for war-time alliance, as well as a recurring image of them as a degraded and vanishing race. These larger patterns, which I'll explore in this first chapter of the Harris family story, form the background for the story of my great-great-great-great-uncle Elijah Harris, whose life illustrates, among other things, the persistence of John Eliot's vision of converting and "civilizing" the Indians, and the continuity of a committed if paternalistic concern for their welfare on the part of a small minority of English settlers.

Elijah Harris was born in the late 1780s or early 1790s in Connecticut, one of eleven children born to Ely Harris and Lucretia Ransom of Colchester, Connecticut; he was the brother of my direct ancestor, James. They were descended from James Harris of Boston, born in 1642, whose wife appears to have been Sarah Eliot, the daughter of John Eliot's brother Jacob.[1] This early James Harris had fought in the Narragansett campaign during King Philip's War and had moved to Mohegan in 1704. His children had married into the Rogers and Stanton families, among others, and like these families the Harrises had enjoyed friendly relations with and often been neighbours of the Mohegans.

But the Harrises also became involved in a bitter power struggle, which began in the 1730s and eventually split the Mohegan tribe. James Harris, Jr., the brother of my ancestor Asa and son of James Harris of Boston, vigorously supported the sachemship of Ben Uncas, the candidate favoured by the Connecticut authorities and considered a puppet candidate by the supporters of John Uncas, who constituted the majority of the tribe. Harris Junior even arranged for Ben Uncas to send an "Address to the King," congratulating the Prince of Wales on the birth of his second child, as a ploy to confirm Ben Uncas's legitimacy. He also solicited donations to support the Connecticut government in its legal battle against the Masons and the majority of the Mohegans in the Mohegan land case.

According to tribal historian Melissa Jayne Fawcett, "the Connecticut assembly and the English overseers (overseers were first appointed in 1719) supported a particular lineage of hereditary sachems who sold, leased and rented tribal lands to whites for individual profit." In fact, in 1745 the Mohegans complained to the General Assembly that James Harris, Jr., and my direct ancestor Asa Harris, Jr., had obtained twenty-year leases on their lands "of which none of ye Indeans knew any thing till after said Leas was obtained but Ben our Sachem who we think hath no Right to Leas our Lands without our Leave . . . and by all which Doings of ye said Harrises we are Exceedingly Distressed impoverished and allmost undone." Asa received a hundred acres of Mohegan land, for which he had only to plough one acre as rent "which we think is but a small rent for a hundred acres." He had fenced and ploughed the land, cutting "a vast deal of timber," and was about to build his house, but the Mohegans apparently succeeded in overturning the lease, for, within two years, Asa moved to Saybrook, where his son Ely, the father of Elijah and James, was born in 1755.[2]

Ely Harris, the great-grandson of James Harris and the great-great-grandson of Thomas Stanton and Jacob Eliot, accompanied his father and mother to Canada in 1761; they were my first ancestors to cross the border as settlers. Asa had joined a large migration of Harris and Denison relatives to settle in Horton Township, Nova Scotia, on lands vacated by the expulsion of the Acadians in 1760. But Asa froze to death in a blizzard in 1762, and six-year-old Ely then went back to southeastern Connecticut with his mother. It would be another forty-one years before he returned to Canada.

At the age of eighteen, Ely Harris had married Lucretia Ransom of Colchester (the town whose land had been acquired for six shillings from Uncas's son Owaneco, while he was intoxicated) and began a family there, acquiring lands in Colchester and nearby Salem. Although he had been a private in the militia just before the Revolutionary War, there is no known evidence that he fought in it, though at least two of his brothers did. He sold his land in 1793 and by 1795 was in the colony of New York for the birth of his tenth child, Elijah Harris's younger brother, John.

The Harrises were among the thousands of Yankees who headed to New York in the late 1700s in search of new land. "Emigrants are swarming into these fertile regions in shoals, like the ancient Israelites seeking the land of promise," observed Elkanah Watson, a Yankee migrant and Albany promoter, for the newly cleared and cultivated farms were free of pests and produced superior yields during the first few years, as much as twenty to twenty-five bushels an acre, compared to the southern New England standard of twelve to sixteen bushels.[3] In addition, New York offered excellent transportation routes for the export market in wheat, which was booming in the late 1780s and early 1790s, as a result of bad harvests and war in Europe. From 1790 to 1820 the population of New York quadrupled, from roughly 340,000 to 1,373,000: by then it was the most populous and dynamic state in the young republic. The new Yankee settlers soon acquired a reputation as hard-working, shrewd, pious, opportunistic, covetous, and hypocritical. To the frequent annoyance of their neighbours, they still saw themselves as God's favoured people and defined their actions in biblical terms.[4]

Ely Harris brought his family to the Otsego patent near Otsego Lake, a two-and-a-half-day journey west from Albany: by 1798 he was listed as ensign of a new militia company in Otsego County. He appeared in the 1800 census near his son Ariel and his brother Asa, with a household, but no land records have been found for him, so he was probably a tenant farmer or living with his oldest children, who had bought farms near Springfield, just north of Otsego Lake.

The history of the Otsego patent exemplifies the rapacious land speculation that fuelled the English settlement of New York. Ownership of the Otsego lands had first passed from the Iroquois to Col. George Croghan, an

Irishman who had been Pennsylvania's foremost fur trader and negotiator with the Indians (a Pennsylvanian version of Thomas Stanton) and a close friend and deputy of Sir William Johnson, the British Crown's powerful northern superintendent of Indian affairs. When, in October 1768, the English had concluded a treaty in which the Iroquois surrendered their lands lying east of the Unadilla River, including all of the country around Otsego Lake, Johnson, Croghan, and their friends met privately with the sachems and, in a move reminiscent of the Atherton Company's acquisition of the Narragansett lands, bought the title to almost all the land acquired within New York, thereby cheating the Crown that they were supposed to serve. In fact, by the Royal Proclamation of 1763, it was illegal for anyone other than the Crown to treat with the Indians. Croghan secured 100,000 acres known as the Otsego patent, as well as four other patents, all for less than one shilling per acre. He paid almost nothing down – he had no money but a lot of connections – and paid instead primarily in promissory notes secured by bonds. These were never honoured and were eventually recognized as worthless. The Iroquois received nothing from their bargain with Croghan or the other patent holders, and they never regained their land.

When the Revolutionary War broke out, the Tuscaroras, Mohawks, and Oneidas at Onoquaga, the largest and most impressive Iroquois village in the vicinity of Otsego, remained loyal to Britain, mostly through the influence of Joseph Brant, brother of William Johnson's Mohawk partner Molly Brant. (Brant had attended Moore's Charity School, a new school for Indians in Connecticut.) From Onoquaga, Brant led Loyalist rangers to attack settlements at Springfield and in the Mohawk Valley. In 1778 the Americans destroyed Onoquaga; a month later Iroquois and English Loyalists retaliated. New York soon became a land of abandoned, plundered, and ruined homesteads, and by 1783, Otsego was virtually depopulated. George Croghan, proprietor of the Otsego patent, was ruined.

In 1782 the British were defeated and the following year gave up all of North America south of the Great Lakes, abandoning their Iroquois allies to the Americans. Refugees from Onoquaga followed Joseph Brant into exile and resettled on the Grand River in Upper Canada, where Elijah Harris would encounter them several decades later.[5]

After Croghan's ruin, the Otsego patent was acquired by an enterprising speculator named William Cooper under extremely questionable circumstances; Cooper paid half of its market value, mostly on dubious credit, and quickly brought in settlers to consolidate his hold on the land. Cooperstown was founded in 1786 and, by the late 1780s and 1790s, Cooper's success in rapidly selling and settling Otsego made him a national, and then international, celebrity. The population of Otsego was 2,700 by 1790, and leaped to 21,343 by 1810. Cooper was named a judge in spite of his scanty education, and three years later he was elected to Congress. His son, the novelist James Fenimore Cooper, chronicled the settling of Otsego in his novel *The Pioneers*; perhaps it is fitting that his novel *The Last of the Mohicans* gave the fullest expression to the myths of the noble savage and the dying race.

For by the time young Elijah and his family arrived in 1795, the Iroquois population of New York had declined to 3,500, about a third of what it had been thirty years earlier. Most of the demoralized survivors were confined to small reservations some distance to the west of Otsego. It's quite possible that members of the Harris family subscribed to another prevailing myth of the time: the myth of the second creation, in which the settlers entered a land they called pure nature or wilderness, a dangerous adversary they were destined to conquer. Such a view of the land implied no human predecessors. "By telling themselves stories of their renewed creation of a wasteland, the victorious Americans erased from memory the accomplishments of the Indians. The newcomers cast the natives as closer to wolves and bears than to civilized human beings."[6] Yet the Six Nations had been a sedentary, agricultural people, whose agriculture was more productive per acre than that of the settlers. They had developed extensive trade networks, sophisticated diplomacy, and a well-established system of laws and individual legal rights, not to mention three levels of government: the village, the nation, and the League of Six Nations Confederacy.

Elijah may well have encountered some of the small groups of Iroquois and Mahicans (not to be confused with the Mohegans of Connecticut or with Cooper's fictional Mohicans) who returned to Otsego annually to hunt or fish, sell venison, fish, brooms, medicines, baskets, and deerskin moccasins, or beg for food. The sole Indian character of James Fenimore Cooper's *The Pioneers*, Chingachgook, was based on one such wandering Mahican basket-maker and hunter named Captain John – it's possible that Elijah knew the very man. Cooper's fictional portrayal reveals the way many settlers would have thought about the Indians they encountered: Chingachgook, once a great warrior, hunter, and sachem, has become an aged, debauched, pathetic basket-maker, who laments his dispossession and degradation when drunk and at the point of death, but can do nothing to change it. As historian Alan Taylor points out in *William Cooper's Town*, a history of the area, this depiction of helpless, hopeless Native victimhood would prove to be a tenacious and convenient stereotype.[7]

Otsego's settlers generally taught their children to hate and fear "Indians." Author Henry Clarke Wright recalled that no child was "allowed to grow up in that region, without imbibing more or less hatred and horror of the Indians. Tales of Indian cruelties were in the mouths of all mothers and nurses."[8]

Young Elijah Harris may have acquired these attitudes, at least to some degree, and his own family's participation in King Philip's War and the later intercolonial wars must have added a few horror stories of their own to the local, one-sided stories of Indian savagery. At the same time, Elijah's perceptions of Native people were likely also shaped by his extended family's long history with the Mohegans, in which real friendships had developed and been remembered over the generations.

Ely and Lucretia did not stay long in Otsego County. They left about 1802 to join in the early settlement of Oxford County, Ontario, taking their younger and unmarried children with them. In this they were not unusual, for most settlers departed Otsego within two decades, selling their farms to repeat the process of settlement farther north or west. Many settlers followed a pattern similar to those people today who buy houses, renovate them, and resell them for a profit. After 1799, there were a growing number of tenant farms in Otsego, as many settlers failed to fulfil their purchase contracts, were issued leases, and evicted if their rent was fifty days late. In fact, one-third of the taxpayers of Otsego Township in 1800 had departed within three years; nearly one-half of the heads of households listed in the census of 1800 had died or departed by the time of the federal census in 1810. For most settler families, Otsego was a temporary stop on the way to somewhere else. Many went to Ontario where, under certain conditions, they could find two-hundred-acre farms for free.

Family tradition has it that Ely Harris came to Canada as a United Empire Loyalist. This does not appear to be true, though politics may well have figured in his decision to leave the United States. It is more likely that he was a Federalist, as was Otsego's patron, William Cooper. Federalists were conservatives who believed in the necessity of a hierarchical and stable social order governed by gentlemen; they predicted anarchy, terror, and tyranny as the probable outcome of the democratic form of government advocated by the Republicans. Although they had fought against the British in the revolution, they favoured reconciliation with the Loyalists, and the mistreatment of Loyalists prompted some to leave the new republic. While Otsego County had been largely Federalist in the election of 1792, with William Cooper pressuring Otsego residents to vote that way, the Republicans won every seat in Otsego County in the 1802 and 1803 elections. Perhaps, deploring this swing to Republicanism, Ely Harris decided to leave.

Ely, Lucretia, and their younger children, including Elijah, arrived at what is now Ingersoll, Ontario, along the Thames River, north of Lake Erie, in 1802. They were the first ancestors of mine to be permanent residents of Canada. There is a family tradition that Ely and his sons came to Oxford County by horseback, though pioneer settlers usually made the journey by wagon pulled by oxen, with the family cow following behind. After leaving New York State, Ely and his family followed the Detroit Path (an ancient Native path) from Niagara north to Ancaster and then westward north of Lake Erie. English settlements were few and far between, and most of the way would have been through dense forest. My ancestor, James Harris, was then about seventeen years of age, and his brother Elijah was probably slightly older.

The Six Nations territory on the Grand River was the last major settlement they passed on their way to Ingersoll, and there the Harrises would have encountered other refugees from New York State. Founded in 1784, it was now home to two thousand displaced Mohawks, Cayugas, Senecas, Oneidas, Onondagas, and Tuscaroras from Onoquaga who had followed Joseph Brant to safety in British North America after losing their homelands in the American Revolutionary War. Their considerable lands in Upper Canada had been purchased by the Crown from the Ojibwa (also known as the Mississaugas, Chippewas, and Anishinabe) in 1784 for £2000. However, in a move deplored by many of his kinsmen – though intended to raise funds for the Six Nations – Brant sold and leased considerable land to white settlers. By 1798, 350,000 acres had been transferred, with the result that a growing British population lived nearby. The Grand River settlement boasted houses, a church, a school, and missionaries. Ironically, the first mission was run by the same Society for the Propagation of the Gospel in New England for which Thomas Weld had raised funds and which had supported the work of John Eliot in the 1600s; the Society, now known as the New England Company, was itself a refugee from the revolution.

Most of the territory north of Lake Erie was very sparsely populated. Except for a handful of French farmers along the Detroit River and a few isolated French trading posts (mainly in the north), what is now Ontario had been occupied exclusively by aboriginal people until the American Revolution. Three successive waves of aboriginal people had occupied the lands north of Lake Erie since the first European contact in the seventeenth century. The Neutrals, who were allied with the Hurons, had been numerous when, in 1615–16, Étienne Brûlé became the first white man to visit the area that later became Oxford County. After the (then) Five Nations defeated and dispersed the Hurons and Neutrals in the mid-1600s, they had used the area as hunting territory. By 1701 the Mohawks had been defeated and displaced by the Ojibwa and allied First Nations, and by 1768 an estimated twenty-five Ojibwa villages were located in southern Ontario.[9]

Most of the land through which the Harris family travelled on their journey to Oxford County, although still used by the Ojibwa and Six Nations as hunting grounds, was no longer in aboriginal hands, but had been sold to the Crown. In a significant departure from the earlier principle of *vacuum domicilium* often cited in New England, by which unimproved lands were considered vacant and available to settlers, the Royal Proclamation of 1763 (which is still seen by many aboriginal people as the Magna Carta of aboriginal rights in Canada) had formally recognized Indian title to their hunting grounds, prohibited the purchase of aboriginal lands by individuals, and stipulated that land must first be surrendered to the Crown. Originally intended as a means of maintaining Britain's strategic alliances with aboriginal peoples, to England's credit the principle continued to be law even when it no longer benefitted England. Significantly, and in contrast to the practice in New England a century earlier, the chiefs alone did not have the power to surrender lands; all members of the band that owned the land had to be called together to consider a surrender before the appropriate chiefs could sign the treaties. In fact, one of the major factors leading to the American Revolutionary War had been the frustration of American settlers whose movement into "Indian country," especially the coveted Ohio Valley, was restricted by this proclamation.[10]

Yet, after the revolution, many of the old patterns of interaction between Natives and newcomers that had developed in the New England colonies were transplanted to Canada along with the new settlers. For example, although the British formally recognized aboriginal title, the end result of the surrenders was much the same as south of the border, for officials of the Indian Department – then a military department of the colonial government concerned with maintaining Indian allies – pressed the Ojibwa to sell their land. In several instances, land surrenders were demanded as a test of Indian loyalty – something the Native people wished to prove because the Americans were their only alternative. Indeed, according to historian Peter Schmalz, the Ojibwa considered the British nearly as bad as the Americans in taking away their land, but they feared the Americans would exterminate them.

Also, aboriginal people were recognized as possessing the land, but, in English eyes, did not fully own it. Indians were regarded as living autonomously under the Crown's protection on lands already part of the Crown's domain. As such, they were not free to sell or give away their own land to whomever they pleased, but could grant lands only to the British government – the European power that had "discovered" the land.

Between 1781 and 1806, as large numbers of United Empire Loyalists sought land in Canada, Britain acquired the waterfront along the St. Lawrence River, Lake Ontario, the Niagara River, Lake Erie, the Detroit River, Lake St. Clair, and the St. Clair River. The area ceded was often incredibly vague, since the land had not been surveyed; the land cessions of one band often included the territory of several other bands, and some aboriginal people surrendered land they did not possess at all. A surveyor encountered trouble on the Thames River, for example, when the local Ojibwa told him that their lands were never sold. The surveyor then informed them that the head chief of the Mississaugas on the Credit River near York (present-day Toronto) had already ceded the land to the Crown. They objected that neither he nor the Indians of Lake Ontario had a right to those lands.[11] In 1792, the land that included the area around Ingersoll had been surrendered by the Ojibwa to the Crown for £1,180 7s.

By the time Ely Harris and his family arrived in Canada in 1802, white settlement extended for nearly twenty kilometres around the Bay of Quinte, at the eastern end of Lake Ontario, then became a narrow strip along the north shore of the lake to York, where farms stretched twenty-five kilometres up Yonge Street, then wended through the good farmland around the base of the Niagara Escarpment and even partway along the Lake Erie shore, where settlement was begun in the early 1790s.[12] By 1791, the non-aboriginal population of southern Ontario exceeded the aboriginal population (by how much is not clear as estimates of the Native population of the time are sketchy) and was nearly twenty thousand.

Early European records tell of Ojibwa, Mohawks, and some Eries in an encampment along the banks of what the English called (once again) the Thames – the French called it "Rivière la Tranche" and the Natives As-kum-e-se-be, or "Antlers like an Elk" – where the trail left the river and travelled southeast towards Brantford. This was the site of the settlement at the junction of two major Indian trails that first came to be known as Oxford on the Thames, later Ingersoll, where the Harris family headed.

Lieut.-Gov. John Graves Simcoe had visited the region in 1793; at that time the British population along the southwestern peninsula fronting on Lake Erie was virtually non-existent, except for small settlements pro-tected by the forts at Niagara and Detroit. He was accompanied by Native guides furnished by Joseph Brant, and had passed through the area where Ingersoll now stands. He formulated a plan of settlement, which called for the provincial capital to be established at the lower forks of the Thames, with the name of London; farther down the Thames would be the town of Chatham, and farther up, at the middle forks, the town of Dorchester. At the upper forks would stand the town of Oxford. Above it a canal would link the headwaters of the Thames with those of the Nith River, which emptied into the Grand; this network of water transportation would open up the region. To encourage rapid settlement, he granted whole townships to companies of associates, in return for a commitment to bring in a fixed number of settlers within a certain length of time.

With the development of American lands bordering on Upper Canada posing a potential military threat to the colony in the late 1700s, Simcoe attempted to lure American land promoters to Canada. By settling the new American settlers inland, leaving the more-strategic lakefront and river frontages for the Loyalists, he hoped to forestall any efforts by the new set-tlers to bring Upper Canada into the United States.

The township of Oxford on the Thames was granted in 1793 to the Rev. Gideon Bostwick "in consideration of [his] well known loyalty" but Bostwick soon died and Thomas Ingersoll took over active leadership of the Oxford grant. Born in Massachusetts in 1749, Ingersoll – the father of Laura Secord – had fought on the rebel side in the Revolutionary War, but later condemned the treatment of the Loyalists in the American states after the war. In 1794, he led forty American families to Oxford on the Thames to begin settlement of the township on two-hundred-acre farms sold at 6 pence an acre. Among these first forty settlers were two with family connections to the Janes and Harris families: James Piper and Samuel Burdick.[13]

These American newcomers, many of whom headed to Canada chiefly for economic reasons, were not welcomed by the Loyalists already there, and legal problems held up large-scale immigration for several years, jeopardizing the commitments of the proprietors. Lieut.-Gov. Simcoe left the province in 1796, his settlement plans largely unrealized. Chief Joseph Brant summed up Simcoe's achievements at settlement when he dryly remarked, "Gen. S. has done a great deal for this province, he has changed the name of every place in it."[14] But just before his departure, Governor Simcoe employed one hundred Natives to build a road along the Indian Trail, later known as the Old Stage Road, after which there was a rapid increase in the local population. There were two hundred settlers in Oxford County by 1798.

My Harris ancestors, arriving in 1802, were typical of the Yankee settlers brought in by Thomas Ingersoll. The Harrises "though physically small of stature were characteristically persistent in holding their own opinions, especially on moral or religious matters and lacking perhaps a keen sense of wit were persevering in the accumulation of wealth." They flourished and acquired a considerable amount of land in Oxford and nearby Dereham counties. Ely Harris became assessor in Oxford on the Thames in 1811 and 1812.[15]

It is likely that any Ojibwa that the Harris family encountered in its first months in Upper Canada were dispirited. In contrast to the Six Nations Iroquois, the Ojibwa had had little experience negotiating with Europeans over land or dealing with settlers. Those who signed the first Ojibwa surrenders, who could not read or write and were unfamiliar with the legalistic terminology of the treaties, had probably believed they were renting the use of their land in exchange for presents in perpetuity, just as the individual members of a band might use a section of a band's territory, without the band as a whole losing ownership of its territory. They believed they were granting the English tenant status, and that the English would establish only a few settlements along the lake. The surrenders seemed like a good idea at the time, because the Ojibwa had grown dependent on European trade goods and had lots of land to spare, given that their population was small – especially after various epidemics. (Along 500 kilometres of lake-front on the north shore of Lake Ontario, for example, Mississauga Ojibwa numbered only about 200 warriors or 1,000 people in the 1780s.) It was only in the 1790s that they realized the true import of the treaties, by which time most of their land had already been ceded to the Crown. Indeed, as his tribal elders told Kahkewaquonaby, later known as Peter Jones, "Our fathers held out to them the hand of friendship. The strangers then asked for a small piece of land on which they might pitch their tents; the request was cheerfully granted. By and by they begged for more, and more was given them. In this way they had continued to ask, or have obtained by force or fraud, the fairest portions of our territory."[16]

Unfortunately, little of the revenue from these surrenders went directly to the aboriginal nations that had surrendered the land, for the policy of the Indian Department was to make the department self-sufficient through these land sales. Thus the Ojibwa received "benefits," paid for out of their own money but had no control over the expenditures of the Indian Department.[17]

In an inducement to part with their land that by now should be famil-iar to the reader, the Indian Department had told the Ojibwa bands that they would be permitted to fish and hunt in their ceded hunting territo-ries as before (which meant among other things, that they would be able to continue to sell their harvested resources commercially), and would be protected from the encroachments of settlers. In fact, they were told that the settlers would help those Indians who wanted to learn farming and would give them access to the services of a doctor and a blacksmith who would repair their guns. But that is not what happened. In 1805, Chief Kineubenaie (Golden Eagle), speaking for the Mississauga chiefs of the Credit River band, told the officers of the Indian Department:

> while Colonel [John] Butler was our Father we were told our Father the King wanted some Land for his people it was some time before we sold it, but when we found it was wanted by the King to settle his people on it, whom we were told would be of great use to us, we granted it accord-ingly. Father – we have not found this so, as the inhabitants drive us away instead of helping us, and we want to know why we are served in that manner. . . . Colonel Butler told us the Farmers would help us, but instead of doing so when we encamp on the shore they drive us off & shoot our Dogs and never give us any assistance as was promised to our old Chiefs.[18]

Indeed, Ojibwa life in southern Ontario changed drastically. As had happened to so many Native people south of the border, European diseases, especially smallpox, had decimated the indigenous population. While the French traders had often lived closely with the indigenous people and intermarried, the Ojibwa found many English traders avaricious and totally ignorant of their culture. The Ojibwa also encountered the popular British belief that cultures could be ranked according to the means of production, and existed at three stages of development: savagery, barbarism, and civilization. In an echo of Puritan attitudes, agricultural society was seen as the pinnacle of civilization and the honest, hardworking farmer as the foundation of civil society. Those who worked the land therefore had a greater right to it than those who did not – it was the destiny of non-agricultural peoples to make way for farmers.[19]

Six years before Ely Harris and his family arrived in Upper Canada, tensions between the Loyalists and the indigenous population came to a head when Wabakinine, head chief of the Credit River band, and his wife were murdered by a white man at York (now Toronto). The murderer was acquitted for "want of evidence"; Indian witnesses had been invited to the trial to give evidence, but not understanding the English judicial system had not attended. (There had also been considerable unrest in 1772 when fur trader David Ramsay received no punishment for murdering – and scalping – several Natives, because the prosecution provided no Indian witnesses.) The situation almost caused an aboriginal uprising, which was only diffused when Joseph Brant, whom the Mississauga Ojibwa had approached to contribute four hundred warriors to the avenging of Wabakinine's murder, convinced them that, with Britain's military strength, such an expedition was doomed to failure.[20]

The government, fully aware of the possibility of a pan-Indian uprising, took advantage of existing divisions among the First Nations to "divide and rule," a policy that had been demonstrably successful in New England. In 1798, administrator Peter Russell had advised officials in the Indian Department "to do everything in [their] power (without exposing the object of this Policy to Suspicion) to foment any existing Jealousy between the Chippewas [Ojibwa] and the Six Nations; and to prevent as far as possible any Junction or good understanding between those two Tribes."[21] The Mississaugas could not turn farther afield to other Native allies south of the Great Lakes, as the Shawnees, Miamis, and Delawares (Lenni Lenapes) who had defeated large American armies in their defence of the Ohio

Territory, had themselves been defeated at the Battle of Fallen Timbers in 1794, and were no longer a significant military force.

It is no wonder that those Ojibwa who lived in close proximity to English settlements were dejected and demoralized. Increasingly they were no longer able to support themselves in traditional ways. Like the aboriginal people Elijah Harris had encountered in Otsego, or those encountered by my Ranney and Janes ancestors in Vermont, they were reduced to begging or selling baskets to the settlers to survive. One commentator has noted: "To a significant degree, the Mississauga and Chippewa [and the Ojibwa generally] financed the foundation of Upper Canada's prosperity at the expense of their own self-sufficiency and economic independence."[22] As virtually all observers, Indian and white, attested, alcohol abuse was also a serious problem, resulting in malnutrition and apathy. (According to historian Peter Schmalz, some of the highest officials of the Indian Department were involved in the whisky trade, knowingly weakening aboriginal morale and physical health.[23]) Soon there was a predictable increase in the instances of Ojibwa killing each other in drunken states. Many settlers came to share the opinion of Elizabeth Postuma Simcoe, wife of the first lieutenant-governor, that aboriginal people were idle, drunken, and dirty – but not all of them reacted with contempt. The terrible situation of the indigenous people in Upper Canada apparently made a deep impression on Elijah Harris, for he would later devote more than a decade of his life to their welfare.

By the time war again broke out in 1812 between the United States and Britain, with the Americans attempting to invade Canada and many of them hoping to finally drive the British from the continent, three out of five men living in Upper Canada were recently arrived Americans who had crossed the border for cheap land and generally did not think of themselves as British. They now faced the very unpleasant prospect of fighting their relatives south of the border. After Oxford's long-time member of Parliament defected to the enemy, along with a number of associates, all the residents of Oxford were viewed with suspicion. Col. Thomas Talbot, the senior military officer in London District, was instructed to "be pointed in his directions to the militia of Oxford," the area being known as a "very turbulent and refractory district." Reports appeared in American newspapers in early 1813 to the effect that the militia of Oxford Township had vowed to pay fines for non-service rather than march against the Americans; in actual fact, there was considerable opposition to militia service everywhere, particularly as it came right in the middle of spring planting.[24] Nevertheless, Ely Harris signed the oath of allegiance to Britain on January 11, 1812, and four of his sons, including both Elijah and James, also fought for Upper Canada. James Harris would even fight at Fort Erie on the British side, while his cousin Asa P. Harris, a native of Erie County, New York, fought as a captain on the American side.[25]

Given the tremendous imbalance in population – there were no more than five hundred thousand settlers in British North America as opposed to six million Americans – the dubious loyalty of the militia and the passively pro-American bias of the bulk of the population of Upper Canada, the British soon realized that the security of this part of British North America depended on the use of well-disciplined British soldiers and the guerilla tactics of aboriginal warriors. Terror would prove to be a useful tactic: the Americans, with their long history of enmity with the Native American nations, were petrified of Indian attack, and the British made the most of this fear – as had the French.

The aboriginal nations, meanwhile, saw alliance with the British as their only hope of survival. Not only the Ojibwa, the Six Nations of Upper Canada and the various aboriginal nations in Lower Canada were allies. A huge army of more than three thousand warriors from south of the border joined the British, in the hope of regaining their lands taken by the Americans, particularly in Ohio, and exacting their revenge on the Long Knives, the frontiersmen who had defeated them and destroyed their villages following the battle of Tippecanoe in 1811. The British promised to assist them in establishing the Ohio Valley as an Indian territory that would be protected against British and American encroachment.

The warriors were inspired by the Shawnee Lalawéthika or "The Prophet," who urged them to go back to their old customs and teachings, give up alcohol, stop inter-tribal warfare, and return to the clothing, implements, weapons, and food of their ancestors. He declared that all aboriginal lands should be held in common, and could not be sold by individuals. His brother Tecumseh ("He Who Walks over Water"), perhaps the greatest orator of his time, hoped to realize Pontiac's dream of an Indian confederacy from Florida to Lake Erie, and became the leader of the Native forces.[26] Appealing to various Native nations to join his cause, he reminded them of the fate of the indigenous nations of New England:

Where today are the Pequot? Where are the Narragansett, the Mohican, the Pokanoket, and many other once powerful tribes of our people? They have vanished before the avarice and the oppression of the White Man, as snow before a summer sun.

Will we let ourselves be destroyed in our turn without a struggle, give up our homes, our country bequeathed to us by the Great Spirit, the graves of our dead and everything that is dear and sacred to us? I know you will cry with me, "Never! Never!"[27]

The role of the warriors under Tecumseh was decisive in several major battles, particularly at Fort Michilimackinac, the Battle of Beaver Dam, and Detroit in 1812. It was at the capture of Detroit that James and Elijah Harris saw Tecumseh's forces close up. Although the British general Isaac Brock had only seven hundred English and Canadian soldiers and militia to the more than two thousand American fighting men under Gen. William Hull, he boldly sent a message to Detroit demanding surrender: "It is far from my intention to join in a war of extermination but you must be aware that the numerous body of Indians who have attached themselves to my troops will be beyond my control the moment the contest commences." The next day, after a full day's cannonade, Tecumseh and his warriors secretly crossed the Detroit River to the American side. While three hundred members of the militia – including James and Elijah Harris? – were issued cast-off crimson tunics to resemble regular British soldiers, Tecumseh and his warriors are reputed to have marched in single file across an open field, out of reach of fire but in full view, then vanished into the forest, only to circle back and repeat the manoeuvre three times, leading Hull's officers to believe there were more than 1,500 "savages." Apparently, even the officers of the British Indian Department dressed and painted themselves as Indians. The ruse worked and General Hull surrendered, writing to his superiors, "I have saved Detroit and the Territory from the horrors of an Indian massacre."[28]

In 1813, when American troops chased the British up the Thames River, the British and their allies were routed in the Battle of Moraviantown (between London and Chatham on the Thames River). When the British fled, Tecumseh's warriors stayed to fight, and Tecumseh was killed. After their victory, the Americans rode eastward, through the Oxford area, burning and plundering, destroying the first meeting house in Ingersoll as they went.

The war ended in a stalemate in 1814, with neither the English nor the Americans conceding defeat. It's clear that the real losers of the war were the First Nations. Tecumseh's confederacy, which had sought to defend Native land, was shattered. In the peace negotiations, the British reneged on their repeated promise to secure an Indian buffer state between Canada and the United States, where neither could purchase land, and Native people south of the border were abandoned to their fate. Most lost their land and were forced to retreat westward, ending up on reservations in the Midwest.

The Ojibwa of Upper Canada, who had been among the strongest supporters of the confederacy, were also devastated. The fighting had driven away wildlife, damaged hunting grounds, and inflicted heavy Native casualties, causing more than two thousand hungry Natives to flee the southwestern region of the colony to the Mississauga territory north and west of Lake Ontario, an area already incapable of sustaining its own indigenous population. Many leaders and tribal elders had been killed, and, as a result, much cultural knowledge was lost. The survivors "were psychologically traumatized, and . . . seem to have lost confidence in themselves as a people."[29]

The spiritual powers that had protected the Ojibwa in the past seemed to have deserted them. Nonetheless, some leaders made valiant efforts to restore confidence in the old ways. During the war, Mississauga Chief Kineubenaie (Golden Eagle) had a dream that he could not be killed by arrow, a tomahawk, or a bullet. Heartened, he gathered his followers together to tell them of his special powers and instructed a man to shoot him, holding only a tin kettle in front of his face to catch the bullet. He died instantly. This poignant incident, reminiscent of those Puritans who believed their Bibles would protect them during Indian raids in King Philip's War, further undermined the confidence of many members of the Mississauga band in their traditional belief system, which was already under considerable stress since the arrival of the Christian settlers, the advent of deadly diseases the shamans couldn't cure, and the decline in the game population in spite of scrupulous observance of traditional ceremonies. Among those whose faith in dreams and spirit helpers was shattered by this incident was the young boy, Kahkewaquonaby, mentioned earlier, who would later gain fame and cross paths with my Harris relatives.[30]

Unfortunately, the settlers of Upper Canada denied the Indian contribution to the war and magnified the role of the militia, as still happens to this day. "The Indians are feeble and useless allies, but dangerous enemies," was one view shared by many. "They were of little benefit to us during the last war, being under no discipline or subordination; and generally taking to flight at the commencement of an action, and returning at its termination, that they might plunder the dead of both armies."[31]

By the end of the war, the non-aboriginal population exceeded the number of aboriginal people in what is now southern Ontario by ten to one. Upper Canada had been transformed from a country where Europeans were seldom seen to a burgeoning agricultural colony under the rule of English laws and institutions. To accommodate the large numbers of immigrants pouring into Upper Canada in the decade after 1815, the Crown arranged several large land purchases, which opened up new areas for settlement north and west of the first surrenders.

Once Native warriors were no longer necessary for defence, aboriginal people were no longer essential to any of the goals pursued by the newcomers; in fact, as had happened earlier in New England, they were now increasingly seen merely as obstacles to economic development. Indeed, their two economies were increasingly incompatible, for with the merger of the Hudson's Bay Company and the Northwest Company in 1821 Montreal was no longer the principal base for the fur trade, and the Native people of eastern North America were no longer needed as partners in the trade – after two centuries of co-operation. Given these circumstances, the British were able to unilaterally change their relationship with aboriginal people, beginning their efforts to dismantle the First Nations and integrate aboriginal people into the new, settler society. The administrators of Upper Canada also wanted to eliminate the expense of the Indian Department, which had seen its budget rise from £60,000 in 1811 to at least £125,000 during the last year of the war.[32]

In the decades following the War of 1812, commercial non-Native fishing and the widespread encroachment of farmers on land formerly used for hunting largely destroyed the traditional livelihood of the Ojibwa in southern Upper Canada. While some managed to find work or survived on meagre earnings from selling baskets, maple sugar, handicrafts, and fish to the settlers, as so many other Natives in similar situations had done, others were reduced to begging, and there was widespread hunger. Annuities from land sales and government assistance prevented mass starvation, but many people suffered a terrible loss of self-esteem and alcohol abuse became an ever more serious problem as demoralization deepened into despair. Others fought back, organizing petitions against white encroachment on Indian fisheries, attempting to secure their land base, and asking for education to help them survive in the new world that had grown up around them.

Many Ojibwa now believed that their world had been transformed to such an extent by Europeans that radical cultural change was necessary to ensure their own survival. Furthermore, their traditional remedies in times of hardship – the spiritual ceremonies that normally restored the equilibrium between humans and the other-than-human world – had not rectified their situation, leading to a crisis of belief that left many aboriginal people even more bereft. It was partly in response to this economic and spiritual crisis that Elijah Harris and other Methodist missionaries were motivated to act.

CHAPTER
17

Sons of the Forest

Elijah Harris may well have been present at the 1823 Methodist camp when Kahkewaquonaby – the son of a Mississauga[1] woman and a Welsh surveyor – and his half-sister Mary became the first aboriginal converts to Methodism in Upper Canada. Harris was a committed Methodist by then and appears to have been an acquaintance, perhaps even a friend, of Alvin Torry, the first Methodist missionary among the aboriginal people of the Six Nations reserve at Grand River. Torry's description of that momentous day in Ancaster provides a fascinating view of the state of mind of both the Native converts and the Methodist preachers:

> Away on the outskirts of the congregation, and leaning against a tree, stood a poor, benighted son of the forest, who, during the day, had been wandering about among the tents and over the ground, and now, drawn by the sound of the minister's voice, he had approached nearer and nearer, till he stood gazing at me. As he listened, the word of truth sunk deep in his heart, and conviction seized upon his soul. The tears streamed from his eyes, and when the call was given for all who wanted religion to come forward and kneel at the altar, he hastened forward and cried aloud for mercy.
>
> Attracted by the same heavenly influence, a sister of this poor red man, came weeping and crying for mercy to the altar. How our hearts

thrilled with joy and thanksgiving to God, as we beheld these benighted youths bowing before the God of the white man.

Here, at last, were the fruits of all our toil and labor, for this had we suffered cold and hunger, privation and want; for this had we given up the comforts of home and friends, and gone forth among strangers; to this end we breasted wind and storm, snow and hail, and made our couch upon the damp earth, with nothing but the sky and stars above us, and the dark, dim woods, like watchful sentinels, around us. . . . We had now unlocked the door of the red man's heart, and thrown back the bolts and bars that superstition and suspicion had placed there; and as we looked forward into the future, we could see crowds of Indians coming from their distant homes from the far West, and bowing down to the gospel of Christ.[2]

Perhaps it was the Ancaster meeting that inspired Elijah to take up the missionary cause, for the conversion of Kahkewaquonaby, later known among the English as Peter Jones, sparked an extraordinary burst of missionary zeal among white Methodists and triggered a wave of conversions among the aboriginal people of southern Ontario.

Even if he did not attend the camp meeting in Ancaster at which Peter Jones was converted, Elijah Harris undoubtedly soon heard through other Methodists of the remarkable events the next Sabbath at a meeting at the house of Mohawk Chief Thomas Davis of Grand River, for, as Alvin Torry recorded in his autobiography:

I commenced the exercises, it was not long before sobs and cries broke from every part of the house; men and women, old and young crying out, "O, my sorry, wicked heart! O, my sorry, wicked heart! I shall go to the bad place!" Scattered all over the room, were eighteen or twenty who were wringing their hands, and crying as though their hearts were breaking under some great grief; while others, crowding up to see what was the matter, looked on in wonder and awe. . . .

We said to them "Jesus, Christ, the son of the Great Spirit, and who lives with the Great Spirit above, will save you. . . . you must believe that Jesus Christ can drive the bad spirit out of your hearts and make them glad and happy, by entering in himself."

Simultaneous with their believing, they fell from their seats either to the floor, or into the arms of some one near by, and to all appearance were dead persons. The Indians at the doors and windows, and those in the house, were very much frightened at this, and ran for water. . . . [A little girl ran home for her father] . . . he arrived to find his wife shouting and praising God, and he was soon rejoicing with his wife. And from all parts of the house was heard the cry, "O Jesus, he make me happy! O Jesus, how I love thee! Glory! Glory!"[3]

Word of these happenings quickly spread among aboriginal people and must have been the subject of considerable discussion. Wary Mohawks who were nominally Anglican said that Methodist preachers threw wolf brains into the air as a medicine, so that the congregation caught the spirit of the wolf and began to cry and shout.[4]

Peter and his half-sister soon became fervent Christians dedicated to converting aboriginal people. Mary, the daughter of the same father but a Mohawk mother, helped the Methodists in their efforts to convert the Mohawks. Peter Jones, who spoke both English and Ojibwa and was comfortable in both cultures, became passionately committed to spreading the gospel among the Ojibwa, convinced that only a spiritual transformation would help them survive in the new world around them. With the aid of the Methodists, Peter Jones began to establish the first schools and churches among the Ojibwa in 1824 and also commenced translating hymns and scripture into Ojibwa. My ancestor Elijah Harris would come to know Peter Jones and would work as a missionary alongside him, devoting a decade of his life to the same cause.[5]

Methodism, the disciplined, "methodical" approach to Christianity developed almost a century earlier by Rev. John Wesley, an Anglican minister in England, had already inspired one of the greatest religious revivals in the history of the English-speaking world in the mid- to late eighteenth century. It was the most dynamic denomination in the newly settled areas of North America. Thomas Ingersoll and most of his early settlers at Oxford on the Thames were Methodists; they had welcomed the itinerant "saddlebag" preachers from the United States who were the first to reach the new settlers of Upper Canada by organizing large outdoor camp meetings that lasted several days. Nathan Bangs, a well-known American Methodist missionary, had visited Oxford (now Woodstock) in 1801 and 1802, and came to Oxford on the Thames (Ingersoll) in 1804. I have no doubt that my ancestors participated in at least the latter meeting: such visits were major social events, attracting settlers and aboriginal people alike. During Bang's nine-day visit in 1801, for example, "Nearly all the settlement consisting of settlers and Indians turned out to hear him."[6]

Camp meetings were very powerful emotional experiences; they brought large numbers of people together for several days, and offered, in addition to confessions, singing, exhorting, and dramatic personal stories of God's presence, "plain truth for plain people" – down-to-earth preaching related to the everyday life of a pioneer, with its hardships, sorrows, illnesses, and deaths. Many experienced Methodism as "a new religion of the heart."[7]

The Harris family was very religious – four of Ely's sons became preachers. Some family members, like my direct ancestor, Ely's son James, were Baptist (the religious faith practiced by their early Rogers ancestors in New London); others joined the Methodists. Some family sources say that Ely Harris became a Methodist; certainly his sons Elijah and Daniel Harris did.[8] Elijah Harris was an exhorter (a layman who spoke after the local preacher gave a sermon or assisted a travelling preacher on his circuit rounds) at the time of Peter Jones's conversion. By 1825 he was an itinerant preacher. This was a challenging vocation, as he was likely away from his growing family five days out of six, he may have had to spend the night in the woods between settlements on occasion and would have endured many hardships in travelling during winter. For his pains he was paid only $80 a year and had to provide his own horses and saddlebags.[9]

That same year – 1825 – Peter Jones also formally joined the Methodist church as an exhorter. His value to the Methodists was immediately apparent. Jones's sermons often had a profound effect on both Native and white audiences. For his Native audiences, "his words went like arrows to their targets. Mississaugas fell to the ground as if dead; some wildly rejoiced, and others cried aloud for mercy."[10] Jones was able to make Christianity comprehensible and appealing to Native people and was able to interpret for white missionaries, establishing Ojibwa equivalents for important Christian concepts. Through his intercultural skills he was able to draw out similarities between Christianity and traditional Ojibwa spiritual beliefs and practices – for example, the biblical forty days and nights in the wilderness was similar to an Ojibwa vision quest.

Methodism began to gain ground among the aboriginal people of southwestern Ontario when Peter Jones made two missionary tours in 1825. It was on the first tour that Peter Jones and Alvin Torry stayed at Elijah Harris's house near Zorra Township, just north of Ingersoll. As Jones recorded in his diary: "We rode about two miles to Brother Harris', where we spent the day. We gave out an appointment for preaching at 4 o'clock p.m. A pretty good congregation assembled, and Brother Torry preached; the people were attentive, and I trust some good was done to the people. I was wonderfully blessed in private prayer in the woods."[11] It is likely that the connection with Harris was initially through Torry, who, like Elijah, had been born in Connecticut and lived in Otsego County, New York, before coming to Upper Canada.

Other families related to the Harrises were also involved with the tour. The previous evening Jones and Torry had stayed at the home of the Pipers (who were related by marriage to Lorrainy Janes, wife of Elijah's brother James) and, a few days later, Jones attended a quarterly meeting at Burdick's chapel, which may also have been within the family connection, for Lorrainy's brother Heman Janes had married a Burdick. Most likely other members of the Harris family came out to hear Jones speak on these occasions, for he generally elicited considerable curiosity and enthusiasm in the communities he visited. A "love feast," held after the quarterly meeting and at which Jones exhorted, attracted six hundred people, one hundred of whom had to listen from outside the overcrowded chapel. It was the largest congregation ever seen in that area. Indeed, the tours were so popular that Jones also began to visit Michigan regularly. The Methodists would soon establish themselves among every aboriginal group in Upper Canada and later also sent travelling missionaries to the First Nations of Lakes Huron and Superior and to the Hudson's Bay Territory. This made them by far the most active of the six missionary churches in Upper Canada before Confederation.

The Methodists' sudden and dramatic success among aboriginal people was partly the result of a new theory about the process of conversion. The Methodists were the first Christian denomination to seriously consider the possibility that Native people could be "Christianized" before being "civilized," the opposite of what had been generally believed for almost two hundred years, since John Eliot had tried to civilize the Massachusetts in the praying towns before admitting converts into full church membership. The innovative approach of the Methodists in Upper Canada was largely due to presiding elder Rev. William Case, who had an unusual empathy with aboriginal people; although his approach was still highly paternalistic, he excelled at identifying and recruiting Native leadership.

It also appears that Methodist Christianity addressed a deep need for spiritual renewal among many traumatized Ojibwa. In contrast to the Puritan belief that only the Elect chosen by God would be saved from hellfire, and that a person could not influence God's decision by a life of good works, John Wesley, the founder of Methodism, had preached the doctrine of atonement – that God had sent his son Jesus Christ to suffer and die on the cross to atone for the original sin, so that humanity could be saved. Methodists held that any seeker could find salvation, since God's grace was freely given to all those who had faith in Jesus.[12] Aboriginal converts expressed their desire to be happy on earth, and to see friends and relatives in heaven – the latter being especially important after so many had died from disease.

After repenting, the sinner had to struggle honestly to overcome the will to sin, and John Wesley laid down a series of rules of behaviour that became a guide strictly adhered to by his followers. Methodists were to observe the Sabbath, avoid alcohol, spurn "costly apparel," and never sing songs or read those books that did not tend to knowledge or love of God.[13] They were to undertake private and public prayer and worship and participate in weekly class meetings in which each member gave personal testimony of his or her spiritual struggle. For many aboriginal people, who had gone through massive social upheaval and, in some cases, terrible personal degradation, Methodism's emphasis on repentance and personal transformation and its strictures against alcohol apparently struck a powerful chord.

From his white audiences, Jones sought assistance for the Methodist missionary project, telling one such audience in the summer of 1826:

If it hadn't been for the Benevolent, who sent the gospel to you, you would, perhaps, now be as we poor Indians are. For we are told that your fathers, the inhabitants of Britain, once lived in tents, wore leggings and were strangers to the religion of Jesus Christ. Now you are clothed, have houses, and the Bible to read. But these people, the former proprietors of your lands, are poor and without houses; and what is more, they are without the knowledge of God and the way of salvation.[14]

His audiences often responded enthusiastically, for progressive members of the colonizing society had become increasingly concerned for the welfare of aboriginal people as they had become aware of the social, economic, and spiritual crisis they were experiencing. In fact, a new force – humanitarianism – was inspiring the establishment of Christian missions, not only in North America but all over the world. Unlike the early missions in New England that had depended upon the financial support of a few wealthy British patrons, such as Lady Armine's support of John Eliot, these missions were financed by small donations from large numbers of less-affluent but sympathetic church members in Canada, the United States, and Britain.[15]

This humanitarianism was truly revolutionary, in its conviction that the problems of other people, no matter how far away or how different, concerned ordinary citizens. It represented a major transformation of the moral imagination of Western societies. Furthermore, the Christian promise of the universality of salvation supported the development of Western ideas about the natural rights and equality of human beings, ideas that would be instrumental in the eventual elimination of the slave trade and later form the basis for the modern Western notion of the universality of human rights. Yet this humanitarianism was also coloured by the ethnocentrism of its time – as it is today. Although genuinely horrified by the poverty, drunkenness, and despair affecting many of the Native people who lived near white settlements, the humanitarians who supported the establishment of the missions did not recognize or could not address the underlying causes of that degradation – the loss of sovereignty, land, and livelihood and the trauma of the epidemics. Like other members of their society, they believed that aboriginal culture was doomed because it was inferior. They saw the "plight" of the Natives as a spiritual condition arising not from a crisis of meaning in a totally transformed world but as the natural result of their non-Christian state, since Christianity was the only true religion.

In contrast to the more extreme racism of eighteenth-century New England, which had characterized Natives as by nature untrustworthy enemies in league with Satan, these reformers perceived aboriginal peoples as backward or less evolved, "different in degree but not in kind from their masters, therefore capable with training and education, to rise ... to a status of equality with the ruling group."[16] So at least ran the rhetoric, though reformers still retained a strong sense of the "natural order" of things, in which those of British descent remained at the top of the hierarchy. While many humanitarians believed Britain had a moral responsibility to assist aboriginal people because of the destructive impact of British contact, most also actively supported a policy of imperialism and shared the conviction that it was Britain's destiny to rule other lands – only by ruling could the British bring civilization to others.

Progressive whites were convinced that aboriginal people had to adopt European culture to survive. They believed that it was the moral duty of administrators and missionaries to give them all possible help in becoming civilized Christians and to teach them such "European" values as sobriety, frugality, industry, and enterprise. Aboriginals were to learn to use European technology, adapt to European economic patterns, and emulate European manners and dress. Christian missionaries, then, were to save aboriginal people from physical extinction by reshaping them culturally, and save their souls from damnation by converting them to Christianity. It is likely that Elijah Harris shared these views and was inspired by considerable idealism, for the missionary became the nineteenth-century ideal of the Christian hero – missionary service was seen as the ultimate expression of dedication to the cause of Christ. "In effect, the missionaries' hope was to create in the Indian communities a utopia, a 'mirror of the ideal world,' with the Indians exhibiting all the virtues of the perfect European."[17]

Another reason for the enthusiasm of Euro-Canadian Methodists for aboriginal conversions was the tenuous legitimacy of Methodism among many whites and especially among the establishment of Upper Canada, who viewed Methodists as radicals with dangerous republican ideas who meddled in politics. The denomination's missionary and expansionist emphasis reflected more than a desire to reach the unchurched; it also revealed a need to establish itself in the face of established Anglicanism, and it sometimes led to a preoccupation with sheer numbers of converts. In the 1820s, Native converts constituted a large proportion of the total number of Methodists in Canada, and their relatively quick and sometimes mass conversions greatly strengthened Methodist aspirations.[18] Also, proselytizing had always been central to Methodism: in England John Wesley had preached in mines and farmers' fields; in Canada, circuit riders ensured that Methodism was the first denomination to reach newly settled areas.

Aboriginal conversions greatly strengthened the faith of many Euro-Canadian Methodists. As Nathan Bangs wrote,

These converts were not merely nominal believers in Christianity. They had felt its renovating and transforming power upon their hearts, and this had produced a corresponding change in their habits, civil, domestic, and religious. By this means they presented in their own lives a living, palpable, and irrefutable evidence to all who beheld them, that the gospel of Jesus Christ in even now the power of God unto salvation to every one

that believeth. These, therefore, were living epistles, written, not with
pen and ink, but by the finger of the living God."[19]

I know nothing of what transpired between Elijah Harris and Peter
Jones during the latter's first missionary tour through southwestern
Ontario. Clearly Elijah was recognized as sympathetic to the cause, for
Jones visited him again on the second tour in August 1825, when he journeyed west with five aboriginal brethren on their way to visit the Munsees
and the Ojibwa on the Thames River. In his diary, Jones noted, "Travelled
about twenty-five miles this day to Westminster, baited our horses in
Oxford, where we visited Mr. E. Harris, who was very low with a fever;
prayed for him and then departed."[20]

Elijah must have recovered fully from his illness, for at the end of the
year he was ordered by his Presiding Elder to leave his circuit and take
charge of the mission the Methodists were establishing at the Munsee
village. There he joined another white Methodist, twenty-four-year-old
John Carey, who had been left behind to establish a school among the
Munsees in the early summer of 1825 after Jones and Torry had visited
them on their first missionary tour.

The Munceytown mission was the third or fourth mission to be established by the Methodists in Upper Canada. "It was a beautiful place, away
there in the wilderness, far from the haunts of civilized men," wrote Alvin
Torry on his first visit.[21] The Munsees were Lenni Lenapes, or "original
people," also known as Delawares, who at first contact had occupied most
of present-day New Jersey, Delaware, eastern Pennsylvania, and southern
New York. For the previous hundred years they had been repeatedly dispossessed, attacked, and driven westward by settlers. The Revolutionary
War had forced them to move again. The majority moved to Ohio, and a
small number (fewer than 150) came north to Upper Canada and settled on
the Grand River in 1784. Some of these then moved to the village that
became known as Muncey, just south of present-day London. (The British
had promised them land in Upper Canada, and Lieutenant-Governor
Simcoe had encouraged them to stay at Muncey. This raised their hopes
that they would be granted land there, but no grant ever materialized, so
the local Chippewas allowed them to occupy a small parcel of land from
their territory.[22])

Carey had been welcomed by two Munsee chiefs, George Turkey and
Westbrook. By the time Jones made a second tour, Carey had eighteen

Munsee children in his school. Since the Methodists had so little money, John Carey's parents in New York State provided all his clothing, books, and school supplies, as well as nearly a hundred dollars' worth of clothing for his pupils. While some Munsees and Chippewas had allowed Carey to set up his school, most were hostile to Christianity and to whites in general, and initially Carey's personal safety was doubtful. In fact, for many years the mission at Munceytown was considered the least promising of the Methodist missions.

The Munsees had good reason to be mistrustful. During the American revolution, the Long Knives had beaten to death, and then scalped and burned the corpses of ninety Christian Lenni Lenape and Mahican Indians at the Moravian mission of Gnadenhütten in Ohio, sixty of them women and children. Some of the survivors now lived fifty kilometres down the Thames River, at Moraviantown, a mission established in the early 1790s (where Tecumseh fell during the War of 1812). The two Munsee chiefs told Peter Jones during his second visit several months later: "The Indians had been murdered after they had embraced Christianity. Many years ago the Moravians preached to the Indians on the other side of the lake, and when they had got a good many to live with them, they so contrived it as to have their own brethren confined to a house, where they were all murdered and burned up."[23] Jones responded that a wicked band of whites had executed the deed, not the Moravian preachers, but most Munsees remained committed to their traditional culture.

Ten kilometres downriver from Munceytown was an Ojibwa encampment of about three hundred people. This Peter Jones had also visited, and it was included in the Muncey mission (a third group, the Bear Creek Ojibwa, would also be included at a later date). These Ojibwa, unlike the Munsees, had no previous knowledge of Christianity, and Peter Jones made no headway when he visited them in 1825. Their head chief, Tommago (written "Tomiko" by the missionaries), told him, "The whites are Christians, and it makes them no better; they have done us much injury. By various pretences they have cheated us out of our lands. We will first retire to the western Indians. We will have nothing to do with the whites or their religion."[24]

Nevertheless, the Canadian [Episcopal] Methodist Missionary Society reported in 1826 that there were about fifteen children attending school, that the opposition to it had lessened, and that "several of the natives had embraced the gospel and experienced a change." The 1827 report stated:

"Mr. Carey has continued to labour with unabated zeal in the midst of privations and opposition. Being assisted by Mr. Harris, who has also voluntarily taken up his residence among the Indians, with a view to their improvement, a house for schools and meetings is now erected, where more regular instruction will be given." In 1828, an article in the *New York Christian Advocate* described a visit to inspect the academic progress of the children: "Three weeks after this, brother Harris met me on Talbot Street, as I was returning from the west, and informed me 'that since my visit there, the number of scholars has trebled. So much had the school increased, that they had no room to accommodate any more.' "[25]

"The Schools to the Missions are as important as a foundation is to a building," a prominent missionary would later write. Because becoming a Protestant required "understanding based on instruction," and prospective converts could not become full church members until a licensed preacher had examined their knowledge of doctrine, the main purpose of the Methodist schools was to give potential converts thorough instruction in Christian teachings. Literacy was vitally important because acceptance of the Bible was the sole standard of faith: children were taught to read so they would be able to read the Scriptures. Thus, the earliest mission schools, such as that at Munceytown, concentrated on reading, writing, Bible study, and singing hymns.[26]

Later the Methodists would become more ambitious, seeing day schools as the training ground for Native missionaries and teachers, through whom Methodists might be able to reach and convert all Ojibwa in Upper Canada and the west. With this goal in mind, the Methodists then developed a more demanding academic curriculum in some schools (though I don't know if they did this at Munceytown), featuring a bilingual English–Ojibwa instruction program, the addition of subjects like geography and astronomy to break down traditional aboriginal cosmology, and the application of progressive teaching philosophies believed to be more suitable to aboriginal children, such as that of Swiss educational reformer Johann Pestalozzi (a pioneer in a more student-centred pedagogy that de-emphasized strict discipline). In her examination of Methodist schooling from 1820 to 1860, graduate student Hope McLean noted that, "in the 1820s and 1830s, the Methodist day schools were attempting a level of instruction for the Indians which was far beyond the level common among the white population, either in Europe or Canada."[27] By the 1830s a considerable proportion of aboriginal children in Upper Canada would be attending school, which was all the more remarkable given that there was no widespread elementary schooling for non-aboriginal children, and 50 per cent of Euro-Canadian adults were illiterate.

Over the next few years, our main source of information about the Munceytown mission comes from Methodist sources, such as the annual reports of the missionary society and the accounts of various missionaries as they appeared in Methodist newspapers. Such reports have to be read with caution, as they were written with an eye for future fundraising and with the need to maintain the missionary zeal of the faithful – successes were sometimes exaggerated and setbacks minimized. The voices of the majority of the Munsees and Chippewas – those who were not interested in Christianity at the time – were usually characterized as "opposers" or sceptics who remained to be convinced, and the stories often ended with the triumph of Christianity. But the traditionalists' point of view is still sometimes discernible. The chief of the Bear Creek Ojibwa, for example, who had fought beside Tecumseh in the War of 1812, explained to Peter Jones that the Indians must honour their own religion. If the Creator had wished the Indians to worship like the whites, He would have made them white. Instead, He presented to the white people across the great waters a religion written in a book. To the Indian He "gave His way of worship written in his heart!"[28]

For the first few years at least, the main interest on the part of many of the Munsees and Ojibwa was in the school, since many parents clearly saw the need for their children to learn how to function in the white man's world. Many aboriginal people were very interested in books, and expressed a strong desire for their children to learn to read and write – perhaps in part because of the Ojibwa tradition of picture-writing on birch-bark scrolls. In the first years of mission work, many aboriginal groups in southern Ontario asked for schools, even when stating adamantly that they did not want Christianity. They apparently assumed that their children could receive an English education without also imbibing the English value system that created it, an assumption that would prove to be problematic.

But even the dubious Munsees and Ojibwa of the Thames began to hear of the startling and extraordinary changes among Peter Jones's relatives and other Christian Mississaugas at the Mississauga village at Credit River. At the time, the Credit River band, where Peter Jones would make his base, was in terrible straits. The population had plummeted by two-thirds to just over two hundred and the band seemed to be facing extinction. In 1818, the Mississauga had sold all their remaining land, except for three small reserves, and in 1820 William Claus, deputy-superintendent-general of Indian affairs, arranged for the Mississaugas to sell all but two hundred acres of the approximately nine thousand acres of their remaining lands on the understanding that the proceeds from the sale would be used to educate their children, instruct them in Christianity, and build houses on the remaining land. The Mississaugas totally misunderstood the treaty they signed; again, none of them could read English or understood the British legal system. They left the negotiations under the impression that the Crown had agreed to protect their land, for they wanted "to keep it for our children forever."[29] They soon discovered that their land had been alienated from them, but they were unable to get it back.

In 1826, the village at Credit River had been re-organized as a model community with the assistance of then Lieut.-Gov. Sir Peregrine Maitland. The four-thousand-acre site lay within their traditional territory, in the vicinity of present-day Mississauga, a western suburb of Toronto. With fertile soil, a large salmon run, an excellent harbour, and a promise that they would soon secure clear title to these hereditary lands, the Mississaugas embarked on a massive social experiment. Peter Jones, now elected chief of the Credit band along with his brother, constantly encouraged the Mississaugas to become "a new race of people."[30] Skilled workmen and teachers were sent to aid in their "civilization." The new Christians moved from widely scattered wigwams on the river flats to log homes set close together in a straight line. Where formerly several families had lived communally in large wigwams, now two families shared a government-built house and adopted the European family pattern Methodists considered essential for the establishment of a moral and respectable family life. Some traditional customs relating to marriage, such as some husbands having more than one wife, were no longer deemed acceptable, and residents adopted European dress. Egerton Ryerson, later a political reformer and the founder of the public school system in Upper Canada, was appointed the first permanent Methodist missionary to the Ojibwa in 1826, and soon became a close and trusted friend of Peter Jones.

Basil Hall, an English traveller, visited the Ojibwa of Credit River in July 1827: "They had all neat houses, made up of beds, tables, and chairs, and were perfectly clean in their persons. . . . Most of the children, and a few of the older Indians, could read English; facts which we ascertained by visiting their school. . . . The whole tribe profess Christianity, attend divine service regularly. . . . They now cultivate the ground. . . . The number of Indians at the Credit village is only 215; but the great point gained, is the fact of reformation being possible."[31]

By mid-1828, the Methodists noted that 1,200 of 5,000 Indians near settlements in southern Upper Canada had received religious instruction from Methodist missionaries and Native helpers, and more and more conversions were reported. At Methodist camp meetings, which often took place in a forest setting, the strong emotion, gripping personal testimony, inspiring hymns, and fervent prayer created a psychological pressure so strong that sometimes whole bands were moved to convert en masse. On June 17, 1828, for example, one hundred and thirty-two Natives were baptized, the greatest number of aboriginal Protestants ever baptized at one time in Canada.[32] The government, which wanted the Indians to join the Church of England, recognized the power of the Methodists' camp meetings and threatened to withhold the Mississaugas' annual presents if they attended them. Even at Muncey, long considered the most challenging of the Methodist missions, the missionaries began to make some progress. Peter Jones returned several times to the Thames River, and in 1827 converted Peter Beaver, Chief Tommago's nephew, which eventually led to the entry of the neighbouring Sable River band into the Methodist church.

There were pragmatic as well as spiritual reasons for this wave of conversions. Some aboriginal people hoped that Christianity would protect them against diseases, as it appeared to do for white people. Many believed that, if they became Christians, the government, the white Methodists, and influential aboriginal converts such as Peter Jones would help them become farmers; similarly, offers of government houses sparked many conversions.

But perhaps most important, many aboriginal people could see nowhere else to turn for the reconstruction of their society. Methodism introduced a completely new social system: its strict rules of conduct and prohibition of alcohol provided new social controls where the old ones had broken down. It offered aboriginal people hope of regeneration and renewal. Many chiefs turned to Methodism because of its strong stand on abstinence, for alcohol was now the greatest obstacle to social and economic progress, leading to poverty, disease, accidental death, and outbreaks of violence. (It was also a serious problem among the settlers.) Jones detested drunkenness for the "evil it had done my poor countrymen, many thousands of whom have had their days shortened by it, and been hurried to destruction."[33]

Methodism made sense of the new world the white people had created – and also left room for aboriginal people. Methodist missionaries stressed that Natives were entitled to the same rights as other British subjects and should be treated as brothers and sisters in Christ. Converts often gained a new respect for themselves and others, for, as historian John Webster Grant has noted, although Methodist conversion demanded a radical personal transformation, it was equally strict and demanding of both Native people and Europeans. Aboriginal converts could maintain their dignity, seeing their former selves as sinners rather than inferiors, and were able to attain positions of leadership.[34]

In fact, much of the reason for this wave of conversions was an extraordinary flowering of Methodist ministers, exhorters, teachers, and interpreters of aboriginal ancestry. Most of these leaders were of mixed European and Native heritage, which enabled them to bridge the two cultures. Peter Jones and David Sawyer of Credit River were the first ordained Native Methodist ministers in Canada, and held positions as teachers, interpreters, writers, and preachers on several reserves. George Copway of Rice Lake, another Methodist preacher and teacher, became the first Canadian Native person to write a book, *The Life, History and Travels of Kahgegagahbow*, published in 1847; he also made a successful speaking tour in Europe, as did Peter Jones, who even visited Queen Victoria. John Sunday (Shawundias) was a Native preacher who did not learn to read or write but who was renowned as an orator. Jones was ordained in 1829, and by 1830 there were seventeen Native teachers, interpreters, and church workers. Over the next decade that number rose to nearly fifty. They served as role models, demonstrating that Christianity was a religion for Natives as well as whites, and they dispelled the notion that God understood only English.

These leaders, many of them well educated, also proved invaluable in protecting aboriginal interests. Peter Jones, for example, protested the raiding of the Indian fishery on the Credit River and challenged Col. James Givens, superintendent general of the Indian Department, when the government did not pay out the full amount of annual land payment that had been specified in the purchase of 1818.

Some Native converts thought it so important to support the work of the Native missionary workers that they donated their jewellery to support the cause; Indian women also made baskets and brooms for sale to raise money for the "blessed work of God."[35] Chief Westbrook of the Munsees, who from the first had been favourable to preaching and teaching, paddled to Detroit, a distance of 120 miles, to obtain nails for the building of a church and school, and the Munsees helped to build them. Native Christian workers were essential in raising funds for over-extended Christian missions; they visited various circuits and profoundly impressed local white congregations, prompting large contributions. On another missionary tour through southwestern Ontario in 1828, Peter Jones was accompanied by George Henry, his half-brother Peter Beaver, and William Jackson (a white man). He preached in Oxford on the way. "Great attention was paid. George Henry related his experience in English, P. Beaver in Indian [Ojibwa], and W. Jackson closed by prayer."[36] Ironically, in these appeals to white settlers and on fundraising tours of the United States and Britain, Peter Jones and other Native Methodists echoed the imaginary Indian plea to "Come over and help us" that the founders of the Massachusetts Bay Colony had so arrogantly and ignorantly affixed to their seal. It was a measure of how much things had changed to the detriment of aboriginal people that this plea was no longer a white fantasy.

So great was the enthusiasm for Native conversions that even Archdeacon John Strachan, later the Anglican bishop of Toronto, appealed to the Church Missionary Society (CMS) in England for aid in providing a program of education for the Indians. In a proposal reminiscent of the failed Harvard Indian College of seventeenth-century Massachusetts, he wanted his planned university, King's College, to extend its benefits to aboriginal students, so that they might be trained as missionaries and then return to their people to teach. He also hoped some white students at King's would learn aboriginal languages and minister among the First Nations. In response the CMS granted $100 annually for the maintenance of two scholarships and $100 for a professorship of Indian languages, but King's College never got off the ground.

Conversions and baptisms may have been numerous elsewhere in Upper Canada, but in 1828 things were not going well at Munceytown. John Ryerson reported in the *Christian Advocate* that

> It appears the Munceytown mission has suffered considerably in consequence of the one of the school teachers [Peter Carey], who has left the mission, and joined the Church of England. The other teacher [Elijah Harris], however, remains at his post, faithfully engaged in the discharge

of his duty, and those of the Indians who had experienced religion remain firm. Brother Jackson, a superannuated preacher, in whom the Indians have much confidence, persevering and enterprising, is now supplying the vacancy occasioned by the departure of Mr. Carey.[37]

Brother Jackson, however, did not work out. Privately, William Case soon expressed his frustration to Peter Jones in this letter: "Munceytown, I expect, is in confusion. Indeed it always has been; and since Mr. Jackson has taken his wild course I presume it is no better. Your visit and advice will be important. In all your understanding pray. The devil and his emissaries can never withstand prayer."[38]

Their prayers were answered with the arrival of the controversial Thomas Hurlburt. Some described him as "an Indian in a white man's skin, who dreamed, thought and taught Ojibwa." But Hurlburt's attitudes to aboriginal people were far more ambivalent than such a description suggests, for he later told a white audience that unChristianized Indians were "devoid of fellow-feeling, superstitious, immoral, imbecile in mind, and degraded in social habits." He also claimed they were cannibals.[39]

Wrote Hurlburt: "I was sent to Munceytown and by stage and on foot made my way westward; and on Oct. 5th 1828 reached Muncey. On April 15th I took charge of the Mission – both the school and the pastoral charge. Lived the first year in a bark shanty, the next in an Indian house, and the next, built the first Mission-house with my own hands between times and at night. When I took this Mission there were about 15 members, just emerging from heathenism; when I left [three years later] there were 85."[40]

That Hurlburt took charge of the mission rather than Elijah Harris is surprising and perhaps telling; Harris appears to have often played second fiddle, to have kept things going through the mission's ups and downs and the comings and goings of various people, but rarely with top billing. Perhaps this was because of the demands of his large family – he had eight children by then – or maybe he was simply not as gifted linguistically, as zealous, or as temperamentally suited to the work. The most important conversions – like that of Chief Tommago's son (also known as Tommago) by Peter Jones in 1829 – appear to have been the work of other men. Yet perhaps Hurlburt wasn't being wholly truthful, for in 1830 Elijah Harris is listed in the treasurer's report as the missionary, Hurlburt as the teacher, and there were other instances where Hurlburt was noticeably competitive with other missionaries.[41]

Harris does seem to have undertaken a new initiative after John Carey's departure, a more practical approach to evangelization that eventually bore fruit. For a few months later, Elijah Harris and one John Phillips, listed as inhabitants of Southwold in the London District, petitioned the government on behalf of the "Moncey-town Relief Society" to aid the Indians on the River Thames by "building some houses and any other means which may be thought necessary for bringing them into a State of Civilization and to the enjoyment of the means of Grace," referring to the "object so glorious, the saving the souls of so many Children of the forest."[42]

In 1830 he wrote to the lieutenant-governor, Sir John Colborne, on behalf of the Munsees and the Chippewas, requesting a meeting, and apparently a second time that same year, petitioning the government to honour its commitment and pay the Chippewas for the land along the Thames that they had sold almost a decade previously. "How and when will they receive future payments?" For "a regular payment of the purchase money is the principal dependence of your red children for a livelihood . . . after giving up their Hunting Grounds for the accommodation of his white children."[43]

Whether because of Thomas Hurlburt's ministrations or Elijah Harris's petitions or some other reason, the Munsees' resistance to the missionaries and their message began to lessen at this time. "Munceytown has been the most unpromising of any of our missions," reported William Case the following winter, reminding readers of the *New York Christian Advocate* of the violent opposition of the chiefs because of the Gnadenhütten massacre in 1782. The Christians had often driven them from place to place, depriving them of their lands, and

certain white men, too, who felt it their interest to preserve a market for their whisky at Munceytown, have continually encouraged the Indians in their opposition. These prejudices have gradually subsided as one and another of the Indians have been converted, and at present there is a great desire among both the Munceys and the Chippeways to settle in one body, and to have our assistance and instruction in erecting their buildings, and instructing their children. . . . Among the principal men are Tomico [Tommago] the father, and Tomico the son, of the lower town; George Turkey, Westbrook, and Captain Snake of the Munceys, and Peter Beaver, of the Chipways on the Saubles. The whole body on the Sables have embraced religion during the past year. Several of the Munceys, among whom are Turkey, have become religious. Young Tomico [Tommago] and several of the lower town have also embraced religion.[44]

Some of the comments recorded by Case and other missionaries are quite revealing of the state of mind of the Munsees and the Ojibwa: Captain Snake said he would worship both ways, for fear that forsaking the old way might displease God; Chief Tommago, the father, agreed with Snake and said that he wanted a deed for their land, he wanted to live with the white people, he wanted a house. The missionaries replied that they would not build houses by themselves, but they would teach the Munsees and Ojibwa how to build houses and how to cultivate lands.

George Turkey told Peter Jones: "Some Munceys he not like it [Christianity] – he say he want worship old way. But I tell him, lost old way. – Old way was good. But now Munceys get their way from all nations, some from the white people, some from the Chippeways, and some from other nations."[45]

William Case related one incident that deeply influenced many residents of Munceytown, given the importance of dreams in traditional aboriginal spirituality. One of the pagans related a dream in which the Christian convert Omik went to "a bad place" after death because he forsook the old religion, and warned Omik that he (Omik) would die first. Omik disputed this, saying that "those who had become Christians at the Credit and elsewhere, were more healthy, prosperous and happy" than the pagans, and that he cared nothing for the man's dreams. When the pagan dreamer went to York that winter, he and his pagan friends became terribly drunk and the dreamer suddenly took sick and died. The fact that Omik continued to live impressed many potential converts. "The death of the false dreamer has given a check to their confidence in the dreams of paganism, and they listen more attentively to Christian instruction."[46]

The following year Peter Jones reported:

When the Indians at Muncey Town became Christians, a white man who used to sell the fire waters to them for their furs and skins, got very angry, because they would buy no more fire waters of him. He swore about the Methodist missionaries, and said that the Indians would not drink as long as the missionaries were among them; but as soon as the Indians were by themselves, he knew he could get them to drink. So when the Indians got alone by themselves this *white heathen* went and placed a keg of whiskey by the side of an Indian path, where he knew they would pass, and then went and hid himself in the bushes in sight of his keg, that he might enjoy the pleasures of seeing the poor Indians tap his keg. Presently four of the Indians came along the path; and the foremost Indian coming up to it, stopped suddenly, and exclaimed, "*Ha! Mahje mundedoo sah oomah chyah*," "So! the evil spirit (the devil) is here." The second came up, and said, "*Aahe, nebejemahinah sah!*" "Yes, me smell him!" The third shook the keg with his foot and said, "*Kagaitnenoondahwah sah!*" "Of a truth, me hear him!" The fourth Indian in passing by the keg, gave it a kick with his foot, and away went the keg of fire-waters, tumbling down the hill, and the Indians went on their way like brave warriors after overcoming their enemy; and the poor disappointed and sadly mortified white man was obliged to come and take up his keg and convey it to his own home; where I suppose he and his friends opened and let out the "*evil spirit*," and swallowed him.

In the same report Jones spoke generally about the changes the missionaries had brought to aboriginal people:

Could the good people of England see and hear what I have seen and heard among my Indian brethren, of the great things which the Lord Jesus has done for their poor souls, I am sure it would make their hearts glad, and they would not be sorry that they helped in saving the poor Indians in the woods from wretchedness and eternal death.

The Indian brethren regularly attend to their class meetings, prayer meetings, and the preaching of the word. They also strictly observe and keep the Christian Sabbath, and will no more hunt or travel on that day. They abstain entirely from drinking ardent spirits, although frequently urged to do so by the wicked white people, who try every means to turn them back again to their old crooked ways. . . . I rejoice to inform you, that, although my countrymen have thus been wronged and oppressed by the wicked whites; yet as soon as they receive the words of the Great Spirit from the hands of the good white people, all angry feelings and jealousies are removed, the sore is healed, and the broken heart comforted; so that the Indian is willing to walk with his white brother in one path, eat out of one dish, and to love as brethren. We desire always to be very thankful to our Christian friends for helping us to become Christians, and for putting us in the way of becoming wise, industrious and useful people.[47]

If the pagan Anishinabe had written reports on the Methodist conversions, what would they have said? That still only a quarter of the five or six hundred were Christians, and of those numbered among Jones's faithful, many likely would have described a syncretistic relationship with Christianity, adding Christian beliefs and practices to their own. That to the missionaries, the traditional ways of aboriginal people appeared to offer nothing of lasting value to the world or to the Natives themselves, and should be abandoned as quickly as possible. That there was never any serious consideration of the idea that Native people might be allowed to remain non-Christians indefinitely. That Christianity had failed to improve corrupt members of white society and had divided their own. That the Christian God protected only Europeans.

During the first half of the nineteenth century, most aboriginal leaders acknowledged that some kind of cultural or spiritual change was necessary, but, as was the case in England during the Reformation, there was no agreement on the nature or degree of change required. Many aboriginal people advocated a revival and reworking of traditional forms of spirituality as an alternative to Christianity. Shamans, especially in more isolated and northerly areas of Ontario, such as west of Lake Superior, were often quite successful in renewing Native culture and resisting missionary initiatives. In southern Ontario, the influence of the missionaries was restricted mainly to the Ojibwa. Among the Iroquois, the teachings of the Seneca prophet Handsome Lake (1750–181?) had spread to Grand River by 1815, and the Longhouse religion became the religion of the majority except among the Anglican Mohawks. Handsome Lake had preached that the Iroquois should simply reform their traditional religious customs and ceremonies and should not become like white men.[48]

One can imagine the tensions that these changes must have engendered in aboriginal communities such as that of the Munsees and the Chippewas at the Muncey mission, tensions between Christian and "traditional" positions, which divide aboriginal people to this day. There were those who believed that radical cultural transformation was the best hope for the community's survival, and others who believed that such changes amounted to giving up aboriginal identity and committing cultural suicide. These differences sometimes led to intense confrontation: Peter Beaver, for example, was continually opposed and taunted by the traditionalists among the Ojibwa of the Thames, and was once almost killed while praying; eventually he broke under pressure, went berserk, threatening to kill everyone around him, and in 1831 committed suicide.

The religious intolerance of the Christians was incomprehensible to most aboriginal people, who did not view different religions or sects as mutually exclusive. They had great difficulty understanding why the missionaries insisted that they could not still follow their traditional religion as well as Christianity. A Munsee chief said, "We Munceys take hold of the white man's worship with *one hand*; with the *other hand* we hold fast our Fathers' worship. Both ways are good."[49] Aboriginal spiritual leaders sometimes integrated compatible elements from Christianity to expand their own teachings, and converts often only followed those practices compatible with their old understanding of God and nature. In adopting Christianity, aboriginal people were not necessarily praying to a new God but recognizing that the Great Spirit now asked them to express their devotion in new ways. The conviction that aboriginal people were really the ten lost tribes of Israel, which Peter Jones and some other prominent aboriginal leaders shared, allowed converts to synthesize their beliefs in the Midewewin (the Ojibwa Grand Medicine Society) and Christianity, since some traditional stories bore similarities to those in the Old Testament.[50]

Native leaders recognized that Christianity had value in preserving the integrity of their communities, especially by encouraging temperance, and that Christians had easier access to government and private assistance. Over time, it became increasingly clear that the government would not protect non-Christian Indians from land-hungry colonists and that, to hold on to their territory, it was necessary, for all intents and purposes, to become Christian and agricultural. Christian converts were able to expand their influence and gain power within aboriginal communities because they were seen as best able to deal with white society – white missionaries could be valuable allies in protecting Native interests both locally and with the imperial government in Britain.[51] Christians were listened to by governments, not traditionalists; traditionalists were labelled "backward" and had to be careful who they talked to. Many went underground.

Some traditionalists today, such as the Ojibwa writer and cultural critic Wub-e-ke-niew, from Red Lake, Minnesota, criticize the role of the mixed-race children of white fathers and aboriginal mothers, such as Peter Jones, noting that they often adopted European values, incorporated into the English social hierarchy, and were usually the ones with whom governments made treaties. Wub-e-ke-niew states that these people of mixed race were not considered fully Ojibwa, as several aspects of ethnic identity had to be passed down through Ojibwa fathers. In his view, such people were crucial in the formation of the white concept of "Indian" as "English subject person," for they depended on the colonizers for their identity, but were kept in their place by a stigmatized identity that could never attain equality with the white settlers.[52]

Part of the reason for the quickening of interest in Christianity at Muncey-town may have been the involvement of a new player – the government – in efforts to transform and civilize the aboriginal population. In 1830, responsibility for the Indian Department was transferred from the military authority to the civil governor in Upper Canada. Formerly, the colonial government had been concerned solely with preventing Indian hostility and maintaining the aboriginal nations as loyal allies of the Crown and active participants in colonial wars. After the War of 1812, however, their usefulness as allies had passed, while the expense of maintaining their allegiance remained. The government was no longer inclined to form alliances with aboriginal nations on a nation-to-nation basis; it now saw its duty as "gradually reclaiming the Indians from a state of barbarism and introducing amongst them the industrious and peaceful habits of civilized life." The Indian Department intended to promote civilization through religious instruction, basic literacy training, and elementary training in agriculture, so that the Indians could be settled on farms and assimilated. As historian Peter Schmalz has noted, "The government project of civilizing the Indians was undertaken partly for humanitarian reasons, but mainly as a method of weaning the Indians from the public purse."[53]

Indeed, by the 1830s, Indians had acquired special legal status: the right to presents (begun by the French) and annuities (dating from 1817), the right to reserved lands, and a special (if inept) government department to oversee settler relations with them. Many of those in power in Upper Canada wanted to end these obligations, to break up reserves, stop the distribution of presents, and disband the Indian Department. The system of annual presents was extremely expensive, and the actual gifts of clothes, ammunition, blankets, and alcohol produced no lasting benefit to the recipients. According to the Colborne Plan, aboriginal settlements would be established at the Coldwater, Lake Simcoe, Amherstburg, Caradoc (Muncey), St. Clair (near Sarnia), and the Grand River reserves. Houses were to be built and superintendents appointed, tools and supplies given out, and numerous support personnel, such as blacksmiths, carpenters, and farmers hired to instruct Indians (the latter never really materialized). With this new government agenda, expenditures on presents dropped from £117,500 to £16,000 and the cost of the Indian Department from £16,200 to £4,400.[54] The plan raised hopes that the entire expenditure of the Indian Department might be eliminated in a few more years.

In its report for 1829–31, the Methodist Missionary Society reported impressive changes at Muncey: "At this station during the Past year the Governor has laid out a village, and is now erecting dwellings for the Indians, as also a commodious house for schools and meetings. In this house the school is now taught, with respect to which the teacher writes as follows: 'The school numbers 25 children, 15 boys and 10 girls; 4 of the scholars can write, and read in the English Reader; 9 more are reading in the Testament.' There are 560 in this station who are receiving religious instruction, 55 of whom are regular members of the Church. Of the Mission generally the Missionary [Elijah Harris?] states 'during the past season several have experienced Religion, 4 have removed, 2 have apostatized and 2 have died.'"[55]

The issue of house-building appears to have been an important inducement, but Case was wrong about the Munsees and the Chippewas wanting to live together in one community. Because of their reluctance to amalgamate their two very different cultures, only a few families would settle permanently in the new settlement, which was named "Colborne."

By 1830, the Methodists counted more than a thousand aboriginal members, nine missionary stations, and eleven schools for Indians in Upper Canada.[56] It seemed that Christianity would indeed rescue demoralized bands of hunter-gatherers and transform them into self-sufficient farmers – that Native people would soon survive and thrive in the new society that had displaced their traditional one.

The future of the missionary project seemed bright, but the particular future of Elijah Harris was in doubt, for Indian agent Joseph B. Clench reported, in February 1831, that "Mr Harris was discontinued as missionary at the last conference without any cause being given." And on December 20, 1830, Elijah Harris of the Township of Southwold had petitioned the government as a "resident in the province of thirty years – the greater part of which period in the Township of Oxford." Describing himself as advancing in years and desiring to retire with his family, he had stated that he had "laboured to do good by his endeavours to meliorate the Conditions of the Indians to the detriment of his family" and petitioned for a grant of land at Caradoc to settle on.[57] The petition was denied.

But Elijah Harris did not retire. Instead, whether out of financial need or vocation, he followed his Elder's instructions to extend his ministry to the St. Clair Ojibwa, an assignment that was to prove even more difficult than that at Munceytown.

CHAPTER
18

St. Clair Mission

Peter Jones and nine others, perhaps including Elijah Harris, had been the first missionaries to visit the Ojibwa along the St. Clair River in August 1829. What they saw was not encouraging. "During the day we saw a great number of the Indians (men and women) so drunk as to be unable to stand, who were lying on the ground, and their poor children almost naked and hungry, and no one to care for them." Later they were visited by two Ojibwa converts, Thomas Smith and Thomas McGee, who reported that "the Indians were universally opposed to Christianity, and that they would hardly enter into any conversation with them. . . . the St. Clair Indians had observed that both religions were equally good but they observed neither."[1] The Methodists apparently concluded that, although they were not wanted, they were needed.

A year later, the missionaries were reporting more favourable encounters. In June 1830, William Case printed the following report from Elijah Harris in the *Christian Advocate*:

> On the fore part of February 1 I left Muncey, accompanied by Peter Beaver, on a tour of the St. Clair Indians. On our arrival at Bear River, we found ten camps of the Indians, who were come to this part for the purpose of hunting and making sugar. After reading some letters, we

proceeded to tell to them what improvements were going on for the benefit of Indians at the Credit and other places.

Harris and Beaver then sang hymns in Ojibwa and prayed, and observed one Ojibwa man who began to weep. In reply to a request by Peter Beaver, the chiefs indicated they had no personal objections to having Methodist meetings and a school, but they had to consult their councils.

After Beaver's departure, Elijah Harris spent three days travelling on his own from camp to camp, holding meetings and conversations with the Indians.

The Indians were very fond of hearing the hymns read. The truths of the gospel which they inculcated appeared to have considerable effect on their minds. After reading the hymns they would ask me to sing them.

As I proceeded from camp to camp, many followed me, listening with much attention, and manifesting some feeling. In this manner I continued to instruct them, reading and singing most of the forty-six Indian hymns. Some of them said, "When the Indian speakers from the Credit were here last summer, we loved to hear them sing; it looked handsome too, to see them all with their books in their hands singing the good words. Although our chiefs don't like it, we love to see and hear."[2]

By the Treaty of 1827 the Ojibwa had surrendered 2.2 million acres in the Western and London districts, bounded on the west by Lake Huron and the St. Clair River. They were gathered on the four-square-mile St. Clair reserve in 1829, and in 1831 the Ojibwa of the St. Clair area were given their choice of reserve: Sarnia for those who wished to be "civilized" and Walpole Island for the others.[3] The new lieutenant-governor, Sir John Colborne, impressed by the Methodist settlement at Credit River, provided financial assistance from provincial funds for a similar settlement at St. Clair (now Sarnia). Houses and schools were to be constructed, teachers supplied, and bands encouraged to settle down and engage in agriculture on thirty-acre farms along the St. Clair River.

The establishment of such reserves suited both the missionaries and the government – the missionaries could exert greater influence when their converts were settled in one place, and the government could more easily make aboriginal people subject to the direction and control of superintendents. A man named William Jones, who had served as a spy for

Tecumseh and General Brock in the Battle of Detroit in 1812, was named the first government agent for the St. Clair reserve. He immediately began preparations to set up a school.

The first entry in his record book, dated June 1, 1831, reads:

a man by name of Harris at Caradoc, whom I had not had an opportunity to see, has been recommended to me by W. Mount [the local member of the Legislative Assembly] and others, as a fit person to be the teacher to the Indians. He is said to talk the Chippewa tongue well, which is very essential in a Teacher, and, though his Education is not very good, may be well enough for a time. He is a Methodist and in the habit of preaching occasionally, but I am told is neither a bigot or enthusiast, and that his manners are such to gain him the confidence of the Indians.[4]

Six months later, Jones reported that he had been visited by a Mr. Vantapel, the missionary teacher of seven hundred Ottawas who had sold their reserve to the American government and moved to Walpole Island.

The Indians [at St. Clair] on seeing Mr Vantapel seemed to be afraid that he wished to be their Teacher and strenuously requested that Mr Harris, who made them a visit some months ago, and with whom they appear to be generally well pleased, might be appointed. I think it will be well to let them suit themselves in the first commencement especially as their choice seems to be a tolerable good one. Mr. Harris appears to understand the Indian character well, and talks the language, which are very essential points. No one, however great his Talents may be, can make much progress in teaching through an Interpreter.[5]

Harris was engaged at $300, or £75 per annum. The Indian agent noted "He is poor and has a large family to support." Jones had encouraged him to come as soon as possible to help visit the Chippewas in their camps "as several of the Indians have evinced a disposition to commence agricultural operation" and he wanted to get to them before the whisky traders dissuaded them. Elijah arrived early in the new year of 1832 and at first lodged in the house intended for "Chief" Wawanosh, intending to move into one of the common Indian houses when these were completed. (Joshua Wawanosh was actually not a chief of the St. Clair Ojibwa at this time and was not even from the area; he gained prominence because he could speak

English and so acted as the intermediary with white people. I was told his name meant "bad egg."[6])

The distribution of houses remained a sore issue, for the Chippewas complained that Harris and the interpreter, François Cadotte, got Indian houses, while the two white men complained of the small size of their habitations – Harris, his wife, and eight children were living in a single 14-by-18-foot room with no place to store anything. "Mr Harris has a claim to land," recorded the Indian agent, and "asks for liberty to locate on a lot adjacent to the reserve where he would build a house for his own family or add to his present house."[7]

Harris began giving lessons in April. Jones reported that he "thinks the prospect of success in his undertaking tolerably good," although he had no books and had to order some. Jones was favourably impressed: "Mr Harris thinks that making the children write the alphabet and spell words on slates will aid them much in learning. Though his Education is limited, he is probably better qualified to bring the children on to the extent of his own knowledge than any other person that can be procured at present." Meanwhile, the Chippewas began clearing land, put up fencing, and planted twenty bushels of potatoes, and six to seven acres of Indian corn.

But Harris's position was soon to be threatened by the arrival at St. Clair of a Wesleyan Methodist missionary, at the invitation of the Anglican Archdeacon of York, John Strachan. The Wesleyan Methodists from Britain were rivals of the American-based Methodist Episcopal Church, to which Elijah Harris and the rest of the early missionaries belonged. The lieutenant-governor of Upper Canada, John Colborne, and other members of the governing clique, who were all members of the Church of England, were deeply suspicious of the Episcopal Methodists; the latter had formed an independent American church after the American revolution and were suspected of promoting republican, democratic political ideas and undermining the loyalty of their Native converts. Worse, they had become actively involved in politics, and were opposing the legislative policies of Upper Canada's Family Compact, as the ruling élite was called.

The members of the Family Compact had initially tried to arrange the replacement of the Methodist missionaries with Anglican missionaries. This was not successful, so Archdeacon Strachan turned to the Wesleyan Methodists, who were much more conservative in outlook and practice than the Episcopals, and whose loyalty to Britain was beyond doubt. The Wesleyans were given a large grant to operate in Canada, in the hope that they would displace the Episcopal Methodists. Their first assignment was the St. Clair mission.

Thomas Turner was the first Wesleyan Methodist missionary to be assigned to Upper Canada and he operated independently of the Episcopal Methodists' local conference. He arrived in Sarnia in July 1832 with a letter of recommendation from John Strachan, but with little experience in North America and none with aboriginal people. He had been warned before he arrived that the local Chippewas were hostile to Christianity, and the Indian agent initially suggested that he not identify himself as a preacher. There was no house ready for him, so he had to lodge across the river on the American side. A cholera epidemic was under way, and the St. Clair Chippewa had deserted the mission and fled into the interior to escape it.

A month later, when Peter Jones visited, he recorded in his diary that "we waited three days to find the Indians sober, so that we could speak to them. But they were drunk all the while." In October, the Indian agent reported that Wawanosh had been continually intoxicated the last two months and "Doing all in his power to counteract His Excellency, plans and operations. . . . Turner complained that he and his family were grossly insulted by one of the Indians last night, which I have reason to believe was done at the instigation of the Chief. Mr Turner's servant maid says she went to Waynosh to complain of the same Indian and that he threatened to beat her."[8] Only when James Givens, the chief superintendent of the Indian Department, wrote directly to Wawanosh did his behaviour improve.

Right from the start Elijah Harris and Thomas Turner did not get along, and Turner disapproved of Harris's teaching methods. Turner wrote in a letter of March 7, 1833:

I exceedingly regret that the man sent here to teach the school is in every Way a most unsuitable Person for such an undertaking. His qualifications, or rather, his entire want of qualifications for teaching a school, could not I think have been known to the Lieut Governor, or I cannot suppose he would have sanctioned this appointment to the situation. . . . [He asks for an interpreter.] Unless something of this kind is done, I fear nothing of importance will ever be done in regard to the education of the Indian children. Without it, the regular attendance of the scholars can never be secured. . . . The Indians themselves seldom or never chasten their children, and never break their will.[9]

The Indian agent was far less critical of Harris's efforts. "Harris has a much fuller school than I had anticipated his getting. 18–26 scholars, all of whom appear to be improving." Among the children at the school were twelve orphans, "who have no person to provide for them, nor any means whatever of getting support," William Jones reported, and asked his superiors for provisions to feed the orphans and provide school books.[10] He also recommended that Mrs. Harris be hired to instruct the Indian women and girls in sewing, spinning, knitting, baking, making soap and candles, and in how to keep their houses clean and in proper order.

Even Thomas Turner eventually had to grudgingly admit that the school was doing better than expected. "They have hitherto attended with much greater regularity than could have been expected. And being very anxious to learn, they have made for the time very pleasing proficiency. We have every reason to believe that a much greater number will shortly attend." He began to petition to have Harris replaced, anyway: "On my arrival at this place last summer, I found that the person who had been sent here under the sanction of the Lieut-Governor to be employed as school master, and who His Excellency supposed would be able to interpret for me [demonstrated] so limited and imperfect a knowledge of the Chippeway tongue as to require an interpreter himself. Thus circumstanced, I was wholly unable to communicate with the Indians."[11]

In response to this missive Turner was authorized to hire an interpreter, and he engaged George Henry, the half-brother of Peter Jones. "To me it appears that it has been by means of the labours of the native teachers especially that the work of God among the Indians has spread with such astonishing rapidity and to so great an extent," wrote Turner. "And therefore, solely with a view to the spiritual good of the Indians here, may I be permitted, respectfully to recommend the appointment of a native teacher to labour here in conjunction with myself; especially as the expense in all probably would not much exceed the salary of an interpreter."

Meanwhile, agriculture was under way but "the Indians get distracted by arriving Indians," and go for a "cheering keg," wrote the Indian agent in his letterbook. Thomas Turner reported that fourteen or fifteen families were now living in the houses that had been erected for them by the government, and had applied themselves to the cultivation of their lands "far beyond our most sanguine expectations." Noting that "ardent spirits" were readily available on American side, he commented that the people were "drunk night and day for weeks altogether."[12] But he had got some "respectable people on the opposite shore to form a Temperance Society which has already been the means of checking intemperance far beyond what was at first anticipated."

When Peter Jones, Thomas McGee, and Thomas Hurlburt (the white missionary who had served at Muncey) visited St. Clair in 1833, the resistance of the Chippewas to Christianity was palpable. Old Chief Yellowbird told them that "although they had agreed to have their children instructed, that they may understand the weights and measures used by the white people, and that they may be able to crib and keep accounts that the white man may not cheat them, yet that they had never engaged, and had no wish to become Christians." Thomas McGee reported "religion at low ebb in these parts, and it was hard work to preach to stone." The Chippewas did not have a very high opinion of government, either: "They frequently say that the Dept has been paid out of their money, merely to be a restraint on them."[13]

The antipathy toward Thomas Turner did not abate, and William Jones, the Indian agent, was confronted by several Ojibwa who wished to see Turner removed. "Some time ago Waywaynosh, with three other chiefs, came to me to tell me that the Government need not go to the expense of building a house for Mr. Turner, as they did not intend to be instructed by him. Waywaynosh, who was the speaker, being somewhat intoxicated at the time, I did not think it expedient to report formally what he said, but replied that Mr. Turner was here to teach only those who were willing to listen to him." The Indian agent himself was suspected of disapproving of Turner and had to "assure his excellency that no intimacy is wanting between Mr Turner and me, and I have no reason to disapprove of any measure that he has heretofore adopted in his capacity of missionary to this establishment."[14]

The hostility to Turner was by no means the only problem at the mission. Although the school was doing well, the provisions for it were nearly exhausted and the Indian agent did not know what to do with the orphan children who relied on the school for food. On top of this, neither Harris or Cadotte, his interpreter, had been paid since the previous October (it was now August 1833). Finally, in September, the Indian agent received approval for an order of rations for the orphans, by which time he had already had to write to his superiors that the chiefs also needed help for the

people, and asked for rations to enable them to keep farming, since with
settlers establishing farms all around them, hunting was less successful, and
their crops were insufficient to provide for the whole tribe over the winter.

It appears that, while they experimented with agriculture, the Ojibwa
had not carried out all their traditional subsistence activities. When, in
November, the rations still had not arrived, the Ojibwa took matters into
their own hands, and set off on hunting trips to keep themselves from starving. In December, William Jones wrote again to his superiors to ask if he
could buy ammunition for the Indians if the goods did not arrive before
freeze-up. When they had still not arrived in January and water navigation
was closed for the season, it was arranged late in the month that the goods
would be transported by road. By then Jones had already had to give the
orphans' rations to the rest of the Chippewas, who were rapidly losing
confidence in the government. The Chippewas went hunting again, taking
their children with them, and school attendance shrank to only five or six
pupils. Although a donation of clothes from the "kind ladies of Bristol"
arrived in January, by March the still-hungry Indians had to eat the potatoes and corn they had been saving for seed.

Meanwhile, Thomas Turner's frustration mounted. In January 1834, he
wrote, "It is to me a subject of deep regret, and I may add of humiliation
too, that it is not my lot to communicate to the Committee the pleasing
intelligence of savages of the wilderness being brought to the obedience of
faith." He reminded them again that he had asked for a Native teacher and
had received no reply. Finally, in April 1834, the Indian agent recorded
simply that "Rev. Thomas Turner withdrew from this station yesterday."[15]

His replacement was an altogether different sort of man. Born in
England, James Evans had emigrated to Lower Canada in 1822. From 1828
until 1830, he had taught at the Rice Lake Mission School, and now came
to St. Clair one year after being ordained. Reverend Evans had a remarkable
aptitude for aboriginal languages and understanding of Indian psychology.
He could write and preach in Ojibwa; in 1830 he had written a letter in that
language to Peter Jones, "the first letter in the Indian language written by a
white man that I have ever seen," Jones recorded. Assisted by Peter Jones
and George Henry, he later prepared many Ojibwa translations of hymns and
scripture, and used the same system of grammar and spelling to develop a
Cree syllabary a few years later when he and Native assistants developed
a written language (syllabics) for the Cree and the Ojibwa to the northwest.

In 1834 Evans reported: "For some months after our arrival, the Indians, with one consent, shunned the house of God, and manifested an utter enmity to Christianity; . . . sometimes entering the mission house, they would tell us, 'This is our house, this is our land, you have no business here, we never sent for you, we will never, while the waters run and the sun shines, become Christians. Go home, go to your own people, preach to the white people.'" The houses were uninhabitable: "The windows and doors having in several instances been completely destroyed; and but few of them was ever occupied as an occasional shelter."[16]

"On my arrival at this station in July," wrote the missionary, "I found that the Indians were not very favorably disposed towards Christianity and that the greater part of them had obstinately resisted every solicitation from my predecessor to hear the gospel. I commenced by calling on the head chief, Wawanosh, who appeared somewhat pleased when I spoke to him in his own tongue. . . . The men were with one exception, drunkards of the most degraded kind, and with one or two exceptions the women were given to the same debasing practice. . . . They were destitute of the common necessaries of life and the payments and presents received by them from the British government were almost invariably lost or sold for whiskey within a few days after their distribution. During the remainder of the year they wandered in rags or nearly naked."

Evans made rapid progress with Wawanosh: "I visited the camp of Wawanosh," Evans wrote in his diary, "and found him at home *sober*, and had a long and serious conversation with him. . . . Since that time I have received several visits from him and have endeavoured, with some degree of success, to influence his mind in favour of Christianity. I regard as a proof of this a few remarks which he made to the interpreter a few days ago. 'I think,' said he, 'it would be a good thing were all the Indians to relinquish the use of liquor. I hope you will let them come to your meetings. I want you to do my young men good.'"[17]

The first baptism was proudly recorded on October 10, 1834, and five Chippewas were baptized that year. In December 1834, Evans persuaded one of the priests of the Midewewin, the Ojibwa Grand Medicine Society, to give Christianity a three weeks' trial, during which time the priest would not drink and would be instructed. During the trial period nine men, including the Mide priest, caught cholera. Only the Mide survived, swearing that it was because he had listened to Christianity; he was soon baptized.

According to the Indian agent, "One of these had been as great a drunkard as any of the tribe, except Waywaynosh, until after recovering from the cholera in August last when he resolved never to taste ardent spirits again. He has kept his word till now and has every appearance of being determined in his resolution and sincere in his profession of religion."[18]

Some Chippewas began to equate conversion with abstinence. Evans reported this discussion:

Another said, "I have tried *four times*, since your talk on that rainy day, which talk I do not forget, to give up drinking; but when I will not drink, the Indians say I am angry, that I dislike them, and they become very *cross* with me, and then I drink again. I think I want something you Methodist Indians have in your hearts, to help me say *No*, and not to drink any more." One old woman observed . . . "I think I must go to where the Indians live who do not drink; perhaps there I will get that religion which will help me not to drink any more."[19]

In a letter to his brother, dated January 26, 1835, Evans reported that Wawanosh, his wife, and son had been converted, and others soon began to follow suit. At a prayer meeting along the St. Clair River in March 1835, 250 Chippewas attended. By 1836, there were 101 Methodist members on or near the Sarnia reserve, while three years later Evans's successor reported 109 and "none given to intoxication." The success of the St. Clair mission – its excellent harvests, well-attended school, neat houses, and regular church attendance – became well known all over the country, and its fame spread even to England. Evans's successor at St. Clair, John Douse, wrote, "The change of habit and character is so great and so striking that many people visit the Mission from far and near to witness it. Many Indians have come and some have been induced to become Christians from beholding the improvement, happiness and zeal here."[20]

In December 1835, John Beecham of the Wesleyan Missionary Society asked Evans to prepare a report, based on his experience at the St. Clair Mission, on the practicability of civilizing the Indians without Christianizing them. Evans vividly illustrated the contrast between the condition of the St. Clair Indians before and after they had accepted Christianity. The statistics that Evans collected to prove the point that "the Gospel in christianizing them civilized them also" were compelling:

Number of deaths during the four years previous to embracing Christianity at St. Clair:

Natural deaths, hastened by drunkenness and other vices	12
Died drunk, from over-drinking	9
Killed in drunken quarrels, etc.	14
Burned to death by falling into the fire when drunk	2
Drowned when drunk	2
Poisoned by Conjurers, to avenge supposed injuries	4
Insane through drink, died in woods and eaten by wolves	1
Run against a pointed stick in woods and killed while drunk	1
Killed by accident when sober	1
Died in childbed	1

Number of deaths since embracing Christianity	
Natural deaths	3

For many, the inescapable conclusion was that Christianity, partly through its missionary programs of education and welfare, had dramatically reduced the death rate and ensured the physical survival of a people who had been doomed to extinction, as an inquiry by Member of Parliament T. J. Baxter concluded in 1836.[21]

James Evans became a popular hero, but my missionary relative Elijah Harris was not there to enjoy this success. Upon his arrival in 1834, James Evans had quickly formed a negative impression of Harris: "the School was so little regarded that the Teacher considered it unnecessary to attend, and during the six months preceding their embracing Christianity, he only gave 13½ days attendance, although receiving a reasonable salary during the whole period." Barely a month later William Jones wrote to his superiors: "I beg leave to state that the school requires a more efficient Teacher. Mr. Harris has hitherto answered the desired purpose as well, perhaps, as any other would have done; but now a man of more Talent, provided one could be got who knows something of the Indian tongue, would do much better."[22]

One senses that the parting was not particularly amicable. In January 1835, the Indian agent received a letter from his superior, Joseph B. Clench, superintendent of the London District, informing him that Clench could recommend a suitable person to teach the school, "as Mr Harris has been absent all the month of December having went to Deleware, and then, as he says, fell sick." This "as he says" is interesting, implying as it does that this was only an excuse for not attending. Had Evans expressed his lack of confidence in Harris to him directly? Or had Harris really given up long before, after the disaster with farming and government bungling left his carefully tended school virtually empty? By February 1835, Harris had not attended to the school for two months and had expressed his intention to give it up altogether, so his salary was discontinued. A new teacher, a Mr. Price, was hired; he was shortly replaced by the same Thomas Hurlburt who had worked at the Muncey mission. Meanwhile, Elijah Harris bought land in Sarnia and then resold it, having apparently decided to head for the United States.

This is all I know about this period of Elijah Harris's life; unfortunately, there is no record of my relative's feelings about any of these events. I imagine it must have been hard to have his own usefulness repeatedly questioned, first by Turner, then by Evans, and to see Evans, a much younger and more energetic man, lionized as the hope of the Methodists, the new apostle to the Indians, the Christian hero, surpassing even Rev. Peter Jones. (Peter Jones may also have felt this, for his mentor William Case now favoured Evans's translations of hymns and scripture over his own.) Despite such personal disappointments, there might have been a happy ending for the missionary encounters I've described if the story ended here – at least from some points of view – with Christianity transforming the lives of dejected Natives, who go on to take a productive place in Euro-Canadian society. But that is not what happened; new pressures would erode all that had been accomplished.

One of these new pressures was the huge wave of European immigration to Upper Canada after the Napoleonic wars, the first wave of which peaked in the 1830s. Between 1830 and 1833, the population of Upper Canada jumped by nearly 50 per cent. In 1826, the town of York counted 1,677 inhabitants, and in 1830 this had increased to 2,860. By 1845 the city's population had mushroomed to 19,706. With this influx, pressure on the Ojibwa's remaining lands intensified. While the government and missionaries had expected the Indians would be quickly assimilated, Native people worried about the security of their land tenure. Peter Jones and others petitioned the government for title deeds to their lands. They could never feel secure as long as their lands remained vested in the Crown, without deeds.[23]

William Jones, the government agent, tried to protect the St. Clair Ojibwa, and wrote in 1835:

I wish his Excellency to understand that a number of speculators have come into the country who are using many unfair means to get possession of the Indians' Land with a view to obtaining grants whenever the Govt may purchase from the Indians, or otherwise speculating upon it – some with a view to cutting and carrying off the most valuable timber, etc. – They are in the habit of making the Indians drunk and then getting them to sign any kind of Instrument they think proper to write.[24]

He referred to a lease on Walpole Island, to two Americans,

which I refused, observing that there had been so many unfair advantages taken of Indians by persons applying for Leases, no more would be let at present. They, however, made one of the Chiefs drunk and got him to sign a lease for a very large Tract. The Indian says that he was so intoxicated that he could not sign and compelled his wife to do it for him, consequently I forbade their taking possession; but I have lately been told that they have not only taken possession, but are dealing out the land in lots to settlers under them.

The situation was similar at the St. Clair mission, where, he wrote, "I have had a good deal of difficulty with the people in keeping them from getting possession of the houses that were built by the Government for the Indians." In fact, the same thing was happening at virtually every reserve in southern Ontario, and the government seemed unable to stop it. At the same time, hundreds of Native people from south of the border arrived in Upper Canada after fleeing President Andrew Jackson's ruthless removals of most of the eastern Native nations to the Great Plains, a policy that caused untold hardship, misery, and death in the United States and created additional pressure on existing aboriginal lands in Canada.

With such population pressures, the ability of aboriginal people to live by hunting was severely curtailed. In 1837, Archdeacon John Strachan observed that "they could no longer live by hunting as the settlements were extending through every part of the Province and unless something was done to induce them to alter their mode of life they must face Inevitable destruction and ruin."

Although several First Nations were attempting to make the transition to farming, they did not become farmers as quickly as the Indian Department wanted. There were many reasons for this, not the least being that traditionally women planted and tended crops, while the missionaries and the Indian Department tried to persuade the men to do it; the Natives were also issued poor tools. Worse, "the greed, incompetence, stupidity or criminality" of those Indian agents involved in selling off reserve land prevented the Indians from having adequate finances in their transition to a farming economy.[25]

Dismissing the achievements of the previous decade, Sir Francis Bond Head, the new lieutenant-governor, declared these experiments "a complete Failure" in 1836 and ridiculed the "Attempt to make Farmers of the Red Men." He argued that "Civilization is against the Indians' nature and they cannot become civilized." (He was obviously ignorant of the fact that, as stated earlier, in the Americas as a whole, far more Native people were farmers than were purely hunters.) He assumed they would soon become extinct as a people; indeed, most people believed they would be gone by the end of the nineteenth century, based in part on their high mortality from imported diseases. In the meantime Bond Head supported total segregation in an isolated area to protect the Indians from whites and he put forward a scheme to move the various First Nations living in the vicinity of Lake Huron and the Thames River to Manitoulin Island, after they had given up their own lands. There he proposed they would live out their last days in peace, without schooling or other interference. He reported to the colonial secretary Lord Glenelg in England: "It is evident to me that we should reap a very great Benefit, if we could persuade those Indians, who are now impeding the Progress of Civilization in Upper Canada, to resort to a place possessing the double Advantage of being admirably adapted to *them* (insomuch as it affords Fishing, Hunting, Bird-shooting, and Fruit), and yet in no way adapted to the White population."[26] This, of course, was what President Andrew Jackson was doing south of the border, even to the agricultural Cherokees, who had their own constitution, public schools, newspaper, and Euro-American-educated leaders. It had also been done much earlier in Ireland, when Oliver Cromwell's army had forced the Catholic Irish to move beyond the Slaney River to less fertile land.

Given the seeming inability or unwillingness of the government to protect the southern reserve lands from white settlers and speculators, the idea of segregation was also one that was popular within church circles –

but for different reasons. The Methodists and also many aboriginal people themselves looked to the last great fertile, unceded territory in Upper Canada, the area south of Georgian Bay and east of Lake Huron known as the Saugeen Tract, as a separate, permanent homeland for all the province's Native people, just as the British and many aboriginal people under Tecumseh had supported the idea of such a territory in the Ohio Valley, until the treaty concluding the War of 1812 put an end to that dream. Many aboriginal people, including Peter Jones, encouraged the southern Ojibwa to use the Saugeen as their homeland.

In July 1836, in an open letter published in the *Christian Guardian*, Wawanosh, now described as the head chief of the Ojibwa nation, proposed that the Saugeen territory be set apart as a homeland for Native people. He argued that the present reserves in southern Upper Canada were too small – especially if the tribes increased in numbers under the Christian religion – and too insecure, given the threat of land-hungry settlers. The Saugeen Tract, which included the Bruce Peninsula and more land to the south, was large, sparsely populated, and surrounded on two sides by water to keep out whites; no roads would be needed. Wawanosh suggested that Indians sell their existing reserves to finance the move, and hoped that if they agreed to do so, the government would give them permanent title to the Saugeen land. "Could we all settle together, separate from the whites; have our own schools, stores, mills, and other requisites in a settlement, all under our own management. . . . Here we can exclude all whose vicious examples would corrupt the morals of our children; while the land being good, we might be encouraged to become farmers and teach our children to draw their bread out of the earth."[27]

Wawanosh's letter clearly illustrates that, while some aboriginal leaders were not averse to adopting certain aspects of a European lifestyle, such as farming and schooling, most aboriginal people were deeply afraid of losing their remaining land. If they had ever supported the idea of assimilation, they no longer did; they did not want to have their reserves broken up or to live among the whites. They wanted to remain separate, with a distinct culture and legal status, and with the power to manage their own affairs as a group. In fact, they were moving toward increasing their segregation from white communities, rather than reducing it.[28]

The Methodists assisted the Ojibwa in their attempts to gain title to the Saugeen Tract and to prevent settlers from encroaching there. At the same time Sir Francis Bond Head was determined to move all aboriginals to rocky Manitoulin Island. In 1836, through intimidation and manipulation, he forced the Saugeen Indians to give up three-quarters of a million acres of territory and agree to move either north to the Bruce Peninsula or west to Manitoulin. He then insisted that the Coldwater and Simcoe Indians surrender their entire tract and arranged major land cessions at Moraviantown and Amherstburg. The lieutenant-governor also obtained title to the land from sixteen Indians on Manitoulin, so the island could be the property of all Indians. Some aboriginal people did move there, particularly those from south of the border, but the whole scheme was strongly opposed by many Ojibwa, the Methodists, and also by the Aborigines' Protection Society, a humanitarian organization that had been established in England in 1836. The latter accused Bond Head of taking three-million acres of arable land from the Ojibwa of Upper Canada and leaving them with twenty-three thousand "barren islands."[29]

In the bitter controversy that followed, Bond Head claimed the Natives' surrender of the Saugeen had been voluntary, but those who had signed the land cession had had a limited, if not dubious, right to the land. In fact, the lieutenant-governor's tactics echoed those used against the Cherokees in the United States ten years earlier. At that time, the American government had made an agreement with a tiny minority of Cherokees – fewer than five hundred – to force the removal of 17,000 people, even though neither the principal chief nor any officials of the Cherokee Nation had signed it.

The Saugeen surrender was also illegal, as Bond Head's actions had contravened both the Royal Proclamation of 1763 and the Additional Instructions of 1794. Certainly his methods were slippery; he recommended putting nothing in writing while negotiating with the Indians. He told his superiors:

> I conceive that the Government of the Indians requires Moral Considerations and elastic Adaptations which are totally incompatible with the straight Railroad Habits of a Public Accountant; . . . I think it highly Politic that we should retain the Advantage as well as the Disadvantage of possessing no written documents, or no fixed rule of Governing the Indians beyond the Will and Pleasure of their Great Father the King.[30]

Bond Head's response to the British colonial secretary regarding Methodist requests for title deeds to the Indian lands that remained was scathing:

Who ever heard of an Indian mainly caring for the Morrow? Who ever heard of his desiring to transmit Arable land to his children? . . . The Methodist Ministers might just as well declare, that when wild Beasts roar at each other it is to complain of the Want among them of Marriage Licenses, for Animals understand these "Documents" just as well as Indians understand Title Deeds.[31]

Both British and Canadian Methodists strongly opposed the Manitoulin resettlement. James Evans launched an attack on Bond Head's policy and especially on a report that Bond Head had sent to the Colonial Office, stating that it was impossible to civilize the Indians, that contact with the white man increased their vices, that many were dying of consumption from being exposed to white civilization, and that Indians would never become farmers. Focussing their efforts on changing policy in Britain, the Methodists repeatedly presented evidence of the successful conversion and civilization of the Mississaugas and the Iroquois to the British Parliament.

Peter Jones, John Sunday, James Evans and Egerton Ryerson met with parliamentary committees, the Colonial Office, and even King William IV and Queen Victoria to impress upon them the injustice of Bond Head's removal policy. They reminded the officials of past promises, pointed out the illegitimate nature of recent land transfers, and published long articles contradicting the lieutenant-governor's assessment of aboriginal conditions and attacking his treaties.[32]

Two influential groups in England, the Aborigines' Protection Society and the Society of Friends (the Quakers) supported them, publishing books on the mistreatment of the Indians in Upper Canada and making strong protests to the Colonial Office. Egerton Ryerson became the Canadian representative of the Aborigines' Protection Society.

All of these efforts increased opposition to the forced removals, but it was sheer luck – the recall of Bond Head to England because of the 1837 rebellion – that ensured enforcement of these particular removals was never completed (though other removals would be carried out in Canada until well into the second half of the twentieth century).

It is important to point out that, laudable as the Methodists' opposition was to the government's forced-assimilation policy, this opposition stemmed from a disagreement about methods, not goals. Both agreed that ultimately there should be no distinct aboriginal culture. The Colonial Office ordered the new lieutenant-governor, Sir George Arthur, to return to the previous policy of gradually changing the aboriginal people through schooling, and instructed him to discontinue the practice of forcing the Indians to surrender their lands. In this, the First Nations of Upper Canada were lucky. In the United States, Native Americans were rounded up at the ends of rifles and bayonets, and many died as a result of the forced removals. For example, at least one-tenth and possibly one-third of the Cherokees died of starvation, exposure, and cholera on their Trail of Tears as they moved to the West.

The Colonial Office further recommended that the Indians of Upper Canada be given permanent title to their remaining lands in the form of title deeds. Aboriginal people of Upper Canada were delighted at the prospect, but, unfortunately, the deeds did not materialize, and the lands already taken, such as the Saugeen Tract, were never returned to them. At Coldwater and Lake Simcoe, the Ojibwa – who had successfully adapted to farming – lost all the land they had cleared, as well as the barns, mills, and houses they had built with their own annuity money, and were never compensated for their losses – they were forced to start from scratch all over again. In 1840, a petition by the chiefs at St. Clair was sent to Queen Victoria herself, pointing out that the Saugeen surrender had been made on the basis of fear and was fraudulent because it was concluded without the consent of a Grand Council of Chiefs and of Wawanosh, the head chief, as had been specified as a requirement in a document sent to Colborne in 1835.[33] Still, the land was not returned.

The effect of this turmoil on the missions was considerable. The missionaries reported that the Indians were depressed and angry, and they feared an uprising if more land was taken. No one knew which group would be next to lose its land. The Saugeen Indians told James Evans, "If we clear fields, build houses, and make orchards, the white man will soon want them, and he must have them." At St. Clair the Chippewas refused to continue farming and declared that they intended to return to a traditional way of life; the response at Munceytown was similar.[34]

I have not been able to find out whether Elijah Harris was involved in any of the Methodist protests against Bond Head's removal policy, or if he kept in touch with events on the St. Clair reserve after his departure. It appears he returned to his earlier vocation of itinerant preacher, for after he left the St. Clair Mission, he "went to the aid of Mr. Flummerfeldt at

Gosfield and Howard [on the Thames circuit], where he remained the following year" (presumably 1836). But because of his large family, he failed to find a charge as an itinerant minister and left for Michigan at the end of the year.[35] Again, I do not know what he was doing or where in Michigan he was for the next while. He was definitely back in Upper Canada by 1840, however, for in that year he was finally received into the ministry on trial at the Grand River Mission. He may have taken this posting to be near his brother, Rev. John Harris, who was a Baptist minister at nearby Mount Pleasant, just southwest of Brantford. Once again he would be ministering to aboriginal people.

The Grand River Mission, as you may remember, had been founded in 1822; Alvin Torry had arrived in 1823 and served as the first Methodist missionary to the Six Nations and the Chippewas of the area. In 1829 headquarters for the mission had moved from Davisville to a new church erected by the Indians at Salt Springs. For a time the mission flourished: John Douse, who was stationed at the mission from 1834 to 1836, wrote that "we have eight preachers and exhorters, nearly as many leaders, & a fine, large, good society . . . we have about 150 thus members of our Society." The mission ran a school as well and had attracted many of the pupils from the schools operated by its main religious competitor on the reserve, the New England Company (the descendant of the Society for the Propagation of the Gospel in New England, founded through the efforts of John Eliot and Thomas Weld).[36]

But the Six Nations of Grand River faced a number of other threats to their welfare. First of all, Joseph Brant and then others had sold off more than half of their lands, and white squatters were continually encroaching on what was left. Much of the land had been sold to raise an endowment fund for the Six Nations, but unfortunately Sir John Colborne had invested much of this without the band's consent in the Grand River Navigation Company, a commercial venture to build canals to make the Grand River navigable for commercial shipping. It would eventually fail when the coming of the railroad rendered the whole plan obsolete and the band would never be compensated for its financial losses, despite many court cases. Even with the failure of the company still in the future, investment in it in the late 1830s and early 1840s absorbed all the funds of the Six Nations, leaving no surplus for distribution in the form of money or provisions. A report on "The Past and Present Condition of the Six Nations," prepared in 1842, reported that "The Indians have frequently complained of the transaction and have petitioned the government to take the Stock off their hands."[37] The construction of dams on the Grand River proceeded in spite of Iroquois protests and flooded some of their lands; the various fevers and agues that afflicted residents were attributed to the unhealthy conditions resulting from it.

I know nothing of Elijah Harris's tenure at Grand River, including whether he was stationed right at the mission's headquarters at Salt Springs church or somewhere else on the reserve. But I do know that he must have had an extremely difficult time there, for once again the rivalry between the Episcopal and the Wesleyan Methodists disrupted his work. The year after the arrival of Thomas Turner at St. Clair in 1832, the impoverished Episcopals had been forced to accept an unequal union with the Wesleyans, and they had been required to withdraw from politics. In 1840 this fragile and unsatisfactory alliance unravelled over several issues, including the disbursement of mission funds. The bitter schism divided many former colleagues: William Case and James Evans, for example, sided with the Wesleyans, while Peter Jones remained loyal to his friend Egerton Ryerson, who, along with his brother William, led the Episcopal faction. William Ryerson was the main minister at Salt Springs in 1840, so Elijah Harris would have been right at the heart of the storm. Unfortunately for Harris, who remained an Episcopal Methodist, Grand River went Wesleyan, as this excerpt from a petition from the chiefs at Salt Springs, dated January 30, 1841, attests:

We have been twelve? Years now with the Methodist. We first join the Episcopal. We suffer great deal for seven years; for many our own brothers say we was Yankee and no good subjects.

We was very glad when Stinson [a Wesleyan Methodist] come. All our pain was taken away. Now it has [come?] about that Stinson and Ryerson part again. We don't wish to draw from the British; but still we wish to be with them.

We now come to High Quarters in religious Things; and beg you would send us a Missionary. Also, we beg for assistance for our children too, to have a School. When the Ryersons forced out we determined to stay with the British; they shut up Chapel against us and now we worship in private houses. We don't know how long we remain so. We very sorry that some of our people gone with the Ryersons. We don't know what we do if you dont help us. We cant go back to the Ryersons.[38]

As a result of the split, the Canada Conference of the Episcopal Methodist Church was left without a missionary treasury, and almost all the remaining missionaries were not paid their half-year's salaries; some were verging on starvation. The church was forced to hold missionary and revival meetings to make money.

It is likely that Harris was thoroughly embroiled in this controversy along with the Ryersons. Their banishment from Grand River, where the Episcopal Methodists had pioneered the whole Methodist missionary movement in Upper Canada, must have been a very painful rejection. It is hard to imagine that he would not feel betrayed and disillusioned after all the Episcopal Methodists had done, after all he had done himself. I do know that this was his last known attempt to work among aboriginal people in Canada.

His next appointment was closer to home and among his own people. In 1842, Harris was finally accepted as a full minister in the London District, and served the Thames circuit of the Methodist Episcopal Church. In 1843, he had the Dereham Forge circuit, but he was without charge the following year. In 1845 he performed marriages in the Brock District, which included Oxford County. In 1849 he was in Huron and Goderich, then from 1852 to 1854 his charge was the W. C. Malahide circuit, and then from 1855 to 1863 he was without charge at Vienna, in Elgin County. After that his whereabouts are unknown, though it's possible he moved to Wisconsin.[39] I don't know where or even when he died.

As I reflect on Elijah Harris's life, I can't help having a certain amount of sympathy for him. It seems he put his ideals and religious commitment before his own material well-being, only to be rejected continually or found wanting and put through the political meat-grinder. He spent his life telling aboriginal people that the colonizing Christian culture was honourable, only to see his life's work repeatedly undermined and undone, betrayed by the actions and inactions of his government, his church, and the other members of the society he tried to persuade aboriginal people to join. It appears that he gave a lot and ended up with little in return. He was certainly a restless soul: for much of his life he moved frequently, for reasons unknown.

And what of the other players in this story? The schism between the Episcopals and Wesleyans deeply disillusioned many aboriginal converts and divided Native communities. Some prominent Native Methodists, like

George Henry, quit the denomination in disgust, some of them subsequently joining the Church of England, as did many former Episcopal Methodists at Grand River. The competition between the Methodists and the Anglicans for aboriginal adherents intensified: in 1846, Robert Alder, the secretary of the Wesleyan Missionary Society in England, wrote to James Evans about just such a situation at the St. Clair Mission:

> The state of a mission in which you feel a special interest has been and is, we fear, very critical. I refer to St. Clair. The Church party [Church of England] had been endeavouring to supplant us and have succeeded in obtaining the removal of Wawanosh from the office of principal Chief there and there is no man who possesses so much influence amongst the Indians there as you do, and who is so well qualified to defeat the machinations of those who are seeking to injure that interesting Mission.

Perhaps in a bid to retain his power, Wawanosh eventually joined the Anglican church, though some Methodists still believed he remained a Methodist "at heart." But the Chippewas were generally doing well, according to Indian agent William Jones, who reported that, by 1840, they were growing Indian corn and potatoes and small quantities of spring wheat, oats, and peas, and fishing extensively. Moreover, he asserted, "As a body they are religious and moral, and will bear a comparison with any Christian communities of the same class. They are deeply sensible of the improvement of their condition and many attribute the preservation of their lives to their conversion." When a series of epidemics struck the reserve in the 1850s, Christian fervour ran high, the missionary reporting, "The altar is now thronged night after night." In 1859 the missionary wrote that two hundred people – most of the adult population – were members of the church, and that "only five old persons attempted to join in the Annual Pagan Holiday Dance, and they were laughed out of countenance by the spectators."[40]

Peter Jones spent most of the 1840s as the missionary at Munceytown, beginning in 1841, though he travelled so much that he devoted little time to the reserve. In 1846, the *Canadian Gazetteer of Canada West* reported that the 378 Chippewas of the Thames were flourishing on 9,000 acres, surveyed into 20-acre farms. They had a schoolhouse, which they also used as a church, 76 log houses and 6 wigwams, 25 barns, four wagons and carts, nine ploughs, and numerous cattle, horses, and swine. Yet despite the fact that a large number of missionaries, including some of the most effective Native preachers, were stationed at the mission, their success in permanently changing the Ojibwa appears to have been minimal. In 1848, there were only 112 members of the Methodist society, and while this increased to 203 when Peter Jones spent one full year at the mission, by 1851, when a non-aboriginal missionary took his place, this number had plummeted to 70. The next year the Ojibwa were quite hostile and did not want services at all. The missionaries lost most of their influence: the less successful ones blamed Ojibwa hostility on drink, but crop failures and flooding also discouraged the residents, and they were forced to hunt and sell baskets and brooms to survive. Attendance at the day school dwindled and it was closed in 1858.[41]

When Joseph Clench, the superintendent and land agent for the London District, which included Munceytown and St. Clair, was finally dismissed in 1854 for embezzling £9,000, or $40,000, from the St. Clair Ojibwa, Egerton Ryerson tried unsuccessfully to have Peter Jones appointed in his place, but the government did not have the kind of vision that the Episcopal Methodists had shown in recruiting Native leadership. Clench was never prosecuted for his criminal activities and, in fact, they were not that unusual, for the Indian Department was "notoriously the worst and most inefficient department in the province." Critics called it "a repository of jobbery and corruption"; as historian Peter Schmalz points out, most of its officials were patronage appointees whose ties to business and the political élite often placed them in conflicts of interest, to the detriment of their aboriginal wards. Although they had sold millions of acres of land to the government, many Ojibwa remained destitute, because the department mismanaged or appropriated their money.[42]

In the early 1840s, the Bagot Commission investigated Indian affairs. Despite its recommendations, many First Nations never secured title deeds, and the government instead consolidated bands on larger, more isolated, reserves. Even the Credit Mission, which had been such an unqualified success in the eyes of the colonizers, was sold in 1847, and the now-agricultural Mississaugas were encouraged to resettle on rocky Manitoulin Island or the infertile Bruce Peninsula. Peter Jones wanted the Credit Ojibwa to move to Munceytown, where there was rich agricultural land, but he was obstructed by Samuel Jarvis, the chief superintendent of the Indian Department. The loss of their lands at Credit River was a devastating blow to the Mississaugas, after all their work to adapt to a new way of life. What was the point of improving land over which you had no control? Although they were given land by the Six Nations at Grand River and established the community of New Credit there, it took six years to eject white squatters from the land.

By mid-century, the famine in Ireland, mushrooming population growth in England, and other forces created a massive influx of land-hungry immigrants (including my Freeman ancestors) into what was now known as Canada West, and the government found it impossible to prevent squatters from settling on Indians lands in more remote areas. Settlers began to crowd into even the Bruce Peninsula, which had been promised as an aboriginal preserve after the surrender of the Saugeen lands, and for which the Ojibwa actually had a deed for 450,000 acres. In 1854, the Ojibwa were forced to sell most of the Bruce Peninsula, under the threat that, if they did not sell, squatters would take it all away anyway, and the Ojibwa would receive no compensation at all. Although the land was sold to settlers at a public auction purportedly for the benefit of the Ojibwa, the government handled the trust funds and the Ojibwa never received all of the money owed to them. Unfortunately, aboriginal communities and their white supporters were too fractured by religious divisions to strongly oppose these developments.

By the 1850s, the missions had lost their momentum, the excitement of the initial conversions had faded, and Native initiative had been largely stifled by these disheartening events. Some prominent Native preachers had fallen into disgrace, running into problems with financial irregularities or alcohol. For a brief time, Christianity and "civilization" had appeared to open up opportunities for aboriginal people, but as it became clear that they still couldn't get clear title to their land and would not be accepted as social or economic partners by whites, Native interest waned.

Partly in response to Bond Head's charges that their instruction had not been successful, the Methodist missionaries in turn felt discouraged that aboriginal people were not turning into Europeans quickly enough. In 1846, Asahel Hurlburt, an elder of the Methodist church, noted: "Yet in some other respects, the nature of the work accomplished, and the people who were the subjects of it, were placed too high – we had thought that more was accomplished, and that less remained to be done than subsequent years have shown actually did remain to be done. We had supposed that almost everything was perfected at once."[43]

The response of Peter Jones, William Case, and other leading Methodists was to turn to a different form of education as the best chance for improvement in the lives of the aboriginal people of Upper Canada. Sir Francis Bond Head's policies had reduced the effectiveness of Indian day schools, for Native people had subsequently refused to farm, and had taken their children out of the day schools to go hunting with them. The Methodists therefore turned to residential schools as the best means of ensuring the children's attendance. The 1844 Bagot Commission Report on the Indians of Upper Canada had recommended the establishment of manual-labour boarding schools, combining academic and practical instruction as the best method of assimilating the Indians, which Euro-Canadians believed to be Natives' only hope of survival. Various aboriginal individuals and bands also requested the establishment of schools, in the hope that a Euro-Canadian education would equip their children to survive in the hostile environment around them – particularly if such schooling could be acquired alongside a traditional education. Peter Jones wrote, "I cannot say much with regard to the prosperity of our Mission School. . . . the children are very backward in their attendance. I am more and more convinced that, in order to effect the *desired* civilization of the Indian tribes, the children *must* be taken for a season from their parents, and put to well-regulated Manual Labour Schools."[44]

The first industrial boarding school in Upper Canada was established by the Wesleyan Methodists at Alnwick, near Belleville, in 1842. In 1844, Peter Jones appealed to the Annual Conference of the Episcopal Methodists for a second industrial school at Munceytown, and was commissioned to go to England to raise funds for the building. Jones also persuaded Indian leaders to support the schools. In 1845 the Grand Council of the Ojibwa Nation at Saugeen petitioned the government for assistance in establishing a school, and the government agreed to provide funding. The chiefs of Munceytown and the Credit drew up a petition authorizing Peter Jones to collect money in England for the school on their behalf, and pledging their support and co-operation. Subsequently, the Ojibwa chiefs donated two hundred acres of land for the school, and the Oneidas, the Ojibwa, and the Munsees agreed to provide funds from their annuity toward the building fund; they apparently agreed to give one-quarter of their annuities for twenty-five years to support the schools, though in later years their annuity payments would be used to maintain the school without their consent.[45] Jones raised

£1,313 in England, and triumphantly returned to Canada with hardware, cooking utensils, bedding, household linens, and crockery.

In 1846, at a conference of chiefs held in Orillia, William Case told the chiefs, "We know not why your young men should not be so educated as to be able to transact your affairs. . . . you may, indeed, live to see some of your sons doctors, attorneys and magistrates. This is a thing not at all improbable. You have already lived to see your warriors become Ministers of the Gospel, Interpreters and Teachers of your Schools."[46]

At the same conference, Thomas Anderson, then chief superintendent of the Indian Department, predicted that, within twenty-five years, Indians would have an independent, Indian-run system of schools. "It is to be hoped in that time, some of your youth will be sufficiently enlightened to carry on a system of instruction among yourselves, and this proportion of your funds will no longer be required."[47]

But Anderson also had an ulterior motive: he attempted to persuade the bands to give up their lands, proposing that the Indians should "abandon their present detached little villages . . . and unite in large settlements" in the three proposed school locations, one of which was Munceytown. In doing so, he promised the leaders that their title to these locations would be secure forever and they could also keep their title to the land left behind. By now, however, such assurances had begun to wear thin, and many chiefs were incensed. Anderson explained that the adults could choose to move or not, but the children would be obliged to attend school, so naturally their parents would have to move if they wanted to be near their children. The missionary society also urged aboriginal people to move near the schools, since this would reduce the cost of missions. In the end, the leaders agreed to give money to support the schools, though they would not consent to the proposal to move.[48]

From the beginning, as Hope MacLean has illustrated in her study of Methodist schooling in Upper Canada, there was a fundamental difference in the nature of aboriginal and white support for the residential schools. Aboriginal people initially supported the schools, not as the means of erasing their separate identity, but as a way to survive in the new world in which they found themselves. Their overall objective remained to retain their lands and their separation from the settlers. Peter Jones envisioned a residential school run by Indians that would turn out "men and women able to compete with the white people, able to defend their rights in English, under English law." The missionaries and the government falsely assumed that schooling could change the attitudes of the majority of aboriginal people and make them want to live among the Euro-Canadian population. They would change just enough to adapt to white settlement and no further. Still the missionaries and government officials persisted in their attempts at total assimilation, in spite of their evident lack of success. The European desire to bring about the assimilation of Indians was too strong to be easily abandoned; instruction in Christianity was still considered the primary means of eradicating Native cultures and instilling the proper moral and social behaviour.[49]

The Indian Department would also use the manual-labour schools to control the Methodists. Because the Methodists required government funding to operate, Anderson used his power over the funding to impose conditions on the operation of the schools. The Methodists could not criticize the government without risking the loss of the government school grant.

The Mount Elgin Industrial School, the second Indian residential school in what is now Ontario, was built at Munceytown on the Caradoc reserve and was completed in March 1850; it soon housed aboriginal students from St. Clair, Thames River, and New Credit as well as other First Nations in southwestern Ontario. Peter Jones wrote to his wife that he expected to superintend Mount Elgin, but he was too sick to take on this position when the school opened in 1851, and his place was taken by a white Methodist who had far less empathy for his students. Unfortunately, an aboriginal person would never again be in charge of the school, and Native teachers would be avoided, since the school's goal quickly became the assimilation of the pupils into Euro-Canadian culture.

The Methodists now focussed on aboriginal children instead of their parents as agents of change in aboriginal society; adult Natives were relegated to the margins of the missionary effort, and aboriginal leadership was no longer encouraged, since aboriginal missionaries were believed to be less effective than white men. It appears that, after 1850, only nine Native missionaries were still active in Upper Canada, and by 1860 there were only two or three.[50] This was a marked change from earlier practice, but in other respects, the Mount Elgin Industrial School – indeed the residential-school system in Canada – was built on the foundations of what devoted Methodists such as Peter Jones and Elijah Harris had started.

THE FREEMAN FAMILY

Six Generations
of the Freeman Family

CHAPTER
19

Shoal Lake

To write about my grandfather is no longer to write of ancestors I've discovered through genealogical records and books, but to write about someone who is real to me in memory and love, though he is no longer alive. Most of his children – my father and his siblings – are still living, and a host of grandchildren and great-grandchildren flourish across Canada. Many of them knew Grandpa far better than I did – I spent time with him on only a few occasions as a small child, since he lived in distant Winnipeg – and the grandfather of my memory may have little to do with the man that others knew. As a child, I thought him the epitome of goodness, and I still carry a lot of that evaluation of him today, though it's tempered now with knowledge of his shortcomings. My grandfather's presence left an indelible mark on my life, as it did on the lives of many others. He and my grandmother Ada were known in United Church circles in Manitoba and beyond for their prodigious energy, compassion, and generosity: they "fed, housed, nursed, counselled or just encouraged" many who crossed their path.[1]

As I've said earlier, I grew up on my father's stories of my grandfather's involvement with aboriginal people, of how my grandmother had taken in various young Native women to live in the family home, of how the family used to meet Ojibwa families in canoes as they made their own summer canoe trips through Lake of the Woods on the Ontario/Manitoba border. I grew up thinking of my grandfather as someone who had been friendly, respectful, and helpful to aboriginal people, someone who cared about their situation and who was culturally sensitive; in fact, he was a role model. So when I first began hearing and reading about the horrors of residential schools and when rereading my grandfather's unpublished memoirs came across his account of his involvement with the Cecilia Jeffrey Indian Residential School at Shoal Lake, Ontario, I was surprised and perplexed. How could someone whom I knew had been an exemplary person have been associated with one of these schools, which are now almost universally condemned for their legacy of suffering? The two pieces didn't fit together, and yet I knew that somehow they must – that for all the potential exaggeration in media reports of the schools' destructive effects on aboriginal culture and individuals, there was a basic truth in the criticism of the schools, and for all of my grandfather's personal virtues and committed work for social justice, he must have indeed become part of an oppressive system. I needed to understand the nature of his involvement.

Edwin Gardner Dunn Freeman's family was Anglo-Irish. His ancestors' story – and the story of the English in Ireland – has many parallels with his wife Ada's ancestors in New England. It appears that he was descended from English settlers who had come to Ireland in the 1600s after Oliver Cromwell's conquest of Ireland in 1649, though it is possible they were related to Freemans who had come to Ireland in the late 1500s as part of the earlier Tudor conquests and plantations; these earlier Freemans were participants in the 1586 English settlement of County Cork and in the 1587 division of County Queens into English shires.[2] Once again, English conquest and colonization of an indigenous population deemed savage, ignorant, incapable, and religiously incorrect (in this case, Roman Catholic) was the context of my ancestors' settlement in a new land. In fact, there were a number of parallels between the English view of the Irish and of the aboriginal people of North America: the English did not comprehend the Irish system of land tenure, thought Irish children were brought up without discipline, disapproved of the freedom and influence of Irish women, and feared the "degeneration" of those English who settled among them.[3]

In 1641, when the Catholic Irish revolted against their English Protestant overlords, their rebellion was brutally put down by zealous English Puritans. (Thomas Weld, as you may recall in chapter 4, had taken part in a punitive expedition against the Catholics after his return from New England in that year.) So devastating was the Puritan campaign that the population actually dropped from 1.5 million to 1 million between 1641 and 1650. At Drogheda in 1649, Cromwell's army slaughtered 3,500 men, women, and children; in an echo of the fate of some Natives after the Pequot and King Philip's Wars, those Irish soldiers who were not killed were shipped to Barbados as indentured servants, their fate little better than that of the Native slaves. Land east of the Shannon River that was owned by Catholics was then expropriated and distributed to Cromwell's soldiers or to those who had financed his campaigns. An early practitioner of "ethnic cleansing," Cromwell ordered that at least 10,000 Irish Catholics move west of the Shannon River to desolate Connaught, which became in essence a reservation; they were threatened with death if found on the eastern side of the Shannon after May 1, 1654. The Irish lost more than a third of their population through war, disease, and famine; by the late 1700s, Irish Catholics, who still made up 75 per cent of the population, owned 5 per cent of the land.

In some respects Catholics faced more severe repression than did North American pagans during this time period; in 1650 a bounty was announced for the capture of priests, and many were killed. But only Catholic landowners, their families, and retainers were forced to relocate beyond the Shannon, their former tenants and landless labourers stayed and became cheap labour for Protestant settlers, including my ancestors.

By the late 1600s, the English had seized more than 85 per cent of Ireland's territory. Before 1600, less than 2 per cent of Ireland was of Scots or English descent, but by the early 1700s that figure had risen to 27 per cent and included the Freemans. My family was certainly in County Wicklow by 1738 and probably earlier, for there are Freeman graves from the 1600s in the graveyard of a ruined church in the parish of nearby Derrylossary, though a genealogical connection between the two Freeman families has yet to be proved. My Freemans likely descended from a landed English family that may have moved into Dublin originally, the younger sons acquiring land southwest of Dublin, near Baltinglass on the River Slaney. They were Anglicans rather than Puritans, and joined the Church of Ireland. Apparently they had a large amount of land and were affluent; they farmed their own land and also were superintendents of the Irish peasants to whom they had leased land. By the late eighteenth century such middlemen were phased out in favour of direct tenancies; in the early 1800s, records show the Freemans had smaller holdings, of about 100 acres each.[4]

This was still far larger than the average Irishman's holding. By the beginning of the nineteenth century, a population explosion had resulted in smaller and smaller plots of land. By 1831, 45 per cent of the Irish had farms of one to five acres. Because of a heavy tax on homes with fireplaces, most people lived in little huts with no heat. In an average year, more than one-quarter of the Irish spent part of the year in semi-starvation, and the average Irish life expectancy was nineteen years, far worse than that even of African slaves in America, who lived only thirty-six years on average. But this was not the case with the family of my grandfather's grandmother, Kate (Catherine) Brien. She was an Irish Protestant who was born in 1829 on a farm adjacent to the Freemans'. Her father was prosperous enough to buy Freeman land when one of the Freemans sold out to pay off debts.[5]

Introduced from North America at least as early as 1606, the potato had become the staple in the diet of millions of poor Irish because of its phenomenal yield per acre; more than half of Ireland's eight million people ate little or nothing else. When the fungus *Phytophthora infestans* caused Ireland's potatoes to rot in the ground, more than one million people died of starvation or of diseases such as typhus and dysentery that decimated the weak and famished. Desperate, more than one million people left Ireland, and thousands of these died during cramped, crowded voyages overseas.[6]

The situation in Wicklow was not as bad as elsewhere in the country, though it was reported in December 1846 that there were 25,000 beggars and no food. "Local evidence is available from a surprising number of well-run estates in east County Wicklow, and this generally indicates that the population was maintained above the level of destitution; the picture in the invaluable diaries of Elizabeth Smith of Baltiboys, in the west of the country [closer to Baltinglass], is more harrowing, though there too, starvation was kept at bay."[7] In Wicklow a number of landlords killed and distributed their livestock to feed tenants, though many landlords faced bankruptcy because of high Poor Law rates imposed by the government in London.

My great-great-grandparents, John Freeman and Catherine Brien, left Ireland for Canada in 1846, during the first year of the famine and before the great rush of poor Irish to the boats. Most who left at that time were comfortable farmers, many of whom had been debating leaving Ireland for some time. In Dublin, "vast numbers of well-dressed countrymen" were to be seen "with baggage and sea-store"; they included bands of young men and women with their children.[8] John and Catherine arrived in Canada in 1846–47, to face the most severe winter in living memory.

They made their way to the vast Huron Tract west of Toronto, which had been opened up by the Canada Land Company in 1828 after being acquired from the Ojibwa almost a decade earlier. They homesteaded near the town of Shakespeare, in Perth County, not far from present-day Stratford. At first they shared land with another family; after several years, John Freeman acquired the title to one acre. Unfortunately, he died of tuberculosis in 1858, leaving Catherine with four children under the age of eight. She remarried, and a cousin, Richard Freeman, who had been living with them, took over nearby Flyndale farm. My grandfather used to go to this farm and help "Uncle Dick" in the summers.

My grandfather's father, the Rev. George Edwin Freeman, was the youngest child of John and Catherine Freeman, born in 1857, the year before his father died. He became the first minister of Deer Park Presbyterian Church in Toronto and married Eliza Price in 1885. He fathered two daughters, both of whom died in infancy of diphtheria, and a son, Gardner – my grandfather – who was born in 1890, four years before George himself died of tuberculosis at the age of thirty-seven.

Meanwhile, my grandfather's maternal ancestors had arrived in Canada in the 1830s. The Prices were a poorer family from County Armagh in northern Ireland, though the family is said to have been originally Welsh. The English had colonized Northern Ireland as well, beginning in 1613. Later, when the Irish rose up and massacred their English landlords in 1641, the records mention one "Elizabeth Prize of Armagh whose five children were taken from her to be pushed from the bridge at Portadown." I have wondered if this unfortunate soul was a relation. At any rate, Eliza Price's father, John, had come to Canada in 1840 as a child of seven, with his mother and seven siblings, his father having died in Ireland the year before. Within three weeks of arrival his mother also died. He then lived with his elder brother on the family farm in Albion township, north of Toronto, until the brother married and sold the farm. John, then almost fourteen, ran away and walked for five days, arriving in Toronto in late November, penniless and knowing no one. Befriended by a Methodist, he joined that church, became a shoemaker, and married one Ann Williams, whose family had arrived several years earlier from Cornwall, England. Ann died of cholera in 1870; Eliza, the eldest daughter, had been forced to leave school and raise her brothers and sisters before marrying George Freeman.[9]

When her minister husband died, Eliza was left with a piano, some old furniture, and $100 cash – until she hid the money in the ash tray of the stove, forgot about it, and lit a fire, burning up her savings. Luckily, her by then well-off brothers found accommodation and a job for her. They arranged for her to run a branch office of the Elias Rogers Coal and Wood Company, for which she received four dollars a week, as well as two large rooms and a kitchen for her own accommodation. She rented out the six rooms on the second and third floor of the house, which was located on Spadina Avenue in Toronto. This was the house in which young Gardner, soon known as "Gard," grew up.

Spadina was a rundown inner-city street, but Gard flourished in its multicultural atmosphere – his immediate neighbours were Chinese, Jewish, Italian, and French families, and he met people of many other backgrounds as well. He was exposed early on to a wide variety of social problems, such as alcoholism and crime. While most of Eliza's tenants were "respectable," one turned out to be a prostitute, four men were gamblers, and one morning the police arrived and charged another couple with theft. Years later my grandfather wrote that he was glad he had grown up in a semi-slum area of a big city, where he had seen just about everything, both good and bad, for he learned that people, no matter what their social class, national or racial origin, were just people. Perhaps because of these early experiences, Gard developed an openness to all kinds of people and opinions – an attitude that was unusual in his generation – as well as a "mischievous, wry sense of humour."[10]

A gifted student, he took every subject offered at high school and came sixth in the province on his matriculation exams. At the University of Toronto he was the only student to graduate in two First Class Honours Courses – Classical Languages and Philosophy – simultaneously, coming first and second respectively.[11] Later he broadened his experience through travels through both western and eastern Canada with his uncle, Alf Price, who, as general manager of the CPR, had a private railway car. He also explored Manhattan thoroughly during a year of graduate studies at Columbia University and the Union Theological Seminary in New York, where he met students from all over the world. He attended several synagogues to learn about Judaism, although, like most Canadians of his day, he apparently had no exposure to or interest in faiths outside the Judeo-Christian tradition, such as Islam, Buddhism, Hinduism, or the spiritual traditions indigenous to North America.

It was in New York that he became committed to the Social Gospel, a new vision of Christianity that was rapidly gaining acceptance among progressive Protestants and creating much excitement and ferment in England, the United States, and Canada. He spent three months teaching an 11 P.M. Bible Class at the All Night Mission, where homeless men slept on chairs all night in a crowded room and another shift slept on the chairs during the day: as he later wrote, the limitations of charity as a solution to social problems were painfully evident. Through this experience and talking to his professors at Union, Gard became convinced that widespread social reform was an essential element of true Christianity: being Christian involved more than concern with personal salvation in another world – it required active involvement in the regeneration of society according to Christian principles. This regeneration was seen as not just the work of humankind alone, for God was immanent in society, at work fomenting a social awakening that would transform society into a living embodiment of the teachings and spirit of Jesus. The Social Gospel "was a call for men to find the meaning of their lives in seeking to realize the kingdom of God in the very fabric of society."[12]

Inherent in this vision was the conviction that Christianity was in essence a social religion, concerned with the quality of human relations on earth. To adherents of the Social Gospel, God was not so much a punishing god of judgment as the source and essence of love. The doctrine drew on the evangelical roots of the early Methodists in Canada with their emphasis on moral regeneration and free will, as well as on their attempts at social engineering through their missions to the Indians and others; it also hearkened back to the older Calvinist and Puritan tradition of society in which social and economic relationships were subject to religious control. Advocates of the Social Gospel believed that, to reform an individual, it was necessary and possible to reform his or her environment. "The demand 'save this man, now' became 'save this society, now' and the slogan 'the evangelization of the world in our generation' became 'the Christianization of the world in our generation.'" The old Methodist stress on Original Sin became the social guilt of living in an imperfect world, and in place of God's forgiveness of those individuals who had repented of their sins, the more radical argued that there could be no personal salvation without social salvation, that, "the only way to be saved was to save someone else."[13]

Many Christians of this persuasion came to view secular social action as a religious rite, and in fact, the Social Gospel was the foundation for the development of the secular practice of social work. In their emphasis on community and collective action, advocates of the Social Gospel also had much in common with socialists and reformers of various other stripes, and there was considerable debate about the relationship between socialism and Christianity – the Social Gospel was a major inspiration for the reform politics of the Progressive political party of the early 1920s and later the Co-operative Commonwealth Federation (CCF), precursor of the New Democratic Party of Canada.

When he married Ada Davis in 1917, my grandfather found a soul-mate who shared his passionate commitment to Christian ministry and his concern for the needs of the disadvantaged. Their idea of a honeymoon in New York was to visit churches, rescue missions, foreign settlement houses, the Bowery, the "red-light" areas, and the Women's Night Court. Back in Toronto in 1917, he accepted a call as minister of Cabbagetown's St. Enoch's Presbyterian Church, where he confronted directly many of the social problems of the inner city. His pastorate was characterized by "vigourous [sic] hands-on leadership with didactic, exegetical preaching. . . . a strong social service thrust . . . and a continuing evangelistic emphasis, a constant drive to reach out to those he termed 'the unchurched and bewildered.' "[14] He visited shell-shocked war veterans once a week and volunteered in the psychiatric clinic of the Toronto General Hospital. In spite of his youth, he was also named convenor of Toronto's Home Mission Committee, which oversaw settlement houses, social-service centres, houses for unmarried mothers, and rescue missions such as Evangel Hall on Queen Street, as well as the foreign-language Presbyterian churches. Rev. J. G. Shearer, the head of the newly formed Social Services Council of Canada, sought to groom the young man as his protégé and eventual successor.

But Gard had other ideas about his future. He had a "pugnacious, almost impudent streak" and enjoyed proving himself in arguments and in taking up challenges that others considered hopeless. He might have ended up as principal of the Church's Theological College in Formosa, a job he was offered in 1919, but instead he accepted the call to King Memorial Presbyterian Church in Winnipeg in 1920, largely because the Winnipeg General Strike of 1919 had severely tested the loyalties and social commitment of the churches and, in the bitter aftermath of the strike, King

Memorial had lost many members. Some of King Memorial's elders had served on the General Strike Central Committee, and many members of the congregation believed the Presbyterian Church had sold out to the capitalists and vested interests of the status quo. What attracted my grandfather was the challenge of proving the relevance of the church to the poor working men who had made up the bulk of the King Memorial's congregation. Gard conducted services in the basement of the not-yet-completed church building, and for four years made fourteen to twenty calls per week to people's homes, to listen to their concerns.

My grandfather was clearly a committed Christian; he was also an open-minded, progressive man for his time. He became interested in psychic research, was a frequent speaker at Jewish organizations, and later became a guest speaker at the organizational meeting of the Lakehead League against War and Fascism, which hosted delegates from fifty-three organizations, including communist groups, labour organizations, church groups, and others. He became a friend of Tim Buck, head of the Communist Party of Canada. He was the kind of man who, during the Depression, asked to have his salary cut by $500 a year in the hope that some of that money might be used to help the unemployed. He and his wife distributed birth-control information to all prospective brides and grooms long before it was legal.

I mention these attributes not to sing the praises of my grandfather, though in many ways I cannot help admiring the man, but to counter the current stereotype that the missionaries and others associated with the residential schools were cruel, insensitive, narrow-minded, and tyrannical. Nothing could have been farther from the truth in my grandfather's case at least, and I do not believe he was an anomaly. In fact, as historian John Webster Grant remarked in *Moon of Wintertime*, his study of Canadian missionaries: "To an extent that is seldom recognized, the assault on Indian culture bemoaned by social activists today was led by social activists of an earlier era."[15] That is a scary thought for me, I must admit, one that tempers any hubris I might have about my own social activism.

As a young man, Gard had developed an appreciation of how happy one could be living simply with nature, with a minimum of worldly goods. He was not alone in this discovery; the first decade of the twentieth century saw a "back to the land" movement among city dwellers, since new railways and roads made Canada's back country more accessible, while over-crowded, unhealthy, and dirty cities gave people second thoughts about the wisdom of industrial progress. This "summering movement," which stressed outdoor activities such as alpine climbing, canoeing, camping, summering at cottages, and sending children to character-building wilderness summer camps, was accompanied by a new, more positive attitude to Native people, for many Canadians suspected they lived a more authentic existence, closer to nature and basic human values. Camping, "the simple life reduced to actual practice," as influential writer and naturalist Ernest Thompson Seton put it, combined the healthful, character-building benefits of outdoor activity with the chance to experience vicariously life as aboriginal people lived it. As such it was an echo of a persistent, if usually unconscious, theme in North American culture – the desire on the part of whites to go Native.[16]

My grandfather and his wife became "demon campers," who went on extended canoe trips every summer of their fifty-odd years of married life. In the summer of 1917, he and Ada made their first camping trip on Lake Couchiching, then the following summer they paddled down the Severn to Georgian Bay and the Thirty Thousand Islands; another year they travelled in a sixteen-foot canoe from Washago to Manitoulin Island and back, with their first child, who was a year and a half old, propped up in the bow.

In 1921 they made their first canoe trip to Lake of the Woods, on the border between Manitoba and Ontario, my grandfather doing all the paddling, as my grandmother was pregnant with my father. Gard later commented that he should have had his head examined, for he didn't have a detailed map and rarely knew exactly where he was, nobody knew where he and Ada were going, and they had no means of communication. Although they occasionally saw Ojibwa families, they saw no other white people (though there certainly were others in the area). But the trip was a success, and the next year, Gard, Ada, and their two small children (the youngest my six-month-old father) first paddled into Shoal Lake, off Lake of the Woods, and sighted a large building, which they thought might be a Hudson's Bay post, on a point of land. They were surprised to discover that it was an Indian boarding school. The nurse and teacher who observed them land at the site of the school were equally surprised, at first mistaking them for Natives, because of their canoe. My grandparents moved off and camped on an island about two miles to the east.

After a couple of days, they returned. Gard found the principal busy making improvements to the basement, so he pitched in and helped mix cement for several days. Meanwhile, Ada got to know the staff and learned about the workings of the school. In addition to accommodations for the staff and the seventy children then in residence, there was a clinic, a dispensary, and classrooms, as well as workshops for the boys and instruction in cooking and sewing for the girls.

Unlike most Presbyterian schools, which were run by the Presbyterian Home Mission Board, the Cecilia Jeffrey Indian Residential School was run by the Women's Missionary Society (WMS), and my grandparents noticed immediately that relations between the WMS and the principal were strained. Though my grandfather thought the principal a hard worker and genuinely concerned for the welfare of the Indians, he could see that he was also autocratic. When the principal spent too much money on repairs without authorization, the WMS fired him a few months after my grandparents' visit. They then asked the Winnipeg Presbytery – the church's governing body for the area – to appoint one of its members to act as a liaison and advisor with the Women's Missionary Society and oversee the installation of a new principal as well as keep an eye on the running of the school. My grandfather was honoured to be chosen for this role.[17] It was in this way that he became involved with the school and the Ojibwa of Shoal Lake.

I doubt that my grandfather knew much about the history or culture of the Anishinabe of the region, or about the history of this school (though he may have been familiar with accounts of earlier Protestant missionary activity in the area), but as both determined the context in which he worked and how his actions would be interpreted by the people of Shoal Lake, it is worth taking a detailed look at this history.

Part of a bountiful river system that has been inhabited for many thousands of years, Shoal Lake was inhabited by Ojibwa or Oji-Cree at the time of first European contact, though these names were not used at the time.[18] In 1670, Shoal Lake became part of Rupert's Land, the sovereign territory of the Hudson's Bay Company established by royal charter – without, needless to say, the consent of the indigenous inhabitants. The explorer Sieur de La Vérendrye, who visited the area after 1726, was the first European to leave a written record of the peoples in the vicinity. Lake of the Woods and Shoal Lake soon became part of the traders' route to the west: La Vérendrye established Fort St. Charles on the former in 1732, which flourished for a while, until abandoned in 1763, after the fall of New France. Later Hudson's Bay forts at Fort Frances and the Dalles on the Winnipeg River north of Lake of the Woods provided outlets for the furs traded by the region's trappers, and the trading post at Fort Frances was a major provisioning centre for the northwest trade. In 1836, the Hudson's Bay post at the Dalles was moved upstream to Fort Island in Lake of the Woods, and then in 1861 to "Rat Portage," the present site of Kenora.

Smallpox epidemics in 1780–82 decimated local populations in the region by one-half to three-fifths; Alexander Mackenzie observed the aftermath of the epidemic during his explorations of 1789, which "destroyed with its pestilential breath whole families and tribes."[19] Yet by the early nineteenth century a large and expanding regional Ojibwa population lived well on bountiful game, wild rice, garden produce, and fish; gathered annually for large national religious and political gatherings; and had developed a tribal government based upon ranked leaders and prominent chiefs drawn from the religious society known as the Midewewin, or Grand Medicine Society.

Although the Ojibwa were "tolerably rich in furs," they did not rely on trapping to survive and the Hudson's Bay Company never dominated them; they received high prices for their furs by playing off American and HBC traders. The Ojibwa were "saucy, and independent of the Hudson's Bay Company, from the fact that they have abundance of sturgeon and great quantities of wild rice, so that they can feed themselves without having recourse to the supplies of ammunition and clothing with which the Hudsons' Bay Company supply their Indians." They were of "an independent, and I should say unmanageable disposition . . . their natural ferocity is not lessened by their constant wars with the Sioux." Some of their strength came from their awareness of their powerful land position – they controlled the gateway to the West and others were forced to seek their permission to pass through their lands. They repeatedly restricted the movements and actions of Euro-Canadian exploring parties in their territory.[20]

Because of this self-sufficiency, the Anishinabe of the Boundary Waters region had little reason to explore alternative world views, unlike the impoverished and traumatized Ojibwa of Upper Canada. They had developed a strong and highly structured organization of shamans, the Midewewin, the purpose of which was to protect individuals against disease and promote long life, to maintain a spiritual balance with the rest of creation, to assist individuals to live well by offering them a code of conduct, and to use spiritual power for the good of the community. In contrast to most other aboriginal cultures, where shamans were essentially self-taught through dreams and visions, a priestly class had begun to develop. Mide priests progressed through eight levels of training, passed on their religious knowledge to other initiates, carried out specific rituals at permanent sites, including large, specially constructed lodges, and were usually rewarded materially for their efforts on behalf of individuals through offerings. To join the Midewewin, one underwent an initiation rite, made offerings, and maintained secrecy.[21]

In Ojibwa society, there were various types of what Euro-Canadians called "medicine men." Not all of these were associated directly with the Midewewin: some were primarily herbalists, while others were Djessakids, who operated independently of the Midewewin and sought to predict events through the Shaking Tent ritual, while the Mide priests and the Wabanos sought to propitiate spirits and promote health through various ceremonies. Because medicine people could both cure illness and harm others through sorcery, they were seen to hold the power of life and death in their hands, and were both feared and revered. Although the Midewewin may have been influenced by Christian beliefs about God and the devil in its beliefs in the Great Spirit, or Gitche Manitou, a master of life responsible for all things, and Matci Manitou, an evil spirit – a dualism unusual in aboriginal religions – the Mide priests were unremittingly hostile to Christian missionaries.[22]

Catholic missionaries had visited the Boundary Waters area at an early date, but with little evident effect. In 1839, the Methodists made their first foray into the region: James Evans and the Ojibwa preacher Peter Jacobs visited Rainy Lake to the east of Lake of the Woods, where huge numbers of Boundary Waters Ojibwa gathered annually to hold Midewewin ceremonies. (These gatherings were also important for the exercise of government by the Grand Council of the Ojibwa.) The Methodists were evidently hoping to reach new bands of Ojibwa before the Catholics did, and Peter Jacobs was left behind as the first permanent resident missionary at Rainy Lake, with orders to found a Methodist mission that was supposed to cover a vast area, including Rainy River, Lake of the Woods, and part of the Winnipeg River, in its circuit.

At first things looked promising. In 1841, a Euro-Canadian missionary, Robert Mason, who had joined Jacobs, reported that he had baptized more than a hundred Ojibwa and people of mixed ancestry. In fact, the people were only humouring the missionaries by taking part in a ceremony that seemed to mean so much to the newcomers; the Anishinabe had no intention of becoming Christians and simply wanted gifts from Mason. Similarly, in 1841–42, a missionary of mixed Ojibwa-European ancestry, Henry B. Steinhauer, spent a winter at Rat Portage on Lake of the Woods, without success. In contrast to the initial receptivity to Christianity of many Ojibwa in Upper Canada, the Anishinabe west of Lake Superior saw no reason to embrace a different religion. They believed their own religious leaders, who said that the missionaries caused some of the illnesses and diseases affecting their people; many also blamed the missionaries for the Hudson's Bay Company's decision in 1840 to curtail the supply of rum.[23] They were also well aware of the treatment of First Nations to the east and south of them.

Although the Anishinabe were not interested in Christianity, they were open to accepting specific knowledge and technology from the Euro-Canadians – on their own terms, with no strings attached. For example, they were interested in sending their children to school to learn to read, if they could have schooling without Christianity. When secular schooling was denied them, they rejected schools altogether. Similarly, they were originally interested in the Hudson's Bay Company's offer of agricultural assistance, since they recognized the need to diversify their food resource base, but the vast majority of Anishinabe vetoed the idea when they realized that accepting the offer to establish an agricultural community would have meant accepting missionaries as well.[24]

Within a decade of the arrival of the Methodists, the leaders of the Boundary Waters Ojibwa had decided together that none of them would accept Christianity. In 1849 the Grand Council of Chiefs of Lake of the Woods had proscribed missionary activity altogether, forbidding a planned mission station and school on the Rainy River; they issued a warning that warriors would dismantle any structures. Even when Allen Salt, an Ojibwa missionary who had been stationed first at the St. Clair Mission (and whose mother was from Rainy River), arrived at Rainy Lake in 1854, he was told that he was not welcome to live among the Anishinabe. If he were Christian, he should continue to live within the confines of the Hudson's Bay Company trading post at Fort Frances and confine his preaching to the people there. When Salt travelled down Rainy River to the edge of Lake of the Woods, he was not permitted to meet Ojibwa there and was told that "some time ago [the Lake of the Woods Ojibwa] had agreed not to embrace Christianity and said that it would be so still let come what may upon us." Although a few individuals did express interest in Christianity, they faced ostracism from their community, and in some cases threats of violence. As Michael Angel has noted, "In attempting to protect themselves from the aggressive proselytization of the EuroAmerican missionaries, the Anishinabeg were forced to relinquish a fundamental tenet of their own world view and become, in turn, exclusivist themselves." As a result of this continuing resistance and their own shortage of mission funds and missionaries, the Methodists decided to abandon all efforts to establish a mission anywhere in the region. Even in 1870, Rev. E. F. Wilson reported that merely mentioning Christianity still provoked anger among the Ojibwa.[25]

But things changed very quickly for the Lake of the Woods and the Shoal Lake Ojibwa after Canadian Confederation in 1867. Canadian politicians, with their vision of one nation from sea to sea, began to cast an acquisitive eye westward. In 1870 the Canadian government paid £300,000 to the Hudson's Bay Company to extinguish the company's charter rights to Rupert's Land, and the territory was ceded to Canada. The changeover in political jurisdiction without the consent of the aboriginal inhabitants or settlers of Red River led to Louis Riel's declaration of the Red River Colony as an independent colony. There had been considerable contact and intermarriage between Ojibwa women and French voyageurs or Scots traders, resulting in a large mixed-race population of Métis, many of whom settled at Red River, not far to the west. There was a real and legitimate fear that the Ojibwa would join Riel. In response, the government of Canada launched the Wolseley expedition, a military force that passed through Lake of the Woods, with permission from the Grand Council of the Ojibwa, on its way to quell the rebellion, an event still part of the area's oral history. The following year, the federal government signed the first of the so-called numbered treaties with the First Nations of the West, Treaty #1, at Red River.

Negotiations with the Lake of the Woods Ojibwa began the same year, but proceeded slowly, owing largely to the solidarity of the chiefs, which made them much tougher negotiators than some of the aboriginal representatives in previous treaties. Treaty #1 had been criticized on the grounds that those Natives who signed it had no authority to do so; the federal government then initiated procedures to have Indians elect representatives on the spot at treaty negotiations. These "chiefs" and "councillors" often had little authority for dealing with local matters with the newly created "bands" they represented. To them, the whole system of governance imposed by the Canadian government was foreign, and subverted traditional systems of authority and decision-making.[26] However, in the case of Treaty #3 the negotiators were legitimate traditional leaders.

The Lake of the Woods Ojibwa finally concluded Treaty #3 with the government negotiators in 1873. In exchange for the surrender of 55,000 square miles, the Ojibwa would receive reserves of no more than one square mile for each family of five, a one-time payment of $12 to each man, woman, and child, $5 per head to each family yearly, and $1,500 a year for each band for ammunition and twine nets, a one-time provision of agricultural tools, seed, and farm animals, the right to hunt and fish throughout unsettled surrendered land, and the provision of schools on the reserves, "whenever the Indians of the reserve shall desire it."[27]

Once again, there was confusion and disagreement over precisely what was agreed to. Negotiations for the numbered treaties were conducted entirely orally; once an agreement was reached, the Indian Affairs Department (as it was now called) produced a text that was supposed to represent the substance of the agreements. In fact, there were often significant differences between the text and the aboriginal negotiators' understanding of what had transpired. For example, the aboriginal negotiators understood that they were being compensated for the use of their lands and had agreed to share it; they did not agree to allow the Crown to take over or control their land. Instead, they had tried to protect and preserve their way of life, which at the time included commercial trade in their resources, and they had been assured, in return, that their freedom, independence, and traditional way of life would not be affected. In their understanding, as they had agreed to share the land and not surrender it, they saw themselves as partners of the Crown,[28] and not as its subjects. But the government assumed that most of the land of the Ojibwa in what would eventually be known as northwestern Ontario had been surrendered.

Meanwhile, the Ojibwa's political rights (and those of other First Nations) were drastically curtailed during the latter half of the nineteenth century. When early attempts at "civilization" didn't work, officials concluded that aboriginal people were by nature lazy, intellectually backward, and resistant to change. When the government became disillusioned about assimilating aboriginal people through education, it turned to legislation to achieve the same end. Section 91 of the British North America Act that created the Dominion of Canada in 1867 took away the First Nations' independent status by making them wards of the federal government, the government even defining who was or was not an Indian. Reserves were established as temporary allocations of land until assimilation would eliminate the need for them. This had been the government attitude since at least 1857, when under the Gradual Civilization Act of that year, any Indian who wished to exercise the right to vote would also have the right to fifty acres of reserve land that he could sell to anyone without the approval of either the band or the Crown. This measure was bitterly protested by the Anishinabe and in practice almost never acted upon. The act destroyed all vestiges of the "partnership for development" that had once existed between the Crown and aboriginal peoples, for it attempted to break up the reserves and attacked the social cohesion of aboriginal nations.[29]

In the Indian Acts of 1876 and 1880, aboriginal self-government was abolished. Band finances, as well as all social services, including education, were placed under federal control. Lands reserved for the use of aboriginal people were to be managed on their behalf, until such time as individual Indians enfranchised themselves or became sufficiently "civilized" to be allowed a measure of self-government, as the federal government determined. Then, in 1889, partly in reaction to the Northwest Rebellion, the government claimed even greater control over education, morality, local government, and land. The latter, it declared, could now be taken without Native consent and leased to non-Indians. Aboriginal rights and freedoms were so circumscribed that for a number of years in the 1880s aboriginal people were not even allowed to leave their reserves without a pass from the Indian agent. No law sanctioned this requirement, yet the North-West Mounted Police enforced it until 1892. Ten years later, the white South African government would study this arrangement when it began to develop a plan for its own pass system to control the movements of indigenous Africans.[30]

At the same time that the government enacted this legislation, the Christian churches enjoyed a resurgence of interest in missions to the First Nations population, partly because the entry of the western provinces into Confederation had greatly increased the aboriginal population of Canada – and hence the number of potential converts. In Ontario, most aboriginal people were now nominally Christian, though Native enthusiasm for Christianity had declined. While the First Nations in Ontario had largely made the transition to a new economy of agriculture, wage labour, and selling produce, in the West the disappearance of the buffalo herds had left Native people destitute and starving, and humanitarians felt compelled to address their situation. The Women's Foreign Missionary Society of the Presbyterian Church was founded in 1876, and in 1883 began to undertake work among aboriginal women and children; soon it was contributing two-thirds of the church's Indian budget. Its president Cecilia Jeffrey toured Western Canada regularly to inspect the administration of the missions.[31]

In 1898 a Presbyterian official, one Professor T. Hart, visited Shoal Lake and later reported to the Toronto Executive Committee meeting of Foreign Missions on the prospects of beginning mission work in that region. He reported that two bands there had asked for and were promised a school.[32] While a Roman Catholic school had been established in Kenora for a number of years, the Native people of Shoal Lake had not had access to education. Nor, aside from the occasional visits of a priest, had they been visited by missionaries. Accordingly, in 1899, Austin G. McKittrick was appointed the first Presbyterian missionary to Shoal Lake. In his inaugural letter to the Foreign Missions Committee, dated December 1, 1900, he counted five hundred pagan Ojibwa on the western side of Lake of the Woods, including Shoal Lake.

"At present the desire is for school work, more than any desire for Christianity," wrote McKittrick.

> As you are no doubt aware a boarding school has been promised for two years and a half and this should be built next summer without fail. . . . So far *our opportunity* [original emphasis] is in the line of *boarding school* work. The Indians, especially at Shoal Lake are not only willing but *anxious* for a boarding school, yes, all of them. But it is now about two and a half years since they asked for our school and since it was promised by Prof. Hart on behalf of the Church, and you can easily see that if this is deferred any longer than next summer they will lose confidence in us and have no further use for us (to use a common and forcible expression) and if that happens, it will be simply useless to try to hold services or do mission work amongst them; our mission would be killed and by ourselves. No doubt you know an Indian well enough to know we must keep our promises with him or we need not go near him.

The Presbyterian missionary saw the offer of education as a powerful means to the end of Christian conversion: "a boarding school could also be a place to dispense medicine . . . from which to cure the sick" and "show *practical* Christianity (which is what wins)."[33]

It is a measure of how much the situation of the Shoal Lake Ojibwa had changed and how strongly they wanted education to protect themselves that they now accepted missionary involvement in the education of their children. By the late 1890s the people of Shoal Lake had seen their world transformed and their power to protect their own way of life seriously hampered by their lack of knowledge of the Euro-Canadian culture and political system. As mentioned earlier, the written version of Treaty #3 differed from their understanding of what had been agreed to in several key areas, notably fishing rights, a situation that they could have avoided had they been able to read English. Although the treaty had promised the Ojibwa material and technical assistance in agriculture, they were given defective tools and their initial successful adaptation to agriculture was stymied by the government's refusal to reconsider its controls on commercial sales of Ojibwa produce. (Ironically, the measure was originally introduced to encourage Native farmers on the Prairies.) Furthermore, many of the islands on which they had gardened since before first contact had only been described and not properly surveyed for Treaty #3 and the Province of Ontario claimed them and then sold them to mining companies or to cottagers. The Ojibwa reverted to hunting and fishing.[34]

Meanwhile, the Shoal Lake Ojibwa faced increasing hardship with the reduction in game and the destruction of most Lake of the Woods wild-rice areas through flooding by dams built to serve lumbering interests and later the hydro demands of the city of Winnipeg. The incorporation of Rat Portage in 1882 attracted an influx of white settlers to the area and the opening of gold mining on Shoal Lake in 1896 had further altered their environment: at the turn of the century, Lake of the Woods mines produced 55 per cent of Ontario's gold. Faced with the necessity of adapting to a wage economy and of defending their rights in unfamiliar legal and political systems, the Shoal Lake Ojibwa eventually became convinced of the need to educate their children in Euro-Canadian schools. McKittrick was therefore received with hospitality, for the Anishinabe were no longer in a position to refuse aid – missionaries would bring benefits such as clothing, medical help, and agricultural training, in addition to schooling. The Shoal Lake chiefs also wanted an alternative to the education currently available at the Catholic school in Rat Portage, for they did not like how the children were treated there.[35]

Yet from the beginning, the aims and objectives of the three partners in the school at Shoal Lake – the Anshinabe, the Presbyterian Church, and the federal government – were fundamentally at odds. The Native population of Canada had actually begun to increase after 1857, and the terrible conditions in which many Native people now lived – particularly on the Great Plains – reinforced the Euro-Canadian conviction that aboriginal people could survive only if they abandoned their culture and assimilated into mainstream society. Many Canadians were also convinced of white racial superiority, an outgrowth of social Darwinism that stated that the different races represented different stages of evolution, the non-white being inferior to the white race, with the inferior eventually dying out and being replaced by the superior. Both the government and the churches equated Christianity with morality and civilization and "heathenism" with sin and barbarism.[36] They agreed that the means to achieve the civilization and assimilation of aboriginal people was education – religious education – even though previous attempts to use education to assimilate Natives, notably the Methodist experiments in Upper Canada, had not been very successful.

In fact, by the 1850s, most day schools in Upper Canada had closed, St. Clair being an exception; the practical instructional programs in farming, trades, and European lifestyles on reserves had been pretty well abandoned; and the early experiments with residential schooling – the manual-labour schools at Alnwick and Munceytown – had been declared failures. Aboriginal parents in Upper Canada had apparently withdrawn their support for the residential schools, sometimes refusing to enroll or withdrawing their children, for the standard of education was abysmal, the number of deaths at the schools appalling, many children ran away, often after having been beaten, and many children were overworked. A student's day lasted from 5 A.M. until 9 P.M. and involved seven and one-half hours of physical work and five and one-half hours of school work each day, leaving only one hour for recreation, as the government wanted the schools either to be entirely self-sufficient or maintain very low per-pupil costs. The missionaries did not understand why their programs did not work. Determined to achieve better results, they resorted to stricter and more coercive practices, such as enrolling pupils at a younger age and preventing children from any contact with other aboriginal people. Yet, in spite of the apparent failure of all three forms of schooling – day schools, practical instruction on reserves, and residential schools – they were exported to the rest of Canada and continued to shape aboriginal schooling for the next hundred years.[37]

By 1880, the federal government had committed itself to a policy of residential education for aboriginal people similar to that already being put in place across the United States. By 1900, out of a total population of

20,000 aboriginal children aged 6 to 16 in Canada, 3,285 were enrolled in 22 industrial and 39 boarding schools (industrial schools tended to be larger than boarding schools and located off reserves) and another 6,349 in 226 day schools. The residential schools marked a new co-operation between church and state with regard to aboriginal people: the churches established the great majority of these schools, with the government induced to support them and provide funds for maintenance. The government approved of the churches' involvement, for they provided dedicated teachers at low cost, who could not only teach reading and writing but also inculcate in their pupils the Protestant work ethic and other habits deemed necessary for "Christian citizenship."[38]

Assimilation appears to have been the only future for aboriginal people that non-aboriginal Canadians could imagine; certainly it was a goal that they could not or would not relinquish. Underlying this attitude was the assumption that Canadians should be homogenous and essentially British in terms of culture. As Duncan Campbell Scott, superintendent of education and later deputy-superintendent-general of the Indian Affairs Department as well as a poet and son of a Methodist minister, saw it, "The happiest future of the Indian race is absorption into the general population, and this is the object of the policy of our government. The great forces of . . . inter-marriage and education will finally overcome the lingering traces of native custom and tradition." "Civilization" was regarded as a gift, an essential for both Native survival and the health of Canadian society – so that others would not be contaminated by heathenism. Indeed, it was the general view that aboriginal people had to be rescued from their traditional practices.[39]

Building the school at Shoal Lake would prove to be a difficult and expensive proposition as it would be the most remote school operated by the Presbyterians. The only access to Shoal Lake was by water. With the necessity of laying in enough food for the long winter, which included the freeze-up and break-up periods, much planning was necessary. But there was also the possibility that the Shoal Lake Ojibwa would turn their attention to the competition if the Presbyterians didn't erect a school quickly.

"The chief is very much pleased that we hope to build this summer," wrote McKittrick.

He said again yesterday that the Roman Catholic Priest – Father Cahill – told him last summer that Shoal Lake belonged only to the Roman

Catholic mission field and Protestants had no business there and that he [Father Cahill] would write to the Ottawa Gov't and see that we were not permitted to work at Shoal Lake . . . Chief Red Sky's sympathies, however, are wholly with us and not with the RC Ch. And he is glad to do anything he can to help on our school and gladly and willingly agreed to your request for 5 days work gratis.[40]

The Shoal Lake chiefs had actually asked for a day school, but McKittrick opposed it because attendance at such schools was too irregular for successful learning – children frequently went out on trap-lines with their parents for months at a time. He did recognize, however, that a distant boarding school was also not appropriate. "We must get in touch with *the parents* as well as the children to have any permanent and spiritual results," McKittrick wrote, noting that the proposed school had to be near the reserve or the Indians wouldn't send their children. "To win them for Christ we should not strive first thing to break family ties and carry the children as far as possible from home, bye and bye to return to the home, which has not been evangelized. I think this has too often been the cause of failure in the Gov't policy."[41] The chiefs had originally indicated that they would set aside reserve land for the school, and had selected one of the islands in Indian Bay, but this was changed to an off-reserve site next to the reserve of the Shoal Lake #40 band.

Indeed, McKittrick appears to have been somewhat more sensitive than most missionaries to the concerns of the parents, for the general Canadian policy was now to deliberately separate aboriginal children and parents by placing the children in large industrial schools far from their home reserves. However, perhaps it was more that he disagreed with the sequence of steps to reach the ultimate goal, as hinted at when he said, "we should not strive *first* thing to break family ties." "Experience convinces us that the only way in which the Indian of the country can be permanently elevated and thoroughly civilized is by removing the children from the surroundings of Indian home life, and keeping them separated long enough to form those habits of order, industry, and systematic effort, which they will never learn at home," was a more typical attitude, here expressed by a prominent Methodist.[42]

Where an earlier generation had tried to develop Native teachers and religious leaders to work among their own people, Native teachers were now rarely hired, because, as one Indian Affairs bureaucrat explained,

"These children require to have the 'Indian' educated out of them, which only a white teacher can help to do." The new missionaries and school-teachers, unlike those of Elijah Harris's time, no longer had to live on aboriginal terms, and did not learn aboriginal ways or languages. In fact, too much interest in aboriginal traditions on the part of a missionary was viewed suspiciously as a flirtation with evil, an echo of the old Puritan fear of "going Indian."[43]

From the beginning, then, although the Anishinabe, the Presbyterian Church, and the federal government agreed on the necessity of formal education for the young people of Shoal Lake, their reasons and objectives for supporting the building of a school diverged sharply and were in fact at cross purposes. As Chief Eli Mandamin would say to the Presbyterian Church on the occasion of the Church's 1994 confession with regard to residential schools: "You used our care and our concern for our most precious possession, our children, and turned our care and our hopes for the future into a process that would attempt to destroy our very foundations as a people."[44]

The Shoal Lake Anishinabe wanted education to help them survive as a distinct people in a changing world, and they put up with the missionaries to that end, though only after all parties signed a written agreement outlining certain conditions for the running of the school. This agreement appears to have been unique to Shoal Lake and was based upon the determination of the Anishinabe to retain control over their children's education and to avoid certain practices common at other residential schools that undermined their children's cultural heritage. The fact that they sought an agreement in writing is a measure of both their distrust and their sophistication in the ways of the Euro-Canadians.

The school's first principal, J. C. Gandier, described the circumstances of this agreement, made in 1902: "The final agreement with the chiefs was made today. They have been made suspicious by the way children were used in Catholic schools (esp at Rat Portage) but they seem very much in earnest and have great faith in Rev. McKittrick. They will send a number of children immediately and if they are well treated they will send us as many as we like to take." The agreement stipulated that young children should not be baptized without the consent of their parents, and when they were older and chose freely to be baptized, relations and friends should be invited to the baptism. Children were not to be transferred to another school without the consent of their parents. Children under eight years of age were not to be given heavy work, and larger children were to attend school at least half the day. If the school should realize a profit from the sale of farm produce, the children were to receive partial remuneration according to their work on the farm. Parents would be allowed to take their children to Anishinabe ceremonies, but only one child at a time, and the child was not to remain overnight. Older children were to get at least three weeks' holiday for berry-picking or the rice harvest, and children were to be allowed to visit sick relatives. If a child ran away, police were not to be used to retrieve him or her, but the parents should bring back the child. Other provisions related to health care and treaty payments. The agreement was signed by Chief Red Sky (also, later, Redsky) and Chief Pagindawind, as well as by McKittrick and Gandier. After a dinner prepared for the chiefs and the "principal" Indians, the Anishinabe gathered together the first nine children. The annual report of the Women's Missionary Society reported that "Miss Nicol writes already that she and Miss Cameron, both of whom have had experience at other schools, think these are the brightest and most promising children they have met with."[45]

Cecilia Jeffrey Indian Residential School opened and the children came, but the parents soon learned they had to remain vigilant, for some aspects of the initial agreement were not always honoured. The Shoal Lake Anishinabe quickly became expert at petitioning Presbyterian officials. In 1902, they protested the actions of the matron, whom they considered too strict; she apparently objected to the agreement that restricted what missionaries could do and resigned. The next year the principal and the matron complained that McKittrick interfered with their work by insisting that the original promise that the children not be taught religion be respected. In 1907, the chiefs protested the removal of McKittrick, who had tried to enforce the wishes of the Anishinabe in the operations of the school; Chief Red Sky threatened that, if the Presbyterian Church removed him, "I will ask the Indian Agent to send the children to another school for we won't have them here at all."[46] Red Sky never carried out his threat – perhaps there wasn't really an alternative school available – and with McKittrick's departure the Anishinabe lost an important protector. The next year the Ojibwa again petitioned against excessive corporal punishment.

The missionaries had their own ideas about what the students required. "It is necessary to have complete control of [native students] to do permanent work," wrote the Presbyterian Women's Foreign Missionary Society in its annual report of 1908–9. While most educators sought the same control over white children, their aboriginal charges were less able to resist or complain to their parents, and there was far more that they were supposed to unlearn, for many aspects of Native society, from the concept of time to customs pertaining to freedom, communication, sharing, authority, religion, and learning itself, were diametrically opposed to the European education system.[47]

Forced to operate in an English-only environment – a policy originally supported by at least some Native parents and leaders as the fastest way for them to learn the language – the children were subjected to corporal punishment when they spoke Ojibwa. When they stepped into the school for the first time, they entered a non-aboriginal world and were expected to leave their own world behind; even aboriginal games were forbidden. Their former identities were transformed, as they were shorn, bathed, and dressed in European clothes. To teachers and administrators, such practices were essential to the job at hand and consistent with their own culture's ideas about education, but to aboriginal children they were bewildering, strange, and profoundly unsettling – for example, in many aboriginal cultures cutting one's hair is a sign of mourning. Even their parents' best efforts could not prevent their receiving the constant message from the missionaries that aboriginal culture was inferior, savage, and backward.

This was particularly true of Native religion. Missionary attitudes at Cecilia Jeffrey are revealed in this excerpt from the 1910–11 WFMS Annual Report:

> Reserve services are held. . . . Usually the attendance is good . . . sometimes, however when they have a dance the attendance is small. We sometimes have a large congregation by going where they are dancing and asking them to stop for a while until we conduct a service. On these occasions they have always consented with a very good grace, while I know that some would rather we had kept away, the medicine man for instance. If they could be suppressed, a great hindrance to the acceptance of the Gospel would be removed, as they are the priests of paganism. . . . The removal by death last summer of Pawawasin [sic] late head chief of all the bands around the Lake of the Woods, was an event that I think will open the way for education and Christianity, as he stood for the old Indian ideals and religion, and was uncompromisingly opposed to change or progress.[48]

Some aspects of the running of Cecilia Jeffrey were not within the control of the teachers or the parents, for inadequate funding was a constant problem. By 1904, the number of residential schools had mushroomed to sixty-four schools from two at the time of Confederation, and the annual government grants were always so low that residential schools couldn't offer competitive salaries, decent accommodation, adequate nutrition, or basic health services. It was hard to obtain qualified teachers, and many didn't stay long – Cecilia Jeffrey suffered from considerable turnover of staff. The missionaries were encouraged to save the taxpayers' money whenever possible, and frugality was the rule in expenditures on food, accommodation, clothing, and equipment. Some schools increased the students' manual labour to two-thirds of the day to ensure the schools' economic survival, though I don't know if this was ever the case at Shoal Lake.

A 1907 report on Canadian residential schools by Dr. Peter H. Bryce described unsanitary conditions and an appalling death rate. The educational achievement of the students was extremely low. Many buildings were unhealthy, and students contracted tuberculosis from living in overcrowded, poorly ventilated dormitories. According to the report, 24 per cent of the children at the fifteen schools surveyed had died of TB, and this figure would have been 42 per cent if the survivors had been monitored for three years after they returned to the reserve. Yet Bryce expressed a common attitude when he wrote, "It has to be carefully considered how far the country can be properly burdened with the cost of giving them superior advantages."[49]

Over time, many Native people became disillusioned with the schools, with reports of mistreatment of students, the high incidence of death and disease, the deliberate policy of cultural transformation, and the fact that assimilation didn't even work, because educated young aboriginals could find no place in "Canadian" society. Massive immigration at the turn of the century had provided an alternative to hiring aboriginal workers, and white workers were generally unwilling to work alongside Natives. Unfortunately, the graduates of the schools were totally unprepared for life in their own communities as well, as they were no longer able to communicate with their own parents or families. A later graduate of a residential school explained the effect of this loss: "Once language disappeared men began to forget their former purpose of life and ideas, they could only understand the thoughts of the adopted culture."[50] Many Anishinabe, their self-image and self-respect profoundly damaged, were comfortable in neither world.

Eventually, the government recognized both the failure of its policy of assimilation and the political irrelevancy of aboriginals now that they constituted only 1.5 per cent of the Canadian population and were safely out of sight on reserves. In 1910, a more frugal and limited education policy was adopted, with the goal now "to fit the Indian for civilized life in his own environment"; segregation now replaced assimilation as the goal. Educational opportunities were cut back, and the curriculum was simplified to practical instruction, thus guaranteeing that aboriginal people would remain at the bottom of Canadian society. The large industrial schools were to be phased out. New contracts were signed the following year between the churches and the government, establishing the government as the senior partner in the management of the schools, with primary responsibility for setting standards of care and education.[51]

New funding formulas increased government grants, with the result that the health of children improved – though, even in 1922, Bryce would publish a pamphlet calling the poor health in the schools "a national crime." Despite the increase, the per-capita grants remained substantially below those of other residential-care facilities: two decades later, the School for the Deaf and the School for Boys in Manitoba received government grants of $642 and $550 per capita, respectively, and even the St. Norbert orphanage received $294 from the Catholic church. The residential schools received only $138 per child.[52]

Throughout the second decade of the twentieth century there were ongoing troubles at Cecilia Jeffrey, many of them centering around the principal, F. R. Dodds. In July 1914 Chief Red Sky complained to Insp. John Semmens of Indian Affairs that the children at the school "were cruelly beaten by the Principal at times," and the Ojibwa refused to send their children until the situation was remedied. "Not one pupil . . . could be obtained for the school at any point," Semmens told his supervisors. After an investigation, he reported that the rumour had been started by a "conjuror, an old time pagan" hostile to the missionaries: "The fact remains that the principal has resorted to corporal punishment at times and the children have reported this."[53] It was agreed that the principal should adopt another method of maintaining discipline.

For several years the school was in a continual state of unrest. Four members of the staff left in 1915. Children began running away. In January 1917, it was reported that "the pupils are rather refractory. . . . The Indian language is still used by pupils to an undesirable extent . . . Indian parents visit frequently and remain for meals and talk a great deal with the children." J. D. McLean, assistant deputy-superintendent and secretary of the Department of Indian Affairs, admonished Reverend Dodds: "The Department will, in future, expect you to take a decided stand and deal firmly with those who transgress the rules, in order that the present abuses in the children's conduct may be corrected." In March 1917, four more runaways were reported; by then the parents were fed up. In late March they sent a letter to Mr. McKenzie, the Indian agent: "A meeting of all the Indians on our reserves was held last night and we decided that a change is necessary in our school for the benefit of the children. Mr Dodds has shown himself incapable of the position that he is holding, and we, in the name of all the Indians on reserves 39 and 40 ask you to report this to the department in Ottawa and at the same time to ask for his dismissal."[54]

This development caused a flurry of official activity. A new assistant principal, a Mr. Matthews, was appointed, but this did not solve the problem of Dodds "and his considerable temper." Gradually his superiors realized a "change should be made." In August, the Indian agent reported "there is also a lot of trouble between the Indians and the Principal," and a series of letters was sent to the Presbyterian Church, urging it to "do something about Cecilia Jeffrey and Dodds." Finally, on February 26, 1918 (a year after the first petition), Presbytery sent a commission to investigate conditions at the school and issued its recommendation that Dodds should be replaced. In a move indicative of their patronizing attitudes, however, the members of the commission suggested that this not be done right away, so that the Indians would not see it "as the direct result of their appeal to the Department and a victory on their part." In April, J. J. Edminson of the Presbyterian Church reported to Indian Affairs that a resolution had been passed asking the government to support Dodds for the time being: "if they stand by him through the present period of unrest, the spirit of disloyalty or rebellion will disappear; and that failing to do so, they are only inviting future difficulty both for the Department and for the next Principal of this School . . . changes in staff will take place during the year that will satisfactorily relieve the situation without conveying to the minds of the Indians the impression that they can control the situation."[55]

Dodds finally resigned, but Mr. Matthews, the new principal, died only a few months later during the 1918 outbreak of the Spanish flu. A telegram recorded that "only matron in charge, things in bad shape, many sick."[56] For a brief period the aging Inspector Semmens took over the school until

P. T. Martin, a lawyer and clergyman, temporarily replaced him in 1919. Publicly available Indian Affairs records for Cecilia Jeffrey are noticeably sparse over the years that followed, when at least one other principal came and went before the hiring of W. J. Cookson, the principal my grandfather met when he canoed into Shoal Lake in 1922.

During the decade before my grandfather's arrival, the parents and families of Cecilia Jeffrey's students had undergone their share of hardships. In 1912–13 a severe epidemic of measles, "a disease very fatal to the Indians," swept through the student body, according to the Cecilia Jeffrey principal F. R. Dodds. Other scourges such as tuberculosis, whooping cough, and influenza attacked the communities and the school over the next few years. When World War I broke out in 1914, several young men from Shoal Lake joined the 141st Battalion, and aboriginals made the region's highest contribution to the armed forces.

The detrimental effects of Euro-Canadian penetration had continued to escalate. In 1911, it was reported that "The industries now in operation on Shoal Lake include two gold mines in operation, the Mikado and the Damascus mine (or Cameron Island Mine) and half a dozen others. . . . the boarding school . . . a fishery with two steamers, scattered farmers."[57] That same year, the city of Winnipeg began to draw its drinking water from Shoal Lake and built a narrow-gauge railway to service the pipeline. From that time on, the Greater Winnipeg Water District (GWWD) had a voice in decisions affecting Shoal Lake. The expropriation of reserve land for the benefit of the GWWD was a clear example of how the needs of distant Euro-Canadians were given priority over those of the local Anishinabe, for it meant the relocation of the community, the loss of some of the best land on the reserve, the loss of the traditional burial area, and, as a result of canal construction, the isolation by water of the community from the mainland – a situation that persists to this day. In addition, Chief Red Sky felt the Anishinabe had received inadequate compensation for the expropriation.

In 1919, the GWWD petitioned Indian Affairs for the right to run summer excursions to the sand beach on Shoal Lake, "to promote business over the railway." Water officials reported, "We have a considerable number of picnics in prospect during the summer and have inaugurated a Saturday train. . . . There is a small Indian graveyard which is a source of great interest to the visitors." These trips to Shoal Lake proved popular: on

July 2, 1926, the *Winnipeg Free Press* reported that six hundred people made the trip, and many others were turned away, because the train was already filled to capacity. Meanwhile, liquor had become available along the railway and, in 1916, Manitoba passed an act enforcing temperance. Shoal Lake and other local Native communities began to feel the effects when Kenora, which was just east of the Manitoba–Ontario border, "blossomed overnight with export liquor stores to serve thirsty Winnipegers."[58]

Frustration with the slow pace of Indian assimilation reached its peak in 1920; in that year, new amendments to the Indian Act further eroded Native control of reserve lands and governance. The federal government imposed an elected system of governance on the reserves, but was able to depose elected leaders of whom it did not approve; it could spend band funds for public works on the reserve without the consent of the band members, lease "non-productive" reserve land to outsiders without a surrender, and force Natives to give up their legal status as Indians under certain conditions. (The latter amendment was an attempt to curb rising Indian militancy, but was itself amended in 1922 by the Mackenzie King government and the coercive element was removed.) Most important, vis-à-vis Cecilia Jeffrey, school attendance was made compulsory for all physically fit children from ages seven to fifteen, a move heartily endorsed and even urged by the missionaries, but successfully resisted by some Ojibwa families. The administration of all Indian schools was assumed by the Department of Indian Affairs, although some were still staffed by the religious denominations. Duncan Campbell Scott, now deputy-superintendent-general of Indian Affairs, summarized the intention of the amendments. "I want to get rid of the Indian problem. I do think as a matter of fact, that this country ought not to continually protect a class of people who are able to stand alone. . . . Our object is to continue until there is not a single Indian in Canada that has not been absorbed into the body politic, and there is no Indian question, and no Indian department, and that is the whole object of this Bill."[59]

Anthropologist Diamond Jenness described the situation in the 1920s: "In many parts of Canada the Indians had no schools at all; in others only elementary mission schools in which the standard of teaching was exceedingly low. A few mission boarding-schools [such as Cecilia Jeffrey], subsidized by the government, accepted Indian children when they were very young, raised them to the age of sixteen, then sent them back to their people, well indoctrinated in the Christian faith, but totally unfitted for life

in an Indian community and, of course, not acceptable in any white one."
The failure of the system was recognized by Capt. Frank Edwards, the
Indian agent for the Shoal Lake bands, who wrote to the Presbyterian
Church in 1923: "I should be glad if the Church could suggest or do something for the pupils leaving the School when discharged, it seems a pity
they should go back to their old life again, after the work done on their
behalf at the School." Across Canada, the standard of aboriginal education
was shockingly low: more than one-third of all residential-school pupils
were in Grade 1; in 1930, three-quarters of Native pupils were in Grades 1
to 3, and only three in every hundred moved past Grade 6. By contrast,
well over half the children in provincial public schools in 1930 were past
Grade 3, and almost a third beyond Grade 6.[60]

But the annual report of the Women's Missionary Society for 1922, as
in most other years, dwelt not upon academic achievement but other
matters: the senior girls had now received sufficient instruction in home
nursing "to enable them to combat the evils attendant upon the medicine
dance. The problem of missionary work on the reserve is not solved, as the
many duties of the principal do not allow the time necessary for this work.
Services have been held in the homes of the Indians occasionally during
the winter months, and many of the Indians attend the regular service in the
school, after which a short service is held in Indian. . . . The senior boys and
girls manifest a deep interest in all the religious work of the school."[61]

The Shoal Lake Anishinabe might have given a different report of the
merits of the school. To them one of the more valuable things about Cecilia
Jeffrey was its nurse; she was the only person from the school who visited
the reserve regularly. In February 1922, Captain Edwards reported that the
Shoal Lake bands had decided to erect a hospital building at Shoal Lake,
close to Cecilia Jeffrey. They proposed to do so at no cost to the Indian
Affairs Department or the Church, and the bands offered free lumber for
the roof, windows, and doors, and Edwards had initially given his permission. But the Indian agent was directed by his superiors to stifle this initiative and "stop the Indians from proceeding."[62]

He was given this instruction because there were already plans afoot to
relocate the school. Besides, as Duncan Campbell Scott pointed out, since
Reserve #40 was under timber licence to the Keewatin Lumber Company,
the lumber no longer belonged to the Ojibwa. Since the school was accessible only by water, and thus inaccessible for periods during spring and fall
when ice was forming or breaking up, the school administrators found it

difficult to keep it well provisioned and adequately maintained. Captain Edwards reported in 1922 that "the Board is not doing their duty in the upkeep of the school." In 1921, the Presbyterian Board of Home Missions was urging Indian Affairs to erect a new, larger school on a new site with more farmland. Although most of the administrators involved seemed to favour this plan, the new principal, Mr. Cookson, cautioned Captain Edwards, "I am not in favour of closing the school without due consideration being given to the feelings of the Indians in this matter. . . . They have stood by the school. There isn't a child with but one exception of school age but is attending school."[63] In fact, by this time, the children of Cecilia Jeffrey's first graduates were attending. Cookson suggested that the existing school be retained for the Shoal Lake bands and a second school be built near Kenora for the many other aboriginal children who had no school to attend.

As the approval and erection of a new school would take some time, Cookson was instructed to make repairs. Evidently taking these directions to heart, and exceeding them, probably in the hope that, with major renovations, the school wouldn't be closed at all, the principal and the larger boys cleared ten acres of land, built an ice house and a boat house, installed electric lights, and worked on the heating and plumbing systems and foundation – the latter with my grandfather's help. But Cookson ended up spending more than $7,000 on repairs and equipment in two years, an astronomical sum in those days, much of it without authorization. His superiors were appalled and noted that the installation of a septic tank costing $1,478.36 – a sum equal to the Presbytery's total annual grant to the school – proved to be a botched job that could have been done for far less. In short, Cookson's accounts were "beyond all reason."[64]

When the Winnipeg Presbytery met on September 11, 1923, the Home Mission Committee recommended "that Mr. Cookson, principal of the Cecilia Jeffrey School, be relieved of his duties at the end of September; that there be a monthly conference between the Indian Committee [a committee of ministers within Winnipeg Presbytery concerned with missions to Indians that was headed by my grandfather] and the School, and that there be no capital expenditure or change in the policy of the School without a recommendation from this Committee for the Women's Missionary Society." Two months later Rev. A. J. Menzies was appointed, to take charge "at once."[65]

Although my grandfather had liked Mr. Cookson, as liaison and advisor to the WMS, his job was to arrange for Cookson's departure and the installation of Rev. A. J. Menzies as the new principal. It was a delicate situation, but my grandfather managed to get the change made without too much hard feeling.

"Mr Freeman is taking a very great interest in the School, and the Staff are very favorably impressed with him, as is also Mr. Menzies," wrote Captain Edwards, adding that he planned to schedule his next visit to coincide with that of my grandfather.[66]

CHAPTER
2 0

Cecilia Jeffrey Indian
Residential School

For the next year my grandfather worked quite intensively on problems at Cecilia Jeffrey, visiting the school once every two months. Then for the next three years he visited for a week to ten days immediately after Christmas. In the summer it was easy to get to the school by boat, but in winter he had to travel the roughly one hundred miles from Winnipeg to Waugh by the Greater Winnipeg Water District (GWWD) narrow-gauge railway and then find a way to get across eight miles of ice to the school – by horse and sleigh if he was lucky. The worst ordeal was coming back from the school to Waugh between midnight and dawn in sub-zero January weather to catch the GWWD for Winnipeg. When a horse and sleigh were not available he would be pulled on a toboggan by boys from the school or men from the reserve.

To his credit, and unlike many administrators of the schools, he tried to get a sense of the community the school was serving. He made a point of visiting every house on the two Shoal Lake reserves to get to know the parents of the schoolchildren.

There he saw the external manifestations of a world view very different from his own – old windows closed up and new ones cut in a house where there had been a death (so neither evil spirits nor ghosts could find a way in), houses surrounded by roughly carved wooden birds on poles painted in bright colours to ward off evil spirits, and the wooden "spirit houses" built over graves and containing money, matches, cooking utensils, decks of cards, packages of snuff, or toys, depending on the age and habits of the person who had died. The Presbyterians, it seems, had not been very effective in stamping out "paganism," at least not among the older Anishinabe.

He also observed traditional healing practices. He watched Little Heaven, a medicine man from Mackenzie Portage, treat a sick woman by slitting open a rabbit and slapping it on the woman's chest (she recovered, he noted), and he spent several hours at ceremonies leading up to a medicine dance. If he saw anything of value in aboriginal healing practices, it is not evident in the brief descriptions that he left in his memoirs, for he commented with apparent frustration that the medicine dance was held in sight of the CJ School where there was a nurse, a hospital, and a dispensary.

My grandfather's reference to the work of the medicine man and the medicine dance is significant in that many traditional religious practices had been outlawed since the 1880s. Regulations outlawed "any Indian festival, dance or other ceremony" in which the giving away "of money, goods or articles of any sort" formed a part, and any celebration or dance that required "the wounding or mutilation of the dead or living body of any human being or animal." In 1922, a man from Fort Frances had been imprisoned for two months for organizing a sun dance at Buffalo Point on Lake of the Woods. Missionaries had actively sought these regulations because they believed that certain cultural practices, especially the West Coast potlatch and the Plains sun dance, were fundamentally incompatible with Christianity and impeded conversion.[1]

Although it was still legal to take part in an ordinary dance – not a sun dance, that is – on one's own reserve, the Department of Indian Affairs tried to discourage aboriginal people from holding any of the old dances or ceremonies. In 1921, for example, Duncan Campbell Scott specifically directed the Kenora Indian agent, Captain Edwards:

> to use your utmost endeavors to dissuade the Indians from excessive indulgence in the practice of dancing. You should suppress any dances which cause waste of time, interfere with the occupations of the Indians, unsettle them for serious work, injure their health or encourage them in sloth and idleness. You should also dissuade and, if possible, prevent them from leaving their reserves for the purpose of attending fairs, exhibitions, etc., when their absence would result in their own farming and

other interests being neglected. It is realized that reasonable amusement and recreation should be enjoyed by Indians, but they should not be allowed to dissipate their energies and abandon themselves to demoralizing amusements.[2]

According to an historian associated with the Treaty #3 First Nations, Captain Edwards was a more lenient Indian agent than most, and he followed this paternalistic advice only partially. He allowed people to wear their regalia and dance, though one elderly woman from another Kenora-area reserve remembered dancers running to hide in the bushes when they saw him coming. "On the reservation they had these shaking tents and sweat lodges and Midewiwin – [the white people] thought it was evil, that's what they thought. We'd be running to the bush to hide if we heard the boat coming; we'd all run to the bush, we didn't want to talk to them, we hid everything."[3] Certainly the round lodges where many ceremonies and dances were held were still in evidence, for my grandparents photographed the interior of one, though they were told it was a council house.

In Duncan Campbell Scott's attitudes we see the paternalism of the era at its height: aboriginal people as primitive children needing the constant care and discipline of the government, the oppression of colonized people rationalized through concepts of "responsibility" and "duty."[4] I do not know to what extent my grandfather shared this outlook, if at all, but it was prevalent in the Indian Department and in missionary circles at that time, not to mention among the general public.

Gard was certainly no blind supporter of the residential schools. In his memoirs he recounted that he soon realized that a terrible generation gap was being created by the school's policy of removing children from their homes, compelling them to live at the school from ages seven to sixteen, and educating them in a culture and religion to which the parents had no access. He noted that the school had little contact with the reserves except through the nurse. It was, he believed, an education guaranteed to complicate life for both the children and parents, and evidence of colossal stupidity.

But although he was able to see that a terrible problem was being created, his solution was still based on the assumption that what the people of Shoal Lake really needed was Christianity, that a missionary working with the parents would narrow the gap he saw developing. He therefore arranged for a full-time missionary, David Cordiner, to be assigned to Lake of the Woods, to pay special attention to the Shoal Lake reserves. Cordiner was stationed at the school. Meanwhile, in contrast to many missionaries who wanted the parents kept as far away as possible, Gard made further efforts to involve the parents in the life of the school. He acquired a four-tube neutrodyne-reflex radio for the school and invited the reserves' residents to come over whenever they felt like it to listen.

As the new missionary was responsible for all of the Lake of the Woods area, he had to spend the summer visiting as many of the reserves as possible and following different bands who were berry-picking, wild-rice harvesting, and fishing. After ensuring that Cordiner knew how to canoe, camp, read maps, and fish, my grandfather took him around to the Lake of the Woods reserves and introduced him to the chief of every band they could locate (the family was left behind on this occasion). They started out from Cecilia Jeffrey in 1924, two days after the ice had left the lake, on a round trip of 150 miles with another man from my grandfather's church and twelve-year-old Archie Redsky as interpreter, in a birch-bark canoe made by Wapiuke of Shoal Lake for $25 and an ounce of one-inch nails. The travellers shot rabbits along the way to supplement their diet. My grandfather thought the missionary had made some progress, for after two years, for the first time in their history, the Anishinabe had buried a corpse at Shoal Lake without painting it with the traditional bright colours that my grandfather was told were supposed to keep evil spirits away.

Here we enter the realm of living memory, for my father and some of his siblings remember leaving from the Indian agent's dock in Kenora in their canoe, with two sets of oars and seven paddles, the infant twins laced up in tikinaagens, or "cradle boards," that were presents from people at Shoal Lake. Sometimes they would camp on Shoal Lake a short distance from the school, and then canoe around the Lake of the Woods with Cordiner, exploring inlets, bays, and streams, and visiting with Anishinabe families who were berry picking or harvesting wild rice. My grandfather got to know a number of people from the Shoal Lake bands and considered some his friends.

Meanwhile, back at the school, the Indian agent, Captain Edwards, had formed a poor impression of the new principal and his wife. In Edwards's view, Menzies was lacking in organizational abilities, and there was bad feeling between the principal and the Indians, for Menzies never set foot on the reserve, and too many pupils were running away from school. Edwards reported that he was trying to discourage Menzies's practice of allowing Shoal Lake pupils to return home for weekends. Furthermore,

Mrs. Menzies, who was matron, didn't like Indians, the staff didn't like her, and, worse, she was "the actual head of the institution." Edwards did form a favourable impression of some of the other staff members, notably one Mr. Gibson, who taught farming and carpentry, and was "a splendid chap with the children," and another teacher whose art classes had inspired a number of students.[5]

Another problem revolved around the nurse. She was so overworked that she was ordered to take a rest. An elder I talked to vividly remembers sick children crying and moaning through the night. But Duncan Campbell Scott, a notorious penny-pincher, directed Edwards not to hire a substitute: "surely they could get along for a couple of months without one."[6] Then a few months later, Scott decided that the services of a nurse could be discontinued altogether because of the expense. This announcement caused a stir on the reserves, because tuberculosis was prevalent and Cecilia Jeffrey was so isolated that there was no other European-style health care available. Scott was finally persuaded to let the nurse remain until the move to the new school, which was scheduled for April 1926.

For the momentous decision to move the school had indeed been made. The two major reasons appear to have been the need for further renovations and expansion of the present building and the isolation of the site, which made obtaining doctors or bringing in supplies very difficult (one year thirteen tons of supplies were taken in by launch and barge before the ice formed). An additional impetus came from the City of Winnipeg, which in 1924 tried to stop navigation in Shoal Lake's Indian Bay and wanted the school relocated to protect Winnipeg's drinking water. (In 1925, the GWWD was informed by the government that the bay could not be closed for navigation, but Indian Affairs granted a portion of the bay to the water authority.)

I do not know exactly what role my grandfather played in the making of the decision to move the school, but as the liaison between the Women's Missionary Society and the Winnipeg Presbytery he was likely involved in it in some way. Once the decision had been made, he was asked to select the new site. In a memo my grandfather wrote as convenor of the Indian Committee for Winnipeg Presbytery in June 6, 1925, he describes the requirements: a water lot giving access to Lake of the Woods, within twenty kilometres of Kenora and preferably near Keewatin, which was west of Kenora and closer to Shoal Lake (presumably so that the parents could visit easily). The site was also to be south of the railway tracks, and include a considerable amount of arable land.[7]

I also do not know if my grandfather consulted the Shoal Lake parents about their preferences for a new site, or if any of the administrators considered their approval of the move necessary, given the pressure from the City of Winnipeg to move the school. (Cookson had written to the GWWD earlier in protest.) Gard would certainly have been aware that the Shoal Lake parents would not be happy with a site in Keewatin, for Captain Edwards, with whom he conferred on possible locations, recorded in a letter to the WMS in 1923 that "if the school was moved to Keewatin, we should have great difficulty in getting the parents to allow their children to attend."

With my grandfather's interest in involving the parents in the school and in improving communication between the school and reserve, he may well have consulted at least the Shoal Lake people. On the other hand, the comments of a chief from Northwest Angle two years later would seem to indicate that many Anishinabe were never asked where they thought the new school should be located. Certainly the initial reaction of the Shoal Lake parents to the news that the school would be moved farther away was dismay. Naturally the parents wished to keep their children nearby and remembered the stipulation in their original agreement with the Presbyterians that their children would not be transferred to another school without their permission, as well as the clause in Treaty #3 promising them on-reserve schooling if they asked for it. Captain Edwards forwarded to his superiors the letters of protest he received from the Shoal Lake Ojibwa – signed by Chiefs Red Sky and Kesick [Kejick] and forty Shoal Lake band members – opposing the proposed move and requesting a day school.[8]

"The whole of the two bands are not agreed with this and they wish you to give the people a report of this. . . . we do not know the reasons why this school is going to be removed," the petition read. If the reason was that freight was costing too much, they suggested moving the school to the end of the GWWD line on Indian Bay, and expressed their fear that, if the school was moved farther away, more children would run away, which would be especially dangerous in cold weather. The people of Shoal Lake would rather have a day school, as had been promised in the first place. "It looks very queer to us why they want to do this," the petition continued, noting all the repairs and hard work done by the two principals, Cookson and Menzies. "We do not know what could cause all this. . . . We want you,

Mr. Edwards, to try and help us. Try and be on our side and fix it so they can understand and you write us and send us a copy of what they say."

From the available records it is not clear how, or even if, the parents were mollified. Were their concerns addressed or were they forced to make the best of a decision they couldn't change? What role did my grandfather play in this dispute? This is a question I wish I could answer, for later events suggest that the parents' concerns about the new school and their desire to keep the old school persisted over a number of years. Also it is evident that their ability to influence decisions affecting their children's education was greatly curtailed once the school was physically removed from their sphere of influence.

Whatever his response to the Anishinabe protest, my grandfather, the Indian Affairs registrar of lands, and Captain Edwards joined forces for two days of searching for a site. Then Gard spent four days further exploring on his own, presumably by canoe. After considering several possibilities, Gard suggested the Carmichael property near Keewatin. It was central to good fishing grounds, had enough land to grow food, had plenty of wood on site, and offered several possibilities for economic enterprises, including the growing of raspberries or strawberries and fur-farming. It was my grandfather's belief that "farming will never be a basic industry for these Indians. The country they live in will not permit it." Edwards and Menzies agreed with my grandfather's suggested site, but when Mr. Carmichael demanded "an exorbitant price" the three men agreed on another property half a mile away.[9]

This second property, of approximately 230 acres, was part of the Rat Portage reserve. Captain Edwards wrote to his superiors that the reserve's residents would have to surrender the land and he presumed "we would have to pay them something." Edwards was instructed to offer $5 an acre, the same as had been paid for the Catholic School in the 1890s. But even though Chief Red Sky advised the Rat Portage Anishinabe to sell at this price, they balked at what they perceived to be too low a figure and demanded $50 an acre. A band vote was taken in February 1926 on the $5 offer but the motion was defeated. However, as twenty-two of the forty-four men on the reserve were out trapping at the time of the vote, Edwards held out hope for another vote at treaty time in June. Before the February meeting broke up, the Rat Portage Anishinabe were informed that the Department had the power to take the land without their consent or surrender, under Section 11 of the Indian Act, and that in all probability that was what it would do. As the Department wanted to get on with construction, Edwards suggested to his superiors that the Department take the land and pay the Rat Portage band $5 an acre; Duncan Campbell Scott soon gave his approval.[10]

The contrast between the ability of a white property owner to ask for whatever exorbitant price he wanted and to refuse to sell at a lower price, and the Rat Portage band's inability to do what they wanted with their own land is a stark reminder of the inequity and lack of power and freedom experienced by aboriginal people at this time. Did my grandfather know about the band's refusal to sell their reserve land at $5 an acre and the Indian Department's threat to seize it unilaterally? What did Edwards tell him? Unfortunately, the records of the Indian Committee of Winnipeg Presbytery have not survived, so it is impossible to know what the church knew of the situation. It's conceivable that my grandfather didn't know what was going on, but I consider it more likely that he knew at least some of it, for he appears to have been working closely with Captain Edwards both in selecting the site, which he knew would require a surrender, and on the plans for its development. Edwards wrote his superiors that "Freeman promises to come choose the best land for the garden, stables, etc." Gard visited the site in early April 1926, two months after the band had refused to sell the land, and suggested clearing only five or six areas. It was assumed that the people on the reserve would do the clearing.

However, the Rat Portage Anishinabe had decided to resist the Indian Department's high-handedness. Shortly after my grandfather had visited the site, the Anishinabe persuaded a lawyer, James Robinson of Kenora, to draw up a petition arguing that the land was worth at least $25 an acre, as it was well timbered and the cordwood was valuable. "Even for cordwood the land would be worth what they claim," the lawyer wrote to Duncan Campbell Scott, and informed the deputy-superintendent-general that the Indians refused to clear the land until their claim was settled.[11]

Scott sent a terse two-sentence reply to the lawyer: "I am directed to acknowledge your letter of the 18th instant, concerning the Cecilia Jeffrey School. In reply I have to state that I propose to deal with this matter in the best interests of the Indians concerned." The band was lucky to have been able to engage a lawyer at all; Scott had proposed to the deputy minister two years earlier that the Indian Act be amended to prevent lawyers and "agitators" from "collecting money from the Indians for the pursuit of claims against the government without departmental approval."[12] This legislation was finally passed in 1927 – one year after submission of the petition.

Since the Rat Portage Anishinabe would not clear the land, Scott directed Edwards to put out tenders for white men to do it, and Edwards received two bids: one for $45 an acre, another for $35 an acre plus $45 for stumping and grubbing. My grandfather knew of this measure, for in a letter Edwards wrote to his superiors, he reported that Freeman had "asked me what had been done about letting the tenders for clearing and construction and was surprised that no action had so far been taken."[13] If he knew about the tendering, he would have known at least that the Anishinabe were refusing to clear the land themselves, and, given the kind of man he was, I find it hard to imagine that he wouldn't have asked why. But I don't know what he thought of this dispute or the government's actions, or if he took any action of his own in response.

In June 1926, Edwards finally succeeded in engineering a vote in favour of surrendering the land – for $5 an acre – with the inviting promise of a cash distribution of $20 a head that summer. But Edwards was also informed that "the new building will not proceed this year as there will be no funds for this purpose."[14]

Meanwhile a crisis in the Presbyterian Church further complicated decisions about the future of the school – and also affected my grandfather's involvement. The Methodist, Congregationalist, and Presbyterian churches had agreed to unite to form the United Church of Canada, and had done so formally on June 10, 1925 – four days after my grandfather's initial letter outlining the requirements for a new site. Those Presbyterians who did not agree to union remained Presbyterians, and it was these "Continuing Presbyterians" who took over Cecilia Jeffrey, though the actual handover of the school appears to have taken place almost two years later. With the changeover, the new school would be operated by the Presbyterians rather than the United Church, and it was decided that they should therefore have a say in selecting a site. The Presbyterians quickly decided not to use the lot on the Rat Portage reserve as it was discovered that the entire property was on a rock formation, and building costs would have been prohibitive. Instead, the Presbyterians selected a 168-acre dairy farm on the far side of Kenora – for which the government paid $12,000, or more than $71 an acre, in November 1928. To the dismay of the Shoal Lake parents, it was inland, and therefore inaccessible by canoe. It was also more than 45 miles from Shoal Lake.[15]

———

As my grandfather had joined the United Church, his official involvement with the school ended at this point, though from his memoirs it appears that he may still have had some contact until the school actually moved to the new Round Lake site in 1929. He certainly remained in occasional contact with some of the Shoal Lake Anishinabe: several people visited him in Winnipeg, and over the years a number of young women from the Shoal Lake reserves lived in his home to help care for his children.

He was probably party to a suggestion put forward in 1926 by "representatives in Winnipeg" of the Board of Home Missions of the United Church that the Shoal Lake school be turned into an isolation hospital for tuberculosis (the GWWD's attempted ban on navigation was no longer an impediment). This suggestion was made because of the prevalence of tuberculosis, which was ravaging entire families. "During the past year our school lost seven pupils through this disease, while five others are now out of the school. . . . The Indians seem to object to their children being sent to Selkirk, as they say they never see them again, because of the distance, and because most of them go there to die."[16] But this suggestion went nowhere.

My grandfather also appears to have been involved in discussions about whether or not Mr. Menzies should continue as principal at the new school, since these began before the Continuing Presbyterians took over. Edwards was convinced that he was "the wrong person to have in charge of an Indian school," and wrote to his superiors that the decision had been made that "this Mr Menzies . . . shall disappear with the old building."[17]

Captain Edwards compiled a report of complaints by some members of the staff against the principal, including that the principal's wife had refused to give a loaf of bread to an old dying woman (the teacher bought a loaf herself and gave it to her) and the nurse had had to do likewise to give eggs to some sick children, although there were plenty of eggs at the school. The principal overcharged the band for hay, and even charged the Indians for clothing that church people donated for them.

The Principal is more of a hard headed businessman than a Principal or Missionary, and I am informed that he practically never visits the Indians on the Reserves, although they live only a few minutes walk from the School. [This had also been my grandfather's complaint about him in his memoirs.] Dr. Cormie informs that when the late Principal Mr Cookson left, the School was in debt about $1500 and that the present principal wiped this off and is now somewhere about $3000 or $4000 ahead. This does not look reasonable, I made enquiries and the children appear to be well fed and nourished and it seems to me the surplus has been made from trading with the Indians, as well as Mr. Menzies being a very close businessman. If he had used any surplus towards helping some of the poor Indians he would have had better feelings between the Indians and himself, a large amount of relief I understand was always previously given by the School to the destitutes.

In fact, some shortcuts may have been made with regard to the food, for when a representative of the Women's Missionary Society visited the school that year she was moved to complain to the superintendent of Indian schools about the menu, exclaiming, "Who could live on such a fare?"[18]

The next summer (1928) the chiefs and councillors in the Treaty #3 region met in Kenora with a representative of Indian Affairs from Ottawa to discuss their concerns about the education of their children. This meeting appears to have been called in response to the bands' concerns about the decision to build the new residential school near Kenora. (Although the new site at Round Lake had been selected, the sale had not yet gone through.) The minutes of this meeting provide an all-too-rare insight into how the Anishinabe felt about the school system at roughly the time of my grandfather's involvement and their feelings about Cecilia Jeffrey in particular.

Chief Gardner of the Wabigoon Band, for example, expressed his grievance about the Catholic School [St. Mary's in Kenora], and contrasted it with what he had heard about Cecilia Jeffrey. His wife and three sons had attended the school, and he felt they had not learned anything useful. It had also been hard to teach his boys hunting and trapping, which they did not learn as children because they were away at school. He said that what the students mainly learned was to pray, rather than to read and write. One son, who began attending school at the age of seven, still could not read or write well when he left at the age of seventeen, and had not been well prepared to find work in Kenora and make a living. He had heard that the boys at Cecilia Jeffrey were taught trades and thought the same should be offered at the Catholic school.[19]

The Shoal Lake representatives were particularly concerned about the move to a more distant school and worried about how the parents would come to see them when there was no reserve or camping ground at Kenora and no house to stay in when they came in winter.

Chief Keesick [Kejick] said the Cecilia Jeffrey School should be kept as it was as there were enough children from the immediate area to fill the present school. They had been told that as long as the Indians were there, the school would be there, and they wished to have it kept there. He agreed that the children "did not know how to make a living when they left school and would like trades taught. In the old days trapping was different. Now the only way the Indians can make a living is to work like the white man and owing to the furs going through white men trapping and the raising of waters, it made it harder for the Indians each year to make a living."

Chief Kejick also complained that when the children left school they did not know anything and could hardly speak English, partly because even very young children were made to work around the school and did not spend enough time in the classroom. Chief Black Hawk of Northwest Angle "could not understand why the Indians were not consulted first as to where the schools should be built, and he was not in favor of it being built at Kenora. He hoped the Dept. would get some land where the Indians could camp and have a house where they could stay to be called an Indian House."[20]

The Indian Affairs minutes record that Mr. Paget of the Department of Indian Affairs replied "they were building a new school at Kenora because they needed a larger school and a larger school near town would be less expensive to maintain and if near town the children would have a better chance to learn the white man's ways. They were looking into finding a place where Indians could camp."[21] If the minutes of this meeting are accurate, this explanation satisfied the chiefs and at least some of them, including Chief Kejick of Shoal Lake, agreed to support the new school.

This may indeed be what happened, or it may have been what Indian Affairs believed had happened, for here we run into questions of cultural differences in the ethics of communication. There is also the possibility that the chiefs were telling Mr. Paget what he wanted to hear out of courtesy or to humour him rather than criticizing him or disagreeing with him to his face, which would have been unacceptable in traditional Anishinabe terms (remember the Ojibwa "conversions" at Rainy Lake). Was Paget aware of this possibility? Did he have any understanding of the behavioural codes that might have led the chiefs to imply an assent they did not really mean? Only Anishinabe oral history about this conference, if it exists, could help us to establish whether or not the chiefs' acquiescence was based on genuine agreement.

By October 1928, the new building at Round Lake was under construction. Early the following spring, Mr. Menzies heard about the complaints against him and the decision not to appoint him principal of the new school. Astounded and outraged by the charges against him, he fought back. The entire staff of the Shoal Lake school signed a refutation of the charges, and Menzies then wrote the Indian agent, Frank Edwards, appealing to him as "an Englishman, with I fancy an Englishman's sense of honor and justice" to reconsider his statements and clear his name. Edwards wrote back, agreeing that his relations with the staff and Indians now appeared quite cordial and had much improved over the years, and he promised to forward the principal's letter to Ottawa. His covering letter accompanying that of Menzies stated: "I consider Mr. Menzies greatly improved of late but still feel that, on account of his wife, that he is not the right man for principal of the new school."[22] A month later Rev. E. W. Byers was hired as principal of the new school.

It was at this point that the Anishinabe were drawn into the dispute over Menzies's dismissal, and their involvement reveals that the issues raised in their petition of 1925, which my grandfather must have been involved in trying to address, had never been adequately resolved. Menzies wrote a letter to the Hon. Peter Heenan, the Minister of Labour and the Member of Parliament for Kenora, saying that he had been directed to do so by the chiefs who were speaking for the Shoal Lake bands, the two Northwest Angle bands, and the Buffalo Bay band. The bands said that they could fill the current school, and would not allow their children to go to the new school, even if they went to jail for their refusal, but they would willingly send all their children to the Shoal Lake school if it were re-opened.[23] They also urged that Mr. Menzies remain in charge, although Menzies stated that he and his wife were leaving in any event.

As the Presbyterian Church prepared its invitation list for the grand opening of the new school in September 1929, Mr. Byers telegrammed the Women's Missionary Society to report that the children had not shown up. "This looks rather serious," the committee's secretary wrote to Duncan Campbell Scott. "Can your Department, through the Agent at Kenora, do anything to reach these Indians and have their children sent in to the new school? . . . I wrote Mr. Menzies as conciliatory a letter as I thought I could, saying that neither the Department nor the church were in funds sufficient for carrying on the two schools."[24]

The bands escalated their protest. A petition signed September 30, 1929, by the Shoal Lake chiefs and councillors to Peter Heenan, the Member of Parliament for Kenora District, asked him to represent their views to the Indian Department: "We very earnestly desire to have the Cecilia Jeffrey Indian School reopened and in this desire are joined by the two North-West Angle Bands and the Buffalo Bay Band." The bands suggested once again that with a few repairs, the school would be serviceable for several more years and offered to provide free land on Indian Bay for a new building when necessary. The site they proposed was two miles from Waugh, and so more accessible by rail than the old site. The bands told Heenan of McKittrick's promise that there should always be a school in the vicinity. They also stated that, with tuberculosis killing so many of their people, it was especially important to have their children nearby, where they could see them often, and that the school's nurse was very helpful to them.

> The School has helped us greatly, giving us wood to cut and other work, buying supplies from us, and furnishing us with clothing at a very low rate, our old people without any charge. Fur has become very scarce here, the high water has spoiled our rice fields and our hay and now they would take the help of the school away. . . . There are more than enough Indian children in Lake of Woods Bands to fill the new school at Kenora without sending our children there. . . . The Department is not providing enough schools to educate all the Indian children in the Agency. Why close Cecilia Jeffrey?[25]

Once again, Duncan Campbell Scott's reply to such outside intervention was curt. He wrote to Heenan, "If you intend to reply directly to these Indians I would take it as a favour if you would tell them that the Department has no intention whatever of reopening this school. . . . For your own information I would say that I have reason to believe that the former principal, a Mr. Menzies, is stirring up the Indians to make this request. I have drawn the attention of the Presbyterian Church authorities to this man's activities and I hope they will be able to control him."[26]

Frank Edwards wrote his superiors in mid-October confirming that it was Menzies who had prepared the petition for the Indians. "Mr. Menzies appears to have been the cause of a lot of the trouble we have had in getting the children back to the new school at Kenora as he was staying there until just lately and I have it on good authority that he has caused most of the dissatisfaction among the Indians."[27]

Is this true? Would the Shoal Lake bands have acquiesced happily to losing contact with their children if Menzies had not objected so strenuously to the termination of his contract? I try to imagine what it must have been like for the parents and elders of Shoal Lake, faced with the prospect of living for months at a time in a community almost totally bereft of young people. Was Menzies's about-face – from supporting a move when my grandfather was choosing a site significantly closer to Shoal Lake to opposing the move to distant Round Lake – based only on self-interest? Even if Menzies used the opposition of the bands for his own purposes, could all five bands in question have been drawn into a contract dispute if they had no major unresolved concerns? Certainly the bands had expressed their worries about the move long before they knew that Menzies would not be principal at the new school, as their comments at the education conference demonstrate in August 1828. If their fears had indeed been allayed by the representative from Indian Affairs at that meeting and they had agreed to send their children to Kenora, was the removal of Menzies the only reason that they changed their minds?

The new Cecilia Jeffrey Indian Residential School opened late in October 1929. It appears that no Anishinabe were on the official guest list for the dedication, which took place November 2, though apparently Chief Cheena of Shoal Lake attended. In late November, the Women's Missionary Society wrote to Duncan Campbell Scott that arrangements had been made for a guest house and place for visiting parents to camp on a piece of land on the shore of Lake of the Woods at Kenora and that this had placated the chiefs. "The rest house arranged for them in Kenora has been a great factor in their becoming more contented."[28]

The contentment of the chiefs, if it ever existed, was short-lived. Soon there were complaints that the children were starving and that Byers should be fired. The very next year a new amendment to the Indian Act was passed that increased the punishment for non-attendance at Indian schools, with penalties such as jail terms for parents who would not comply – penalties which were of course far harsher than those for non-Native parents – and so the pattern of complaints and coercion continued – for decades. In 1939, officials from the Department of Indian Affairs and from the Ontario

Provincial Police visited Cecilia Jeffrey school to investigate rumours of sexual immorality among students and between students and a female staff member, and allegations of misappropriation of government funds. No official action was ever taken with regard to these complaints (the incidents of sexual abuse by a female staff member were independently confirmed to me by a witness). In 1940, Byers was removed as principal; his replacement proved to be such a harsh disciplinarian that one of the teachers complained to the Women's Missionary Society about the severe beatings he administered and his extremely abusive language; she left a few months later, declaring that she could no longer work in that kind of environment. Another principal, although generally considered more sympathetic to the Anishinabe and more respectful of their culture, refused to let the children return to their homes for the Christmas holidays unless their parents could guarantee they would provide them with proper sanitation, lighting, ventilation, and nutrition in their homes.[29]

Looking back on his involvement with Cecilia Jeffrey fifty years later, my grandfather wrote that he found it difficult to assess the value of his own work there. He had enjoyed his contact with the school and felt he had learned a great deal, but he had been frustrated by inadequate resources (I'm not sure whether he meant to run the school or evangelize the area or both). He had seen the terrible gulf being created between aboriginal children and their parents, and had attempted to bridge that gap by encouraging parents to have more contact with the school and by assigning a missionary to them, but the missionary had left his post after a couple of years. My grandfather certainly valued the friendships he had made, particularly with one Cecilia Jeffrey graduate, Cora Mandamin, who converted to Christianity and lived with his family while she studied nursing in Winnipeg. She remained a long-time family friend and was the great-aunt – grandmother in Anishinabe terms – of Chief Eli Mandamin, who would accept the formal apology of the Presbyterian Church many years later. My grandfather took great satisfaction in Cora's record of thirty years as a practical nurse in Home Mission hospitals and in her statement that the biggest thing Christ had done for her was deliver her from fear.

Cora was living proof that the successful transformation of a young aboriginal woman into a satisfied convert and trailblazing Native professional was possible. And it is undeniably true that some aboriginal graduates of the schools were able to gain access to the mainstream culture in ways that enabled them to advance the concerns of Native people and fight more effectively to protect their rights, just as their parents had hoped they would when they had originally asked for schooling. Yet Cora stands out in part because she was one of Cecilia Jeffrey's very few "success" stories – her experience was not the norm, and even her success had its personal cost.

While teachers and administrators delighted in the handful of students who became nurses or successful farmers or even just high-school graduates, Indian residential schools in general failed to provide a useful education for the vast majority of those who attended them. For many former students became marginalized human beings, "lacking the necessary skills of both White and Indian cultures, confused over their identity, and left to their own devices after their failed school experience." Or, as a former student at another residential school wrote in 1923, "For those who do live [through the experience], who survive and who graduate from the school at the age of eighteen, during every day of their training they have acted under orders. They have never needed to use their own minds and wills. . . . When suddenly given their freedom they do not know how to use it. Their initiative is lost. . . . [They] sit on the fence between the whites and the Indians, belonging to neither, fitting into neither world." Many of those who attended residential school internalized their teachers' attitudes that they were untrustworthy, inferior, incapable, and immoral, and that their culture was useless in the modern world. Graduates were often more troubled and less able to lead productive lives than those who stayed on the reserve. Many aboriginal people who attended residential schools developed a long-lasting sense of alienation toward Canadian society.[30]

I know little about how students were treated at Cecilia Jeffrey during the time my grandfather was involved with the school – for example, whether or not there was physical or sexual abuse then as there was at various other times during the school's history. I also do not know what proportion of Cecilia Jeffrey students felt that their school experience was positive or negative or how many were traumatized by it. Only a handful of those who attended the Shoal Lake school are still living, and their testimony cannot fully represent that of all the students who went there, for evidence from other schools shows that even individuals who attended the same school at the same time may have had widely different experiences.[31] (In fact, to my knowledge there is no statistically accurate survey of the experiences of students from any Indian residential school in Canada, though there is voluminous first-person testimony revealing serious mistreatment and negative experiences at many schools.) But it is certainly safe to say that, in general, even when the students did not suffer physical or sexual abuse, the schools were destructive of aboriginal languages, cultures, and families, and as a result often caused serious psychological harm to individuals as well as long-lasting damage to communities.

Walter Redsky, a respected elder at Shoal Lake, was eighty-three when I interviewed him in 1999. He is a former chief of Shoal Lake First Nation #40 and the brother of the Archie Redsky who guided my grandfather and the missionary David Cordiner around Lake of the Woods in the mid-1920s. He was the only person I was able to talk to who had attended the Shoal Lake school at the time of my grandfather's involvement – most former students from the mid-1920s have died. When I visited him at the seniors' residence at Shoal Lake, I asked him how the parents of the students had viewed the school; he recalled that his own elders had told him that the school was stealing their children. Speaking emphatically, he stated that the school had "hurt all the people, not just some." To him, the worst aspect of the school was the relentless pressure to abandon traditional Anishinabe spirituality and convert to Christianity.[32]

I have often wondered why my grandfather felt so sure that the Anishinabe of Shoal Lake would be better off if they became Christians. Cora Mandamin's comment about deliverance from fear was obviously very significant to him, for it proved that some aboriginal people did find Christianity a welcome alternative to certain aspects of traditional spirituality, such as fear of bad medicine or of spirits that could cause harm. It was a very significant comment to my grandmother also, for she used it on more than one occasion thirty years later in missionary slide-show scripts she wrote and circulated widely among members of the United Church. In these she portrayed aboriginal religion as based on fear, not love, whereas the opposite was true of Christianity. Aboriginal people, she wrote, felt themselves surrounded by evil spirits and lived in complete subjection to the "conjurors" and medicine men, who held the power of life and death over them.[33]

My grandparents evidently considered aboriginal religion to be the result of superstition, fear, and ignorance, and hoped that it would be completely abandoned and replaced with Christianity. Indeed to most Euro-Canadians, aboriginal spirituality had no redeeming value or moral worth and was only a hindrance to successful adaptation to Euro-Canadian society – those who attempted to help aboriginal people abandon their old ways and convert to Christianity were doing valuable, necessary, even heroic work. I believe these were attitudes that underlay my grandfather's involvement with Cecilia Jeffrey.

These have been common themes since the seventeenth century, when John Eliot believed that aboriginal people worshipped the devil and were controlled by the powwows. They have been used for centuries to justify Christian attempts to convert pagan Indians, sometimes forcibly. In the Boundary Waters region, William Mason, the first white missionary stationed in the area, wrote that "the conjurors hold all the others in servile subjection; were it not for this circumstance many who are even desirous would long ere this have embraced the religion of a crucified Jesus."[34]

Such oversimplifications distorted aboriginal beliefs and ignored much of Native religious practice that was life-affirming, visionary, and focussed on respect, balance, harmony, and connectedness with all creation. The many "conjurors" who worked only for the good of their communities went unrecognized. However, it was also true that, in some areas, corrupt Mide priests did generate an undercurrent of fear among the Anishinabe, exercising a considerable degree of power over band members through sorcery, intimidation, and ostracism, though I do not know how widespread this corruption was. Like many missionaries and other members of the churches at the time, my grandparents may have believed that Christianity would liberate the Anishinabe from this apparent tyranny (disregarding the instances of corruption and abuses of power in Christianity). Yet, as graduate student Michael Angel comments in his thesis on the missionary–Ojibwa encounter at Rainy Lake, despite their different methods such Mide priests and the missionaries, in exercising their power over the Anishinabe, were more alike than either group would have cared to admit.[35] The missionaries apparently did not recognize that their own spiritual power was as double-edged as that of the Mide priests they criticized – or that, in "civilizing" small children from a different culture and alienating them from their parents and communities, they themselves were far more destructive in the end.

My grandfather's legacy is one I struggle to come to terms with. He was a good man by the standards of his culture and time. He did not shirk what he believed to be his responsibility toward aboriginal people or his concern for their welfare, and he had a very real interest in and appreciation of aboriginal people as people. But all of us are prisoners of our own time and its limited understanding, and he was evidently ignorant of the positive teachings of aboriginal spirituality. In a society in which cross-cultural education did not exist, his conviction of the superiority of Christianity facilitated his involvement in a school system that was designed not just to educate aboriginal children but to root out their own culture and replace it with that of Euro-Canadians, an agenda that would adversely affect the lives of several generations of aboriginal people.

PART III

REVERBERATIONS

CHAPTER
21

Revisiting the Past

Hampton, New Hampshire, is a testament to just how much can change in three hundred and fifty years. Little remains of the Puritan town where my ancestor John Wheeler lived, and where his daughter and her husband, Aquila Chase, got into trouble for picking peas on a Sunday. Most of the oldest houses are gone; the grassy town green where Aquila Chase is honoured as one of the town's founders is an out-of-the-way anomaly, a quiet oasis in a resort town full of gas stations and fast-food outlets. Down the road a couple of miles, in Salisbury, I find the place where John Wheeler's house once stood, somewhere under the parking lot of a Dunkin' Donuts.

Now, every summer, crowds flock to the long strip of sandy beach along the New Hampshire coast. On a Sunday afternoon, the chrome fixtures of an endless ribbon of slowly moving cars glint in the sun along the coastal highway; the aroma of french fries and gasoline mingles with the salty, seaweed tang of sea air. Music blares. Scantily clad and deeply tanned young men and women on roller blades ogle each other outside The Puritan, a beach hotel. One stretch of sand has been turned into an amusement park, complete with Ferris wheel. Huge souped-up motorcycles line the street. Pedestrians are everywhere, ducking into candy stores and tourist shops, stepping over puddles of spilled ice cream. It is one big midway, one giant party. The only incongruity is the number of people,

411

most of them older and wearing more clothes, standing at the railing on the sea wall and staring silently out to sea, momentarily caught by a vision of the infinite.

Even less remains to remind one of the original owners of the land here – the Pawtuckets. When I visited New Hampshire, I did find a Native American gift shop along an inland highway that sold arts and crafts – turquoise jewellery, arrowheads, moccasins, and so on – most of it made elsewhere by other tribes. The owner of the shop told me that there is a population of Native Americans in the area, but that many have come from other states. I picked up a copy of *The Spike*, a Native-American newspaper, and checked out the listings of local powwows. Aboriginal people are here, as they always have been, but they are largely invisible to non–Native Americans.

I visited New England twice on summer-time car trips in search of my ancestors. Even before we crossed the border into the United States, I found myself contemplating the land itself – how beautiful the eastern woodlands are and how much this land where I have lived virtually all my life is home to me. I know now that my family has been on this continent for thirteen generations, going on fourteen if I count my children, a mere scratch on the surface of time compared with the history of aboriginal people here. How deep the bond with this land must have been before so many people were pushed off their ancestral territories; how deep it must still be for many today who still live where countless generations lived and died. What struck me as we sped along the highway was that the land is the grounding for all my stories, the repository of so much history, yet how little the land itself reveals; most of the history I have written of leaves no physical trace. Looking at beautiful Lake Champlain, driving down the narrow ribbon of North and South Hero Islands and through the mountains of Vermont, I saw no trace of all the misery that had been experienced there, of the Abenaki families who were pushed farther and farther into the mountains or were forced to flee their ancestral land, of the mixed European–aboriginal raiding parties that traversed this land so many times in both directions to kill and plunder, of the suffering of the war captives like Elisha Searl and Esther Jones and the Williams family of Deerfield as they trekked along beside their Abenaki captors, of the terrible naval battles on Lake Champlain during the Revolutionary War and the War of 1812 – so much blood spilled, so much anguish, so much fear and hatred.

While it is not in its pristine state, the land today is still green and beautiful, a joyful repudiation of all that human cruelty.

New England must be the only place in the world where "colonial" is not
a dirty word. You see the word everywhere, unself-consciously affixed to
every kind of business venture, along with names like Abenaki Country
Club, Uncas Bottled Gas Co., Passaconaway fire station, Pequot Properties
Real Estate. While the story of the Mayflower Pilgrims finding freedom in
America is a founding myth of the nation – even in a tiny museum on South
Hero Island there is a fragment of undistinguished rock said to be a piece of
Plymouth Rock – that other history of dispossession, war, and subjection of
the indigenous population is largely unacknowledged, relegated to a prehis-
toric past no longer of any consequence, it seems, in the public mind.

Yet the remaining aboriginal people of eastern North America have survived and tenaciously clung to their own sense of history – indeed, memory
has been the key to their survival. Among the Abenakis of Vermont, for
example, families passed down the stories of dispossession and a fierce
determination to see the land returned. Nearly every generation appealed
to the courts for justice, even as their numbers dwindled – a 1980 U.S.
Census reported an Indian population of a mere 983 in Vermont, with
another 1,297 in New Hampshire. In the 1970s, the Abenakis finally began
to make political gains and formed a tribal council, the St. Francis–Sokoki
Band of the Abenaki nation, and an Abenaki Self-Help Association. But so
much depends on the vagaries of electoral politics or individual judges:
although on Thanksgiving Day, 1976, Vermont Gov. Thomas Salmon
issued an executive order recognizing the Abenakis as a tribe, that vitally
important recognition was rescinded a few months later when a new governor was elected. In 1989, a court ruling that had upheld Abenaki title and
rights to part of their ancestral land in northwest Vermont was overturned
by the State Supreme Court on the grounds that the "weight of history" had
extinguished their aboriginal title. A decade later, the Abenakis are still
doggedly fighting court battles to gain federal recognition.

Nevertheless, everywhere I went while researching this book, I encountered this slow but absolutely determined process of renewal among the
Native nations I visited.[1]

The First Congregational Church of Roxbury, where Thomas Weld thun-
dered against sin and tolerance and where John Eliot ministered while he
tried to convert the Massachusetts, was derelict when I passed through in

1996, though apparently due for restoration. This beacon of the New Jerusalem sat forlornly on a unkempt lot in an area of Boston that was rumoured to be dangerous for white people; the many vacant storefronts on the streets in the surrounding neighbourhood spoke of hard times and poverty. The Society for the Propagation of the Gospel in New England, for which Weld had helped to raise funds, and which had supported Eliot's proselytizing, had long since deserted America for fresh prospects in Canada; two years after my trip to Roxbury, I would interview a Mohawk historian in his office in the Mohawk Institute, a former residential school in Brantford, Ontario, that had been run for more than a hundred years by the New England Company. Would John Eliot turn over in his grave if he knew that former students of that school have now launched a class-action suit against the Canadian government and the Anglican Church for the physical and emotional harm they suffered at the school?

As for the Native people to whom Eliot had first ministered, while there are undoubtedly descendants of the seventeenth-century Massachusetts alive today, the last Massachusett speaker died at the end of the nineteenth century, and the nation no longer has a distinct tribal identity. Similarly, the Nipmucks and Pennacooks were also largely dispersed. The Congregation-alists themselves are still around; some of the Canadian ones joined the Methodists and Presbyterians to form the United Church of Canada in 1925, the church of many of my paternal relatives.

As I conducted my research I was struck by this phenomenon of groups or families reappearing in various guises, in various places, through the centuries. Sometimes these reappearances were just coincidental, like Gersholm Bulkley, the doctor who tended Hannah Janes in northern Massachusetts after she was scalped in 1704. He had known and even stayed at the home of Thomas Stanton in southeastern Connecticut a quarter-century earlier, and his son James later ministered to my Harris and Ransom relatives in Colchester, Connecticut. At other times the web of action and interaction, of act and consequence, is far larger, deeper, and more long-lasting than we often realize; events in faraway places or long ago can influence our lives today in surprising ways. For example, I real-ized with sadness that the French and English in Canada are still using aboriginal people in their struggles with each other, just as they did in the seventeenth and eighteenth centuries.

History has a way of looping round and doubling back on itself through the bizarre twists and turns of human choice. We can't escape it, but it's never fixed; every generation makes it new. There's always a new convolution that changes or reaffirms the meaning of what went before. This was especially evident on my first research trip to Connecticut. One night, as my husband and I drove along a dark and deserted rural highway, we saw a huge complex of lighted buildings glowing in the distance. It seemed to float in the air like a fairy-tale castle. And incredible it was, for it was Foxwoods Casino, the largest gambling mecca in the world, now edging towards thirteen thousand employees and rumoured to be drawing in more than a billion dollars a year – and owned and run by the descendants of those Pequots my ancestors had tried to exterminate. I find it the greatest irony – and perhaps the most fitting justice – that the Pequots are now the most powerful, rich, and publicly visible aboriginal nation in New England today. Clearly, total genocide is a lot harder than one might think: a few survive in spite of everything one does to them; toughened, they struggle and defiantly resist. Not only have they successfully resisted genocide, they have rejuvenated their nation, and they have done it on their own.

Theirs is a story of incredible spirit and perseverance, for in the 1960s, government officials counted a mere twenty-one Pequots in all of Connecticut, and the Mashantucket Pequot reservation where my ancestor Thomas Stanton visited and accepted tribute from Robin Cassacinamon had dwindled to a mere two hundred acres occupied by two elderly sisters. After their deaths, the state was poised to turn the reservation into a park, but Richard A. "Skip" Hayward, the grandson of one of these women, began to stubbornly re-organize the Pequots and, as more Pequots returned to the reserve, became their chief. Living in trailers, because they were not even allowed to build houses on their own reservation, members of the tribe doggedly pursued the restoration of their rights. The federal government finally recognized the tribe officially in 1983, by which time it boasted about a hundred members, and the Pequots received a U.S. grant to recover lost land. Sadly, only the Western or Mashantucket Pequots gained this recognition; the Pawcatuck Pequots, who live near Stonington and for whom Thomas Stanton first selected a reservation, still have some of their land, but are not yet federally recognized as a tribe.

The incredible turnaround in the Mashantucket Pequots' fortunes came when they secured a multi-million loan from foreign investors (no one in America would lend them the money) to open a large bingo hall. Foxwoods opened in February 1992 and has been open twenty-four hours a day ever since. It is now the most profitable casino in the Western Hemisphere, attracting more than twenty thousand gamblers a day; a million dollars a day passes through the slot machines alone. The complex features 5,500 slot machines, four casinos, Tai Gow Poker, roulette, a high-stakes bingo hall, a Wampum Club nightclub, several hotels, restaurants, movie theatres, shopping malls, and virtual adventures. Linda Ronstadt was playing there the night we visited. The place was full of glitter and swank, including cigarette sellers in tiny miniskirts with coloured feathers in their hair Hollywood Indian-style; there was monumental Native-American art everywhere. People I talked to in southeastern Connecticut, many of whom were ambivalent about gambling, conceded that Foxwoods was "first class" and "a clean operation," known for its progressive hiring of women and minorities.

As the Pequots pay the state of Connecticut 25 per cent of the slot-machine take, pumping more than $100 million a year into state coffers, the now six-hundred-member tribe has once again become a major political and economic force in Connecticut, a development that has caused resentment among some of the Puritans' descendants. At the Indian and Colonial Research Center in Mystic, I saw a political cartoon from a newspaper showing a farmer in a pickup truck driving by a huge sign that read "Welcome to Connecticut!! A Subsidiary of Foxwoods Casino." Another cartoon showed a tour guide at the Smithsonian Institution commenting on a statue of a businessman in a three-piece pinstriped suit, holding a briefcase in one hand and a cell phone in the other: "Here we have the Pequot Indian in Full Battledress."[2] As the Pequots have learned, money is power in modern America. Skip Hayward and the Tribal Council have poured more than $1 million into political lobbying for various Native-American causes and campaign contributions and had lunch with Bill Clinton; the tribe pledged $10 million to the Smithsonian Institution for the new Museum of the American Indian, the Smithsonian's largest donation ever. The Pequots also make substantial donations to many local charities and public organizations in Connecticut.

Profits from the casino have been used to buy back tribal land, create more jobs, and improve the reservation's infrastructure. Things are so good that now people are proudly returning to the reservation, rather than downplaying or even hiding their ancestry, as was often the case in the past. For many of the families returning to Mashantucket, their new affluence is a decided change from their previous circumstances. Now they live comfortably, and in some cases luxuriously, they work in gleaming new offices, use a $17-million community centre, and receive free medical care, post-secondary education, and many social programs.

But the Pequot renaissance is not just about money – it's also about history and how it's understood. In the summer of 1998, I visited the newly opened and brilliantly realized $100-million Mashantucket Pequot Museum and Research Center, which researches, documents, and brings vividly to life the history of the Pequots, providing museum visitors with a rare public opportunity to see American history from a Native American point of view. There, wandering through the meticulously detailed reconstruction of a Pequot village, and watching a film that graphically portrayed the horror of the massacre at Mystic, I was able to imagine more clearly what Thomas Stanton might have seen and experienced and how he in turn might have been perceived.

Even before the completion of this facility, the increased public presence and political clout of the Pequots had resulted in challenges to the accepted settler view of their shared history. In Mystic, Connecticut, where the massacre of the Pequots took place, the Pequots demanded that a statue honouring Capt. John Mason, who led the slaughter, be removed, while local white residents vehemently resisted. For the first time in many, many years, Americans and Native Americans publicly debated the meaning of that history together. A committee that was struck to deal with the dispute spent a year embroiled in heated arguments about racism and revisionism, and finally agreed to move the offending statue to Windsor, Connecticut, where Mason was an early settler.[3] I wonder if the same fate awaits the statue of my relation Hannah Dustin, who still stands proudly on her forgotten island in New Hampshire, clutching her bloody Abenaki scalps?

While the Pequots have revived their nation and insisted upon a reassessment of their history, some aspects of traditional culture are lost forever. The translation of the Bible by Rev. Abraham Pierson and Thomas Stanton is one of the few surviving sources of information about the now-extinct Mohegan-Pequot language.

The Pequots have also helped their ancient rivals, the Mohegans, who had joined the English in almost wiping out the Pequots four hundred years earlier, to gain federal recognition, which they achieved in 1994. Despite their support for the English, the Mohegans subsequently suffered a fate similar to that of the Pequots: their lands and numbers dwindled to the point that, by 1910, there were only about twenty-six Mohegans in

Connecticut according to the census, and only a small fraction of their original land base remained in Mohegan hands, for much of it had been sold by non-Native tribal overseers, and the remaining reservation was broken up into individual lots. Diseases and destitution were the main reasons for their decreasing population; from 1649, they suffered at least seven smallpox epidemics, as well as outbreaks of influenza, diphtheria, and measles, and then in the 1700s many Mohegans left Connecticut to re-establish themselves on Oneida land in New York. But as with the Abenakis, a handful of dedicated Mohegans maintained Mohegan traditions, and when the Mohegans finally won tribal recognition they also gained the right to pursue their own economic development. They now have a membership of about 1,200, of whom roughly 600 live in Connecticut. In 1996 the Mohegan Sun Casino opened; it was then the third-largest casino facility in the United States and, with huge expansion in the works, may soon rival Foxwoods, its neighbour ten miles down the road. You can now drive all the way from Boston or New York to the Mohegan Sun without ever hitting a red light.

Naturally, casino fever has hit many of the area's Native nations. The Narragansetts of Rhode Island, who merged with the Niantics in 1680 and now number 2,400, and the Wampanoags of Massachusetts (whose leader Metacom started King Philip's War) also hope to build casinos, but have so far been stymied in their efforts. The Narragansetts were unilaterally deprived of their tribal status in 1880 and 3,200 acres of their reservation was taken, leaving them with just two acres, until 2,500 were returned in 1978 after a lengthy lawsuit. In the 1990s, a gaming agreement was signed with Gov. Bruce Sundlun, but the agreement's legality was successfully challenged the next year by the new governor, who has refused to negotiate a new one. The ruling, which denied the tribe its right to pursue economic development on its lands, is now being appealed. A councilman for the Narragansetts described this state of affairs as "the typical baloney we go through whenever we try to do anything."[4]

The new Mashantucket Pequot museum will give Native American history a new prominence and legitimacy, but when I visited Connecticut in 1996, I came across the Tantaquidgeon Indian Museum, the oldest Native-run museum in the United States. This small museum in Mohegan, in the area of Uncas's former stronghold of Fort Shantok, has played a key role in keeping Mohegan identity and history alive. The curator, Gladys Tantaquidgeon, a venerated Mohegan elder and medicine woman who was ninety-six when I visited her in 1996, showed me treasured Mohegan baskets and an eighteenth-century ceremonial beaded Mohegan belt, and recounted to me the story of the friendship between Uncas and my ancestor Samuel Rogers, which is part of Mohegan oral tradition. She also directed me to her niece, the current tribal historian, who had just published a book of Mohegan history and tradition called *The Lasting of the Mohegans*, an ironic echo and counter to James Fenimore Cooper's *The Last of the Mohicans*, with its main character Uncas and its myth of the dying race.

That day I was struck forcefully by the contrast in the material remains of aboriginal people and white North Americans, for I had spent the morning with another keeper of history, John Whit Davis, a "cousin" of mine, as genealogy buffs refer to people to whom they are distantly related. Another direct descendant of Thomas Stanton, he owns Thomas Stanton's third house in Pawcatuck, Connecticut, built sometime in the 1670s and before Stanton's death in 1677. I believe this is the house Thomas Stanton was living in during King Philip's War – the very house where Stanton hosted the Niantic sachem Ninigret and countless others, including Dr. Gersholm Bulkley, surgeon for the Connecticut forces, who many years later would tend poor scalped Hannah Janes. This house has been in the Stanton and related Davis families ever since, and is still in its original condition. As Davis told me ruefully, his family never threw anything out. I saw the "Christian" front door, with its bronze knocker and butterfly hinges, the original three-foot shingles on the ends of the house, the kitchen fireplace fifty-seven inches high and more than seven feet long, and many architectural details that reflected Stanton's prosperity and social standing. I sat at Thomas Stanton's table, examined the paddle owned by Garner, an Indian who worked on the farm in the late 1700s or early 1800s, and saw the grave of Cuff, the African slave, in the family burial ground. The land was also rich with history, for countless Native American artifacts have been discovered on the farm, many during an excavation in 1931. For me, to be able to step into my ancestor's house and hear the family stories, to walk where he walked and look out windows he looked out of, was an incredible experience. I will always carry an image of that house in my mind as part of "where I came from."[5]

Remarkably, the positive relationship between Thomas Stanton and Native Americans, especially the Mohegans, has been remembered and renewed at various times over many generations. Davis's father and grandfather were interested in Native culture and maintained an ongoing connection with local Native Americans. During the archeological excavation in the 1930s, Davis's father did not allow human remains to be removed from the site, and, years later, Whit Davis arranged for a traditional reburial by the Mohegans of a child's skeleton found on his land. Even more remarkable, nine members of the Mohegan tribal council attended the Stanton family reunion in 1995; they showed their respect for Stanton by leaving tobacco at his grave, and participated with other visiting Native Americans in a mini-powwow on the Stanton farm, organized for the occasion by the Connecticut River Powwow Society. "I just thought it'd be nice if the remnants of the Stantons and the remnants of the [tribes] could get together one more time," said Davis. When I told him that I too have been involved with Native people, he slapped me on the shoulder and exclaimed, "That's the Stanton in you, kid!" Is it? I'll never know, but I was surprised by the kinship I felt with this man.

On my second visit to New England I made a pilgrimage to Rhode Island, to the memorial erected to commemorate the Great Swamp Fight in King Philip's War, where, on a bitterly cold day in December 1675, three hundred to one thousand Narragansett men, women, and children non-combatants were surprised and killed by the English and their allies. Many of my ancestors and relations – members of the Wheeler, Stanton, Harris, Chase, Denison, and Ranney families – participated in that slaughter, and I wanted to see where it had happened and how it was remembered. For that battle had been a pivotal moment when the English lust for Narragansett land and the English need to ensure their security after a summer and fall of humiliating and terrifying defeats collided with the Narragansetts' refusal to become English allies and their determination to pursue an independent (and apparently neutral) agenda in the war. I think of that day as a black hole of the spirit.

The site was almost impossible to find, despite its historical significance. It was literally no longer on the map, though I was fairly certain it had been mentioned in a guidebook I'd read a few years earlier. After various enquiries I found a very small sign that indicated the turn-off from the highway and followed a dirt road until it petered out into a circular dead end. An unmarked path then led off into the thick woods, but whether or not it led to the memorial, and whether or not the memorial still existed I didn't know. I walked uncertainly and alone along this desolate path for a considerable distance, and after about fifteen minutes was just about to shrug my shoulders and turn back when I spotted the top of a stone obelisk above the trees. As I drew closer, I was overwhelmed by the heavy scent of a flowering bush that grew profusely around the obelisk and the four boulders that surrounded it in a small clearing. Funereal was the only word to describe its effect, there in the stillness and silence of that place. I peered closer to read the inscription on the monument and saw that it had been defaced almost completely. But it was clear that it had been a paean to English victory, and the stones around it commemorated the four colonies that shared the glory: Connecticut, Rhode Island, Massachusetts, and Plymouth. Nothing there commemorated the fallen Narragansetts or even the Native American allies of the English. I stood for some time before the monument, until at last persistent flying insects forced me away. I walked back to the twentieth century with a heavy heart, turning back only once to leave as an offering a branch of heady white-flowered pepperbrush along the trail. Like so much of the unpleasant side of our history, the memorial lies abandoned and forgotten, tucked away out of sight and mind, though the repercussions of that history are with us still.

Later I talked to Lucille Dawson, the Narragansetts' tribal historian, about the site, which is now owned by the state of Rhode Island. She told me that the memorial is not on the actual site of the battle, because the stones had to be hauled in by oxcart and could not have made it into the actual swamp. The Narragansetts gather at the memorial once a year to commemorate their dead, but at present they have no plans to publicize their historic sites or open them to the public, as they have frequently been vandalized in the past, and the Narragansetts do not have the resources to protect them.

Dawson and I were linked by more than our connection to the Great Swamp Fight, as it turned out. She too was interested in the Stanton family, but for different reasons. Stanton had been her maiden name, but she was no blood relation, at least not in the usual sense: according to her family's oral history, she is descended from one of the Indian slaves of General Joseph Stanton.

In Canada, the interactions between my family and aboriginal people have been far more recent. Visiting the First Nations with which Elijah Harris or my grandfather had been involved was an intense experience, for their history with missionaries and residential schools is still felt on a raw, visceral level, and I, in turn, felt more accountable, more fearful of rejection, and more defensive about my family's role. What struck me forcefully was how differently the various First Nations communities I visited –

the Munsee-Delaware Nation and the Chippewas of the Thames on the
Caradoc reserve, the Chippewas of Sarnia, the Six Nations near Brantford,
and the Shoal Lake #40 and Iskatewizaagegan First Nations at Shoal Lake
– had reacted to the missionaries and their Christian message and how
widely their present circumstances varied.

At the Caradoc reserve just south of London, Ontario, where Elijah
Harris had been missionary to the Munsees and the Chippewas, I had
expected no one would remember the early missionaries of the 1820s,
but, in fact, their actions were very pertinent to Jody Kechego, land-
claims researcher, and to Chief Kelly Riley of the Chippewas of the
Thames First Nation, for they had several land claims under way that were
based on events of that period. In fact, one smaller land claim, recently
settled in the band's favour after a twenty-year legal case and a century of
dispute, was to the farm of John Carey, Elijah Harris's colleague and the
first schoolteacher at the Methodist mission; the band proved that his farm
had been illegally patented (that is, severed from the reserve) in 1831.
Although the Chippewas (or the Munsees, depending on who you talk to)
had allowed Carey to use the land, it was never their intention to surrender the land.[6]

Today, on or near the site of Carey's house and the original building used
as a Methodist school and church, sits the Nimkee Nupigawagan ("the thun-
derbird's necklace") Healing Centre, an aboriginal treatment centre for drug
and solvent abuse, its clients children aged five to twelve from across
Canada. Two domed sweat lodges sheathed in plastic sit outside the building, near where Elijah Harris and others once ministered to effect the spiritual and psychological transformation of the Munsees and the Chippewas
through Christianity. The treatment centre uses traditional aboriginal spiritual and healing practices to restore Native children's psychological health
and pride in their own heritage – among those who have come here for help
are the children from Davis Inlet, Labrador, who tried to commit suicide as
a group by inhaling gasoline. It's a sobering place for a descendant of missionaries. Prospective employees of the centre may be Christians, I was
told, but they must feel comfortable with traditional spiritual practices.

These days, few members of the Caradoc reserve actively follow any
religion. Only a handful attend the sole surviving church on the reserve
– an Anglican one dating back to a later Anglican mission among the
Munsees. Christianity never really caught on here. Traditional Ojibwa spiritual practices have also been largely forgotten; although some traditions,

such as the sweat lodge, are being re-introduced, they are only slowly gaining acceptance.

The site of the Mount Elgin Industrial School, operated first by the Methodists and then by the United Church, which the Ojibwa–Welsh preacher Peter Jones helped to establish, is a place most members of the reserve avoid. Mount Elgin operated for almost one hundred years as a residential school, housing children from all over Ontario, while children from the Munsees and the Chippewas of the Thames were often sent to distant schools in Brantford and Sault Ste Marie to discourage them from running away. Closed in 1946, it was refurbished by the Department of Indian Affairs in 1957 and run with an "equally punitive system of discipline"[7] as a local school, with resident students and Euro-Canadian teachers; the current chief, Kelly Riley, was among those who attended. Finally in 1991 it was condemned by the Chippewas, and soon after an unknown arsonist destroyed the main building. It lies abandoned and ruined, overgrown with thick, matted grass, a place haunted by the misery of generations of lonely children.

People on the reserve hold the school responsible for the devastation of their culture and language; a recent survey showed there were no fluent Ojibwa speakers on the reserve.[8] Chief Riley tells me Ojibwa language classes will soon be offered at a new band-run school, Wiiji Nimbawiyaang, ("Together We Are Standing") in a newly completed building in an attractive complex that houses the nation's office, library, and health and social services for the thousand-member First Nation. The Chippewas of the Thames are also working on a large land claim to much of southwestern Ontario, which, if settled in their favour, would radically transform their economic prospects.

The Caradoc reserve, with its valuable and rich arable land, is already one of the more prosperous reserves in Canada but, as I drove back to London after my visit, I felt surprisingly sombre; it hurt to see these very able men devoting themselves to rebuilding their nation. They were doing it with wonderful spirit and energy, but it hurt that they had to do it at all.

Today the Chippewas of Sarnia are an aboriginal enclave in the poorer south end of the southwestern Ontario city of Sarnia, their three-thousand-acre reserve an oasis of green in a stinking chemical valley. Although surrounded by chemical plants and oil refineries, split in two by the main highway, and carved up by a network of secondary roads, two-thirds of the reserve is still undeveloped and people still hunt deer there. Health is a major issue, because of the unknown effects of living so close to industrial plants. The reserve has had to be evacuated on one occasion because of the risk of a major explosion, and there have been other scares, such as the time a large storage tank was struck by lightning. The reserve is much smaller today than it was in Elijah Harris's time; the cash-strapped band sold land to industry, but never acted on various plans to sell the entire reserve and relocate the community. The site of the reserve's first church is now home to Dow Chemical; the old cemetery is dwarfed and completely surrounded by industrial plants. Many of the Chippewas of Sarnia now work in the petrochemical industry, or in construction or steelwork, either in Sarnia or across the river in the United States.

Compared to many northern First Nations, the Chippewas of Sarnia live in material comfort. Although housing is still in short supply, the homes in the new subdivision built by band members are large and attractive. There's a new health centre and a new senior-citizens complex designed by a committee of seniors. The reserve has its own industrial park, but its focus is on non-polluting small industries: Chippewa Industrial Development oversees the development of the park and ensures that band members put up the buildings and are offered employment. The establishment of the industrial park and a comprehensive community plan developed in 1982–83 marked a real turning point for the First Nation, according to Janice Rising, the co-ordinator of social services for Chippewas of Sarnia. "It's only in the last twenty or thirty years that people have gained some sense of control over their lives," she said. Although the Chippewas of Sarnia must still contend with the social and health problems endemic to most reserves, not to mention the challenges of serving a population in which 66 per cent are under the age of twenty-five, I came away with the impression that things are going relatively well.

St. Clair United Church, which celebrated its 150th anniversary in 1982 and traces its roots back to the Methodist mission that Elijah Harris and Thomas Turner initiated, sits right next door to the Chippewas of Sarnia band office; the current chief is the president of the board of the church, and other people I met at the band office were also active Christians. On the walls inside the church are old photographs of Thomas Turner, the first missionary, and of James Evans. There's another old photograph showing a St. Clair Indian Methodist camp meeting with Thomas Hurlburt and Allen Salt, the Ojibwa minister who served at St. Clair in 1854 and from

1868 to 1872 and who wrote, "The Gospel has been the means of good to my people."

According to a long-time non-Native minister at the church who retired a few years ago, there has been a strong tradition of Native evangelizing at St. Clair United, not only with Allen Salt,[9] who served at Muncey, St. Clair, and Parry Island and also tried (without success) to proselytize the Ojibwa in the Rainy Lake–Lake of the Woods district in the 1850s, but more recently with Native evangelists such as Alex Bird, who died in 1985. The church still holds summer-time camp meetings, and every Sunday church members still sing the old Ojibwa hymns translated by Peter Jones and James Evans – perhaps even the same ones that Elijah Harris sang on his first visit to the region. The current minister, Aleace Davidson, the daughter of a Tyindinaga Mohawk mother and white father, told me that she had always wanted to be a missionary. This was a comment that intrigued me, given the very mixed legacy of the Native missions. Elaborating on this desire, she wrote, "But to think that there were areas for missionary work within Canada had never occurred to me. To be a missionary to my own people seemed ironic for it was from my native mother that I learned the great depth of spirituality. Then I realized my understanding of mission has always been that missionary work is not a mission of conversion – it is a mission of unity and mutual spiritual growth, respect, and love for one another."

The Chippewas of Sarnia First Nation is the only aboriginal community I visited during my research in Canada that was still strongly connected to its missionary history; most band members there still have ties to Christian churches. (The other First Nation I visited that still has a large Christian population is the Six Nations reserve, although a large minority follow traditional Iroquois spirituality.) While only about thirty-five people regularly attend St. Clair United Church, most claim the United Church as their home church, and this church has long played a central role in the community. According to Nicholas Plain, the author of *History of Chippewas of Sarnia and the History of the Sarnia Reserve* (himself a Methodist preacher, former elected chief, and son of the last hereditary chief), "religion was the real life of the tribe, permeating their activities and institutions."[10]

Yet so successful were the missionaries that the Chippewas of Sarnia have lost most of their traditional culture, including the language, and, of the various First Nations I visited, they seemed to have the least interest in their own history. What they have retained are their aboriginal values and identity. As Nicholas Plain wrote, "When the Chippewas embraced Christianity as their religion, they did not cast off their moral laws but added the Christian principles to their principles of community living."[11] Gradually some aspects of traditional culture are being revived: traditional dancing was re-introduced about thirty or forty years ago, and the community hosts an annual powwow. Ojibwa is taught in the daycare, at local elementary and secondary schools, and in adult evening classes, and a more comprehensive community language program is under development. In the church Sunday School, a new Native-themed church resource, "The Dancing Sun" is used to teach traditional stories and crafts. The new health clinic has a room for traditional healing – but the room still sits empty and unused, because there has been no money to develop a traditional healing practice. At the New Year's Feast, held at the dawning of the year 2000, the Chippewas of Sarnia announced that the band would reclaim its old name and henceforth be officially known as Aamjiwnaang.

Not surprisingly, a contentious issue is the resurgence of traditional spiritual practices. Reverend Davidson spent two years at the United Church's Francis Sandy Centre for Aboriginal Ministry before coming to Sarnia in 1996; there she gained an appreciation for the traditional spiritual teachings and practices of aboriginal people. She has tried to incorporate some elements of traditional spirituality into her ministry and is convinced that much can be synthesized with Christianity: "There is a need for us to explore beyond the literal teachings of Christianity to the spiritual, and there we will find our native heritage," she wrote to me, and added diplomatically, "Many are willing to take this journey, while others remain firm in the teachings of the first missionaries." In fact, some members of the congregation have left St. Clair United, and gone elsewhere for Christian services that do not incorporate Native teachings.

The United Church has responded to the unique situation and expressed needs of Native congregations and church members by establishing an All-Native Circle Conference, a new conference of aboriginal congregations and ministers, where Davidson says, "native people find their voice as members of the wider church." Davidson is active in the ANCC, although St. Clair United is not at present a member of the new conference. Members of the St. Clair congregation are still learning of its existence and purpose, Davidson says; the church remains at present within the London Conference of the United Church.

As in other Ojibwa communities, there are also members of the Chippewas of Sarnia who follow traditional spiritual practices associated with the Midewewin, who are not interested in a synthesis of Christian and aboriginal traditions. They seek to regain and follow the teachings of their ancestors. The differences between the different religious groups at St. Clair were highlighted when the band was faced with the question of how nineteenth-century aboriginal human remains that were dug up during construction of the Bluewater Bridge should be reburied – according to Christian or traditional customs?

According to Reverend Davidson, "the key to the resurgence of traditional spiritual teachings is the first teaching: 'to live in respect.' The community put this teaching into practice when faced with the reinterment." After much discussion and joint planning, a group of traditional men and the minister were able to "respectfully return the ancestors to mother earth," and a subsequent survey of the community supported this joint approach and laid the groundwork for future ceremonies should more ancestors be returned for burial.

Clearly, it is not easy to overcome the divisions that are one aspect of the legacy of European involvement in aboriginal communities. "Being native, being white, being Christian, and respecting traditions is a part of the history of our nation," Davidson writes. "We seek to change attitudes that foster division and denial of who we really are. To respect ourselves is to accept ourselves completely, then we can walk together in the spirit the Creator intended."

At the end of my visit to Sarnia, Janice Rising takes me down to the shore of the St. Clair River to see if we can find an old marker commemorating the site of the Methodist mission. We find it between storm sewage–holding tanks, the railroad tracks, and Dow Chemical. It is a simple stone put up by the United Church in 1932, with an inscription honouring Thomas Turner and James Evans, the first two missionaries at the St. Clair Mission. In front of the marker is a low evergreen bush, and fastened to the bush is something fluttering in the breeze. As I move closer, I am startled to see that it is a dream catcher – a small webbed hoop with a hole in the centre, which, according to some Native traditions is supposed to catch good dreams and let bad dreams slip out through the middle, protecting the sleeper. It seems a perfect metaphor for the aboriginal Christians I have met here and their attitude to the missionaries: neither accepting nor rejecting all of that experience, but keeping and valuing the best and letting go of and trying to protect themselves from the worst.

Shoal Lake, just west of Kenora, Ontario, at the Manitoba border, is another world away from Sarnia or Caradoc. Although the two First Nations communities at Shoal Lake are also Ojibwa, or Anishinabe, as they call themselves, life in these more remote and inaccessible territories is vastly different from that of the reserves in southwestern Ontario. My first trip there was fraught with anxiety, because it was my own grandfather I was now researching, just another one of the missionaries in the eyes of the people there, though no one I met remembered him by name. I wouldn't have had the nerve to go there at all without the help and encouragement of a number of aboriginal friends. Al Hunter, an Anishinabe writer I worked with on the "Beyond Survival" conference, who is from the Manitou Rapids area, southeast of Lake of the Woods, arranged a place for me to stay with friends of his, an aboriginal family who live on a beautiful lake just east of Kenora. I boarded the plane with much trepidation, not only because Winnipeg, my destination, was threatened by the Red River flood and no one knew what would happen when it crested in a day or two, but also because one of the reserves, Shoal Lake #40, was almost totally inaccessible. The ice was just beginning to break up on the bay that separates it from the road. The chief had told me that I was coming at the worst possible time of year and that it would be very difficult to cross the bay, that I might not be able to, that a vehicle had gone through the ice just the week before.

I landed safely in Winnipeg and drove east for two hours in a rented car. Al showed up at our meeting place driving a car with the licence plate "Aneen" – "hello" in Ojibwa. He took me to the supermarket, where we bought food – a traditional gift – to give to my hosts, Mary Alice Smith and Joe Morrison. Al was my advisor on Ojibwa protocol: he had already told me to write to the chiefs of the two reserves – Iskatewizaagegan #39 First Nation (formerly Shoal Lake #39) and Shoal Lake #40 – explaining my mission, to follow up with phone calls, and to bring lots of tobacco and gifts to show my respect for the people I talked to. We drove to the other side of Kenora and arrived at Mary Alice and Joe's house, set on the shore amid the spectacular scenery of Longbow Lake. As we talked on the deck, while Joe barbecued our dinner, Al sighted two eagles, a very good omen in Ojibwa terms. There were also cormorants, loons, and beaver within view, and a few days later I saw three deer on the front lawn. It was early spring, and the clear air was something this Torontonian was not used to, a reminder of the land as it used to be.

The Shoal Lake school that my grandfather was involved with was just on the trailing edge of memory among the people at Shoal Lake, and disappearing fast. On my first visit, I did not locate anybody still alive who had attended it, though I later made contact with Walter Redsky, who had attended the school in the 1920s, during my grandfather's time there, though he did not remember my grandfather. Because of the state of the ice, I was unable to visit the site of the school, but I was told that the foundations are still there, as well as some bricks and odds and ends of debris. It was either torn down or burned down, depending on whom I talked to. The Presbyterian Church still owns the site, but the Shoal Lake Anishinabe want it back.

It was clear to me as I visited people at Shoal Lake that they did not want to be interfered with, and were wary of white strangers – particularly white writers – asking questions. I learned quickly that although I was treated politely, there were many things I would not be told and that I would have to earn people's trust. Even aside from the obvious historical reasons for this caution, Anishinabe culture has a secretive aspect: an Ojibwa friend married to a Métis woman told me that there were some cultural things he would never tell his wife, even though she was aboriginal. His wife commented that it would take more than one lifetime to really understand Ojibwa culture. Although the people I talked with speak English and live in the same country that I do, I was always conscious of being a guest in a cultural environment vastly different from my own. The effort to transcend these differences and communicate clearly was often exhausting. Yet many people helped me in my search to understand more about my grandfather and his time at Cecilia Jeffrey.

Everywhere I went I showed the old family photographs I had brought. It was the one thing I could offer people, a glimpse of their past, even if from a foreign perspective. The chief of Iskatewizaagegan #39 First Nation asked me for a copy of a photograph of my father's family standing in front of the abandoned school at Shoal Lake in 1939 – it was one of the few photos he'd seen of it. I showed photos of a young Cora Mandamin, who had lived with my father's family in Winnipeg while she attended nursing school and on a couple of other occasions, to several of her relatives, including her surviving sister; there Cora sat at my grandfather's table during Christmas dinner in 1947. In return, one of her nieces and a number of women in the Band Office at #39 moved an entire wallful of stacked plastic water bottles (the reserve had recently suffered an outbreak of cryptosporidiosis and had to use bottled water) so that I could see their collection of old photographs mounted on the wall behind. I saw pictures of many of the people mentioned in my grandfather's memoirs, and Cora's picture in the fur coat that one of her nieces remembered with awe and which I later discovered had been a hand-me-down from my great-grandmother.

One incident involving the photographs was particularly significant to me. The man who had ferried me across Indian Bay to Shoal Lake #40 had been particularly kind to me, and I offered him his choice of photograph in gratitude. He looked at them all, then pointed to one that was rather dim and out-of-focus, but showed the interior of some kind of building. It had been labelled by my grandmother as a "council house" and dated 1922. When I said he could have it, I saw that he was deeply moved, to the point of tears. Then he told me it was actually the interior of a round house for dances and ceremonies – my grandmother may have been deliberately misled about its function – and he had never before seen what the inside of one had looked like from the time before they disappeared.

For in the decades following the time of my grandparents' photographs, aboriginal spirituality apparently suffered a precipitous decline. Already, by 1930, the number of initiations into the Midewewin at Shoal Lake had fallen off sharply. According to the late Shoal Lake medicine man James Redsky, as recorded by Selwyn Dewdney, this was because few could afford even "first-degree curing" and the high cost of apprenticeship ($10,000 for apprentice James Redsky) meant that detailed knowledge of the rituals was being passed on to fewer and fewer people.[12] This only worsened during the Depression when a deep poverty "ate its way into Ojibwa communities" and most apprentices could not afford thorough training and dropped out. This explanation for declining membership in the Midewewin has been questioned by one of James Redsky's nephews, former chief and elder Walter Redsky, who emphasized that Mide priests were not paid a fixed amount but customarily given offerings, which were not necessarily monetary. Nevertheless, it appears that for a while visionary shamanism, which cost nothing, began to become more popular and, according to James Redsky, bad medicine – and the secrecy and suspicion it engendered – also became more prevalent at Shoal Lake.[13]

Meanwhile, a Presbyterian church had been built at Shoal Lake and that mission was reinforced by a steady flow of former students of Cecilia

Jeffrey who had lost much of their language fluency and culture and had acquired varying degrees of Christian beliefs; both school and mission undermined the power and influence of the Midewewin. But, as Selwyn Dewdney recorded, the new religion could not restore the sinking morale of the people of Shoal Lake; drinking and violence became more widespread, and many Anishinabe suffered a loss of identity.[14] In 1972, James Redsky was described as the last of the Mide masters in the Lake of the Woods area, and Dewdney reported that the "corrupting influence of zealous missionaries . . . caused its demise, and few Ojibwa groups now practice this ritual."[15] James Redsky, who was both a Presbyterian elder and a medicine man, could find no one to whom he could pass on his medicine knowledge. He sold eight sacred birch-bark scrolls, which recorded Midewewin songs, ceremonies, and Ojibwa history, and had been handed down for generations, to Calgary's Glenbow Foundation to ensure that they would not be lost altogether.[16] Today, the loss of these scrolls to the community is deeply felt, and efforts have been made to have them returned.

The Midewewin declined for many years, but like the predictions of the extinction of the race, its anticipated demise didn't occur; Midewewin traditions have proven far stronger than most outsiders anticipated. As my host Mary Alice reminded me, the Anishinabe are fiercely independent in this area, and most have always resisted Christianity, unlike the Cree farther north, many of whom converted. Even when missionaries thought they had successfully made conversions, many Anishinabe who embraced Christianity did so within the context of an Ojibwa world view, while today an increasing number of people either continue to observe the tenets of the Midewewin or have returned to its practices.[17] For example, Walter Redsky was at one time a Presbyterian elder, but eventually left the church and joined the Midewewin; he regards the students' acceptance of Christianity at Cecilia Jeffrey as largely superficial: "The [Christian] teachings went in one ear and out the other. They didn't accept Christianity. . . . It was useless. It didn't accomplish anything. . . . Even when your grandfather was here, this Mide society, it kept on going! It was as if your grandfather was working for nothing, people didn't accept it."

Today, Anishinabe spirituality and culture are enjoying somewhat of a resurgence, particularly among the older generations at Shoal Lake. There are now new round houses for ceremonies and dances, like the one in my grandmother's photograph, and no less than three active Midewewin societies. Medicine people from Shoal Lake travel to many different aboriginal communities to participate in ceremonies and share their knowledge. Clearly, the Midewewin was, and is, much more than the tyranny of evil shamans that so many missionaries believed it to be. But much has also been lost. According to Walter Redsky, "There are no more [fully qualified] Mide priests, all the old guys are gone and there is nobody following. The only priest that's living is in Ponemah near Red Lake, Minnesota." Also, according to Redsky, most young people are not seeking out the cultural knowledge of the elders at Shoal Lake: "I have a friend here, across the bay. [She says] 'everyday I sit by my window hoping for some young person to come, and ask me to share what knowledge I have – medicines, songs – I'm willing to share, but I don't see anybody come.' Our Anishinabe young people, they don't search, nobody searches for that culture."

One of the main reasons for this disruption in culture is not hard to see. Walter Redsky, in a written version of his own teachings, has noted of aboriginal young people, "the more they are in school, the more they seem to be un-educated and illiterate by Indian standards. They know very little about our history, our religion, and our way of life. . . . Many of them end up as suicides, drunks or just roaming the streets in juvenile gangs."

While at Shoal Lake and in nearby Kenora, I talked with several people of different ages who attended the replacement for the Shoal Lake school that was built at Round Lake. In fact, one interview was conducted in the main building of the second Cecilia Jeffrey Indian Residential School, which is now used as the main office for the Grand Council of Treaty #3 First Nations. There I talked with Albert Mandamin, one of Cora Mandamin's nephews, who is about my age, about his experiences there. The anguish in his voice was so palpable that I believed him utterly when he told me that he still bore the scars, as do so many others, and that the effects of that trauma will not be healed for generations. He was so angry that he could barely look at me and struggled to remain polite as he described how he had been hungry all the time and had had to steal turnips and potatoes from the root cellar. "Those 'Christians'" – he spat out the word – "taught us to lie, cheat, and steal." He told me about the thick strap the missionaries used "when we spoke our language," about the boy who lost several toes to frostbite when he tried to escape in the winter. It sounded like prison, or a concentration camp. "What I don't understand is, how did those people get away with what they did?" he asked me. I winced, thinking of course of my grandfather, for, although he had been involved at the earlier school, at a different time, and had not been a teacher or principal, he had still been part of that system. "The only way for the Anishinabe to heal is to go back to our own traditional ways, our own religion," Mandamin told me. To him, Christianity was a form of brainwashing that wiped out the past – or, worse still, a part of his soul.

Albert Mandamin's words reverberated through me for days. They had not conveyed the detailed history I had sought to document, though they were the product of that history – they exuded present pain. They wrenched me from any emotional detachment I might have pretended to and reminded me forcibly that what I am really concerned with is the present, and my own relationship with aboriginal people. I hope he's right, that a revival and re-integration of the old ways will help heal the wounds so many aboriginal people bear. But it is a monumental task to repair the damage, to restore health to entire communities that have been traumatized repeatedly over several generations.

Ada Morrison, the mother of my host Joe Morrison, began attending Cecilia Jeffrey in 1929, the first year the Round Lake school opened. Although not from Shoal Lake herself, Mrs. Morrison knew many of the same people my grandparents had known, for some of the staff and most of the children who had been at Shoal Lake transferred to the new school. This elderly woman, who is now in her late seventies and the same age as my own father, described being put on a boat at the age of six, as was her four-year-old brother, and taken hours away to the new school. "We were all afraid, we had never seen a big building like that," she recalled. Even though she did not understand a word of English, she and the other children were forbidden to speak Ojibwa and the staff used the strap on those who were caught disobeying. She too learned to steal food to keep hunger at bay, and to adopt other surreptitious strategies to survive. But unlike some of the other former students I talked to, Ada remembered a number of positive experiences at the school, including one teacher who had been particularly sensitive to the needs of her culture-shocked students. She was thankful that she had learned to read, write, cook, and play music there.

The original agreement with the Shoal Lake parents not to convert the children without their parents' permission was obviously long forgotten by 1929. Although she is a Christian to this day, and thankful that she learned about the Bible and Christianity at the school, Mrs. Morrison had no idea what was happening the day she was accepted into the church. "When we were baptized, we didn't even know what baptized meant. I thought we were lining up because we were going outside to play and [the teacher]

said, 'Whoever wants to be baptized, get in line against the wall.' We all
ran and stood in line and then we were all taken to the chapel. . . . I didn't
know what was going on, other kids too, they didn't know. The minister
was baptizing us with water! and I said, 'It's cold!' in Indian. We tried to
stop it, but they couldn't understand what we were saying. That's how I
became baptized!"

   Mrs. Morrison also described how, when she first arrived at the school,
a staff member told them what their "Christian" names were, and then gave
them name tags to wear. "There was a lady there who must have been a
supervisor, and she told us what our names were, and then you put your
name tags on." When Mrs. Morrison told me that the staff at the school later
arbitrarily changed her name to Ada, I stiffened, for Ada was my grandmother's name and otherwise uncommon. Joe's mother did not know where
this name had come from, but I consider it a real possibility that this elderly
aboriginal woman was named after my grandmother, Ada Freeman, by staff
members who had known her. There in stark simplicity was my relationship
to colonialism, there in the attempt to blot out the aboriginal identity of a
small child, to rename and remake her in the image of my grandmother!

   While visiting Kenora, I also met Emma Paishk, the first former student
to write publicly about her experiences at Cecilia Jeffrey at Round Lake,
and the first to challenge the Presbyterian Church to deal with this aspect
of its history. When she was seven years old, a Cecilia Jeffrey staff member
hit her so hard for playing with a light switch in the bathroom that her
hearing and sense of balance were permanently damaged. This incident,
she said in a ground-breaking article, was mild compared to the stories of
many other children. Paishk described the psychological effects of attending Cecilia Jeffrey and called on the church to negotiate a financial settlement for those who had been abused at the school:

> I was abducted from my safe, familiar environment and plunged into a
> stark, cruel existence that was as foreign to me as the language. I began
> to regress into a very quiet little girl, terrified of the new world around
> me, using gestures and facial expressions to communicate with others
> because I was not allowed to use my God-given language. . . . I withdrew,
> living in fear of making a mistake. I lived in a silent world of hurt, rejec-
> tion, and most of all loneliness, which was so indescribable that at times,
> it still brings tears to my eyes to remember. . . . I often experienced the
> lashes of those studded hard brown leather straps when I was caught

speaking my own language or making an attempt to run away. I lived in such fear of those people that ran the school, that my throat was always constricted with unshed tears. All the crying in the world did not help me so I began to suppress my emotions. I became the shell of a once beautiful creation of God.[18]

Clearly, it was not only physical and sexual abuse at residential schools that was so devastating – though that was obviously tremendously damaging to the individuals concerned – but the everyday wearing down of the spirit, when children were told that everything their parents had taught them was wrong. Or, as I read somewhere, "you were told you shouldn't be an Indian but you knew you'd always be one."

The Anishinabe learned various things in the residential schools, my host Mary Alice remarked to me one day, but perhaps the most important was the spirit of resistance. Some learned that lesson well: the little property on the Kenora waterfront – now known as Anicinabe Park – which was bought to appease the Shoal Lake parents so they would send their children to the new school at Round Lake, was the site of an armed occupation by the Ojibwa Warrior Society in 1974. It was the first armed confrontation, the first large radical action, of the modern Red Power movement in Canada.

In 1994, largely in response to the efforts of Iskatewizaagegan #39 First Nation, the Presbyterian Church of Canada made a confession "Regarding Injustice Suffered by Canada's First Nation Peoples" at its 120th General Assembly. The Confession acknowledged the role of the Church in cooperating with the government policy of assimilation, and in encouraging the government to ban important spiritual practices. It recognized the cultural arrogance of the Church in trying to turn aboriginal people into Euro-Canadians and acknowledged that, in its two residential schools, Cecilia Jeffrey and Birtle (at Birtle, Manitoba), the Presbyterian Church had used disciplinary practices foreign to aboriginal peoples and open to "exploitation in physical and psychological punishment beyond any Christian maxim of care and discipline." The Church further admitted that sexual abuse also took place in its schools, that the effect of all these abuses was a loss of cultural identity and a secure sense of self, and that many students' lives had been deeply scarred by the effects of the mission and the ministry of the Church. The Church then committed itself to seeking opportunities to "walk with aboriginal people to find healing and wholeness together as God's people."[19]

Phil Fontaine, then head of the Manitoba chiefs and later Grand Chief
of the Assembly of First Nations (1997-2000), accepted the Confession,
but reminded all present that it was only a first step toward healing, that the
Church was not absolved of responsibility for what had happened. In fact,
in 1998, the courts began to settle the question of legal responsibility for
abuses at the residential schools when the Supreme Court ruled that the
Canadian government and the United Church shared legal liability for
abuses at another residential school at Port Alberni, British Columbia.
This ruling, which is now being appealed, opens the door for other suits
for damages. There are so many potential lawsuits from former students
across the country that the churches fear bankruptcy, and there is now talk
of negotiating a blanket settlement for abused former students.

One night I was alone at Longbow Lake as my hosts had gone to a wedding
in Fort Frances. While perusing Joe and Mary Alice's books, I came across
a centennial history of Kenora, which in its account of the town made virtually no mention of the history of aboriginal people in the area, including
instead what was purported to be Ojibwa "mythology." Even that was
grotesquely, horribly wrong: the Ojibwa creator was called a Windigo, a
terrible insult, for even I know a windigo is a cannibalistic monster. The
book was twenty years old, but the attitudes are still so prevalent: History
begins when the white people got here, history is what the white people
did. Aboriginal people are the people we have never bothered to know.

That night I was overwhelmed by the enormity of it all, what my ancestors and others had been part of. For the first time I acknowledged the
shame I felt, the burning weight of it. It was hard to admit that even my
grandfather had contributed to this process. I had been trying to differ-
entiate his actions and attitudes from those of the "real" colonizers, but it
was clear that, from an aboriginal perspective, he was still one of them.
Whatever his private qualms, his actions had supported the system that
oppressed them. And mine?

Almost a year after my first trip to Shoal Lake, I sat with the chief, two
councillors, and an advisor from Iskatewizaagegan #39 First Nation around
a table in a meeting room at the Indian Affairs building on St. Clair Avenue
in Toronto. Fraser Greene, the chief of Iskatewizaagegan #39, had invited
me to join them in their attempt to have the Round Lake site of the Cecilia
Jeffrey school, to which Indian Affairs has title, officially recognized as
Anishinabe land jointly owned by all the First Nations of Treaty #3. Only

a month before, the new federal Minister of Indian Affairs, Jane Stewart, had formally apologized for the residential school system's treatment of aboriginal people, set up a healing fund, and called for "a new relationship" between the government and the First Nations, and between aboriginal people and the citizens of Canada. Her actions had given the Shoal Lake First Nations hope that a breakthrough could be made with regard to ownership of the site, after a decade of stonewalling.

Chief Greene spoke first:

CJ Round Lake simply *is* and always will be "Indian land." By the nature of its creation; by the nature of its use; by the experiences suffered there; by virtue of, – as one elder has put it – the children's tears that soak the soil; by the fact that the bodies of our children and our families are buried there; by its history as one of the sites of the concerted, willful attack of the colonial church and state, this is, and always will be Anishinaabe land. . . . CJ Round Lake is a site made sacred by the lives of our children. There is no way that we could allow this place to be put to any purpose than one directed by the Anishinaabe . . . CJ Round Lake is a part of Anishinaabe heritage.[20]

He said that they will use the land for the benefit of the First Nations, to heal and move forward, to celebrate their survival and renewal and to honour the memory of those who did not survive. Acquiring title to the Round Lake site is one of several initiatives that the Shoal Lake First Nations are pursuing in their efforts to heal from the residential-school experience. They are also negotiating to acquire title to two other pieces of land, one of which is the site of the original Cecilia Jeffrey school at Shoal Lake, and they are requesting that the Presbyterian Church and the federal government set up a healing-trust fund to finance counselling and other activities.

I had been invited by the First Nations to make a supporting statement as a descendant of one of the people involved in the administration of Cecilia Jeffrey. I had hoped to make a statement on behalf of my family, but I did not have time to consult everyone fully, and some of my relatives vehemently disagreed with what I was trying to do. So in the end I spoke as an individual, acknowledging that my grandfather was party to the decision to move the school away from Shoal Lake, apparently against the wishes of the communities. I said that, although he believed he was acting in the best interests of the Anishinabe, others should never again presume to know what is best for the First Nations. And I stated that the site of Cecilia Jeffrey belongs to the aboriginal people of the Treaty #3 First Nations because it was bought for their supposed benefit.

The meeting ended hopefully but, in true bureaucratic style, was not conclusive. After the meeting, the chief and the other members of the Shoal Lake group, several of whom I had met for only the first time, hugged me and thanked me for my contribution. We went out for lunch afterwards and I commented to Fraser Greene that I never dreamed that my research trip to Shoal Lake would lead to such a meeting. He smiled and spoke appreciatively of my effort to help. I was honoured by his thanks, but a part of me was also sad, for I thought of my grandfather and all the good he had tried to do and all the good that the other missionaries had tried to do, and how so much of it did not turn out as they hoped and is viewed so differently now. And I knew with hindsight my own good intentions might prove equally problematic.

Afterwards I was struck by various ironies: it was because of my grandparents and their interest in and involvement with aboriginal people that I was not utterly indifferent to Native people myself. It was because of them that I have been open to learning about aboriginal ways. It was because of them that I grew up with a sense that one could actively resist injustice and had spent a decade working in solidarity with aboriginal people, however imperfectly I have done so. This has been true for other members of my extended family, too: several members of my family descended from my paternal grandparents have worked with or interacted with aboriginal people in a variety of capacities, as doctors or ministers or community development workers on reserves, or as community workers of various kinds in urban areas with large aboriginal populations. My uncle helped to design a bilingual Cree–Ojibwa typewriter and was instrumental in closing down the Norway House residential school in Manitoba; a cousin made a film about Cree syllabics; and there have been two adoptions of aboriginal children into my family. And yet, some of these well-intentioned efforts, as well as some of my own, have had ambiguous, unfortunate, or even tragic results. I turned these contradictions, these twists and turns, over in my mind. My investigation of the past had led me now into the contentious territory of the present.

CHAPTER
2 2

Judgment Day

History is not the past but a map of the past drawn from a particular point of view to be useful to the modern traveller.
  – Henry Glassie, *Passing the Time in Ballymenone:*
      Culture and History of an Ulster Community

Men cannot become fully human or whole without coming to terms with their relation to the suffering of others.
  – Joseph Amato II, *Guilt and Gratitude*

When I began this book, I knew nothing of my family's history with aboriginal people. I thought that the land had already been acquired from the indigenous people of this continent long before my ancestors arrived on the scene (which I erroneously believed to be sometime in the nineteenth century) and that they had merely accepted a fait accompli. I imagined the taking of the land as something that happened over a short period of time hundreds of years ago. I had no idea what an ongoing process Native dispossession has been, or how deeply my family or I might be implicated. Over the years, as I conducted my research, I gradually traced my family's involvement in that process almost generation by generation, from the arrival of the Puritans in New England, right to my own doorstep.

Sometimes my ancestors acquired land through conquest, especially after the Pequot War, King Philip's War, and the defeat of New France, but more often this dispossession was gradual and far more subtle. In some cases, the taking of the land was legitimized by the concepts of the indigenous people as "heathen" and "savage" and by the doctrine of *terra nullius*, or *vacuum domicilium* – "the belief that the discovery of empty, uninhabited barren land gave the discovering nation immediate sovereignty and all rights and title to it . . . a concept that was extended by European lawyers and philosophers to include lands not in possession of 'civilized' people or not put to proper 'civilized use.'" Ordinary European settlers like my ancestor John Wheeler then felt free to disregard aboriginal title and settle on lands claimed by European governments without the consent of aboriginal people. Religion was used to justify the taking of the land; biblical precedents such as Psalm 2:8: "Ask of me, and I shall give thee the heathen for thine inheritance, and the uttermost parts of the earth for thy possession" buttressed the conviction of my Puritan ancestors that God intended them to take over the land and establish a new Christian community.[1]

It was not only the Puritans who justified taking land through *vacuum domicilium*. Even when governments attempted (often half-heartedly) to protect Native lands in the nineteenth century – in what is now southern Ontario, for example – thousands of individual settlers invaded aboriginal hunting territories and simply squatted on the land, then had their occupation of the land legally recognized after the fact by governments that served their interests.[2]

Vacuum domicilium was only one way that my ancestors and others acquired Native lands. In other cases, Native rights were recognized, but only as English colonists attempted to extinguish them; for example, colonists in New England often acquired land deeds retroactively from Native Americans so they could protect land they had squatted on against other English claimants. In most cases, aboriginal people gave up legal title to the land on the understanding that they would retain the rights that were more critical to them, the rights to hunt and fish or use other resources from the land. But these usufructuary rights were not recognized and honoured after the legal deeds were drawn up, or they were honoured for only a short time, or the land was transformed in such a way that the exercise of these rights was no longer possible. Thus, as historian Peter Leavenworth has commented, "The [promised] continuation of usufruct rights was . . . a critical condition of Indian dispossession."[3]

Sometimes my ancestors were directly involved in taking the land; at other times – such as when my Ranney and Janes ancestors moved to Vermont – they simply followed the tide of history and accepted what had been done, without questioning its justice or validity. The economic and social structures of their society fostered imperialistic processes that guided and even overwhelmed individual choices, just as still happens today. They also reflected basic values that most individuals shared, although I have come across the equivalent of "righteous Gentiles," such as Roger Williams, who denounced the Puritan appropriation of Indian land. I could easily attribute ignorance to my ancestors or say that they were simply sharing the attitudes of the day, but it took me longer to acknowledge the self-interest in their blindness, that they stood to profit if they did not recognize the full humanity of aboriginal people, just as we do today. Tragically, the alienation of Native lands and resources was a more permanent and invasive change – thus more damaging to Native people – than perhaps any other consequence of the European invasion of America.[4]

There are many parallels in the ongoing dispossession of the indigenous peoples of Canada and the United States, but over time the treatment of Native people by the society of my direct ancestors in Canada diverged from that of my relatives who remained in the United States, particularly over the course of the nineteenth century. Although large-scale removals were contemplated in Canada, they never took place on the same scale of those in the United States, where, except for a few tiny enclaves (mainly in New England), the Native nations east of the Mississippi River such as the Cherokees, Choctaws, Creeks, and Seminoles, were deported to the West.

Physical violence against Native people was far more common in the United States, from the bloody Indian wars involving the U.S. Cavalry in the western territories to openly condoned murders by settlers who coveted their land, as in California, where Indians were killed for sport. The fact that the Colonial Office in England retained ultimate responsibility for Indian affairs in Canada until 1860 provided some check on the rapaciousness of settlers, whose local governments might otherwise have proved as deadly to aboriginal people as those south of the border. Many Native people living in Canada today are the descendants of peoples who were forced to flee their traditional tribal territories in the United States.

Lastly, although Canadian authorities attempted to break up reserves through the Gradual Civilization Act of 1857 and other tactics, the government of the United States was far more successful at doing so through "allotment," where collectively owned reservation lands were broken up into individually owned farms. These then often ended up in white hands because of the economic circumstances of the Native owners. As a result of allotment, many tribes were declared extinct; today, numerous groups, such as the Pawcatuck Pequots, are still struggling to regain federal recognition of their existence.

While I don't fully understand the reasons for these differences in our histories, I do recognize that, paradoxically, the end result has been much the same in both countries. The Cherokees and the Mississaugas of New Credit both ended up dispossessed of their land, even though they both adapted creatively to the presence of the settlers and became "civilized," as the colonists said they wanted Native people to become. I also recognize that in both countries, some Native nations – such as the Mohegans, Narragansetts, and Six Nations at Grand River, lost considerable amounts of land because of poor judgment or corruption on the part of some of their leaders.

As I gained a deeper understanding of my ancestors' sense of entitlement to aboriginal land, it has become clearer to me that this process is far from over; the basic pattern of behaviour toward Native people has not changed fundamentally, even as we sign new land-claims agreements. Think of the recent violence and public outrage directed against Mi'kmaq lobster fishers in New Brunswick when the Supreme Court of Canada recognized that rights to hunt, fish, and gather, retained by aboriginal people in a 1760 treaty, were still valid. Or of the situation of the Innu of northern Quebec and Labrador, who have spent a decade fighting the assumption that NATO military aircraft can repeatedly fly at low altitudes over Innu land, no matter what the effect on the Innu or on the wildlife they depend on, and who are also threatened by hydro-electric development and nickel mining that will permanently damage their land and their ability to live off its resources. Or of the James Bay Agreement, signed only twenty years ago, the terms of which we have already violated.[5] Or the Native communities in the United States whose land, water, and food resources are being contaminated by uranium mining over which they have no control. Or of Dudley George, who died trying to assert the Stoney Point First Nation's right to an ancient burial ground that had been appropriated and incorporated into an Ontario provincial park. Even my own house in Toronto sits on land that was supposedly ceded by the Mississaugas in 1787, but their intention was not to "surrender" it, only to share it; today the Mississaugas of New Credit – the descendants of Peter Jones's people, who by 1820 were deprived of all but two hundred acres of land – have put a new claim before the Indian Claims Commission for compensation.[6] It is in my lifetime that these things are happening, and yet they are part of such a long process.

Many of the attitudes that justified the dispossession of aboriginal people are still readily observable. Recently, a man wrote the following in a letter to the editor of the *Toronto Star*:

North America was settled by the process of taking land that was there for the taking. Many of the natives of that time were nomadic, which hardly gives them claim of ownership to land. Even the argument that natives were here first is being disputed by archeological findings. It is interesting to contemplate what North America would be like had not the non-natives come here. We owe nothing to the natives unless they can demonstrate a willingness and ability to earn it. Seldom is that the case.[7]

Even the modern Canadian doctrine of "aboriginal" title holds that aboriginal people possess but do not "own" their lands, although they now have the legal right in Canada to demand compensation if they are dispossessed of them by the government ("historically, because they were neither Christian nor 'civilized,' they were not regarded as a nation capable of exerting sovereign ownership").[8] It is still the case that aboriginal rights are most often recognized when we wish to extinguish them: the First Nations are only sovereign enough to give their sovereignty away.

Historically, many Native people fought against the loss of their land and the erosion of their sovereignty. A number of my ancestors were involved in these wars, especially in King Philip's War and then in the conflicts that flared between the competing European-derived polities in northeastern North America – first New England and New France, then the United States and Canada. Some Native nations tried to play off Europeans against each other, hoping that, by backing the French, they could retrieve land taken by the English, or by backing the English against the Americans that they could regain the Ohio Valley. This scenario was replayed over and over, in the four intercolonial wars, the American Revolutionary War, and the War of 1812. For some indigenous peoples, such as the Abenakis, their lands were the battlegrounds in wars not of their making, though they became embroiled in them as allies, with devastating results both for them and for some of my ancestors, such as Hannah Janes. The differing Canadian and American relations with Native people have contributed to the shaping of relations between the two nations: for example, before the War of 1812, American resentment of the British grew when they discovered that Indians fighting westward expansion in the United States had British muskets and ammunition.

Canadians tend to pride themselves on the fact that, for the most part, our ancestors made peaceful, negotiated land deals with the indigenous peoples, rather than conquering them, as happened numerous times in the United States. Because in the eighteenth and nineteenth centuries the British needed aboriginal allies to hold their territory in North America against first the French and then the Americans, members of my ancestors' culture signed treaties with various First Nations, and ended by finding themselves legally and morally obligated to "people they no longer wanted to deal with."[9] The First Nations who signed these agreements were generally not beaten and defeated, nor did they simply give their territories away, although initially, some, like the Mississaugas, appear to have been involved in a process they did not fully comprehend.

Later treaties were signed by First Nations in the Canadian West who, like the Boundary Waters Ojibwa, had numeric superiority in the area and literally stood in the way of the national dream. They had a very good sense of where the future was leading and what they needed in order to survive as a people within the new environment. They insisted on treaty clauses that secured the resources, opportunities, and tools to enable them to participate fully in the new nation. Their concept of sharing resources is clearly expressed in the speeches of the chiefs and headmen who represented the people of the First Nations, including the people of Shoal Lake, who signed Treaty #3 in northwestern Ontario.[10]

But in both Canada and the United States, many of the treaties and agreements our ancestors made with the First Nations – from huge treaties concerning thousands of acres of land to the agreement between the missionaries and the Ojibwa parents of Shoal Lake – were not honoured. The reason, I believe, is because of our historic disregard for the First Nations as peoples, cultures, and often even as individuals – and because of their lack of power to force us to comply. Although Native people protested our violation of these agreements on numerous occasions, non-Natives were in control and thought they didn't need to address aboriginal complaints or renegotiate; they believed the process of assimilation would soon ensure that the complaints died away. Our ancestors regarded the treaties as one-time business deals rather than agreements furthering an ongoing relationship between our peoples, and so they denied our nations the ability and the advantage of evolving a partnership that would be productive for both parties.

My friend Cuyler Cotton has worked for years in support of the claims of the First Nations of Treaty #3 in northwestern Ontario. He wrote to me:

> The generations that preceded us have evolved a huge falsehood. . . . We promised to protect the rights and interests of the First People in order that we might share the wealth of this part of the earth. We solemnized our promises in sacred ceremonies and written agreements. But as the colonists' numbers grew in strength, we began to ignore these promises and set about marginalizing the people to whom they were made. Over the years, we fell into a national mind set, a way of going about our business that ignored the rights and interests of the very people who first granted us the privilege of sharing the beauty and bounty of this land. Our words, now enshrined in our laws, said that we respected the Treaties but our historic actions demonstrated the lie. . . . The colonists and the successive governments presumed to themselves rights, privileges, and resources that had not been granted by the First People.[11]

While non-Natives have largely forgotten the true nature of the relationship between our peoples, the Native peoples did not. And while we may rightfully congratulate ourselves on concluding ground-breaking modern-day treaties, such as those that establish the Nisga'a territory in British Columbia and the Nunavut territory in the eastern Arctic, our agreements are still only as good as our word.

But as Native traditionalists say, the circle comes around. Today, our words have caught up with us, in the form of court judgments affirming the validity of these "impossible, static and anachronistic pieces of paper." The judges of our highest courts – who act as the conscience of the nation – have confirmed in several recent decisions that we must live up to the legal agreements made by our ancestors.[12] It is sad that Native people have had to go to the courts to force us to live up to our word, but at least we created such avenues for appeal, and the courts now appear to be more willing then they were in Metacom's time to support the rights of Native people.

We can no longer dismiss these obligations, however difficult it may be to face up to them. Fundamentally it's a question of justice. It's also a matter of honour, not just in terms of our relationship to the First Nations, but also to ourselves and the world. Speaking of the situation in Canada, Cuyler Cotton says, "All Canadians need to be clear about the true place the First People secured for themselves in the founding of this country. This is our historic Canadian truth. It is our confirmed legal truth. It is also [in the light of these recent court judgments] the new Canadian reality."[13] A similar process is under way in the United States, where court judgments confirming various powers of Native-American "domestic, dependent nations" have meant that many non-Natives find themselves "living in a new country."[14]

There is another fundamental concept that has driven the colonization of North America: "the conviction that Native people require the guidance of Europeans to live successful lives and that European intervention in aboriginal people's lives, even when forcefully applied, is ultimately in the best interests of aboriginal people." This is a concept that has motivated many of my ancestors and which is definitely still alive today – witness Canada's Indian Act, that paternalistic anachronism that still controls so much of aboriginal life. Many of my ancestors and other members of their society believed that the bestowing of their culture and religion on aboriginal people was a priceless gift, but, as American historian Brian Dippie put it, civilization has been "a gift more appreciated by the donor than the recipient."[15]

Christian missionaries from the time of John Eliot have taken the lead in seeking to transform Indians into Europeans. Their racism was high-minded and condescending – the need to save aboriginal people was based on a view of them as a childlike, primitive, and inferior race without knowledge of the true religion and with an inferior code of ethics. The missionaries' heartfelt spiritual message of peace, love, and justice was undercut by the material reality of Indian wars, the taking of ancestral lands, and the increasing restriction of aboriginal rights and freedoms, not to mention the missionaries' own inability to value the strengths and teachings of traditional indigenous cultures.[16] Their genuine efforts to find a place for aboriginal people in the new settler societies were ultimately unsuccessful because most settlers would not accept Native people on any terms, whether Christianized and civilized or not.

Most missionaries did not subscribe to the generally accepted view that aboriginal people were doomed to extinction, and were willing to resist the most destructive aspects of white society, sometimes becoming the closest thing many aboriginal people had to allies in their struggles. However, the missionaries also shared the government's view that assimilation was the only future for aboriginal people. Gradually they assumed the role of paternalistic guardians of aboriginal people and the missions became almost extensions of the Indian Department, thus bolstering the legitimacy of European expansion.[17]

As I saw in the case of my grandfather, the relationship between the missionaries and the government's Indian policy became even more intertwined with the establishment of a system of residential schools, which Canada copied from the United States. The Indian residential schools became isolated "total institutions," designed to re-socialize aboriginal children along European lines. The Canadian and American governments were explicitly committed to eradicating aboriginal culture – one of the aims of residential schooling was to "kill the Indian in the child."[18]

Although many Native leaders initially supported residential schooling, the government never provided adequate funding to run the schools properly. Native communities withdrew their support when they became aware of the thinly veiled "missionary" agenda, mismanagement, chronic underfunding, the provision of inferior educational and health services, and the mistreatment, neglect, and abuse of many children.[19] In the first decade of the twentieth century, the number of student deaths at Canadian Indian residential schools was so high that Duncan Campbell Scott himself commented that "fifty percent of the children who passed through these schools did not live to benefit from the education they received therein," and Toronto social reformer and lawyer Samuel H. Blake warned "that because the department had done nothing to obviate the preventable causes of death, [it] brings itself within unpleasant nearness to the charge of manslaughter."[20]

In both Canada and the United States, many situations of neglect and abuse were known to government departments and the churches throughout the history of the school system, yet very few spoke out against them or attempted to reform the system. When Native parents tried to withdraw their children, the Canadian and American governments legislated compulsory attendance and legal penalties to ensure compliance. The result was the "neglect, abuse and death of incalculable numbers of children, and immeasurable damage to aboriginal communities."[21] Although many teachers were motivated by religious conviction, self-sacrifice, and concern for the future of aboriginal children, many aboriginal people experienced the residential schools as coercive institutions that treated them with profound cruelty. To many aboriginal children, the education they received was "training for self-destruction."[22]

Today it is generally recognized that forced assimilation – the destruction of the specific characteristics of a group – is cultural genocide. Canadians and Americans understand more clearly today than in my grandfather's day that culture is not something that can be stripped off and changed like a suit of clothes, that a person's identity, feelings of self-worth, and sense of meaning are rooted in one's culture, and that forced deculturation can cause profound psychological harm, including the loss of meaning in one's life and the will to live. Some would say cultural genocide is just genocide, that if you destroy a people's culture, you destroy the people as well – the current rate of suicide in many aboriginal communities suggests there is definitely something to this argument.

Of course, cultures, including aboriginal cultures, change all the time; this was certainly evident during the several hundred years of the fur trade in the West. And one shouldn't underestimate the power of a new idea – such as Christianity was for Native people – to stimulate profound change. But contrary to the wholesale replacement of aboriginal culture and religion envisioned by the missionaries, individuals adapting to new circumstances or ideas in a healthy way are generally able to choose what new ways they will accept and not accept. They have the opportunity to integrate new beliefs and behaviours with old ways of acting and thinking in a manner consistent with their own world view.

"Genocide" is a loaded word, I know, and one which many people think of only in terms of the deliberate mass murder of the Jews by Adolf Hitler's Nazis. In fact, the word has as yet no generally accepted definition. Raphael Lemkin, the man who originally coined it and prepared the original draft of the United Nations Genocide Convention for the UN Secretariat, intended the word to be used broadly. He defined genocide as "the destruction of a human group, as such, whether wholly or in part, and by whatever means." While some have termed cultural destruction (as opposed to physical destruction) "ethnocide" and have seen it as entirely

distinct from and far less serious than genocide, Lemkin saw genocide as
having three distinct but often interactive modes: physical genocide
(killing or depriving a group of the means of life), biological genocide (preventing reproduction), and cultural genocide (the "destruction of specific
characteristics of the group, forced transfer of children, forced and systematic exile of individuals representing the culture of the group; the prohibition of the use of the national language, or religious works, or the
prohibition of new publications; systematic destruction of historical or
religious monuments or their diversion to alien uses; destruction or disper-
sion of documents and objects of historical, artistic and religious value and
of objects used in religious worship.")[23] Aboriginal peoples in North
America have experienced many of these forms of persecution over the
past five hundred years.

The United Nations adopted the final draft of the UN Convention on
Prevention and Punishment of the Crime of Genocide in 1949, and Canada
ratified it in 1952. The United States successfully blocked the inclusion of
cultural genocide, except for the clause about the transfer of children, in
the final draft of the Convention in a deal with the Soviet Union that also
saw political groups deleted from groups protected by the Convention. The
United States gave the Convention only a very conditional ratification in
1988.[24] The current Convention defines genocide as "(a) Killing members
of the group; (b) Causing serious bodily or mental harm to members of the
group; (c) Deliberately inflicting on the group conditions of life calculated
to bring about its physical destruction in whole or in part; (d) Imposing
measures intended to prevent births within the group; (e) *Forcibly trans-
ferring children of the group to another group* [italics mine]." So blind have
Canadians been to the harmful effects of their own policies that compulsory attendance at residential schools continued for another thirty years
after the signing of the UN Genocide Convention.[25]

I can't speak for Americans, but I know that we Canadians like to consider
ourselves benevolent defenders of human rights. It is hard to admit that our
modern liberal democracy has been built upon the destruction of aboriginal
nations and cultural identity. In fact, the historian Robert Melson charac-
terizes countries such as Canada, the United States, New Zealand, and
Australia as "settler states," based upon an invading group supplanting an
indigenous population on its own land base. "Since wholesale displacement,
reduction in numbers and forced assimilation of native peoples is virtually

a requirement for the existence of any settler state, Melson suggests that they are properly construed as being inherently rather than potentially genocidal in their makeup."[26]

As Daniel Francis argues in *The Imaginary Indian: The Image of the Indian in Canadian Culture*, while Canadians tell themselves that at least they did not share the widespread American view that "the only good Indian was a dead Indian," "in practice that is exactly what they did believe." In the long run, assimilation amounted to the same thing as outright extermination – "the only good Indian was a non-Indian."[27] Rev. R. G. MacBeth expressed the softer, more polite, Canadian vision of the vanishing Indian when he wrote in 1931, "It is inevitable in the progress of human history that higher civilizations should supersede the lower – but within the context of British justice, this process would take place without injustice or hardship."[28] Today the similarities in the Native struggle for self-determination in both countries are far greater than any differences in their particular circumstances.

In Canada, the process of nation-building led to the marginalization of aboriginal communities and resulted in Confederation as a federation between two peoples, English and French, completely excluding Native people as participants.[29] Today, in maintaining paternalistic control over their lives and lands, in not settling land claims, in expecting aboriginal people to assimilate, we continue this oppressive tradition. While we trumpet human rights abroad, at home we are still in a colonial relationship.

Since visiting Shoal Lake I have realized that my research – this book – has been partly a process of mourning. If you are of European heritage, and particularly if you are, like me, the descendant of families who have been in North America for some time, the question of your relation to the history of this continent is a difficult and painful one – should you be brave enough to consider it at all. It is far easier to hear about disasters in faraway places than the disasters our loved ones have created and we perpetuate.

I have wondered a lot about what relatedness entails. I don't feel guilty in the sense of personally responsible for what happened before I was born or for what other family members have done, but I do feel connected to these events. Perhaps it is a lingering remnant of the old concept of family responsibility that, if a family member of mine kills someone, for example, I cannot simply say it is none of my business and deny my connection to that act. It's a concept of justice and of family from before the time when punishment and restitution were left to the state, and I acknowledge that it often led to blood feuds. But my family, whatever the intentions or understanding of individual members, has been involved in the oppression of aboriginal people for hundreds of years, and because of this, and because this oppression still continues – and because I continue to benefit personally from this oppression – I feel a responsibility to address the wrong that has been done.

I started out by saying that I began this project because I wanted to understand the feeling of amorphous guilt I had. Surprisingly, after finding out some of the things my ancestors did, I no longer feel this way. I have a better sense of what they actually did, and why, and understand that I am not responsible for their actions, though I have inherited their legacy. Now I can more easily catch the traces of their thinking in my own; I can more easily recognize my own instances of arrogance or disrespect. I can listen to the grievances expressed by aboriginal people with greater clarity and openness, because I know that much of what I once dismissed as hyperbole and exaggeration is actually true. Yet in conducting my research, I was surprised to discover the same sense of nebulous guilt described by the children or even grandchildren of German Nazis, "this feeling guilty for something one hadn't done oneself yet which also hadn't been done by just anybody, but one's own father" (or in my case, one's own ancestors and culture).[30]

I believe that many North Americans feel this vague guilt because our ancestors and our society have remained silent about the treatment of aboriginal people or did not tell the full truth. We know something bad happened, but most of us shy away from examining it too closely. While it is not my intention to suggest a simplistic equivalency between the Jewish Holocaust and the treatment of aboriginal people over five hundred years, I have learned from German writers who have reflected on how a culture deals with guilt. I find it interesting that in Germany, almost none of the perpetrators ever expressed feelings of guilt or shame. "For decades their parents had told them that they did not feel responsible for what had happened, but they themselves, the children of the 'innocent' often reacted altogether differently."[31] Indeed, "the memory of a whole country disappeared in a bout of amnesia and was replaced by a calamitous silence."[32] The children always wondered about the "nebulous identity of the mysterious phantoms who were really guilty"[33] and whether or not their parents were implicated, for they had no sense of the perpetrators: it was a crime that had apparently happened all by itself. In North America, I think, a similar process of denial of responsibility across the generations has been at work; I suspect that amorphous guilt arises when we participate in that conspiracy of silence, when no one takes responsibility for what has been done.

But just who is responsible for what has happened? Are colonization, land theft, and cultural obliteration the work of certain morally reprehensible individuals or a collective guilt? What I have seen in researching this book is that the colonization of North America has been the result of millions of actions, or non-actions, great and small, by thousands, even millions, of people over hundreds of years. It is not a case of a few immoral leaders committing crimes that the general populace is ignorant of or of the particular cruelty of certain individuals. Ordinary people have been part and parcel of the process, making decisions that deny another people's being or that allow a destructive process to continue. Within the norms of a culture, "decent people" can do indecent things; they are conditioned to be insensitive to another people's pain. It is easy to see this in another cultural context – the insensitivity of many white South Africans to the suffering they caused black South Africans, for example – or in the more distant past – such as the slave trade or the treatment of women in many societies – but harder to recognize in ourselves. With regard to the taking of Native land, the breaking of treaties, and cultural genocide, Canada as a whole is implicated – as is the United States. Everyone benefited except the indigenous people.[34] It was, and to a very large degree remains, a culturally sanctioned injustice.

In the case of the residential schools, hundreds, if not thousands, of people were involved – church members, school staff, government bureaucrats, police, Indian agents, social service agents, all with the support of the institutions they represented, as well as the population at large. The belief in assimilation was embedded in the dominant culture; few non-aboriginal people questioned it or anticipated the personal disintegration or social chaos that would result. While the government and the churches were the major players in residential schooling, they were collective entities. The government in particular acted in the name of the general population, and the mainstream churches also reflected the beliefs and priorities of the vast majority of the population. As Canadian historian J. R. Miller has commented, "The reality is that in a democracy it is the citizenry that ultimately has to accept the responsibility for what its government does. If people in a democracy get the government they deserve, then in the ultimate sense the Native policy that emerges is their responsibility too."[35]

———

But it's also dangerous to blame an entire people for past wrongs. Not everyone shared the general consensus about how Native people should be treated: some vehemently protested the generally accepted cruelty and injustice and were not listened to, such as John Eliot when he denounced Indian slavery, or the lawyer who wrote the letter to Duncan Campbell Scott about the price the Indian Department was offering the Rat Portage band for its land. Such critics were even sometimes in positions of power. In 1841, for example, the dangers of the government's paternalistic Native policy were articulated by Gov.-Gen. Charles Thomson, Lord Sydenham, when he spoke of "the general truth that a government undertaking to assume a parental relation to adult men and women is sure to do itself and them unmixed harm."[36] Similarly, no less a personage than Frank Oliver, the Minister of Indian Affairs in 1908, wrote to the General Synod of the Anglican Church, "I hope you will excuse me for so speaking but one of the most important commandments laid upon the human by the divine is love and respect by children for parents. It seems strange that in the name of religion a system of education should have been instituted, the foundation principle of which not only ignored but contradicted this command."[37]

In fact, over the generations quite a number of people criticized and resisted what was being done to Native people as best they could, but they were marginalized, ignored, or ridiculed; most (but not all) of them were Native people themselves, and their voices didn't count. Others may not have spoken out for fear of the consequences. Even today it is difficult to speak out: witness the attempt in the 1990s by the multinational company Daishowa (which was clear-cutting unceded traditional lands subject to a land claim by the Lubicon of Alberta) to outlaw the citizens' boycott of their forest products and to silence the organizers of Friends of the Lubicon through lawsuits claiming damages against individual protesters.

My exploration of family history has also given me a deeper sense of the complexity of moral judgments of individual players in any historical event. What has been most revealing to me has been the contour of individual ancestors' lives, and the various kinds of interactions with Native people, both positive and negative, that one person could have over the course of a lifetime. What to make of Thomas Stanton, for example, who took part in an attempted genocide but who later argued with his neighbours and the colonial authorities to secure decent land for a Pequot reservation, and who, over the course of his career, generally managed to retain the trust of both Native and non-Native leaders? Or of John Eliot, who was a cultural imperialist but also a lone voice speaking out against injustices done to the Christian Indians? Similarly, institutions also played a variety of roles in this history: while the Christian churches have played a major role in the destruction of Native cultures, among some Native groups such as the Narragansetts in Rhode Island or the Chippewas of Sarnia in Ontario, Christianity, once embraced, became a source of strength for many and helped hold fragile aboriginal communities together during difficult times.[38] Today some churches, including the United Church that my grandfather belonged to, provide substantial political and financial support for aboriginal-rights solidarity work.

In the case of my own family, there wasn't a single period of time when certain "bad" ancestors colonized aboriginal people; in fact, it was often not the worst but the best of my relatives who were involved in actions or institutions that would prove to be destructive – the ones who tried the hardest to act ethically, to honour truth as they perceived it. This was particularly true of those ancestors involved in missions or residential schools. As Terry Anderson, an ethicist and member of the United Church, wrote in the magazine *Touchstone*, "Our best efforts may contain destructive distortions or be harnessed for wrong ends. It is not easy to acknowledge that the best intent and effort of the Church proved destructive, not just its neglect and shortcomings."[39] There have of course been many other examples of good intentions leading to unforeseen results: "The residential schools were an idealistic experiment based on faulty assumptions, that went drastically, tragically wrong – like Communism," was one comment I heard and I was also reminded of the attempts by Western aid groups to build wells in India in the 1980s, which ended up pumping to the surface water that contained so much fluoride it crippled an estimated 60 million people. As one of my relatives quite rightly admonished me, "Don't think that your generation is any smarter or that you would have acted any differently!"

Of course, it was not good intentions per se that harmed Native people; it was the conviction of cultural and religious superiority that convinced the missionaries and government officials that they could and should make decisions on behalf of aboriginal people and blinded them to the human suffering they engendered. Furthermore, the benevolence of the missionaries and of Indian Department officials served an additional purpose: "the lingering guilt arising from conquest and expropriation was assuaged by the myth of duty and the delusion of paternal responsibility."[40]

From the point of view of a victim's family, a victim is still dead, the loss is still felt, whether the action that caused the death was premeditated murder or accidental manslaughter, though there may be more forgiveness of the offence and hope of reconciliation if the killing was not intended. Similarly, in the case of the Native nations, the fact that some of the harm done to them was unintentional does not change the fact that, as a society, we almost destroyed a people. Indeed, as Roland Chrisjohn, Sherri Young, and Michael Maraun, the authors of *The Circle Game: Shadows and Substance in the Indian Residential School in Canada*, point out, we taught aboriginal people to hate themselves, destroyed their livelihood, stole their children, and took their land. We have never respected what an Indian was or is. Aboriginal forms of life have never mattered to us. Indeed, we did everything we could politely do to ensure that there would be no more Indians.[41]

What is an ethical relation to this history? I like what Marguerite Duras, the French novelist and playwright, wrote in 1945 in contemplating the Holocaust: "The only possible answer to this crime is to turn it into a crime committed by everyone. To share it, just like the idea of equality and fraternity. In order to bear it, to tolerate the idea of it, we must share the crime."[42] Terry Anderson of the United Church describes a similar response: "It doesn't mean that we are now personally culpable, but that we acknowledge the wrong done and mournfully own that these perpetrators are part of our community . . . and that we take responsibility for rectifying as much as we can the harms done. We try to ascertain why 'our people' went astray, and in what ways we might still be exhibiting in different ways the same underlying problem." In Anderson's view, a "free sharing of the burdens and shame" is different from collective guilt.[43]

This is a stance that is sure to annoy many people. "The past is gone. I can't change what happened and I'm not responsible for it," is a typical reaction I've encountered. "My ancestors were also conquered by the English but I'm not crying about it four hundred years later," one man told me. In a letter to the *United Church Observer* a woman wrote: "Are we always going to be paying or apologizing for things we had no control over, or what our ancestors did forty, fifty or even a hundred years ago? We are all sorry it ever happened, but to keep digging up all these misdoings gets a bit much. It is a shame people didn't see what was going on then, and we need to know it did happen, now let's get on with our lives."[44]

Unfortunately, it's not over. Until I embarked on this book, I did not comprehend how cumulative was the effect of generation after generation of assault on aboriginal people. Native people today experience more than racism and oppression in their own lives; they carry the burden of generations of pain, generations of losses, that are passed on from parents to children, often wordlessly. The assault has not stopped; there has rarely been justice, or the freedom and opportunity to rebuild, so they have had few opportunities to heal.

This was all brought painfully close to home for me in a conversation with a friend from a First Nation in western Canada. She is often perceived, by both Native and non-Native people, as one of the "success stories" in Indian country – university-educated, successful in her career, politically active – one of those who, like Cora Mandamin in my grandfather's day, is seen as a pioneer. But the demons she has had to live with and come to terms with are horrific: as a child on her reserve in the chaotic 1950s, she witnessed the beatings of her grandparents and rapes of her mother and aunts, and a murder committed by someone who lived in the same foster home that she did. She endured years of sexual abuse by her stepfather, the breakup of her family when she went to the police and reported it, years of foster care in non-Native homes, the suicide of a family member, and deep alienation from and mistrust of her own people and culture – this extreme social disintegration the legacy of residential schools, the Indian Act, and all the other forms of oppression that have killed or traumatized so many Native people. It has taken her years of therapy, treatment programs, spiritual healing, and political action to overcome this personal history, to understand the origin of such violence and abuse, and to let go of her own inner shame at being aboriginal. For the most insidious consequence of these generations of assault has been the internalization of racist attitudes, wherein Native people themselves come to believe all that has been said about them.

Unfortunately, I know that my friend's experiences are by no means unusual; there are similar stories on most reserves in Canada and the United States. The Innu, according to recent reports, have the highest suicide rate in the world.[45] And while most non-aboriginal Canadians are all too familiar with stories of drinking and violence and suicides among aboriginal people – as Rev. Stan McKay says, "the dominant society has succeeded in turning aboriginal communities themselves into part of the problem"[46] – there does not appear to be a lot of understanding of what aboriginal people's lives are really like. Most non-Native people have no idea of the personal struggle most aboriginal people must go through simply to survive, let alone to break the cycle of abuse, violence, and despair, which, remarkably, many aboriginal people are now doing. Non-Native people often reveal a curious lack of empathy; in our society's collective mind, Native people are still non-persons. Perhaps we do not mourn the terrible waste of so many lives because mourning requires sadness and a sense of loss: "A person can only mourn something that was valuable to him and with which he has an emotional relationship."[47] It is said that Canada's reserve system was an inspiration for the architects of apartheid in South Africa, and it's often said that a form of apartheid still exists in Canada today; this is true, but it is less about reserves or separate status than an apartheid of suffering.

"History is what hurts." That's another definition of history I've come across. I wonder, how can we heal from this history? Can it ever be healed? Can we even agree on what happened?

I don't know if it is possible to move beyond what Calvin Martin refers to as "five hundred years of mutual incomprehension, of mutually unintelligible thoughtworlds," to change the plot – there is still such a stark mental border between Native and non-Native people on this continent. We might regret the past, but we can't undo it; what we are accountable for is what we do with our inheritance – this legacy of pain, cruelty, and misunderstanding.

My hope is that as Canadians and Americans – as North Americans – we will work to change our relationship with Native people, to de-colonize the colonizers as well as the colonized, just as is beginning to happen in South Africa. It's harder for us because non-Native people are now the majority on this continent. In many ways, we can just keep on acting as we always have, and it's easier to keep doing so, because to stop requires systemic change and political will, and there are no simple solutions to the problems we have created. Non-Native people still profit from the weakness and disorientation of North America's indigenous peoples. If they are weak and powerless, we can do what we want; we don't have to take them into account or compensate them for their losses. As *The Circle Game* asks, "Who wants a crowd of secure, focused, determined and knowledgeable Aboriginals looking at treaties, land claims, damage suits and the like?"[48]

In Canada, racism is institutionalized in the Indian Act. Hard as it is to accept, all of us living in Canada today are complicit in the ongoing oppression of aboriginal people, and the situation is similar in the United

States. Nobody has clean hands. As an aboriginal participant in a panel discussion replied to a person from the audience who asked how long the pan-
elists expected him to feel guilty for what his ancestors had done, "I don't
expect you to feel guilty for what your ancestors have done. However, if
things haven't changed in twenty years, then I expect you to feel guilty."[49]

Today, whenever a Native person meets a non-Native person, the
wrongs of the past take up a lot of space between them. The Canadian
Royal Commission on Aboriginal People concluded that "a great cleansing" of these wounds must take place before any reconciliation is possible.
Can we strip away the layers of pain, anger, guilt, and suspicion that separate us? My hope in writing this book is to assist in the acknowledgement
of the destruction we have wrought – not for the purposes of assigning
blame and guilt, but as a necessary foundation for trust. The basic facts –
and the terrible results – of the oppression of aboriginal people are well
documented: to deny them is akin to denying the Jewish Holocaust. Understanding why these things happened is crucial to decolonize and restruc-
ture our own thinking and behaviour, so that we do not simply find new
outlets for our colonialist impulses.[50] Native people need to understand this
history as well. As Marius Tungalik said at a public hearing for the Royal
Commission, "We need to know why we were subjected to such treatment
in order that we may begin to understand and heal." To know where we are
now, we have to know how we got here. Then perhaps we will be able to
"reopen the doors which the fait accompli has closed."[51]

As my own family story illustrates, aboriginal people have had to fend
off attempts at assimilation, control, intrusion, and coercion for hundreds
of years. Remarkably, they have steadfastly refused to live within our
stereotypes. They have not disappeared; they did not assimilate; and they
have not gone away. Our attempts at conquest have failed.

What would a just relationship between our two peoples look like? I certainly don't have a blueprint for the future, but I know we can't continue to
deny Native people their history, culture, right to be here, and right to make
their own decisions, nor abandon them to lives of poverty on the fringes of
mainstream society.[52] Can we give back what has been stolen – the right
of aboriginal people to make their own decisions and to husband the
resources they retained for themselves? Can we counteract, as best we can,
the negative effects of past treatment and ensure that we are not exploiting
aboriginal people or their lands today? Can we imagine respectful mutual

co-existence, the one possibility my ancestors and their compatriots never seriously considered?

Unfortunately, my sense is that most non-Natives in Canada and the United States still want to see Native issues settled by having Native people assimilate. In Canada, where "multiculturalism" is official government policy, most people see Native people as just another ethnic group. It's all right if they do traditional singing and dancing and take pride in their heritage, but it's harder to understand why they should have rights different from those that other Canadians have. Similarly, in the United States, many non-Native people fear the consequences of sovereignty for "hundreds of semi-independent 'tribes' . . . with special privileges that are denied to other Americans."[53] Yet, in both countries, Native people now have different legal rights from other citizens, as the courts affirm.

One of the hardest things for non-Natives to accept is that insisting on one law for everybody, including aboriginal people, can be a form of discrimination – it goes against all our treasured notions of equality. However, as Associate Chief Judge Murray Sinclair of the Manitoba Aboriginal Justice Inquiry wrote in 1991, "the application of uniform standards, common rules, and equal treatment of people who are not the same . . . may result in adverse consequences, hardship or injustice, and in the case of aboriginal people may be considered a form of racism."[54]

In Canada, aboriginal people are not the same as other Canadians. They did not join Canada under the same terms – in fact, the ancestors of most Native people never agreed to join Canada at all. They agreed to share the land, but not to give up their sovereignty; the way they saw it, European and Native nations would follow separate but parallel paths in a mutually beneficial way.[55]

Perhaps again, the circle is coming round, for we may be returning to a form of the "covalent" society that flourished in the initial years of contact between Europeans and indigenous North Americans before King Philip's War – in which various Native and non-Native polities of different sizes and strengths were linked through trade and mutual obligations. It certainly requires creativity to envision a workable society under these terms, particularly in Canada, where there is also the question of relations with Québec, but if we succeed in doing so, not only will we have rectified a long-established injustice at home, we also will have made a valuable contribution to solving a problem with which many countries are struggling – how to develop a truly post-colonial state.

In the seventeenth century, New Englanders realized that Native communities – Pequots, Mohegans, Pennacooks – varied enormously. They had different relations with each local group. It is still true that there are no generic "Indians," and indeed there never have been. So, today, Native nations will vary considerably in the means they use to achieve and exercise self-government, and Native individuals and groups will adopt or reject non-Native North American culture to varying degrees. There is no single way to be Native, no right way or wrong way: there are only people struggling to find a balance between the past and the present, their cultures and ours, often finding in this juggling act a creative synthesis that can benefit all of us.

A people is not defined solely by blood or even by material culture, but also by self-identity, history, culture, and values. Canada is a good example of this: the ethnic and racial make-up of Canadians has changed considerably even in my lifetime, yet Canada's right to exist is not questioned. Although our lives do not differ materially from those of our far-more-numerous American neighbours, Canadians perceive themselves as different and maintain their right to express their own values on a range of issues, such as gun control or medical insurance. Similarly, although Native people are greatly outnumbered in modern North America, and although there has been considerable interracial mixing and adoption of Western material culture, the descendants of the indigenous people still see themselves as distinct, and many I talked to, such as Janice Rising of the Chippewas of Sarnia – the Aamjiwnaang – see different values as the most important aspect of their Native identity. That Native people, like non-Natives, have undergone dramatic change since the seventeenth century does not alter their identity: to "see change as failure, as some kind of cultural corruption . . . [is] to condemn Indians to solitary confinement in a prison of myth."[56]

I have no illusion that renewing our relationship will be easy. In fact, the complexity of the project is staggering. As costly as it will be to settle land claims, there is no just alternative. Similarly, no one knows the ultimate cost of compensating the victims of abuse at residential schools; in Canada there are already more than six thousand former students suing the government or churches (not just for physical or sexual abuse, but also for "cultural genocide"), and the number grows daily. The cost of settling these lawsuits in the courts could run into billions of dollars. A 1999 Indian Affairs estimate of the total cost of settling all Native claims against the government was $11.8 billion, though an alarmist, worst-case scenario created headlines when the Finance Department proclaimed Native demands would cost $200 billion.[57] The financial consequences for the churches are very serious: the United Church – the church of my relatives – may be facing national bankruptcy; the Presbyterian Church, because it ran only two schools (one of them Cecilia Jeffrey) is in a slightly better position. Some have argued that the churches are taking an unfair share of the blame and financial burden for institutions that were ultimately the responsibility of the federal government, and hence of the general population; there is now talk of government assistance to forestall the financial ruin of the Christian denominations in Canada.

I do know that it is not enough to simply give aboriginal people money, though money is certainly necessary for healing and reconstruction. That would be akin to an abusive husband making donations to a battered women's shelter or paying for his wife's counselling (or perhaps just buying her make-up to hide the bruising). It would not address the real problem, which is his own behaviour. Money is no substitute for changing our human relations with the indigenous people of this land. As a German writer wrote of the relationship between post-war Germans and Jewish people, "It is our obligation – and ideally a desire – to move toward the people who were callously pushed out of our consciousness for so long and offer them the respect and spiritual and emotional retribution that our parents' generation denied them by having their government open the wallet, instead of offering them their hearts."[58] Ironically, given all my culture's attempts to suppress and deny the validity of aboriginal spirituality, it is to its emphasis on showing respect, giving thanks, sharing, and maintaining appropriate relationships that we could turn for guidance.

But even in attempting reconciliation our good intentions can still go astray, particularly if our own attitudes or assumptions are unexamined or we know little about Native cultures. The more I've talked to family members and friends of my own or my father's generation, the more I've become aware of the hidden reservoirs of pain that some of us carry from encounters and experiences with Native people that ended badly, that foundered in misunderstanding, accusations, bitterness, feelings of betrayal, and culminated in the rupturing and destruction of relationships. I've experienced some of these painful encounters too, and sometimes it's taken me years to understand what went wrong. This is also the pain of colonization, and one of the few ways that it is felt by non-Native people. Even as we try to dismantle the effects of colonization and our culture's racism, even as we offer what we believe is friendship, the past impedes our efforts to know Native people now, to see each other clearly. It distorts and booby-traps our relations, and makes it so much harder for them to flourish.

In conducting my research, I've learned that one of these boobytraps is seeing Native people only as victims, for this too is a form of paternalism. In so doing, we deny them agency of their own. While their options may have been limited in the past, the stories in this book have shown that Native people have always actively made choices and tried to make the best of whatever situation they were in – think of the Pequots stubbornly reasserting themselves on their traditional land after the Pequot War. If they are mere victims, we cannot respect them, we see them only as pitiful beings who "lost" their culture and have nothing of value to offer the rest of the world.

In recognizing Native agency, we also see that the ancestors of Native people bear some responsibility for where we all are today. This is not to blame the victim and say that their colonization was their own fault. But just as my ancestors may not have anticipated the long-term consequences of the fur trade or have seen their individual land purchases as part of a huge movement of Native dispossession, Native people of long ago did not anticipate the consequences of some of their choices, such as allying themselves with the English to attack Native enemies, or selling pieces of land they didn't need at the time, or buying alcohol when they brought their furs to the trading posts. It is often only with hindsight that we can see in the choices of our ancestors the patterns that would prove so destructive.

I think of the aboriginal and non-aboriginal children in my story and what they did or didn't learn about each other. I think of John Wheeler, probably raised according to what seem to me to be barbaric English traditions of physical violence and authoritarianism, which he and others brought to North America, the same traditions that were later imposed on aboriginal children in residential schools. I think of his daughter Ann Wheeler's children, who probably played with Pawtucket children in the streets of seventeenth-century Newbury, though Lord knows what they thought of each other. I think of John Sassamon, the young Indian convert raised by Puritans, whom John Eliot taught so well to be English that he lost the trust of many of his own people and used his knowledge of English to his own advantage, though he also tried to pass on his skills of reading and writing to other Native children. And young Elisha Searl, who at the age of eight crossed the cultural divide in the other direction – becoming a Frenchman and a "white Indian" – and then as an adult crossing back again and resuming the identity of a New England Puritan, for it was impossible to reconcile these ways of being. Or Hannah Janes, who grew up on hatred and violence and became a victim of it herself. I think of my father as a boy, playing on the dock at Shoal Lake with Ojibwa children attending Cecilia Jeffrey Indian Residential School, remembering their names seventy years later, and of my own children, Claire and Ariel, and their friend Danielle, the granddaughter of Ada who also attended Cecilia Jeffrey and may have been given my grandmother's name. And I wonder what we will pass on to the next generation and the ones that follow, to the aboriginal and non-aboriginal children who will share this continent, this Turtle Island.

My fear is that we will not teach them the truth. Most North American children have no direct knowledge of aboriginal people and are exposed mainly to images of "Indians" created by non-Natives, many of which still promulgate the "imaginary Indian" of our fantasies, "simultaneously savage, noble and pathetic."[59] In Ontario, where I live, the Grade 3 curriculum teaches children about "pioneer life" and "the contributions of aboriginal peoples to early settlement," without addressing the real relations between the two peoples in this period. The Grade 6 "Heritage and Citizenship" curriculum that is supposedly teaching my daughter about Native/Euro-Canadian interactions guides teachers to focus on the early contact period between Native people and explorers, and then to jump ahead three hundred years to modern aboriginal people and their "concerns," conveniently ignoring three hundred years of colonization. There is absolutely no obligation to discuss the role of settlers, missionaries, governments, or supremacist ideologies in depriving aboriginal people of their lands, rights, and culture – and such an analysis is essential if we are to understand the present. Isolated topics in later academic years do address aspects of the relations between aboriginal peoples and other Canadians, such as the Northwest Rebellion and the Indian Act, yet this history and the development of this relationship is never studied systematically.[60] How can we prepare our children for responsible citizenship with respect to Native people if they do not understand what has shaped this relationship they will inherit?

Our relations today, as in the past, depend on the myths or histories Native and non-Native peoples construct to define themselves and each other; we must be so careful in the stories we tell ourselves and pass on. I think of the Puritans telling themselves that they had treated Indians fairly in land dealings, and how, in King Philip's War, the "cultural gestalt of the colonists allowed them to carry out effectively genocidal policies while steadfastly believing to the end that they stood upon the moral high ground."[61] (The English published fifteen thousand books about King Philip's War in the first five years after the war to buttress those beliefs.) I think of the heroic stories that New Englanders told for at least a hundred years about noble Hannah Dustin scalping her savage Abenaki captors and their children, or of the myth perpetuated by settlers in Vermont who pretended that the Abenakis had never lived there at all. Today the stories we non-Natives tell ourselves may be different – they may be about totally wicked white oppressors and saintly Native victims, or about Native people as the fount of all things spiritual – but the tendency to fictionalize is just as strong.

Native people do this too – in their attempts to create a pan-Indian identity, sometimes imagining their ancestors as always resisting the English, when in fact their ancestors may have fought on the side of the English against other Native Americans in King Philip's War,[62] or mythologizing the lives of their ancestors before the coming of Europeans as their own idyllic Golden Age, or denying that scalping was an indigenous practice. We lose the true complexity of this history at our peril.

As I've tried to suggest, there is a lot that non-Native people can do to address our legacy with Native people. It's equally important, however, to recognize what we can't do, where we don't belong, and where it is inappropriate to act. We can't heal Native people of the traumas they have endured, though we can give them hope that we will treat them with respect now and in the future. We can commit ourselves to listening to and respecting Native definitions of their issues and solutions, which may differ from what we ourselves would choose, and we can be open to learning from the many unique and enriching aspects of Native culture. We can recognize that non-Natives are often afraid of the very thing that Native people need to heal – greater power.

Most of the aboriginal people I've talked to see the restoration of key elements of aboriginal culture as the most important factor in the healing of aboriginal individuals and communities. It is something they must do themselves. Stan McKay, a Cree United Church minister and former moderator of that church, speaks of colonization as "the captivity of the imagination, the very spirit of who we are" and foresees "a long journey of working to overcome our people's loss of confidence in our own stories." "We have to reprogram our people into believing in themselves again," says Beverley Sellars, chief of the Soda Creek First Nation in British Columbia.[63] How terribly ironic that the surviving traditionalists, those who clung so stubbornly to their cultures in spite of the concerted efforts of the Church and State, those who for so long were reviled as backward, pagan and evil, who were shunted aside and ignored, are now the ones who seem best qualified to help Native communities heal, rebuild, and flourish.

I will end with a story:

When I travelled to Shoal Lake, the Red River flood was about to crest in Winnipeg and was on everyone's mind, and I saw immediately the differences in the ways Native and non-Native people interpreted its significance. Among non-Native Canadians, the flood was being talked about as a freak of nature and, while it was causing tremendous dislocation and damage, what was most evident was the spirit of co-operation in a time of crisis – the Red River Rally on CBC Radio's *Morningside* program, for example, raised two million dollars for flood victims and demonstrated tremendous good will among Canadians for fellow Canadians in need. The Anishinabe experienced the flood quite differently. The people I talked to blamed the flood on all the dams that had been built, and saw the disaster as the predictable outcome of not respecting and honouring nature, of not being in the right relation with it. The Anishinabe of Lake of the Woods and Shoal Lake have a long experience of raised water levels: many of their ancestors' graves are now under water, and the level in the lakes is so high now that there is often no wild rice to harvest in a region long famed for this bounty.

One night when I was visiting the Kenora area, my host Mary Alice told me of a speech Ovide Mercredi had given as head of the Assembly of First Nations, in which he used the flood as a metaphor for the experience of aboriginal people in Canada. They have been overwhelmed by the newcomers' culture; it is an endless flood always coming at you, he said. It never seems to crest. You are always struggling to keep your family intact; you can never live normally, your environment is transformed beyond recognition. You have lost so much, which you never get back. You get so tired and worn out, but you are on your own. It seems no one tries to help. No one else notices or cares.

This, I think, is an accurate expression of what many Native people feel. But I've also heard another flood analogy, which is more hopeful. It was

related by the Mohegan writer Melissa Jayne Fawcett, who heard it from
elder Bill Wakole of the Sac and Fox Nation in Oklahoma:

> When the Europeans first came to the eastern shores, it was as if a giant
> tidal wave had hit the Native people and knocked them all flat. As the
> wave made its way west, the devastation was not as great; for the wave
> was not as strong. As the waters subsided, there were no obvious signs
> of life along the eastern shore, so it was assumed that all the creatures
> who had lived there, before the wave came, were dead and gone. But
> after a while, tiny bubbles were seen on the surface of these eastern
> waters, and it was realized that the creatures of the eastern shore had not
> died at all. They had simply learned to live underwater. These creatures
> – among whom are the Mohegans – are now rising to the surface. They
> are wise creatures, for they have learned to live well within the wave that
> now surrounds them. Their experience beneath the wave has made them
> strong, and they are destined to grow and prosper.[64]

A few months after I heard these stories, an aboriginal friend of mine
in Toronto, who makes her living as a cross-cultural educator, used the
wave image again. She was describing an incident at work in which she had
failed to confront a non-Native person about her blatant prejudice. My
friend was conscious of her own feeling of failure and betrayal of responsibility. Then she described how another aboriginal person had come
forward and dealt with the situation, and she suddenly realized there would
always be another person behind her to carry on the work. Wave after wave
of aboriginal people will always come forward to confront those who deny
them and to assert their right to be themselves. And, while I do not wish to
imply that it is the responsibility of aboriginal people to change the rest of
us – it is our responsibility to decolonize ourselves – this is another hopeful
image of aboriginal strength, for we all know the effect of waves on even
the hardest rock. I think, too, of a statement an Okanagan writer made at a
conference I attended years ago: "You're not here to change us – we're here
to change you!"[65]

For me, these stories convey a truth that my research and travels
confirmed many times over. Native people are regrouping and rebuilding;
it is their determination, courage, imagination, and spirit that will bring
true healing – if a matching determination, courage, imagination, and spirit
on our part will enable us to meet them as equals and respect their desire

and need to be themselves. We now have another chance to know each other. If colonization was the product of the attitudes and incremental actions of thousands of people, including my ancestors and perhaps yours, it can also be undone through many small changes and actions.

Writing this book has been such a journey of joy and pain, knowledge and self-knowledge, such a huge, huge learning, and massive undertaking. Writing my own history has been invigorating and empowering: I've made my own judgments of my ancestors. I know how I got here. Sometimes I feel I can't hold it all in my heart.

I believe it is possible to move beyond this ugly and often violent history, to be a society that is founded not on mere "tolerance," but on respect, a society that lives up to its word. But I know we can't move forward until we look the past in the eye, until we understand ourselves more deeply, acknowledging and exploring even the darker aspects of our history – not to damn our forebears, but with hope for a more humane world.

A portion of the author's royalties from this book will be used to support projects furthering justice for aboriginal people and healing and rebuilding in their communities.

Notes

Abbreviations

CHS	Connecticut Historical Society
CHSC	Connecticut *Historical Society Collections*
MHS	Massachusetts Historical Society
MHSC	Massachusetts *Historical Society Collections*
NAC	National Archives of Canada
NEHGR	*New England Historical and Genealogical Register*
NYCA	New York *Christian Advocate and Zion's Herald*
N.Y. Col. Docs.	*Documents Relating to the Colonial History of the State of New York,* 15 vols. – 12-335 (n2, 7)
NYHSC	*New York Historical Society Collections*
OA	Archives of Ontario, Toronto
RIHS	Rhode Island Historical Society
RIHSC	*Rhode Island Historical Society Collections*
Belknap Press	Belknap Press of Harvard University Press
RCAP	*Report of the Royal Commission on Aboriginal Peoples,* 5 vols.
UCA	United Church of Canada Archives, Toronto
VUL	Victoria University Library, University of Toronto
WMS	Women's Missionary Society
WFMS	Women's Foreign Missionary Society

Introduction

1. Edward Spicer's comment came to me second-hand, and I have not been able to locate it, though it may come from *A Short History of the Indians in the United States* (N.Y.: Van Nostrand Reinhold Co., 1969.) I've reworked a phrase of Richard Drinnon's from *Facing West: The Metaphysics of Indian-hating and Empire-building* (Minneapolis: University of Minneapolis Press, 1980), xxiv.
2. Ibid., xiii.
3. "Ahnishinahbaeóᵗjibway" is his own designation for his ethnic and cultural identity.

4. Wub-e-ke-niew, *We Have the Right to Exist: Translation of Aboriginal Indigenous Thought* (N.Y.: Black Thistle Press, 1995), pp. 97–130; p. 202.

5. Ibid.

6. Carl Jung, *Memories, Dreams, Reflections*, recorded and edited by Aniela Jaffé, trans. by Richard and Clara Winston (N.Y.: Vintage, 1963), p. 233.

7. I've borrowed this phrase from Kerwin Lee Klein, *Frontiers of Historical Imagination: Narrating the European Conquest of Native America, 1890–1990* (Berkeley: University of California Press, 1997). Other sources on historiography as it pertains to Native people and the colonization of North America are Calvin Martin, ed., *The American Indian and the Problem of History* (Oxford: Oxford University Press, 1987); James Axtell, "History as Imagination," in *Beyond 1492: Encounters in Colonial North America* (N.Y.: Oxford University Press, 1992), pp. 3–22; Wub-e-ke-niew, *We Have the Right to Exist*; Angela Cavender Wilson, "Power of the Spoken Word: Native Oral Traditions in American Indian History," in Donald L. Fixico, ed., *Rethinking American Indian History* (Albuquerque: University of New Mexico Press, 1997); Jennifer S. H. Brown and Elizabeth Vibert, eds., *Reading Beyond Words: Contexts for Native History* (Peterborough: Broadview Press, 1996); David Stineback, "The Status of Puritan–Indian Scholarship," *New England Quarterly* 51: 80–90; and Olive Patricia Dickason, "Toward a Large View of Canada's History: The Native Factor," in David Alan Long and Olive Patricia Dickason, eds., *Visions of the Heart: Canadian Aboriginal Issues* (Toronto: Harcourt Brace Canada, 1996).

8. I have found some biographical information on early Native Americans my ancestors knew in Carl Waldeman, *Who Was Who in Native American History: Indians and Non-Indians from Early Contacts through 1900* (N.Y.: Facts on File, 1989), and Samuel G. Drake, *Biography and History of the Indians of North America from Its First Discovery* (Boston: Benjamin B. Mussey & Co., 1848).

9. The Mohegan oral version of this story is also recorded in Melissa Jayne Fawcett, *The Lasting of the Mohegans* (Uncasville, Conn.: The Mohegan Tribe, 1995), p. 12.

10. Quoted in Celia Haig-Brown, *Resistance and Renewal: Surviving the Indian Residential School* (Vancouver: Tillacum Library, 1988), p. 141.

11. Robert F. Berkhofer, Jr., "Cultural Pluralism Versus Ethnocentrism," in Martin, ed., *The American Indian and the Problem of History*, p. 40.

12. Quoted in Axtell, *Beyond 1492*, p. 17.

13. L. P. Hartley quoted in Axtell, *Beyond 1492*, p. 10; Steiner quoted in ibid., pp. 6–7.

Chapter 1: *Home*

1. *Wiltshire Parish Register Marriages*, 13:43. Most of the personal information about Mercy Jelly, Dominick Wheeler, John Wheeler, Ann Wheeler, and Aquila Chase can be found in John Carroll Chase and George Walter Chamberlain, comps., *Seven Generations of the Descendants of Aquila and Thomas Chase* (Derry, N.H.: Record Publishing Co., 1928), including the wills of John and Dominick Wheeler. Birth, death, marriage, and other records pertaining to the family in Salisbury can be located through Barbara J. Carter, *Location of Documents for Wiltshire Parishes* (Swindon, Eng.: B. J. Carter, 1981), and M. G. Rathbone, ed., *Records of Wiltshire Boroughs Before 1836* (Wiltshire Archeological and Natural History Society Records, Branch V, 1951). Additional genealogical information comes from the records of the Church of the Latter Day Saints, now available on-line via Ancestry.com. John Wheeler's passage to North America is documented in "Passengers of *Mary AND John* 1634," *NEHGR*, IX (1855): 265–68.

2. *Oxford English Dictionary* (Oxford: Oxford University Press, 1971). Compact edition, p. 1773.
3. *Essex Institute Historical Collections* 44: 292.
4. My chief source for information about Salisbury in the late sixteenth and early seventeenth century is Paul Slack, "Poverty and Politics in Salisbury, 1597–1666," in *Crisis and Order in English Towns, 1500–1700: Essays in Urban History*, eds. Peter Clark and Paul Slack (Toronto: University of Toronto Press, 1972). Other sources of information specific to Salisbury were Robert Benson and Henry Thatcher, "History of Old and New Sarum," *Salisbury and Winchester Journal*, and D. H. Robertson, *Sarum Close: A History of the Life and Education of the Cathedral Choristers for 700 Years* (London: Jonathan Cape, 1938). More general sources for social conditions and Puritanism in Wiltshire and in England during the sixteenth and seventeenth centuries are Anthony Fletcher and John Stevenson, eds., *Order and Disorder in Early Modern England* (Cambridge: Cambridge University Press, 1985); Keith Wrightson, *English Society, 1580–1680*, Hutchinson Social History of England (London: Hutchinson, 1982); Wallace Notestein, *The English People on the Eve of Colonization, 1603–1630* (N.Y.: Harper, 1954); David Underdown, *Revel, Riot and Rebellion: Popular Politics and Culture in England, 1603–1660* (Oxford: Oxford University Press, 1987); Barry Coward, *The Stuart Age: England, 1603–1714*, 2nd ed. (London: Longman, 1994); Christopher Hill, *Society and Puritanism in Pre-Revolutionary England* (N.Y.: Schocken Books, 1964); David Stannard, *The Puritan Way of Death: A Study in Religion, Culture and Social Change* (N.Y.: Oxford University Press, 1977), and Hugh Trevor-Roper, *Archbishop Laud, 1573–1645* (London: Macmillan, 1940). Additional information about the life of women comes from D. E. Underdown, "The Taming of the Scold: The Enforcement of Patriarchal Authority in Early Modern England," in *Order and Disorder in Early Modern England*, pp. 116–36, and Carroll Camden, *The Elizabethan Woman* (Houston: Elsevier Press, 1952).
5. Celia Fiennes, *The Illustrated Journeys of Celia Fiennes, 1685–1712*, ed. Christopher Morris (London and Exeter: Macdonald, Webb & Bower, 1982), p. 36.
6. *Essex Institute Historical Collections* 44: 292, quoted in Chase and Chamberlain, comps., *The Descendants of Aquila and Thomas Chase*, p. 521.
7. For Puritanism in England, my chief sources are, in addition to the general sources listed in note 4 above: Theodore Dwight Bozeman, *To Lead Ancient Lives: The Primitivist Dimension in Puritanism* (Chapel Hill and London: University of North Carolina Press, 1988), Larzer Ziff, *Puritanism in America: New Culture in a New World* (N.Y.: Viking, 1973), and Max Weber, *The Protestant Ethic and the Rise of Capitalism*, trans. Talcott Parsons (N.Y.: Scribner's, 1930).
8. Bozeman, *To Lead Ancient Lives*, pp. 14–18.
9. Slack, "Poverty and Politics," p. 186.
10. Salisbury Municipal Archives, Box 4, File "Various 1600–30," doc. 65A. Quoted in Slack, "Poverty and Politics," p. 171.
11. David Cressy, *Coming Over: Migration and Communication between England and New England in the Seventeenth Century* (Cambridge: Cambridge University Press, 1987), p. 68.
12. Bozeman, *To Lead Ancient Lives*, p. 98; William Haller, *The Elect Nation: The Meaning and Relevance of Foxe's Book of Martyrs* (N.Y.: Harper & Row, 1963), p. 20.
13. Trevor-Roper, *Archbishop Laud*, pp. 109–10.
14. Ibid., p. 103.
15. "Henry Sherfield," *Dictionary of National Biography*, 18: 74. See also *The Proceedings in the Star Chamber against Henry Sherfield Esq* (1713) and Trevor-Roper, *Archbishop Laud*, pp. 110–11.

16. *The Proceedings in the Star Chamber against Henry Sherfield Esq* (1713). The bishop had been summoned before the Privy Council, and after listening to a tirade from Archbishop Harsnet submitted and was dismissed with a caution, as described in Thomas Fuller, *Church History of Britain, from the Birth of Jesus Christ until the year 1648*, ed. J. S. Brener (Oxford: Oxford University Press, 1845), p. 77.

17. Quoted in Bozeman, *To Lead Ancient Lives,* p. 95.

Chapter 2: *Dreaming of America*

1. See for example, in addition to the writings of Columbus, those of Amerigo Vespucci in Clements Markham, ed., *The Letters of Amerigo Vespucci and Other Documents Illustrative of His Career* (N.Y.: B. Franklin, 1964); also Edward Alber, ed., *The First Three English Books on America, 1511–55* (Birmingham, 1885), xxvii. For early English attitudes to aboriginal people and the justifications for colonization, I draw upon James Axtell, *The Invasion Within: The Contest of Cultures in Colonial North America* (N.Y. and Oxford: Oxford University Press, 1985) and *The European and the Indian* (N.Y. and Oxford: Oxford University Press, 1981); H. C. Porter, *The Inconstant Savage: England and the North American Indian, 1500–1660* (London: Gerald Duckworth & Co., 1979); Olive P. Dickason, *The Myth of the Savage and the Beginnings of French Colonialism in the Americas* (Edmonton: University of Alberta Press, 1984, 1997); Francis Jennings, *The Invasion of America: Indians, Colonialism, and the Cant of Conquest* (Chapel Hill: University of North Carolina Press, 1975); and Frederick Turner, *Beyond Geography: The Western Spirit Against the Wilderness* (New Brunswick, N.J.: Rutgers University Press, 1983). L. C. Green and Olive P. Dickason's *The Law of Nations and the New World* (Edmonton: University of Alberta Press, 1989) examines the actions and beliefs of Europeans in relation to America in the context of the development of international law. Carolyn Foreman's *Indians Abroad, 1493–1938* (Norman, Okla.: University of Oklahoma Press, 1943) describes the experiences of aboriginal visitors to England during the sixteenth and seventeenth centuries.

2. Paul Le Jeune, "Brief Relation of the Journey to New France," in Reuben Gold Thwaites, ed., *The Jesuit Relations and Allied Documents*, Vol. VI (N.Y.: Pageant Books, 1959), p. 27, quoted in Alden T. Vaughan, *New England Frontier, 1620–1675* (Boston: Little, Brown, 1965), p. 27.

3. Vaughan, *New England Frontier*, p. 20; Thomas Morton, *New English Canaan; or, New Canaan . . .* (1637; facsimile edition, N.Y.: Da Capo Press, 1969), p. 19; Richard Cogley, *John Eliot's Mission to the Indians before King Philip's War* (Cambridge and London: Harvard University Press, 1999), pp. 15–18.

4. From George Abbot, "De America sive orbe novo," *Briefe Description of the whole World* (London 1599; facsimile edition, Amsterdam and N.Y.: Da Capo Press, 1970), p. 1605, quoted in Porter, *The Inconstant Savage*, p. 118.

5. Julius Caesar, *The Conquest of Gaul*, trans. S. A. Handford (Harmondsworth, Eng.: Penguin, 1951), p. 136.

6. Jennings, *Invasion of America*, p. 6.

7. The Bull Romanus Pontifex, Jan. 8, 1455, in Frances Gardiner Davenport, ed., *European Treaties Bearing on the History of the United States and Its Dependencies*, Carnegie Institution of Washington Publication 254: I (Washington, D.C., 1917), p. 23, quoted in Jennings, *Invasion of America*, p. 4.

8. See, for example, Green and Dickason, *The Law of Nations*, p. 247, and Heather Lechtman, "Pre-Columbian Surface Metallurgy," *Scientific American* 250, no. 6 (June

1984): 56–63, on the differing philosophical and ideological orientation of metalwork between the two cultures. In the Old World, metallurgy was directed toward practical goals of improving warfare, transportation, and agriculture; in the New World, it was associated with religious beliefs, political power, and social status. My other major sources on the technological differences between Europeans and the indigenous peoples of North America are Thomas Sowell, *Conquests and Cultures: An International History* (N.Y.: Basic Books, 1998), p. 255, and Jared Diamond, *Guns, Germs and Steel: The Fates of Human Societies* (N.Y. and London: W. W. Norton, 1999).

9. Sowell, *Conquests and Cultures*, p. 255.

10. Quoted in Green and Dickason, *The Law of Nations*, p. 188; see also pp. 146, 244–45.

11. [Christopher Columbus], *The Journal of Columbus*, tr. Cecil Jane, ed. L. A. Vigneras (London, 1960, 1968), p. 28, quoted in Porter, *Inconstant Savage*, p. 8.

12. Jennings, *Invasion of America*, p. 7. For the actions of the English in Ireland and the ideology of English colonization, my main sources were Robert Kee, *Ireland: A History* (London: Weidenfeld & Nicolson, 1980); Peter Berresford Ellis, *Hell or Connaught: The Cromwellian Colonization of Ireland* (London: Hamish Hamilton, 1975); and Nicolas P. Canny, "The Ideology of English Colonization: From Ireland to America," *William and Mary Quarterly*, 3rd Series, XXX (1973): 575–98.

13. Montaigne quoted in James Axtell, *Beyond 1492: Encounters in Colonial North America* (N.Y.: Oxford University Press, 1992), p. 30.

14. Richard Hakluyt, *A Discourse of Western Planting*, in E. G. R. Taylor, ed., *The Original Writings and Correspondence of the Two Richard Hakluyts*, 2 vols., Series 2, Nos. 76, 77 (London: Hakluyt Society, 1935), pp. 214–15.

15. Letters patent found in Hakluyt, *Divers Voyages touching the discoverie of America*, London 1582, facsimile reprint, in D. B. Quinn, ed., *Richard Hakluyt* (Amsterdam: Theatrum Orbis Terrarum, 1967), ed. J. W. Jones, Series 1, No. 7 (London: Hakluyt Society, 1850), pp. 19–22; Green and Dickason, *The Law of Nations*, pp. 244-49.

16. D. B. Quinn, ed., *The Voyages and Colonizing Enterprises of Humphrey Gilbert*, Vol. 1, Series 2, no. 83 (London: Hakluyt Society, 1940), pp. 188–94.

17. D. B. Quinn, ed., *The Roanoke Voyages, 1584–1590: Documents to Illustrate the English Voyages to North America Under the Patent Granted to Walter Raleigh in 1584*, Vol. 1, Series 2, no. 104 (Cambridge: Hakluyt Society, 1955), p. 110, quoted in Porter, *Inconstant Savage*, p. 229.

18. Hakluyt in *Roanoke Voyages*, p. 478.

19. Louis B. Wright, ed., *The Elizabethan's America: A Collection of Early Reports by Englishmen on the New World, 1565–1630* (London: E. Arnold, 1965), pp. 160–62.

20. Philip L. Barbour, ed., *The Jamestown Voyages Under the First Charter, 1606–1609* (Cambridge: Hakluyt Society, 1969), p. 354, quoted in Porter, *Inconstant Savage*, p. 324. There is, however, both historical and archaeological evidence for the pre-contact practice of human sacrifice, both of adults and children, among some other indigenous nations in the Americas.

21. Susan Myra Kingsbury, ed., *The Records of the Virginia Company of London*, (Washington, D.C.: Gov't Printing Office 1906 and 1933), Vol. 3, pp. 14–15, in Porter, *Inconstant Savage*, p. 391.

22. De Bry in Kingsbury, *Records of the Virginia Company*, 399–400, quoted in Porter, *Inconstant Savage*, p. 256; Richard Eburne, *A Plain Pathway to Plantations*, 1624, ed. L. B. Wright (Ithaca, N.Y.: Cornell University Press, 1962), p. 56, quoted in Porter, *Inconstant Savage*, p. 257; Hayes, MS. Dd.III.85, No. 4., published as appendix to John Brereton, *A Briefe and True Relation of the Discoverie of the North Part of Virginia*

(London, 1602; facsimile edition, Amsterdam and N.Y.: Theatrum Orbis Terrarum, Da Capo Press, 1973), quoted in Porter, *Inconstant Savage*, p. 264.

23. Sermon, Nov. 13, 1622. John Donne, *Sermons*, ed. George R. Potter and Evelyn M. Simpson, Vol. IV, No. 10 (Berkeley, Calif.: University of California Press, 1953) quoted in Porter, *Inconstant Savage*, p. 358; John Smith quoted in Porter, *Inconstant Savage*, p. 341; John Smith, *Advertisements for the Planters of New England* (London, 1631; facsimile edition, N.Y.: Da Capo Press, 1971), p. 10.

24. Edward Waterhouse, *A Declaration of the State of the Colony in Virginia* (London, 1622; facsimile edition, Amsterdam: Theatrum Orbis Terrarum and N.Y., Da Capo Press, 1970), and Kingsbury, *Records*, III, No. CCX, p. 558, in Porter, *Inconstant Savage*, p. 463.

25. An earlier attempt had been made in March 1597, when a group of Puritan separatists had been allowed permission to plant a colony in the Province of Canada, on Amherst Island in the Magdelan Islands in the Gulf of St. Lawrence. When the plan failed because of French opposition, they went to Holland instead.

26. Nathaniel B. Shurtleff, ed., *Records of the Governor and Company of the Massachusetts Bay in New England*, 5 vols. (Boston: W. White, 1853–54), Vol. 1, p. 17.

27. Robert Beverley, *The History and Present State of Virginia*, 1705, ed. L. B. Wright (Chapel Hill: University of North Carolina Press, 1947), p. 29.

28. John Webster Grant, *Moon of Wintertime: Missionaries and the Indians of Canada in Encounter since 1534* (Toronto: University of Toronto Press, 1984), p. 21.

29. Jennings, *Invasion of America*, p. 105.

Chapter 3: *Along the Merrimack*

1. *NEHGR*, IX (July 1855): 265.

2. Richard S. Dunn, James Savage, and Laetitia Yeandle, eds., *The Journal of John Winthrop, 1630–1649* (Cambridge: Belknap Press, 1996), p. 88; Joshua Coffin, *Sketch of History of Newbury* (Boston: Samuel G. Drake, 1845), p. 10. It was only in 1637 that the English acquired a quitclaim for Ipswich from the Pawtucket sachem Masconomo; this payment was for land already settled by the English based on grants from the General Court. As Neal Salisbury points out, "these deeds make clear that Massachusetts Bay's reputation for having purchased titles from Indians in the same manner as it would have done from Europeans is unjustified" (Salisbury, *Manitou and Providence: Indians, Europeans, and the Making of New England, 1500–1643*. [N.Y.: Oxford University Press, 1982], p. 200).

3. See John Anthony Scott, *Settlers on the Eastern Shore* (N.Y.: Knopf, 1967). See also Thomas Morton, *New English Canaan; or, New Canaan*, (Amsterdam, 1637; facsimile edition, N.Y. and Amsterdam: De Capo Press, Theatrum Orbis Terrarum, 1969); and William Wood, *New England's Prospect* (London, 1634), ed. Alden T. Vaughan (Amherst: University of Massachusetts Press, 1977); James Axtell, *Beyond 1492: Encounters in Colonial North America* (N.Y. and Oxford: Oxford University Press, 1992); and Francis Jennings, *The Invasion of America: Indians, Colonialism, and the Cant of Conquest* (Chapel Hill: University of North Carolina Press, 1975).

4. Axtell, *Beyond 1492*, p. 32. My information on the initial contacts between Native Americans and Europeans comes chiefly from T. J. C. Brasser, "Early Indian-European Contacts" in Bruce Trigger, ed., *Northeast*, Vol. 15, *Handbook of North American Indians* (Washington, D.C.: Smithsonian Institution, 1978); James Axtell, *The Invasion Within: The Contest of Cultures in Colonial North America* (N.Y. and Oxford: Oxford

University Press, 1985), *Beyond 1492*, and *The European and the Indian* (N.Y. and Oxford: Oxford University Press, 1981); Jennings, *Invasion of America*; Salisbury, *Manitou and Providence*; Calvin Martin, *In the Spirit of the Earth* (Baltimore and London: Johns Hopkins University Press, 1992); John Webster Grant, *Moon of Wintertime: Missionaries and the Indians of Canada in Encounter Since 1534* (Toronto: University of Toronto Press, 1984).

5. Wood, *New England's Prospect*, 55.

6. Dean Snow, *Archaeology of New England* (N.Y.: Academic Press, 1980), pp. 32, 31.

7. My sources of information about the aboriginal nations of New England before English colonization are Howard S. Russell, *Indian New England before the Mayflower* (Hanover, N.H., and London: University Press of New England, 1980); Burt Salwen, "Indians of Southern New England and Long Island," in Trigger, ed., *Northeast*, pp. 160–63; William S. Simmons, *Spirit of the New England Tribes: Indian History and Folklore, 1620–1984* (Hanover, N.H., and London: University Press of New England, 1986); Snow, *Archaeology of New England*; William S. Simmons, "Southern New England Shamanism: An Ethnographic Reconstruction," in *Papers of the Seventh Algonquian Conference*, 1975, ed. William Cowan (Ottawa: Carleton University, 1976), and T. J. C. Brasser, "The coastal Algonkians," in Leacock and Lurie, eds., *North American Indians in Historical Perspective* (N.Y.: Random House, 1971), pp. 64–91.

8. Wood, *New England's Prospect*, pp. 100–1. Other information about the Pennacooks and the Pawtuckets comes from Gordon Day, "Western Abenakis," in *Northeast*, ed. Bruce Trigger, pp. 148–49; Salwen, "Indians of Southern New England," pp. 154–56; and Peter S. Leavenworth, "'The Best Title That Indians Can Claime': Native Agency and Consent in the Transferral of Penacook–Pawtucket Land in the Seventeenth Century," *New England Quarterly*, 72(2) (June 1999): 279–80. More information, not all of it reliable, about Passaconaway, the Pennacooks and the Pawtuckets, can be found in Chandler Potter, "Memoir of Passaconaway," *The Farmer's Monthly Visitor*, vol. XXII, no. 2 (Manchester, N.H., 1852); Charles Edward Beals, *Passaconaway in the White Mountains* (Boston: Richard G. Badger; Toronto: Copp Clark, 1966); Nathaniel Bouton, *History of Concord . . . with a History of the Ancient Pennacooks* (Concord: Benning W. Sanborn, 1856); B. B. Thatcher, *Indian Biography, or an historical account of those individuals who have been distinguished, etc.* (N.Y.: Harper Bros., 1848); and "Passaconaway, the Great Bashaba, An Address delivered by George Calvin Carter before Molly Stark Chapter, D.A.R. [Daughters of the American Revolution]," n.d. Manchester, N.H.

9. Morton, *New English Canaan*, pp. 34–36.

10. Ibid., p. 58.

11. John White, *Planter's Plea, or the Grounds of Plantations Examined, and usuall Objections Answered* (1630; facsimile edition, Rockport, Mass.: Sandy Bay Historical Society and Museum, 1930), p. 14. My sources on the impact of the epidemics on the Pawtuckets in particular and the New England Natives generally are S. F. Cook, *The Indian Population of New England in the Seventeenth Century* (Berkeley: University of California Press, 1976); Sherburne F. Cook, "The Significance of Disease in the Extinction of the New England Indians," *Human Biology* 45: 485–508; Alfred Crosby, "God would Destroy Them, and Give their Country to Another People . . ." *American Heritage* 29 (6): 38–43; Thomas Sowell, *Conquests and Cultures: An International History* (N.Y.: Basic Books, 1998), p. 255; Jared Diamond, *Guns, Germs and Steel: The Fates of Human Societies* (N.Y. and London: W. W. Norton, 1999); Richard Drinnon, *Facing West: The Metaphysics of Indian-Hating and Empire-Building* (Minneapolis:

University of Minnesota Press, 1980); and Colin G. Calloway, *The Western Abenakis of Vermont: War, Migration and the Survival of an Indian People* (Norman and London: University of Oklahoma Press, 1990).

12. John Winthrop to John Endecott (Jan. 3, 1634), in Allyn Forbes, ed., *The Winthrop Papers*, 5 vols. (Boston: Massachusetts Historical Society, 1929–47), III, p. 149; Cotton Mather, *Magnalia Christi Americana* (1702), ed. Kenneth B. Murdock (Cambridge: Belknap Press, 1977), p. 129.

13. Robert Cushman, "Cushman's Discourse" (1622), in Alexander Young, ed., *Chronicles of the Pilgrim Fathers of the Colony of New Plymouth from 1602–1625*, 2nd ed. (Boston: C. Little and J. Brown, 1844; reprint Baltimore: Genealogical Publishing Co., 1974), p. 258. A similar decline in traditional beliefs would occur later in Ireland during the Potato Famine, when many Irish abandoned their ancient magical practices. See R. F. Foster, *Modern Ireland, 1600–1972* (London: Allen Lane/Penguin, 1988), p. 340.

14. William Bradford, *History of Plymouth Plantation*, ed. S. E. Morison (N.Y.: Modern Library, 1952), p. 25; Cotton Mather, quoted in Axtell, *The European and the Indian*, p. 160.

15. Quoted in Scott, *Settlers on the Eastern Shore*; Morton, *New England Canaan*, p. 57.

16. Roger Williams, *A Key to the Language of America* (London: Gregory Dexter; reprinted in *RIHSC*, 1: 64. 1643), p. 133.

17. Jennings, *Invasion of America*, p. 49. See also Axtell, *The Invasion Within*, Chapter 7, and Larzer Ziff, *Puritanism in America: New Culture in a New World* (N.Y.: Viking, 1973), p. 18, for a discussion of these differences.

18. Leavenworth, "'The Best Title That Indians Can Claime,'" and Salisbury, *Manitou and Providence*, provide my information about Pawtucket land sales.

19. Henry Bowden and James Ronda, eds., *John Eliot's Indian Dialogues: A Study in Cultural Interaction* (Westport, Conn.: Greenwood Press, 1980), p. 12.

20. My information about the settlement of Newbury, Hampton, Salisbury, and Newburyport and details about the Chase and Wheeler families are drawn from David Hoyt, *Old Families of Salisbury and Amesbury, with some related families of Newbury, Haverhill, Ipswich and Hampton* (Providence, R.I.: Snow & Farnham Co., 1919); Joseph Dow, "History of Hampton," Vol. I (Salem: Salem Press, 1893) in *History of Hampton, 1638–1988* (Hampton: Peter Randall, 1988); *Hampton Tercentenary, 1638–1938 Official Pictorial Magazine*, Complete Program; Joseph Merrill, *Amesbury, History of, including the first 17 years of Salisbury, to the separation in 1654; & Merrimac, from its incorporation in 1876* (Haverhill: Press of F. P. Stiles, 1880); John J. Currier, *A History of Newbury Mass., 1635–1902* (Boston: Damrell & Upham); Joshua Coffin, *A Sketch of the History of Newbury; Celebration of the 250th Anniversary of the Settlement of Newbury (1885), Newburyport* (Historical Society of Old Newbury, 1885); *Salisbury 350th, 1638–1988*; Victor Channing Sanborn, "The grantees and settlement of Hampton, N.H.," *Essex Institute* 53 (1917): 228–49; Fanny Louise Walton, *Historic Nuggets of Newburyport* (Newburyport: Newburyport Press, 1958); Mrs. E. Vale Smith, *History of Newburyport: From the Earliest Settlement of the Country to the Present Time* (Newburyport, s.n. 1854). More general information about the settlement of New Hampshire comes from Jeremy Belknap, *History of New Hampshire*, Vol. I (Phila., 1784; reprint, Dover, N.H.: J.Mann and J.K. Remick, 1812); and Edwin Charlton, *New Hampshire as It Is* (Claremont, N.H.: Tracy and Co., 1856). Information on homesteading comes from Douglas Edward Leach, "The Life of the Pioneer," in *The Northern Colonial Frontier, 1607–1763* (N.Y.: Holt, Rinehart and Winston, 1966), pp. 74–79.

21. See Chapter Six, "These Now Insulting Pequots," and Chapter Seven, "Destroy Them . . . and Save the Plunder" in the Stanton Family section.

22. Nathaniel E. Shurtleff, ed., *Records of the Governor and Company of the Massachusetts Bay in New England*, 5 vols. (Boston: William White, 1853–54), Vol. 1, p. 167.

23. Wood, *New England's Prospect*, 64–65.

24. Roger Williams, *Complete Writings* (N.Y.: Russell & Russell, 1963), Vol. 2, pp. 46, 47; Joke quoted in Jennings, *Invasion of America*, p. 83.

25. Dow, "History of Hampton," p. 2.

26. Dunn, Savage, and Yeandle, eds., *Journal of John Winthrop*, p. 407.

27. Nathaniel E. Shurtleff, *Records of Massachusetts*, 2: 24.

28. Ibid., p. 73.

29. William Hubbard, *The History of the Indian Wars in New England from the First Settlement to the Termination of the War with King Philip, in 1677, from the Original Work by the Rev. William Hubbard* (1677), ed. Samuel G. Drake, 2 vols. (Roxbury, Mass., 1865; N.Y.: Kraus Reprint Co., 1969), I, pp. 48–49.

30. Coffin, *Sketch of History of Newbury*, p. 91.

31. *Records and Files of Quarterly Courts of Essex County*, 1: 110, 113, 139.

32. C.E. Potter, *History of Manchester* (Manchester, N.H.: C.E. Potter, 1856), pp. 61–63, quoting Massachusetts Archives.

33. William Little, *History of Warren* (Manchester, N.H.: W.E. Moore, 1870), quoted in Beals, *Passaconaway in the White Mountains*, pp. 46–47.

Chapter 4: *The Saints*

1. The wife of James Harris of Boston was first identified as Sarah Denison, daughter of Edward Denison and Mary Weld, by Nathaniel Harris Morgan in *A History of James Harris of New London, Conn., and His Descendants from 1640 to 1878* (Hartford, Conn., 1878). She would thus be descended from the daughter of Thomas Weld's brother Joseph Weld and from George Denison's brother Edward (see George Denison in the Stanton Family section). This connection, though still widely repeated, is no longer tenable, as Margaret Harris Stover demonstrated in an article in *Harris Hunters: Newsletter of the Harris Family*, ed. Richard G. Boyd (Jan. 1996): 2. Stover showed that Sarah would have been ten years old in 1667, by which time James Harris was known to be married. The case for identifying Sarah Harris with Sarah Eliot, daughter of John Eliot's brother Jacob, has been researched exhaustively by Gale Ion Harris and published in his article "James and Sarah (Eliot?) Harris of Boston and New London," *NEHGR*, 154 (Jan. 2000): 3-32. Although entirely circumstantial, his evidence is considerable and compelling, and there is at present no other identification as likely.

My sources for biographical information about John and/or Jacob Eliot are Richard Cogley, *John Eliot's Mission to the Indians before King Philip's War* (Cambridge and London: Harvard University Press, 1999); Richard Cogley, "John Eliot's Puritan Ministry," *Vides et Historia*, 21(1) (Winter/Spring 1999); Ola E. Winslow, *John Eliot, "Apostle to the Indians"* (Boston: Houghton Mifflin, 1968); *Life of the Rev. John Eliot, the Apostle to the Indians* (London: Religious Tract Society [18?]); W. Winters, "The Pilgrim Fathers of Nazing," *NEHGR* 28 (1874): 140–45; William B. Transk, "Rev. John Eliot's Records of the First Church in Roxbury, Mass.," *NEHGR* 33 (1879) pp. 62–68; Hamilton Andrews Hill, *History of the Old South Church* (Boston: Houghton Mifflin); and Cotton Mather, *Magnalia Christi Americana, or, the Ecclesiastical History of New England*

(London: Thomas Pankhurst, 1702). Information about Thomas Weld and/or his brother Joseph comes from Isabel Weld (Perkins) Anderson, *Under the Black Horse Flag: Annals of the Weld Family* . . . (N.Y.: Houghton, 1926); *NEHGR* (1891) 45: 115; "Thomas Shepard's Memoir of His Own Life," in Alexander Young, ed., *Chronicles of the First Planters of the Colony of Massachusetts Bay, from 1623–1636* (Boston, 1846), pp. 521–22; *Appleton's Cyclopedia of American Biography*, eds. James Grant Wilson and John Fiske (N.Y.: D. Appleton, 1889); and *Dictionary of American Biography*, ed. Dumas Malone (N.Y.: Charles Scribner's Sons, 1936).

2. Winslow, *John Eliot, "Apostle to the Indians,"* p. 1; Alden T. Vaughan, *New England Frontier, 1620–1675* (Boston: Little, Brown, 1965), pp. 245–46; Samuel Eliot Morison, *Builders of the Bay Colony* (Boston: Houghton Mifflin, 1930), p. 292.

3. John Eliot at his wife's funeral, "John Eliot" in *Appleton's Cyclopedia*, 2, p. 323.

4. S. R. Gardiner, *Reports of Cases in Courts of Star Chamber and High Commission* (1886), p. 260; "Thomas Weld," *Dictionary of American Biography*, IX, p. 628.

5. Anderson, *Under the Black Horse Flag*, p. 5; "Thomas Shepard's Memoir of His Own Life," pp. 521–22.

6. Francis S. Drake, "Roxbury in the Colonial Period," in Justin Winsor, ed., *The Memorial History of Boston* (Boston: Ticknor and Co., 1880–1881), I, p. 407. My information on the settlement of early Boston and Roxbury is also drawn from Darrett B. Rutman, *Winthrop's Boston: Portrait of a Puritan Town, 1630–1649* (Chapel Hill: University of North Carolina Press, 1965); Morison, *Builders of the Bay Colony* and *Harvard College in the Seventeenth Century*, 2 vols. (Cambridge: Harvard University Press, 1936, 1962); C. M. Ellis, *History of Roxbury Town* (Boston: S. G. Drake, 1847); Richard S. Dunn, James Savage, and Laetitia Yeandle, eds., *The Journal of John Winthrop, 1630–1649* (Cambridge: Belknap Press, 1996); and Samuel Gardner Drake, *The History and Antiquities of Boston* . . . (Boston: L. Stevens, 1856).

7. Quoted in Rutman, *Winthrop's Boston*, p. 12.

8. "Thomas Welde to his Former Parishioners in Tarling, June/July 1632," in Everett Emerson, ed., *Letters from New England: The Massachusetts Bay Colony, 1629–1638* (Amherst: University of Massachusetts Press, 1976), pp. 94–98, from British Museum MS Sloane 922, Folios 167–74.

9. "John Eliot to Sir Simonds D'Ewes," Sept. 18, 1633, reprinted in Emerson, *Letters from New England*, p. 106, from British Museum MS Harley 384, Folios 256–57.

10. Theodore Dwight Bozeman, *To Lead Ancient Lives: The Primitive Dimension in Puritanism* (Chapel Hill and London: University of North Carolina Press, 1988), pp. 114–19. My other secondary sources on Puritanism in early colonial America include Vaughan, *New England Frontier*; Larzer Ziff, *Puritanism in America: New Culture in a New World* (N.Y.: Viking, 1973); Albert E. Van Dusen, *Puritans against the Wilderness* (Chester, Conn.: Pequot Press, 1975); Neal Salisbury, *Manitou and Providence: Indians, Europeans, and the Making of New England, 1500–1643* (N.Y.: Oxford University Press, 1982); Perry Miller, *The New England Mind: The Seventeenth Century* (N.Y.: Macmillan, 1939); Peter N. Carol, *Puritanism and the Wilderness: The Intellectual Significance of the New England Frontier, 1629–1799* (N.Y.: Columbia University Press, 1969); David Stannard, *The Puritan Way of Death: A Study in Religion, Culture and Social Change* (N.Y.: Oxford University Press, 1977); David D. Hall, *Worlds of Wonder, Days of Judgment: Popular Religious Belief in Early New England* (N.Y.: Knopf, 1989); Francis Jennings, *The Invasion of America: Indians, Colonialism, and the Cant of Conquest* (Chapel Hill: University of North Carolina Press, 1975); James Axtell, *The Invasion Within: The Contest of Cultures in Colonial North America* (N.Y. and Oxford:

Oxford University Press, 1985) and *The European and the Indian* (N.Y. and Oxford: Oxford University Press, 1981).

11. Tyler, quoted in Morison, *Builders of the Bay Colony*, p. 197.

12. *Bay Psalm Book*, quoted in Louis B. Mason, *The Life and Times of Major John Mason of Connecticut* (N.Y.: G. P. Putnam's Sons, 1935), p. 195.

13. Darren Staloff, *The Making of an American Thinking Class: Intellectuals and Intelligentsia in Puritan Massachusetts* (N.Y.: Oxford University Press, 1998), pp. 36, 43, 91–94; Dunn, Savage, and Yeandle, *Journal of John Winthrop*, pp. 136–37.

14. Cogley, "John Eliot's Puritan Ministry," 4–5. This article and Cogley, *John Eliot's Mission*, are my chief sources on Eliot's religious views.

15. Theodore Dwight Bozeman, quoted in Cogley, "John Eliot's Puritan Ministry," p. 7.

16. Eliot, *The Christian Commonwealth* (London, 1659), in Massachusetts Historical Society, 3rd Ser. 9 (1846): 139.

17. My sources on the Antinomian Controversy are Charles Francis Adams, ed., *Antinomianism in the Colony of Massachusetts Bay, 1636–1638* (Boston, 1894); Charles Francis Adams, Jr., *Three Episodes in Massachusetts History*, 2 vols. (Boston, 1896); and David Hall, *The Antinomian Controversy, 1636–1638* (Middletown, Conn.: Wesleyan University Press, 1968), which includes "A Short Story of the Rise, Reign, and Ruine of the Antinomians, Familists & Libertines," sometimes attributed to Thomas Weld.

18. Max Weber, *The Protestant Ethic and the Rise of Capitalism*, trans. Talcott Parsons (N.Y.: Scribner's, 1930), p. 104.

19. Joshua Coffin, *A Sketch of the History of Newbury* (Boston: Samuel G. Drake, 1845), p. 22.

20. "A Report of the Trial of Mrs Anne Hutchinson before the Church in Boston, March 1638," in Adams, ed., *Antinomianism in the Colony of Massachusetts Bay*, p. 336; also *Life of John Mason*, p. 175.

21. Dunn, Savage, and Yeandle, eds., *Journal of John Winthrop*, p. 244.

22. The following discussion is based primarily on M. J. Tooley, "Political Thought and the Theory and Practice of Toleration," in *The New Cambridge Modern History*, Vol. III, ed. R. B. Wernham, pp. 480–506, and G. L. Mosse, "Changes in Religious Thought," in ibid., Vol. IV, ed. J. P. Cooper (Cambridge: Cambridge University Press, 1968), pp. 169–201.

23. Michael Zuckerman in foreword to Avihu Zakai, *Theocracy in Massachusetts: Reformation and Separation in Early Puritan New England* (Lewiston: Mellen University Press, 1994), no pagination.

24. Henry W. Bowden and James P. Ronda, *John Eliot's Indian Dialogues: A Study in Cultural Interaction* (Westport, Conn.: Greenwood Press, 1980).

25. This doctrine is described in some detail in Bozeman, *To Lead Ancient Lives*, pp. 198–217.

26. Marjorie Reeves, "History and Eschatology: Medieval and Early Protestant Thought in some English and Scottish Writings," *Medievalia et Humanistica*, IV (1973); 109, quoted in Bozeman, *To Lead Ancient Lives*, p. 206.

27. Nathaniel E. Shurtleff, *Records of Massachusetts*, I: 332, June 2, 1641.

28. Robert C. Black, *The Younger John Winthrop* (N.Y.: Columbia University Press, 1966), p. 113.

29. *Dictionary of National Biography*, s.v. "Peters or Peter, Hugh."

30. For Thomas Weld's subsequent career in England, my sources are *The Dictionary of National Biography*, s.v. "Thomas Weld"; "Rev. Thomas Welde's Letter, 1643," *NEHGR* 36 (1882): 36–39; William L. Sachse, "Migration of New Englanders to England,

1640–1660," *American Historical Review* 53 (1948): 251–78; Thomas Weld to John Winthrop, *Winthrop Papers*, III: 365–67; Rev. Denis Murphy, *Cromwell in Ireland: A History of the Cromwell's Irish Campaign* (Dublin: M. G. Gill & Sons, 1890); A. G. Matthews, *Calamy Revised: Being a Revision of Edmund Calamy's account of the ministers and others ejected and silenced, 1660–62* (Oxford and N.Y.: Oxford University Press, 1988); and William Fordyce, *The history and antiquities of the county palatine of Durham, comprising a condensed account of its natural, civil and ecclesiastical history* (London: T. Fordyce, 1857). Weld's encounter with William Laud is recorded in Laud's diary, *The History of the Troubles and Tryal of the most Revernd father in God, and blessed martyr, Archbishop Laud*, ed. Henry Wharton (1694).

31. Fordyce, *The history and antiquities of the county palatine of Durham*, p. 761, quoted in *NEHGR* 36 (1882): 406.

32. Henry Wharton, ed., *The History of the Troubles and Tryal of the most Revernd father in God, and blessed martyr, Archbishop Laud* (London, 1694), p. 213.

Chapter 5: *First Fruits*

1. Thomas Lechford, *Plain Dealing; or, News from New-England* (1642), ed. J. Hammond Trumbull (1867), new intro. Everett Emerson (N.Y.: Garrett Press, 1970), p. 56 (p. 21 of original edition).

2. [Thomas Weld and Hugh Peter], *New England's First Fruits, in respect to the progress of learning, in the Colledge at Cambridge in Massachusetts-bay . . .* (1643) (Boston, 1792), *MHSC*, 1st Series, I:249. Weld's fundraising efforts on behalf of the Harvard Indian College and the founding of the New England Company are documented in Weld and Peter, "New England's First Fruits . . . 1643," pp. 242–50; Thomas Welde, "Innocency Cleared," in *NEHGR*, 36 (1882): 62–70; [——] "The Society for the Propagation of the Gospel in New England and the Rev. Thomas Welde," in *NEHGR* 34 (1885): 179–83; Raymond Phineas Stearns, "The Weld–Peter Mission to England," in *Publications of the Colonial Society of Massachusetts, Transactions* 32 (1933–37): 188–246; William Kellaway, *The New England Company, 1649–1776* (London: Longmans, 1961); Samuel Eliot Morison, *Harvard in the Seventeenth Century* (Cambridge: Harvard University Press, 1936, 1962); and *Winthrop Papers*, "Daniel Weld to John Winthrop, Jr.," *MHSC*, 5th Series, VI: 409.

3. Weld and Peter, *First Fruits*, pp. 242–50.

4. Henry Warner Bowden, *American Indians and Christian Missions: Studies in Cultural Conflict* (Chicago: University of Chicago Press, 1981), p. 112. Puritan missions to Native Americans have engendered considerable scholarship. The major secondary sources I have consulted are Richard Cogley, *John Eliot's Mission to the Indians Before King Philip's War* (Cambridge and London: Harvard University Press, 1999); Henry W. Bowden and James P. Ronda, *John Eliot's Indian Dialogues: A Study in Cultural Interaction* (Westport, Conn.: Greenwood Press, 1980); James Axtell, *The Invasion Within: The Contest of Cultures in Colonial North America* (N.Y. and Oxford: Oxford University Press, 1985) and *The European and the Indian* (N.Y. and Oxford: Oxford University Press, 1981); Daniel Mandell, "Standing by His Father: Thomas Waban of Natick, circa 1630–1722," in Robert S. Grumet, ed., *Northeastern Indian Lives, 1632–1816* (Amherst: University of Massachusetts Press, 1996); Francis Jennings, *The Invasion of America: Indians, Colonialism, and the Cant of Conquest* (Chapel Hill: University of North Carolina Press, 1975); Neal Salisbury, "Red Puritans," *William and Mary Quarterly*, 3rd Series 31 (1974): 27–54; James P. Ronda, "We Are Well as We Are: An Indian Critique of

17th Century Missions," *William and Mary Quarterly*, 3rd Series 34: 66–82; Kenneth Morrison, "'That Art of Coyning Christians': John Eliot and the Praying Indians of Massachusetts," in *Ethnohistory* 21(1) (Winter 1974): 77–92; Francis Jennings, "Goals and Functions of Puritan Missions to the Indians," *Ethnohistory* 18(3) (1971): 197–212; and Alden T. Vaughan, *New England Frontier, 1620–1675* (Boston: Little, Brown, 1965).

5. Quoted in editorial note, Lechford, *Plain Dealing*, ed. Trumbull, p. 54, in Jennings, *Invasion of America*, pp. 235–36.
6. Andrew Delbanco, *The Puritan Ordeal* (Cambridge: Harvard University Press, 1989), p. 105.
7. John Winthrop, quoted in Cogley, *John Eliot's Mission*, pp. 3–4.
8. Bowden, *American Indians and Christian Missions*, pp. 115–16.
9. Thomas Shepard, *The Day-Breaking, If not the Sun-Rising of the Gospell with the Indians in New-England* (London, 1647). In *MHSC* 3rd series, 4 (1834): 15.
10. "The Letter of Mr. Eliot to T. S. concerning the late work of God among the Indians," Sept. 24, 1647, in Thomas Shepard, *The Clear Sun-shine of the Gospel Breaking Forth upon the Indians in New-England . . .* (1648), *MHSC*, 3rd Series, IV (1834): 50.
11. Jennings, *Invasion of America*, pp. 239–53.
12. Nathaniel E. Shurtleff, ed., *Records of the Court of Assistants of the Colony of Massachusetts Bay, 1630–1692* (Boston, 1853–54), II, p. 55.
13. Shurtleff, ed., *Records of Massachusetts Bay*, II, pp. 176–77, 178.
14. Quoted in Jennings, *Invasion of America*, p. 244.
15. Cogley, *John Eliot's Mission*, p. 5.
16. John Cotton in Everett Emerson, ed., *Letters from New England: The Massachusetts Bay Colony, 1629–1638* (Amherst: University of Massachusetts Press, 1976), quoted in ibid., p. 20.
17. John Winthrop quoted in Cogley, *John Eliot's Mission*, p. 40.
18. [John Wilson?], "The Day Breaking, If Not the Sun-Rising of the Gospell with the Indians in New England," in *MHSC*, 3rd Series, IV (1834): 8–14.
19. Jennings, *Invasion of America*, p. 247.
20. Weld, "Innocency Cleared," pp. 69–70.
21. Louis B. Mason, *The Life and Times of Major John Mason of Connecticut* (N.Y.: G. P. Putnam's Sons, 1935), p. 193. For more information about Native students at Harvard, see Morison, *Harvard in the Seventeenth Century*.
22. William Wood, *New England's Prospect* (London, 1634), ed. Alden T. Vaughan (Amherst: University of Massachusetts Press, 1977), p. 102.
23. Edward Winslow, "The Glorious Progress of the Gospel amongst the Indians in New England . . ." (1649), *MHSC*, 3rd Series, IV (1834): 82.
24. Weld and Peter, *First Fruits*, quoted in *Spirit of the New England Tribes*, p. 38.
25. This story is told in William Hubbard, *The History of the Indian Wars in New England from the First Settlement to the Termination of the War with King Philip in 1677*, ed. Samuel G. Drake, 2 vols. (Roxbury, Mass.: 1865), I, pp. 289–90.
26. John Eliot, quoted in Ronda, "We Are Well as We Are," pp. 32, 67.
27. John Josselyn, "An Account of Two Voyages to New-England" (1675), *MHSC*, 3rd Series, III (1833): 299.
28. Josselyn, "An Account of Two Voyages," p. 310.
29. Bowden, *American Indians and Christian Missions*, p. 115.
30. Cotton Mather, *Magnalia Christi Americana: or, the Ecclesiastical History of New-England from Its First Planting in the Year 1620, unto the Year of our Lord, 1698*, 2 vols. (1702, reprinted Hartford, Conn., 1820), Vol. 2, pp. 479–80.

31. Axtell, *The European and the Indian,* pp. 42–43.

32. Bowden and Ronda, *Indian Dialogues,* p. 34.

33. Kenneth Miner, quoted in Cogley, *John Eliot's Mission,* p. 123.

34. Ronda, "We Are Well as We Are," p. 67.

35. Henry Whitfield, ed., "The Light appearing more and more towards the perfect Day" (London, 1651). In *MHSC,* 3rd Series, IV (1834): 139–40, quoted in Jennings, *Invasion of America,* p. 248; George Cartwright, "Account of Massachusetts" (1665) in "Clarendon Papers," *NYHSC,* 1869, p. 86, quoted in Jennings, *Invasion of America,* p. 248; Daniel Gookin, "Historical Collections," *MHSC,* 1st Series, I: 208–9.

36. Eliot, "Light Appearing," p. 139; Eliot, *Christian Commonwealth,* p. 133; Letter to Winslow quoted in Cogley, *John Eliot's Mission,* p. 91.

37. In fact, he believed that Native Americans were the descendants of two Hebrew peoples, the Gentile sons of Eber and the lost tribes of Israel, who had migrated to North America and mingled, reaching the eastern shores of the Atlantic, the biblical "utmost ends of the earth eastward." He believed they deserved to be redeemed before the Jews, because they had lived in ignorance of Christianity, while the Jews had supposedly lived in contempt of it. See Cogley, *John Eliot's Mission,* pp. 87–90.

38. Cogley, *John Eliot's Mission,* p. 247.

39. Cotton Mather, *Triumphs of the Reformed Religion,* p. 85, quoted in ibid., p. 103.

40. Bowden and Ronda, *Indian Dialogues,* p. 33.

41. Statistics from Bowden and Ronda, *Indian Dialogues,* 40; Gookin, "Historical Collections," p. 182.

42. Ronda, "We Are Well as We Are," p. 68; Bowden and Ronda, *Indian Dialogues,* p. 30.

43. Reuben Gold Thwaites, ed., *The Jesuit Relations and Allied Documents,* 73 vols. (N.Y.: Pageant Books, 1959), 1: 31.

44. Edward Winslow, "The Glorious Progress of the Gospel amongst the Indians in New England," p. 85, quoted in Ronda, "We Are Well as We Are," p. 71.

45. Bowden and Ronda, *Indian Dialogues,* p. 71.

46. Ibid., pp. 49, 71–73.

47. Ronda, "We Are Well as We Are," p. 81; P. F. S. de Charlevoix, *History and General Description of New France,* ed. and trans. John Gilmary Shea, II (N.Y., 1870), p. 79, quoted in Ronda, "We Are Well as We Are," p. 81.

48. Bowden and Ronda, *Indian Dialogues,* pp. 64, 45, 87.

49. Roger Williams to Mass. General Court, Oct. 5, 1654, in David Pulsifer, ed., *Acts of the Commissioners of the United Colonies,* 2 vols. Published as part of *Records of the Colony of New Plymouth,* IX–X (Boston, 1859), II: pp. 43–49.

50. Letter of John Eliot, Dec. 1, 1671, *Mass. Hist. Soc. Proceedings,* 1879–80, 17: 250, quoted in Jennings, *Invasion of America,* p. 249.

51. Morison, *Builders of the Bay Colony* (Boston: Houghton Mifflin, 1930), p. 306.

52. "Peters or Peter, Hugh," *Dictionary of National Biography;* William L. Sachse, "Migration of New Englanders to England 1640–1660," *American Historical Review* 53 (1948): 276.

53. John Ford, ed., *Some Correspondence between the Governors and Treasurers of the New England Company in London and the Commissionaers of the United Colonies in America . . .* (N.Y.: B. Franklin, 1970), pp. 74–76.

Chapter 6: *"These Now Insulting Pequots"*

1. Genealogical and biographical information about the Stanton family comes from William A. Stanton, *A Record Genealogical, Biographical, Statistical of Thomas Stanton, of Connecticut, and His Descendants, 1635–1891* (Albany, N.Y.: Joel Munsell's Sons, 1891); Frances Manwaring Caulkins, *History of New London, Connecticut* (New London, 1852); and Richard Anson Wheeler, *History of the Town of Stonington* (New London: Press of the Day, 1900). Additional family lore comes from Thomas Stanton descendants John Whit Davis and Bernard J. Stanton (including the latter's speech at the dedication ceremony for the new monument to Thomas Stanton on Aug. 4, 1995); William W. Bower, "The Thomas Stanton Story" (Conn. Translation Service, 1969); Emily H. Lynch, "The Robert Stanton/Davis Homestead," Stonington Historical Society, *Historical Footnotes* 24(3) (May 1987): 10–11; Henry Robinson Palmer, "The Beginnings of the Town," Stonington Historical Society, *Historical Footnotes* 23(1) (Nov. 1986): 8–9; and R. R. Hinman, *A Catalogue of the Names of the First Puritan Settlers of the Colony of Connecticut* (Baltimore: Genealogical Publishing Co., 1968). Thomas Stanton's will can be found at the State Library, Hartford, Conn. Private Controversy Collections, Series #2, 24:148 a, b, c, d. Sources for related families were the chapter on the Lord family in Edward Elbridge Salisbury and Evelyn McCurdy Salisbury, *Family Histories and Genealogies* (New Haven, 1892), pp. 247–72; James Swift Rogers, *James Rogers of New London, Ct., and His Descendants* (Boston, 1902); and E. Glenn Denison, *Denison Genealogy: Ancestors and Descendants of Captain George Denison* (Baltimore: Genealogical Society Co., 1978).

2. According to Bernard Stanton, family historian of the Stanton Society.

3. Alfred A. Cave, *The Pequot War* (Amherst: University of Massachusetts Press, 1996), p. 64. My primary sources for the Pequot War are the contemporary accounts found in Charles Orr, *History of the Pequot War: The Contemporary Accounts of Mason, Underhill, Vincent and Gardiner* (Cleveland: Helman-Taylor Co., 1897). My main secondary sources are Cave, *The Pequot War* and "Who Killed John Stone?: A Note on the Origins of the Pequot War," *William and Mary Quarterly*, 3rd Series, 49 (3) (July 1992); Francis Jennings, *The Invasion of America: Indians, Colonialism, and the Cant of Conquest* (Chapel Hill: University of North Carolina Press, 1975); Laurence M. Hauptman and James D. Wherry, eds., *The Pequots in Southern New England: The Fall and Rise of an American Indian Nation* (Norman and London: University of Oklahoma Press, 1990); and Kevin McBride, "The Pequot War and Massacre," in Melissa Jayne Fawcett, *The Lasting of the Mohegans* (Uncasville, Conn.: Mohegan Tribe, 1995). See also Louis B. Mason, *The Life and Times of Major John Mason of Connecticut, 1600–1672* (N.Y.: G. P. Putnam's Sons, 1935); Alden Vaughan, *New England Frontier: Puritans and Indians, 1620–1675* (Boston: Little, Brown, 1965); Neal Salisbury, *Manitou and Providence: Indians, Europeans, and the Making of New England, 1500–1643* (N.Y.: Oxford University Press, 1982) and "The Hartford Treaty with the Narragansetts and the Fenwick Letters," *NEHGR* 46 (1892): 354–56.

4. William Wood, *New England's Prospect* (London, 1634), ed. Alden T. Vaughan (Amherst: University of Massachusetts Press, 1977), p. 80.

5. William Bradford, *Of Plymouth Plantation, 1620–1647*, ed. Samuel Eliot Morison (N.Y.: Modern Library, 1952), p. 291.

6. Jennings, *Invasion of America*, p. 193.

7. John Winthrop to John Winthrop, Jr., Dec. 1634, Allyn Forbes, ed., *The Winthrop Papers*, 5 vols. (Boston: Massachusetts Historical Society, 1929–47), III, p. 177. This is

one of two published sources I used for the correspondence of the Winthrops; the other is several volumes of *MHSC*, series 3, 4 and 5. Unpublished letters are held in the Winthrop Family Papers, Massachusetts Historical Society, Boston.

8. Salisbury, *Manitou and Providence*, p. 216. I have consulted the following books about the early settlement of the Connecticut Valley: Sherman W. Adams and Henry R. Stiles, *The History of Ancient Wethersfield*, 2 vols. (Somersworth: New Hampshire Publishing Co., 1904-1974); Charles M. Andrews, *The River Towns of Connecticut*, Johns Hopkins University Studies in Historical and Political Science, VII (Baltimore, 1889); William DeLoss Love, *The Colonial History of Hartford* (Chester, Conn.: Centinel Hill Press, 1974); "Original Distribution of the Lands in Hartford among the Settlers, 1639, Hartford," *CHSC* (Connecticut Historical Society, 1912), Vol. XIV.

9. Melissa Jayne Fawcett, *The Lasting of the Mohegans* (Uncasville, Conn.: The Mohegan Tribe, 1995), p. 11.

10. Jonathan Brewster to John Winthrop, Jr., June 18, 1636, Forbes, ed. *Winthrop Papers*, III, p. 270.

11. Cave, *The Pequot War*, p. 101.

12. "Commission and Instructions from the Colony of Massachusetts Bay to John Winthrop, Jr., for Treating with the Pequots," Forbes, ed., *Winthrop Papers*, III, p. 285.

13. Calvin Martin, "The Metaphysics of Writing Indian-White History," in Martin, ed., *The American Indian and the Problem of History* (N.Y.: Oxford University Press, 1987), p. 33.

14. Richard S. Dunn, James Savage, and Laetitia Yeandle, eds., *The Journal of John Winthrop, 1630–1649* (Cambridge: Belknap Press, 1996), p. 183; Cave, *The Pequot War*, p. 168.

15. Dunn, Savage, and Yeandle, *Journal of John Winthrop*, p. 183.

16. John Underhill, *Newes from America, or a New and Experiemental Discoverie of New England* (1638), in Orr, *History of the Pequot War*, p. 55; translation in Cave, *The Pequot War*, p. 114.

17. Roger Williams to Major John Mason and Governor Thomas Prence, June 23, 1670, in Glenn W. LaFantasie, ed., *The Correspondence of Roger Williams*, *RIHS*, 2 vols. (Hanover and London: Brown University Press / University of New England, 1988), 2: 611–12; Roger Williams to Sir Henry Vane and John Winthrop, Sr., Forbes, ed., *Winthrop Papers*, III, p. 414.

18. Lion Gardiner, *Relation of the Pequot War* (1833), in Orr, *History of the Pequot War*, pp. 131–33.

19. Thomas Hooker to John Winthrop, Sr., May 1637, Forbes, ed., *Winthrop Papers*, III, pp. 407–8; John Higginson to John Winthrop, May 1637, Forbes, ed., *Winthrop Papers*, III, pp. 404–5, quoted in Cave, *The Pequot War*, p. 169.

20. Edward Johnson, *WonderWorking Providence of Sion's Savior in New England, 1628–1651*, ed. J. Franklin Jameson (N.Y.: Charles Scribner's Sons, 1910), pp. 105–6; Hinman, *A Catalogue of the Names of the First Puritan Settlers of the Colony of Connecticut*, p. 75.

21. John Mason, *A Brief History of the Pequot War* (1736), in Orr, *History of the Pequot War*, pp. 23–24.

22. Mason, *Brief History*, p. 26.

23. Ibid., pp. 27–29.

24. Underhill, *Newes from America*, pp. 80–81.

25. Cave, *The Pequot War*, p. 153.

Chapter 7: *"Destroy Them . . . and Save the Plunder"*

1. Bernard Stanton, family historian for the Thomas Stanton Society, personal communication, Nov. 1999.
2. Underhill, *Newes from America* (1638), in Charles Orr, *History of the Pequot War: The Contemporary Accounts of Mason, Underhill, Vincent and Gardiner* (Cleveland: Helman-Taylor Co., 1897), p. 81.
3. Underhill in Orr, *History of the Pequot War*, 82; John Mason, *A Brief History of the Pequot War*, (1736), quoted in Orr, *History of the Pequot War*, p. 41.
4. Mason and Underhill in Orr, *History of the Pequot War*, pp. 28, 84. My main secondary sources on the aftermath and consequences of the Pequot War are Alfred A. Cave, *The Pequot War* (Amherst: University of Massachusetts Press, 1996), p. 151; Laurence M. Hauptman and James D. Wherry, eds., *The Pequots in Southern New England: The Fall and Rise of an American Indian Nation* (Norman and London: University of Oklahoma Press, 1990); and Francis Jennings, *The Invasion of America: Indians, Colonialism, and the Cant of Conquest* (Chapel Hill: University of North Carolina Press, 1975).
5. Edward Johnson, *WonderWorking Providence of Sion's Savior in New England, 1628–1651*, ed. J. Franklin Jameson (N.Y.: Charles Scribner's Sons, 1910), p. 263.
6. Underhill in Orr, *History of the Pequot War*, p. 81.
7. Ibid., p. 83.
8. Mason in Orr, *History of the Pequot War*, p. 30.
9. Roger Williams quoted in Cave, *The Pequot War*, p. 158.
10. Gardener, "Relations," in Orr, *History of the Pequot War*, pp. 137–38.
11. John Winthrop to William Bradford, May 28, 1637, Allyn Forbes, ed., *The Winthrop Papers*, 5 vols. (Boston: *MHSC*, 1929–47), III, p. 457.
12. Ibid.
13. Almon Wheeler Lauber, *Indian Slavery in the Colonial Times within the Present Limits of the United States* (N.Y.: Columbia University Press, 1913), pp. 122–23. See also Ethel Boissevain, "Whatever Became of the New England Indians Shipped to Bermuda to be Sold as Slaves?" *Man in the Northeast* 21 (1981): 103–14; Bernard C. Steiner, *History of Slavery in Connecticut* Johns Hopkins University Studies in Historical and Political Science, Series 11, Nos. 9-10 (Baltimore: The Johns Hopkins Press, 1893).
14. The text of treaty is reprinted in Alden Vaughan, *New England Frontier: Puritans and Indians, 1620–1675* (Boston: Little, Brown, 1965), pp. 340–41.
15. Quoted in Samuel Eliot Morison, *Builders of the Bay Colony* (Boston: Houghton Mifflin, 1930), p. 121.
16. Cave, *The Pequot War*, pp. 170–71.
17. Ibid.
18. Cotton Mather, *Magnalia Christi Americana* (1702), ed. Kenneth B. Murdock (Cambridge: Belknap Press, 1977), p. 166, quoted in Cave, *The Pequot War*, p. 170; Mason in Orr, *History of the Pequot War*, p. 43.
19. George Madison Bodge, *Soldiers in King Philip's War* (Baltimore: Genealogical Publishing Co., 1967), Appendix A, p. 466.
20. Mason in Orr, *History of the Pequot War*, p. 43.
21. Lynn Ceci, "Wampum as a Peripheral Resource," in Laurence M. Hauptman and James D. Wherry, eds., *The Pequots in Southern New England: The Fall and Rise of an American Indian Nation* (Norman and London: University of Oklahoma Press, 1990), pp. 60–61.
22. J. Hammond Trumbull, *Public Records of the Colony of Connecticut*, 3 vols. (Hartford:

Brown and Parsons, 1850), I, p. 19, Apr. 5, 1637; Richard Anson Wheeler, *History of the Town of Stonington* (New London: Press of the Day, 1900), pp. 576–77.

23. William A. Stanton, *A Record Genealogical, Biographical, Statistical of Thomas Stanton, of Connecticut, and His Descendants 1635–1891* (Albany: Joel Munsell's Sons, 1891), p. 15; Albert E. Van Dusen, *Puritans against the Wilderness: Connecticut History to 1763* (Chester, Conn.: Pequot Press, 1975), p. 40.

24. Charles J. Hoadley, ed., *Records of the Colony and Plantation of New Haven* (Hartford: Case, Tiffany and Co., 1857), pp. 1–5.

25. Bernard Stanton, personal communication, Nov. 1999.

26. Stanton, *Thomas Stanton*, p. 13.

Chapter 8: *Ambassador to the Indians*

1. Frances Manwaring Caulkins, *History of New London, Connecticut* (New London, 1852), p. 101.

2. Hezekiah Usher, quoted in George Parker Winship, ed., *The New England Company of 1649 and John Eliot* (Boston: Publications of the Prince Society, 1920), p. 34.

3. Sources on interactions between Native Americans and the English in Connecticut before and after the Pequot War include Francis Jennings, *The Invasion of America: Indians, Colonialism, and the Cant of Conquest* (Chapel Hill: University of North Carolina Press, 1975); Neal Salisbury, *Manitou and Providence: Indians, Europeans, and the Making of New England, 1500–1643* (N.Y.: Oxford University Press, 1982); Laurence M. Hauptman and James D. Wherry, eds., *The Pequots in Southern New England: The Fall and Rise of an American Indian Nation* (Norman and London: University of Oklahoma Press, 1990), especially Jack Campisi, "The Emergence of the Mashantucket Pequot Tribe, 1637–1975"; and Neal Salisbury, "Indians and Colonists in Southern New England after the Pequot War: An Uneasy Balance"; George Sheldon, *1636 – Pocumtuck – 1886: A History of Deerfield, Massachusetts . . . with a special study of the Indian Wars of the Connecticut Valley*, 2 vols. (Deerfield, 1895–96); John W. De Forest, *History of the Indians of Connecticut* (Hartford: W. J. Haersley, 1852); Edward S. Johnson, "Uncas and the Politics of Contact" and Kevin A. McBride, "The Legacy of Robin Cassacinamon: Mashantucket Pequot Leadership in the Historic Period," in *Northeastern Indian Lives, 1632–1816*, ed. Robert S. Grumet (Amherst: University of Massachusetts Press, 1996). "Pequot Indians" in Richard Anson Wheeler, *History of the Town of Stonington* (New London: Press of the Day, 1900); Arthur Peale, *Uncas and the Mohegan Pequot* (Boston: Meador Publishing, 1939); and William L. Stone, *Uncas and Miantonomo* (N.Y.: 1842) provided some information, but are less reliable. For a modern Mohegan perspective, see Melissa Jayne Fawcett, *The Lasting of the Mohegans*, Part I (Uncasville, Conn.: Mohegan Tribe, 1995).

4. LaFantasie, *The Correspondence of Roger Williams*, Roger Williams to Gov. John Winthrop, Feb. 28, 1637–38, I, p. 145; Roger Williams to John Winthrop, Jan. 10, 1637–38, I, p. 140; Roger Williams to John Winthrop, May 27, 1638, I, p. 157.

5. Robert C. Black, *The Younger John Winthrop* (N.Y.: Columbia University Press, 1966), p. 135; Daniel Gookin, "Historical Collections," *MHSC*, 1st Series, I: 208; John Mason, "Brief history," in Charles Orr, *History of the Pequot War: The Contemporary Accounts of Mason, Underhill, Vincent and Gardiner* (Cleveland: Helman-Taylor Co., 1897), p. 25.

6. Thomas Stanton to John Winthrop, Feb. 16, 1657, *Winthrop Papers. MHSC*, 5 Series, I: 135.

7. David Pulsifer, ed., *Acts of the Commissioners of the United Colonies*, Vols. IX and X, *Records of the Colony of New Plymouth* (Boston, 1859), IX, pp. 17–18.

8. Emanual Downing to John Winthrop, Sr., [ca. Aug. 1645] in Allyn Forbes, ed., *The Winthrop Papers*, 5 vols. (Boston: 1929–1947), V, pp. 38–39.

9. Sheldon, *History of Deerfield*, p. 58.

10. Aug. 12, 1657, J. Hammond Trumbull, ed., *Public Records of the Colony of Connecticut*, 15 vols. (Hartford, 1850–1890), I, p. 300.

11. Pulsifer, *Acts of the United Colonies*, X: p. 94, Sept. 20, 1653.

12. Ibid., X: p. 223, Sept. 10, 1659; sachems' message quoted in Sheldon, *History of Deerfield*, p. 67.

13. Pulsifer, *Acts of the United Colonies*, X: p. 285, Sept. 16, 1662.

14. Caulkins, *History of New London*, p. 99.

15. Judd, "The Fur Trade on the Connecticut River," pp. 217–19; James Axtell, *Beyond 1492: Encounters in Colonial North America* (N.Y.: Oxford, 1992), p. 130.

16. Jennings, *Invasion of America*, p. 85.

17. Ibid., p. 103.

18. His brother-in-law Richard Lord, for example, owned shares in the ships *Society* and *Desire*, and his son was part-owner of the ship *America* in 1661 and *Hartford Merchant* in 1676. Thomas Stanton also may have owned shares in ships.

19. See notice for 1670, William Haynes, *Stonington Chronology, 1649–1976* (Stonington: Globe Pequot Press, Stonington Historical Society, 1976); Caulkins, *History of New London*, p. 21.

20. John Whit Davis, personal communication, July 1996; Trumbull, ed., *Recs. of Conn.*, III, p. 298; Bernard C. Steiner, *History of Slavery in Connecticut* (Baltimore: Johns Hopkins University Press, 1893), p. 12.

21. Willys Papers, *CHSC* 21 (1924), pp. 255–57.

22. Trumbull, *Recs. of Conn.*, Oct. 11, 1666, II, 53; Pulsifer, *Acts of the United Colonies*, II: 281–2, Sept. 16, 1662.

23. Connecticut State Library, Hartford. Connecticut Records, Indian Papers, 1st Series [1]: 10.

24. Connecticut State Library, Hartford. Connecticut Records, Indian Papers, 1st Series [1]: 9.

25. George P. Winship, ed., *The New England Company of 1649 and John Eliot*, Publications of the Prince Society, XXXVI (Boston: 1920), p. 34; Vaughan, *New England Frontier*, p. 300; Caulkins, *History of New London*, p. 103.

26. Vaughan, *New England Frontier*, p. 281; Pulsifer, *Acts of the United Colonies*, September 1659, II, p. 228.

27. Daniel Gookin, "Historical Collections," *MHSC*, 1st Series I: 208.

28. "The Indian Powwow," *NEHGS*, 2 (1848): 44.

Chapter 9: *Land*

1. George Madison Bodge, *Soldiers in King Philip's War* (Baltimore: Genealogical Publishing Co., 1967), Appendix A, p. 466.

2. Bernard Stanton, "Dedication Ceremony for the Monument to Thomas Stanton and Anna Lord" (speech), Pawcatuck, Conn., Aug. 4, 1995.

3. My main sources on the disputes over the Narragansett country are Richard S. Dunn, "John Winthrop, Jr., and the Narragansett Country," *William and Mary Quarterly*, 3rd Series, 13 (1956): 68–86; Robert C. Black, *The Younger John Winthrop* (N.Y.: Columbia

University Press, 1966); Clarence Winthrop Bowen, *The Boundary Disputes of Connecticut* (Boston: J. R. Osgood, 1882); Elisha R. Potter, Jr., *The Early History of Narragansett* (*RIHSC*, III) (Providence: Marshall, Brown and Co., 1835); and Francis Jennings, *The Invasion of America: Indians, Colonialism, and the Cant of Conquest* (Chapel Hill: University of North Carolina Press, 1975).

4. Dunn, "John Winthrop, Jr.," p. 74.

5. Text of the spurious charter, Dec. 10, 1643, C.O. 1/10, pp. 257–58, Public Record Office, London, England.

6. General Court of Massachusetts Bay to Roger Williams, Aug. 27, 1645, in Glenn W. LaFantasie, ed., *The Correspondence of Roger Williams*, 2 vols. *RIHS* (London and Hanover: Brown University Press/University Press of New England, 1988), pp. 226–27; Nathaniel E. Shurtleff, ed., *Records of the Court of Assistants of the Colony of Massachusetts Bay, 1630–1692* (Boston, 1853–1854), III, pp. 48, 49.

7. John Winthrop, Jr., to Humphrey Atherton, Nov. 10, 1650, *Winthrop Papers*, *MHSC*, 5th Series, VIII: 42.

8. "Cartwright's Answer to the Massachusetts Narrative of Transactions with the Royal Commissioners," Jan. 5, 1666; "Clarendon Papers," *NYHSC*, 1869, pp. 90–91. Dunn, "John Winthrop, Jr., and the Narragansett Country," p. 72; "Trumbull Papers," *MHSC*, 5th Series, IX: 10–12; 98, 11.

9. Richard Anson Wheeler, *History of the Town of Stonington* (New London: Press of the Day, 1900), p. 586; *Suffolk Deeds* (Boston, 1880–1906), III, p. 482.

10. Sept. 1659, Pulsifer, *Acts of the United Colonies*, II, p. 227. See "Letter to the Commissioners of the U. Colonies, complaining of Affronts Received from the Narragansetts," J. Hammond Trumbull, ed., *Public Records of the Colony of Connecticut*, 15 vols. (Hartford: 1850–90) I, Appendix VIII, pp. 576–77; Dunn, "John Winthrop, Jr.," pp. 72–73; Pulsifer, *Acts of the United Colonies*, Sept. 1660, II, pp. 247–49; Trumbull, *Recs. of Conn.*, Oct. 4, 1660, I, p. 355; review of documents, Trumbull, *Recs. of Conn.*, I, p. 300; Trumbull, *Recs of Conn.*, II, Appendix VII, pp. 541–45.

11. Quoted in Dunn, "John Winthrop, Jr.," p. 73; Trumbull, *Recs. of Conn.*, II, Appendix VII, pp. 541–45; *MHSC*, Series 5, IX: 12–13, 25–26; Black, *The Younger John Winthrop*, p. 198.

12. Wheeler, *History of Stonington*, p. 34; Potter, *The Early History of Narragansett*, III, pp. 242–47; Letter from Southerton townsmen to General Court of Massachusetts, p. 19 Jan. 1662, Massachusetts Archives, II, p. 34, quoted in Wheeler, *History of Stonington*, p. 15 note.

13. Dunn, "John Winthrop, Jr.," pp. 80–82; *CHSC*, 21, pp. 144–45; Trumbull, *Recs. of Conn.*, I, p. 407; Daniel Denison et al., "In Behalf of the Atherton Proprietors, to John Winthrop," Trumbull Papers, *MHSC*, 9, pp. 27–29.

14. Connecticut State Library, Hartford, Connecticut Records, Col. Boundaries, I, p. 32.

15. Pulsifer, *Acts of United Colonies*, Sept. 14, 1663, II, pp. 304–5. Trumbull, *Recs. of Conn.*, May 10, 1666, II, 33 and note; 36; July 26, 1666, 44 and note; Oct. 11, 1666, 50, 56.

16. George Denison to John Winthrop, Jr., Oct. 27, 1666, *Winthrop Papers*, *MHSC*, 10: 64–65.

17. E. Glenn Denison, *Denison Genealogy: Ancestors and Descendants of Captain George Denison*, The Denison Society (Baltimore: Genealogical Publishing Co., 1978), p. xii; James Noyes to John Winthrop, Jr., Mar. 25, 1666–67, *Winthrop Papers*, *MHSC*, 10, pp. 67–69.

18. Deposition of John Stanton, Connecticut Records, Indians, I, p. 20, quoted in Trumbull, *Recs. of Conn.*, II, Appendix IX, p. 551.

19. Connecticut State Library, Hartford, Connecticut Records, Indians, I, Doc. 13, 14; See also Trumbull, *Recs. of Conn.*, II, Appendix IX, "The Rumored Indian Plot, of 1669," p. 549. Louis B. Mason, *The Life and Times of Major John Mason of Connecticut, 1600–1672* (N.Y.: G. P. Putnam's Sons, 1935), p. 312.

20. Stonington Town Records, July 8, 1669; Connecticut State Library, Hartford, Connecticut Records, Indians, I, Doc. 13.

21. Arthur L. Peale, *Uncas and the Mohegan-Pequot* (Boston: Meador Publishing, 1939), p. 24. The deed is reprinted in John W. De Forest, *History of the Indians of Connecticut . . .* (Hartford: W. J. Haersley, 1852), p. 495. Uncas is quoted on p. 398 of David W. Conroy, "The Defence of Indian Land Rights: William Bollen and the Mohegan Case in 1743," *Proceedings of the American Antiquarian Society* 103 (2) (1993): 395–424, which provides a thorough description of the Mohegan land case. Other sources on the struggle over Mohegan land are Frances Manwaring Caulkins, *History of New London, Connecticut* (New London, 1852); Melissa Jayne Fawcett, *The Lasting of the Mohegans* (Uncasville, Conn.: Mohegan Tribe, 1995); and William S. Simmons, *Spirit of the New England Tribes: Indian History and Folklore, 1620–1984* (Hanover and London: University Press of New England, 1986).

22. The quote about Uncas comes from John Sainsbury, "Miantonomo's Death and New England Politics, 1630–1645," *Rhode Island History* 30 (4) (1971): 122. For details about James Rogers, see Caulkins, *History of New London*, and James Swift Rogers, *James Rogers of New London, Ct., and His Descendants* (Boston, 1902).

23. Fawcett, in *The Lasting of the Mohegans*, p. 12, says Uncas "allowed Rogers to use" this land, while English sources refer to the grant as a gift.

24. Arthur Peale, *Uncas and the Mohegan Pequot* (Boston: Meador Publishing, 1939), pp. 60–61, based on Caulkins. This story can also be found in Caulkins, *History of New London*, p. 425, and, as told by Mohegan elder Gladys Tantaquidgeon, in Fawcett, *Lasting of the Mohegans*, p. 12.

25. Neal Salisbury, "Indians and Colonists in Southern New England after the Pequot War: An Uneasy Balance," in Laurence M. Hauptman and James D. Wherry, eds., *The Pequots in Southern New England: The Fall and Rise of an American Indian Nation* (Norman and London: University of Oklahoma Press, 1990), pp. 91–92.

Chapter 10: *God's Wrath*

1. The population statistics and description in the following paragraphs of New England on the verge of King Philip's War come largely from James D. Drake, *Civil War in New England, 1675–1676* (Amherst: University of Massachusetts Press, 1999), pp. 14–62.

2. My chief sources for information and analyses of King Philip's War are Drake, *King Philip's War*; Jill Lepore, *The Name of War: King Philip's War and the Origins of American Identity* (N.Y.: Alfred A. Knopf, 1998); Douglas Edward Leach, *Flintlock and Tomahawk: New England in King Philip's War* (N.Y.: Macmillan, 1958); George Madison Bodge, *Soldiers in King Philip's War* (Baltimore: Genealogical Publishing Co., 1967); Michael J. Puglisi, *Puritans Besieged: The Legacies of King Philip's War in the Massachusetts Bay Colony*, Institute for Massachusetts Studies, Connecticut Valley Historical Museum (Lanham, Md.: University Press of America, 1991); Francis Jennings, *The Invasion of America: Indians, Colonialism, and the Cant of Conquest* (Chapel Hill:

University of North Carolina Press, 1975); and Philip Ranlet, *Enemies of the Bay Colony*, American University Studies, Series IX, Vol. 157 (N.Y.: Peter Lang, 1995). Other sources included Russell Bourne, *The Red King's Rebellion: Racial Politics in New England, 1675–1678* (N.Y.: Atheneum, 1990); George Sheldon, *1636 – Pocumtuck – 1886: A History of Deerfield, Massachusetts . . . with a special study of the Indian Wars of the Connecticut Valley*, 2 vols. (Deerfield, 1895–96); George W. Ellis and John E. Morris, *King Philip's War* (N.Y.: Grafton Press, 1906); Patrick M. Malone, *The Skulking Way of War: Technology and Tactics among the New England Indians* (Lanham, Md.: Madison Books, 1991); and Richard R. Johnson, "The Search for a Usable Indian: An Aspect of the Defense of Colonial New England," *Journal of American History* 64: 623–51.

    Primary sources that I consulted include Daniel Gookin, "An Historical Account of the Doings and Sufferings of the Christian Indians in New England, in the Years of 1675, 1676, 1677," in *Transactions and Collections of the American Antiquarian Society (Archaeologia Americana)*, II (1836), pp. 429–534; Benjamin Church, *Diary of King Philip's War, 1675–76*, intro. by Alan and Mary Simpson (Chester, Conn.: Pequot Press, 1975); William Hubbard, *A Narrative of the Troubles with the Indians in New England, From the First Planting thereof to the Present Time*, ed. Samuel G. Drake under the title *The History of the Indian Wars in New England from the First Settlement to the Termination of the War with King Philip, in 1677*, 2 vols. (Roxbury, Mass., 1865); Samuel G. Drake, *The Old Indian Chronicle, Being a Collection of Exceeding Rare Tracts, Written and Published in the Time of King Philip's War* (Boston: Dranke, 1867); John Easton, *A Relacion of the Indyan Warre, 1675*, reprinted in Charles H. Lincoln, *Narratives of the Indian Wars, 1675–1699* (N.Y.: Charles Scribner's Sons, 1913); Nathaniel Saltonstall, *The Present State of New England with Respect to the Indian War* . . . (London, 1675) and *A New and Further Narrative of the State of New-England; being a Continued Account of the Bloudy Indian War* . . . (London, 1676), in Lincoln, *Narratives*; Increase Mather, *A Brief History of the Warr with the Indians in New-England* . . . (London, 1676), reprinted in *The History of King Philip's War*, ed. Samuel G. Drake (Albany, N.Y.: J. Munsell, 1862; Bowie, Md.: Heritage, 1990); Richard Slotkin and James K. Folsom, eds., *So Dreadfull a Judgment: Puritan Responses to King Philip's War, 1676–1677* (Middletown: Wesleyan University Press, 1973); Cotton Mather, *Magnalia Christi Americana: or, the Ecclesiastical History of New-England from Its First Planting in the Year 1620, unto the Year of Our Lord, 1698*, 2 vols. (1702; reprinted Hartford, Conn., 1820); and Mary Rowlandson, *Sovereignty and Goodness of God . . .* (1682), in Alden T. Vaughan and Edward W. Clark, eds., *Puritans Among the Indians: Accounts of Captivity and Redemption* (Cambridge and London: Belknap Press, 1981).

3. Easton, *Relacion*, p. 10.

4. I've unfortunately misplaced the reference to the historian who made this point.

5. Easton, *Relacion*, pp. 9–11, quoted in Leach, *Flintlock and Tomahawk*, pp. 4–5.

6. Quoted in Puglisi, *Puritans Besieged*, p. 4.

7. Quoted in Ranlet, *Enemies of the Bay Colony*, p. 102.

8. My information about the life of John Sassamon is derived chiefly from Lepore, *The Name of War*, and Drake, *King Philip's War*.

9. Hubbard, *History of the Indian Wars*, I, p. 60.

10. Ibid.

11. Mather, *Magnalia, Christi Americana: or, the Ecclesiastical History of New-England from its First Planting in the Year 1620, unto the Year of our Lord, 1698*, 2 vols. (1702; reprinted Hartford, Conn., 1820), I, p. 559.

12. John Eliot to the commissioners of the United Colonies, Aug. 25, 1664, David Pulsifer,

ed., *Acts of the Commissioners of the United Colonies* (*Records of the Colony of New Plymouth*, vols. IX–X) (Boston, 1859), II, pp. 383–84.

13. Daniel Gookin, "Historical Collections of the Indians in New England . . ." (1674) in *MHSC*, 1st Series, Vol. 1 (Boston, 1792) pp. 141–226.

14. Cotton Mather, *Magnalia* p. 514.

15. John Eliot quoted in Ranlet, *Enemies of the Bay Colony*, p. 101.

16. Quoted in Jennings, *The Invasion of America*, p. 296.

17. Mather, *A Brief History of the Warr*, pp. 49–50; Gookin, "An Historical Account," p. 440; Saltonstall, *The Present State of New England*, pp. 24–25.

18. Easton, *Relacion*, pp. 10–11.

19. Unattributed quote in Ellis and Morris, *King Philip's War*, pp. 65–66; see also Hubbard, *History of the Indian Wars*, I, p. 71.

20. Edmund Randolph, "A short narrative of my Proceedings an Several Voyages to and from New England to White Hall . . .," in *Hutchinson Papers* (Albany, N.Y.: Prince Society, 1865) Vol. 2, p. 226.; John Eliot to John Winthrop, Jr., July 24, 1675, *Winthrop Papers*, *MHSC*, 5th Series, I (1871):424; [Edward Wharton], *New England's Present Suffering Under Their Cruel Neighboring Indians* . . . (London, 1675), p. 4; John Bishop to Increase Mather, July 8, 1676, *MHSC*, 4th Series, VIII (1868):299.

21. Hubbard, *History of the Indian Wars*, I, p. 59.

22. Lepore, *The Name of War*, p. 68.

23. Rowlandson, *The Sovereignty and Goodness of God* . . ., p. 35.

24. Quoted in Lepore, *The Name of War*, p. 104.

25. Bodge, *Soldiers in King Philip's War*, p. 139. The incident is described in Leach, *Flintlock and Tomahawk*, p. 87.

26. Hubbard, *History of the Indian Wars*, I, pp. 98–99; Joshua Coffin, *Sketch of History of Newbury* (Boston: Samuel G. Drake, 1845), p. 388; Leach, *Flintlock and Tomahawk*, pp. 87–88. Thomas Chase was pressed into service Aug. 27, 1675, in Capt. Samuel Appleton's company. See Bodge, *Soldiers in King Philip's War*, p. 154.

27. Bodge, *Soldiers in King Philip's War*, p. 69.

28. Gookin quoted in Leach, *Flintlock and Tomahawk*, p. 146; Ellis and Morris, *King Philip's War*, p. 134. The major primary sources on the experience of the praying Indians during King Philip's War are Gookin, "Historical Account," and Mather, *Magnalia*. My secondary sources include Lepore, *The Name of War*; Drake, *King Philip's War*; Leach, *Flintlock and Tomahawk*; "Boston in Philip's War," in Justin Winsor, ed., *Memorial History of Boston* (Boston: Ticknor, 1880–81); and Almon Wheeler Lauber, *Indian Slavery in the Colonial Times within the Present Limits of the United States* (N.Y.: Columbia University Press, 1913).

29. Gookin, quoted in Puglisi, *Puritans Besieged*, p. 34.

30. Gookin, "Historical Account," pp. 427, 473–74, 485.

31. John Lyne and Numphow to Thomas Henchman, c. Nov. 15, 1675, reprinted in Gookin, "Historical Account," p. 483.

32. Order of the Massachusetts Council, Aug. 30, 1675, Grafton, Massachusetts, Local Records, AAS (note about Tukapewillin's is written at the end of the order), quoted in Lepore, *The Name of War*, p. 143; see also Gookin, "Historical Account," pp. 504–5.

33. "Rev. John Eliot's Records of the First Church at Roxbury, Mass.," *NEHGR* 33 (1879): 413; Gookin, *Historical Account*, pp. 527–29; Lepore, *The Name of War*, pp. 143–45.

34. Lepore, *The Name of War*, pp. 153, 162.

35. John Eliot to the Massachusetts Governor and Council, Aug. 13, 1675, Pulsifer, *Acts of United Colonies*, II, pp. 451–52.

36. Thomas Church, "Entertaining Passages Relating to Philip's War which began in the Year 1675," in Slotkin and Folsom, eds., *So Dreadfull a Judgment*, pp. 411–12.

37. Increase Mather, *The Day of Trouble is Near* (Cambridge, 1674), p. 6. See also Puglisi, *Puritans Besieged*, p. 14.

38. *Laws & Ordinancies of Warre, Pass'd by the General Court of the Massachusets* (Cambridge, 1675), p. 32.

39. Nathaniel G. Shurtleff, ed., *Records of the Governor and Company of Massachusetts Bay in New England* (Boston: William White, 1854), V, pp. 59–63. The following discussion of Puritan attitudes owes much to Puglisi, *Puritans Besieged*.

40. Saltonstall, *A New and Further Narrative*, p. 86.

41. Hubbard, *History of the Indian Wars*, I, p. 244.

Chapter 11: *Thomas Stanton's War*

1. Henry Stephens to Mr. Stanton, June 29, 1675, *Winthrop Papers*, MHSC, 3rd Series, X, p. 117. The *Winthrop Papers*; *Wyllys Papers*, ed. Albert C. Bates, CHSC (Hartford, 1924); William Hubbard, *The History of the Indian Wars in New England from the First Settlement to the Termination of the War with King Philip, in 1677*, ed. Samuel G. Drake, 2 vols. (Roxbury, Mass.: 1865; Kraus Reprint Co., N.Y., 1969); and J. Hammond Trumbull, ed., *Public Records of the Colony of Connecticut*, 15 vols. (Hartford, 1850–1890), are my main sources of information about Thomas Stanton's involvement in the war. My main secondary sources on the campaign against the Narragansetts are Douglas Edward Leach, *Flintlock and Tomahawk: New England in King Philip's War* (N.Y.: Norton, 1958); George Madison Bodge, *Soldiers in King Philip's War* (Baltimore: Genealogical Publishing Co., 1967); Francis Jennings, *The Invasion of America: Indians, Colonialism, and the Cant of Conquest* (Chapel Hill: University of North Carolina Press, 1975); James D. Drake, *Civil War in New England, 1675–1676* (Amherst: University of Massachusetts Press, 1999); and Jill Lepore, *The Name of War: King Philip's War and the Origins of American Identity* (N.Y.: Alfred A. Knopf, 1998).

2. Wait Winthrop to John Winthrop, Jr., July 4, 1675, *Winthrop Papers*, MHSC 5th Series, VIII: 401–2.

3. Drake, *King Philip's War*, p. 106.

4. Leach, *Flintlock and Tomahawk*, p. 114; Thomas Stanton to Wait Winthrop, Nov. 4, 1675, *Winthrop Papers*, MHSC 5th Series, VIII; Thomas Stanton to John Allyn, May 1676, Document 69, Journal of the Council, in *Recs. of Conn.*, p. 411.

5. Daniel Witherell [Wetherell] to John Winthrop, Jr., June 29, 167[5], *Winthrop Papers*, MHSC 3rd Series, X: 118; Daniel Witherell [Wetherell] to John Winthrop, Jr., June 30, 1675, *Winthrop Papers*, MHSC, 3rd Series, X: 119.

6. George Madison Bodge, *Soldiers in King Philip's War* (Baltimore: Genealogical Publishing Co., 1967), p. 369.

7. Wait Winthrop to Gov. John Winthrop, July 8, 1675, *Wyllys Papers*, ed. Albert C. Bates, CHSC (Hartford, 1924), XXI, pp. 209–11.

8. Jennings, *Invasion of America*, p. 305.

9. Coddington to Andros, July 21, 1675, E. B. O'Callaghan, ed., *Calendar of Historical Manuscripts in the Office of the Secretary of State, Albany, New York*, 2 vols. (Albany, N.Y. 1865–1866) in *New York Col. Manuscripts*, XXIV, p. 128; Testimony and order about Mr. Gold, July 14, 1675, *Wyllys Papers, Recs. of Conn.*, 21, p. 212.

10. Quotations in Leach, *Flintlock and Tomahawk*, pp. 58, 59.

11. Jennings, *Invasion of America*, p. 306.

12. Leach, *Flintlock and Tomahawk*, p. 112, n. 8.

13. Thomas Stanton to John Winthrop, Jr., Sept. 22, 1675, *Winthrop Papers*, XVIII, p. 140; Leach, *Flintlock and Tomahawk*, p. 115, note 5.

14. See Bodge, *Soldiers in King Philip's War*, for details on the participation of these various ancestors. Massachusetts Archives, Boston 67: 293.

15. Thomas Stanton and Tobias Saunders to John Winthrop, Jr., Dec. 10, 1675, *Winthrop Family Papers*, Massachusetts Historical Society, Boston.

16. John Winthrop, Jr., to Thomas Stanton, Dec. 12, 1675, *Winthrop Papers*, MHSC 5 Series, VIII, Pt 2: 175–76.

17. Leach, *Flintlock and Tomahawk*, p. 126.

18. Samuel Gorton to Winthrop, Sept. 11, 1675, *Winthrop Papers*, MHSC, 4th Series, VII (1865): 629–30.

19. Resolution backdated to Nov. 2, 1675, David Pulsifer, ed., *Acts of the Commissioners of the United Colonies*, Volume IX and X of *Records of the Colony of New Plymouth* (Boston, 1859), July 1645, II, p. 357; Jennings, *Invasion of America*, p. 310.

20. Richard Anson Wheeler, *History of the Town of Stonington* (New London: Press of the Day, 1900), p. 22.

21. Manuscript of Rev. W. Ruggles, quoted in George W. Ellis and John E. Morris, *King Philip's War* . . . (N.Y.: Grafton Press, 1906), p. 152.

22. As Francis Jennings points out, the fact that Philip's forces initially fired on the Narragansetts when they came to join them suggests that the supposed conspiracy between them was more an English fear than reality: *Invasion of America*, p. 312. See also Samuel G. Drake, *Biography and History of the Indians of North America* . . . 11th ed. (Boston, 1856), pp. 272–73.

23. E. Glenn Denison, *Denison Genealogy: Ancestors and Descendants of Captain George Denison* (Baltimore: Genealogical Publishing Co., 1978), p. xiii.

24. Wheeler, *History of Stonington*, p. 337.

25. Ibid., p. 592 note. See also William Hubbard, *The History of the Indian Wars in New England from the First Settlement to the Termination of the War with King Philip, in 1677*, ed. Samuel G. Drake, 2 vols. (Roxbury, Mass.: 1865, Kraus Reprint Co., N.Y., 1969), II, p. 60.

26. N[athaniel] S[alstonstall], *A New and Further Narrative of the State of New-England; being a Continued Account of the Bloudy Indian War* . . . (London, 1676), reprinted in Charles H. Lincoln, ed., *Narratives of the Indian Wars, 1675–1699* (N.Y.: Charles Scribner's Sons, 1913), pp. 90–91.

27. Hubbard, *The History of the Indian Wars*, I, p. 209; John Winthrop, Jr., to William Leete, Governor of Connecticut, Feb. 29 1675/76. *Winthrop Papers*, MHSC 5th Series, VIII, Pt. 2: 176–77; William A. Stanton, *A Record Genealogical, Biographical, Statistical of Thomas Stanton, of Connecticut, and His Descendants, 1635–1891* (Albany: Joel Munsell's Sons, 1891), p. 27; *Recs. of Conn.*, II, April 18, 1676, p. 435.

28. Excerpt of letter from Thomas Stanton to John Allyn, May 10, 1676, in *Recs. of Conn.*, Vol. II, Journal of the Council, &c., 441 note; *Recs. of Conn.*, Vol. II, Journal of the Council, &c., p. 441.

29. Bodge, *Soldiers in King Philip's War*, p. 251; Leach, *Flintlock and Tomahawk*, pp. 201–4; George Sheldon, *1636 – Pocumtuck – 1886: A History of Deerfield, Massachusetts . . . with a Special Study of the Indian Wars of the Connecticut Valley*, 2 vols. (Deerfield, 1895–96), p. 157.

30. Bodge, *Soldiers in King Philip's War*, p. 251; John Carroll Chase and George Walter Chamberlain, *Seven Generations of the Descendents of Aquila and Thomas Chase* (Derry, N.H.: Record Publishing Co., 1928), p. 39.
31. Instructions, May 24, 1676, Trumbull, *Recs. of Conn.*, II, p. 444.
32. Hubbard, *The History of the Indian Wars*, I, p. 281; Nathaniel B. Shurtleff, *Records of the Governor and Company of the Massachusetts Bay in New England*, 5 vols. (Boston: William White, 1854), V, p. 136.
33. Account book of Maj. John Talcott, which includes his accounts as treasurer of the colony during King Philip's War, printed in Samuel Orcutt, *The History of the Old Town of Derby, Connecticut, 1642-1880* (Springfield: Press of Springfield Printing Co., 1880), p. lvii.
34. Drake, *King Philip's War*, pp. 136–39.

Chapter 12: *Among the Ruins*

1. Thomas Hutchinson, *The History of the Colony and Province of Massachusetts-Bay*, ed. Lawrence Shaw Mayo (Cambridge: Harvard University Press, 1936), p. 240. My description of the transformation of the Puritan landscape draws heavily on Jill Lepore, *The Name of War: King Philip's War and the Origins of American Identity* (N.Y.: Alfred A. Knopf, 1998). My other major sources for the consequences of King Philip's War are Michael Puglisi, *Puritans Besieged: The Legacies of King Philip's War in the Massachusetts Bay Colony* (Lanham, N.Y., and London: University Press of America, 1991); and James D. Drake, *Civil War in New England, 1675–1676* (Amherst: University of Massachusetts Press, 1999). Much of my information about Native refugees comes from Colin G. Calloway, *The Western Abenakis of Vermont, 1600–1800: War, Migration and the Survival of an Indian People* (Norman and London: University of Oklahoma Press, 1990) and Colin G. Calloway, ed., *After King Philip's War: Presence and Persistence in Indian New England* (Hanover, N.H.: University Press of New England, 1997). My main sources on the praying Indians during and after the war comes from Henry W. Bowden and James P. Ronda, *John Eliot's Indian Dialogues: A Study in Cultural Interaction* (Westport, Conn.: Greenwood Press, 1980); and Daniel Gookin, "An Historical Account of the Doings and Sufferings of the Christian Indians in New England, in the Years of 1675, 1676, 1677," in *Transactions and Collections of the American Antiquarian Society (Archaeologia Americana)*, II (1836): 429–534.
2. Randolph's report, Oct.12, 1676, in E. B. O'Callaghan and Berthold Fernow, eds., *N.Y. Col. Docs.*, 15 vols. (Albany, N.Y., 1856–87), III, pp. 243–44.
3. William Hubbard, *A Narrative of the Troubles with the Indians in New England, From the First Planting Thereof to the Present Time*, ed. Samuel G. Drake under the title *The History of the Indian Wars in New England from the First Settlement to the Termination of the War with King Philip, in 1677*, 2 vols. (Roxbury, Mass., 1865), I, p. 122.
4. This incident is described in Rev. Frederic Janes, *The Janes Family: A Genealogy and Brief History of the Descendants of William Janes* (N.Y.: John H. Dingman, 1862), pp. 41–45, 87–94; see also Douglas Edward Leach, *Flintlock and Tomahawk: New England in King Philip's War* (N.Y.: Norton, 1958), p. 87.
5. Bodge, *Soldiers in King Philip's War*, p. 413; John J. Currier, *A History of Newbury, Mass., 1635–1902* (Boston: Damrell & Upham), p. 511. Stanton's will can be found in the State Library in Hartford, Conn., under Private Controversy Collections, Series #2, Vol. 24, pp. 148a-d.

6. E. Glenn Denison, *Denison Genealogy: Ancestors and Descendants of Captain George Denison* (Baltimore: Genealogical Publishing Co., 1978), p. xiii.

7. "Governor Andros' Answer to Enquires of the Council of Trade," April 9, 1678, *N.Y. Col. Docs*, III, p. 263.

8. Drake, *King Philip's War*, p. 169.

9. Hubbard, *History of the Indian Wars*, II, p. 55.

10. Appleton's *Cyclopedia of American Biography*, p. 322; Cotton Mather, *Magnalia Christi Americana* (Hartford: Silus Andrus and Son, 1855), I, p. 577; Samuel Eliot Morison, *Builders of the Bay Colony* (Boston: Houghton Mifflin, 1930), p. 319.

11. Richard Anson Wheeler, *History of the Town of Stonington* (New London: Press of the Day, 1900), p. 578.

12. John Mason, *A Brief History of the Pequot War* (1736), in Charles Orr, ed., *History of the Pequot War: The Contemporary Accounts of Mason, Underhill, Vincent and Gardiner* (Cleveland: Helman-Taylor Co., 1897), p. 25.

13. Jennings, *Invasion of America*, p. x; Puglisi, *Puritans Besieged*, p. 176.

14. Nathaniel Knowles, "The Torture of Captives by the Indians of Eastern North America," extract from the *Proceedings of the American Philosophical Society*, 82 (2), March 22, 1940, reprinted in *Scalping and Torture: Warfare Practices among North American Indians* (Ohsweken, Ont.: Iroqrafts Ltd. Indian Publication, 1985), pp. 186–11, 213.

15. Louis B. Mason, *The Life and Times of Major John Mason of Connecticut, 1600–1672* (N.Y.: G. P. Putnam's Sons, 1935), p. 116; Knowles, "The Torture of Captives," p. 151; John Demos, *The Unredeemed Captive: A Family Story from Early America* (N.Y.: Vintage, 1994), p. 130.

16. William L. Sachse, *The Diurnal of Thomas Rugg, 1659–1661* (London, 1961), p. 116, quoted in Axtell, *The European and the Indian* (N.Y., Oxford: Oxford University Press, 1981), p. 144; Mason, *Life and Times of John Mason*, p. 117.

17. Axtell, *The European and the Indian*, p. 145.

18. Increase Mather, *A Brief History of the War with the Indians in New England* (1676), reprinted in Richard Slotkin and James K. Folsom, eds., *So Dreadfull a Judgment: Puritan Responses to King Philip's War, 1676–1677* (Middletown: Wesleyan University Press, 1978), p. 141; Cotton Mather, *Magnalia Christi Americana: or, the Ecclesiastical History of New-England from Its First Planting in the Year 1620, unto the Year of Our Lord, 1698*, 2 vols. (1702, reprinted Hartford, Conn.: 1820), I, p. 215; Puglisi, *Puritans Besieged*, p. 180.

19. N[athaniel] S[altonstall], "The Present State of New England with Respect to the Indian War, 1675," in Charles H. Lincoln, ed., *Narratives of the Indian Wars, 1675–1699* (N.Y.: Charles Scribner's Sons, 1913), p. 44; Puglisi, *Puritans Besieged*, pp. 185–90, 192; Cotton Mather, "A Brand Pluck'd Out of the Burning," in George L. Burr, ed., *Narratives of the Witchcraft Cases, 1648–1706* (N.Y.: Charles Scribner's Sons, 1914), pp. 281–82.

20. Janes, *The Janes Family*, pp. 36–37 note.

21. Increase Mather, *Brief History*, p. 48, cited in Puglisi, *Puritans Besieged*, p. 190.

22. Mary Rowlandson, *The Sovereignty and Goodness of God* (1682), in Alden T. Vaughan and Edward W. Clark, eds., *Puritans among the Indians: Accounts of Captivity and Redemption* (Cambridge and London: Belknap Press, 1981), pp. 31–75.

23. Arthur Peale, *Uncas and the Mohegan Pequot* (Boston: Meador Publishing Co., 1939), p. 69.

24. David W. Conroy, "The Defence of Indian Land Rights: William Bollen and the Mohegan Case in 1743," *Proceedings of the American Antiquarian Society* 103 (2)

(1993): 395–424; William S. Simmons, *Spirit of the New England Tribes: Indian History and Folklore, 1620–1984* (Hanover and London: University Press of New England, 1986), p. 32; see also Melissa Jayne Fawcett, *The Lasting of the Mohegans*, Part I (Uncasville, Conn.: Mohegan Tribe, 1995), pp. 17, 22; and Frances Manwaring Caulkins, *History of New London, Connecticut* (New London, 1852), pp. 424–31.

25. See Jack Campisi, "The Emergence of the Mashantucket Pequot Tribe, 1637–1975," in Laurence M. Hauptman and James D. Wherry, eds., *The Pequots in Southern New England: The Fall and Rise of an American Indian Nation* (Norman and London: University of Oklahoma Press, 1990).

26. Mason, *Life and Times of John Mason*, p. 148; Larzer Ziff, *Puritanism in America: New Culture in a New World* (N.Y.: Viking, 1973), pp. 289–90; See also Elizabeth Donnan, *Documents Illustrative of the History of the Slave Trade* to America, 4 vols. (N.Y.: Octagon Books, 1969), III, p. 16n, and Lorenzo Johnston Greene, *The Negro in Colonial New England, 1620–1776* (N.Y., 1942; Baltimore, 1893). The Stonington statistics come from the Stonington Town Treasurer's Records, p. 34, quoted in Barbara W. Brown, *Black Roots in Southeastern Connecticut, 1650–1900* (Detroit: Gale Research Co., 1980), p. 615; the legend is repeated on placemats at the Wilcox Tavern, the former home of Gen. Joseph Stanton, Charlestown, Rhode Island.

27. "Inventory of the Estate of Mr. James Rogers, Sr.," from 3rd Book of Wills, New London County, July 22, 1703, reprinted in James Swift Rogers, *James Rogers of New London, Ct., and His Descendants* (Boston: James Swift Rogers, 1902), pp. 33–34.

28. Venture Smith, *A Narrative of the Life and Adventures of Venture, a Native of Africa, but Resident above Sixty Years in the United States of America* (New London: C. Holt, 1798); revised and republished with traditions by H. M. Selden, 1896, republished in *Five Black Lives: The Autobiographies of Venture Smith, James Mars, William Grimes, the Rev. G. W. Offley, and James L. Smith*, intro. Arna Bontemps (Middletown: Wesleyan University Press, 1971), pp. 1–34.

29. Lepore, *The Name of War*, p. 166.

30. Nathaniel Harris Morgan, *A History of James Harris of New London, Conn., and His Descendants, from 1640 to 1878* (Hartford, Conn., 1878), p. 22.

31. For a discussion of this shadow self, see, among others, Richard Drinnon, *Facing West: The Metaphysics of Indian-hating and Empire-building* (Minneapolis: University of Minneapolis Press, 1980).

Chapter 13: *Hannah's Scalp*

1. Other sources say four children were murdered: Hannah, aged eight, Miriam four, Benjamin three, Nehemiah one. My main source on the life of Hannah Janes is Rev. Frederic Janes, *The Janes Family: A Genealogy and Brief History of the Descendants of William Janes* (N.Y.: John H. Dingman, 1862), pp. 41–45, 87–94. Other sources include James Trumbull, *History of Northampton, Mass., from Its Settlement in 1654*, 2 vols. (Northampton, 1898–1902), Vol. 1, pp. 171–83, 491–514; George S. Roberts, *Historic Towns of the Connecticut River Valley* (Schenectady, N.Y.: Robson & Adee, 1906), pp. 330–33; Payson W. Lyman, *History of Easthampton, Its Settlement and Growth*: . . . (Northampton: Trumbull & Gere, 1865; facsimile edition by Heritage Books, 1985); Lawrence E. Wikander et al., *The Northampton Book: Chapters from 300 Years in the Life of a New England Town, 1654–1954* (Northampton: Northampton, Mass., Tercentenary Committee, 1954).

2. James Axtell, *The European and the Indian* (N.Y. and Oxford: Oxford University Press,

1981), pp. 16–35. My other sources on scalping are James Axtell, "Who Invented Scalping?" *American Heritage* 28 (3); Axtell and Sturtwevant, "The Unkindest Cut, or Who Invented Scalping?" *William and Mary Quarterly*, 3rd Series, 37 (1980): 451–72; Nathaniel Knowles, "The Torture of Captives by the Indians of Eastern North America," *American Philosophical Society Proceedings* 82 (1940): 151–225, reprinted in *Scalping and Torture: Warfare Practices among North American Indians* (Ohsweken, Ont.: Iroqrafts Ltd. Indian Publications, 1985); Georg Friederici, "Scalping in America," *Annual Report of the Smithsonian Institution*, 1906, reprinted in *Scalping and Torture: Warfare Practices among North American Indians*; Gabriel Nadeau, "Indian Scalping: Technique in Different Tribes," *Bulletin of History of Medicine*, 10 (2) (July 1941), reprinted in *Scalping and Torture: Warfare Practices among North American Indians*. The medical treatment of scalping victims is discussed in James Robertson, "Remarks on the Management of the Scalped Head," *Philadelphia Medical and Physical Journal* 2 (2) (1805–6): 27–30; Eric Stone, "Medicine among the American Indians," in *Clio Medica: A Series of Primers on the History of Medicine*, ed. E. B. Krumbhaar, M.D., Vol. VII, pp. 76–87; and Laurence Heister, M.D., *A General System of Surgery*, 2nd ed., (London, 1745), I, pp. 83–87.

3. John Demos, *The Unredeemed Captive: A Family Story from Early America* (N.Y.: Vintage, 1994), p. 20.

4. Janes, *The Janes Family*, p. 89.

5. Roberts, *Historic Towns*, p. 331; Janes, *The Janes Family*, p. 90.

6. Janes, *The Janes Family*, p. 38.

7. Recorder's Book for Old Hampshire County, printed in *New England Historic and Genealogical Register* 9 (1855): 161.

8. For example, in the Janes family history, it is mentioned only in a footnote to the second description of the incident, on p. 88, the first having been given forty pages earlier, and not at all in Roberts, *Historic Towns*.

9. E. B. O'Callaghan and Berthold Fernow, eds., *N.Y. Col. Docs.*, 15 vols. (Albany, N.Y., 1856–87), IX, p. 762, quoted in Emma Lewis Coleman, *New England Captives Carried to Canada, 1677–1760* (Portland: Southworth Press, 1925), p. 318.

10. John Williams, *The Redeemed Captive Returning to Zion* (1707), 6th ed., 1795, 1909 (N.Y.: Kraus Reprints, 1969), p. 58.

11. Richard R. Johnson, "The Search for a Usable Indian: Aspects of the Defense of Colonial New England," *Journal of American History* 64 (1977): 641. The following paragraph on Abenaki warfare draws heavily on this source.

12. Colin G. Calloway, *The Western Abenakis of Vermont, 1600–1800: War, Migration and the Survival of an Indian People* (Norman and London: University of Oklahoma Press, 1990), p. 18. My other sources on the Abenakis are Kenneth Morrison, *The Embattled Northeast: The Elusive Ideal of Alliance in Abenaki-Euroamerican Relations* (Berkeley: University of California Press, 1984); Douglas Leach, *The Northern Colonial Frontier, 1607–1763* (N.Y.: Holt, 1966); and Colin G. Calloway, ed., *Dawnland Encounters: Indians and Europeans in Northern New England* (Hanover and London: University Press of New England, 1991).

13. Quoted in Calloway, *Abenakis of Vermont*, p. 159.

14. Axtell, "Who Invented Scalping?", p. 97.

15. Axtell, *The European and the Indian*, p. 22; Friederici, "Scalping in America," p. 424; Reginald and Gladys Laubin, *Indian Dances of North America: Their Importance to Indian Life* (Norman, Okla.: University of Oklahoma Press, 1977), p. 152.

16. Axtell, *The European and the Indian*, p. 229.

17. Ibid., p. 234.
18. Cited in ibid., p. 142.
19. Friederici, "Scalping in America," pp. 107–8.
20. The Judd Manuscripts, Forbes Library, Northampton, Mass., quoted in Trumbull, *History of Northampton*, p. 496; Janes, *The Janes Family*, p. 93.
21. Steiner, "The Rev. Gersholm Bulkley, an Eminent Clinical Physician," *Johns Hopkins Hospital Bulletin*, 1906: xvii.
22. Heister, *A General System of Surgery*, pp. 86–87.
23. Robertson, "Remarks on the Management of the Scalped-Head," pp. 27–29.
24. Unfortunately, I have lost track of the citation for this wonderful remedy! But similar remedies can be found in Louis B. Mason, *The Life and Times of Major John Mason of Connecticut, 1600–1672* (N.Y. and London, 1935).
25. *Bulletin des Recherches Historiques* (Quebec) 38 (1932): 569–72, quoted in Calloway, *Western Abenakis of Vermont*, p. 106.
26. Friederici, *Scalping in America*, p. 425; Janes, *The Janes Family*, p. 89.
27. Charles H. Lincoln, ed., *Narratives of the Indian Wars, 1675–1699, Original Narratives of Early American History* (N.Y., 1913), p. 34.
28. Axtell, *The European and the Indian*, p. 224; Massachusetts Archives, Boston, Mass., 73, 278, quoted in Emma Louise Coleman, *New England Captives Carried to Canada between 1677 and 1760 during the French and Indian Wars*, 2 vols. (Portland, Me.: Southworth Press, 1925), I, p. 52.
29. *The Acts and Resolves . . . of the Province of the Massachusetts Bay . . .*, 21 vols. (Boston, 1869, 1922), I, pp. 530, 558, 594; II, p. 259; Samuel Penhallow, *The History of the Wars of New-England with the Eastern Indians . . .* [1726] (Cincinnati, 1859), pp. 48, 93.
30. Quoted in Axtell, *The European and the Indian*, p. 313.
31. Clifford K. Shipton, *Sibley's Harvard Graduates* (Cambridge: Charles William Sever, University Bookstore, 1873–), 7: 176–77, quoted in Coleman, *New England Captives*, p. 53.
32. All the major versions of Hannah Dustin's story are collected in *The Indian Captivity Narrative: A Woman's View*, comp. Frances Roe Kestler (N.Y. and London: Garland Publishing, 1990), pp. 79–106. The preceding paragraphs are based on this source.
33. Betty Brook Messier and Janet Sutherland Aronson, *The Roots of Coventry, Connecticut* (Coventry, Conn.: 275th Anniversary Ctte., 1987), pp. 10–12.
34. Janes, *The Janes Family*, p. 93.
35. John Demos, *The Unredeemed Captive*, p. 47; Vaughan and Clark, eds., *Puritans among the Wilderness*, pp. 5, 9–10; Judges 2:3; Demos, *The Unredeemed Captive*, p. 41; Stoddard quoted in Puglisi, *Puritans Besieged*, p. 190.
36. Demos, *The Unredeemed Captive*, p. 47.
37. Mary Rowlandson, *The Sovereignty and Goodness of God*, 2nd ed. (Cambridge, Mass.: 1682), p. 9.
38. Barbara G. Walker, *The Woman's Encyclopedia of Myths and Secrets* (San Francisco: Harper & Row, 1983), pp. 367–70, is the source for most of my information about the significance of hair.
39. Axtell, *The European and the Indian*, pp. 59–60.
40. Ibid., p. 60.
41. Ibid., p. 214, *n.* 59.

Chapter 14: *Gone Indian*

1. The situation of the New England captives in New France is vividly recreated in John Demos, *The Unredeemed Captive: A Family Story from Early America* (N.Y.: Vintage, 1994), and a first-hand account of the Deerfield captives is found in John Williams, *The Redeemed Captive Returning to Zion, or the Captivity and Deliverance of Rev. John Williams of Deerfield* (1707), 6th ed., 1795, 1909 (New York: Kraus Reprints, 1969), pp. 83–84. James Axtell, "White Indians of Colonial America," *William and Mary Quarterly*, 3rd Series, XXXII, 1975: 55–88 and *The European and the Indian* (N.Y. and Oxford: Oxford University Press, 1981) are major sources of information about their captivity and transculturation, as is Alden T. Vaughan and Daniel K. Richter, "Crossing the Cultural Divide: Indians and New Englanders, 1605–1763," *Proceedings of the American Antiquarian Society* 90: Pt. 1 (Oct. 1980), from whom most statistics are quoted. Other sources include Norman Heard, *White into Red: A Study of the Assimilation of White Persons Captured by Indians* (Metuchen, N.J.: Scarecrow, 1973); Emma Louise Coleman, *New England Captives Carried to Canada between 1677 and 1760 During the French and Indian Wars* (Portland, Me.: Southworth Press, 1925), I, pp. 79–97; C. Alice Baker, *True Stories of New England Captives Carried to Canada during the Old French and Indian Wars* (Cambridge: Stanton House, 1897); and Richard I. Melvin, *New England Outpost: War and Society in Colonial Deerfield* (N.Y.: W. W. Norton, 1989).
2. Williams, *The Redeemed Captive*, pp. 83–84.
3. Rev. Frederic Janes, *The Janes Family: Genealogy and Brief History of the Descendants of William Janes* (N.Y.: John H. Dingman, 1868), p. 84. Other sources concerning Elisha Searl are Coleman, *New England Captives*, pp. 79–97; George Sheldon, *1636 – Pocumtuck – 1886: A History of Deerfield, Massachusetts* (Deerfield, 1895); and Baker, *True Stories of New England Captives*.
4. Axtell, *The European and the Indian*, p. 162; Vaughan and Richter, "Crossing the Cultural Divide," pp. 23–95. While Vaughan and Richter show through statistical analysis that the number of captives who became "white Indians" over the entire period from 1675 to 1763 was lower than previously thought – only 3.2 to 4.1 per cent underwent complete cultural transition – the rate of transculturation during the first two wars was substantially higher, and more in accordance with the estimates of Baker and others; Janes, *The Janes Family*, pp. 44–45.
5. *A Narrative of the Captivity of Mrs. Johnson* [Walpole, N.H., 1796]; reprint of 3rd rev. ed. [1814] (Springfield, Mass., 1907), pp. 76–77, quoted in James Axtell, *The Invasion Within: The Context of Cultures in Colonial North America* (N.Y. and Oxford: Oxford University Press, 1985), p. 316.
6. J. Hector St. John [Crevecoeur], *Letters from an American Farmer; Describing Certain Provincial Situations, Manners, and Customs . . . of the British Colonies in North America* (London, 1782), pp. 214, 215.
7. Major T. Lloyd, "Names and conditions of all English prisoners taken this year," Oct. 3, 1709, in *Calendar of State Papers (Great Britain), Colonial Series: America and the West Indies, 1677–1733, Preserved in the Public Record Office*, 30 vols. (1896–1939) 1710–June 1711, p. 76.
8. Louis Franquet, *Voyages et Mémoires sur le Canada en 1752–53* (Toronto, 1968), p. 38, quoted in Demos, *The Unredeemed Captive*, p. 144.
9. P. F. X. Charlevoix, *Journal of a Voyage to North America*, trans. Louise Phelps Kellogg, 2 vols. (Chicago, 1923), II, p. 29; J. C. B. *Voyages au Canada dans le Nort d'Amerique*

septentrionale, fait depuis l'An 1751 à 1761 (Quebec, 1887), p. 228, quoted in Demos, *The Unredeemed Captive*, p. 144; Joseph Kellogg, MS. document "When I was Carryed to Canada . . .," in the Gratz Collection, The Rev. John Williams and Family, Case 8, Box 28 (Historical Society of Pennsylvania, Phila.), quoted in Demos, *The Unredeemed Captive*, p. 144.

10. Benjamin Franklin to Peter Collinson, May 9, 1753, in Leonard W. Labaree et al., eds., *Papers of Benjamin Franklin* (New Haven, 1961), 4, pp. 481–82, quoted in Axtell, *The Invasion Within*, p. 303.
11. Quoted in Vaughan and Richter, "Crossing the Cultural Divide," p. 46.
12. Crevecoeur, *Letter from an American Farmer*, p. 215.
13. See Vaughan and Richter, "Crossing the Cultural Divide," pp. 23–95; Roger Williams to John Winthrop, Jan. 10, 1637/38, *The Correspondence of Roger Williams*, ed. Glenn W. LaFantasie, RIHS 2 vols. (Hanover and London: Brown University Press/University Press of New England, 1988), Vol. 1, p. 140; J. Hammond Trumbull, *The Public Records of the Colony of Connecticut*, 15 vols. (Hartford, 1850–90), Vol. 1, p. 78. Vaughan and Richter, "Crossing the Cultural Divide," pp. 46–47; R. F. Foster, *Modern Ireland, 1600–1972* (London: Allen Lane, Penguin, 1988), p. 12.
14. Williams, *The Redeemed Captive*, p. 51; Demos, *The Unredeemed Captive*, p. 164.
15. Janes, *The Janes Family*, p. 53. My other sources on Northfield's history are Josiah Temple and George Sheldon, *History of the Town of Northfield* (Albany: Joel Munsell, 1875), and Herbert Collins Parsons, *A Puritan Outpost: A History of the Town and People of Northfield, Mass.* (N.Y.: Macmillan, 1937).
16. Colin G. Calloway, *The Western Abenakis of Vermont, 1600–1800: War, Migration and the Survival of an Indian People* (Norman and London: University of Oklahoma Press, 1990), pp. 12, 76.
17. Janes, *The Janes Family*, pp. 53–58, 7–74.
18. Coleman, *New England Captives*, p. 323; Janes, *The Janes Family*, pp. 44–45 n., 83–84 n.; Aug. 17, 1722, Prov. Laws. X, p. 216, quoted in Coleman, *New England Captives*, p. 323.
19. Mary Cabot, comp. and ed., *Annals of Brattleboro, 1681–1895*, 2 vols. (Brattleboro, Vt.: E. L. Hildreth & Co., 1921–22), Vol. 1, pp. 11–12. Kellogg had been captured at the age of twelve, with his brother and two sisters, and taken to Canada, where he was adopted by a Mohawk. He lived for a year with the Kahnawake Mohawks and with the French for ten, learning how to hunt and trap, and speak French, Mohawk, and other aboriginal languages. One of his sisters, like Eunice Williams, refused to return to New England.
20. Cabot, *Annals of Brattleboro*, p. 6; A. McCorison Marcus, "Colonial Defence of the Upper Connecticut Valley," *Vermont History*, Proceedings of the Vermont Historical Society, 30 (1962): 54.
21. Governor Vaudreuil, quoted in Calloway, *Western Abenakis*, p. 114.
22. Deerfield historian George Sheldon, quoted in Calloway, *Western Abenakis*, p. 116.
23. Massachusetts Archives 46:32; James Trumbull, *History of Northampton, Mass., from its Settlement in 1654*, 2 vols. (Northampton, 1898–1902), II, p. 19; Calloway, *Western Abenakis*, pp. 117–18; Letter of Col. John Stoddard to Lieut.-Gov. William Dummer, quoted in George Sheldon, *1636 – Pocumtuck – 1886: A History of Deerfield, Massachusetts* (Deerfield, 1895), I, pp. 405–6.
24. William Dummer, quoted in Sheldon, *History of Deerfield*, I, p. 405. My other sources on Elisha's service at Fort Dummer include Myron O. Stachiw, *Massachusetts Officers and Soldiers, 1723–1743: Dummer's War to the War of Jenkin's Ear* (Boston: Society of Colonial Wars in the Commonwealth of Massachusetts and the New England Historic

Genealogical Society, 1979), p. 223; Sheldon, *History of Deerfield*, I, p. 406–7; and Cabot, *Annals of Brattleboro*, p. 8. Further information was found in Parsons, *A Puritan Outpost*, and Egbert C. Smyth, "Papers Relating to the Construction and First Occupancy of Fort Dummer, and to a Conference with the Scatacook Indians Held There," *Mass. Hist. Soc. Proceedings*, 2nd Series, 6 (1891): 375–76.

25. Cabot, *Annals of Brattleboro*, 1, pp. 8–10; see also Temple and Sheldon, *History of Northfield*.

26. George S. Roberts, *Historic Towns of the Connecticut River Valley* (Schenectady, N.Y.: Robson and Adee, 1906), p. 333; Trumbull, *History of Northampton*, II, pp. 26–27; Baxter MSS 10: 222, 227–29, reprinted in Temple and Sheldon, *History of Northfield*, pp. 206, 213; Cabot, *Annals of Brattleboro*, 1, p. 11.

27. Demos, *The Unredeemed Captive*, pp. 193, 201, 206; Richard Storrs to Rev. Romeyn, Apr. 6, 1811, reprinted in *The Christian Magazine*, June 1811: 344, quoted in Demos, *The Unredeemed Captive*, p. 212.

28. Solomon Williams, *A Sermon Preach'd at Mansfield, Aug. 4, 1741* (Boston, 1742), p. 1; Demos, *The Unredeemed Captive*, p. 202.

29. Jonathan Edwards, *The Great Awakening: A Faithful Narrative. . . .*, ed. C. C. Goen (New Haven: Yale University Press, 1972), p. 120.

30. "Diary of Steven Williams," typeset copy, Richard R. Storrs Memorial Library (Longmeadow, Mass.), III, pp. 374–75, quoted in Demos, *The Unredeemed Captive*, p. 199.

31. William S. Simmons, "Pequot Folklore," in Laurence M. Hauptman and James D. Wherry, eds., *The Pequots in Southern New England: The Fall and Rise of an American Indian Nation* (Norman and London: University of Oklahoma Press, 1990), p. 198; William S. Simmons, "Red Yankees: Narragansett Conversion in the Great Awakening," *American Ethnologist* 10 (1983): 253–71.

Chapter 15: *Vanishing*

1. Rev. Frederic Janes, *The Janes Family: A Genealogy and Brief History of the Descendants of William Janes* (N.Y.: John H. Dingman, 1862), p. 123.

2. Colin G. Calloway, *The Western Abenakis of Vermont, 1600–1800: War, Migration and the Survival of an Indian People* (Norman and London: University of Oklahoma Press, 1990), pp. 175, 160.

3. Alan Taylor, *William Cooper's Town* (N.Y.: A. A. Knopf, 1995), pp. 89–90; Calloway, *Western Abenakis*, p. 188.

4. Charles Collard Adams, *Middletown Upper Houses* (N.Y.: Grafton Press, 1908), pp. 11, 55–56, 174, 198–99; M. Elizabeth Minard Simonds, *History of Westminster, 1791–1981* (Westminster: Town of Westminster, 1941; rev. ed., 1983), pp. 26, 27. Additional information about the Ranney family in Vermont comes from John Ellsworth Goodrich, *Rolls of the Soldiers in the Revolutionary War, 1775–1783* (Rutland, Vt.: Tuttle Co., 1904); Frank Miller and Bertha Miller Collins, *Vignettes of Westminster, Vermont*, comp. and ed. Rachel V. Duffalo (1993); *Vermont Quarterly*, 22 (1) (Jan. 1953): 118–20.

5. Colin Calloway, "Surviving the Dark Ages," intro. in Colin G. Calloway, ed., *After King Philip's War: Presence and Persistence in Indian New England* (Hanover, N.H.: University Press of New England, 1997), p. 11.

6. Calloway, *Western Abenakis*, p. 185; Charles E. Clark, *The Eastern Frontier: The Settlement of Northern New England, 1610–1763* (N.Y.: Alfred A. Knopf, 1970), pp. 352–59.

7. Simonds, *History of Westminster*, pp. 8–16, from Rev. F. J. Fairbanks, "History of East Parish"; Charles Collard Adams, *Middletown Upper Houses*, pp. 59–60, 199.

8. Calloway, *Western Abenakis*, p. 226.

9. Allen Stratton, comp., *History of South Hero Island, Being the Towns of South Hero and Grand Isle, Vermont*, 2 vols. (Burlington, Vt.: Queen City Printers, 1980), I, p. 593.

10. Primary sources for the Janes family in Vermont include: *Vermont State Papers, Vol. 5*, Petitions for Land Grants for South Hero and the *Vermont Census, 1790*; and Ira Allen, *The Natural and Political History of Vermont* (London, 1798). The history of South Hero Island can be found in Stratton, comp., *History of South Hero Island*, I; and Lewis Cass Aldrich, *History of Franklin and Grand Isle Counties* (N.Y.: D. Mason and Co., 1891). More general Vermont histories include William Chambers, *Atlas of Lake Champlain, 1779–1780* (Bennington, Vt.: Vermont Heritage Press, 1984); David Mansell, *Gazetteer of Vermont Heritage* (Chester Vt.: National Survey, 1974); David Ludlum, *Social Ferment in Vermont, 1791–1850* (N.Y.: AMS Press, 1966).

11. Champlain's quote translated from George E. Desbarats, ed., 1870, in Stratton, comp., *History of South Hero Island*, I, p. 2; ibid. I, pp. 5, 225.

12. Calloway, *Western Abenakis*, pp. 207, 220; Gordon Day, *The Identity of the St. Francis Indians*, Canadian Ethnology Service Paper, No. 71 (Ottawa: National Museums of Canada, 1981), p. 55; Aldrich, *History of Franklin and Grand Isle Counties*, p. 28.

13. See Janes, *The Janes Family*; Stratton, comp., *History of South Hero Island*, pp. 33, 42, 43, 52, 782.

14. Quote from Arthur D. Woodrow, ed. and comp., *Metallak: The Last of the Cooashaukes* (Rumford, Me.: Rumford Publishing Co., 1928), pp. 16–17, quoted in Calloway, *Western Abenakis*, p. 231.

15. Calloway, *Western Abenakis*, p. 237.

16. Ibid., p. 239.

17. John Moody, "The Native American Legacy," in Jane C. Beck, ed., *Always in Season: Folk Art and Traditional Culture in Vermont* (Hanover, N.H.: University Press of New England, 1982), p. 59, and "Annals of the St. Francis Indians," John B. Perry Papers, Bailey/Howe Library, University of Vermont, p. 242; Calloway, *Western Abenakis*, p. 234.

Chapter 16: *Repeating Patterns*

1. See footnote 1 in Chapter 4, "The Saints." My main genealogical source on the Harris family is Margaret Harris Stover, *Ely Harris and Lucretia Ransom of Connecticut, New York, and Ontario* (Decorah, Iowa: Anundsen Publishing Co., 1990) and *Supplement*, comp. Margaret Harris Stover and Margaret Luno Naby, ed. Margaret Harris Stover (Decorah, Iowa: Anundsen Publishing Co., 1995). See also Gale Ion Harris, "James Harris and Sarah [Eliot?] of Boston and New London," in *NEHGR*, 154 (Jan. 2000): 3-32. An interesting, but older and less accurate, genealogy of the family can be found in Nathaniel Harris Morgan, *A History of James Harris of New London, Conn., and His Descendants, from 1640 to 1878* (Hartford, Conn., 1878). My sources on the history of Colchester were John Warner Barber, *CHSC*, 2nd ed. (New Haven: Durrie & Peck and J. W. Barber, 1837), pp. 303–6, and a typed manuscript, "The Settlement of Colchester" [no date, no author], sent to me by Bessie Moroch of the Colchester Historical Society. For information on early Connecticut emigration to Nova Scotia, see Jean Stephenson, "The Connecticut Settlement of Nova Scotia Prior to the Revolution," in *Aids to Genealogical Research in Northeastern and Central States* (Washington, D.C.: National Genealogical Society, 1957), pp. 1–8.

2. *The Law Papers: Correspondence and Documents during Jonathan Law's Governorship of the Colony of Connecticut, 1741–1750,* 3 vols. (Hartford: CHS, 1907-1914), I: 287. (Vol. II, CHSC), quoted in Harris, "James and Sarah (Eliot?) Harris," pp. 20, 29.

3. Quoted in Alan Taylor, *William Cooper's Town* (N.Y.: A. A. Knopf, 1995), p. 92.

4. Taylor, *William Cooper's Town,* pp. 4, 92–93. The following paragraphs on the settlement of the Otsego patent are derived from this source.

5. My main sources of information on the Six Nations Iroquois in Canada are Charles M. Johnston, ed., *The Valley of the Six Nations: A Collection of Documents on the Indian Lands of the Grand River,* Champlain Society for the Government of Ontario (Toronto: University of Toronto Press, 1964); Bruce Hill, Ian Gillen, et al., *Six Nations Reserve* (Markham, Ont.: Fitzhenry & Whiteside, 1987); Charles Hamori Torok, "The Iroquois of Akwesasne, Mohawks of the Bay of Quinte, Onyota'a:ka (the Oneida of the Thames), and Wahta Mohawk, 1705–1945," in *Aboriginal Ontario: Historical Perspectives of the First Nations,* ed. Edward S. Rogers and Donald B. Smith (Toronto: Dundurn, 1994); Susan Padmos, "Muncey and the Six Nations: A Comparative Study of Acculturation on Two Reserves," M.A. thesis, Carleton University, 1985, as well as personal communication with Mohawk historian Keith Jamieson.

6. Taylor, *William Cooper's Town,* p. 39.

7. Ibid., p. 54.

8. Henry Clarke Wright, *Human Life, Illustrated in My Individual Experience as a Child, a Youth and a Man* (Boston, 1849), quoted in Taylor, *William Cooper's Town,* p. 112.

9. Peter Schmalz, *The Ojibwa of Southern Ontario* (Toronto: University of Toronto Press, 1991), p. 32. Other sources on aboriginal people in Ontario are Donald B. Smith, *Sacred Feathers: The Reverend Peter Jones (Kahkewaquonaby) & the Mississauga Indians.* (Toronto: University of Toronto Press, 1987); Olive Dickason, *Canada's First Nations* (Toronto: McClelland & Stewart, 1992); Tony Hall, "The Red Man's Burden: Land, Law and the Lord in the Indian Affairs of Upper Canada, 1791–1858," Ph.D. thesis, University of Toronto, 1984; Canada, Dept. of Citizenship and Immigration, Indian Affairs Branch, *Indians of Ontario: An Historical Review* (Ottawa: Queen's Printer, 1966); Tony Hall, "Native Limited Identities and Newcomer Metropolism in Upper Canada," in *Old Ontario: Essays in Honour of J. M. S. Careless,* ed. David Keanes and Colin Read (Toronto: Dundurn, 1990).

10. My main sources on Ojibwa land surrenders and the legal issues involved are Schmalz, *Ojibwa of Southern Ontario;* Hall, "The Red Man's Burden"; Smith, *Sacred Feathers;* and Canada, Royal Commission on Aboriginal Peoples, *Looking Forward, Looking Back,* Vol.1, *RCAP,* 5 vols. (Ottawa: Supply and Services Canada, 1996).

11. Schmalz, *Ojibwa of Southern Ontario,* pp. 126, 108.

12. Smith, *Sacred Feathers,* p. 26.

13. James Piper's daughter Olive married Heman Janes, the brother of my ancestor Lorrainy Janes of South Hero, Vermont. Lorrainy would marry Ely Harris's son James Harris in 1810. I believe Samuel Burdick was a relative of Abigail Burdick, the wife of Heman Janes, Sr., and mother of Lorrainy. Lorrainy's brother Heman and possibly also her parents moved to the Ingersoll area, but I don't know when or what prompted their migration. My sources for the early settlement of the Ingersoll area are Brian Dawe, *"Old Oxford Is Wide Awake!": Pioneer Settlers and Politicians in Oxford County, 1793–1853* (Woodstock: B. Dawe, 1980); James Sinclair, *History of the Town of Ingersoll* (private printing, 1924); H. W. Whitwell, *Ingersoll, Our Heritage* (Ingersoll: H. W. Whitwell, 1978); *History, Gazetteer and Directory of the County of Oxford* (Peterborough, Eng.: R. Gardner, 1852); Woodstock Public Library and Susan Start,

comps., *History of Oxford County Resource Kit* (Woodstock: Oxford County Bd. of Ed., 1986); Wadsworth, Unwin & Brown, *Illustrated Historical Atlas of Oxford County* (1876; reprint, Belleville, Ont.: Mika, 1972); Thomas A. Shenston, *The Oxford Gazetteer* (1852; reprinted 1965, Woodstock: Council of Corp. of County of Oxford Court House); and genealogical and town history papers from the Salford Museum, Salford, Ontario.

14. P. C. T. White, ed., *Lord Selkirk's Diary, 1803–4* (Toronto: McClelland & Stewart, 1972), p. 38, quoted in Dawe, *"Old Oxford Is Wide Awake!"*, p. 8.

15. Rev. Alex Harris, quoted in "Harris Picknic" in *Tillsonburg Liberal Newspaper*, Tillsonburg, Ont., Sept. 8, 1910, quoted in Stover, *Ely Harris and Lucretia Ransom*, p. 4. For Harris family history in Ontario, my primary sources are the publications "Oxford Militia," "Index to . . . census of Oxford County," "Oxford County Land Abstract," "Muster Roll of Volunteers," "Wills of Oxford County" of the Oxford County Branch of the Ontario Genealogical Society. My secondary sources are Stover, above. For some hilariously bad poetry about my Harris and Ranney ancestors, see James McIntyre, *"Musing on the Banks of Canadian Thames . . ."* (Ingersoll: H. Rowland, 1884).

16. Peter Jones, *History of the Ojebway Indians: With Especial Reference to Their Conversion to Christianity* (London: A. W. Bennett, 1861; reprinted, Freeport, N.Y.: Books for Libraries, 1970), p. 27.

17. *RCAP*, I: 156, 194, n. 28; Schmalz, *Ojibwa of Southern Ontario*, pp. 165–69.

18. Kineubenaie (Quinepeno), quoted at a meeting with the Mississaugas at the River Credit, Aug. 1, 1805, RG10, 1:294 NAC; Quoted in Smith, *Sacred Feathers*, p. 27.

19. Hope MacLean, "The Hidden Agenda: Methodist Attitudes to the Ojibwa and the Development of Indian Schooling in Upper Canada, 1821–1860," M.A. thesis, University of Toronto, 1978, pp. 67–68. The notion that God intended the land to be farmed can be found in Emerich de Vattel's *Le Droit des Gens* (1758).

20. Schmalz, *Ojibwa of Southern Ontario*, pp. 93, 108–10.

21. Peter Russell to the Duke of Portland, Mar. 21, 1798, quoted in Smith, *Sacred Feathers*, p. 29.

22. Ian Johnson, "British Tribal Relations in the Colonial Period," unpublished MS (Union of Ontario Indians), 1986, quoted in RCAP, I: 156.

23. Schmalz, *Ojibwa of Southern Ontario*, p. 85.

24. J. S. Carstairs, "The Late Loyalists of Upper Canada," in U. E. Loyalist Association, *Transactions* IV (1901–1902): 119, quoted in Dawe, *Old Oxford*, p. 24. Other sources on the War of 1812 include George F. G. Stanley, *The War of 1812: Land Operations*, Canadian War Museum Historical Publication #18 (Ottawa: National Museums of Canada and Macmillan, 1983); Pierre Berton, *Invasion of Canada* (Toronto: McClelland & Stewart, 1980); and the Oxford County sources mentioned in note 15 above.

25. Stover, *Ely Harris and Lucretia Ransom*, pp. 3, 19, 23.

26. See John Sugden, *Tecumseh* (N.Y.: Henry Holt & Co, 1997).

27. "Tecumseh's Speech to the Choctaw Council, 1811," in C. F. Cline, ed., *Tecumseh: Fact and Fiction in Early Records* (Ottawa: The Tecumseh Press, 1978), pp. 91–92.

28. E. A. Cruikshank, ed., *Documents Relating to the Invasion of Canada and the Surrender of Detroit*, Canadian Archives Publications, No. 7 (Ottawa: Government Printing Bureau, 1912), p. 144, Brock to Hull, Aug. 15, 1812, quoted in Berton, *Invasion of Canada*, p. 171; [William Hull] *Report of the Trial of Brigadier-General William Hull . . .* (N.Y.: Eastburn, Kirk, 1814), p. 103, quoted in Berton, *Invasion of Canada*, p. 183.

29. Neil Semple, *The Lord's Dominion: The History of Canadian Methodism* (Montreal and Kingston: McGill-Queen's University Press, 1996), p. 151.

30. VUL, Peter Jones Collection, Anecdote Book, Anecdote No. 53, "Powwowiska Quene-Henaw's Death," Peter Jones Collection; Smith, *Sacred Feathers*, pp. 36–37.
31. John Howison, *Sketches of Upper Canada* (Edinburgh, 1821), pp. 151, 33, quoted in Schmalz, *Ojibwa of Southern Ontario*, p. 117.
32. *RCAP*, I: 137–38; Schmalz, *Ojibwa of Southern Ontario*, p. 148.

Chapter 17: *Sons of the Forest*

1. There are several different names used to refer to these people: Ojibwa, Mississauga, Chippewa, and Anishinabe. In Elijah's time, the term Mississauga was used to refer to Ojibwa in southern Ontario, particularly those in the central region; Chippewa was the term used for Ojibwa in the southwestern part of the province and in Minnesota and Wisconsin. Both groups spoke Ojibwa. Anishinabe was and is a term used by Ojibwa people (and sometimes their allies the Ottawas and Pottawotamies) to refer to themselves.
2. Alvin Torry, *Autobiography of Rev. Alvin Torry: First Missionary to the Six Nations and the Northwestern Tribes of British North America*, ed. Rev. William Hosmer (Auburn: W. J. Moses, 1864), pp. 75–76.
3. Ibid., pp. 79–81.
4. VUL, Peter Jones Collection, Anecdote Book, Anecdote No. 33, quoted in Donald B. Smith, *Sacred Feathers: The Reverend Peter Jones (Kahkewaquonaby) and the Mississauga Indians* (Toronto: University of Toronto Press, 1987), p. 62.
5. The major primary sources I used for information about the Methodist missions are Peter Jones [Kahkewaquonaby], *Life and Journals of Kahkewaquonaby (Rev. Peter Jones), Wesleyan Missionary*, published under the direction of the Missionary Committee, Canada Conference (Toronto: Anson Green, 1860); the *Annual Reports* of the Methodist Missionary Society of the Methodist Episcopal and Wesleyan Methodist Churches; the two Methodist newspapers of the time, the *New York Christian Advocate and Zion's Herald* and the *Christian Guardian*. My secondary sources on the missions in Ontario are John Webster Grant, *Moon of Wintertime: Missionaries and the Indians of Canada in Encounter since 1534* (Toronto: University of Toronto Press, 1984); Smith, *Sacred Feathers*; Neil Semple, *The Lord's Dominion: The History of Canadian Methodism* (Montreal and Kingston: McGill-Queen's University Press, 1996); John Carroll, *Case and His Contemporaries*, 5 vols. (Toronto: Wesleyan Conference Office, 1874); Hope MacLean, "The Hidden Agenda: Methodist Attitudes to the Ojibwa and the Development of Indian Schooling in Upper Canada, 1821–1860," M.A. thesis, University of Toronto, 1978; Jean Barman, Yvonne Hebert, and Don McCaskill, eds., *Indian Education in Canada*. Volume 1: *The Legacy* (Vancouver: UBC Press, 1986); Elizabeth Graham, *Medicine Man to Missionary: Missionaries as Agents of Change among the Indians of Southern Ontario, 1784–1867* (Toronto: Peter Martin Associates, 1975); Methodist Missionary Society (Canada), *Faith of Our Fathers: A Century of Victory, 1824–1924* (Toronto: The Society, 1924); Annie Davina (Swinton) Stephenson, *One Hundred Years of Canadian Methodist Missions, 1824–1924* . . . (Toronto: Missionary Society of the Methodist Church, 1925).
6. Ruth Ellis, comp., *Methodist Churches in Oxford County, 1800–1900* (Woodstock: Ontario Genealogical Society, Oxford County Branch, 1988), p. 17.
7. Smith, *Sacred Feathers*, p. 56.
8. Daniel's son, Daniel Harris, Jr., became a Methodist exhorter, nicknamed "Exhauster," who was so keen to convert people that he even exhorted in bars. He was "rather short,

a little stooped, but his eyes bright and keen, vivacious in his every movement, and a
man consecrated to God from the crown of his head to the soles of his feet." Dorothy M.
Currie, *Heritage Renewed: A History of the West Oxford United Church and Cemetery*,
quoted in Margaret Harris Stover, *Ely Harris and Lucretia Ransom of Connecticut, New
York and Ontario* (Decorah, Iowa: Anundsen Publishing Co., 1990), p. 47. He was
severely injured in 1848 when a whirlwind picked him up and dropped him on a pile of
rails. My sources for the history of the churches in the Ingersoll area are Douglas
Flanders, *Settlement Patterns and the Evolution of Methodism in Dereham Township,
Oxford County* (London: Oxford County, 1976); Ellis, *Methodist Churches in Oxford
County, 1800–1900*; and Stuart Iveson and Fred Rosser, *The Baptists in Upper and
Lower Canada* (Toronto: University of Toronto Press, 1956).

9. NAC, RG1 L3, Upper Canada Land Petitions, 1831, Southwold, Vol. 233A, H16/80, Reel
 C-2051; Semple, *The Lord's Dominion*, p. 43; Ellis, *Methodist Churches in Oxford
 County*, p. 17.

10. Smith, *Sacred Feathers*, p. 70.

11. Jones, *Life and Journals of Kahkewaquonaby* (entry for May 25, 1825), p. 25.

12. Smith, *Sacred Feathers*, p. 55; Semple, *The Lord's Dominion*, pp. 15–16.

13. John Wesley, quoted in Smith, *Sacred Feathers*, p. 55.

14. Peter Jones, quoted in Methodist Episcopal Church in Canada, *Annual Report of the
 Canada Conference Missionary Society* (York, 1826, p. 18).

15. Grant, *Moon of Wintertime*, pp. 73, 85. The following paragraphs on the development of
 humanitarianism also draw on the work of Michael Ignatieff, *The Warrior's Honour:
 Ethnic War and the Modern Conscience* (Toronto: Penguin Canada, 1999), pp. 5, 12–15;
 Semple, *The Lord's Dominion*, p. 150; Maclean, *The Hidden Agenda*, pp. 72–74.

16. R. A. Schermerhorn, *Comparative Ethnic Relations* (N.Y.: Random House, 1970),
 pp. 73–74.

17. Robert J. Berkhofer, Jr., *Salvation and the Savage: An Analysis of Protestant Missions
 and American Indian Response, 1787–1862* (Lexington: University of Kentucky Press,
 1965), p. 10, quoted in MacLean, "The Hidden Agenda," p. 52.

18. Grant, *Moon of Wintertime*, p. 83; Semple, *The Lord's Dominion*, p. 167; MacLean, "The
 Hidden Agenda," p. 25.

19. Nathan Bangs, *A History of the Methodist Episcopal Church*, 4 vols. (N.Y.: Mason and
 G. Lane, 1840) vol.1, pp. 55–56, quoted in Tony Hall, "The Red Man's Burden: Land,
 Law and the Lord in the Indian Affairs of Upper Canada, 1791–1858," Ph.D. thesis,
 University of Toronto, 1984, p. 380.

20. Jones, *Life and Journal* (entry for Aug. 24, 1825), p. 40.

21. Torry, *Autobiography*, p. 114.

22. Later the ownership of this land would be disputed and subject to litigation, according
 to Mark Peters, councillor of the Munsee-Delaware Nation, and Jody Kechego, land-
 claims researcher for Chippewas of the Thames First Nation.

23. Alvin Torry letter, Grand River, Sept. 28, 1825, *Methodist Magazine* 9 (1826): 38–39.

24. Quoted in ibid.

25. Methodist Episcopal Church in Canada, *Annual Report of the Canada Conference
 Missionary Society* (1826), p. 7; *Annual Report* (1827), p. 6; John Ryerson, *New York
 Christian Advocate*, Apr. 4, 1828, p. 122.

26. Egerton Ryerson, *Christian Guardian*, Feb. 22, 1832, p. 59. My source on the curriculum in Methodist schools is MacLean, "The Hidden Agenda," especially pp. 33–34,
 41–43, and 51.

27. MacLean, "The Hidden Agenda," p. 51.

28. Kanootong, quoted in Jones, *Life and Journal*, p. 123.

29. NAC, RG10, 5:47, Joseph Sawyer, John Jones to Sir John Colborne, River Credit, Apr. 3, 1829; Smith, *Sacred Feathers*, pp. 39–40.

30. VUL, Peter Jones Collection, Peter Jones to Samuel Martin, River Credit Mission, Jan. 18, 1830, quoted in Smith, *Sacred Feathers*, p. 78.

31. Basil Hall, *Travels in North America in the Years 1827 and 1828*, 3 vols. (Edinburgh: Cadell and Co., 1829), I, p. 259.

32. Meth. Miss. Soc., *Faith of Our Fathers*, p. 41.

33. Jones, *Life and Journal*, p. 8. My chief sources on the reasons for the Ojibwa conversions were Grant, *Moons of Wintertime*, pp. 88–90; Semple, *The Lord's Dominion*, pp. 155–56; Smith, *Sacred Feathers*, pp. 95–96; and MacLean, "The Hidden Agenda," p. 131.

34. Grant, *Moons of Wintertime*, p. 90.

35. VUL, Peter Jones Collection, Peter Jones, Anecdote Book, Anecdote No. 63, quoted in Smith, *Sacred Feathers*, p. 83.

36. The Chief Westbrook anecdote is told in Annie Davina Stephenson, *One Hundred Years of Methodist Missions* (Toronto: Missionary Society of the Methodist Church, 1925), p. 61; Jones, *Life and Journal*, p. 117.

37. John Ryerson, *NYCA*, Oct. 3, 1828, p. 18; Jones, *Life and Journal*, May 7, 1828, p. 117.

38. Carroll, *Case and His Contemporaries*, III, p. 221.

39. John Morrison, *The Central Methodist Church* (Sarnia, Ont.: s.n., 1919), p. 46; *Christian Guardian*, Mar. 15, 1843, quoted in Smith, *Sacred Feathers*, p. 186.

40. Carroll, *Case and His Contemporaries*, III, p. 266.

41. See Smith, *Sacred Feathers*, pp. 185–87; Hurlburt became notorious for a series of public attacks on Peter Jones and the quality of his translations.

42. NAC, RG10, Vol. 3, 1829–1830, 2037.

43. NAC, RG10, Vol. 5, File C10997, Lieutenant Governor's Office Correspondence, pp. 2334–36, Letter to John Colborne, Feb. 19, 1830.

44. William Case, *NYCA*, Feb. 19, 1830, p. 97.

45. Peter Jones, *Christian Guardian*, 7 Aug. 1830: 300.

46. Ibid.

47. Peter Jones, *NYCA and ZH*, Dec. 2, 1831, 54.

48. Anthony F. C. Wallace's *Death and Rebirth of the Seneca* (N.Y.: Alfred A. Knopf, 1970) provides an in-depth review of the rise of the longhouse religion; Semple, *The Lord's Dominion*, pp. 153–54.

49. *Christian Guardian*, June 5, 1830: 229.

50. Semple, *The Lord's Dominion*, p. 158; Hall, "The Red Man's Burden," pp. 221–22.

51. Hall, "The Red Man's Burden," p. 221; Semple, *The Lord's Dominion*, pp. 158–59.

52. See Wub-e-ke-niew, *We Have the Right to Exist: Translation of Aboriginal Indigenous Thought* (N.Y.: Black Thistle Press, 1995).

53. Sir George Murray to Sir J. Kempt, Jan. 25, 1830, Great Britain, Sessional Papers (Commons), "Papers Relative to the Aboriginal Tribes in British Possessions (North America, New South Wales, Van Diemen's Land, and British Guiana)" 1834, 44: 300–499; Schmalz, *The Ojibwa of Southern Ontario*, p. 148.

54. Viscount Howick to J. K. Stewart, Feb. 14, 1832; Great Britain, Sessional Papers (Commons), 1834, 44: 300–499, "Papers Relative to the Aboriginal Tribes in British Possessions" quoted in Maclean, "The Hidden Agenda," p. 138.

55. Methodist Episcopal Church in Canada, *Report of the Missionary Society of the Methodist Episcopal Church in Upper Canada,* Sept. 1, 1824 – Sept 1, 1831, p. 6.

56. Ibid.
57. NAC, RG10, Vol. 441, R1 C9636, Feb. 7, 1831; Upper Canada Land Petitions (RG1 L3); 1831, Southwold, Vol. 233A, H16/80, Reel C–2051.

Chapter 18: *St. Clair Mission*

1. Entry for Aug. 2, 1829, Peter Jones [Kahkewaquonaby], *Life and Journals of Kahkewaquonaby (Rev. Peter Jones), Wesleyan Missionary*. Published under the direction of the Missionary Committee, Canada Conference (Toronto: Anson Green, 1860), p. 244; Smith and McGee quoted in ibid., May 25, 1830, p. 273.

2. Elijah Harris's letter is included in an article by William Case in the *New York Christian Advocate*, June 4, 1830, p. 158. The Ojibwa hymns can be found in [Peter Jones,] *A Collection of Chippeway and English Hymns for the Use of the Native Indians . . .*, trans. Peter Jones (N.Y.: Lane and Scott for the Missionary Society of the Methodist Episcopal Church, 1851).

3. Most of those at Walpole Island had come from the American side; many had been companions of Tecumseh, and one was a grandson of Pontiac. See John Webster Grant, *Moon of Wintertime: Missionaries and the Indians of Canada in Encounter since 1534* (Toronto: University of Toronto Press, 1984), p. 80.

4. Ontario Archives, William Jones, Indian Agent, Baldoon, Upper Canada, 1831–39, Letterbook, June 1, 1831, William Jones to Col. James Givens. The major primary sources I use for information about the Methodist mission at St. Clair are Peter Jones, *Life and Journals*; the annual reports of the Methodist Missionary Society of the Methodist Episcopal and Wesleyan Methodist Churches; the two Methodist newspapers of the time, *New York Christian Advocate and Zion's Herald*, 1826–33, and *The Christian Guardian;* and Charles How Phelps, ed., "The St. Clair Mission Register," *Western Ontario Historical Notes*, 17 (2), (Sept. 1961): 92–114. Missionary correspondence is another major source, especially the letters of Thomas Turner in the United Church Archives and of James Evans in the same depository and at the University of Western Ontario. A government perspective on the missions and the founding of the reserves can be found in the Letterbook of William Jones, Indian Agent, Baldoon, Upper Canada, 1831–39, and in the files of the Western (Sarnia Superintendency) Correspondence, 1825–64, at the Ontario Archives. My secondary sources on the St. Clair mission include Aylmer Nicholas Plain, *A History of the Chippewas of Sarnia and the History of the Sarnia Reserve* (Bright's Grove: George L. Smith, 1975); George Smith, *History of Sarnia to 1900* (Bright's Grove, Ont.: G. L. Smith, 1970); Margaret Kay, "An Indian Mission in Upper Canada," *Bulletin of United Church Committee on Archives* (Toronto: United Church Publishing House, 1954); John Morrison, *The Central Methodist Church* (Sarnia, Ontario: s.n., 1919); and James Johansen, *Indian Preacher: The Life and Teachings of Rev. Allen Salt* (Sarnia: St. Clair United Church, 1985 and 1988). General sources on early missions in Upper Canada include Grant, *Moon of Wintertime*; Donald B. Smith, *Sacred Feathers: The Reverend Peter Jones (Kahkewaquonaby) & the Mississauga Indians* (Toronto: University of Toronto Press, 1987); Neil Semple, *The Lord's Dominion: The History of Canadian Methodism* (Montreal and Kingston: McGill-Queen's University Press, 1996); John Carroll, *Case and His Contemporaries, or the Canadian Itinerants' Memorial: Constituting a Biographical History of Methodism in Canada*, 5 vols. (Toronto: Wesleyan Conference Office, 1874); and Hope MacLean, "The Hidden Agenda: Methodist Attitudes to the Ojibwa and the Development of Indian Schooling in Upper Canada, 1821–1860," M.A. thesis, University of Toronto, 1978.

5. OA, William Jones, Letterbook, Nov. 27, 1831.
6. Janice Rising, Chippewas of Sarnia, personal communication. There seems to be some dispute about where he was originally from. According to Plain, *A History of the Chippewas of Sarnia*, p. 5, he was from the district of Michipicoten, on the northeast shore of Lake Superior. In the early 1800s he became involved in some unknown offence to his tribe and had to flee for his life. He ended up hiding in a swamp and supplied with food by the Chippewas of Sarnia. "Because he knew some English he was adopted into the tribe and also made friends with early settlers." According to Plain, he may have been a Christian before the arrival of the Methodists. However, Rev. James Evans later described him as the hereditary head chief of the Saugeen Ojibwa, a fact which he said was attested to by William Jones and other Indian agents.
7. OA, William Jones, Letterbook, June 15, 1832.
8. Peter Jones, *Life and Journal*, Aug. 1832; OA, William Jones, Letterbook, Oct. 10, 1832.
9. UCA, The Wesleyan Methodist Church (Great Britain) Missions: America. The British Dominions in North America. The Canada District Correspondence, Fonds 3/2, 78.128C (Henceforth Miss. Corr.), File 106, Box 17, Roll 9, #18, Letter of Thomas Turner, Mar. 7, 1833.
10. OA, William Jones, Letterbook, May 1, 1833; April 19, 1833.
11. UCA, Miss. Corr., File 106, Box 17, Roll 23, Thomas Turner, May 30, 1833.
12. OA, William Jones, Letterbook, May 1, 1833; UCA, Miss. Corr., File 106, Box 17, Roll 23, Letters of Thomas Turner, May 30 1833, May 31, 1833.
13. OA, William Jones, Letterbook, July 1, 1833.
14. OA, William Jones, Letterbook, Aug. 1, 1833.
15. UCA, Miss. Corr., File 113, Box 18, Roll 9, Letter of Thomas Turner, Jan. 15, 1834; OA, William Jones, Letterbook, Apr. 23, 1834.
16. *Christian Guardian*, Sept. 9, 1835, p. 174; UCA, Miss. Corr., File 128, Box 20, Roll 22, James Evans to Rev. John Beecham, Mar. 29, 1836.
17. *Christian Guardian*, Sept. 24, 1834, p. 182.
18. UCA, Miss Corr., File 120, Box 19 Roll 22, James Evans to John Beecham, Sept. 1, 1835; OA, William Jones, Letterbook, Nov. 20, 1834.
19. *Christian Guardian*, Sept. 24, 1834, p. 182.
20. UCA, Miss. Corr., File 128, Box 20, Roll 22, James Evans to John Beecham, Mar. 29, 1936; Box 23, Roll 11, John Douse to Joseph Stinson, Apr. 1, 1839; Semple, *The Lord's Dominion*, p. 169; Margaret Ray, "An Indian Mission to Upper Canada," *United Church Bulletin* 7 (1954): 14; Methodist Missionary Society, *Annual Report*, 1839.
21. *Christian Guardian*, May 9, 1938, pp. 105–6; Grant, *Moon of Wintertime*, p. 91.
22. UCA, Miss. Corr., File 128, Box 20, Roll 22, James Evans to John Beecham, Mar. 29, 1936; OA, William Jones, Letterbook, Aug. 1, 1834.
23. Schmalz, *The Ojibwa of Southern Ontario*, pp. 150, 184.
24. OA, William Jones, Letterbook, Jan. 21, 1835.
25. Schmalz, *Ojibwa of Southern Ontario*, pp. 165–66.
26. Quoted in Schmalz, *Ojibwa of Southern Ontario*, p. 132; *Christian Guardian*, Mar. 21, 1838, p. 78, quoted in *The Lord's Dominion*, p. 169.
27. *Christian Guardian*, July 20, 1836, p. 146; Maclean, "A Hidden Agenda," p. 118.
28. MacLean, "A Hidden Agenda," pp. 119, 129.
29. Quoted in Schmalz, *The Ojibwa of Southern Ontario*, p. 134.
30. Smith, *Sacred Feathers*, p. 162; Schmalz, *The Ojibwa of Southern Ontario*, pp. 136–37; Great Britain, Parliament, *Sessional Papers* (Commons), 34: 2000-2399, "British North American Provinces. Return to an Address of the Honourable The House of Commons,

dated 11 June 1839; – for, Copies or Extracts of Correspondence since 1ˢᵗ April 1835, Between the Secretary of State for the Colonies and the Governors of the British North American Provinces, Respecting the Indians in those Provinces," (*BNA Provinces*), pp. 136–137, Francis Bond Head to Lord Glenelg, Apr. 4, 1837.

31. *BNA Provinces*, p. 149, Francis Bond Head to Lord Glenelg, Aug. 15, 1837, quoted in MacLean, "A Hidden Agenda," p. 120.

32. Semple, *The Lord's Dominion*, p. 170.

33. MacLean, "A Hidden Agenda," pp. 122, 128; *Christian Guardian*, Sept. 2, 1840.

34. *Christian Guardian*, Apr. 25, 1838, p. 98; *Christian Guardian*, Jan. 4, 1837, p. 34; *Christian Guardian*, Apr. 25, 1838, p. 98; UCA, Miss Corr., File 168, Box 24, Roll 23, Joseph Stinson to Robert Alder, July 24, 1838.

35. John Carroll, *Case and his Contemporaries*, IV: 344.

36. Rev. John Douse to Rev. Richard Reece, in Charles M. Johnston, *The Valley of the Six Nations: A Collection of Documents on the Indian Lands of the Grand River* (Toronto: The Champlain Society for the Government of Ontario, University of Toronto Press, 1964), pp. 260–61; Jacob H. Busk to Sir George Grey, Great Britain, Colonial Office, British North American Provinces . . ., Parliamentary Papers, 1839, No. 323, pp. 115–17, reprinted in Johnston, *The Valley of the Six Nations*, pp. 300–2.

37. "The Past and Present Condition of the Six Nations," 1842, P.E.O., X.O. 42, c. 515, Report on the Affairs of the Indians in Canada, 1844, Part ii, pp. 142–56, reprinted in *The Valley of the Six Nations*, pp. 305–11.

38. UCA, Miss. Corr., Box 25, Roll 23, Petition of Jan. 30, 1841.

39. Carroll, *Case and His Contemporaries*, IV, pp. 344, 362.

40. University of Western Ontario, James Evans Papers, Robert Alder to James Evans, Mar. 31, 1846; Allen Salt, in Rev. James Johansen, *Indian Preacher: The Life and Teachings of Rev. Allen Salt, 1818–1911* (Sarnia: St. Clair United Church, 1985, 1988), no page; *Evidence of William Jones, Superintendent of Indians for Sarnia, 1844-45* (Bright's Grove, Ont.: George L. Smith, 1977), no page; *Missionary Notices*, May 1856, p. 98; Wesleyan-Methodist Church of Canada, *Annual Report of the Missionary Society of the Wesleyan-Methodist Church of Canada*, Toronto, 1859, p. xiv.

41. W. H. Smith, *Canadian Gazetteer* (Toronto, 1846), quoted in Schmalz, *The Ojibwa of Southern Ontario*, pp. 176–77; Maclean, "A Hidden Agenda," pp. 209, 219–21. For other information on Munceytown, see Government of Canada, Indian Claims Commission, *Chippewas of the Thames Inquiry: Report on Muncey Land Claim*, Dec. 1994, "Appendix A: Historical Background"; and Susan Padmos, "Muncey and the Six Nations: A Comparative Study of Acculturation on Two Reserves," M.A. thesis, Carleton University, 1985.

42. NAC, RG10, 802:10 File C-13625, J. B. Clench Defalcation, Dismissal and Inquiry, 1854–55, Related Papers, ca. 1828–1905, and Smith, *Sacred Feathers*, p. 225; James Douglas Leighton, "Compact Tory as Bureaucrat: Samuel Peter Jarvis and the Indian Department, 1837–1845," *Ontario History* 73 (1) (1981): 46–47, quoted in Schmalz, *Ojibwa of Southern Ontario*, p. 165; ibid., p. 166.

43. *Christian Guardian*, May 6, 1846, p. 113.

44. Ibid., Sept. 29, 1841, p. 194.

45. Wesleyan-Methodist Church of Canada, *Annual Report of the Missionary Society of the Wesleyan-Methodist Church of Canada*, Toronto, 1846, p. viii; Semple, *The Lord's Dominion*, p. 171; MacLean, "A Hidden Agenda," p. 146; Chief Kelly Riley of the Chippewa of the Thames, personal communication, May 1998. The following account of the development of Indian residential schools draws heavily on the work of Hope MacLean.

46. Indian Chiefs and Principal Men, General Council, Orillia, Minutes *of the General Council on the Proposed Removal of the Smaller Communities and the Establishment of Manual Labour Schools* (Montreal: Canada Gazette Office, 1846), p. 10.
47. Ibid., p. 23.
48. Ibid., pp. 5–8; MacLean, pp. 147–49.
49. Smith, *Sacred Feathers*, p. 160; MacLean, "A Hidden Agenda," pp. 234–45.
50. VUL, Peter Jones Collection, Peter Jones, Letterbook, Peter Jones to Eliza Jones, June 7, 1846; Grant, *Moon of Wintertime*, pp. 94–95; Schmalz, *Ojibwa of Southern Ontario*, pp. 190–91; MacLean, "A Hidden Agenda," p. 188 and Appendix. By 1860, most Native people in what is now southern Ontario had found ways to adapt to Euro-Canadian settlement, and most Ojibwa were at least nominally Christian, so the prospects for new converts were not encouraging. The Methodist Missionary Society then turned its attention to the Northwest, where there were thousands of unconverted Indians in Rupert's Land, and most remaining aboriginal missionaries were sent there.

Chapter 19: *Shoal Lake*

1. Dorothy Wyman, "E. G. D. Freeman: An Intentional Life," *Touchstone* (Sept. 1990): 34. My primary sources for biographical information about Rev. E. G. D. Freeman come from his unpublished memoirs (typescript), which were written in the early 1970s; my aunt Lois Wilson's autobiography *Turning the World Upside Down* (Toronto: Doubleday, 1989); the above-mentioned article by Dorothy Wyman; and conversations and correspondence with his children. To respect the wishes of some of his children, I have not quoted directly from his memoirs, as my grandfather did not intend them for publication.
2. Much of my information about the Freemans in Ireland is based on the genealogical research of my aunt, Jean Harvey. Any errors are my responsibility.
3. My main sources on Irish history during this period were R. F. Foster, *Modern Ireland, 1600–1972* (London: Allen Lane, Penguin, 1988); Robert Kee, *Ireland: A History* (London: Weidenfeld & Nicolson, 1980); and Peter Berresford Ellis, *Hell or Connaught: The Cromwellian Colonization of Ireland* (London: Hamish Hamilton, 1975).
4. National Archives of Ireland, Tithe Aplotment Book, Kiltegan Parish, County Wicklow, 1824–1827.
5. Cecil Woodham-Smith, *The Great Hunger: Ireland, 1845–9* (London: Hamish Hamilton, 1962), pp. 34–36; Thomas Sowell, *Conquests and Cultures: An International History* (New York: Basic Books, 1998), p. 65. Joseph Brien bought land from William Freeman, who came to the Ottawa area in Ontario in the 1830s.
6. For a vivid and detailed exploration of the potato famine, see Woodham-Smith, *The Great Hunger*.
7. Foster, *Modern Ireland*, p. 322.
8. Woodham-Smith, *The Great Hunger*, p. 214.
9. Robert Kee, *Ireland: A History*, p. 43; unpublished letter of John Davis, Dec. 9, 1901.
10. Wyman, "E. G. D. Freeman: An Intentional Life," 36.
11. Ibid., 36–37.
12. Richard Allen, "The Social Gospel and the Reform Tradition in Canada, 1890–1928," *Canadian Historical Review*, 49 (1968): 382. The following discussion of the Social Gospel draws heavily on Allen's work.
13. Richard Allen, *The Social Passion: Religion and Social Reform in Canada, 1914–1928* (Toronto: University of Toronto Press, 1971), p. 5; Allen, "Social Gospel and Reform Tradition," p. 384; Allen, *The Social Passion*, p. 29.

14. Wyman, "E. G. D. Freeman," 36.

15. John Webster Grant, *Moon of Wintertime: Missionaries and the Indians of Canada in Encounter since 1534* (Toronto: University of Toronto Press, 1984), pp. 185–86.

16. Daniel Francis, *The Imaginary Indian: The Image of the Indian in Canadian Culture* (Vancouver: Arsenal Pulp Press, 1992), pp. 153–57.

17. E. G. D. Freeman, Unpublished memoirs; Presbyterian Church in Canada, Synod of Manitoba, Synod's Committee on Home Missions and Social Services Minutes, 1922–1925, July 3, 1923; Sept. 11, 1923.

18. Adolph M. Greenberg and James Morrison, "Group Identities in the Boreal Forest: The Origin of the Northern Ojibwa," *Ethnohistory* 29, (2) (1982): 75–102. My sources on the Anishinabe include Michael Angel, "Discordant Voices, Conflicting Visions: Ojibwa and Euro-American Perspectives on the Midewewin," Ph.D. thesis, University of Manitoba, 1997; Michael Angel, "The Ojibwa-Missionary Encounter at Rainy Lake Mission," M.A. thesis, University of Manitoba, 1986; J. A. Lovisek, "The Political Evolution of the Boundary Waters Ojibwa," *Papers of the 24th Algonquian Conference*, ed. William Cowan (Ottawa: Carleton University, 1993); Joan A. Lovisek, Leo G. Waisberg, and Tim E. Holzkamm, Treaty and Aboriginal Rights Research, Grand Council Treaty #3, "Deprived of Part of Their Living: Colonialism and Nineteenth-Century Flooding of Ojibwa Lands," *Papers of the Twenty-Sixth Algonquian Conference*, ed. David Pentland (Winnipeg: University of Manitoba, 1995); Leo G. Waisberg and Tim E. Holzkamm, "'Their Country Is Tolerably Rich in Furs': The Ojibwa Fur Trade in the Boundary Waters Region, 1821–71," *Actes du Vingt-Cinquième Congrès des Algonquinistes/Papers of the 25th Algonquian Conference*, ed. William Cowan (Ottawa: Carleton University, 1994); Leo Waisberg and Tim E. Holzkamm, Treaty and Aboriginal Rights Research, Grand Council Treaty #3, "'A Tendency to Discourage Them from Cultivating': Ojibwa Agriculture and Indian Administration in Northwestern Ontario," *Ethnohistory* 40, (2) (Spring 1992), pp. 175–211; Leo G. Waisberg and Tim E. Holzkamm, "The Ojibway Understanding of Fishing Rights under Treaty 3: A Comment on Lise C. Hansen, 'Treaty Fishing Rights and the Development of Fisheries Legislation in Ontario: A Primer,'" *Native Studies Review* 8 (1) (1992), pp. 47–55; James Redsky, *(Esquekesik) Great Leader of the Ojibway: Mis-quona-queb* (Toronto: McClelland & Stewart, 1972); Selwyn Dewdney, *The Sacred Scrolls of the Southern Ojibway* (Toronto and Buffalo: University of Toronto Press, 1975); Elizabeth Hornbeck Tanner, ed., *Atlas of Great Lakes Indian History* (Norman: University of Oklahoma Press, 1987); A. Irving Hallowell, *The Ojibwa of Berens River, Manitoba: Ethnography into History*, ed. with preface and afterword by Jennifer S. H. Brown, Case Studies in Cultural Anthropology; gen. eds. George and Louise Spindler (Fort Worth, Texas: Harcourt, Brace Jovanovich, 1992); Jennifer S. H. Brown and Robert Brightman, *"The Orders of the Dreamed": George Nelson on Cree and Northern Ojibwa Religion and Myth, 1823*, Manitoba Studies in Native History III (Winnipeg: University of Manitoba Press, 1988); Rupert Ross, *Dancing with a Ghost: Exploring Indian Reality* (Toronto: Octopus Publishing, 1992); Wub-e-ke-niew, *We Have the Right to Exist: Translation of Aboriginal Indigenous Thought* (N.Y.: Black Thistle Press, 1995); and Basil Johnston, *Ojibway Heritage* (Toronto: McClelland & Stewart, 1976).

19. Lovisek, "Political Evolution," p. 287; Alexander Mackenzie, *Voyages from Montreal on the River through the Continent of North America to the Frozen and Pacific Oceans in the Years 1789 and 1793* (London: T. Cadell, June and W. Davies, 1801), p. 22, quoted in Lovisek, "Political Evolution," p. 288.

20. Richardson, in Simon J. Dawson, "General Report on the Progress of the Red River

Expedition," pp. 11–41, in *Report on the Exploration of the Country Between Lake Superior and the Red River Settlement, and between the Latter Place and the Assiniboine and the Saskatchewan*, ed. Simon J. Dawson (Toronto: Legislative Assembly of the Province of Canada, 1859), p. 15; Waisberg and Holzkamm, "Tolerably Rich in Furs," p. 500.

21. Angel, "Discordant Voices," p. 29; Angel, "Ojibwa-Missionary Encounter," p. 62.
22. Angel, "Ojibwa-Missionary Encounter," p. 53; Hallowell, *The Ojibwa of Berens River*, pp. 37, 44.
23. Ibid. p. 121; Grant, *Moon of Wintertime*, p. 87; Angel, "Ojibwa-Missionary Encounter," p. 145.
24. Angel, "Ojibwa-Missionary Encounter," pp. 150–51.
25. Hudson's Bay Company Archives, Provincial Archives of Manitoba, Gov. George Simpson, Correspondence Inward D.5/26, Fol. 194–95, 660; Waisberg and Holzkamm, "Tolerably Rich in Furs," p. 500; Allen Salt MSS, Journal, 49; Angel, "Ojibwa-Missionary Encounter," p. 151; Grant, *Moon of Wintertime*, p. 87; Angel, "Discordant Voices," p. 47.
26. Hallowell, *The Ojibwa of Berens River*, p. 35f.
27. Alexander Morris, *The Treaties of Canada with the Indians of Manitoba and the North-west Territories: including the negotiations on which they were based, and other information relating thereto* (Toronto: Belfords, Clarke & Co, 1880), p. 323.
28. RCAP, I, p. 159–75.
29. Hope MacLean, "The Hidden Agenda: Methodist Attitudes to the Ojibwa and the Development of Indian Schooling in Upper Canada, 1821–1860," M.A. thesis, University of Toronto, 1978, pp. 195–97; Olive Dickason, *Canada's First Nations* (Toronto: McClelland & Stewart, 1992), p. 251; RCAP 1, p. 146.
30. E. Brian Titley, *A Narrow Vision: Duncan Campbell Scott and the Administration of Indian Affairs in Canada* (Vancouver: UBC Press, 1986), p. 201; F. Laurie Barron, "The Indian Pass System in the Canadian West, 1882–1935," in *The Native Imprint*, ed. Olive Patricia Dickason, Vol. 2 (Athabasca, Alta.: Athabasca University, 1996), pp. 184–204.
31. Maclean, "Hidden Agenda," pp. 219–20; Grant, *Moon of Wintertime*, pp. 156, 163.
32. UCA, Presbyterian Church of Canada, Foreign Mission Fonds, Records Pertaining to Missions to the Aboriginal People in Western Canada, Correspondence, Fonds 122/14, 79.199C, Box 2, File 14. (Henceforth Missions to Aboriginal People in Western Canada.) Professor T. Hart, Indian Boarding School to Rev. Wm. Moore, Foreign Missions Committee, 09/12/1898. Primary sources on Cecilia Jeffrey Indian Residential School are the National Archives (NAC), Indian Affairs, School Files, Record Group 10, especially Vol. 6190, File 461–9, Parts 1 and 2; Vol. 6187, File 461–1, Parts 1 and 2, Reels C7922; File 461–5, Reel 7923; Letterbooks of Duncan Campbell Scott, C9009; and interviews with Emma Paishk, Albert Mandamin, Ada Morrison, Florence and Frank Redsky, Walter Redsky, and others at Shoal Lake and Kenora, Ontario. Foreign Mission Fonds, Records Pertaining to Missions to the Aboriginal People in Western Canada, Correspondence, Fonds 122/14, 79.199C, Boxes 2 and 3. Early correspondence concerning the founding of the school can be found in UCA, Presbyterian Church of Canada, Foreign Mission Committee, Western Section, Boxes 2 and 3; and the annual reports of the Presbyterian Church in Canada, WFMS (to 1914), can be found in the archives of the Presbyterian Church and United Church. Secondary sources were J. R. Miller, *Shingwauk's Vision* (Toronto: University of Toronto Press, 1996); I. R. Brooks, comp., *Native Education in Canada and the United States: A Bibliography* (Calgary: University of Calgary Office of Educational Development, Indian Students University

Program Services, 1976); RCAP; Jean Barman, Yvonne Hébert, and Don McCaskill, eds., *Indian Education in Canada:* Volume 1: *The Legacy* (Vancouver: UBC Press, 1986); Canada, Department of Indian Affairs. *The Education of Indian Children in Canada: A Symposium Written by Members of Indians Affairs Education Division with Comments by the Indian Peoples* (Toronto: Ryerson Press, 1965); Elizabeth Graham, *The Mush Hole: Life at Two Indian Residential Schools* (Waterloo, Ont.: Heffle Publishing, 1997).

33. UCA, Presbyterian Church in Canada, Missions to Aboriginal People in Western Canada, Box 2, File 20, Austin G. McKittrick to Rev. R. P. McKay, Dec. 1, 1900; McKittrick to McKay, Jan. 30, 1901.

34. Waisberg and Holzkamm, "A Tendency to Discourage Them from Cultivating," pp. 176–211.

35. According to Cuyler Cotton, who has researched the early history of Cecilia Jeffrey Indian Residential School for the Shoal Lake First Nations.

36. Donald B. Smith, *Sacred Feathers: The Reverend Peter Jones (Kahkewaquonaby) & the Mississauga Indians* (Toronto: University of Toronto Press, 1987), p. 241; Grant, *Moon of Wintertime*, p. 190.

37. MacLean, "Hidden Agenda," pp. 153–54, 159–60, 172, 243.

38. Barman, Hébert, and McCaskill, *Indian Education in Canada*, I, p. 7; Grant, *Moon of Wintertime*, p. 186.

39. D. C. Scott, "Indian Affairs, 1867–1912," in Adam Shortt and Arthur G. Coughty, eds., *Canada and Its Provinces: A History of the Canadian People and Their Institutions by One Hundred Associates* (Toronto: Glasgow, Brook & Co, 1914), vol. 7, pp. 622–23, quoted in Titley, *A Narrow Vision*, p. 36; Grant, *Moon of Wintertime*, p. 184.

40. UCA, Presbyterian Church of Canada, Missions to Aboriginal People in Western Canada, Box 2, File 23, McKittrick to McKay, Mar. 15, 1901.

41. Ibid., Box 2, File 21, McKittrick to McKay, Jan. 30, 1901.

42. Rev. Alexander Sutherland, general secretary of the Methodist Church of Canada, Missionary Dept., to Laurence Vankoughnet, Dept. of the superintendent general of Indian Affairs, quoted in *RCAP* summary, p. 181.

43. Quoted in Robert J. Surtees, *The Original People* (Toronto: Holt, Rinehart & Winston, 1971), p. 74; Grant, *Moon of Wintertime*, p. 162.

44. Eli Mandamin, Address to the 120th General Assembly of the Presbyterian Church in Canada on the Occasion of the Church's Adoption of Its Statement of Confession, June 4, 1994.

45. UCA, Presbyterian Church of Canada, Foreign Mission Fonds, Records Pertaining to Missions to the Aboriginal People in Western Canada, Correspondence, Fonds 122/14, 79.199C, Box 2, File 33, J.C. Gandier to R.P. MacKay, Jan. 14, 1902, and "agreement"; UCA, Presbyterian Church in Canada, Women's Foreign Mission Society, *Annual Report*, 1901–2.

46. UCA, Presbyterian Church in Canada, Missions to Aboriginal People in Western Canada, Box 5, File 95, Petition dated Shoal Lake, March 4, 1907 to Foreign Mission Society, Toronto, quoted in Miller, *Shingwauk's Vision*, pp. 347, 516n.

47. UCA, Presbyterian Church of Canada, WFMS, *Annual Report,* 1908, p. 53; Peter Schmalz, *The Ojibwa of Southern Ontario* (Toronto: University of Toronto Press, 1991), p. 185.

48. UCA, Presbyterian Church in Canada, Women's Foreign Missionary Society, *Annual Report*, 1910–11.

49. *RCAP*, I, p. 357; Government of Canada, Department of Indian Affairs, *Annual Report*, 1898, p. xxvii.
50. Barman et al., *Indian Education in Canada*, I, p. 8; Basil H. Johnston, "The Four Hundred Year Winter," *The Northian* 9, No. 1 (1972): 36–42.
51. Barman et al., *Indian Education in Canada*, I, pp. 8–9; Duncan C. Scott, "Indian Affairs, 1867–1912," p. 616; *RCAP*, I, p. 355.
52. *RCAP*, I, pp. 355–56.
53. NAC, RG10, Vol. 6187, File 461–1, Pt. 1, July 8, 1914.
54. Ibid., Report of Inspector Semmens on Cecilia Jeffrey Boarding School, Jan. 22, 1917; J. D. McLean, asst. deputy and secretary to Rev. F. T. Dodds, principal, Feb. 1, 1917; Petition, Mar. 29, 1917.
55. Ibid., Apr. 4, 1917; J. D. McLean to Rev. J. H. Edminson, Sec., Board of Home Missions, Aug. 25, 1917; Report of Commission of Presbytery to Investigate Conditions at Cecilia Jeffrey Boarding School, Feb. 26, 1918; J. H. Edminson, to J. D. McLean, Apr. 2, 1918.
56. Ibid., Telegram to Deputy and Sec, Department of Indian Affairs, from R. S. McKenzie, Nov. 24, 1918.
57. Ibid., Andrew B. Baird to Hon. Frank Oliver, July 28, 1911.
58. Ibid., R. D. Waugh to Rev. John Semmens, Department of Indian Affairs, June 21, 1919; James H. Gray, *Booze: The Impact of Whisky on the Prairie West* (Toronto: Macmillan, 1972), p. 88.
59. Miller, *Shingwauk's Vision*, pp. 169–70; NAC, RG10, Vol. 6810, File 470–2–3, Pt. 7, evidence of Scott before the Committee of the House, quoted in Titley, *A Narrow Vision*, p. 50.
60. Diamond Jenness, "Canada's Indians Yesterday. What of Today?" *Canadian Journal of Economics and Political Science* 20, (1) (Feb. 1954), quoted in Barman et al., *Indian Education in Canada*, I, p. 9; NAC, RG10, Vol. 6187, File 461–1, Pt. 1, Frank Edwards to Mrs. Adelaide Clarke, WMS, Nov. 19, 1923; Barman et al., *Indian Education in Canada*, I, p. 9.
61. UCA, Presbyterian Church in Canada, WMS, *Annual Report*, 1922.
62. NAC, RG10, Vol. 6187, File 461–5, Frank Edwards to J. D. McLean, Feb. 8, 1922; J. D. McLean to Frank Edwards, Feb. 17, 1922.
63. NAC, RG10, Vol. 6187, File 461–5, Frank Edwards to J. D. McLean, Feb. 6, 1922; NAC RG10, Vol. 6187, File 461–1, Pt. 1, W. J. Cookson to Frank Edwards, Apr. 11, 1922.
64. United Church in Canada, Manitoba and Northwestern Ontario Conference Archives, Presbyterian Church in Canada, Synod of Manitoba, Synod's Committee on Home Missions and Social Services, Minutes 1922–25, July 3, 1923; NAC, RG10, Vol. 6187, File 461–1, Pt. 1., Frank Edwards to Mrs. Adelaide Clarke, Nov. 19, 1923.
65. UCA, Presbyterian Church in Canada, Synod of Manitoba Fonds, Records of the Presbyteries, Fonds 146/2, 79.221C, Presbytery of Winnipeg Minutes, Vol. 5, MRG, Sept. 11, 1923; Nov. 6, 1923.
66. NAC, RG10, Vol. 6187, File 461–1, Pt. 1, Frank Edwards to Mrs. Adelaide Clark, WMC, Nov. 19, 1923. (The Women's Missionary Committee was the Women's Missionary Society.)

Chapter 20: *Cecilia Jeffrey Indian Residential School*

1. An Act further to amend the Indian Act, S.C. 1895, c.35 (58–59 Vict.) assented to July 22, 1895, quoted in E. Brian Titley, *A Narrow Vision: Duncan Campbell Scott and*

the Administration of Indian Affairs in Canada (Vancouver: UBC Press, 1986), p. 166; ibid., p. 15. (The original amendment was made in 1884.)

2. NAC, RG10, Vol. 3226, File 60, 511–4A, Duncan Campbell Scott circular Dec. 15, 1921.

3. Leo Waisberg, personal communication, May 1996; Ada Morrison, personal communication, May 1996.

4. Titley, *A Narrow Vision*, p. 36.

5. NAC, RG10, Vol. 6187, File 461–1, Pt. 1, Frank Edwards to J. D. McLean, Feb. 9, 1923; Ibid., Sept. 19, 1924, "Memorandum for File"; Ibid. Extract from Agency Report for Month of April, Frank Edwards, original in File 75–129, May 7, 1923.

6. Ibid. D. C. Scott to Frank Edwards, Feb. 10, 1925.

7. NAC, RG10, Vol. 6190, File 461–9, Pt. 1, E. G. D. Freeman, Memo re. new location for Cecilia Jeffrey School, June 6, 1925.

8. NAC, RG10, Vol. 6187, File 461–1, Pt. 1, Frank Edwards to Mrs. Adelaide Clarke, Nov. 19, 1923; Ibid., Part 2, Memorandum to Mr. Ferrier from Mr. Paget, Aug. 21, 1928, Comments of Chief Black Hawk of Northwest Angle; Ibid., Frank Edwards to Asst. Deputy and Secretary, April 6, 1925.

9. NAC, RG10, Vol. 6190, File 461–9, Pt. 1, E. G. D. Freeman, Memo re. new location for Cecilia Jeffrey School, June 6, 1925; Ibid., Memo of E. G. D. Freeman, Aug. 4, 1925.

10. Ibid. Frank Edwards, Aug. 6, 1925; Ibid., Frank Edwards to Asst. Deputy and Secretary, Indian Affairs, Feb. 6, 1926.

11. Ibid., James Robinson to Duncan Campbell Scott, April 12, 1926.

12. Ibid., Duncan Campbell Scott to James Robinson, April 29, 1926; Titley, *A Narrow Vision*, p. 59. The amendment was to section 149a of the Indian Act, later section 141.

13. NAC, RG10, Vol. 6190, File 461–9, Pt. 1, Frank Edwards to Asst. Deputy and Secretary, May 20, 1926.

14. Ibid. J. D. McLean to Frank Edwards, May 26, 1926.

15. NAC, RG10 Vol. 6187, File 461–1, Pt. 2, Frank Edwards to Asst. Deputy and Secretary, Apr. 27, 1927.

16. Ibid., J. H. Edmison to D. C. Scott, Apr. 28, 1926.

17. Ibid., Frank Edwards to Asst. Deputy and Secretary, July 8, 1927; Frank Edwards to Asst. Deputy and Secretary, Feb. 12, 1927; Duncan Campbell Scott to Mr. Pratt, May 6, 1927.

18. Ibid., Frank Edwards to Asst. Deputy and Secretary, Feb. 12, 1927; Ibid., Margaret Pierce to Superintendent of Indian Schools, Dept. of Indian Affairs, Sept. 19, 1927.

19. Ibid., Memorandum to Mr. Ferrier from Mr. Paget, "What Transpired at the Conference of Chiefs and Councillors of the Various Bands in the Kenora and Savanne Agencies in Connection with Indian Education," Aug. 21, 1928.

20. Ibid.

21. Ibid.

22. Ibid., A. Menzies to Frank Edwards, Feb. 27, 1929; Ibid., Frank Edwards to A. D. Menzies, Feb. 28, 1929.

23. Ibid., A. D. Menzies to Hon. Peter Heenan, Minister of Labour, Aug. 9, 1929.

24. Ibid., Mary McKerroll, Secretary, Indian Department, Women's Missionary Society, to Duncan Campbell Scott, Sept. 10, 1929.

25. Ibid., Petition of Shoal Lake Chiefs and Councillors to Hon. Peter Heenan, Sept. 30, 1929.

26. Ibid., Duncan Campbell Scott to Hon. Peter Heenan, Oct. 8, 1929.

27. Ibid., Frank Edwards to Asst. Deputy and Secretary, Indian Affairs, Oct. 18, 1929.

28. Ibid., Mary McKerroll, Secretary, Indian Department, Women's Missionary Society, to Duncan Campbell Scott, Nov. 23, 1929.
29. "The Presbyterian Church in Canada and Native Residential Schools, 1925–1969," in the *Presbyterian Record* (Nov. 1994): 17–18.
30. J. Donald Wilson, "Indians in Nineteenth-Century Ontario," in Jean Barman, Yvonne Hébert, and Don McCaskill, eds., *Indian Education in Canada*, Volume 1: *The Legacy* (Vancouver: UBC Press, 1986), 83; Rev. Edward Ahenakew, *Voices of the Plains Cree*, ed. Ruth M. Buck (Toronto: McClelland & Stewart, 1973), p. 133; Miller, *Shingwauk's Vision*, pp. 136, 151–82.
31. See Elizabeth Graham, *The Mush Hole: Life at Two Indian Residential Schools* (Waterloo, Ont.: Heffle Publishing, 1997) for examples of very different testimony from the same school at the same time.
32. Walter Redsky, personal communication, July 23, 1999.
33. Ada Freeman, slide-show scripts: "Conflict of Cultures," pp. 4–5, "The Church and the Indian," pp. 1–2.
34. UCA, Wesleyan Methodist Church Collection, Correspondence from Ministers, Statesmen, Layreaders, and others in mission areas, Fonds 3–1; 78.128C, William Mason to Society secretaries, Aug. 11, 1841, Roll 13.
35. Michael Angel, "The Ojibwa-Missionary Encounter at Rainy Lake Mission," M.A. thesis, University of Manitoba, 1986, p. 172.

Chapter 21: *Revisiting the Past*

1. Some of my sources on the resurgence of Native American nations in the United States are William Apess, *On Our Own Ground: The Complete Writings of William Apess*, ed. and with intro. by Barry O'Connell, in the series *Native Americans of the Northeast: Culture, History and the Contemporary*, ed. Colin G. Calloway and Barry O'Connell (Amherst: University of Massachusetts Press, 1992); Melissa Jayne Fawcett, *The Lasting of the Mohegans*, Part I (Uncasville, Conn.: Mohegan Tribe, 1995); *Pequot Times* (a Publication of the Mashantucket Pequot Tribal Nation in Conn.), 5 (7) (July 1996); "Return of the Natives: The Northeast's Indians Rise Again," 28-page special supplement to the *Hartford Courant*, June 1994; Merja Lehtinen, "Return of the Indian Nations," *Discover CT & The Connecticut Chronicles*; *Ni Ya Yo* (an official Publication of the Mohegan Tribe), 1 (5); John Mason Statue Advisory Committee, *Final Report*, Oct. 20, 1993.
2. *Hartford Courant*, Oct. 26, 1994.
3. Final Report, John Mason Statue Advisory Committee, Groton Town Council, Groton, Conn., Oct. 20, 1993.
4. Navajo Hopi Observer Online, Oct. 21, 1997.
5. Sources on the Thomas Stanton Society and the surviving house of Thomas Stanton include: Emily H. Lynch, "The Robert Stanton/Davis Homestead," Stonington Historical Society, *Historical Footnotes* 24 (May 1987): 3, 10–11; Robert Rodriguez, "Tribal Drums, Dances Return to Homestead," *The Day*, Sunday, Aug. 6, 1995; "Denisons, Stantons to Hold Joint Reunion," *The Day*, Wed., Aug. 2, 1995 (New London); John Lawrence Davis, "The Davis Homestead," unpub. MS at Indian and Colonial Research Center, Old Mystic, Conn.; Thomas Stanton Society, *Newsletter* #1, Jan. 1997.
6. Jody Kechego, personal communication, May 1998.
7. "History," Chippewas of the Thames First Nation Web site, 1997, 2.

8. Sweetgrass First Nations Language Council Inc., "Speakers of Aboriginal Languages Survey," Oct. 1995, Web site of the Woodland Cultural Centre, Brantford, Ont.

9. Rev. James Johansen, *Indian Preacher: The Life and Teachings of Rev. Allen Salt, 1818–1911* (Sarnia: St. Clair United Church, 1985, 1988), n.p.

10. Aylmer Nicholas Plain, *A History of the Chippewas of Sarnia and the History of the Sarnia Reserve* (Bright's Grove: George L. Smith, 1975), p. 4.

11. Plain, *Chippewas of Sarnia*, p. 28.

12. Selwyn Dewdney, *The Sacred Scrolls of the Southern Ojibway* (Toronto: University of Toronto Press for the Glenbow–Alberta Institute, 1975), p. 177.

13. Ibid., p. 177.

14. Ibid., p. 178.

15. James Redsky, *Great Leader of the Ojibway: Mis-quona-queb*, ed. Selwyn Dewdney (Toronto: McClelland & Stewart, 1972), p. 21.

16. Ibid., p. 20.

17. Michael Angel, "Discordant Voices, Conflicting Visions: Ojibwa and Euro-American Perspectives on the Midewewin," Ph.D. thesis, University of Manitoba, 1997, p. 23.

18. Emma Paishk, "To the Presbyterian Church in Canada from a former student of Cecilia Jeffrey Indian Residential School, Kenora, Ont.," *Glad Tidings* (October 1994), pp. 12–13.

19. *Presbyterian Record*, Nov. 1994: 19.

20. Fraser Greene, "Statement concerning the former Cecilia Jeffrey Indian Residential School Property, Round Lake, Ontario," Feb. 25, 1998.

Chapter 22: *Judgment Day*

1. *RCAP*, Vol. 1, p. 43; Francis Jennings, *The Invasion of America: Indians, Colonialism, and the Cant of Conquest* (Chapel Hill: University of North Carolina Press, 1975), p. 83. See, for example, Daniel Gookin, "Historical Collections of the Indians in New England (1674)," *MHSC*, 1st Series, I (1792): 141.

2. Roland Chrisjohn and Sherri Young with Michael Maraun, *The Circle Game: Shadows and Substance in the Indian Residential School Experience in Canada* (Penticton, B.C.: Theytus Books, 1997), p. 46.

3. Ibid., p. 282.

4. Peter Leavenworth, " 'The Best Title That Indians Can Claime': Native Agency and Consent in the Transferral of Penacook–Pawtucket Land in the Seventeenth Century," *New England Quarterly* 72 (2) (June 1999): 299.

5. See Billy Diamond, "Villages of the Damned: The James Bay Agreement Leaves a Trail of Broken Promises," *Arctic Circle* (Nov./Dec. 1990): 24–34; Daniel McCabe, "James Bay Governing Scheme Leaves Natives Uneasy," *The McGill Reporter*, 28 (17) (May 23, 1996); and "Grand Chief Coon-Come Speaks to the Sioux on Treaty Implementation, Human Rights and Development," news release, Winnipeg, Jan. 28, 2000, Canada Newswire.

6. Margaret Sault, Mississaugas of New Credit, personal communication, Jan. 2000.

7. Murray Philp, "We Owe Nothing to Natives," *Sunday Star, Toronto Star*, Nov. 7, 1999.

8. Canada. Royal Commission on Aboriginal Peoples, *People to People, Nation to Nation: Highlights of the Report of the Royal Commission on Aboriginal Peoples* (Ottawa: Supply and Services Canada, 1996), pp. 455–46.

9. Chrisjohn et al., *The Circle Game*, p. 46.

10. I am indebted to Cuyler Cotton for many of the ideas and much of the wording in this discussion of the history of treaties in Canada in this and the following two paragraphs.

11. Cuyler Cotton, personal communication, Dec. 1999.
12. Recent court judgments affirming aboriginal rights include *R. v. Marshall*, 1999, and *Delgamuukw v. British Columbia*, 1997.
13. Cuyler Cotton, personal communication, Dec. 1999.
14. Gus M. Bordewich, *Killing the White Man's Indian: Reinventing Native Americans at the End of the Twentieth Century* (N.Y.: Doubleday, 1996), p. 337.
15. *RCAP, People to People, Nation to Nation*, p. 16; Brian W. Dippie, *The Vanishing American: White Attitudes and U.S. Indian Policy* (Middletown, Conn.: Wesleyan University Press, 1982), p. 61.
16. Stan McKay and Janet Silman, *The First Nations: A Canadian Experience of the Gospel-Culture Encounter*, Gospel and Cultures Pamphlet 2 (Geneva: World Council of Churches Publications, 1995), p. 8.
17. John Webster Grant, *Moon of Wintertime: Missionaries and the Indians of Canada in Encounter since 1534* (Toronto: University of Toronto Press, 1984), pp. 185–88, 205, 236–37.
18. "Total institution" is a concept of Irving Goffman's, cited in Chrisjohn et al., *Circle Game*, p. 70; *RCAP*, Vol. I, p. 365.
19. Hope MacLean, "The Hidden Agenda: Methodist Attitudes to the Ojibwa and the Development of Indian Schooling in Upper Canada, 1821–1860," M.A. thesis, University of Toronto, 1978, pp. 159–65; J. R. Miller, *Shingwauk's Vision: A History of Native Residential Schools* (Toronto: University of Toronto Press, 1996), pp. 343–59. See also Elizabeth Furniss, *Victims of Benevolence: The Dark Legacy of the Williams Lake Residential School* (Vancouver: Arsenal Pulp Press Cariboo Tribal Council, 1992 and 1995); Celia Haig-Brown, *Resistance and Renewal: Surviving the Indian Residential School* (Vancouver: Arsenal Pulp Press, Tillacum Library, 1988); and Basil Johnston, *Indian School Days* (Toronto: Key Porter, 1988).
20. D. C. Scott, "Indian Affairs, 1867–1912," in *Canada and Its Provinces: A History of the Canadian People and Their Institutions by One Hundred Associates*, ed. Adam Shortt and Arthur G. Coughty, 23 vols. (Toronto: Glasgow, Brook & Co, 1914) vol. 7, p. 615; Anglican Church of Canada, General Synod Archives, S. H. Blake Files, G.S., pp. 75–103, "To the Honourable Frank Oliver, Minister of the Interior, 27 January 1907," quoted in Memo to the Members of the Board of Management of the Missionary Society of the Church of England, Feb. 19, 1907; *RCAP*, I: 358.
21. *RCAP*, I: 337, 353.
22. Beverley Sellars, quoted in Furniss, *Victims of Benevolence*, p. 125.
23. Quoted in Ward Churchill, *A Little Matter of Genocide: Holocaust and Denial in the Americas, 1492 to the present* (San Francisco: City Lights, 1997), p. 366.
24. Ibid., 365.
25. The United Nations Genocide Convention, quoted in Appendix A, Chrisjohn et al., *Circle Game*, p. 150; ibid., p. 41.
26. Churchill, *A Little Matter of Genocide*, pp. 421–22, quotes Robert Melson, "Provocation or Nationalism: A Critical Inquiry into the Armenian Genocide of 1915," in Richard G. Hovannisian, ed., *The Armenian Genocide in Perspective* (New Brunswick, N.J.: Transaction, 1986).
27. I heard this phrase from Cuyler Cotton.
28. Rev. R. G. MacBeth, *Policing the Plains; being the real-life record of the famous Royal North-west Mounted Police* (Toronto: Musson Book Co., 1931), p. 66, quoted in Daniel Francis, *The Imaginary Indian: The Image of the Indian in Canadian Culture* (Vancouver: Arsenal Pulp Press, 1992), p. 72.

29. *RCAP*, I: 334. The *Report of the Royal Commission on Aboriginal Peoples* provides an excellent summary of Canada's history with respect to aboriginal people, a useful discussion of the issues arising from the residential schools, and excellent recommendations for future action. Recent official responses and initiatives of the federal government are outlined in Government of Canada, Indian and Northern Affairs Canada, *Gathering Strength: Canada's Aboriginal Action Plan*, Jan. 7, 1998, and Hon. Jane Stewart, "Statement of Reconciliation," Jan. 7, 1998.

30. Peter Sichrovsky, trans. Jean Steinberg, *Born Guilty: Children of Nazi Families* (London: O. B. Tauris & Co, 1988), p. 154; Sabine Reichel, *What Did You Do in the War, Daddy? Growing up German* (N.Y.: Hill and Wang, 1989), p. 198. My thoughts on guilt, accountability, and responsibility have been further enriched by Joseph Anthony Amato II, *Guilt and Gratitude: A Study of the Origins of Contemporary Conscience*, Contributions in Philosophy Number 20 (Westport, Conn.: Greenwood Press, 1982) and the works of Chrisjohn, Young and Maraun, and Churchill.

31. Sichrovsky, *Born Guilty*, p. 168.

32. Reichel, *What Did You Do?* p. 6.

33. Ibid., p. 150.

34. Chrisjohn et al., *The Circle Game*, pp. 56–57.

35. J. R. Miller, "Native Residential Schools in Historical Context." Paper presented at the annual meeting of the Canadian Catholic Historical Association, University of Calgary (June 14, 1994), p. 32.

36. Cited in George Mellor, *British Imperial Trusteeship, 1783–1859* (London: Faber and Faber, 1951), p. 413.

37. Anglican Church of Canada, General Synod Archives, GS 75–103, Series 1–14, Box 15, MSCC Blake Correspondence, To S. H. Blake from F. Oliver, Jan. 28, 1908.

38. William S. Simmons, "Red Yankees: Narragansett Conversion in the Great Awakening," *American Ethnologist* 10 (1983): 253–71.

39. Terry Anderson, "Lessons from the Residential Schools: Some Beginning Reflections," *Touchstone* (May 1998): 26. Other contemporary reflections from a Christian, and largely United Church, perspective on Christian missionary activity among aboriginal people in Canada and the churches' involvement in residential schools can be found in other essays in the same issue of *Touchstone* as well as in McKay and Silman, *The First Nations*; Muriel Duncan, "The Lessons of the Alberni School Trial Go Far Beyond the Courtroom Walls," *United Church Observer*, July/Aug. 1998; "The Missionary Vision of the Heart," in *Visions of the Heart: Canadian Aboriginal Issues*, eds., David Alan Long and Olive Patricia Dickason (Toronto: Harcourt Brace Canada, 1996); Motion passed by the United Church of Canada at the 36th General Council in Camrose, Alberta, 14–21 Aug. 1997, Apology Statement to Native Congregations in the United Church of Canada, General Council, Aug. 15, 1986; "Why the Healing Fund? The United Church Response," pamphlet published by The Healing Fund, United Church of Canada, n.d.; "The Healing Fund: In Response to the Hurt of Native Residential Schools," brochure produced by the United Church of Canada, n.d.; and Katharine B. Hockin, "My Pilgrimage in Mission," *International Bulletin of Missionary Research*, Jan. 1988. For Presbyterian perspectives, see Peter G. Bush, "The Presbyterian Church in Canada and Native Residential Schools, 1925–1969"; "Our Confession: The 1994 Confession of the Presbyterian Church in Canada Regarding Injustice Suffered by Canada's First Nations People"; James Marnoch, "The Way We Saw It: A Personal Remembrance of the Native Residential Schools"; Michael Farris, "Moderator Presents Confession"; and John Congram, "Stan McKay Reflects," in *Presbyterian Record*, Nov. 1994.

40. E. Brian Titley, *A Narrow Vision Duncan Campbell Scott and the Administration of Indian Affairs in Canada* (Vancouver: UBC Press, 1986), p. 201.

41. Chrisjohn et al., *Circle Game*, p. 80.

42. Reichel, *What Did You Do?* p. 149.

43. Anderson, "Lessons from the Residential Schools," p. 24.

44. Ethel Meachem, Carrot River, Sask., *United Church Observer* (Sept. 1997): 6.

45. "Innu Suicide Rate Highest in World," *Toronto Star*, Mon., Nov. 8, 1999, A1.

46. Stan McKay, "Calling Creation into Our Family," in Diane Engelstad and John Bird, eds., *Nation to Nation: Aboriginal Sovereignty and the Future of Canada* (Toronto: Anansi, 1992), p. 33.

47. Reichel, *What Did You Do?* p. 183.

48. Chrisjohn et al., *Circle Game*, p. 105.

49. Drew Hayden Taylor, "Reflections on the White Man's Burden," *Toronto Star*, Wed., Oct. 7, 1998, A27.

50. This danger is real, as the varying present-day actions of the Christian churches toward aboriginal people illustrate. Most of the mainstream churches in Canada have made or are in the process of making various apologies for their role in the spiritual, cultural, and physical abuse of aboriginal people and have begun to recognize the validity of aboriginal spirituality. Some of the churches are rethinking their concept of missionary activity at the same time and are voluntarily making or are being forced to make restitution. Yet a number of Native people have told me that some fundamentalist Christian groups active in aboriginal communities continue to aggressively denounce traditional aboriginal culture and spirituality as evil. See Norman Lewis, *The Missionaries* (London: Arrow Books, 1988) for an account of how evangelical Christian groups in Latin America, Asia, and Africa are destroying other, indigenous cultures at a dizzying pace. A group called Cultural Survival in Cambridge, Mass., (617–441–5400 or FAX 617–441–5417 or www.cs.org) is a clearing-house for information on such issues faced by tribal peoples world-wide.

51. *RCAP*, I: 384; Hugh Trevor-Roper, "History as Imagination," in Hugh Lloyd Jones, Valerie Pearl, and Blair Worden, eds., *History & Imagination: Essays in Honour of Hugh Trevor-Roper* (N.Y.: Holmes & Meier, 1982, c. 1981), p. 365.

52. *RCAP* I: 7. The following questions are based on issues enunciated in RCAP's final report.

53. Bordewich, *White Man's Indian*, p. 324.

54. Judge Murray Sinclair, quoted in the Report of the Aboriginal Justice Inquiry of Manitoba/Public Inquiry into the Administration of Justice (Winnipeg: The Inquiry, 1991).

55. *RCAP*, I: 159–60; 173–76.

56. Bordewich, *White Man's Indian*, p. 324.

57. "Ottawa Prices Native Demands at $200-Billion," *Globe and Mail*, Tues., Oct. 26, 1999, A3.

58. Reichel, *What Did You Do?* p. 148.

59. Bordewich, *White Man's Indian*, p. 324.

60. For a cogent analysis of the Ontario social studies curriculum as it relates to the First Nations, see Susan Dion Fletcher, "Moulded Images: First Nations People, Representation, and the Ontario School Curriculum," in *Weaving Connections: Educations for Peace, Environmental and Social Justice*, forthcoming from Second Story Press, Toronto.

61. James D. Drake, *King Philip's War: Civil War in New England, 1675–1676* (Amherst: University of Massachusetts Press, 1999), p. 139.

62. See Bordewich, *White Man's Indian*.

63. McKay and Silman, *Gospel-Culture Encounter*, p. x; Bev Sellars, quoted in Furniss, *Victims of Benevolence*, p. 126.

64. Quoted in Melissa Jayne Fawcett, *The Lasting of the Mohegans*, Part I (Uncasville, Conn.: The Mohegan Tribe, 1995), p. 6.

65. Jeannette Armstrong at "Women and Words/Les femmes et les mots" Conference, Vancouver, B.C., June 1983.

Index